# The Diaries of
# Beatrice Webb

BOOKS BY BEATRICE WEBB

*The Co-operative Movement in Great Britain* (London, 1891)
*My Apprenticeship* (London, 1926)
*Our Partnership* (London, 1948)

BOOKS BY SIDNEY AND BEATRICE WEBB

*The History of Trade Unionism* (London, 1894)
*Industrial Democracy* (London, 1897)
*English Local Government* (London, 1906–29)
*A Constitution for the Socialist Commonwealth of Great Britain*
(London, 1920)
*The Consumers Co-operative Movement* (London, 1920)
*The Decay of Capitalist Civilization* (London, 1923)
*Methods of Social Study* (London, 1932)
*Soviet Communism: A New Civilization* (London, 1935)

# The Diaries
## of
# Beatrice Webb

Edited by
Norman and Jeanne MacKenzie

*Abridged by Lynn Knight*
*Preface by Hermione Lee*

Published in association with
The London School of Economics and Political Science

A *Virago* Book

First published by Virago Press 2000 in association with
The London School of Economics and Political Science

A CIP catalogue record for this book
is available from the British Library.

ISBN 1 86049 823 X

Typeset in Garamond by M Rules
Printed and bound in Great Britain
by Clays Ltd, St Ives plc

Virago
A Division of
Little, Brown and Company (UK)
Brettenham House
Lancaster Place
London WC2E 7EN

# Contents

# Preface

In her early thirties, Beatrice Potter (currently researching conditions for workers in the East End) admits to her diary that she is 'haunted by a longing to create characters and to move them to and fro among fictitious circumstances – to put the matter plainly, by the vulgar wish to write a novel!' This 'intensely attractive' vulgar longing will recur, for instance in 1896, when Beatrice Webb is busy collaborating with Sidney on *Industrial Democracy,* and she erupts in the diary: 'The truth is I want to have my "fling". I want to imagine anything I damn well please without regard to facts as they are.' But these desires are firmly stifled, and, indeed, whenever Beatrice Webb mentions novels in her diary, it is disapprovingly. *Jane Eyre* is impure and disagreeable, Balzac is a disgusting cynic, *To the Lighthouse* is objectionable, and the modern novel (Huxley, Lawrence) is morbid and ugly. Instead of writing fiction, Beatrice Webb wrote a history of the Co-operative Movement, and, with Sidney Webb, a large number of important books of social analysis – on trades unions, the Poor Law, local government, socialism, capitalism, and Soviet Communism.

But she also, famously, wrote her autobiography, for which she mined her life-long volumes of diaries. It was in her diary that she could create a secret place or 'Other self', where she could express the feelings she didn't allow into her public writings and 'rid her mind' of things that troubled her, and where, to an extent, she could exercise her stifled novelistic leanings.

Of course Beatrice Webb's diaries are historical and social documents of high interest. Even in this abridged version, there are rich pickings for anyone interested in the public, political and cultural history of late nineteenth- and early twentieth-century Britain, and particularly in the history of socialism in this country. Charles Booth and the Co-operative Movement, slum reform in the 1890s, Fabians, Trades Unionists and the Labour party, the suffrage movement and the Salvation Army, local government, the founding of the London School of Economics and the *New Statesman,* England in the First and Second World Wars, the monarchy, the strikes, the attitudes to communism: there is an enormous swathe of subjects covered here, vigorously argued over and vividly embodied. And there is, as well, a great deal of plotting and conspiracy, shifting allegiances and feuds (which the Webbs throve on), and a large gallery of (often highly critical and disapproving) portraits of Shaw, Wells, Russell, and many others.

This material in itself makes the diaries well worth reading. But what makes them as gripping as any novel is the struggle they reveal in this beautiful, driven, clever, egocentric, powerfully assertive and high-minded woman between two kinds of self, two possible ways of living. From her twenties, Beatrice was quoting Goethe to herself on the need for a great career, a 'life occupation' which could 'keep your heart and mind open to the outer world'. She always knew that she needed an aim in life and a philosophy of life. (She thought that Virginia Woolf killed herself because she had, as she told Beatrice on their last meeting, 'no living philosophy'.) Beatrice's own philosophy was that she needed (without, or instead of, a religious faith) to dedicate herself analytically and intelligently to the improvement of the world she lived in. (That was the point of her marriage to Sidney Webb.) She was always telling herself this, rather grandly, in her diaries: 'We have to go straight for an object – to clean up the base of society, single-mindedly, without thought of ourselves or what people think of us or our work.' 'Someone must begin to think things out, and our task in life is to be pioneers in social engineering.'

But these redoubtable aims involved the suppression – or sublimation – of another part of her nature: sensual, passionate, emotional and turbulent. She was well aware of this, but could not allow that there might be anything valuable in the sensuality. As a young woman, she thought that the 'enthusiast for Truth' and 'lover of thought' was 'the highest expression of her Ego', and that the 'sensual nature' could only be a trouble to her. If she dedicated herself to her work, then that side had to remain 'controlled and unsatisfied'; if she married, it would mean 'destruction of the intellectual being'. This painful conflict (what she called 'constant friction') was agonisingly acted out in her long, obsessive passion for Joseph Chamberlain, which certainly did not end with their separation and his marriage: 'It is strange that a being who will henceforth be an utter stranger to my life should be able to inflict such intense pain.' It also came out in her confused and contradictory feelings about women's roles, which involved some hostility to feminism and the suffrage movement. Her marriage to Sidney Webb began in a spirit of compromise and dubiousness: 'Marriage to me is another word for suicide'. Yet it turned into one of the most impressive and satisfying working partnerships of the century.

But the cost of the compromise shows up in her depressions, 'morbidness' and illnesses, and in the punishingly disciplinarian regimes she imposed on herself, like her ferocious dieting in her early forties: 'If only I can have a steadfast mind in a healthy body my life will approach the ideal.' Beatrice Webb's diary is a staggering record of determination and endeavour. At sixteen, she is reproaching herself for laziness; at nearly seventy, she is telling herself: 'Courage, old woman, courage: be game to the end.'

*Hermione Lee*
*Oxford, 2000*

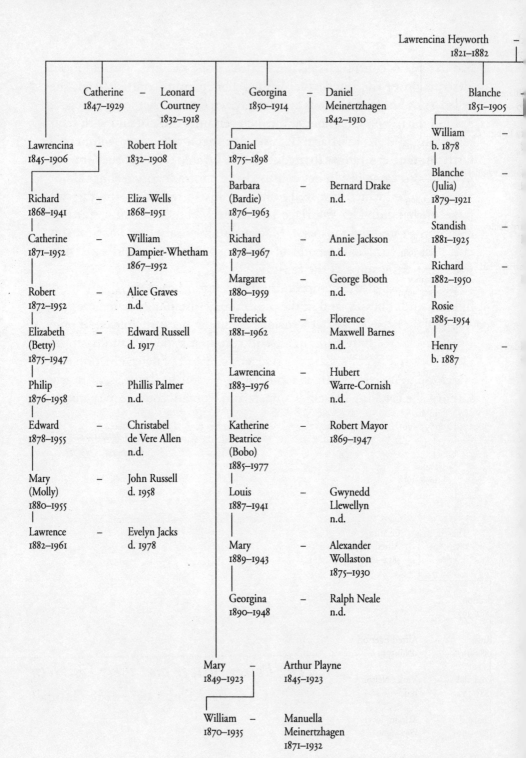

Lawrencina Heyworth
1821–1882

Catherine – Leonard
1847–1929 Courtney
1832–1918

Georgina – Daniel
1850–1914 Meinertzhagen
1842–1910

Blanche
1851–1905

Lawrencina – Robert Holt
1845–1906 1832–1908

Richard – Eliza Wells
1868–1941 1868–1951

Catherine – William
1871–1952 Dampier-Whetham
1867–1952

Robert – Alice Graves
1872–1952 n.d.

Elizabeth – Edward Russell
(Betty) d. 1917
1875–1947

Philip – Phillis Palmer
1876–1958 n.d.

Edward – Christabel
1878–1955 de Vere Allen
n.d.

Mary – John Russell
(Molly) d. 1958
1880–1955

Lawrence – Evelyn Jacks
1882–1961 d. 1978

Daniel
1875–1898

Barbara – Bernard Drake
(Bardie) n.d.
1876–1963

Richard – Annie Jackson
1878–1967 n.d.

Margaret – George Booth
1880–1959 n.d.

Frederick – Florence
1881–1962 Maxwell Barnes
n.d.

Lawrencina – Hubert
1883–1976 Warre-Cornish
n.d.

Katherine – Robert Mayor
Beatrice 1869–1947
(Bobo)
1885–1977

Louis – Gwynedd
1887–1941 Llewellyn
n.d.

Mary – Alexander
1889–1943 Wollaston
1875–1930

Georgina – Ralph Neale
1890–1948 n.d.

William
b. 1878

Blanche
(Julia)
1879–1921

Standish
1881–1925

Richard
1882–1950

Rosie
1885–1954

Henry
b. 1887

Mary – Arthur Playne
1849–1923 1845–1923

William – Manuella
1870–1935 Meinertzhagen
1871–1932

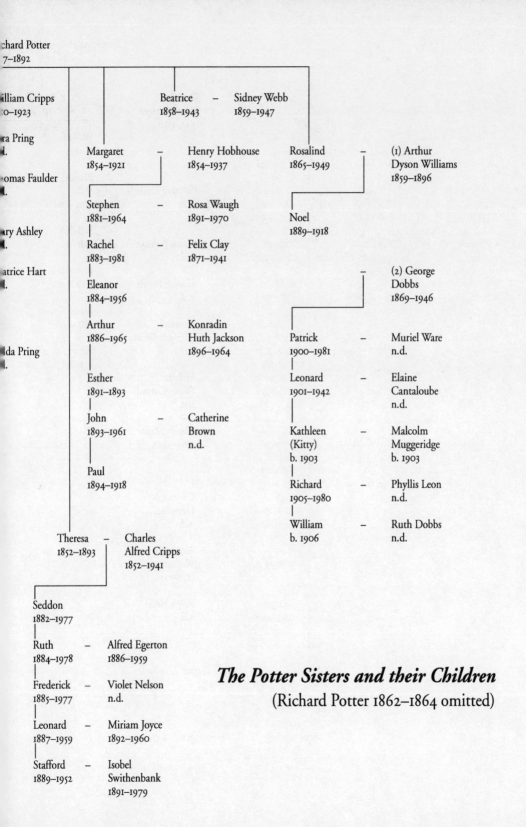

chard Potter
7–1892

illiam Cripps
0–1923

ra Pring
.

omas Faulder
.

ry Ashley
.

atrice Hart
.

da Pring
.

Beatrice – Sidney Webb
1858–1943   1859–1947

Margaret – Henry Hobhouse     Rosalind – (1) Arthur
1854–1921   1854–1937       1865–1949   Dyson Williams
                                         1859–1896

Stephen – Rosa Waugh
1881–1964   1891–1970        Noel
                             1889–1918
Rachel – Felix Clay
1883–1981   1871–1941
                                    – (2) George
Eleanor                               Dobbs
1884–1956                             1869–1946

Arthur – Konradin
1886–1965   Huth Jackson      Patrick – Muriel Ware
            1896–1964         1900–1981   n.d.

Esther                        Leonard – Elaine
1891–1893                     1901–1942   Cantaloube
                                          n.d.
John – Catherine
1893–1961   Brown             Kathleen – Malcolm
            n.d.              (Kitty)     Muggeridge
                             b. 1903     b. 1903
Paul
1894–1918                     Richard – Phyllis Leon
                             1905–1980   n.d.

                             William – Ruth Dobbs
Theresa – Charles            b. 1906     n.d.
1852–1893   Alfred Cripps
            1852–1941

Seddon
1882–1977

Ruth – Alfred Egerton
1884–1978   1886–1959

Frederick – Violet Nelson
1885–1977   n.d.

Leonard – Miriam Joyce       *The Potter Sisters and their Children*
1887–1959   1892–1960        (Richard Potter 1862–1864 omitted)

Stafford – Isobel
1889–1952   Swithenbank
            1891–1979

# Introduction

## The Long Record of a Life

Martha Beatrice Potter was born on 22 January 1858 at Standish House, on the edge of the Cotswolds, where she spent much of her childhood and youth. She began life with many advantages. Her father, Richard Potter, was a wealthy railway promoter with cultivated habits, who filled his house with books and intelligent friends; and her mother, Lawrencina Potter, also valued things of the mind. They were both of liberal provincial background, and their nine daughters, almost all of whom married able and eminent men, were permitted to read widely and to discuss candidly, and their father's encouragement gave them a sense that all things were possible. 'He admired and loved his daughters,' Beatrice recalled many years after his death: 'He was the only man I ever knew who genuinely believed that women were superior to men, and acted as if he did.'

In such a home Beatrice was free to let her natural talent roam far beyond the subjects and accomplishments considered suitable for girls of her class in mid-Victorian society. In *My Apprenticeship*, the only volume of her planned autobiographical trilogy which she completed, and also in the pages of this diary, she describes an eclectic education in which speculation about religion and philosophy played as large a part as the study of literature and the classics, modern languages, history, mathematics and science. Yet she was not merely the earnest bluestocking that

such high-mindedness suggests. She was strikingly handsome, unconventional, and sociable. After her mother's death in 1882, indeed, she
became her father's close companion, running his households in London
and in the country, and delighting to share in the stimulating conversation round his dinner-table.

Well-to-do, intelligent and attractive, Beatrice was apparently set for
a conventionally successful marriage. But appearances were deceptive.
Her odd upbringing, she said, left her with 'a tireless curiosity together
with a double dose of will-power'. It also left her with a profound inner
conflict between emotion and intellect, between her feminine instincts
and her desire to be independent and successful in a man's world; and
that ambivalence led to the first great crisis of her life, when she conceived an obsessive passion for the Radical politician Joseph
Chamberlain.

It came to nothing, but it left an enduring mark upon her. All
through the 1880s she sought relief from that self-tormenting attachment
in the anodyne of work in the East End of London. In its poverty-rav-
aged slums Beatrice discovered a craft and a creed. As a rent-collector for
a philanthropic housing association, a researcher for the great survey of
London poverty launched by her cousin-in-law Charles Booth, and
then as the author of a book on the Co-operative movement, she
painstakingly taught herself to be a social investigator; and, though she
had abandoned formal Christianity when she was still an adolescent, she
was sustained by a vague deism and she found spiritual comfort in
prayer and in a vocation for public service. She had the makings of a
great *religieuse*, but the circumstances of her life made her a great social
scientist instead.

She had already settled on her career when she met Sidney Webb, the
fast-rising civil servant and Fabian ideologist; and, with no idea in her
mind beyond a professional collaboration based upon common interests
and complementary abilities, she struck up a friendship that was to
end in marriage two years later, on 23 July 1892. It was a troubled
courtship, in which Sidney had both to win her reluctant affection and
to satisfy her that marriage would not be 'an act of *felo de se*', as she put
it, but, rather, a working partnership which would enhance their usefulness to society quite as much as their personal happiness – the only
line of argument, as their fretful correspondence shows, which had any
prospect of success. 'One and one, placed in a sufficiently integrated
relationship', Sidney said repeatedly in his letters, 'make not two, but
eleven.'

So it proved, despite the superficial incongruity of a match between the beautiful heiress, seemingly headed for spinsterhood at the age of thirty-four, and the dumpy, dowdy and infatuated son of a Soho shopkeeper. 'The world will wonder,' Beatrice understandably wrote in her diary when they became engaged, and Sidney felt much the same. 'I can't help it being "Beauty and the Beast",' he told her, 'if only it is not a case of Titania and Bottom.' Within seven years the Webbs had published *The History of Trade Unionism*, which was their first joint work, and two other books on industrial problems. They had become, with George Bernard Shaw, the dominant personalities in the Fabian Society, and Sidney was its most prolific pamphleteer. They had founded the London School of Economics, which was to become their most enduring legacy to the social sciences. Through Sidney's membership of the London County Council they had made themselves into experts on educational and municipal reform, and they had committed themselves to a series of monographs on English local government which took them thirty years to complete.

As Beatrice remarked, they were 'curiously well combined' in so many ways. Her flair as an investigator was matched by his extraordinary capacity for work; her private income supported them, modestly but in quite sufficient comfort for their austere tastes, so that Sidney was able to leave the Civil Service and devote his days to research, writing and politics and they were able to dine and be dined by prominent politicians, administrators, academics and writers; her febrile vitality was sustained by his unremitting affection; and while she beguiled he persuaded. Long before they decided to take a working holiday in 1898, and set off across the United States on their way to New Zealand and Australia, their partnership had become a marvel to everyone who knew them and a professional phenomenon that had already made them famous.

During the next phase of the Webb partnership, which coincided with the Edwardian decade, Beatrice was in her prime, and full of energy and ideas. She was a striking, if austere, hostess, who used her *salon* so effectively to promote Webbian policies that she deservedly earned a reputation for political intrigue; she was a forceful and uncompromising member of the Royal Commission on the outmoded Poor Law; and it was she, rather than Sidney, who controlled the national campaign which the Webbs subsequently launched to promote their own proposals for the break-up of the Poor Law and the creation of a welfare state.

The Webbs, in this period, were in an ambiguous position. They were among the best-known socialists in the country, but they were at odds with many of their fellow-Fabians; they disliked the new Independent Labour Party led by Keir Hardie, and they were opposed to the formation of a national Labour Party as an alliance of individual socialists and affiliated trade unionists. They also fell out with the anti-imperialists in the Liberal Party over the Boer War, with the Nonconformists over their support for the Conservative government's education policies, and with Lloyd George and Winston Churchill over the Liberal plans for reforming the Poor Law. While those differences kept them out of the mainstream of progressive politics, and certainly reduced their direct influence on events, they also made for a varied and lively public life, as the voluminous entries in Beatrice's diary reveal.

In the summer of 1911, when the Webbs found themselves without significant allies in any of the parties, and without any notion what they should do next, they set off on another journey across the world, starting in Canada and going on through Japan, China, Burma and India; they were therefore abroad when the Liberal struggle to reduce the power of the House of Lords was at its height, when the suffragette movement was gathering momentum, and when a great wave of industrial unrest swept across the country. On their return to London in 1912 they immediately began to plan two new ventures. The first was designed to restore their political base in the Fabian Society, which had fallen away into squabbling factions: the remedy, Beatrice decided, was to enlist the younger and more able members into a Research Department, and to produce a new set of policies for social reconstruction to replace those devised by the founding Fabians thirty years before. The second venture was intended to give them their own means of publicizing their ideas, and creating a cross-party current of collectivist opinion. In 1913, with the help of Bernard Shaw, they founded the weekly *New Statesman* as an independent radical journal.

Both these schemes were scarcely launched when the First World War began, and the Webbs were at a loss what to do with their talents. There was a moratorium on political activity and, though the Webbs were invited to serve on a number of committees, they both felt frustrated; the only serious piece of work that Beatrice produced in these four years was a minority report to one of these committees arguing the case for equal pay, and for much of the war she was ill and depressed – feelings that were intensified by the collapse of her working partnership with Sidney. They continued with their research into the history of local government, and soon after the war they produced two theoretical books, *A Constitution for the Socialist Commonwealth of Great Britain* and

*The Decay of Capitalist Civilization;* but after 1916, when the Webbs were at last converted to the idea of a Labour Party, Sidney was increasingly drawn into its affairs, working with Arthur Henderson and Ramsay MacDonald to reorganize it and drafting the manifesto, *Labour and the New Social Order,* which marked its emergence as the main opposition party in post-war years.

For the next ten years, indeed, Beatrice had to subordinate her own interests to the claims of Sidney's career as a Labour politician. In 1922 he was elected to Parliament, and in 1924 he became a cabinet minister in the first Labour government. Beatrice again became a political hostess, though much more reluctantly, for she now preferred to spend her time at Passfield Corner, the country home in Hampshire which the Webbs acquired in 1923; and her main concern was the revision of her diaries, with the aim of publishing one or more volumes of autobiography. In 1926 she published *My Apprenticeship,* but the advent of another Labour government in 1929, in which Sidney once more sat as a member of the Cabinet, was a fresh distraction.

So, too, was the fascination of the Soviet Union, which dominated the last years of the Webb partnership. Beatrice had already begun to draft the second volume of her autobiography, which was to describe the busy years between her marriage and the First World War, but after the collapse of the Labour government in 1931 she became disillusioned with the gradualist socialism that had been so distinctively Fabian. Turning towards Moscow, and what she saw as a new creed that reminded her of Auguste Comte's Religion of Humanity, she carried Sidney along with her enthusiasm; and in 1932 they set off to the Soviet Union to collect the material on which they based *Soviet Communism: A New Civilization.* The book was a last and immense effort, for both the Webbs were over seventy-five when it appeared in 1935, and its optimism about the Soviet regime, though qualified by Sidney's natural caution, was the one gleam in the growing darkness which Beatrice saw descending on the world.

Their last years were indeed a time of sadness. After Sidney's stroke in 1938, from which he never really recovered though he lived until 1947, the Webbs were housebound in the country, and they became even more cut off when the outbreak of war a year later made it difficult for their friends to visit them. Beatrice tried to keep in touch with events, and especially with those that affected the Soviet Union, to care for Sidney, to run a house under wartime conditions, to maintain her diary, and to go on with the book she proposed to call *Our Partnership.* But her own health was failing. On 19 April 1943 she wrote a last entry in her diary: eleven days later she was dead.

Beatrice Webb's long life thus spanned a whole epoch. Born just before Darwin published the *Origin of Species*, and dying two years before the atom bomb was dropped on Hiroshima, she saw the transition from mid-Victorian individualism to the modern collectivist state, from a society in which people grew up with the certainty of a revealed religion to one in which they sought for secular creeds to replace it.

Although the Webbs knew more about poverty, trade unionism and public administration than anyone else in England, imperial and foreign policy meant very little to them; they were not greatly interested in cultural pursuits; and they preferred work to social intercourse, unless there was some useful point to it. Yet they lived close to great people and great events, and in the confidence of her diary Beatrice displayed her 'tireless curiosity' about them. They knew nine prime ministers – Lord Rosebery, Arthur Balfour, Sir Henry Campbell-Bannerman, Herbert Asquith, David Lloyd George, Bonar Law, Ramsay MacDonald, Winston Churchill and Clement Attlee – as well as members of all their Cabinets. Beatrice had learnt much from her father's friend, the individualist philosopher Herbert Spencer. She had known the great housing reformer Octavia Hill, worked with Charles Booth, and been deeply attached to Joseph Chamberlain, the most controversial politician of his day. The Webbs knew the early trade union leaders, such as Henry Broadhurst, Tom Mann and John Burns, as well as all their successors in the first half of the twentieth century; they had close academic and literary friends, including Bernard Shaw, H. G. Wells, Graham Wallas, Bertrand Russell and Harold Laski; they were professionally involved with some outstanding public servants, of whom Robert Morant and William Beveridge are the best known; and on their travels they met Woodrow Wilson, Theodore Roosevelt, Maxim Litvinov, Grigori Zinoviev and Lazar Kaganovitch.

Their travels were just as varied. They were in Washington when the United States declared war on Spain in 1898; they arrived in Hawaii on the day the island was annexed; they visited New Zealand and Australia when these two distant countries were the first to experiment with democratic socialist governments. They travelled through Japan when few intellectuals from the West had ever been there; they reached Peking at the height of the revolution which overthrew the Manchu dynasty in 1911, and they were in the Soviet Union on the eve of Stalin's great purges.

It is thus scarcely surprising that Beatrice's diary names over four thousand persons, a thousand places and more than six hundred institutions and organizations. It is an extraordinary compendium, running to close on three million words of scrawled and notoriously illegible handwriting, and though it is not a daily record – for Beatrice often let a week and sometimes a month or more go past without an entry – it is continuous and very comprehensive. The more one reads it, the more this long record of a life begins to assume a life of its own, as if a second self were writing with perfect freedom and extraordinary verve.

*My Apprenticeship* in fact shows what a stylist was submerged by the pedestrian prose in which Sidney wrote their books, and the pages of this diary repeatedly mention Beatrice's belief that she was a talent lost to literature. 'This last month or so', she wrote on 30 September 1889, 'I have been haunted by a longing to create characters and to move them to and fro among fictitious circumstances: to put the matter plainly, by the vulgar wish to write a novel.' At one point she proposed writing a utopian novel in collaboration with her literary friend, Auberon Herbert, and three years after she married, when she and Sidney were just completing their first book together, she came back to the idea. 'For the last three months', she noted on 1 February 1895, 'an idea has haunted me that after we have finished our stiff work on trade unions I would try my hand at pure "Fiction" in the form of a novel dated *60 Years Hence*. . . . The truth is, I want to have my "fling". I want to imagine anything I damn please without regard to facts as they are. I want to give full play to whatever faculty I have for descriptive and dramatic work. . . . I am sick to death of trying to put hideous facts, multitudinous details, exasperating qualifications, into a readable form.'

It was only in her diary, however, that she could release that impulse; and even there, when she reflects on the contrast between fiction and fact she dismisses fiction as 'vulgar' because it does nothing for 'the advancement of society', and persuades herself that the craving for 'a day's fame' was merely vanity and an unworthy aspiration for one who might otherwise be discovering 'the truths about social organization'. Leonard Woolf remarked in his autobiography that Beatrice had the soul of an artist but suppressed her passion and her imagination.

Beatrice had all the talents a great diarist needs. She was a well-informed, well-connected and reflective person, and she lived an active life; she had a sharp eye, a turn of mordant wit, and a knack for catching a character in a telling phrase; and all through these thousands of pages of self-analysis and self-explanation she was as critical of herself as she was of others – the gift a diarist needs above all, for a diary ultimately depends upon its truth to art, its autonomy. There are many passages where she explicitly recognizes that the denial of instinct emotionally impoverished her and cramped her sensibilities, especially when she describes how she recoiled from the prospect of marriage to Joseph Chamberlain: a woman's choice between suffocating domesticity and independence has seldom been more insightfully expressed, or recounted with such vigorous honesty. She was as frank about the willpower and sense of duty which she saw as the strengths of her character as she was about the vanity and self-indulgence for which she repeatedly chastised herself. And even in small things she did not deceive herself or those who now read what she wrote. She knew that she had only received opinions about the visual arts, and that music meant very little to her until, late in life and living in the country, the B.B.C. programmes helped her to discover it. She usually judged books by a utilitarian rule of thumb. She disliked Virginia Woolf's novels, for instance, because the characters had 'no predominant aims, no powerful reactions from the mental environment', and because 'one state of mind follows another without any particular reason'. Beatrice always wanted reasons for things; and whenever she found herself preferring enjoyment to usefulness a twinge of guilt would quickly remind her of her lapse from grace.

Such double-mindedness, in which feeling struggles in vain against duty, was Beatrice's tragedy, and she knew it. She even began *My Apprenticeship* with a memorable sentence that expresses it precisely. 'Beneath the surface of our daily life, in the personal history of many of us, there runs a continuous controversy between an Ego that affirms and an Ego that denies.' That inner dialogue points the contrast between her physically attractive, light-hearted and worldly father and her frustrated, intellectually ambitious and puritanical mother, and the diary is full of paradoxes that echo two very different parental voices, setting self-indulgence against self-sacrifice, impulse against self-control, affection against the urge to dominate. These paradoxes, moreover, are not merely the dialectic of Beatrice's private life. The same moral calculus controlled her attitude to public affairs. If one believes that spontaneity is wrong, then regulation must be right; if individualism is a social evil, collectivism must be a social good.

As Beatrice said many times, the diary personifies the Other Self. Like the 'secret sharer' in Conrad's story of that name, it is always at hand, expressing the ideas that have been suppressed in consciousness and giving haunting reminders of an alternative life which can be glimpsed but never grasped. She began it as so many young girls begin a diary, treating it as a secure place for the confidence of an unhappy child, and it always served as a confidante of last resort for a woman who found it difficult to talk openly about her feelings. In adolescence she began to make notes on her foreign holidays, to record impressions of relatives and friends, and to summarize books that interested her; and by the time she was twenty she was beginning the experiments with structure and style which give the mature diary its extraordinary texture. It was already more than a habit: Beatrice was becoming dependent upon it, as if the Other Self compensated for some deficiency in her personality, just as the Other One (as she came to call Sidney) later supplied what she needed to sustain her everyday life.

There were, in effect, two partnerships. One was the lifelong colloquy with the diary, which kept her sane and helped her to cope with the self-destructive impulses that punctuated her career: the laudanum bottle was never far away, she said more than once in her youthful years, and she was subject to bouts of depression whenever she had finished a book or some other substantial piece of work. The other was with Sidney, who kept her effective, and steadied the erratic rhythms of her work.

This personal ambivalence was to some extent related to the ambivalent position of women in late-Victorian society, which still elevated the domestic virtues and deprecated attempts by women to copy or compete with men, in the professions and in public life. Beatrice was actually in revolt against the feminine ideal of her day, and breaking new paths for women who wanted satisfying and useful careers, but she did not see her own struggle for independence in that light. She was in no sense a conventional feminist. She was long opposed to women's suffrage; she always saw women as the weaker sex; she favoured special legislation to protect them against exploitation and to improve their working conditions; and she never made an issue of legal, political and educational discrimination on grounds of sex. On the contrary, finding little or no difficulty in doing what she wanted to do, she failed to appreciate that she had exceptional advantages and that most women were not so fortunate. She had money, she was charming, intelligent and good-looking, and she was well connected. Whether she was visiting slums in the East End, or sitting smoking in a hotel lounge with delegates to a trades union congress, travelling without a chaperone, or sitting on a committee, she had the style of effortless superiority which enabled energetic women from the upper classes to get their way. Lady Bountiful and Lady Researcher were not so different when it came to dealing with the cap-in-hand masses of the late-Victorian age.

It was not that Beatrice was insensitive to the constraints and dis-
qualifications which made it difficult for other women to follow her
emancipated example. She wrote sympathetically about women who
chose or were obliged to choose a career rather than marriage; she saw
spinsters forming a 'working sisterhood'; she took it for granted that
men should treat women as equals; and she noted the rare occasions
when a man was rude or deliberately unhelpful to her. But she never
addressed her mind to the differences between the sexes in the same way
that she thought about the differences between the classes; and she had
very little influence on the women's movement in her own lifetime. It is
only as one reads on through her diary that one sees how much her
struggle to find herself was, in some measure, a woman's struggle in a
man's world, and that a diary which begins as an intensely personal
document can become a testament for a whole generation of women.

*Norman and Jeanne MacKenzie*

There are three different versions of the unpublished diary. The first is
the original manuscript which is written in Beatrice's slapdash and
scarcely legible hand in fifty-seven exercise-books. In addition to the text
it contains two wills, letters, newspaper clippings, fragments of poetry,
and even pressed flowers. The other two versions are typescripts, typed
partly by Beatrice herself, partly by her secretaries and partly in the
British Library of Political and Economic Science when it was found
that there were no transcripts of some of the volumes in the Passfield
Papers which were handed over after Sidney Webb's death.

The types versions differ from the original, and from each other,
though only in minor respects. The variations are either simply errors of
transcription, because Beatrice as well as her typists found it hard to read
what she had written many years before, or her corrections when she was
going through the manuscript to prepare extracts for her volumes of
autobiography – corrections which occasionally introduced misdating as
well as grammatical improvements. Though she sometimes added a
later note where she thought she had been harsh or inaccurate, she was
scrupulously honest and generally resisted the temptation to censor the
text with hindsight. There are a few pages torn out, and these may once
have contained entries she found too painful to keep, but in later years
she inserted confidential material which she had withheld from earlier
typists. Most of the corrections, in fact, are simply stylistic.

The diary was published in four volumes between 1982 and 1985,
edited by Norman and Jeanne MacKenzie. The four-volume edition is

based on the first typescript which Beatrice used as a working text, with reference back to the original manuscript in cases where the meaning is uncertain, and with slips of the pen, careless punctuation, ampersands and abbreviations silently converted as Beatrice herself converted them in the extracts she reprinted. Square brackets show additional interpolations, and the addition of a query indicates a doubt about a date, place or word. Brief omissions are indicated by ellipses.

Substantial cuts were made in the diary in order to produce the four-volume edition. Further cuts have been made to create this abridgement. These are also indicated by ellipses and, in order to ensure readability, are not distinguished from the ellipses in the full-length edition. The original paragraphing has been maintained where possible, but in some instances it has been necessary to create new paragraphs. The aim throughout has been to stay faithful to the substance of Beatrice's life, if not always its detail, and to the spirit and rhythm of her prose. Norman and Jeanne MacKenzie's notes have sometimes been reduced, and occasionally re-written in consideration of space.

Explanatory notes about individuals, included at the first significant mention, can be found by reference to the index. Organizations are a different matter, since Beatrice was prone to use initials for bodies familiar to her but not to modern readers. Where clarification is most needed these initials have been expanded where they occur, but for convenience a list of the most common is given below.

*The Charity Organization Society* (C.O.S.) A philanthropic body which sought to systematize alms-giving in London and to prevent benevolence 'demoralizing' the beneficiaries.

*The Fabian Society* (F.S.) Founded in 1884 by a small group which sought to combine self-improvement with social reform, by 1893 it had become the most influential (and also the most respectable) of the small socialist societies. It was known for its moderate and anti-Marxist views, and for its distinctive 'Fabian' tactic of permeating other organizations with its ideas.

*The Independent Labour Party* (I.L.P.) Founded in 1893 to promote parliamentary candidates in the labour interest, and to campaign for trade union support of this policy, its philosophy was an amalgam of ethical socialism and class consciousness. It was one of the groups which (with the Fabians and a number of trade unions) formed the *Labour Representation Committee* (L.R.C.) in 1900, and until 1918 it was the usual means through which individuals joined a Labour Party (L.P.) dominated by affiliated trade unions.

*The Liberal Imperialists* ('Limps') The group of Liberal M.P.s, especially H. H. Asquith, Edward Grey and R. B. Haldane, who, together with Lord Rosebery, inclined to imperial expansion abroad and social improvement at home. Distinct from the Radical and predominantly Nonconformist faction of pacifist inclinations which formed the left of the Liberal Party.

*The Liberal Unionists* The large group of Liberal M.P.s who followed Joseph Chamberlain when he broke with his party in 1886–87 in protest against Gladstone's proposal to give Home Rule to Ireland. They formed a coalition with the Conservatives under Lord Salisbury, and then under Arthur Balfour. A few returned to the Liberal Party when Chamberlain began to campaign for protective tariffs but the majority were absorbed into the Conservative Party.

*The Local Government Board* (L.G.B.) The civil service department responsible for the central administration of the Poor Law (P.L.), for the reorganization of local government that began with the creation of county and county borough councils in 1888, and for relations between Whitehall and these local authorities.

*The London County Council* (L.C.C.) First elected in 1889, the Council soon brought municipal reform to a capital city that had been singularly ill-governed. In its early years the Council was dominated by the Progressive Party (Progressives), which was a loose electoral alliance of Liberals, philanthropists and administrative reformers such as Sidney Webb. The Moderate Party (Moderates) was a local variant on Conservative politics, though the organization included some independently-minded persons who could be induced to support particular improvements. After 1903 it became responsible for elementary, secondary and further education in London, and was given a supporting role in higher education as well.

*The London School of Economics and Political Science* (the L.S.E. or 'the School') Founded by Sidney and Beatrice Webb in 1895, it grew rapidly from very modest beginnings to be a centre of social science research and teaching that attracted students from all over the world.

*The Social Democratic Federation* (S.D.F.) Established as the Democratic Federation in 1881 (with a change of name in 1883), it was the first Marxist party in Britain. It was doctrinaire and schismatic, but it played a significant part in the unemployed marches of the 1880s and in the great dock strike of 1889.

*The Technical Education Board* (T.E.B.) This body, chaired by Sidney Webb and including both elected members of the L.C.C. and representatives of the main educational interests, grew out of the *Technical Education Committee* (T.E.C.) which was originally set up to allocate the 'whisky money' or liquor tax which the government had decided should be used to promote technical education. The T.E.B. was the means whereby Sidney Webb won control of secondary, and then elementary, education away from the independent *London School Board* (L.S.B.) and gave invaluable help to the London School of Economics and the reorganized University of London.

*The Trades Union Congress* (T.U.C.) A confederal body of affiliated trade unions which held an annual conference in September. Successive attempts to win a majority for the independent representation of labour culminated in the motion which led to the creation of the Labour Representation Committee in 1900. The Parliamentary Committee of the T.U.C. (P.C.) was the body which traditionally expressed the political interests of organized labour. A stronghold of Liberal supporters, with a scattering of Conservatives, it was consistently hostile to socialist attempts to win trade union support.

For a fuller account of the Webbs' life and political activity, see:

*The Diary of Beatrice Webb*
Volume I 1873–1892 *Glitter Around and Darkness Within*
Volume II 1892–1905 *All the Good Things of Life*
Volume III 1905–1924 *The Power to Alter Things*
Volume IV 1924–1943 *The Wheel of Life*

# The Search for a Creed

## September 1873–December 1882

The diary begins when Beatrice was fifteen. It was her father's custom, whenever he inspected his railway interests in Canada and the United States, to take some of the family with him. On this occasion he took Beatrice, her sister Kate, and Arthur Playne, who was married to her sister Mary.

We left England on the 13 September, two days after Georgina's marriage. I only enjoyed our passage pretty well, the people not being anything particular. . . .

*25 September*
We landed at New York. . . . I was delighted with New York, there is such a cleanliness and elegance about the town, with trees all down its streets and no smoke, and then Central Park is so lovely, beats all our town parks to pieces. . . .

*1 November*
Salt Lake City is not to be compared with any town in England or America; it is so utterly different from anything I have ever seen. The streets are very wide, and on both sides of them flow beautiful streams of crystal water brought from the mountains ten to twenty miles off. It is through this water that Brigham Young and his few followers

transformed this sandy desert into a fertile farm. . . . The houses are for the most part low, built rather in the French style, and of wood white-washed over, with green shutters and doors. This gives the city a fresh innocent appearance, especially as . . . each house has its garden and orchard. The Tabernacle is by far the most important building . . . then come Brigham's two houses, 'The Lion' and 'The Beehive', and a very pretty villa he is building for Mrs Amelia Young, his last and most beloved wife. Most of his other wives either live in one of his two houses, or else have small houses round them in his garden. . . . In the afternoon we went to hear Anson Pratt, an Apostle, and one of the original founders of the Mormon creed. The congregation was mostly of the working men's class. They seemed to be very attentive and earnest in their devotions. I noticed here particularly the dejected look of the women, as if they had continually on their mind their inferiority to their lords and masters. . . .

*Chicago. Arrived 6 November, left 3 December*
Four weeks spent in getting through scarlet fever and measles, accompanied by a severe attack of rheumatism . . . nursed by Kate, spoilt by Papa, feared by everybody except a stranger.

Tuesday – the day before we leave New York! . . . It seems a long time since I passed through the hall at Standish, feverish with excitement and longing to see the world, with sisters kissing us, and giving us a tearful goodbye, and with a file of wedding guests on each side. . . . I wonder if I have altered? And if altered, whether for the better or the worse. I shall find my own level when I get home, that is one good thing in a large family. . . . Hitherto I have lived a great deal too much apart from my sisters, partly from indolence and partly from my unfrank disposition. Dear Kitty, I have got quite fond of her, she has been such a dear, kind devoted sister. I can't imagine why she does not get on better at home. . . .

### ～ 1874 ～

Ludwig Tieck (1773–1853) was a German romantic novelist and poet. Miss Mitchell was a governess in the Potter household. Joaquin Miller (1837–1913), American poet of frontier life, had a great success in England with *Songs of the Sierras* (1871). Sir Francis Galton (1822–1911) founded the doctrine of 'eugenics'.

*18 January. Standish*

I am now busily engaged in studying. I am translating *Faust* and reading a novel of Tieck's. [Goethe's] *Faust* is wonderfully clever and often very beautiful. Putting the introductory piece out of the question, which is fearfully blasphemous, it might almost have been written by a good man, as a satire of the philosophers of the present day. . . . I have left off music almost entirely. I practise exercises and scales for half an hour, half because Mother wishes it, and half because I do not want to leave it off entirely. Drawing is what I should like to excel in, and now in the evenings before I go and read Shakespeare to Miss Mitchell, I make a point of copying one of the patterns in the School of Art book . . .

Maggie and Blanche are very much improved the last four months. Maggie has become much softer and much more charitable towards the world. Blanche is now a practical, kind, cheerful girl, working hard at German and becoming quite useful in household matters. Theresa is as dear a girl as ever . . .

*25 January.* [Standish]

I am not thoroughly contented with the way that I have passed this week. I have been extremely irregular in all my duties. I have not worked as much as I ought to have done, I have been lazy about my religious duties, I have been lazy in getting up; altogether I have been totally devoid of any method. Now I must really try and be more regular, go to bed early, get up early, practise and not be lazy about my drawing, else I shall never get on. I don't think it hurts at all, now and then to read some of St Paul's life, instead of studying German, say twice a week. . . . I am in a complete muddle about politics. I think they are one of those things of which you cannot see the 'right' or the 'wrong'. I can't help having a sort of sympathy with the Radicals, they are so enthusiastic, but I don't think that their time is come yet. They require a much more perfect state of society than that at present. But it is ridiculous for me to waste my time in scribbling about politics, when I am so ignorant on all those questions.

*6 March.* [Standish]

Sometimes I feel as if I must write, as if I must pour my poor crooked thoughts into somebody's heart, even if it be into my own. I am fascinated with that book of Joaquin Miller's . . . It's queer after reading of nothing but the influence of civilization . . . to hear a man boldly stand up and declare that civilization often is degradation, that the savage is often better, wiser and 'nearer God' . . . and that too from an American.

Dear me! my trip to America seems to have opened a new world to me, and into which I seemed to have had a glimpse, a glimpse long enough to make one wish for another.

*13 March.* [Standish]
. . . I am altogether unsettled and discontented. What if my trip to America has made me so? I think that the spoiling I received from Kate and Father has had something to do with it. Then I was *the* important person but now I am the least important of six or seven others, and naturally my interests and my health cannot be considered first, and I am a great fool to think so. . . .

Now if I am a wise girl I shall go away at Easter, especially if F.G. [F. Galton?] comes – ten to one if I see him again I shan't be able to resist making a lot of silly castles in the air about him; and that is what I want to avoid. And now, my dear friend, I want to tell you something seriously, because nobody else will have the chance of telling it you. You are really getting into a nasty and what I should call an indecent way of thinking of men, and love, and unless you take care you will lose all your purity of thought, and become a silly vain self-conscious little goose. . . . I often think you are something like Rosamund in *Middlemarch*. . . . Oh that I had thorough command over you.

*24 March.* [Standish]
What is this feeling between Mother and me? It is a kind of feeling of dislike and distrust which I believe is mutual. And yet it ought not to be! She has always been the kindest and best of mothers, though in her manners she is not over-affectionate. She is such a curious character I can't make her out. She is sometimes such a kind, good affectionate mother, full of wise judgement and affectionate advice, and at other times the spoilt child comes out so strong in her. But whatever she is, that ought not to make the slightest difference to my feeling and behaviour towards her. . . .

*3 August.* [Standish]
It is a long time since I last wrote in my diary. [Since] then the whirl of the London Season [has] included me, though a schoolroom girl, in its rush. I enjoyed it immensely. It is seldom I have had so much pleasure in so small a space of time. . . . The theatricals were the climax of all the pleasure and excitement. The getting up of them was in itself great fun, though I was only a looker on. And then that

tremendous excitement the week before them, the thought of my having to act Kate Hardcastle [in Goldsmith's *She Stoops to Conquer*] before two audiences of two hundred people! But, however, that never came to pass, Maggie got well in time and carried off the laurels. The Dance, oh how I did enjoy that! It was the first dance I had ever been at as a grown-up lady, and I felt considerably satisfied with myself, as I had two or three partners for each dance. Ah vanity! vanity! unfortunately for me my ruling passion. . . .

*27 September.* [Standish]
Here we are alone, Mother, Blanche and myself. Poor Mother, she has two rather broken crutches to lean upon. Blanche is a dear good girl, but she is unpractical and rather inclined to bore you; and as for me, I am, as Mother says, too young, too uneducated and, worst of all, too frivolous to be a companion to her. But, however, I must take courage, and try to change, and above all I must guard against that self-satisfaction which I consider is one of my worst faults. . . . the only way to cure myself of it is to go heart and soul into religion. It is a pity I ever went off the path of orthodox religion, it was a misfortune that I was not brought up to believe that to doubt was a crime. But since I cannot accept the belief of my Church without inward questioning let me try and find a firm belief of my own, and let me act up to it. That is the most important thing. God help me to do it!

*11 December.* [Standish]
. . . Since I have been poorly this autumn I have been thinking of nothing but myself, and I am sure that it is the most unhealthy state of mind. . . . I have never felt so low spirited . . . I have felt for the first time in my life how much unhappiness there is in life. . . . I have come to the conclusion that the only real happiness is devoting oneself to making other people happy. . . .

Beatrice was now sent for a short time to Stirling House, a fashionable Bournemouth school for girls, where she spent much time 'in lonely study and religious meditation'. Here she briefly found 'mental security in traditional Christianity' and decided to be confirmed. When the Potter family was in London for the Season it was Richard Potter's habit to take his daughters to hear the most interesting speakers on Sundays, whether they were in a Catholic church, a Nonconformist chapel or a Positivist meeting-room. 'Except for this eclectic enjoyment of varieties of

metaphysical experience', Beatrice wrote years later, 'the atmosphere of
the home was peculiarly free-thinking'.

## ∼ 1875 ∼

*27 March. Easter Eve.* [Stirling House]
The day before I receive for the first time the holy sacrament. The last
month or two has been a very solemn epoch in my life, and may God
grant that I may never cease remembering the vows which I have made
before God and man, that I intend to become a true Christian, that is,
a true disciple and follower of Jesus Christ, making Him my sole aim in
life. . . . There are many things which remain still mysteries to me, like
the doctrine of the Atonement. The idea that God demanded that some
innocent person should die for the sins of men . . . is repugnant to me.
I firmly believe that Jesus Christ has and will save the world, but not so
particularly by His death, as by His Word . . .

*11 July. Stirling House*
. . . The first weeks here were not very happy ones, though I think I
might have been more contented. But now that I have a room to myself
I do not think there could be a happier and more peaceful life. I have
enjoyed the little reading I have been able to do immensely . . . Though
I have hardly read *Jane Eyre* carefully enough to be able to judge of it
fairly, I must say it impresses me disagreeably. I do not think it a pure
book. The author's conception of love is a feverish, almost lustful passion. Her hero is frankly speaking a bad and immoral man, whom she
endeavours to render attractive by giving him a certain force of character and much physical and intellectual power.

*19 September.* [Standish]
I must confess I am much more sorry to leave Standish than I
expected. . . . But I hope at Bournemouth to grow much stronger . . . I
must try and not become egotistical in my thoughts, for that is a great
danger when one leads a solitary life, for my life with regard to thought
is completely solitary at Stirling House. . . . I must also above everything
endeavour not to think myself superior to the other inmates . . . because
I have been brought out more by circumstances and encouraged to reason
on subjects which other girls have mostly been told to take on faith. . . .
But perhaps the mistake I felt most was joining gossiping conversations.

And [to correct] this is certainly most difficult because it in a great way necessitates keeping myself aloof from the girls' society.

*21 September.* [Stirling House]
The first day at Stirling House. I must confess I feel rather wretched. I feel wrenched from a home which for the first time this year agreed with me and where I have been thoroughly happy, and a family who I was beginning to appreciate and love. . . . The continual din of the pianos, the want of interesting conversation, the absence of small comforts, and the little restraints on one's actions are all circumstances which require to be got accustomed to. On the other hand I have a greater certainty of health and have perfect peace and very little responsibility. These advantages I hardly appreciate, because my family knowing that I should soon leave them made rather a pet of me.

But if I compare my life here for the next thirteen weeks with my life last autumn at Standish I shall see how much happier I am. Then I . . . had all the responsibility of Mother's happiness on my shoulders, at the same time continuing lessons with Mademoiselle with whom I did not agree. I shall never forget the agony I suffered; the dreadful feeling of unfitness and incompetency for the work which was forced upon me . . . that period between Father's return and going to Bournemouth was a black blank. No health, no God, no love, nothing but moping, wounded vanity, desperation. . . .

*4 October.* [Stirling House?]
Lied again today. I will make a practice of noting these lies, by putting a cross for every one to the day of the month. I am quite convinced that it is a most disagreeable habit.

There are, in fact, no 'lie' crosses in the succeeding entries.

*9 December.* [Stirling House]
The reason why I tell so many stories is pride and vanity. It is very often from the wish that people may think me or my people better in one way or another that I exaggerate so fearfully. . . .

*17 December.* [Stirling House]
I hope when I return home I shall not lose the little earnestness I have gained; that I shall be diligent in the study of religion. I do not want to 'come out', and I hope I shall have enough determination and firmness

to carry my point. The family does not really want another come-out member; they are almost too many as it is. . . .

## ∽ 1876 ∽

Beatrice decided, after all, to 'come out' that summer. 'I joined my sisters in the customary pursuits of girls of our class,' she wrote in *My Apprenticeship* fifty years later, 'riding, dancing, flirting and dressing-up, an existence without settled occupation or personal responsibility, having for its end nothing more remote than elaborately expensive opportunities for getting married.' With this round of 'restless and futile activities', she lost her feeble hold on orthodox Christianity. Her intellectual curiosity led her to study the religions of the Far East and the 'religion of science'.

*16 August.* [Standish?]
. . . I see now that the year I spent at Bournemouth I was vainly trying to smother my instinct of truth in clinging to the old faith. And now that I have shaken off the chains of the beautiful old faith, shall I rise to something higher or shall I stare about me like a newly liberated slave, unable to decide which way to go, and perhaps the worse for being freed from the service of a kind of master? Do I look on death and trouble with less calmness than I used?

## ∽ 1877 ∽

Herbert Spencer (1820–1903), the social philosopher, a friend of Beatrice's father, became her mentor.

*19 March.* [Standish]
As for my religious opinions they are as Mr Spencer's *Social Statics* left them. I am afraid I may say that I have no religion whatever, for I have not yet grasped the religion of science. Of one thing I am quite certain, that no character is perfect without religion.

*31 March.* [Standish?]
. . . I at present believe (by no means without inward fear at my audacity) that Christianity is in no way superior in kind, though in degree,

to the other great religions . . . That the idea of working out your own salvation, of doing good and believing blindly in order to arrive at eternal bliss is, through its intense selfishness, an immoral doctrine. . . . what seems to me clear is that we are at a very early period of man's existence and that we have only just arrived at the true basis of knowledge . . .

*15 December.* [Standish]

Mr Spencer's *First Principles* has had certainly a very great influence on my feelings and thoughts. It has made me feel so happy and contented. . . . One has always feared that when the orthodox religion vanished, no beauty, no mystery would be left . . . but instead of that each new discovery of science will increase our wonder at the Great Unknown and our appreciation of the Great Truth.

⁓ 1878 ⁓

*8 March.* [Standish]

The religion of science has its dark side. It is bleak and dreary in sorrow and ill-health. And to those whose lives are one continual suffering it has but one word to say – suicide. If you cannot bear it any longer, and if no ties of duty turn you from extinguishing that little flame of your existence, depart in peace, cease to exist. It is a dreadful thought. It can never be the religion of a 'suffering humanity'. The time may come, and I believe will come, when human life will be sufficiently happy and full to be unselfish. But there are long ages yet to be passed, and generations of men will still cry in their misery for another life to compensate for their life-long sorrow and suffering.

In June, Beatrice went with Mary and Arthur Playne and their adopted daughter Polly on an extended tour of Germany and Hungary. Carrie Darling was the governess for the Playne children and the first woman outside her family with whom Beatrice formed a friendship.

*15 June.* [Ems?]

Our life here is a modest one, but with the German lessons as a *raison d'être* pleasant, if one only had tolerable health. The people we know at present are decidedly dull; I don't know how the Americans will turn out. Mr Barclay has brought a certain amount of fun into the *ménage*. Yesterday evening we spent at Dr Geiser's drinking and smoking and talking and laughing in a very rowdy way. I had got up a mock flirtation with Mr Barclay, which Mary thought proper to reprove, in not the gentlest of language. However, she was right; one can't be too careful in this comical existence where half of one's time must be spent in considering and working for the good opinion of the little world mannikins that surround us. Thank Heavens one has books – a society whose good opinion you need never consult, and which is always there and infinitely varied. . . .

*3 July. Marienburg* [North Holland]
. . . I think on the whole at present I have settled that I am sorry to miss the Season. That the pleasure of seeing new countries does not compensate for the intimate companionship of one's family and the society of London. On the other hand, one must remember that, though I feel inclined for gaiety now and sorry on the whole to have missed it, yet it would most probably have knocked me up. . . .

*15 July.* [Boppard, on the Rhine]
The last two or three days have been very amusing. We have made friends with all the inhabitants. It has been an odd experience, chumming with a set of people from all nations and classes. They certainly have very much better manners and understand sociability much better than the English. There is a nice feeling of unexclusiveness and general goodwill. . . .

Mary and I are very good friends now that I let her lead the conversation and follow. In order to get on with her you must be content to talk of nothing but personalities, particularly about those individuals who are nearest to her. We have really led such different lives, have lived in such a completely different atmosphere, that it is impossible for us to talk on any serious subject. When I attempted to do it, we disagreed, and disagreed without understanding each other. Mary's great fault is jealousy and vanity. She has a grudge against 'intellectual people' and 'learning' because she feels that she is 'inferior' or, rather, that they think her inferior. She has the same grudge against the family, particularly Mother. In spite of that, she is a charming woman, and most kind and considerate. She is also a clever, shrewd woman. Had she been led by a fine strong character and brain instead of leading a weak one, she would probably have lost that self-complacent jealousy which prevents her from taking a true and just view of the people surrounding her.

*9 November.* [Wiesbaden]
Our party is broken up. Arthur and Mary left this morning and, as is usual where the feeling has not been quite what it should be, when one has parted one begins to regret not having made more of the opportunities for friendship. . . . On the whole, this trip to Germany was a mistake, that is to say from a worldly point of view – but still the last two months I have enjoyed, and I was wise to stay once I had missed the London Season. At any rate I can read German quite easily.

Poor Arthur has been miserable and Mary has not enjoyed herself nearly as much as she expected. How she can be happy with such an inferior man I cannot understand. Still, he is a most affectionate devoted husband and I suppose love covers a multitude of sins. . . . Miss Darling is a dear little woman, a person it is impossible not to be intimate with. . . .

> Rusland Hall, in Cumberland, was taken for a time as a holiday home convenient to Barrow-in-Furness where there was a branch of the timber firm which was the foundation of Richard Potter's fortune. Beatrice was much affected by Goethe's autobiographical novel *Wilhelm Meister.* Her interest in drawing and watercolour led her to a study of John Ruskin.

*30 March. Rusland Hall*
. . . The first two months after my return I was altogether wrong – and the quiet and perfectly lonely life here was not calculated to shake me right again. The old story of anaemia; want of employment, which makes life almost torture, a silent misery, all the more painful because apparently causeless. But the last month has been spent very happily with my dear Goethe and my dearest old Father in quiet reading and long rambling walks in this lovely country. I feel I am not appreciating this time of perfect freedom and without care. . . . I shall look back on these days, in a happy home, with envy and regret that I had not been more content to enjoy the simple pleasures of living. . . .

*14 December. Rusland*
This autumn has been a very happy one for me. And the secret of my happiness has been plenty of occupation of a varied description. . . . I do believe, independently of being in better health, I have started on a brighter path of existence . . . I have gained immensely by taking up drawing and music with a spirit of love instead of with a spirit of jealous ambition; and this I owe to Ruskin and to Goethe. . . .

Some parts of this autumn have been very sweet. We three sisters have seen much of each other, and Maggie and I particularly have had a perfect communion of pursuits and ideas. We had a delightful little trip among our sublime little hills, and read through the first two volumes of *Modern Painters* together, and this little experience has inspired us with a wish to go [on] sketching and reading tours together, should we remain lonely spinsters. . . .

One thing is clear. Goethe wishes to impress on his reader the advantage of liberty, of unrestrained liberty in thought and deed. . . . it is better to develop the whole of your nature, looking upwards to a noble ideal, and allowing perhaps some ugly weeds to grow, than to repress the good with the bad. . . . you should seek a really congenial career, as a life occupation, and then you should keep your heart and mind open to the outer world. . . . Until you have found this career you should wander up and down regarding no place as too low and dirty, no society too licentious or too frivolous – perhaps in the lowest society you may light on some human soul who will impart to you some vital truth. . . .

*20 September.* [Standish?]
The London Season passed with a happy result, and Theresa and I are left to divide the honours of the Potter sisterhood! . . .

> In October, after the marriage of her sister Margaret to Henry Hobhouse, Beatrice embarked on a six-month trip to Italy. An elderly couple, the Cobbs, and a Mr Watson were travelling companions for the first part of the journey. She then met Theresa and the Hobhouses, who were honeymooning in Italy. During the winter, Beatrice was ill with congestion of the lungs. She joined her parents on the Riviera in the spring.

*24 October.* [Florence?]
A glimpse of Paris – a perfect modern city. . . . The morning we spent in Notre-Dame. It a little disappointed me. The building is beautiful, but after the romantic vision I had formed of it, from Victor Hugo's description, it seemed more like other cathedrals, and not so devotional in its feeling as some. . . . I was struck very much by Paris itself with its peculiar and unique charm. So much that one had felt about the French character was here pictured. . . .

I can't help smiling at finding myself settled down with this very elderly trio, with none of whom have I had the slightest previous connection. They are none of them persons to whom I should naturally have taken. They are exceedingly kind, and I think they like me, which is pleasant, but I do not feel as if I were one of them.

That feeling has disappeared. One cannot be in the constant companionship of kindly people, with sincere and warm-hearted natures, without a tie springing up between you and them. . . .

*7 November.* [Rome]
The journey to Rome was not pleasant for me nor the first few days there, but the idea of being actually in the Eternal City sustained me through the worst of it. On Sunday we had a delicious drive out on the Campagna. The view looking towards the Alban Hills, with the broken line of aqueduct arches and stone pines, was very lovely. There was a sweet, soft feeling in the air, the birds were singing, butterflies flying, and flowers blooming. Yet we were surrounded by the tombs of Roman, Jew and Christian. In their great city, crowded with the memories and memorials of bygone worlds, the great mystery of the why and the wherefore seems ever more pressing. . . .

*Sunday, 14 November* [Rome]
I cannot write down what I felt on this Sunday morning watching the silent mass in St Peter's. Perhaps there was a good deal of mere emotion in it but it made me look back with regret on those days when I could pray in all sincerity of spirit to my Father in Heaven. . . . My intellectual or logical faculty drives me to the conclusion that, outside the knowledges of the relative or phenomenal, I know nothing except perhaps that there must be an absolute, a something which is unknowable. But whether the very fact that it is unknowable does not prevent me from considering it . . . is a question which Mr Spencer's logic has not set at rest. My reason forces me to a purely negative conclusion, but I see very darkly before me and feel that my logical faculty is very insufficient to the task I set it. Nor do I feel that its present decision is a final one. But I possess another faculty, the emotional, which is the dominant spirit in all my better and nobler moments. This spirit unceasingly insists that there is something above and around us which is worthy of absolute devotion and devout worship. . . . Could not the agnostic, if he felt that his nature was not sufficiently developed to live without an emotional religion, could he not renounce his freedom to reason on that one subject. . . .

*21 November.* [Rome?]
Our party has broken up and the first chapter of my Italian trip is

finished! It seems but yesterday since we four were feeling miserable together in that very stuffy hotel at Dover. . . . With Mr Cobb I soon became fast friends. It is always so much easier to get on with men; they seldom criticize a girl who is willing to make herself pleasant to them. And then their wider knowledge of human nature makes them more interesting as companions, and enables one to be freer in one's conversation with them. With a highly respectable matron I always feel rather conciliatory and frightened lest I should let loose any of my bohemian sentiments. That feeling of constraint on my part soon passed away with Mrs Cobb when I felt that she was certain that I was not insincere. . . . One can never have too many true friends in one's own class, even if they are not so attractive or as well bred, as bohemian friends.

*28 November.* [Florence]
Settled with Theresa in this very airy house, looking over the golden and brown-tiled roofs of Florence. . . . Henry and Margaret are here, silently happy. One would hardly know her to be the same woman as the discontented, original, interesting young person who used to be so fascinating to me. As these books are more or less an autobiography I ought to have mentioned the great influence she has had on my life, for good chiefly, but also for evil. With a powerful nature like hers, her influence on a weaker one was complete, even when one secretly knew that she was mistaken. But on the whole, her principles of life were strong and wise, and she had a vigorous and straight intellect. Now she has found in Henry Hobhouse just the man to complete her, a man utterly without worldliness or power to compromise with evil. . . .

*19 December.* [Florence]
The time has flown while we have been at Florence. I have hardly enjoyed it as much as I ought to have done; my health has been bad, and I have not been able to give the enthusiasm and time to the glorious works of art that I should if I had been quite up to the mark. . . . This is the close of the second chapter of my Italian trip. . . . Rome again is before me, with its entangled net of interests and associations.

~ 1881 ~

Margaret Hobhouse was pregnant with her son Stephen.

*22 January.* [Rome]

... the Roman climate is detestable, varying daily, almost hourly, between depressing heat and intense cold. Xmas week, with all the museums closed and those dismal farces of church services, does not leave a happy impression, especially as Maggie was seedy and miserable, the natural result of the conditions of married existence. It was painful to see her so poorly, and now since her marriage, since the necessary break in our absolute intimacy it is rather painful to me to be with her. She was such a complete companion to me, and as such she is not to be replaced. ...

*2 February.* [Rome]

Alas, we must away. This wretched climate has undone me, and the only thing is flight. Poor Theresa who has been a most devoted nurse is torn away from unfinished sightseeing. ... I feel quite remorseful for being such an unlucky travelling companion. The time for me, chiefly spent in the queer-shaped room, has been by no means without its charm. There have been hours of depression and many of physical discomfort, but I have never had that utter, hopeless melancholy, which has come upon me when ill at home. Whether this is due to the difference of lung and liver complaints, or whether the happy change comes from a new faith that has crept into my heart I cannot tell. Certain it is, that life seems nobler and more worth living, even if one rests incapable of much action. It is impossible for a woman to live in agnosticism. That is a creed which is only the product of one side of our nature, the purely rational, and ought we persistently to refuse authority to that other faculty which George Eliot calls the emotive thought? ...

There was another mind that I really became better acquainted with through this illness – George Eliot's. Perhaps it was her noble influence which made me feel happier and more contented. In her stories of life, she always takes the deep earnest view. ... I know no author who is so sad and so uncynical – consequently her sadness is ennobling and not discouraging. ... *Daniel Deronda* interested me deeply, because in it she seems to express her last thoughts, the conclusions of her experience of life. One sees from it the preference she gives to emotive over purely rational thought, and also her conception of the ideal human being. ...

*20 March.* [Rome]

... I have given myself up to Balzac for the last five weeks, which has perhaps not contributed to my happiness. ... He is an utter cynic and complete disbeliever in the progress of human nature. . . . I have never read such disgustingly true analysis of mean, base thought and feeling. Perhaps his most revolting type is the *célibataire* . . . especially women. Her only nobility is in self-immolation to her lover and child – if these two feelings are undeveloped there is no chance for her. And in his analysis of these two feelings, it is purely the instinctive and not the spiritual love that he describes. . . . French society, if Balzac is as true a portrait painter as one would judge from the manner of the pictures, must be a sink of impurity and dirt. . . .

*28 April.* [San Remo]
Father arrived at San Remo and found us in not a very happy condition. . . . It has been sadly disappointing, this finale of 'our trip in Italy', begun with so much enthusiasm and promise of interest and pleasure, and ending in ill-health and self-disgust, with increased estrangement between me and Mother. Too utterly discouraged to think with any hopefulness of the future – too pluckless to take up any pursuit – and yet suffering acutely from absence of any occupation and from irritating restlessness. However, all things must end, and misery after a certain time consumes itself or its subject.

Theresa is a sweet girl . . . For Rosy, in spite (perhaps because) of her nobility of character, I see rocks ahead if she does not quickly leave her state of spinsterhood on emerging from the schoolroom. Dearest old Father – it adds to one's self-disgust, the thought that some day one will regret bitterly having added to his worries. I write this, Friday evening, our last day in Italy after a fortnight spent at this most enchantingly lovely place – Ah me! . . .

*14 May. Standish*
The English country looks perfectly enchanting clothed in its spring loveliness. No foreign land, however exquisite it may be, can have the same power of calling out the sympathy and affection of the beholder as the native country with its manifold associations of happiness and struggles which sum up one's past existence. So entirely are we creatures of ideas and not of the senses.

All those miserable egotistical feelings are for the time fled, and, though from lack of health a not altogether pleasant prospect is before me, still I am determined to set again cheerfully to work . . . With this immense amount of leisure, with this perfect comfort, one ought to add to one's power of usefulness . . . The course of reading I propose for myself this autumn is English history and literature, with Shakespeare as the aim and centre. . . . Not a moment of my time, except what is required for positive rest, shall be unemployed . . . No more foolish trifling with health, but a steady perseverance in the path of duty – alas! the only straight way left to us poor children of the nineteenth century.

*12 June.* [Standish?]
Quite recovered from the extraordinary state of mind into which I had fallen. A really pleasant four weeks at Standish and a complete re-establishment of pleasant relationship to Mother.

Theresa Potter married Alfred Cripps in the summer of 1881.

*8 September. Rusland*
The last of the sisterhood, at least of those of my generation, pledged herself!

Dear Theresa . . . never meant to live alone, or without devotion and love given and returned. Still it is sad this last final break-up of the home life with all its ups and downs . . . Now I am left alone, with this 'problematical' younger sister. Shall I rise equal to the occasion, and casting aside all self-consciousness and miserable morbidness, make the best of the materials at hand for the good of all? As Mary says, it is on these occasions that the true stuff of a character is tested, whether it is one which moulds or is moulded by circumstances.

*12 September.* [Rusland]
Mr Spencer's visits always interest me, and leave me with new ideas and the clearing up of old ones. He leaves me too with a due realization of the poverty of my intellect . . . One thing seems clear to me both from my own experience and from Mr Spencer's theoretical demonstration, that there is a fatal mistake being made in the 'improved education of women', in that it is a purely intellectual one, and restricted even in its intellectuality in as much as it neglects one great faculty of the intellect, the observation.

Also there seems to me little doubt but that women should have a real knowledge of the different branches of household work, at least for them to understand the difference between bad and good work, that they should be taught to apply *method* to the practical duties of life and not allowed to be content with covering the very slight demands made by society on their usefulness. But then comes the personal question – how am I to remedy this in myself, I who fully recognize the evil? I dislike all mechanical work and have an instinctive feeling that it is a waste of time. . . .

These twenty-four years of my life now are nearly past and gone. I know now pretty clearly what I ought to *do* (though less than ever what I ought to think) and yet I cannot maintain my reason as the ruler of my nature, but am still constantly enslaved by instinct and impulse. . . .

## ∽ 1882 ∽

Mary Booth (1847–1939) was a first cousin. Her mother was a sister of Richard Potter, and her father a younger brother of the historian Thomas Babington Macaulay. Her husband, Charles Booth (1840–1916), did well in the shipping business at Liverpool before a crisis in physical and mental health made him turn away from business and use his capital to underwrite a seventeen-volume study of *The Life and Labour of the People in London*.

*9 February.* [London]
The last six weeks spent in London with friends and sisters. The Booths' house dark, dull and stuffy and somewhat smelly, but the inmates exceedingly charming and lovable. Mary really a remarkable woman, with an unusual power of expression, and a well-trained and cultivated mind. She makes one feel, in spite of her appreciative and almost flattering attitude, a 'very ignoramus'. To me there is a slight harshness in her literary judgements; they are too correct, too resting on authority and not the result of original thought. Perhaps it is this very orderliness of mind and deference to authority which makes her so attractive as a woman; and to this culture and polish of intellect add a deep vein of emotion, of almost passionate feeling.

Charlie Booth has a stronger and clearer reason, with a singular absence of bias and prejudice. It is difficult to discover the presence of any vice or even weakness in him. Conscience, reason, and dutiful affection, are his great qualities; what other characteristics he has are not to be observed by the ordinary friend. But he interests me as a man who has his nature completely under control, who has passed through a period of terrible illness and weakness, and who has risen out of it, uncynical, vigorous and energetic in mind and without egotism. Many delightful conversations I had with these two charming cousins, generally acting as a listening third to their discussions. . . .

*13 February.* [Standish]

My stay with the Hobhouses was not a very fortunate one. . . . The old intimacy with Maggie is quite broken . . . I shall never be really friends with Henry. He has not the gift of drawing out what is best in you, nor does he understand anyone's thoughts but his own. And this deficiency in him is at present acting like a wet blanket on Maggie's intellect. His own inferiority makes him disapprovingly suspicious of her great freedom, originality and variety of thought. His mind is better trained and better stocked than hers; this superiority he is conscious of, and she assents to it, but her greater superiority is not yet acknowledged by either. . . . By the time I left London I was rather weary of conversation and had a distaste for second-rate 'interesting people'. . . .

> Lawrencina Potter died unexpectedly on 13 April from pleurisy and kidney failure. Margaret Harkness (1854–1923) was Beatrice's second cousin. A socialist and feminist, she wrote novels and articles under the pseudonym 'John Law'. She had some training as a nurse and was called when Beatrice's mother was brought from The Argoed, the Potter holiday home in the Wye Valley, to die at Standish.

[Undated note.] *Mother's Last Illness*

On Thursday, 6 April, Kate received a telegram from Father asking her to meet them at Gloucester and if they were not there to go on to Monmouth. When she had left I had a glorious walk through the young larch and round by the park, standing for some time under those beeches with that magnificent stretch of sky, river, hill and valley. All seemed very bright and hopeful. I had been very happy at home these last weeks. Mother had been very affectionate and we had had much intimate conversation and we were both full of plans for the London Season. I felt we were on the verge of a true and complete intimacy – perhaps it would never have come – we were both proud.

Soon after I returned, the carriage drove up and Mother was helped out by Father, Kate and I. She looked in pain, but neither Kate nor I thought much of it. We got her to bed and that night I slept with her. She seemed to have a fairly good night, but in the morning the pain returned, Dr Walters was sent for, and I saw him with her. There was then no question of danger. He said it was a rheumatic affliction, sent her some mixture and promised to return in the evening. But by the afternoon Mother had become very anxious and restless and so sent for Dr Washbourne who arrived before Dr Walters. After their consultation they injected morphia to alleviate the pain, and decided that Dr Walters should give her an injection to relieve if possible the bowels, which were very much distended with wind and caused her what I fear now was great agony. Kate remained with her until five. The injection did not act. After I came to her she seemed quieter. That morning about 11 o'clock she told me she thought she was mortally ill, begged me to write down instructions about jewellery, hoped that we should all of us take care of Father and attend to all his little comforts, look after the interests of Blanche and Rosy and not entirely desert her relations. I was very much affected, but was too anxious not to appear so, and too certain that her fear was a delusion to encourage her to tell me more; perhaps now I regret it. One thing I proposed, as I lay by her side and petted her, that we should give Carrie some little thing; she was pleased at that. A trained nurse had been recommended by Dr Washbourne and we decided that she should stay the night with her (Saturday). I slept in the dressing-room, getting up at intervals to see Dr Walters and hear his report. She did not like the nurse; she was a roughish woman. I regretted afterwards I allowed her to be with Mother, but I did it for the best. The whole of the next morning Kate stayed with her – in the afternoon we sent for Maggie Harkness. Theresa and Alfred had come on the Saturday and Mary drove over and stayed the night.

After that afternoon there seemed to be no division of day and night. It was one continual strain to think and act. I was continually with Mother until Wednesday at 3 o'clock in the morning, when I left her for good, and only returned twice again for two short moments to give her the last farewell kiss and to take poor little weeping Rosy to her deathbed. During the whole time I nursed her she was always tender and loving and grateful. It was Tuesday at two o'clock, when I returned to her after 24 hours' rest from nursing, that I first lost hope and began to realize that I was in the presence of coming death. All that afternoon I sat and watched her; she was lying in a half-conscious state, muttering and thinking (as she said) incoherently. She picked and clutched nervously at the bed-clothes – she seemed in no pain, and was perfectly willing to take and do everything ordered by the doctors. I asked her, towards supper time, whether she would like anyone besides the new nurse from London to stay with her through the night. She asked me to stay with her. The last words she spoke to me, about 11 o'clock that Tuesday night, were to beg me to ask Dr Washbourne to see her first, before she saw Dr Walters – and to tell him that if she took more food she would die of inflammation of the bowels. I do not think that she despaired of her life. When I returned to her after Dr Washbourne had left she was under morphia and appeared to me quieter. The nurse from London was most successful with her and Mother took to her from the first. About 3.30 I went to bed; the next morning at seven I saw Dr Walters. She was worse; they had thought her dying in the early morning.

Wednesday was the blackest day. None of us went in to her. Maggie Harkness and the nurse stayed with her. There was really no hope, but it was thought wiser to avoid exciting her in any way. That afternoon and evening brought all the sisters. On Thursday morning about four o'clock we were called up and spent a miserable hour waiting for death. There was a slight improvement towards six; she asked for food. She lasted until a quarter to twelve; her spirit passed away without struggle and without pain after half an hour of quiet sleep.

Maggie was with her for those last six hours and told me afterwards that Mother had asked after little Stephen [Maggie's son] and Hadspen [the Hobhouse estate] and old Mrs Hobhouse. Poor girl, she was terribly grieved and felt the awfulness of death tragically. Once again we were very perfectly intimate and in the middle of the night of Friday she told me much about her married life and all its troubles.

Sunday at Longfords was spent in sleep and walking in those lovely woods – body and soul were weary. The next day the house was full of half-intimate relations; there was little time for thought.

*Sunday, 23 April.* [Standish]
We all joined with Father in that beautiful communion service. Now that I have experienced what the death of a dear one is, and have watched it and waited for it, a deep yearning arises for some religion by which to console grief and stimulate action. I have, if anything, less faith in the possibility of another life. As I looked at our mother dying, I *felt* it was a final dissolution of body and soul, an end of that personality which we call the spirit. This was an instinctive conviction; on this great question we cannot reason. But though my disbelief in what we call immortality was strengthened, a new and wondrous faith has arisen within me – a faith in goodness, in God. I must pray, I do pray and I feel better for it, and more able to put aside all compromise with worldliness and to devote myself with single-heartedness to my duty. . . . In this spirit I took the holy communion, for the first time for six years, years of more or less dreary materialism. Rationally I am still an agnostic, but I know not where my religious feeling will lead me, whether I may not be forced to acknowledge its supremacy over my whole nature. . . .

My duty now lies clearly before me – to Father and Rosy first, secondly to the home as a centre for the whole family.

Rosy has picked up wonderfully with complete rest to her intellect and yet with a fully occupied day and more responsibility and call on her affections. She has the making of a fine woman if we can add to her great nobility, joyousness of character and briskness of action and thought.

On 13 June, in a few hastily scribbled and roughly corrected lines, Beatrice wrote the first of two informal wills she included in her diary. 'In case of my death', she wrote, 'my little property' was to go to her nephew Alfred Standish Cripps, Blanche's son born in 1881. She wanted each of her sisters to have an item of jewellery; and she hoped that her father would make a small settlement 'on my only two great friends', Carrie Darling and Margaret Harkness. On 26 September she added a codicil, which began by asking her father to burn the diary-books when he had read them, and ended by asking him to send them to Carrie Darling. 'I don't want any of the *sisters* to see them.' Her distressed state of mind was epitomized in one sentence. 'If I do die I hope no one will regret it for me', she wrote, 'as I shall not regret it myself.'

Herbert Spencer had left Beatrice a copy of a letter in which he outlined his doctrine of evolution. Spencer's *First Principles* was published in 1862.

### 13 *August*. [London]

Alfred [Cripps] and I had a long discussion over Mr Spencer's résumé of his philosophy, resulting in my taking it up to bed and spending a couple of hours over it, eventually rushing downstairs and plunging into *First Principles*, a plunge producing such agreeable sensations that I have since continued the practice every morning before breakfast.

So far I seem to be able to work my brain with greater ease than hitherto, and so long as I do not neglect the duties nearest to me, I think I may indulge in dreams of attainment . . . Now I have within me a definite ambition, perhaps a foolish and vain one. Still, it has taken possession of me and filled a vacancy with – wind? Anyhow, I know more decidedly than ever what materials and what tools I want – the mastery of some sympathetic philosophy to bind together isolated groups of ideas and experiences, experiences of human nature by careful observation and experiment, and certain necessary tools such as a fair knowledge of numbers and their relation, and some power of correct expression. I feel sadly the lack of a good groundwork. . . .

Theresa gave birth to a son, Alfred Henry Seddon, in August.

*27 August.* [London]
This time last year I had recognized the inevitable; and now poor
Theresa is suffering the inevitable.

A woman gives much when she consents to become mother and wife.
I put the mother first because it is *the* relationship which absorbs her life,
for which she suffers and should be loved. Poor little Mother. Looking
back I see how bitterly she must have felt our want of affection and sympathy and for that I feel remorse. . . . I never knew how much she had
done for me, how many of my best habits I had taken from her, how
strong would be the impress of her personality, when the pressure had
gone, a pressure wholesome and in the right direction, but applied
without tact. . . .

Poor little Mother! Her death was so sad – so inexpressively sad in its
isolation. Is all death like that? Can we not in that supreme moment
bind the past with the future . . . and our last mortal act be one of
prayer and blessing? And who knows that Mother did not bless us with
her last breath and that we, that I, am not now feeling the working of
that blessing within me. It is strange, how I now feel the presence of her
influence and think of her as an absent friend who does sympathize
with my new life, but cannot tell it me. I never asked for her sympathy
when she lived, but now she, through the medium of my memory, gives
it me. When I work, with many odds against me, for a far distant and
perhaps unattainable end, I think of her and her intellectual strivings,
which we were too ready to call useless, and yet will be the originating
impulse of all my ambition, urging me onward towards something
better in action or thought. When I feel discouraged and hopeless,
when I feel that my feeble efforts to acquire are like a blind grasping in
space for the stars, the vision of her will arise persistent always in action
and in desire. Persevere.

And I *will persevere* . . . the struggle is for good (God help me) and for
truth, and the direction right. Why I have written this I know not. This
morning I took the sacrament, and again solemnly vowed 'to endeavour
to lead a new life, following the commandment of God and walking
henceforth in His holy ways'. I get so much comfort, help and peace
from this service. How strange it is. . . .

*31 August.* [London?]
A day of terrible anxiety. Theresa lying between life and death. Poor Alfred

bearing up with grand courage. How deeply illness and death impresses on one that life in itself is worthless; only what it achieves is enduring. . . .

*10 September.* [Standish]
That evening I walked through the fields, after a day spent with Arthur [Playne] at The Argoed. There was a glorious sunset. Masses of cloud, wonderful in colour and form, more solemn than lovely, swept across the sky, here towards the south, built up in ominous layers of dark blue and grey, tossing wildly waves of fiery gold to meet the glory of the west. . . . I paused, from above seemed to come some inspiration, I bowed my head. . . . Strange these feelings are, of an outward presence, this sense of downcoming help, this real answer to prayer. Where does this 'peace' come from, which was absent before, this rest in endeavour, this hope in despair? . . .

*20 September.* [Hadspen]
Three or four days spent with Henry and Margaret. I was wrong in my estimate of Henry. He has a sweet and gentle nature, great refinement of feeling and great persistency in it. Lives in a world of ideas, chosen by his moral sense. . . . Self-culture is a duty to him and has been all through his scholar's life. No desire to see things as they are, but a will to see them as he thinks they should be. . . . from all one hears he has good abilities and better industry but no original thought and great intellectual nervousness. . . .

Margaret is the same strong genuine woman. A fine intellect and robust imagination, warped by want of faith. . . . This cynicism arose partly from a breadth of intellectual vision, and partly from a narrowness of moral nature . . . All good impulses, apart from those generated by instinct, were to her mind foolish and unnecessary. She never made a *friend*, except within her own family. 'I do not care to give or to receive.' This was her feeling towards the world. . . . There is no sacrifice Margaret would not make for her husband and children – no effort she would grudge for her family; their relative rights would be determined by the degree of blood relationship. 'The Family' is to her the only 'holy thing'; all individual and all social life should be based on it. . . .

*22 September.* [Standish]
The individual here to be described [Alfred Cripps] is a short man with broad shoulders, clear-cut features and imposing chin. His first nickname in our family was 'Chin Chin', afterwards increased in dignity and

length to [Thomas] Carlyle's epithet for [Francis, Lord] Jeffrey, 'The Little Jewel of an Advocate'.

You are struck at first sight by the self-complacency of his expression . . . but with increasing intimacy the careful observer will trace it to the simple amiability of his disposition, to the absence of struggle in his nature and no doubt partly to a very justifiable satisfaction at his own success in life. . . . Intellectually he is the genius of common sense. . . . He *is* in most things, and believes himself to be in all, reasonable. In the many talks I had with him I always stumbled on two persistent ideas – a practical belief in the wisdom of sincerity and an equally practical hatred of control. . . . His principal intellectual interest is the constitution of society and his ambition the government of men. . . .

*15 October. Rusland*
Rather a weary fortnight spent in entertaining. . . . Hobhouses, Leonard and Kate, and large party of unattractive Americans. Leonard Courtney is no doubt an excellent and an able man, but not companionable to an ignorant young woman. His conversation bores me. It is made up of a certain measure of facts, given out in an assertive tone, and quotations from English poets, which from his ugly pronunciation are difficult to catch. He never argues (with his inferiors, i.e. with us) but denies and quotes. . . . As Father says, 'Politics are with him a trade secret'. . . . However, I will get to know him. His evident contempt for my 'scattered' ideas will be valuable – and who knows how much the evident contempt has to do with my dislike? . . . With Maggie I had many delightfully doleful talks, reminding me of old times (only three years ago) when we wandered over moor and moss, gossiped cynically and talked tragically, and enjoyed and suffered *Weltschmertz*. . . .

*4 November.* [Rusland]
Two or three weeks passed in the mental contortions consequent on attempting mathematics . . . The geometrical side is the most pleasing – it is always easier to prove the existence of something which you *see* exists. . . . How subjective women are. Does it belong to their education or their nature? Certainly if psychology is to be advanced by self-analysis, women will be the great psychologists of the future. A perfectly frank account of the inner workings of our brain would be interesting . . . there is much that goes on within one, which one, as a prudent mistress winks at and overlooks. . . .

*25 November.* [Rusland]

. . . What a blessing I can write in this little book without fearing that anyone will ever read and ridicule the nonsense and half-sense I scribble. That has been the attraction of a 'diary-book' to me . . . sometimes this is a necessary safety-valve to save one from that most painful operation, watching one's most cherished chicks hatched by unwearied persever-ance coolly trodden underfoot. Now my honest desire is to appear commonplace and sensible, so that none of my dear kind family will think it necessary to remark to themselves or to me that I am otherwise than ordinary; to be on the right side of ordinary is the perfection of prudence in a young woman, and will save her from much heartburning and mortification of spirit. . . .

*3 December.* [Rusland?]

. . . looking back on the past month I see much unwholesomeness. That bad old habit which as a child took such possession of me, build-ing castles in the air, so nourishing to vanity, has again cropped up. . . . most of these castles are essentially vulgar in their nature . . . No doubt their somewhat sudden reappearance is due to the sterility of my present intellectual life, fatiguing and straining as it is to the mind and yet absolutely barren of ideas.

Again I am not at rest with my own conscience. I know I might have done better by Rosy and made this autumn more healthful to her. My difficulty lies in her imitativeness. She will learn only by example, and yet it is well nigh impossible for me to live as she ought to live. I cannot order my diet either physical or mental to suit her constitution. I acknowledge that I am not equal to the position of mother to her, per-haps I confess, too, that my effort is rather a half-hearted one – that I am not willing to sacrifice my own interests to hers. . . . And alongside of this inner conflict is a recognition that (probably owing to this egotism) I am losing ground in the affections of my sisters. Of course there will be unavoidable criticism, and some of it will be unjustified. It is no use being over-sensitive, but if one wishes to feel philosophically towards it, one must be honestly convinced of the rightness and thoroughness of one's own intentions.

# A Multiple Personality

## January 1883–December 1885

*2 January. Rusland Hall*

. . . Mother's death opened a new world to me in thought and action. . . .
A position of responsibility was forced upon me and I accepted it
heartily and threw myself into active work. Two months at Standish were
spent in clearing the ground and establishing myself as mistress. I
thought of little but my duties and prayed earnestly that I might fulfil
them. . . . Driving through the streets of London on my way from
Paddington I had that curious 'sensation' of power which I suppose
comes to most people who have lived within themselves, who have
seldom had their self-estimate righted by competition with others. Every
face in the crowded streets seemed ready to tell me its secret history, if
only I would watch closely enough. . . . In most of us there is a desire to
express our thought, feelings or impressions. Women generally choose
music or drawing, but there is really no more pretension in writing, so
long as one does not humbug oneself as to the value of the stuff
written. . . .

*1 February.* [Standish]

Again at this old (I cannot say dear old) place where I have droned out
so many years of existence, twenty-five. Much the same surroundings as
last year, but one gone for ever and I in her place, at least not in the
hearts of those who loved her – (I was not made to be loved, there must
be something repulsive in my character) – but outwardly holding the

same position. The family becoming middle-aged, all but the pet lamb, and the father becoming aged. The family is successful and the children thriving. A hateful feeling of unreality clouds all things. I can understand insanity. An experience of death undermines one's faith in the reality of life which after all is dependent on the persistence of individual life in one's consciousness.

Richard Potter rented 47 Prince's Gate, Kensington, for the Season. As a girl Beatrice had greatly enjoyed the summer whirl of smart entertainment. When she became her father's hostess, however, she saw a different side of things. 'I realized', she wrote in *My Apprenticeship*, 'that the pursuit of pleasure was not only an undertaking, but also an elaborate, and to me a tiresome undertaking, entailing extensive plans, a large number of employees and innumerable decisions on insignificant matters. There was the London house to be selected and occupied; there was the stable of horses and carriages to be transported; there was the elaborate stock of prescribed garments to be bought; there was all the commissariat and paraphernalia for dinners, dances, picnics and week-end parties to be provided.'

*22 February.* [Standish]
One word before leaving. . . . A conflict has been going on within me. Shall I give myself up to Society, and make it my aim to succeed therein, or shall I only do so as far as duty calls me, keeping my private life much as it has been for the last nine months? On the whole the balance is in favour of Society. It is going with the stream, and pleasing my people; it is doing a thing thoroughly that I must do partially; it is taking opportunities instead of making them; it is risking less and walking on a well-beaten track in pleasant company. . . . and lastly, and perhaps this is the reason which weighs most with me, there is less presumption in the choice.

Therefore, I solemnly dedicate my energies for the next five months to the cultivation of the social instincts, trusting that the good daemon within me will keep me from all vulgarity of mind, insincerity and falseness. . . .

*26 February. Prince's Gate*
A pleasant bedroom in front of the house and looking towards the west. In the afternoon I can sit here and watch the sun slowly setting behind the Museum buildings and gardens. . . . undisturbed by the rushing life of the great city; only the brisk trottings and even rollings of the well-fed horses and well-cushioned carriages. Altogether we are in the land of

luxury, we are living in an atmosphere of ease, satiety and boredom, with prospect and retrospect of gratified and mortified vanity. . . .

*1 March.* [Prince's Gate]
Huge party at the Speaker's [House of Commons] – one or two of such would last one a life-time. Find it so difficult to be the 'universally pleasant'. Can't think what to say. Prefer on the whole the crowd in Oxford Street, certainly the feminine part of it. 'Ladies' are so expressionless. Should fancy mental superiority of men greatest in our class. Could it be otherwise with the daily life of ladies in society? What is there in the life which is so attractive? How can intelligent women wish to marry into the set where this is the social regime?

> Catherine Potter married Leonard Henry Courtney, M.P., at St Jude's Church, Whitechapel, on 15 March 1883. She was thirty-six; he was fifty-one. The son of a Cornish banker, Courtney had made his mark at Cambridge before becoming a barrister and journalist.

*17 March.* [Prince's Gate]
Kate's wedding. The pleasantest wedding I have ever been at. . . . He [Courtney] is a thoroughly true-hearted strong-minded man. Every day one respects him more. His eldest sister, though she has little pretension to refinement, has a genuine ring about her. The evening before the marriage Kate goes up to her and says, sentimentally, 'I am afraid Leonard has a cold on his chest'. 'Cold!' says Miss Courtney in a hearty emphatic tone. 'Cold! Rubbish! Stomach cough. Look after the champagne', and the advice is not altogether unneeded. Leonard was nervous that night and much excited. No wonder. Marriage at their ages is rather a leap in the dark – curious to see how it turns out. . . .

*20 March.* [Prince's Gate]
Thursday before Good Friday. London deserted and a bitter cold wind blowing. Father, Rosy, Polly and myself alone. Others of the family scattered. Father naturally depressed at this anniversary of Mother's death. Have much conversation with him now on social and economic subjects. He, a strong political economist, not from the theoretical point of view, but from a practical acquaintance with a great variety of commercial undertakings. . . . I have read nothing on Political Economy, but all these problems are beginning to fascinate me and I want to think them over before reading about them.

*24 March.* [Prince's Gate]
Reading Herbert Spencer's *Psychology* diligently every morning. Those quiet three hours of study are the happiest ones in the day. Only one trouble continually arises – the stimulus a congenial study gives to my ambition, which is continually mortified by a gleam of self-knowledge. Meeting with the most ordinarily clever person forces me to appreciate my own inferiority. And yet, fool that I am, I can't help feeling that could I only devote myself to one subject, I could do something. . . . All my duties lie in the practical direction; why should I, wretched little frog, try and puff myself into a professional? If I could rid myself of that mischievous desire to achieve, I could defend the few hours I devote to study by the truly satisfactory effect it has on my physical nature. . . .

It's extraordinary the improvement in Margaret Harkness since she has given herself up to work. When I first remember her . . . she was an hysterical egotistical girl with wretched health and still worse spirits. Her clerical and conventional parents tried to repress her extraordinary activity of mind, causing a state of morbid sensibility and fermentation which gave almost a permanent twist to her nature. Now that she has broken loose from all ties, supporting herself by literary piecework . . . she is blossoming out into a clever, interested and amusing young woman. . . . Whenever she visits me we have delightful talks. . . .

Rosy Potter was sent to an advanced school at Fontainebleau in France, run by Marie Souvestre (d. 1905), who later opened a similar establishment in Wimbledon, noted for its intellectual standards and its advanced attitude to the education of girls.

'The circumstances of my life did not permit me to seek out one of the few university institutions then open to women,' Beatrice remarked in *My Apprenticeship* and, though she met enlightened and stimulating men, she realized that their 'casual conversations at London dinner-parties' could not take the place of disciplined training. She was thus obliged to make what she called 'pitifully ineffectual attempts' to educate herself in algebra, geometry, and then physiology, the last of these by 'casual attendance' on her brother-in-law William Harrison Cripps, who was at that time studying cancerous cells in the hope of discovering a carcinogenic bacillus.

*31 March.* [Prince's Gate]
Rosy left for school. She has a sweet touching character which already is the centre of much love and will be of more. By no means deficient in

strength of a passive kind – a certain solidity and steadfastness of feeling. Intellectually she has been much damaged by overstraining. . . . No imagination, no spirit of adventure has been developed. . . . What is so very attractive about her is her humility and the refreshing absence (for our family) of a hard self-assertiveness, of a determination to make our view of things felt and if possible noted upon. . . . Her ideal, intellectually, is like that of many of us. Rather too high for her capacity. . . . That is the worst of having no real aim and occupation, one loses the capacity for true recreation. One goes into society to learn and not to amuse and when one loses the charm of youth one becomes an unmitigated prig, a future which I myself firmly foresee and which is confidently prophesied for me by Mary. At present I feel like a caged animal, bound up by the luxury, comfort and respectability of my position. I can't get a training that I want without neglecting my duty. . . .

*24 April.* [Prince's Gate]
. . . Now my life is divided sharply into the thoughtful part and the active part, completely unconnected one with the other. . . . it is a curious experience, moving about among men and women, talking much, as you are obliged to do, and never mentioning those thoughts and problems which are your *real life* and which absorb, in their pursuit and solution, all the earnestness of your nature. This doubleness of motive, still more this dissemblance towards the world you live in, extending even to your own family, must bring with it a feeling of unreality; worse, a loss of energy in the sudden transitions from the one life to the other. Happily one thing is clear to me. This state of doubtfulness will not be of long duration. . . . I shall surely some day have the veil withdrawn and be allowed to gaze unblinded on the narrow limits of my own possibilities.

> Beatrice was becoming increasingly aware of the contrast between her own life and that of the poor. She was not alone in this feeling. Though William Ewart Gladstone (1809–98) had led the Liberal Party to a sweeping victory in 1880, promising peace and prosperity, his government was plagued by foreign crises, colonial wars and domestic problems. There was a slump of such severity that the word 'unemployment' was coined to describe its effects; it was matched by deteriorating conditions in the countryside and by an appalling situation in Ireland, where the problem of the land fed the rising tide of nationalism. A sense of social failure and responsibility among the comfortable classes was the spring of many reforming movements. Private philanthropy was an obvious response, but there was also a

doctrinaire reaction against indiscriminate alms-giving, exemplified by the Charity Organization Society, set up years before to co-ordinate London charities on strictly utilitarian lines. Though at first Beatrice found its harsh philosophy congenial, she soon saw that the C.O.S. neither sought the real causes of poverty nor had any cure for them.

*30 April.* [Prince's Gate]
The time rushes and I accomplish nothing. Only three months more and I am only *beginning* work – joined the C.O.S. (Charity Organization Society) and about to make arrangements for physiology lessons, with but a poor prospect of much doing, considering all the social duties that are fast absorbing time and energy. If I can only get well started in laboratory work, it would be easy to continue it in the country. It is hopeless to attempt to do much connected work in London . . . As for the C.O.S. . . . the experience I shall gain from it will work in well with my 'human' studies. One learns very little about human nature from society. It is too much clothed with the 'conventionalities and seemings'.

*5 May.* [Prince's Gate]
. . . Spent the whole day with Herbert Spencer at [a] private view. He worked out, poor man, a sad destiny for one whose whole life has been his work. There is something pathetic in the isolation of his mind, a sort of spider-like existence; sitting alone in the centre of his theoretical web, catching facts, and weaving them again into theory. . . . I see what it is in him which is repulsive to some persons. It is the mental *deformity* which results from the extraordinary development of the intellectual faculties joined with the very *imperfect* development of the sympathetic and emotional qualities, a deformity which, when it does not excite pity, excites dislike. There is no life of which I have a really intimate knowledge which seems to me so inexpressibly sad as the inarticulate life of Herbert Spencer, inarticulate in all that concerns his own happiness. . . .

*15 May.* [Prince's Gate]
Spent a dreary three days at The Argoed and Standish. Miserably seedy, walked about as if in an unpleasant dream reminding me of olden days when headache was habitual and life weariness my ordinary frame of mind. Fear I was not much good as companion to darling Father. His great and tender devotion to her who has gone and to those she has left behind strikes me every day more strongly. . . . Read to me yesterday

some of his journal in Rome, when he was courting Mother. Just the same mind as now – uncritical reverence for what was beautiful and good, no trace of cynicism or desire to analyse and qualify. . . . With him the instinctive feelings are paramount. He would sacrifice all, to some extent even his self-respect, if he thought the happiness of some loved one were at stake. He is far away the most unselfish nature and most unselfconscious nature I know.

The Argoed building looked most melancholy, *actually* ugly and made still more dismal by the feeling that it was the work of a *dead will*, uncared for by any living person, rising up defiantly. All associations there are now painful. . . . Poor little Mother clung to that place as something which belonged to her *exclusively*, which was to be *for her* entirely, to make up to her for much self-devotion to her family; and yet it was in this place that she met with death. . . . Poor little Mother, in her youth twisted, and yet for all that her course was straight towards the good, in direction, with some swaying of the pendulum of motive. Only one year dead!

*18 May.* [Prince's Gate]
Have seen a little into the working of the C.O.S. . . . One thing is clear to my mind, it is distinctly *advantageous to us* to go amongst the poor. We can get from them an experience of life which is novel and interesting; the study of their lives and surroundings gives us the facts wherewith we can attempt to solve the social problems; contact with them develops on the whole our finer qualities. . . . Perhaps the worst result for us is that our philanthropy is sometimes the cause of pharisaical self-congratulation. I have never noticed this in the real philanthropist; he is far too perplexed at the very 'mixed result' (even if he can recognize any permanent result) of his work, to feel much pride over it.

*20 May.* [Prince's Gate]
Visited this morning Pavey (C.O.S. case). Had been dispenser, took to opium eating, now unfitted for work. Wife earning 15s a week, has to support him and three children, two provided for by relations, one boarded out at 4s per week. Still clings to her baby, poor woman. 'Why should I be separated from my children as if I were a bad woman? What will they think of me? They will hear whispers against me and I slaving all the while, night and day. I cannot bear it much longer; I must give way.' The wretched man, standing sulkily in the corner, twisting his thumbs, cursing the existing order of things, talking of his better days

and good education, could write well, talk and translate French, had a smattering of Greek and Latin. All to no purpose! One is tempted to a feeling of righteous indignation against the man, but did he not make himself wretched and is he not on the whole more pitiable? Look at the two faces. An expression on the one of dogged discontent and misery, ever present disgust of the world and himself; marking the woman's face, deep lines of unselfconscious effort, of perhaps agonizing struggle, agonizing in those moments when she felt herself face to face with the fact that in the end she *must* succumb; but still she loved, and the little one for whom she is giving away strength, and maybe life, smiles sweetly and stretches its tiny arms longingly towards her.

I walk back down Piccadilly, meeting the well-dressed young men and young women who had been praying to Jesus of Nazareth that he should forgive them having twirled and whirled and chattered through the last week – 'sensitively' ignoring the huge misery around them. . . .

Eleanor Marx (1855–98), the youngest child of Karl Marx, was much interested in the theatre and politics. The noted free-thinker Charles Bradlaugh (1833–91) was President of the National Secular Society.

*24 May (early morning).* [Prince's Gate]
Went in afternoon to British Museum and met Miss Marx in refreshment rooms. Daughter of Karl Marx, socialist writer and refugee. Gains her livelihood by teaching 'literature', etc., and corresponding for socialist newspapers. . . . In person she is comely, dressed in a slovenly picturesque way with curly black hair flying about in all directions. Fine eyes full of life and sympathy, otherwise ugly features and expression, and complexion showing the signs of an unhealthy excited life, kept up with stimulants and tempered by narcotics. Lives alone, is much connected with Bradlaugh set, evidently peculiar views on love, etc., and I should think has somewhat 'natural' relations with men! Should fear that the chances were against her remaining long within the pale of 'respectable' society. Asked me to come and see her. Exactly the life and character I should like to study. Unfortunately one cannot mix with human beings without becoming more or less *connected* with them. If one *takes* one must also *give* and a permanent relationship gradually rises up.

Beatrice met Joseph Chamberlain (1836–1914), the rising star of the Liberal Party, at a dinner party given by a wealthy neighbour, Miss

Williams. A powerful demagogue, 'Radical Joe' was, in private, reserved and saddened by domestic misfortune. In October 1863, his wife of two years died in childbirth, leaving him with a daughter, Beatrice, and a son, Austen (a future Foreign Secretary). Married again in 1868, he was widowed for a second time seven years later, with four more children – one of them, Neville, a future Conservative Prime Minister. As success and public acclaim revived his spirits, Chamberlain was seen more in society and, as a very eligible widower, was said to be on the lookout for a wife. Herbert Spencer gave an annual picnic near Weybridge for his friends. Miss Chamberlain was Chamberlain's younger sister Clara. She and his daughter Beatrice were then part of his household.

*3 June.* [Prince's Gate]
Wretchedly wasted week. No hard work done. Sick headache from over-eating and under-exercising. Met sundry distinguished men, among others Joseph Chamberlain. I do, and I don't, like him. Talking to 'clever men' in society is a snare and delusion as regards interest. Much better read their books. . . .

Lessons most interesting. . . . Before us on the table diagrams, microscopic sections, and various dissections – these last do not distress me but give me genuine pleasure to pick to pieces. One leaves behind all personalities, and strives to ascertain the constitution of things.

*27 June.* [Prince's Gate]
Last Saturday spent at St George's Hill with a large party of somewhat elderly persons. . . . Spent most of the afternoon with Miss Chamberlain – a really genuine woman, who is somewhat perplexed and bored by London Season life. Essentially provincial in the good and the bad sense. Mr Chamberlain joined us in the evening and I had much conversation with him. His personality interested me. . . .

Gradually sinking into a do-nothing worthless life. Ah me!

*7 July.* [Prince's Gate]
. . . Seen more of C.O.S. work, visited various cases. What is wanted in London is a body of persons who would make it their business to know thoroughly each district, the capabilities and wants; and would have the means of getting at like information about other districts. London is so huge, and the poor are so helpless and ignorant, do not know even of those advantages which are open to them. The clergy, as an adequate organization, are worked out. Some secular body must take their place.

Why do these hundreds and thousands of cultivated people go on boring themselves with unrealities when there is near to them this terrible reality of tortured life? If I could only devote my life to it I might do something, but that is not my fate! Perhaps I stand now on the eve of a new life. . . . If it is to be so, there is work and the influence that work brings, but not happiness. Am I strong enough to face that?

*Sunday, 15 July.* [Prince's Gate]
If a future Francis Galton should ever invent a machine for registering thoughts as they rush through the brain, many humiliating reflections will be forced upon us during the London Season. He speaks in his *Enquiry into Human Faculty* of the mind 'mumbling over the old stories' but in the Society life one leads in this Babylon one's brain is for the most part engaged in 'chattering over its newest impressions'. Conversation becomes a mania, and a most demoralizing one. Even when alone, it is continued in a sort of undertone. . . . When I am not organizing, I am either talking with my tongue, or a lively conversation is going on within the 'precincts of my skull'. Reading and meditating are equally impossible. A train of thought is an unknown experience. . . . Certainly 'Society' has carried the day – my own pursuits have gone pretty well to the dogs, but oh, how I long for rest. And for time to digest!!!!!!!!!!

Interesting dinner here on the 18th. A Whig peer on one side and Joseph Chamberlain on the other. Whig peer talked of his own possessions, Chamberlain *passionately* of getting hold of other people's – for the masses. Curious and interesting character, dominated by *intellectual passions* with little self-control but with any amount of *purpose*. Herbert Spencer on Chamberlain: 'A man who may mean well, but who does, and will do, an incalculable amount of mischief.' Chamberlain on Herbert Spencer: 'Happily, for the majority of the world, his writing is not intelligible, otherwise his life would have been spent in doing harm.' No personal animus between them, but a fundamental antipathy of mind. In what does it originate? I understand the working of Herbert Spencer's reason, but I do not understand the reason of Chamberlain's passion. . . . How I should like to study that man!

*23 July.* [Prince's Gate]
What is to be my work this autumn? I have got hold of a certain number of physiological facts but what am I going to do with them? What do I want with physical facts when my real interest is in psychology? . . . Certainly the scientific mind seems to me the fairest, the most *purely*

*rational.* The only test it acknowledges is *truth* (in its most literal and perhaps narrowest sense), a demonstrable accordance of idea with fact. . . .

*27 July.* [Prince's Gate]
Last evening at Prince's Gate. Alone. Looking from this dismal back room on to the square garden. From behind those trees and distant houses I have watched many a sunrise, when sleepless from excitement. One in particular which I superstitiously remember.

'And so ends the London Season!' Beatrice wrote to Mary Playne at the end of July, 'and I shall return with a clear "social" conscience to my dowdy dress (black lace and all!), early hours, and dear books.' Number 10 Rutland Gate, Knightsbridge, was the London home of Beatrice's sister Georgina Meinertzhagen.

*15 August. Rutland Gate*
Alas! Alas! the whirlpool!

*27 August.* [Standish]
The whirlpool is past for the present – the current of my life may bring me again within the sphere of its attraction but now I again swim freely. . . . My own individual life may be worthless, and if I am ever absorbed into another life I shall no doubt appreciate the pettiness of past existence, but today I feel as if I should regret it bitterly were I once to renounce it.

*22 September.* [Standish]
I intend to work up those physiology papers and read [John] Stuart Mill's *Logic* [*A System of Logic*, 1843] and do as much practical work in the way of dissection and microscopic investigation as may be. In the meantime . . . refusing even to receive the impress of those pictures which are constantly passing before me, some of them passing away into the dimness of the irretrievable past. One such scene: in the Standish garden and the family life therein during the warm summer months. . . . It has been our nursery, and our playground, afterwards the place of our suffering, the half-hated, the half-loved, companion and confidant in our *ennui* and melancholy *dénouement*. . . . And then the brighter days; and these more frequent as one grew in strength, when one revelled in delicious sensations and brooded over exciting thoughts arising from a sympathy with minds deeper and nobler than one's own –

thought over past argument and dreamt of future achievement or perchance of – love. . . .

Beatrice was invited to stay in Chamberlain's London house.

*26 September.* [London?]
Spent the whole week with Miss Chamberlain. A quiet, genuine woman not attractive or interesting in person or intellect, sympathetic in character, valuing things truly and attempting honestly to guide herself and others by high principles. Threw more light on Joseph Chamberlain's character. Coming from such honest surroundings he surely *must* be straight in intention. He is one of many able minds who are all working for the same end and choosing the same means, yet all is darkness when I try to discover their meaning. Much might be learnt in studying the life and thought of such a man, discovering how *representative* he was, how much his convictions were the result of individual characteristics and how much they were the effect of surrounding circumstances. They are *convictions* passionately held, his whole energy is thrown into the attempt to realize them. Is the basis of those convictions honest experience and thought or were they originally the tool of ambition, now become inextricably woven into the love of power, and to his own mind no longer distinguishable from it? What is his principle? . . .

*5 November.* [The Argoed]
Three weeks thoroughly enjoyed at The Argoed, and some good work done. Solitude too has matured my plans for the future. *If* I remain free (which alas is a big if) I see pretty clearly where the work is which I *would* do. Whether I have sufficient faculty remains to be seen. Proof of incapacity will not be wanting if I am strong enough to see it. At present, in this phase of my work, my duties as an ordinary woman are not interfered with by the pursuit of my private ends. I doubt whether they would ever need be, if one chose to remain unmarried. It is almost necessary to the health of a woman, physical and mental, to have definite home duties to fulfil: details of practical management and, above all things, someone dependent on her love and tender care. So long as Father lives and his home is the centre for young lives, I have mission enough as a *woman*. If to this *most* important work I could join another work and work that would satisfy the restless ambition of my nature, then possibly I might remain content to know only through sympathy those feelings which absorb the energies of most women. . . .

There had clearly been some discussion within the family about Chamberlain's intentions, for Beatrice wrote to Mary Playne in October in a manner that revealed her ambivalence. 'If, as Miss Chamberlain says, the Right Honourable gentleman takes "a very conventional view of women", I may be saved all temptation by my unconventionality. I certainly shall not hide it. He would soon see that I was not the woman to "forward" his most ambitious views.' At the same time, and despite the fact that both her father and Herbert Spencer disliked the man, she invited Chamberlain and two of his children to visit the Potters at the New Year.

*24 November.* [Standish]
Alas! the whirlpool. Only two months and I shall be sailing past it for weal or for woe.

*7 December.* [Standish]
. . . One thing I will *not* do. I will not give way to a feeling, however strong, which is not sanctioned by my better self. I will not desert a life in which there are manifold opportunities for good for a life in which my nature is at war with itself.

*27 December.* [Standish]
Rather a miserable dinner-party. Old philosopher very low, feeling his pulse and looking suspiciously at every morsel of food, speaking grudgingly every word. . . .

Yesterday better. 'It would never have done for me to marry,' he said. 'I could not have stood the monotony of married life and then I should have been too fastidious. I must have had a rational woman with great sympathy and considerable sense of humour.' 'Rather difficult to find,' I observed. 'Rational women are generally odiously dull and self-centred.' 'That is a very erroneous generalization; George Eliot was highly rational and yet intensely sympathetic, but there the weak point (which appeared a very important one to me) was physique.' 'I could not have married a woman who had not great physical attraction,' added the withered old philosopher, stretching his bony limbs out and leaving that patent theory-making machine on the side of the armchair, his upper lip appearing preternaturally long and his eyes preternaturally small.

Father, what between past remembrances and future prospects, was excited and really unhappy, though he did his best to appear genial and happy. Slight feeling of jar in the whole party, and consciousness of wide difference of opinion on a possibly *coming* question. When host and hostess are not at peace with themselves and the world there is not much chance of real geniality. However, my tortured state cannot long endure. The 'to be or not to be' will soon be settled.

> Beatrice had decided to test her powers of social diagnosis by visiting Bacup, a town of textile mills and terraced streets near Rochdale, the seat of the Co-operative Movement, to which she was connected through her mother. Although her richer Hayworth relatives had long since moved away, several poorer connections – Ashworths and Akeds – remained. To avoid mutual embarrassment, Beatrice travelled as 'Miss Jones'. She stayed in Bacup from 7 to 20 November; the visit made a great impression upon her, but was not recorded in her diary at the time. Sir James Knowles (1831–1908) was the founder and editor of the *Nineteenth Century*.

*New Year's Eve. Standish*
Rosebud and I alone.

It is indeed an Eve for me. Two distinct ways open to me, one of which, it seems inevitable, that I must take. Herbert Spencer's last words: 'It is not only foolish but absolutely wrong of you not to publish your Bacup experiences. . . . I shall arrange with Knowles about publishing an article from you.' And while the old philosopher is discussing with the editor of the *Nineteenth Century* the desirability of encouraging a beloved disciple to come into the literary arena, the same beloved disciple is entertaining with no *un*tender feeling the arch-enemy. . . .

And this horrible dilemma which appears to threaten me (principle versus feeling) renders all my thought egotistical. My own immediate fate stares me in the face wherever I turn. I seem to be moving onward amidst a company of phantoms, some pushing others restraining; but both parties equally ghostly in their powers, equally immaterial in their influence on the result. I, too, seem to be as in a dream, acting a part with my own family as audience, a part which *makes itself* as I go on, the final scene of which lies not within the healthy region of free-willing foresight. And as the time approaches I *dare* not *think*, but trust that the energy stored up in days of thought*lessness* will suffice for the last struggle; or that perchance some current arising within the 'whirlpool' will drift me outward. This truly is my last hope; if I do hope for continued independence of mind and body.

~ 1884 ~

*12 January. The Argoed*
Another small episode of my life over. After six weeks of feverish indecision, the day [of Chamberlain's arrival] comes. House full of young
people and the three last days passed in dancing and games: I feel all the
while as if I were dancing in a dream towards some precipice. Saturday
5th remainder of the ball party chatting round the afternoon tea table,
the great man's son and daughter amongst them. The door opens – 'Mr
Chamberlain', general uprising. I advance from amongst them, and in
my nervousness almost press six pounds just received into his hand.
General feeling of discomfort; no one quite understanding the reason of
Mr Chamberlain's advent. There exists evidently no cordiality between
him and his host, for Father in a few minutes returns to play patience
with an absent and distressed look, utterly disgusted at the *supposed*
intentions of his visitor.

At dinner, after some shyness, we plunged into essentials and he
began to delicately hint his requirements. That evening and the next
morning till lunch we are on 'susceptible terms'. A dispute over state
education breaks the charm. 'It is a question of authority with women;
if you believe in Herbert Spencer you won't believe in me.' This opens
the battle. By a silent arrangement we find ourselves in the garden. 'It
pains me to hear any of my views controverted', and with this preface he
begins with stern exactitude to lay down the articles of his political
creed. I remain modestly silent; but noticing my silence he remarks that
he requires 'intelligent sympathy' from women. 'Servility, Mr
Chamberlain,' think I, not sympathy, but intelligent servility: what
many women give men, but the difficulty lies in changing one's master,
in jumping from one *tone* of thought to the exact opposite – *with intelligence*. And then I advanced as boldly as I dare my feeble objections to
his general proposition, feeling that in this case I owe it to the man to
show myself and be absolutely sincere. He refutes my objections by re-
asserting his convictions passionately, his expression becoming every
minute more gloomy and determined. He tells me the history of his
political career, how his creed grew up on a basis of experience and
sympathy, how his desire to benefit 'the many' had become gradually a
passion absorbing within itself his whole nature. 'Hitherto the well-to-
do have governed this country for their own interests; and I will do them
this credit, they have achieved their object. Now I think the time is
approaching for those who work and have not. My aim in life is to make

life pleasanter for this great majority. I do not care in the process if it becomes less pleasant for the well-to-do minority.' . . .

And so we wandered up and down the different paths of the Standish garden, the mist which had hid the chasm between us gradually clearing off. Not a suspicion of feeling did he show towards me. He was simply determined to assert his convictions. If I remained silent he watched my expression narrowly, I felt his curious scrutinizing eyes noting each movement as if he were anxious to ascertain whether I yielded to his absolute supremacy. If I objected to or ventured to qualify his theories or his statements, he smashed objection and qualification by an absolute denial, and continued his assertion. He remarked as we came in that he felt as if he had been making a speech. I felt utterly exhausted, we hardly spoke to each other the rest of the day. The next morning, when the Playnes had left, he suggested some more 'exercise'. I *think* both of us felt that all was over between us, so that we talked more *pleasantly*, but even then he insisted on bringing me back from trivialities to a discussion as to the intellectual subordination of women. 'I have only one domestic trouble: my sister and daughter are bitten with the women's rights mania. I don't allow any action on the subject.' 'You don't allow division of opinion in your household, Mr Chamberlain?' 'I can't help people *thinking* differently from me.' 'But you don't allow the expression of the difference?' 'No.' And that little word ended our intercourse.

Now that the pain and indecision are over, I can't help regretting that absorption in the peculiar nature of our relationship left me so little capable of taking the opportunities he gave me of knowing him. The political creed is the whole man; the outcome of his peculiar physical and mental temperament played upon by the experiences of his life. He is neither a reasoner nor an observer in the scientific sense. He does not deduce his opinions by the aid of certain well-thought-out principles, from certain carefully observed, ascertained facts. He aims, rather, at being the organ to express the *desires* of those he believes to be the majority of his countrymen. His power rests on his intuitive knowledge of the wishes of a certain class of his countrymen, his faculty of formulating the same and of re-impressing these wishes forcibly on a mass of indifferent-minded men, who, because these desires are co-existent with their apparent or real interests, have them latent within them. Whether these desires are normal, and the gratification of them consistent with the health and well-being of the English body politic, is a question upon which I certainly do not presume to have an opinion. . . .

And now that it is all over, I have a stunned feeling as I gradually wake up to the old surroundings. . . . Plenty of practical work immediately in front of me. . . . The time is now come for some defined object towards which all my energies must be bent. . . .

It was towards the end of January that Beatrice received her invitation to Highbury, the house which Chamberlain had recently built. The meeting at Birmingham was on 29 January. John Bright (1811–89), a Birmingham M.P. and leader of the Free Trade movement, was a member of three of Gladstone's cabinets. The Kenricks were related to the Chamberlains; Joseph had married two of them. Arthur Chamberlain was Joseph's brother.

*16 March.* [Standish]
Receiving a pressing letter from Miss Chamberlain, and feeling convinced that the negotiation was off, I saw no harm in going for two days to Birmingham to watch the great man at home. I am afraid there is a dash of the adventuress about me . . .

Highbury is a very elaborately built red-brick house with numberless bow windows and long glass orchid-houses stretching along the brow of the hill upon which it is placed.

Inside there is very much *taste* and all very bad. At first you admire the bright softness of the colouring and general luxurious comfort of the rooms and furniture, but after four and twenty hours the whole palls on you, and you long for a bare floor and plain deal table. The two Miss Chamberlains sit ill at ease in the midst of the luxury. They are dressed with the dowdiness of the middle class . . . From the great man they get conversation but little sympathy; possibly they don't give it. He comes and goes, asks his friends and entertains them and sees little of his womenkind. In Birmingham they make kindly homely hostesses and are useful to him; in London they are glum and sit silently between the distinguished men who dine with the future 'Prime Minister' and try in vain to interest and be interested in the fashionable worldly-wise wives who stay the correct time in the drawing-room. . . .

In spite of the luxury and brightness of the house, a gloom overhangs the 'Home'. The drawing-room with its elaborately carved marble arches, its satin paper, rich hangings and choice watercolours has a forlornly grand appearance. No books, no work, no music, not even a harmless antimacassar, to relieve the oppressive richness of the satin-covered furniture. Here on Tuesday afternoon, 29 January, I find the whole family assembled (except its head) ready to receive me. Presently the great man himself emerges from his glass houses and gives me a constrainedly polite welcome. Are we about to take part in a funeral procession? think I, and sink oppressed into a perfectly constructed armchair. Enter John Bright. 'Miss Potter, I think you know her.' 'Not me,' say I humbly, 'but I think you knew my grandfather, Lawrence Heyworth.' 'Lawrence Heyworth,' replies the old man with slow emphasis, 'yes. Then you are the daughter of Lawrencina Heyworth – one of the two or three women a man remembers to the end of his life as beautiful in expression and form.' With this introduction our intercourse becomes naturally of the most kindly description. Immediately he dives into the memories of the past . . . and describes the girl-hostess, who charmed the teetotal and Anti-Corn Law League enthusiasts who visited her father. . . . presently he leaves the room. 'There is one consolation for me,' remarks Mr Chamberlain as he gets up to follow him, 'Bright in a terrible fidget is a good deal worse than I.' 'Miss Potter, I shall reserve the orchid-house for tomorrow and then I shall do the honours myself. I don't want my sister to take you there', and he forthwith retired to his library.

At dinner we are all subdued. The only stranger a certain George Melly from Liverpool, intimate friend of the Holts [Robert and Lawrencina], who fawns upon and flatters Chamberlain till I feel inclined to shriek with nervous irritation. Austen Chamberlain, a big fair-haired youth of handsome feature and open countenance and sunny sympathetic temperament, is deputed by his father to escort us womenkind to the town hall. We are placed in the front seats of the balcony overlooking the platform. A long row of Chamberlains and Kenricks continue our line. The men look earnest and honest, the great man's brothers perhaps have a bit of the cad in dress and manner; the women are plain and unpretentious, essentially ungraceful, might be labelled 'for use and not for ornament' and are treated accordingly. . . .

Below us, packed as close as may be, stand some thousands of men. Strong barriers divide the hall into sections, and as a newcomer tries to push himself in or a faint-hearted one attempts to retire, the whole section sways to and fro. . . . Chamberlain, the master and the darling of his town, is received with deafening shouts. The Birmingham citizen (unless he belongs to the despised and downtrodden minority) adores 'Our Joe', for has he not raised Birmingham to the proud position of one of the great political centres of the universe! . . .

As he rose slowly and stood silently before his people, his whole face and form seemed transformed. The crowd became wild with enthusiasm. Hats, handkerchiefs, coats even were waved frantically as an outlet for feeling. The few hundreds of privileged individuals seated in the balcony rose to their feet. There was one loud uproar of applause and, in the intervals between each fresh outburst, one could distinguish the cheers of the crowd outside, sending its tribute of sympathy.

Perfectly still stood the people's tribune, till the people, exhausted and expectant, gradually subsided into fitful and murmuring cries. At the first sound of his voice they became as one man. Into the tones of his voice he threw the warmth of feeling which was lacking in his words, and every thought, every feeling, the slightest intonation of irony and contempt was reflected on the face of the crowd. It might have been a woman listening to the words of her lover! . . .

His diplomatic talent is unquestioned . . . the only case in which he does not show it is in *la recherche d'une femme*; but then possibly he does not consider our sex worthy of manipulation.

Is it cold-blooded to write truthfully of one's relationship to a man? If one tells anything one should tell all. . . . All the small *affaires de coeur* of past years I have left unmentioned, simply because they have not interested me. The commonplaces of love have always bored me. But Joseph Chamberlain with his gloom and seriousness, with absence of any gallantry or faculty for saying pretty nothings, the simple way in which he assumes, almost asserts, that you stand on a level far beneath him and that all that concerns you is trivial; that you yourself are without importance in the world except in so far as you might be related to him: this sort of courtship (if it is to be called courtship) fascinates, at least, my imagination. His restrained politeness gave way this morning after the first meeting. I had no longer any desire to dispute with him. I no longer cared to adjust my mind to his: I wished only to watch him. We wandered amongst his orchids and he seemed curiously piqued because I said that the only flowers I loved were wild flowers, and at dinner apologized to me for my own want of taste! That evening after the second meeting, I felt that susceptibility was increasing. It did not show itself in any desire to *please me*, but in an intense desire that I should *think and feel like him* (even in small details of taste), by a jealousy of other influences, specially that of the old philosopher, and in his serious attempts to drag me into his interests. I have not met him since except for a few minutes at an evening party.

I don't know how it will all end. Certainly not in *my happiness*. As it is, his personality absorbs all my thought and he occupies a too prominent position for me not to be continually reminded of him. At the best he will leave a present blank though a past interest. And if the fates should unite us (against *my will*) all joy and lightheartedness will go from me. I shall be absorbed into the life of a man whose aims are not my aims; who will refuse me all freedom of thought in my intercourse with him; to whose career I shall have to subordinate all my life, mental and physical . . . my temperament (if it be not ridiculous to compare the nature of an ordinary young woman with that of an extraordinary man) is exactly opposite to his. I hate every form of despotism. My admiration first for Goethe, then for Herbert Spencer, rested on their great faith in natural development. If I married him I should become a cynic as regards my own mental life. I should become *par excellence* the mother and the woman of the world intent only on fulfilling practical duties and gaining practical ends. And that, Mary would say, is a consummation devoutly to be wished for.

> Richard Potter now gave up the family home at Standish and moved his London house from Prince's Gate to York House, a fashionable residence in Kensington Palace Gardens.

*8 April.* [Longfords]
This afternoon I drove from Longfords to settle up everything at Standish. . . . The early spring months have always been sweet at Standish and the loveliest memories of my childhood gather round the first long days, when the dreary walks along the muddy roads directly after the midday meal were replaced by the scramble among hyacinths and ferns, the gathering of primroses and violets and the building of grottoes in the hours of sunset and dusk.

My childhood was not on the whole a happy one; ill-health and starved affection and the mental disorders which spring from these, ill temper and resentment, marred it. Hours spent in secret places, under the shade of shrub and tree, in the leaf-filled hollows of the wood and in the crevices of the quarries, where I would sit and imagine love scenes and death-bed scenes and conjure up the intimacy and tenderness lacking in my life, made up the happy moments. But long dreary times of brooding and resentfulness, sharp pangs of mortified vanity and remorse for untruthfulness, constant physical discomfort and frequent pain absorbed the greater part of my existence – and its *loneliness* was absolute.

It is only lately that I have known the true childish happiness, that I have experienced the *deliciousness* of life, known what it was to revel in my own sensations. But as I wandered this afternoon along the Standish walks and picked these flowers all memories, whether bitter or sweet, were clothed with the beautiful sadness of the setting sun. . . . The flowers and birds and the soft light . . . seemed to say . . . 'You stand on the threshold of active life: ways open before you, each step must decide you. Fear not, but judge by the true light which is given you. Work and pray.'

### 22 April. York House

. . . My nature is like a strong wilful ship; unless I keep it occupied it gives me endless trouble. . . . And lately I have allowed it free play, and must have a struggle with it, before I can again have peace. Can I begin this struggle bravely and instantly? . . . My own mind is not made up. I have been meditating over the question for five months, have done little else but think about it; now I am no nearer solving it. Practically I have resisted, have refused to take the line of subordination and absolute dependence which would have brought things to a crisis. Possibly my refusal to consent to the conditions will have cured all desire on the other side. Then, though mortified, I shall be relieved. I shall have been only decently truthful and honest and can abide by the consequences. But if the question be put in another form?

Let me look facts clearly in the face and take counsel with myself. Ambition and superstition began the feeling. A desire to play a part in the world, and a belief that as the wife of a great man I should play a bigger part than as a spinster or an ordinary married woman. Let me analyse the part I should play. He has taken his line for better or for worse in politics; he has an overpowering ambition, he will not hesitate much as to the means of gaining his ends. He has told me distinctly that he will not bear his opinion being 'controverted' or his action criticized. He desires a woman who is personally attractive to him, who will sympathize and encourage him, be a continual rest to him, giving him the uncompromising admiration which the world withholds. His temperament and his character are intensely attractive to me. I feel I could relieve the gloom, could understand the mixed motive and the difficulties of a nature in which genuine enthusiasm and personal ambition are so curiously interwoven. The outward circumstances of the life of a politician's wife would be distasteful to me or, rather, they would be supremely demoralizing, unless they were accepted as a means to an end in which I myself believed. And here is really the kernel of the question. Do I believe in the drift of his political views and do I believe that the means employed are *honest*? If I do not . . . I should be selling my soul and should deserve misery. . . . Once married, I should of course subordinate my views to my husband's, should, as regards his own profession, accept implicitly his views of right and wrong. But I cannot shirk the responsibility of using my judgement before I acknowledge his authority. . . .

I should *not* influence him. He has shown me that distinctly. He has been straightforward all through, has told me distinctly his requirements. When I have been absolutely honest with him he has turned away. That is not what he wants and *I know it.* It is only when I have simulated *la femme complaisante*, turned the conversation from principles to personalities that he has desired me. He has pointed out to me plainly the hardships in the life of the wife of a man absorbed in public life, has not wished me to be influenced by any glamour that may surround it, has said in so many words 'only devotion to my aims would justify you in accepting it'. And I have not only no devotion to these aims, but have to twist my reasoning in order to *tolerate them.*

And now, what is the straightest course? Is it not to cut the knot by refusing all further intercourse? . . . now I can make a fresh start; force my thoughts from their dwelling-place of the last five months, and devote myself vigorously to my duties and to the natural and true development of my own nature. . . . I shall look about me for some permanent work, some sphere of practical usefulness. . . .

*9 May.* [York House]
. . . It is the close of a period with me. I began it with my old ambition strong upon me; working my little faculties to their utmost, in the full belief that some day I should have somewhat to tell to the world. This strange conceit was fostered by the retirement of a woman's life, living and striving by herself, shielded from all tests as to the real worth of her work. Midway in this period, another path seemed opened to me, another highway to prominence. That also is closed. I remain weakened and discouraged, my old ambition fallen irretrievably. I prayed for light and I *have it.* I see clearly that my intellectual faculty is only mirage, that I have no special mission. . . .

Strength too fails me now. I look hopelessly through the books on my table and neither understand nor care to understand what I read. My imagination has fastened upon one form of feeling. The woman's nature has been stirred to the depths; I have loved and lost . . . Let me look that fact bravely in the face and learn by it. I may not again trifle with my nature: and yet – I would not be without the experience of the last months. It has broadened the basis of sympathy, as all true experience does, even if it be the experience of our own gains, of our own craving for devotion of another being. One must *feel with* (*mitgefuhl*) in order to understand, and to feel with, one must have felt before. . . .

There is glitter all around me and darkness within, the darkness of blind desire yearning for the light of love. All sympathy is shut from me. I stand alone with my own nature now too strong for me. I clutch desperately at *my duty* to those around me, that last hope for the soul despairing of its own happiness. . . . Still there rises up before me, the misty forms of three maidens: Humility, Tenderness, Discretion, and they beckon me with loving pity to follow them. Amen.

*28 July.* [York House]
One last word. I have seen the great man once or twice this Season – there was a little flicker of feeling and then it died, died a natural death from the unfitness of things, and he was the wiser of the two. Perhaps I shall soon hear of his marriage to a woman who would suit him and his conditions. *I* was not equal to it. But we have parted friends and understand each other. A few years, possibly a few months, and I shall be a name to him, one of the many women he has liked, examined, found wanting in qualities and pliability of nature and dismissed from his thoughts. . . . I might have been his helpmate. It would not have been a happy life; it might have been a noble one. Of the simple spontaneous love, there was naught between us. He has it not to give, and my feeling for him was gradually created within me by many mixed motives. . . . I shall watch his career, and whether he rises or falls in the world's estimation I shall know that I am watching the struggle of an earnest mind.

On the back page of her manuscript diary Beatrice wrote yet another testamentary note which emphasized her state of depression.

*1 August.* [York House]
In case of my death I should wish that all these diary-books, after being read (if he shall care to) by Father, should be sent to Carrie Darling.
                                                                BEATRICE POTTER

In an effort to raise her spirits Beatrice went on holiday to Bavaria with Margaret Harkness.

*8 September. Munich*
'Our harmony as moral beings is impossible on any other foundation but altruism. Nay more, altruism alone can enable us to live in the

highest and truest sense. To live for others is the only means of developing the whole existence of man. . . . Our thoughts will be devoted to the knowledge of Humanity, our affections to the Love, our actions to her service.' Auguste Comte.

In 1884 Richard Potter rented a house at Summerhill, a few miles south of Coniston Water and close to his business interests in Barrow-in-Furness.

*15 October. Summerhill*

I don't suppose I shall ever again take that interest in myself to make me much care to tell my thoughts and feelings to this impersonal confidant – my diary. At any rate there is a long lapse in my habit of writing down what I see, think and feel. . . . It would be curious to discover who it is to whom one writes in a diary. Possibly to some mysterious personification of one's own identity, to the Unknown. . . . This unknown one was once my only friend, the being to whom I went for advice and consolation in all the small troubles of a child's life. Well do I remember, as a small thing, sitting under the damp bushes and brooding over the want of love around me (possibly I could not discern it) and turning in upon myself and saying – 'Thou and I will live alone, and if life be unbearable, we will die'. Poor little meagre-hearted thing! And then I said – 'I will teach thee what I feel, think and see, and we will grow wise together. Then shall we be happy.' . . . Today I say humbly, 'we have learnt, poor thing, that we can neither see, think nor feel alone, much less live, without the help of others; therefore we must live *for* others and take what happiness comes to us by the way'.

And all the time I was travelling in Bavaria this was the eternal refrain running through my mind. I saw things; I wrote about them; I lived with an intimate friend, but day and night I cried secretly over the past, and regretted the form which my past life had given me. For who can undo the moulding work of years? We must bear with the self we have made.

The storm has swept over. I can once again go on my way, if I knew only which way to turn.

Beatrice was reading G. H. Lewes's *History of Philosophy*, and making notes on the works of Bacon, Descartes, Spinoza, Hobbes, Locke, Leibnitz and Berkeley.

*24 October.* [Summerhill]

Got back to books again: and stopped as usual by poor health. The whole of my life, from the age of nine (when I wrote a priggish little note on the right books for a child to read) has been one continuous struggle to learn and to think, sacrificing all to this, even physical comfort. . . . Why should a mortal be born with so much aspiration, so much courage and patience in the pursuit of the ideal, and with such a beggarly allowance of power wherewith to do it.

And even now . . . my only peaceful and satisfactory life lies in the old lines of continuous inquiry. Endless questionings of the nature of things . . . At times I pour before me my little hoard of facts – a tiny little heap it is – some of it base coin too. I pass them through and through my brain, like the miser passes the gold through his hands trying to imagine that before me lies the wealth of the world wherewith I may untie the knots of human destiny. Since I have been suffering from neuralgia and have been sitting up hours through the night, I have thought – this cannot long continue, thoughts are the shadows of actions. Where in thy life is the reality?

*24 October. Midnight.* [Summerhill]

Up with pain. The last sleepless nights I had were those terrible ones at York House. Sitting in blank misery on my sofa looking at the two candles burning lower and lower. Darkness is unbearable when in pain. But how much more difficult to bear mental misery than physical pain.

*6 November.* [York House]

A week in London and Winchester. Stayed with the Alfred Cripps. Theresa, fascinating as ever, slightly depressed with poor health, but sweetly happy with that good husband of hers. Alfred keeps up his success at the Bar. Bought the family place and taken to farming in these bad times as a recreation! Evidently will not go into politics except as 'a scholar and a gentleman'. . . .

I have seen something of Leonard Courtney lately. He and Kate stayed with us for a fortnight or so this autumn. A character you learn to admire and reverence for its high integrity of purpose and honesty of means. . . . The Playnes stayed a fortnight with us . . . Arthur is now a hard-worked manufacturer, fighting for existence in these days of over-production. Mary full of schemes, not of social advancement, but of work amongst the millhands trying to inspire them with an *esprit de corps*. Polly married, Bill [Playne] at school, establishment reduced to women servants, interests commercial and rightly *social*. This man and woman are fighting their battle bravely. . . .

Becoming every year more intimate with the Booths, knowing now pretty well the story of their life. Their children, too, growing up with each character known to me and gradually unfolding itself. Indeed if it were not for a morbid horror of a certain physical deformity overtaking me, I could lead now a full and happy life, even without those closer ties which make a woman's life blessed. I have health – liberty – and love; with fair faculties to understand and sympathize with what goes on around me. . . . Perhaps, should all ways to the simple happiness of wifehood and motherhood close, I shall turn again and struggle onwards on the path chosen by my nature in the first enthusiasm of youth.

But nature is strong and cries out for its natural fulfilment [some words deleted in the original MS] while I suffer, I console myself with the faith that pain must have some equivalent in force; it rests with the will to direct this force rightly. We cannot triumph over difficulties, we cannot accept discipline with meekness and courage, without rising out of it more powerful for good.

*26 November.* [York House]
Have seldom felt more strangely ominous than I do now; as if death were approaching. Personally it would be welcome. Had a strange dream. Mother, looking beautiful and young, put out her hand and then kissed me. I, sobbing the while, begged her forgiveness for lack of tenderness. 'It was my nature, Mother, I could not help it.' Then she bent over me and kissed me a second time. What would I give for a mother now; just to lay my head down, tell all – and cry. Perhaps the earth will be my mother – I sometimes think so – hope and pray so, but I would like to have someone by my side when I go. . . .

Then I get up and look at myself: a strong healthy body looking as if it had centuries before it. No release yet; years of health before you. How is it that anyone cares for life? I have always hoped for better, and better has never come except perhaps those eighteen months after Mother's death when duty and faith still burnt clearly.

Tonight is as the end of the year – a year spent in much misery – and little action. Tomorrow will begin a new time for me. A life of noble usefulness . . . I once longed for power; I have it now. . . . Shall I sink under the very vastness of my opportunities – or rise to them and fulfil them?

For many months my thoughts have wandered over and over the same old ground. Perhaps the terrible time of tortured feeling will after all transform itself into good as all pain rightly taken should do. God grant it may be so.

> Before Beatrice's sister Kate married Leonard Courtney she worked as a voluntary rent-collector in an experimental housing scheme for 'the poorest of the poor' just off Tower Hill, behind the Royal Mint. Beatrice now took over this charitable work, collaborating with Ella Pycroft in a newly built block called Katherine Buildings. Five floors high, it had 281 rooms and about 600 tenants; none of the rooms had running water and there were 18 trough-like closets in common use. 'In short,' Beatrice wrote afterwards, 'all amenity, some would say all decency, was sacrificed to the two requirements of relatively low rents and physically sanitary buildings.' The lady rent-collectors, working to the principles of the housing reformer Octavia Hill (1838–1912), had to act as welfare workers and moral guardians of their tenants.

[December? York House]
If I take to this work, might as well keep account of it. Breakfasted with Kate. Of course her first thoughts are for Leonard. Met directors at the buildings, amongst them stumbled on an old lover. Discussion as to stoves and other fittings. Crowder, cut and dried philanthropist, with little human nature, determined that tenants *should* like nothing but what was *useful.* Paint and finish all rooms alike. Kate mildly suggests that tenants *have* taste, are immensely influenced by small things. . . .

## ∾ 1885 ∾

> Edward Bond (1844–1920), a wealthy leader of the Charity Organization Society, was much interested in housing reform. He was said to be the model for Daniel Deronda in George Eliot's novel of that name.

*16 January.* [York House]
Another day at Whitechapel. Met Mr Bond there, looked over fittings. . . . Afterwards talk with Mr Barnett. He is anxious that I should spend this unoccupied time in getting more general information, and find out particulars about medical officer, sanitary officer, relieving officer, School Board visitor, Voluntary Sanitary Committee – and their powers and duties. . . . Miss Pycroft spent three days with me. Daughter of country doctor and one of two families, step-mother died. Plain, very

strong-looking, and unattractive except for sincerity of expression. Free thinking – had somewhat similar life to ours, isolated from other country neighbours by opinions. Decided business capacity and strong will and placid temper. Devoted to her father, with whom she has same intimate companionable relationship as we have, and fond of all her step-sisters. Evidently suffered from feeling herself unattractive in comparison to a pretty sister. Very anxious for work and indifferent to life! We shall get on and we are anxious to have no other workers on the block.

Beatrice kept insisting that her relationship with Chamberlain was over, yet she was unable to break it. In November she had been visited by Clara Chamberlain, who told her much about the family, including anecdotes about 'little Joe's' childhood. 'It is a comfort to have come out of a painful affair with the respect and affection of his family,' Beatrice wrote to Mary Playne afterwards, 'and to have done no harm anyway.' She was whistling in the dark, for her depression was deepening and there was a new crisis in the Chamberlain affair. On 29 January, he delivered a powerful speech at the Birmingham Town Hall on 'The Fruits of the Franchise', the third in a campaign to launch a 'Radical Programme' of reform. It is not clear whether Beatrice went to Birmingham for this meeting or whether it merely reminded her of the occasion she recorded in January 1884.

George Eliot's Life as Related in Her Letters and Journals by J. W. Cross was published in January 1885. 'He is a good, delightful creature and I always feel better for being with him,' George Eliot wrote of Herbert Spencer in April 1852. Two months later she wrote: 'We see each other every day and have a delightful *camaraderie* in everything. But for him my life would be desolate enough.'

29 *January*. [?]
A warm moonlight night with soft west wind, thinking of a crowded hall, deafening shouts, dead silence except for one voice – the voice of the people's tribune; and between those vividly representing thoughts, reading snatches of George Eliot's letters, whose life has been curiously linked through the affection of one great man with mine. . . .
A strange calm over me, though tomorrow I shall know how my fate is to be unravelled. No longer in my hands. If the answer be yes I am in honour tied. If no, I am free and *will be* free in body and mind, free until another binds me. I will not bind myself again and wake up and find myself unbound. Do most people shut their eyes wilfully as *I* have done

and drift, drift, drift they know not whither even with a dim dark dread of a whirlpool ahead. God help the child: this will be thy last childish day – tomorrow will make thee a woman, a woman to love or a woman to work while others love. . . .

*Sunday* [1 February. Birmingham?]
Long talk with Clara Chamberlain. Leaving her great position for a quiet working life with a man who has loved her for years past. 'At first I had a lonely life of it, very little companionship, Beatrice away, my brother absorbed in his sorrow and his politics, and only the little child to care for.'

My relationship to her is a peculiar one – intimacy begun on both sides for different reasons than mere natural affinity, but now grown into a steady friendship. Whether it will endure will practically depend on me. . . . To me this morning's talk seemed like the dropping of the curtain over the tragic end of strong feeling.

George Eliot's letters disappointing. Dull and pretentious in their style, wanting in spontaneity; strengthens the doubt I felt the other day in reading one of her books whether some of her grand paragraphs were not rubbish. But worse than falling short intellectually, they give me a painful impression of her character. It may be narrow-minded prejudice, still I feel that a woman who left the beaten track of morality should have some 'inward searching' – apparently not; posed as the great and good woman. Really self-indulgent? Took to herself all the good things of this world and, if one judges from J. Cross's *Life*, which of course may be quite misleading, did not seek the less gifted and fortunate, but chose from the first those for friends who could benefit her by thought, word or deed. Perhaps genius is always selfish – has a voracious appetite for the material and spiritual good things of this world. . . .

*8 March.* [York House]
. . . Work is the best of narcotics, providing the patient be strong enough to take it.

All is chaos at present. Long trudges through Whitechapel after applicants and references, and tenants tumbling in anyhow. A drift population, the East Enders, of all classes and races – a constantly decomposing mass of human beings, few rising out of it but many dropping down dead, pressed out of existence in the struggle. A certain weird romance, with neither beginning nor end, visiting amongst these people in their dingy homes; some light-hearted enough, in spite of misery and disease. More often feel envy than pity. . . . Earnestly hope I shall never get conceited again, or look upon any work I do as more than a means for remaining contented and free of pain. Relief to be alone, and have poor little Rosy off my hands and out of my thoughts for a short time. . . . Society constantly increasing – have none of that terrible nightmare feeling about it of last year. Real work brings society into its proper place – as a rest and relaxation, instead of an effort and an excitement. Trust I shall never make social capital out of my work. . . . Perhaps this past year of suffering will decrease my egotism, and instead of that cold observation and analysis, all done with the egotistical purpose of increasing knowledge, there will be the interest which comes from feeling, and from the desire humbly to serve those around me.

*13 March.* [York House?]
Feel rather depressed by the bigness of my work. When I look at those long balconies and think of all the queer characters – occupants, would-be occupants – and realize that the characters of the community will depend on our personal power, and that, again, depend not only on character but on persistent health, I feel rather dizzy. The home life and Rosy add to the strain. Have cleared away all 'instructive books'; taken to poetry and beautiful prose. Find the restfulness of *beauty* now that I have hard practical work and constant frictions. Emerson's essays delight me. . . .

*12 April. The Argoed*
Here for two or three days' rest. . . . Feel so utterly *done* when I come back from Whitechapel. Too tired to think or feel, which possibly under present circumstances is the most comfortable state. So long as I have strength enough to go on, don't much care, but dread idleness as if it were Hell. Wonder how it will all end, or whether it will end me. . . . Among the East Enders, in spite of their misery, misery which makes me sick to see, there seems little desire to leave life, on the whole a value in it. Perhaps they *expect* less than we do. What will the next entry be – in the rapids – or out of them? either *for ever*.

George Peabody (1795–1869), an American philanthropist settled in London, spent large sums on schemes for housing the artisan class.

*4 June.* [York House?]
Working hard. Buildings unsatisfactory. Caretaker hopelessly inadequate. Tenants, rough lot – the aborigines of the East End. Pressure to exclude these and take in only the respectable – follow Peabody's

example. . . . May have some rough work to do, but am gaining experience. When over-tired, the tenants haunt me with their wretched, disorderly lives. Wish I had started with more experience, and had taken the thing more regularly in hand. Half-hearted work is always bad. Altogether my life, though not so completely wasted as it was last year, has not turned into much good for others; the rapids are too dangerously near. But there must be an end to that.

Towards the end of July, in an effort to settle the matter one way or another, Kate Courtney arranged a picnic in Buckinghamshire, inviting Chamberlain to meet Beatrice. It was a disastrous occasion. 'The great man and I are painfully shy when we are alone and very anxious that nothing shall be noticed when others are there – a state of affairs which seems destined to lead to endless misunderstandings,' Beatrice wrote to Mary Playne afterwards. 'It certainly brings a good deal of unhappiness to me – and I can't imagine *he* finds much amusement in it. I should think that one or the other of us would break off this enigmatical relationship this autumn, by refusing to see more of each other.' When Beatrice later reflected on the picnic she was even more explicit. 'That day will always remain engraved on my memory as the most painful one of my life,' she recalled. (See entry for 12 May 1886.) The Courtneys shared her disgust. 'I wonder what you thought of yesterday,' Kate wrote to Beatrice; 'to me there was no sign or trace of any other feeling than an intense personal ambition and a desire to dominate at whatever cost to other people's rights. I do not even see any room in his nature for such an affection as would satisfy one of us. It would be a tragedy – a murder of your independent nature.' Leonard Courtney wrote to similar effect, and so did Mary Booth, in whom Beatrice had confided. 'You could never be happy and would be increasingly unhappy with that man. . . .' Beatrice then went to Rusland to stay with her father and Rosy. 'During my fortnight's holiday', she wrote to Mary Playne, 'I have thought very seriously about my own future, especially about my relationship to Mr Chamberlain, and I think I have arrived at definite conclusions. I certainly do not intend to be forlorn. Heaven knows there is enough work to be done . . . to make life worth living even without personal happiness. . . .'

*7 August.* [Rusland]
I return to London tomorrow for five weeks' hard work. Exhausted and very miserable the first two days of my holiday. The old delusion

returned in the spring – had a rude shake to awaken me. Now must face a working life bravely and make the best out of it. . . .

Emma Cons (1838–1912), Beatrice said, was 'one of the most saintly, as well as the most far-sighted of Victorian women philanthropists'.

*12 August.* [London]
Visited Miss Cons at Surrey Buildings. . . . Working-class tenements, shops and cottages, outside stair-case, balconies round pleasure-ground, water closets together, one to each tenement with keys, *no* sinks. Wash-house and drying-ground on roof.

Miss Cons trained by Octavia Hill. Not a lady by birth, with the face and manner of a distinguished woman, a ruler of men. Absolute absorption in work, strong religious feeling, very little culture or interest in things outside the sphere of her own action. Certainly not a lover of fact or theory. Was not clear as to total number of rooms, unlets or arrears. No description of tenants kept. Did not attempt to theorize on her work.

Kept all particulars as to families in her head, spoke to her people with that peculiar mixture of sympathy and authority which characterizes the modern class of *governing women.* I felt ashamed of the way I cross-questioned her. . . . She lives on the premises; collects other blocks, but devotes much time to other work in connection with the amusement and instruction of the people. A calm enthusiasm in her face, giving her all to others. 'Why withhold any of your time and strength?' seemed to be her spirit. . . . These 'governing and guiding women' may become important factors if they increase as they have done lately; women who give up their lives to the management of men, their whole energy of body and mind absorbed in it.

Unlike the learned woman, the emotional part of their nature is fully developed, their sympathy kept almost painfully active. . . . They have the dignity of habitual authority. Often they have the narrow-mindedness and social gaucherie of complete absorption, physical and mental, in one set of feelings and ideas. The *pure organizer* belongs to a different class. She is represented by the active secretary to a growing society or the matron of a big hospital – is to a certain extent unsexed by the justice, push, and severity required. Not that I despise these qualities; the former is indispensable in any work, but with the manager it is more moral; with the organizer more technical justice. Push and severity are not *prominent* qualities of the governing and guiding woman. For the *guidance* of men by personal influence, *feeling* more than thought is required. . . .

Haselour Hall, in Shropshire, was a temporary home of the Booths.

*Saturday, 22 August.* [Haselour Hall?]
Delightful two days with Booths. Charles and I [took a] long walk among pines and Spanish chestnuts. Discussed the possibility of social diagnosis. He, working away with [a] clerk on the Mansion House Inquiry into unemployed, and other work of [a] statistical sort. . . .

Working very hard. Now that I have more or less mastered detail I can do with less time and energy. The idea of developing self-government among the tenants has to be gradually introduced. Should like for that purpose to go back to Bacup and learn Co-operative spirit.

*10 September.* [Cheyne Walk]
Oh so tired. Struggling through the end of my work with painful effort. The old physical longing for the night that knows no morning.

Beatrice was currently staying in the Courtney house at 15 Cheyne Walk, Chelsea, and travelling down to Tower Pier by the regular river service.

*15 September.* [Cheyne Walk]
. . . Outside my work, I ha[ve] a pleasant life at Cheyne Walk. Journeys down the Thames in the ferry steamers, especially back by the evening light; the picturesque side of London lower-class life, the background of grand public buildings with their national historical associations. And then once back in that perfect house, Maggie Harkness fresh from her novel-writing to greet me to chat on all subjects, human and divine, and to play snatches of good music on the parliamentary piano; I, lying the while on the sofa, watching the river and the barges on it creeping by. Happy fellowship in work, rest, and also in memories. 'Who would have thought it', we said constantly to one another, 'when we two as schoolgirls stood on the moorland near Bournemouth, watching the sunset and the trees against it, discussed our religious difficulties and gave vent to all our world-sorrow, and ended by prophesying we should in ten years be talking of cooks and baby linen, boys going to their first school and other matronly subjects, who would have thought of our real future?' She, struggling for her livelihood with queer experiences of a working woman's life; of another with her cook and big establishment but also

absorbed in work outside home duty; both passed through the misery of strong and useless feeling. . . . Will another ten years bring as great a change or have we settled down in the groove we are destined to run in?

On 8 October, Clara Chamberlain (now married to Frederick Ryland) wrote inviting Beatrice to visit her in Birmingham on 2 November. 'The election fever is absorbing everyone and I have, I fear, nothing more lively to offer you in the way of entertainment than a big meeting at the Town Hall when my brother addresses his constituents. . . .' Beatrice went to visit the Rylands, and while she was there broke down and openly expressed her feelings about Chamberlain – only to be deeply mortified when Clara Ryland claimed that she had been mistaken about the whole affair, and that the 'brother had never thought of me'. (See the diary entry for 6 March 1886, when Beatrice recorded this visit.) Much distressed, she sought consolation in a three-day visit to Mary Booth.

*23 October.* [Crosthwaite?]
Tomorrow to London town to begin a new year of work. . . . I am back on the old lines, when shall I run off again?

In early November, Beatrice wrote to her father (who was visiting Tadcaster, the original home of the Potters) that she was 'working hard at a book of all the tenants, past and present, with description of occupation, family, etc.' She seemingly abandoned the project when she had to leave London suddenly a fortnight later. She had prepared a proposal for the better man-agement of Katherine Buildings, and she was beginning to think of an association to co-ordinate the various agencies concerned with housing the poor: a body which would give the lady collectors better professional prospects. 'I admire and reverence women most who are content to be among the "unknown saints", but it is no use shutting one's eyes to the fact that there is an increasing number of women to whom the matrimonial career is shut and who seek a masculine reward for masculine qualities,' she told her father. 'There is in these women something exceedingly pathetic, and I would do anything to open careers to them in which their somewhat abnormal but useful qualities would get their own reward. . . . I think these strong women have a great future before them – in the solution of social questions. They *are not* just inferior men. They may have masculine faculty but they have the *woman's temperament* – and the stronger they are the more distinctively feminine they are in this. I only hope that, instead of trying to ape men and take up men's pursuits, they will carve out their own careers, and not be satisfied until they have found the careers in which their particular form of power will achieve most.'

*8 November.* [York House]
. . . The past fortnight I have been struggling against headache and physical depression: spent first three days with Mary Booth and the continual conversation upset me. . . . Two long conversations with Mr Barnett: I, making my suggestion of associating all agencies for housing the poor in one body. Have not thought this out and was rather astounded at the way he took it up and wanted me to elaborate a plan and to become the moving spirit. Shall I always disappoint myself and others when my strength comes to be tested – or will my strength increase and enable me to carry out what I initiate? . . .

And I am constantly weary; life is a continual struggle, a real battle-field, both physically and mentally. Still, if Rosy will only get strong, there is interest enough in life, and affection too, and this gnawing pain will cease in time. I have not fully realized the uselessness of it. As for work, I have done only my bare duty at Katherine Buildings, and have begun a careful account of tenants – but oh! for more energy. . . .

*15 November.* [York House]
Worked well. Monday, Katherine Buildings, one to nine o'clock. Afterwards saw over Whittington Club. . . . Tuesday at Katherine Buildings book, 4 hours. Wednesday Albert and Victoria Docks from 10 p.m. to 6 a.m. Thursday, idle morning castle-building – afternoon, Katherine Buildings. Friday, 7 hours' work at Katherine Buildings book. Saturday, Katherine Buildings 12 to 7 o'clock. Forty hours' work including railway journeys.

On Thursday, 26 November, Richard Potter suffered a stroke while on his way to vote in the General Election. Sir Andrew Clark (1826–93), chief physician at the London Hospital, was a personal friend. Richard Potter was taken to stay with the Playnes at Longfords, then in the New Year Beatrice took him to Bournemouth. Her father's collapse, when her own emotions were under strain and her sister Rosy appears to have been suffering from *anorexia nervosa*, threw Beatrice into the profound depression in which she wrote the informal will she included as the first entry in her diary for 1886. The Miss Darling mentioned here, and in ensuing entries until 1888, was presumably a sister of Carrie Darling (who was now in Australia) but is not otherwise identified.

*19 December.* [York House]

A month ago today Father and Rosy returned from their little trip to York and Tadcaster. I had written to beg them not to take it, on Rosy's account. The reports of her state, physical and mental, brought to me by the servants and Miss Darling were most alarming and I had made up my mind to offer to take her away for six months. They came back both looking very ill – but apparently enamoured of each other. However, the next morning I broached the question with Father. I explained to him I felt very miserable about her and convinced that nothing short of separation from him would do much good. He, poor man, seemed quite relieved about the idea of getting rid of the responsibility and acquiesced in my vague suggestion I should take her away.

On Thursday, 26th, Father came down to breakfast late, very unusual for him. He looked to me strange, seemed so curiously slow in his movements. Still there was nothing to cause me much anxiety. He read the papers, but did not open his letters. I found them afterwards lying on the table. I had arranged an appointment with Dr Gee for Rosy at 11 o'clock. Father and she went out, he with the intention of voting. I watched him from the dining-room window fumbling with the lock of the dog's kennel. It struck me suddenly that he was fast becoming an old man. Then I went about my business – with a heavy heart, for six months' *tête-à-tête* with Rosy was not a refreshing prospect. Half-past ten and they had not come back – another twenty minutes I became nervous, opened the front door and walked to the big gate. There, some yards down the street, Father leaning heavily on poor little Rosy, dragging his leg, his face drawn down, but seemingly quite unconcerned at the change that had befallen him. I helped him into the house, hurried Rosy, who was pale and trembling, away with Miss Darling and sent for the doctor. Dr Tyrell, when he saw him, said immediately it was a stroke of paralysis and advised me to send for Sir A. Clark. His mind was not touched – it was as active as ever on politics, he talked in an excited manner with Sir A. Clark. . . .

The 'beloved physician' spoke seriously to me that evening. 'The greatest proportion of these cases do not recover.' He seemed to get better the first three days, then a relapse. His mind became more affected, he was extravagant in his ideas and wishes. Saturday, 5th, was the '*black day*'. He dictated an extraordinary letter to Rosy and sent out for fifty or sixty pairs of slippers from different shops. Andrew Clark evidently thought the worst was coming, he feared softening of the brain and a rapid ending. Since then his tone of body and mind has become steadily healthier. He is happy and contented, slightly irritated with small things, but on the whole sweet and gentle to do for. It is a month now since he was struck down. His intelligence is singularly lucid on some questions and he is extraordinarily cheerful. But there is something gone – some part of his mind sleeping or dead? Tomorrow we move him to Longfords for the New Year.

Poor little Rosy had a terrible time of it. She reproached herself for worrying him into his illness, and she was not far wrong. But, as I told her, it was as much my neglect as her worry. . . . the future does look gloomy indeed. Companionizing a failing mind – a life without physical or mental activity – no work. Good God, how awful. This time last year I was suffering from the same feeling – with other circumstances. There was hope for me then in work. Now I am *hopeless*. Except that this year I feel as if the end of my pain *must* come. Surely my cup is full.

# The Dead Point
# of My Career

## January 1886–December 1887

*1 January.* [Longfords]
In case I should not outlive the year, I will that the £600 odd in
Father's or his executors' hands should be given to Leonard Courtney
towards the expenses of his political career. That the diamond brooch
should be given to Margaret Hobhouse, to whom Mother really left it.
The rest of my properties may be distributed, every member of the
family taking that which they care for most in the following order:
Mary, Kate, Georgie, Theresa, Blanche, Margaret, Rosy (I don't suppose Lallie would wish for anything). To Margaret Harkness I leave
any books that belong to me and any of the pictures in my room she
cares for.

In case my diary-books and letters are not destroyed I earnestly beg
they may be destroyed immediately on the reading of this – and I should
prefer that no one had looked into them.

I am grateful to all those who have shown a love and interest.

If Death comes it will be welcome – for life has always been distasteful to me.

If Father be still alive I should earnestly advise him to beg the
Courtneys or some other couple to have him – and if Rosy is wise she will
press for this. The position of unmarried daughter at home is an unhappy
one even for a strong woman: it is an impossible one for a weak one.

BEATRICE POTTER

*28 January.* [Longfords]

I intend to acquire a general knowledge of English history with a special view of the conditions of the poorer classes, in different times, leading up to a study of my own subject, the question of state interference in the housing of the lowest class. For this purpose I shall abstract the books I read.

When Beatrice settled in lodgings (Kildare) in Bournemouth with her father, she reported to Mary Playne, there was 'nothing and nobody to distract my attention and no chain of excitement for him'. This commitment meant that she had to abandon her career in London; and her father's illness, together with heavy losses he had lately incurred by speculation, meant that York House had also to be given up as a measure of economy.

*11 February.* [Bournemouth]

Ah. Life seems to my consciousness a horrible fact. Sometimes I wonder how long I shall support it. I am never at peace with myself now – the whole of my past life looks like an irretrievable blunder, the last two years like a nightmare! I have mistaken the facts of human life as far as my own existence is concerned, and I am not strong enough to live without happiness. What tie have I to life, except the melancholy one of a fast-ageing parent, gradually losing his grasp on all things, material and spiritual? I struggle through each new day, waking with suicidal thoughts early in the morning, trying with determined effort to force my thoughts on to the old lines of continuous inquiry, to beat back feeling into the narrow rut of duty. . . . When will pain cease? . . . I look out tonight on the beating of that hateful grey sea, the breaking and the vanishing of the surf on the shore; the waves break and vanish like my spasms of feeling, but they return again and again – and behind them is the bottomless ocean of despair. Eight and twenty! Living a life without hope. . . . No future but the vain repetition of the breaking waves of feeling.

On 8 February a riot of the unemployed in Trafalgar Square stirred up much public discussion. When Beatrice sent a letter to the *Pall Mall Gazette* on 18 February, entitled 'A Lady's View of the Unemployed', the editor proposed instead to publish it as a short article. Beatrice was so pleased that she wrote 'a turning-point in my life' across the letter of acceptance. The letter was also the cause of a new and frustrating exchange with Chamberlain, then President of the Local Government

Board and responsible for the administration of Poor Law relief. After he read her article he wrote to solicit her views on unemployment and suggest that they might meet. Beatrice replied at once explaining that she was now living out of London, that she thought her knowledge of the situation in the East End was superficial, and that she believed there was so much ignorance of the facts that it would be useful to launch a thorough inquiry into labour problems in London. Chamberlain sent a friendly answer, assuring Beatrice that he valued her advice and repeating his opinion that a 'rather crude' scheme of public works might be part of the price 'the rich must pay to keep the poor alive'.

Beatrice, quick to sense a slight, sent a frigid reply. 'As I read your letter', she wrote, 'a suspicion flashed across me that you wished for some further proof of the incapacity of a woman's intellect to deal with such larger matters.' She told him, in terms that showed how much she was still influenced by Spencer's strict individualism, that she had nothing to suggest in this crisis 'except sternness from the State, and love and self-devotion from individuals', and she came back to a mock-modest reproof for his original request. 'But is it not rather unkind of you to ask me to tell you what I think? I have tried to be perfectly truthful. Still, it is a ludicrous idea that an ordinary woman should be called upon to review the suggestions of Her Majesty's ablest minister, especially when I know that he has a slight opinion of even a superior woman's intelligence in these matters (I agree with him) and a dislike of any independence of thought.'

Chamberlain was stung to a tart reply. 'You are quite wrong in supposing that I undervalue the opinion of an intelligent woman,' he wrote on 5 March. 'There are many questions on which I would follow it blindly.' Yet he now realized that there was no point in continuing the correspondence. 'I hardly know why I defend myself', he wrote, 'for I admit that it does not much matter what I think or feel on these subjects.' He ended curtly. 'I thank you for writing so fully and do not expect any further answer.'

Beatrice had brought this snub upon herself, but she was so upset by it that she broke through conventional niceties and sent him the note which is included in the following entry.

*6 March.* [Kildare]
And so the agony of two years ends. I thought it was ended, that evening at Clara Ryland's, when I broke down utterly and she told me I was mistaken. The brother had never thought of me. And this after she had talked to me and examined me as to my intentions a year since. Anyhow

when I came here I felt for the first time free in thought and feeling.

I was slowly recovering from that terrible nightmare of absolute despair which had haunted me since Father's illness. When I saw the Great Man's handwriting I was ominously excited. I knew it was the old torture coming back again. In my first letter I told him he would find my experience incomplete and quite useless. . . . I was not such an arrant fool as to think I could inform him; I thought that he wished to know my mind literally to see whether it would suit him. So I told him I would try and be truthful and that I was the first to admit that my thought was worthless – only if he asked me for it I was in honour bound to give it him in its true form. No doubt my expression was pedantic – I was far too intent on being honest to think much of my manner.

In the agony of the moment I wrote and posted the following words. 'Now I see I was right not to deceive you. I could not lie to the man I loved. But why have worded it so cruelly, why give unnecessary pain? Surely we suffer sufficiently – thank God! that when our own happiness is destroyed there are others to live for. Do not think that I do not consider your decision as *final* and destroy this.'

Is it ended now? I think so. Double-mindedness has run right through – a perpetual struggle between conscience on the one hand and feeling on the other. I had not the courage to follow either to the bitter end, hence my misery. And on his side hatred of insubordination and personal attraction possibly tinged with pity, for I believe the man believed I loved him – so I did! Anyhow these last words from me close it. God help me. What decision!

Mary Booth again sought to console Beatrice. 'A man so dependent on flattery, so impatient of contradiction, so sensitive with regard to his own feelings, and so indifferent to those of others, must be at bottom a very poor and shallow creature,' she wrote. 'You are well rid of him.' Beatrice thanked her for a 'sweet letter' but was not persuaded. 'I am afraid I shall never think of him as you do,' she said. 'I shall always be ready to help him even if I *do* get a slash in the face in return. I have no proper pride!'

### 15 March. Kildare

It is curious that old associations with this place, perhaps other causes, have brought me again under the influence of religion. I lost that holy influence as a persistent feeling when first I gave way to that delusion about the Great Man. Sometimes I have tried to pray, when I have thought it possible I should be united to him, but I have failed. In the agony of my grief, I have implored comfort. And this last time before I answered that letter, I prayed earnestly for help to do what was right and truthful. Now I feel comforted: for the first time I live harmoniously with myself. My great love for him is acknowledged before God, but it is chastened by truthfulness and absolute honesty. And I can turn with earnestness to my own aims in life – to a loving care of that darling old Father, to a persistent pursuit of truth by the light of the faith that is in me. This morning I take the sacrament – the great symbol of sacrifice, of the sacrifice of individual life and happiness. I take it in the old church where I made that holy vow that I would love Christ and follow His commandments. God knows I have not kept it. I have passed through months and months of hardness and vain endeavour after foolish things, years of materialism. And the last two years I have been striving after the fulfilment of my lower nature, have been haunted by petty fears for my personal fate. *Now*, surely I am humbled? . . .

Mrs Thompson was companion and nurse to Richard Potter.

*29 March. Kildare*

As I wrote these words, dear Father came – 'Good morning, dear child,' he said in his cheery tone, 'how are you this morning?' (he always said this though I had always seen him directly after breakfast). And he sat down looking as bright and happy as if he had not known illness. Mrs Thompson remarked, 'Isn't he looking smart this morning?' 'Yes, and I feel smart too – why, it's the 1st April today – I hope it isn't April fool's smartness.' The words struck me, for though he was looking beaming, his mouth was more drawn down than usual. He wrote a few letters, and kept his promise to me to enter some of his other investments in his ledger. I noticed, as I had noticed all along since the stroke in November, that his mind was weak and incapable of ordinary business.

It was out walking that the change came over him. I cannot tell when, but I felt instinctively that he was changed as he leaned heavily on my arm. His eyes were glazed, his mouth more than ever pulled down – he was quite unconscious of it. He ate his lunch mechanically, his cigarette tumbled from his left hand, and his mind was dull and unconscious of movements around him. At tea Dr Falls came. As he had not seen him before he said he could not appreciate the amount of the change. He could only say: he saw an old man before him, suffering from the effects of partial paralysis of the left side.

He soothed our anxiety I think, said (what we knew from experience) that nothing could be done except to keep him absolutely quiet, with light food and a slight aperient. Except for the increase of weakness he seems in perfectly sound condition. No tension of pulse, no indigestion, good appetite, clean tongue. His mind not in any way excited, but perhaps *clouded* and disinclined to exert itself. More than his usual absence of mind, in not noticing his surroundings. Towards evening he complained for the first time in the day. He felt weary and weak – he said in the clearest way, 'Un pas en arrière pour mieux sauter'. He dreads the idea of being an invalid again and won't think it possible. . . .

Whatever happens, I shall look back to those days here, to the peace and restfulness, to his loving dependence on me, the quiet thought and reading, with a sad regret. It has been one of the resting-places of life, so few and far between in this constant and painful struggle.

If only I had not seen that handwriting!

*4 April.* [Kildare]
Father slightly better though still much changed. Sits the whole day apathetically in his armchair, twiddling the fingers of his right hand. Dr Falls advises me to move him to London. It is sad watching the slow decay. And yet I am perhaps happier than I have been since the first beginning of that miserable affair. Now it is irretrievably settled – and also laid bare, so that there can no longer be any misunderstanding. . . . It will be a sad life; God grant it may be a useful one, that I may dedicate myself earnestly and without trembling to a search after the truths which will help my people.

There is no inflation now. I have not despised the simple happiness of a woman's life; it has despised *me* . . . My way in life has been chosen for me; let me walk on it with an open mind and a single heart. God grant it! . . .

*17 April.* [York House]
Charles Booth's first meeting of the Board of Statistical Research at his City office. Present: Charles Booth, Maurice Paul, Benjamin Jones (working man, secretary to Wholesale Co-operative), Radley (working man, secretary to a trade society) and myself.

Object of the Committee [is] to get a fair picture of the whole of

London society – the 4,000,000 – by district and employment, the two methods to be based on census returns. We passed Charles Booth's elaborate and detailed plan for the work, and a short abstract of it for general purposes.

At present Charles Booth is the sole worker in this gigantic undertaking. If I were more advanced in knowledge of previous conditions, just the sort of work I should like to undertake – and if I were free! But I intend to do a little bit of it while I am in London, not only to keep the Society alive, but to keep me in touch with *actual facts* so as to limit my study of the past to that part of it useful in the understanding of the present. . . .

### 4 May. [York House]

Early morning, looking over the sunlit mist at the Kensington Gardens. What an untold blessing to me, my small intellectual life in my present surroundings. At least other things are kept in their due proportions. Thinking that I might do well to explain thoroughly what I mean by social diagnosis and publish it as an article in the autumn. If it were well written it would help C. Booth's survey.

### 17 May. [York House]

Spent yesterday afternoon with the Benjamin Jones'. Aristocrats of the working class who have stuck to their own class. Originally millhands in some North Country town. Benjamin married early, not only from principle (thinking that it was better for a man to marry 'with the bloom and innocence on him') but also because there was a great practical difficulty of keeping his earnings from the grasp of his parents. . . .

I should like to know more of these intelligent working men. They have their own side of the question, and it is a quite different side from the rose-coloured vision of the capitalist, and yet it is not the socialist view. But the point I should like to get clear is whether there is actually more selection of workers of a given trade, whether work has been harder and more straining to those who are fully employed, and more and more intermittent to those who are constantly unemployed.

Chamberlain and a large group of supporters, who called themselves Liberal Unionists, had defected from the government in March over Gladstone's proposals for Home Rule. The defection brought down Gladstone's government; their votes put Lord Salisbury in office.

*12* [?22] *May.* [York House]

I have seen Beatrice Chamberlain once or twice this season. She is depressed with the condition of things – is interesting to me, because she reflects her father's state of mind. Mr Chamberlain has acted in the high-minded patriotic way, but, in his misfortune, he is reaping the fruits of his high-handed arbitrariness in the day of his glory. He has offended many persons and many classes by the injustice of his imputations . . . He has so many great qualities it is a pity that his career should be damaged by this small petulance and intolerance of the views of others . . . This time last year, all through the summer, he was preparing for a great triumph. [He] thought the Democracy once established would show itself his true follower. . . .

That evening in July the Great Man dined with us. . . . A week after, the Courtneys arranged a picnic on purpose we should meet. They had asked Mr Chamberlain for a day, the week before, but he had begged them to change it, so that he might come. And he came! That day will always remain engraved on my memory as the most painful one of my life. The scene under the Burnham beeches, forcing me to tell his fortune – afterwards behaving with marked rudeness and indifference. The great reception given to him at the station, returning back in the evening, we all running after him like so many little dogs . . .

Still, now the Great Man himself is down, I *would* like to give him one word of sympathy. Perhaps he would think my sympathy impertinent! Since that day, among the Burnham beeches, I have not seen him. Neither do I intend to. Our correspondence this spring has made it impossible, though apparently he thinks not.

I met Miss Octavia Hill the other night at the Barnetts'. . . . The form of her head and features, and the expression of the eyes and mouth, show the attractiveness of mental power. A peculiar charm in her smile. We talked on Artisans' Dwellings. I asked her whether she thought it necessary to keep accurate descriptions of the tenants. No, she did not see the use of it. 'Surely it was wise to write down observations so as to be able to give true information?' I suggested. She objected that there was already too much 'windy talk'. What you wanted was action . . . I felt penitent for my presumption, but *not convinced.*

*24 May.* [York House]

Do not get on much with the accumulation of useful knowledge for my article. It is absolutely necessary that I should get a proof from history that we *do* act from the thoughts and sentiments formed by descriptions of social facts. To a large extent, as Charles Booth remarked the other day, legislation is founded on class feeling, religious or anti-religious feeling, and uses facts to prove its points, gives facts as data when they are really illustrations. . . .

Frederic Harrison (1831–1923) was president of the Positivist community in London and founder of the *Positivist Review*.

*28 May.* [York House]
Dined out, night before last, for the first time since I have been in London. Frederic Harrison, with whom for some mysterious reason I am always being mated at London dinners. . . . The conversation was mostly personal. First he said he had heard that 'I had taken an important step' or was about to take it. The step turned out to be my 'conversion to Catholicism'! Then we fell into politics. . . . He thought a little discipline of adversity would improve Chamberlain and lessen the jealousy of and antagonism to him. That seems to be the general feeling of those who wish him well. . . . It is curious to watch the wind of opinions turning against Chamberlain now he has lost favour with the ruling power, the Democracy – makes one long to offer him humbly anything in one's possession that would please him.

Then we talked of unmarried life, especially for women; agreed it could not be happy, in one sense of the word, though we disagreed as to the usefulness of it. Frederic Harrison taking the extreme contrast view that marriage was absolutely essential to the development of character, that it alone gave the restfulness necessary for true work. I maintaining that if unmarried women kept their feelings alive, did not choke them with routine idleness, practical work, or with intellectualism, though they must suffer pain, they were often for that very reason more sympathetic than married women. . . .

*28 May.* [York House]
A quiet little dinner. Mr Barnett, Alfred Cripps, Beatrice Chamberlain, dear old Father, who thoroughly enjoyed it, and myself. Mr Barnett told me much about Octavia Hill. How, when he had met her as a young curate just come to London, she had opened the whole world to him. A cultivated mind, susceptible to art, with deep enthusiasm and faith, and a love of power. *This* she undoubtedly has and shows it in her age in a despotic temper. . . . I remember her well in the zenith of her fame; some

14 years ago. I remember her dining with us in Prince's Gate, I remember thinking her a sort of ideal of the attraction of woman's power. At that time she was constantly attended by Edward Bond. Alas! for we poor women! Even our strong minds do not save us from tender feelings. Companionship, which meant to him intellectual and moral enlightenment, meant to her 'Love'. This, one fatal day, she told him. Let us draw the curtain tenderly before that scene and inquire no further. She left England for two years' ill health. She came back a changed woman. . . . She is still a great force in the world of philanthropic action, and as a great leader of woman's work she assuredly takes the first place. But she might have been more, if she had lived with her peers and accepted her sorrow as a great discipline.

After dinner I talked to Beatrice Chamberlain. Of course we talked of her father. . . . She told me he was much changed. These last months had aged him more than the past ten years. . . .

Did we smoke? Heaven forbid the unholy thought! I am an old-fashioned woman and hate these mannish ways. But I would whisper a small truth in the reader's ears. Let men beware of the smoking woman. For the pretty dress and the sweet-smelling cigarette unite the outward tokens of a woman's sympathy and a man's ease. I would urge earnestly on the defenders of man's supremacy to fight the female use of tobacco with more sternness and vigour than they have displayed in [fighting?] the female use of the vote. It is a far more fatal power. It is the wand with which the possible women of the future will open the hidden stores of knowledge of men and things and learn to govern them. Then will women become the leading doctors, barristers and scientists. They may even learn the touch of the rhetorical politician. And a female Gladstone may lurk in the dim vistas of the future. . . .

*9 June. York House*

Poor Herbert Spencer. Since I read his autobiography I often think of that life given up entirely to philosophy, now given up to feeling his pulse and analysing his sensations, with no near friends to be all in all to him . . . 'I was never in love' he announced when I put the question straight: 'Were you never conscious of the wholesale sacrifice you were making, did you never long for those other forms of thought, feeling, action, you were shut out from?' Strange, a nature with so perfect an intellect and little else, save friendliness and the uprightness of a truth-loving mind. . . .

*29 June. The Argoed*
A long hot journey with my two poor invalids and with my capable nurse. . . . These my companions. And yet for all that I am happy, happier than I have been for three long years. . . . The struggle is over. Last time I stayed here for any time is November, 1883. I was on the eve of all my trouble. I was full of enthusiasm for the idea that is now the leading motive of my life – but then the thought was without form. Between that time and this I have thought little of it – I have passed through the agony of strong but useless feeling. . . . Many a time during those ghastly days I almost prayed for Father's death so that I might feel free to die. But I conquered; and now though I feel humbled and weak, I will go straight on my way. I live in the summer air, in the sounds and the scents – in the freshness of early-morning hours devoted to reading, in the calm of the twilight, devoted to thought and to prayer. The day spent with my two poor invalids. And that old idea! Ambition and vanity are not dead, though sadness has blunted them. . . . But the old idea is no longer without form. With tiresome effort I am hewing it out of the stone. It is no slight work for my slight faculties. It is a persistent desire only that has done what is already there and will do what *must* come. It is *truth* – a little bit of truth for me to unveil. Ah! but Love, how much sweeter than Truth.

*2 July.* [The Argoed]
Oh! my head aches and my ambitious idea looms unreachably large and distant.

Political economy is *hateful* – most hateful drudgery. Still, it is evident to me I *must* master it, and what is more, I must master the *grounds* of it . . .

*18 July.* [The Argoed]
I have broken the back of economical science as far as I want it . . . In the meantime I am thoroughly enjoying my life. . . . I am living in the present and preparing for the future. . . .

*20 August.* [The Argoed]
My bad days come on. Not that I suffer much, but I am always stupid at them and practically incapable of thought. . . .

*30 August.* [The Argoed]
Beatrice Chamberlain has stayed a week with me. She interests me for her own as well as for her father's sake. It is still of the nature of a

painful happiness to be with her and to listen to the details of their past
and their present life. . . . One great devotion absorbing every day more
her whole life – a passionate feeling for her father, a desire to protect him
from all pain and to share with him every pleasure. . . . Ah! what a struggle idealism is in a woman's nature. I could not have idealized that man,
though I loved him so passionately. Only to a *faith* could I bring the
whole devotion of my nature. Still, for all that, God bless him!

*14 September.* [The Argoed]
Finished my essay on 'The Rise and Growth of English Economics'. I
am satisfied with it. . . . I wonder whether, if it is published, it will be
thought very conceited? It isn't so. I can't help my ideas taking a positive
form . . . It is this hopeless independence of thought that makes my
mind so distasteful to many people; and rightly so, for a woman *should*
be more or less dependent and receptive. However, I must perforce go
through the world with my mind as it is – and be *true to myself*. . . . I
shall rest for a few days now – and then I shall . . . finish up political
economy. . . . The winter is to be devoted to German socialism . . . and
then for English history but this time with a definite intention of writing a History of Industrialism or something of the sort.

I should like, however, to write one more article on 'Research in
Social Questions' . . . Ah! Work, what a grand comfort it is.

*18 September.* [The Argoed]
Sent the 'little thing of my own' out into the world to meet its fate in the
hands of strangers. First it goes to those who will love it for the sake of
its mother – the Charles Booths and then on to Maurice Paul, possibly
Ella Pycroft. But after that it is either rejected at the extreme gate or it
goes into the world and stands to be judged of by all men, and I in it
meet my judgement. . . . Adieu, little one. If you come back to me in
printed proof I will welcome you as a successful child; if you return
rejected – well, many that are better than you have suffered likewise. My
daydreams will be destroyed but perhaps I, myself, will be all the better!

Charles and Mary Booth wrote kindly letters. 'I think much of the
paper,' he said. 'It is good wine, but new, and needs to mature in the
bottle.' His wife made a similar comment: 'I am not sure whether the
paper is yet as good as you can make it,' she told Beatrice, who was in no
mood for qualified approval. Mary Booth thought more of the paper
than Beatrice believed. 'The more I think of that paper the more I like it,'

she wrote to Charles, who was away in Liverpool, 'and feel that it has an inspiring ring and force of its own; which I hope it will not lose in the revision which I recommend. Beatrice has the power which is to my mind one of the most characteristic notes of great ability, the power of investing what she takes up with charm.'

*Monday evening.* [The Argoed]
So my little one is rejected, even at the private gate! Still there is encouragement in the rejection – and I shall get to work all the harder. After all, it savours something of ignorant self-confidence to have attempted a critical essay after two months' study! What a blessing true friends are.

*28 September.* [The Argoed]
Very tired and weary with my summer's work. Spent two days castle-building about the great man at Highbury and re-read that episode of six months ago. He either has a courteous wish to show that he has forgotten, or he does not wish to lose all hold on me; for he half asked through Beatrice for an invitation here (which of course he did not get) and sent for my opinion about an East End charity. I hold to the 'courteous wish' explanation; and shall always treat his advances as such, give him back respectful courtesy and no more. For me, it would be happier if I never heard more of that family. They have been black friends for me. But faithfulness, pride, and sentiment hold me from a complete separation.

I doubt whether I shall ever see that man again. At least for a time, I have made it impossible and in spite of the deep humiliation it is happier so – for it limits my horizon to *work*.

But at times a working life is weary work for a woman. The brain is worn and the heart unsatisfied, and in those intervals of exhaustion the old craving for love and devotion, given and taken, returns and an idealized life of love and sympathy passes before one's eyes; little ones, too, of flesh and blood, dependent on one and upon whom one might in old age depend. God grant that I may not see old age! . . . Ah! me. The years are passing – from painful childhood into an unhealthy youth, two years of brilliant girlhood and then a working womanhood with friendship and not love. Work, work, work, how does it differ from stitch, stitch, stitch? In one element, that of growth, new *power*.

Beatrice had an agreement with her sisters that one of them would care for her father for part of each year so that she could take a working holiday in London.

*9 October.* [The Argoed]

The day before I leave for my holiday. . . . Dear Father lives on in perfect content and happiness. His dying life is like the autumn tints, a beauty that tells decay. One painful episode in which I had to openly disobey him, to use force, refuse to post a letter ordering his brokers to buy more Northern Pacific ordinary stock. It is a mercy to have settled all responsibility on Daniel Meinertzhagen, with whom I keep up a steady business correspondence. Dear old Father, he was hurt at the tone though even in the evening he said to Mrs Thompson: 'She does it for my good, but it is rather hard.' Of course speculation would mean another stroke, as well as loss of money.

Rosy is springing up to health and beauty. She has spent the whole time in work and occupation of all sorts, cooking, work among the poor on the hill. There is now nothing to dislike in the child; there is even a certain sweetness and dependence that is lovable and attractive. This place has been most successful for her. . . . I shall never be an intimate friend; indeed it is better that I should not be so for my nature is too exciting in its aims, too profoundly unconventional in its methods not to strain her in friendship. And then, poor dear child, she bores me intensely when she attempts to be intellectual. She will be far more interesting as a practical woman; may indeed develop the dry wit of an observant and indifferent mind.

*16 October.* [York House]

Flew down to see Clara Ryland at Highbury where she is in charge, while the great man and his daughter are away. I was glad to see the house again, the home of my hero. Poor woman, she feels the physical ills of married life keenly! Suffered 29 hours in her confinement. She misses too the comfortable ease of her old life. . . . I love that woman though she is not in any way clever and in spite of my personal grudge against her – for I think she used me badly in her anxiety to give her brother just what he wanted, when he wanted it and to throw it overboard when he found it did not suit. But personal grudges seldom stick with me. . . .

The house is gorgeous, soft and easy to live in. The society genuine and respectable, the family life affectionate and well ordered. Mr Ryland I like, a warm-hearted man with plenty of practical intelligence. Between us there is a kindly feeling; for I, unwittingly, was the cause of his happiness. It was the report that the great brother was to be married to me that brought him to the point as the sister's suitor. And I think he knows my story. That evening last winter when I was sobbing so bitterly, I heard Clara talking to him in a low voice below – and at the time I little doubted that he was told all. I don't think I resented it – what is pride beside true, deep feeling? . . . Will the pain of it ever cease? Now I can think of the whole story calmly, and see how I was led away by the excitement around me long before there was any need for decision. It is better as it is: and the great man was right in his final word, though cruel in the way he said it. And I wish him nothing but good and, if I believed in prayer, would pray for his success and happiness.

Herbert Spencer often went to stay in Brighton.

*18 October.* [York House]
Ran down to Brighton to see the old philosopher – a pious journey. A great mind run dry. But I love the poor old man, and my warm feeling gladdens his life. . . . Ah! me, there come times in life when one would recommend universal suicide, for the whole business of living seems too horribly tiresome to all concerned. And I feel seedy today, sick and headachy and discouraged, but my spirit will return. I need a change, and think the world is going to the Devil because I am ailing in body and mind. Courage, my friend, courage.

*31 October.* [York House]
Returned yesterday from Bacup: a visit full of interest. . . . I shall write a short account while the impression is still clear. Three years ago I meant to do it but was overwhelmed by the approach of the Great Man. Now I am safely hid from his view, in profound obscurity. . . .

Bacup, in spite of municipal life and Co-operative industry, is spiritually still part of the 'old world'. It knows nothing of the complexities of modern life, and in the monotony of its daily existence likens the hand-loom village of a century ago. The restless ambition, the complicated motives, and the far-stretching imagination of cosmopolitanism find no place in the gentle minds of Bacup folk. . . . Sitting by the hands at work, watching the invigorating quickness of the machinery, the pleasant fellowship of men, women and children, the absence of care and the presence of common interest, the general well-being of well-earned and well-paid work, one was tempted to think that here, indeed, was happiness – unknown to the strained brain-worker, the idle and overfed rich, or the hardly pressed very poor. Young men and women mix freely;

they know each other as fellow-workers, members of the same or kindred chapels; they watch each other from childhood upwards, live always in each other's company. They pair naturally, according to well-tested affinity, physical and spiritual. Public opinion, which means religiously guided opinion, presses heavily on the mis-doer or the non-worker, the outcasting process, the reverse of the attracting force of East End life, seen clearly in this small community ridding it of the ne'er do well and the habitual out o' work. There are no attractions for those who have not sources of love and interest within them; no work for those who cannot, or will not work constantly.

On the other hand, ill-success and unmerited failure are dealt with gently, for these people are in the main thinking of another world, and judge people not according to the position they have scrambled into in this, but according to their place in a future heaven ... this class eats too little and, above all, sleeps too little – growing boys getting only six or seven hours' bed – and their unfortunate mother who calls them lying awake half the night so as to be in time, and sitting up for the latest and oldest to get to bed. But overtime is forbidden for women and children, and it is here that one sees the benefit of the Factory Acts and consequent inspection. *Laissez-faire* breaks down when one watches these things from the inside. . . .

### 7 November. York House

Is it this house with all its painful associations that drags me down again into this spiritless melancholy, or is it discouragement or ill-health? The dark autumn weather, the garden lonely and strewn with leaves, all the kith and kin out of London, the sight of the old work and the companionship of fellow-workers all bring a rush of the old memories. And of late I have given way to the old old feeling which sometimes I despair of ever shaking off. . . . The lot I have drawn in life is an evil-omened number. Still, there is freedom, freedom to do, to think and to feel the highest possible to one's nature. Happiness is a closed book – work is hardly opened. . . .

This undated entry was written when Beatrice was looking after the second pair of buildings she managed with Ella Pycroft, who was away.

### Wentworth Dwellings

It would not do for me to live alone. I should become morbid. I miss terribly the dependence of others on me, the happy necessity to seem bright, forcing one to put down depression sternly. And the East End life, with its dirt, drunkenness and immorality, absence of combined effort or common interest, saddens me . . . I could not live down here. I should loose heart . . . practical work does not satisfy me; it seems like walking on shifting sand . . .

Where is the wish for better things in those myriads of beings hurrying along the streets night and day? Even their careless, sensual laugh, the coarse jokes and unloving words depress one as one presses through the crowd, and almost shudders to touch them. It is not so much the actual vice, it is the low level of monotonous and yet excited life, the regular recurrence of street sensations in quarrels and fights, the greedy street bargaining, and the petty theft and gambling.

The better natures keep apart from their degraded fellow-citizens and fellow-workers, live lonely and perforce selfish lives. . . . These buildings too are to my mind an utter failure. In spite of Ella Pycroft's heroic efforts, they are not an influence for good. . . . The lady collectors are an altogether superficial thing. Undoubtedly their gentleness and kindness bring light into many homes, but what are they in face of this collected brutality . . . And how can one raise these beings to better things without the hope in a better world, the faith in the usefulness of effort? Why resist the drink demon? A short life and a merry one. Why not? . . .

The bright side of East End life is the sociability and generous sharing of small means. . . . there are glimpses into better homes – sights of love between men and women and towards little children – and rarely enough, devotion to the aged and the sick. And possibly it is this occasional rest from dirt and disorder that makes the work more depressing; for one must hear unheeded the sickening cry of the sinking man or woman dragging the little ones down into a poverty from which there is no rising. . . .

*1 December. Kildare*
I have been so wretched during most of my seven weeks away that I am glad to get back to my home and my home duties. Intellectual work is the only occupation that absorbs my mind, prevents the constant brooding over the mistakes of the past and the dreary possibilities of the future. Perhaps too I was discouraged with the ill-success of my writing, though the idea was hailed as a good one. I must to it again. . . .

There was as yet no English translation of Karl Marx's *Capital.* Frederick Myers (1843–1901) was one of the founders of the Society for Psychical Research in 1882.

*10 December.* [Kildare]

Ten days' hard work at Karl Marx ending in a cold in bed. Finished the first volume, that one translated into French.

Certainly our little party is not an enlivening one. Dear Father – merely a shadow . . . Sleeps, eats, is read to, and sleeps again; spending most of the 24 hours in a half-comatose state. Little Miss Darling, depressed and small-minded, melancholy, cross with her meaningless little life; still she is a loving little body and would have grown through love. And then Rosy! That sodden weight. Poor child, how I pity her life companion! . . . But have I a right to criticize? For my life is contracted into a ceaseless regard for self, a petty regret for the past and fear of the future. Why this ceaseless grasping after that phantom – happiness? And as the only alternative why this desperate clutch at *Power* – power to impress and to lead? No wonder I gain only a powerless unhappiness.

Frederick Myers wrote an interesting article in one of the reviews the other day on multiple personality, giving pathological cases in which absolutely different personalities appeared in the same person according as different parts of their brain were physically acted upon. . . . And certainly in my own case I have noticed a duplex personality, and have been happy or unhappy as one or the other got uppermost. The sadness and suffering of my early life brought out the *nether* being in me; the despondent vain, grasping person – (the Heyworth) – doomed to failure. Linked to this nethermost being was the phantom of Mother, the gloomily religious – affecting asceticism and dominated by superstition. Left under the dominion of this personality my natural vacation and destiny was the convent . . .

But there is in me another person. An enthusiast for Truth, regarding self only as a means to further Truth. . . . a lover of thought and ready to sacrifice all things to it. Essentially a *realist* in intellectual questions, a rationalist in metaphysics and therefore a sceptic of religion. This is the happiest and perhaps the highest expression of my Ego. But alas! this being has its life and origin in my sensual nature: it springs from vigorous senses and keen perceptions. If I were a man, this creature would be free, though not dissolute, in its morals, a lover of women. . . . as I am a woman: these feelings, unless fulfilled in marriage, which would mean destruction of the intellectual being, must remain controlled and unsatisfied, finding their only vent in one quality of the phantom companion of the nethermost personality, religious exaltation.

And so, in this ill-sorted round of disjointed circles, there is constant friction. And my intimacy with the great man brought about a deadly fight between the intellectual and the sensual . . . The battle was long and terrible . . . But now – Fate, that term for outside and independent forces, has built strong barriers and forced Will to be at least passive. And womanly dignity and reserve side with Fate and forbid the inroads of Passion. . . .

Two days in London with the Booths. Charlie absorbed in his inquiry, working all his evenings with three paid secretaries. I have promised to undertake the docks in my March holiday. Dear sweet little Mary, with her loving ways and charming motherhood. They become each year more near to me. Perhaps they are the only persons who really *love* me. It is sad, that my family for whom I have a strong affection, are so distant from my real aims in life. . . . With none of my sisters can I talk in the perfectly unconstrained way I talk to my friends – for they all secretly condemn my want of success and think my aim absurdly out of proportion to my capacity – that is to say, if they know my aim. . . . This old year wears out sadly – but it began *desperately*. Courage. . . .

*23 December.* [Kildare]
Made up my mind to do it. Anything would be better than this constant torture. Cut them [the Chamberlain family] all off. . . . But the next month must be lived through and maybe I shall be obliged to entertain Clara Ryland. Then it shall be over.

∼ 1887 ∼

*22 January.* [Kildare]
Written to put off my visit to the Arthur Chamberlains. It is like a load off my mind . . . Only Clara to whom I owe aught; and I will see the last of her this time. Why should my life be spoilt simply from a feeling of loyalty? I shall always have a gentle feeling towards that family . . . And perhaps I have misunderstood them. Anyhow let them rest in peace.

*5 February.* [Kildare]
An unpleasant week in London, broken down with neuralgia and weakness, both of which still oppress me. Perhaps I needed this terrible lesson of pain and weakness to teach me the suicidal effect of giving way to intellectual ambition and to strong feeling. Sometimes I have said to

myself – these dreams are but dreams, why not indulge in them, why deny myself this harmless gratification? I have not counted the cost – the waking up, perhaps with weakened energies, to the dull routine of daily life. I wonder whether I shall bear my life through or whether, when the last remaining ice is broken, I shall break with life and end it in a sleep. How willingly I would yield it.

*25 February*. [Kildare]
Three weeks absorbed in my review of Karl Marx, which I have now nearly ended. It has cleared my own ideas, but whether it is written in a form that will be accepted and 'take' I do not know. . . . If only I could work from the pure love of my work and not need to stimulate my effort by vulgar ambition!

My spirits have risen into youthfulness. It is rare for me to feel youthful but just now I do! and am looking forward to my month in London. . . .

Began investigation of docks. . . .

Edward Spencer Beesly (1831–1915), professor of history at University College, London, was a well-known Positivist, and was much interested in labour problems.

*12 March*. [London]
The Booths are delighted with my article. Charlie enthusiastic. They sent it to Professor Beesly. . . . He overlooks the whole point of the article, which is to distinguish between the labour that is useful and the labour that is useless. . . . However, if my idea is true it is unlikely that it will be accepted all at once, especially by men who are pledged by past utterances to contrary opinions. . . .

Long day at the docks. . . .

Sir George Otto Trevelyan (1838–1928), historian and politician, had been Chief Secretary in Dublin 1882–84. Beatrice accompanied Sir George and the Courtneys to Leonard's Cornish constituency. She was reading Emile Zola's *Bonheur des dames*. *Princess Casamassima*, by Henry James (1843–1916), had been published the previous year.

*15–17 March. Visit to Liskeard*
Leonard, Kate, Sir George Trevelyan and I left London on 15 March for Liskeard. Sir George Trevelyan is a tall, thin, nervous man, with a

delicately courteous manner; one of the 'charming persons' of London society. . . . The Trevelyans are one of the oldest English families, distinguished for lack of distinction and for their luck in marrying heiresses . . . the present representative married early in life a Manchester girl with a rent roll of £12,000 a year.

But Sir George is a Macaulay as well as a Trevelyan: his mother was the beloved and gifted sister of the great historian. He was born under the shadow of the great 'Uncle Tom' [Thomas Babington Macaulay], and trained by him in literary and political life. . . . Political personalities, to me the most tiresome of subjects, were the order of the day. . . .

. . . Sir George Trevelyan, Kate and I journeyed to Plymouth . . . Kate left us at Exeter and I looked forward with some constraint to 6 hours' *tête-à-tête* with the 'charming person'. I was not the 'colleague's wife' but a 'Miss Potter' with whom he had unfortunately to travel. I begged him to go into a smoking carriage – and my prayer was genuine – for had I not in the pocket of my sealskin not only a volume of Zola, but my case of cigarettes! neither of which could I enjoy in his distinguished presence. . . . But it was a case of 'no go' with the model man – and we both subsided into our corners, he to read *Princess Casamassima* (with which he was highly delighted) and I to pretend to sleep and amuse myself with picturing the past two days . . . Sir G. Trevelyan, agreeably surprised by my modest silence, thought at least he ought to address me, and read at short intervals bits from the paper about the snowstorm and an exhibition at Rome – to all of which I returned a polite 'How very interesting' and subsided back into my meditative doze. . . .

Beatrice occasionally stayed at the house of her brother-in-law William Cripps.

*30 March. 2 Stratford Place* [Marylebone, London, W.1.]
Thoroughly enjoyed the last month. . . . inquiring into social facts is interesting work, but it needs the devotion of a life to do it thoroughly. I feel that the little bit of work I do will be very superficial . . . In the meantime I am enjoying my life. I see more reason for believing that the sacrifices I have made to a special intellectual desire were warranted by a certain amount of faculty. . . . And the old faith in individual work is returning. . . . When I gave up my nature to the great passion of my life I denied this faith though I could not rid my nature of the effect of it. Even in those moments when I believed the time was come, when I looked forward to the joys of satisfied passion, a blank 'and after?' stared

at me in the background. 'And after?', that cynical question asked by conscience of triumphant love.

The morning breaks and the cock crows, awakening the mortal paralysed by fear, or soothed by passion, to the old, old, question – And Peter is not the only man who turns round and weeps.

[22 April. Brighton?]
Paid Mr Spencer a visit. Found him in a pitiable condition. Perfectly hopeless, thinks that he can neither eat, walk nor talk. . . . he wished to discuss an important business matter . . . that of Beatrice Potter as literary executor. I was taken aback, but it was evident that he had set his heart on it and longed, poor old man, that someone who loved him should complete his life. I was very much touched by his confidence in me, though I suggested he might find a fitter person from a literary point of view. I can quite understand his feeling. He instinctively feels that . . . the world will look back upon him as a thinking machine and not as a man with all a man's need for a woman's love and devotion and for the living affection of children. And my relationship to him represents in a way both the absent elements. . . .

Millicent Garrett Fawcett (1847–1929) became the president of the National Union of Women's Suffrage Societies in 1897. The movement for women's rights had been gathering momentum for half a century; its legislative successes included the Married Women's Property Act (1882). Suffrage resolutions had been presented in Parliament (in the Lords in 1851 and the Commons in 1870), and John Stuart Mill's *Subjection of Women* (1869) was a powerful argument in their support. There were now local groups all over the country. John Morley (1838–1923) was a Liberal statesman and man of letters.

*6 May.* [London]
. . . This morning I walked along Billingsgate from Fresh Wharf to the London docks. Crowded with loungers smoking bad tobacco, and coarse, careless talk with the clash of a halfpenny on the pavement every now and again. Bestial content or hopeless discontent on their faces. The lowest form of leisure – senseless curiosity about street rows, idle gazing at the street sellers, low jokes – and this is the chance the docks offer. . . .

Dinner in the evening with the Courtneys. John Morley, Mr Arthur Balfour (Secretary for Ireland), Mr E. Russell (editor of *Liverpool Post* and rising politician), Mrs Fawcett and Mrs Dugdale (Sir G. Trevelyan's sister). . . . The conversation, though easy and pleasant, was all froth. No one said what they thought and everyone said what they thought to be clever. But the individual who interested me most was Mrs Dugdale. She had asked to meet me and evidently wished to make my acquaintance. She is the fascinating widow sister of Sir George Trevelyan and lives for distinguished and interesting society. She is supposed to be a friend and possibly the future wife of Chamberlain, and that was the reason she wished to know me. I felt it instinctively, and as I looked at her charming person, with all the daintiness of a well-bred lady, I felt her superiority to me in attractiveness. She would suit him, but she would not suit his family. . . . She is a thin-natured woman, superficially sympathetic and with admirable tact – no vices or even queer faults – but with little generosity or depth of feeling. But she is adaptable, without conviction, and worshipping distinction.

She tried to book me to go to the House with her, but I would not. Even if she were not connected with me in that subtle way, I should not care to know her. It is not worth my while to know 'Society' – to meet it occasionally at the house of my distinguished brother-in-law refreshes me, makes me feel how little I lose in being out of it.

*12 May.* [London]
Docks early morning. . . . Robinson, socialist dock labourer, originally tobacconist. Emigrated, and returned to England because he became homesick. . . . Complains that women of working class are no companions to their husbands. 'When I was courting my wife I could not get a word out of her – it was just walking by her side and giving her an occasional kiss. If a working man gets a good mother, and a woman that doesn't drink, as his wife, that's as much as he can expect. And my wife wasn't the first woman I courted – they're all alike in not talking of anything but details.'

T. R. Malthus (1766–1834), an influential English economist, maintained that poverty was unavoidable because the population would always increase faster than the means of subsistence. 'Neo-Malthusianism' was the polite phrase for the advocacy of birth control. *The Fruits of Philosophy, or the Private Companion of Young Married Couples* (1832) was a pioneer work on contraception written by an American physician named Charles Knowlton. He was sentenced to three years in prison when it was published. In 1877 Charles Bradlaugh and his collaborator Annie Besant were prosecuted in London for selling the book.

*13 May.* [London]

Most amusing afternoon with Kerrigan, in Victoria Park. Victoria Park lies in the extreme east of London. It is surrounded by streets of small two-storied houses of the genteel type; a porch and one bow-window, venetian blinds and a lace curtain. These are inhabited by the lower middle class. Now and again there is a row of more modest little dwellings, without the bow or the porch, or with a bow of less publicity and consideration, the abode of the aristocrats of the working class, mechanics or permanent labourers.

Sunday afternoon is a great time in Victoria Park . . . the meeting-place of the enthusiasts and the curious-minded of the whole East End district. The first group we came to were congregating round a small organ. . . . the Elder Branch of the ancient sect of Primitive Methodists. Verily they looked like the adjectives of their title! The second group, larger and more within the combative spirit of the age, 'The Christian Association of Young Men' [Y.M.C.A.], composed of city clerks, spotty, seedy and smelly, but one or two among them inspired with living enthusiasm. They were singing loudly, when we reached them, of the Blood of Jesus, and that eternal happiness which is . . . to compensate for an existence of dreary half-starved drudgery. . . .

. . . facing another crowd there was a messenger from the Hall of Science. He was explaining to an attentive audience of working men that man was an animal, and nothing but. . . . He used scientific phrases, quoted freely from Huxley, Darwin and German physiologists, and assumed a certain impartiality in his treatment of rival religious theories of man's development. But the thickest crowd surrounded the banner of the Socialist Democrat. From a platform a hoarse-voiced man denounced the iniquities of the social system. His hearers were also working men, on their faces earnest attention. In one hand he held Malthus, in the other *The Fruits of Philosophy*. The subject was a delicate one, the two rival methods of checking the growth of the population – late marriage versus preventive checks. But he joined issue with both methods, for he declared that neither was needed. There was bread enough for all if it was equally distributed. Men starved while ware-houses were stocked to overflowing – it was the commercial system that was at fault, not the laws of nature. The crowd was not enthusiastic, only interested and eager to listen to new suggestions. But for the most part they were men in full employment whose speculative interest in social reform was not whetted by positive hunger. . . .

Some yards from these in the open grass space, a circle of the strangest individuals. 'Latter Day Saints' was inscribed on their banner. They seemed like beings from another world. Bearded, soft, illogical and illiterate, they stood there preaching alternatively, listened to by a scoffing crowd. . . . They offered, meekly, the other cheek, remained silent with closed eyes, or struck up a feeble hymn to drown opposition. . . .

We wended our way back between the groups and crowds to Mr Kerrigan's lodgings. . . . Ah! what would the conventional West End acquaintance say to two young women smoking and talking in the bed, sitting, working, smoking and bath room of an East End School Board visitor? It is quite sad leaving the homely Quakers' hotel. Ella Pycroft and I have found each other excellent company. We have entertained freely and thoroughly enjoyed our life in working-class society. . . .

> The next section of the diary deals with Beatrice's final exchange with Chamberlain. Chamberlain had been in touch with Beatrice intermittently through his sister and daughter, and on 19 May wrote saying he had met Charles Booth at breakfast at the Courtneys' and that he had subsequently read a paper written by Booth, for the Statistical Society, on 'The Inhabitants of the Tower Hamlets'. Once again he asked Beatrice what might be done, since he was equally sceptical about large-scale charity, state employment schemes and emigration. It is clear from the following diary entry that Beatrice responded to this letter and agreed to visit Birmingham again. The second Chamberlain letter, dated 5 June, accepted an invitation from Richard Potter to visit The Argoed on 23 July; and in a third letter Chamberlain, who wished to go to the Queen's golden jubilee naval review, postponed the visit until 30 July – a decision confirmed by the fourth letter on 21 June.

*9 June. The Argoed*
I spent a week with the poor old philosopher in Brighton. . . . Most of the time I spent sleeping or wandering by the uninteresting sea. I meant to have worked but I dreamt instead.

I dreamt of the scene I was soon to see; another act of old, old story. A week from the day I left the old philosopher lying wearily in bed, I sat in a crowded hall in Birmingham. Within a few steps of me stood the great man on the platform. . . . He was white and agitated, for this was a crucial time, whether or not these meetings would be successful. He has lost none of his old charm of voice and manner, less arrogance and a touch of stern sorrow at the defection of friends . . . But his speech showed no hesitation. Resist unto death was his true motto. And after he sat down it was natural our eyes should meet in the old way. . . . [however] the speech had a different flavour. Sentimental sympathy for the wrongs of the down-trodden masses was exchanged for a determination to preserve law and order. The statesman had overcome the demagogue.

. . . Met the great man and his daughter at the Arthur Chamberlains'. Result – invited him to come and see Father and enjoy bracing air and beautiful scenery. In six weeks the great man comes, and before then I must have my article written. Now to work, try to forget that which it is useless to remember . . . In his relation to me there has been a strange lack of chivalry and honour. In mine to him, of womanly dignity.

Beatrice could not contain her misery any longer, and when Chamberlain visited The Argoed she told him how strongly she felt, at the same time insisting that they should not meet again. Chamberlain kept his emotional distance, saying that they could remain friends, but Beatrice wrote to say this was impossible. On 7 August he sent his last letter:

> I thank you sincerely for your kind letter. I cannot help feeling depressed and discouraged at times and I value greatly the sympathy which you have shown me.
>
> The concluding part of your letter has given me much pain. Did I indeed do wrong in accepting your invitation? If so forgive me and allow me to tell you frankly what I feel. At your own request I destroyed your letter of March 1886. There was one passage in it on which I did not presume to put a definite interpretation, and which I thought at the time was rather the outcome of a sensitive mind, overstrained by suffering and work, than the expression of settled feeling. I thought you had forgotten it and wished me to forget it also.
>
> So much for the past – now as to the future. Why are we never to see each other again? Why can not we be friends – 'comrades' – to use your own expression? I like you very much – I respect and esteem you – I enjoy your conversation and society and I have often wished that fate had thrown us more together.
>
> If you share this feeling to any extent why should we surrender a friendship which ought to be good for both of us?
>
> I have so much confidence in your generosity as well as in your good sense that I am encouraged to make this appeal to you in what I feel to be a very delicate matter.
>
> The circumstances of my past life have made me solitary and

reserved, but it is hard that I should lose one of the few friends whose just opinions I value and the sense of whose regard and sympathy would be a strength and support to me.

I cannot say more. You must decide, and if it is for your happiness that we should henceforth be strangers I will make no complaint.

I return your letter, as you wish it, but there is surely no reason why you should be ashamed of feelings which are purely womanly and for which I have nothing but gratitude and respect.

I am always

Yours very sincerely
J. CHAMBERLAIN

At the end of this letter Beatrice wrote the following comment.

This letter after I had, in another moment of suicidal misery told him I cared for him passionately. This after he had pursued me for 18 months and dragged me back into an acquaintance I had all along avoided. To insist on meeting a woman who had told you she loved you in order to humiliate her further.

*8 August.* [The Argoed]
A week's unhappiness added on to the long chain of misery already forged – seemingly impossible to break. But I have health and intelligence and a warm heart and I have suffered pain – surely these shall not be wasted. And after all, all my crime has been being too much a child of nature, saying what I thought and felt too simply. Feeling has overridden dignity. And now to work again. . . .

Gracedieu was the Booths' country estate in the Charnwood Forest, Leicestershire. Beatrice and Charles Booth visited Manchester Art Gallery.

[August?]. *Manchester*
I shall not forget the misery of that day's journey up to London. The nerve was not killed! And added to pain was the feeling that I could no longer respect the man. Since that correspondence of 1886, he has tried every means to renew the acquaintance. Six or seven times in the year I have refused his overtures, made directly or through his family. At last I gave way. If he had treated me with simple respect when we met at his brother's house, there would have been a reason in his advances. He could well have said – you told me to forget and I thought you wished

me to mark my continued respect for you. But he behaved towards me as the triumphant lover, as a man who is sure of his conquest. And then after that visit to The Argoed with another proof that I cared for him deeply and desired that we should not see each other again, to appeal to my 'generosity' to be his friend; of course I was weak and gave way again, weak and romantic. But he did not like the tone of my letter. Perhaps that has saved me from more entanglement.

The visit to the Booths followed up by two days here has recovered my spirits. The beautiful old place, filled to overflowing with happiness and youth, checked my egotistical suffering. The Booths' home life at 'Gracedieu' is perfect. Mary says her life is one continual sunshine. Charlie has the three sides of his existence complete – profession, home, intellectual interest. His business, he says, is the most important to him of the three, but I expect he under-rates the constant happiness of satisfied affection. He and I have spent two evenings here alone, principally at the pictures. We are very fond of each other, a close intimate relation between a man and woman without sentiment (perhaps not without sentiment but without passion or the dawning of passion). We are fellow-workers, both inspired by the same intellectual desire. Only in his life it is only an etc.; in my life if it becomes anything it would become the dominating aim.

The exhibition of pictures is well worth seeing. . . . Undoubtedly the pre-Raphaelites stand out as the greatest individualists. Walker, Burne-Jones, Rossetti, Watts – all expressing suffering in one form or the other, significant of the passion or weariness of mental development . . . No age which has produced these men as the leading artists can be called materialistic. . . .

Settled with Charlie on the autumn's work. The sweating system is to be the subject of my next paper. I have it in my mind to make it more of a picture than my article on 'Dock Life' – to dramatize it. . . . I could not get at the picture without living among the actual workers. This I think I could do. . . .

*21 August. The Argoed*
Spending these days in reading English literature with a view to gain the ease and simplicity of style which Leonard says I lack; also in order to discover the secret of great writing, whether prose or poetry. To me it seems as if the art of presenting pictures to the mind were the aim of writing. . . .

*29 August.* [The Argoed]

Visit of three days from the Barnetts, which has confirmed my friendship with them. Mr Barnett distinguished for unself-consciousness, humility and faith. Intellectually he is suggestive, with a sort of moral insight almost like that of a woman. And in another respect he is like a strong woman; he is much more anxious that human nature should *feel rightly* than that they should *think truly, being* is more important with him than *doing*. . . . He was very sympathetic about my work and anxious to be helpful. But evidently he foresaw in it dangers to my character, and it was curious to watch the minister's anxiety about the *morale* of his friend creep out in all kinds of hints. He held up as a moral scarecrow the 'Oxford Don', the man or woman without human ties, and with no care for the details of life. He told his wife that I reminded him of Octavia Hill, and as he described Miss Hill's life as one of isolation from superiors and from inferiors, it is clear what rocks he saw ahead. . . .

Mrs Barnett is an active-minded, true and warm-hearted woman. She is conceited. She would be objectionably conceited if it were not for her genuine belief in her husband's superiority . . . But the good in Mrs Barnett predominates . . . Her personal aim in life is to raise womanhood to its rightful position; as equal, though unlike, to manhood. The crusade she has undertaken is the fight against impurity as the main factor in debasing women from a status of independence to one of physical dependence. The common opinion that a woman is a nonentity unless joined to a man, she resents as a 'blasphemy'. Like all crusaders, she is bigoted and does not recognize all the facts that tell against her faith. I told her that the only way in which we can convince the world of our power is to show it! And for that it will be needful for women with strong natures to remain celibate, so that the special force of womanhood, motherly feeling, may be forced into public work. . . .

A week staying with the Courtneys. It is delightful to watch their happiness. Success has made Leonard more cordial and open-minded. As chairman of committees all the finest points of his character are brought into play, and his deficiencies are not seen. . . . Kate has become 'the wife of Leonard Courtney'. She basks in the sunshine of happiness. Her life is a purely social one and not demanding much self-sacrifice or self-devotion. . . . She has lived a good deal apart from her family but since her happy and successful marriage she has always tried to welcome them, though she has been unwilling to take more than her share of family duty, and perhaps even to shirk this. She is benevolent and worldly, a good citizen of the world but not a heroine. . . .

*30 September. The Argoed*
The day (yesterday) we gave up York House, my article on 'Dock Life'
appeared in the *Nineteenth Century*. . . . Goodbye, little home, with your
picturesque surroundings and all-expressing scenery, goodbye, summer
of 1887 with your cross-purposes and crooked ways. Enter, persistent,
patient work, with faith but no hope! Next year we shall be here again,
not altered in one condition, but *grown*.

> Beatrice now had no London home. She stayed with relatives and friends,
> but usually took a room in the Devonshire House Hotel, a Quaker estab-
> lishment near Liverpool Street Station. In October she started to research
> into conditions in the boot, shoe and tailoring trades, interviewing offi-
> cials and workers. It was part of her inquiry into the sweating system,
> which was to lead into a wider, sympathetic study of Jewish life in the
> East End, undertaken in the course of the Booth investigation and pub-
> lished as part of it. She was encouraged by the Chief Rabbi and helped by
> prominent members of the Jewish community. Olive Schreiner
> (1855–1920), author and feminist, was best known for *The Story of an
> African Farm* (1883).

*14 October.* [Devonshire House Hotel]
The Akeds, mother and son, have been staying with me. They are
simple, true-hearted people, strong Christians. I love these Lancashire
folk. I showed them all over London; the one thing they delighted in was
the endless galleries of books in the British Museum. Olive Schreiner
was staying here. She is a wonderfully attractive little woman, brimming
over with sympathy and thought. Titus Aked lost his heart to her; her
charm of manner and conversation bowled over the true-hearted
'Lancashire laddie' . . .
    Very favourable notice of my article in the *Daily Telegraph*. . . .

*19 October.* [Devonshire House Hotel]
First morning learning how to sweat; Mrs Moses, 78 Oxford Street,
Stepney. Four rooms and a kitchen, one room let for 3*s*. Deserted street
during the daytime. Public house at each corner. Small back yard. Three
rooms on ground floor, two used as workshop. Large room with two
machinists – Polish Jews – and master who acts as presser.
    In back room, mistress, first hand who was a Scotch woman and two
girls learning the trade. Coats turned out at 1*s* 2*d* each, trimmings and
thread supplied by the sweater. Buttonholes 4 1/2*d* a dozen by woman

outside. Mistress said the women by working very hard could earn 10s a week, with 2s deducted for silk. Evidently these people worked tremendously hard, a woman working from 8 a.m. to 10 p.m. without looking round, and master working up to 2 o'clock and often beginning at five in the morning. The mistress was too busy to give me much information and I did nothing but sew on buttons and fell sleeves in. They all seemed very pleasant together. . . .

*20 October. Devonshire House Hotel*
Spent over a fortnight here. . . . At times terribly despondent and disgusted with my own, impulsive, mad behaviour. At other times enjoying my spectator's life and successful in my attempts to forget the immediate past. After all, it will soon be like a dream – to him and to me.

*1 November. Kildare, Bournemouth*
Again the comfortable lodgings. Father's step on the landing with the drag of the foot on the oil-cloth. From the sitting-room windows the broad cliff walk; immediately behind it, the sea, the same everlasting beat of the waves on the shore . . . The pine-wooded town, smart young ladies and delicate narrow-chested men, and an occasional weather-beaten admiral or retired general, men and women, for the most part, whose interest is centred in gossip over five o'clock tea. The social life of Bournemouth is not invigorating, even to look at from the outside; to live in would be purgatory. But I come down to rest . . . the struggle is finally over. Passion lies at my feet, dead. At first, I stood over it and wept bitter tears. Now, I have buried it and think of it tenderly. I have lived through my youth – it is over. But I am only on the threshold of working womanhood . . .

I see before me clearly the ideal life for work. . . . Love and cheerfulness in my home life; faithful friendship with a few . . . and lastly charity and sympathy towards women of my own class who need it, whether they be struggling young girls, hard-pressed married women or disappointed spinsters. Every woman has a mission to other women – more especially to the women of her own class and circumstances. It is difficult to be much help to men (except as an example in the way of persistent effort and endurance in spite of womanly weakness); do what one will, sentiment creeps in, in return for sympathy. Perhaps as one loses one's attractiveness this will wear off – *certainly* it will. At present it is only with working men one feels free to sympathize without fear of unpleasant consequences. . . .

On the whole I am encouraged by the publication of my article. It made no great sensation and was snubbed by the *Spectator* and ignored by the other papers except the *Daily Telegraph*. But it was thought *painstaking and thorough*, and showed that I understood my subject. . . .

*13 November.* [Kildare?]
A very happy peaceful fortnight, with one drawback, tooth-ache. Wrote out my notes and shall tomorrow decide on my plan of campaign with Charlie for the coming month in London. Read four volumes of Macaulay's history. It interests me, not only as a standard work, but as the writing of Mary Booth's uncle. In the seven volumes there is only one chapter devoted to the 'condition of the people' question. Not one word, except in this chapter, about home industry, the growth of foreign commerce, literature, art, or the habits and occupations of the various classes of the English people. . . .

*16 November.* [Devonshire House Hotel]
Delightful evening with the Booths. Charlie looked tired and worried. . . .
   Dined at Toynbee Hall and attended conference on women's wages. . . . I was induced to speak in spite of my dreadful nervousness. I *must* conquer it – it is necessary for me to be able to speak on occasions.

   Annie Besant (1847–1933), Secularist, Fabian, trade union organizer,
   Theosophist and later a founder of the Indian nationalist movement, had
   a disastrous marriage with the nephew of Sir Walter Besant.

*27 November.* [Devonshire House Hotel]
Nearly half my month past. A certain amount of definite information and a confused impression of men, women and places, a jostling of images each seeking to efface the other. I am sorry I have not seen Mrs Besant again. We met and [I] felt interested in that powerful woman, with her blighted wifehood and motherhood and her thirst for power and defiance of the world. I heard her speak, the only woman I have ever known who is a real orator, who has the gift of public persuasion. But to *see* her speaking made me shudder. It is not womanly to thrust yourself before the world. A woman, in all the relations of life, should be sought. It is only on great occasions, when religious feeling or morality demand it, that a woman has a right to lift up her voice and call aloud to her fellow-mortals. . . .

*6 December.* [Kildare]
Father's illness has taken a turn for the worse. He has completely lost his memory. He asks question after question: whether Mother is dead, where he lives, and why he is living here.

*13 December.* [Kildare]
Father much better: memory returning. . . . Intend to spend these two months in reading history and studying composition. Hope to read through Gardner, Lecky, Walpole; to translate Chaucer into modern prose; and to write from dictation selections of various writers.

*Christmas Day.* [Kildare]
The first Xmas for five years that I have been in a peaceful happy frame of mind. . . . Then my ambition was individual work . . . the scientific description of society. If only I had been true to my ambition! . . . Even now a foolish, quixotic generosity urges me not to turn my back on the figures of the past. Happily a feeling of contempt for dishonourable and unchivalrous conduct has killed all other feelings except sadness that the same qualities which wounded me have, perhaps irretrievably, injured his career. 'Let him rest in peace.' . . .

. . . A very pleasant feeling to all my family – my position with them improved by the success (relative to their appreciation of me) of my article. So the old year dies, and the new year, with her yet unbroken promises, steps on to the scene. . . .

# The Working Sisterhood

## January 1888–December 1889

Auberon Herbert (1838–1906), younger brother to the Earl of Carnarvon, the Colonial Secretary, had himself been a politician. A friend and disciple of Herbert Spencer, he was later one of the philosopher's three trustees.

*8 February.* [Ashley Arnewood, Hampshire]
In the midst of the most beautiful part of the New Forest there are a few acres of poor pastureland enclosed by a wooden fence. . . . On the higher part of this ground stands a little colony of queer red-painted buildings, two large cottages and various small outhouses, huddled together, yet distinct from one another, and quite free from architectural plan. No attempt at a drive or even a path, not even a gate. To enter the back yard the visitor must needs dip under a wooden paling. But once inside the larger cottage, there is comfort, even taste. The floors are bare and clean-scoured; here and there warm-coloured rugs thrown across; while the monotony of the panelling is broken by draped eastern hangings. . . . Refined eccentricity, not poverty, lives here. . . .

Mr Auberon Herbert, head of this little home, is a tall, stooping man; he is already quite grey (though only fifty years of age) and the look of failing physical strength is stamped on his face and figure. His bearing, manner, voice – all tell the courtesy and sensitiveness of good breeding; his expression is that of an intellectual dreamer . . . The younger son of a great English peer, he was brought up to the amusements and occupations of his own class – the quick succession of public school, university, Army, sport and racing, and lastly politics, with a background of big country houses and sparkling London draw-ing-rooms. But his choice was not here. He married a woman of his own caste, but, strangely enough, sharing his own tastes; and these two refused to move in the groove of aristocratic custom . . . Strange stories floated up to 'London Society' of their doings – Shaker settlements, gypsy vans, spirit rapping and medium-hunting and, to the horror of Mrs Grundy, eating with their own servants! . . . Now the life-compan-ion is dead. Two little girls, one thirteen, the other seven, a boy away at grammar school, are the beloved of this solitary man. . . .

Across the forest and moor we rode on that February day, the man, the elder girl and I myself, to this home in the wilds. . . . lunch over, we sank into comfortable chairs round the blaze of peat and wood fire, sipped coffee and smoked cigarettes. Religiously minded individualism disputing with scientific fact-finding! . . . 'A woman without a soul,' said Auberon Herbert playfully, 'looking on struggling society like a young surgeon looks on a case, as another subject for diagnosis.' . . .

*12 February.* [Kildare]
Last days at Bournemouth; hardly expect to return here. If Father lives we shall move to Wimbledon for next winter. Very happy during these peaceful months . . . now I enjoy my life. I have fair health, faith in my own capacity to do the work I believe in, and I have regained my old religious feeling without which life is not worth living to one of my nature. Intend to spend ten days of my holiday in the West End before I settle in to work . . . Thirty years is a good deal of sand in the hour-glass; I must justify all this long period of silent intellectual seed-time . . .

. . . So mighty is even a small success! Great ladies want to know me . . .

*22 February.* [London]
Staying with the Hobhouses and wasting time! Spent afternoon and evening with Benjamin Jones in their happy little home at West Norwood. They live on £400 and are as happy as others on £4000. Three boys and a girl; have taken measures to prevent others from coming, and advise others to do so. . . . The question of Neo-Malthusianism is coming to the fore; the underground growth of it is unquestioned; the open discussion of it is every day more permitted. I

see it practised by men and women who are perfectly pure. I cannot see *reasons* against it; yet my moral instinct is not with it.

Beatrice prepared herself for work in an East End sweatshop by training at a Co-operative tailoring workshop.

*28 March. Good Friday.* [Devonshire House Hotel]
So the first six weeks of my inquiry ends. . . . Most of my time spent in training as a 'plain hand' . . . has given me an insight into the organiza-tion, or, in this case, into the want of organization, of a workshop, and into the actual handicraft of tailoring. I am more than ever assured that, *if I have capacity*, I have found the life that suits me. . . . My work now absolutely absorbs me. When I am too tired to work I pray; when I am too exhausted to pray I simply rest in the faith that my work is useful if I give it my best energy and my whole heart. . . . Of my family I see less and less but that is unavoidable in my present hurried life – every bit of spare time must be devoted to work.

Arthur Dyson Williams (1859–96) was a barrister and nephew of the Miss Williams in whose house Beatrice first met Chamberlain.

*9 April.* [Devonshire House Hotel?]
Rosy engaged to Mr Williams. He is a respectable young man with fair abilities and I should think a good fellow. A barrister, not likely to do brilliantly, with a small income of his own. He is not up to the mark of the other brothers-in-law, but then Rosy is the least gifted, mentally and physically, of the whole sisterhood. I wonder how her little nature will thrive under it; whether this the greatest crisis of a woman's life will make her grow into a 'Soul', whether it will lift her out of the tiny part played by a little Ego grasping after personal happiness. . . .

*11 April.* [London lodgings]
Settled at 56 Great Prescott St, to begin life as a working woman. With a very queer feeling I left the house in my old clothes and walked straight off to Princes Street and Wood Street, a nest of tailors. No bills up, except for 'good tailoress', and at these places I daren't apply, feeling myself rather an imposter. I wandered on, until my heart sank with me, my legs and back began to ache, and I felt all the feelings of 'out o' work'. At last I summoned up courage and knocked at the door of a tailor wanting a 'good tailoress'. A fat and comfortable Jewess opened the door.

'Do you want a plain 'and?' said I, trying to effect a working-class accent.

'No,' was the reply.

'I can do everything except buttonholes,' I insisted.

'Where have you worked?'

'With my father, a master tailor. I've come from Manchester.'

'Rebecca,' shouted the fat Jewess to her daughter down the street, 'do you want a hand?'

'Suited,' shouted back Rebecca, to my mingled disappointment and relief. 'You will find plenty of bills in the next street,' she added in a kindly voice.

So I trudged on, asked at one or two other places, but all were 'suited'. Thought I, 'Is it because it's the middle of the week, or because they suspect I'm not genuine?' and looked sensitively into the next shop window at my reflection; certainly I looked shabby enough. . . . in a fit of listless despair I take the top of the tram down Mile End Rd. It is warm and balmy, and with a little rest from that weary trudge I pick up my pluck again. A large placard strikes my eye. 'Trouser and vest hands wanted immediately.' I descend quickly and am soon inside the shop. A large crowded room with a stout, clever-looking Jewess presiding at the top of the table, at which some thirty girls are working.

'Do you want trouser hands?'

'Yes, we do,' answers the Jewess.

'I'm a trouser finisher.'

The Jewess looks at me from top to toe; and somewhat superciliously glances at my draggled old dress.

'Call tomorrow half-past eight.'

'What price do you pay?' say I with firmness.

'Why, according to the work; all prices,' answers she laconically.

'Then tomorrow, half-past eight', and I leave the shop feeling triumphant to have secured a place, but a little doubtful of my power of finishing trousers. So I hurry back to my little room, throw off my disguise, gulp down a cup of tea and rush off to a friendly Co-operative workroom to 'finish a pair of trousers' which I accomplish without difficulty in two hours. If they only expect 'finishing' I'm safe. . . .

*12 April.* [London]

Thursday morning I reappear at 198 Mile End Road. It is a long irregular-shaped room running backward from the retail shop to the kitchen. Two small tables by the gas jets (used for heating irons) serve for the two pressers. Then a long table with forms on either side and chairs at top and bottom, for the trouser finishers. Two other tables for machinists and vest hands and a high table for the trouser-basters complete the furniture . . . It is barely 8.30 but the 30 girls are crowding in and taking their seats in front of their work and boxes on the tables. The 'missus' has not yet come down; the two pressers, English lads of about 22, saunter lazily into the room a little after the half-hour. The head woman calls for a pair of trousers and hands them to me. I look at them puzzled . . . I have no materials wherewith to begin. The woman next to me explains: 'You will have to bring trimmings, but I'll lend you some to begin with.' 'What ought I to buy?' say I, feeling very helpless. At this moment the 'missus' bustles into the room. She is a big woman, enormously developed in the hips and legs, with strongly Jewish features and only one eye. Her hair is crisp and has been jet black; now in places it is quite grey. Her dress is stamped cotton velvet of a large flowery pattern; she has a heavy watch-chain, plentiful rings; and a spotlessly clean apron.

'Good morning to you,' she says good-temperedly to the whole assemblage. 'Esther, have you given that young person some work?'

'Yes,' replied Esther. '3 1/2 trousers.'

'I have not got any trimmings. I did not know that I had to supply them. Where I worked before they were given,' I ejaculate humbly.

'That's easily managed; the shop is just around the corner, or Esther,' she calls out across the table, 'you're going out; get this young person her trimmings. The lady next you will tell you what you want,' she says in a lower tone bending over between us. The lady next me is a good-tempered married woman of a certain age. She, like all the other trouser-hands, works piecework; but in spite of that she is ready to give me up a good deal of time in explaining how I am to set about my work.

'You'll feel a bit strange the first day. Have you been long out 'o work?'

'Yes' I answer abruptly.

'Ah, that accounts for your feeling awkward like. One's fingers feel like so many thumbs at first.'

And certainly mine do. The work is quite different from the Co-operative shop [in which I learnt the work?]; much coarser and not so well arranged. And then I feel nervous, very much 'on trial' . . . However, happily for me, no one pays much attention. There is plenty of row, what with the machines, the singing of the girls at the other end of the room, the chattering that goes on at the upper end of one table, at which sits the mistress. Chaff and bad language is freely thrown from the two lads at the pressing-tables to the girls at our table. Offers of kisses, sending to the Devil and his abode, and a constant repetition of the inevitable adjective form the staple of the conversation between the lads and the workgirls; the elder women whisper bits of gossip or news . . . There is a free giving and taking of each other's trimmings, and a general supervision of each other's work, altogether a hearty geniality of a rough sort. The missus joins in the chatter, encourages or scolds as the case may be.

'The missus has 16 children,' says the Mrs Read (the woman next me), '8 of her own and 8 of her husband's. All those girls at the last table are her daughters.'

I look down the room: the girls there are smartly dressed, but are working quite as hard as the others and appear on terms of equality.

'They are a nice-looking set,' say I in a complimentary tone.

'Yes, it's a pity some of the girls are not like them,' mutters the woman. 'They're an awful bad lot, some o' them. Why bless you, that young woman just behind us has had three babies by her father, and another here has had one by her brother.'

'Yes,' remarks the person next to her (a regular woman of the slums), 'it's ill thinking of what you may have to touch in these sort of places.'

'Well,' replies Mrs Read, 'I've worked here these eight years and never yet had any words with anyone. . . .'

'One o'clock,' shouts a shrill boy's voice. 'Stop work,' orders the missus.

'I wish I could finish this bit,' say I to the woman next me.

'You mustn't. It's dinner-time.'

So I put on my bonnet and jacket and go out into the Mile End Road heartily glad to get a breath of fresh air and a change from the cramped position. I take the tram up and down to Aldgate and end by turning into a clean shop for a cup of tea and a bun. Back again at two.

'You must work a little quicker for your own sake,' says the missus . . . 'We've had worse buttonholers than this,' she says in a kindly voice, 'but it don't look as if you have been 'customed to much work.' . . .

At last tea-time breaks the working day. All, or nearly all, the women have their own teapots on the gas stove and have with them bread as a relish. The women on either side of me offer me tea, which I resolutely refuse. An hour afterwards I have finished my second pair of trousers.

'This won't do,' says the missus, pulling the work to pieces. 'Here, take and undo that one. I'll set this one to rights. Better have respectable persons who know little to work here than blackguards who know a lot . . .'

'Eight o'clock by the Brewery clock,' cries out the shrill voice.

'Ten minutes to,' shouts the missus, looking at her watch. 'However, it ain't worth while breaking the law for a few minutes. Stop work.'

This is most welcome to me. The heat, since the gas has been lit, is terrific and my fingers are horribly sore and my back aches as if it would break. . . .

*13 April.* [London]

. . . this morning I feel hopelessly tired, my fingers clammy and a general shakiness all over. The needle will not pierce the hard shoddy stuff; my stitches will go all awry and the dampness of my fingers stretches the linings out of place. Altogether I feel on the brink of deep disgrace. . . .

'This will never do,' says the missus. . . . 'This work won't suit me. You want to go and learn somewhere first.' . . . All the women at the table look at me pityingly and I retire to my place feeling very small. There is a dead silence, during which I arrange my trimmings so as to be ready to take my leave if the missus persists. Presently she beckons to me. 'I'll see what I can do with you. You sit between those two young ladies and they'll show you. You must help one another,' she says to the two girls. . . .

Tea-time the missus addresses me: 'Now I am very much interested in you; there is something in your face that is uncommon. The women here will tell you that I have made an exception for you. I should have bundled you out long ago if it had not been for your face and your voice. Directly you open your mouth, anyone can see that you are different from the others. What have you been?'

'I used not to have to work for my living,' I reply, evading the question. 'I am looking out for different work now, but I had to take to something.'

'A nice-looking person like you ought to get married to a respectable man, you're more fit for that than to earn your living,' says the shrewd Jewess. 'But since you have come here, I'll see what I can do with you.'

I have my cup of tea. The pale weary girl is munching her bread and butter.

'Won't you have some?' she says, pushing the paper towards me.

'No, thank you,' I answer.

'Sure?' she says. And then, without more to-do, she lays a piece on my lap and turns away to avoid my thanks. A little bit of human kindness that goes to my heart and brings tears into my eyes. Work begins again.

My friend has finished her trousers and is waiting for another pair. She covers her head with her hand and in her grey eyes there is an intense look of weariness, weariness of body and of mind. Another pair is handed to her and she begins again. She is a quick worker but, work as hard as she may, she cannot make much over a 1s a day, discounting trimmings. A shilling a day is about the price of unskilled woman's labour.

Another two hours and I say 'goodnight' to the mistress and leave this workshop and its inhabitants to work on its way day after day and to become to me only a memory. . . .

*15 April.* [London]
An interval. Spent the afternoon in the Speaker's Gallery. Debate on local government. Eloquent speech of Leonard's . . . Followed by Chamberlain . . . What a change in that man's position! Only three years ago he was the idol of the democracy and the *bête-noire* of the well-to-do classes. Now he is the darling of the aristocracy and the much abused 'traitor' to the people's cause. . . . And socially he is absorbed by the aristocratic set. He is flattered and spoilt by all the fine ladies of London Society; and has a pleasant enough life of it – if he is satisfied with Society and does not awaken to the consciousness of loss of real power. Society is a magic looking-glass; it often reflects past and not present position . . . And so a man lives on in a fool's paradise . . . It did me good to hear these two men this afternoon. The contrast between Leonard's tone and his was another death-knell to feeling. Courage, courage. My present life, though lonely and at times wearisome, is better than it would have been by his side. For there is growth in it. Only I must keep humble and devoted. Humility, devotion and truth-desire – my three guardian angels. *True to myself.* . . .

Mary Endicott (b. 1864), the daughter of the American Secretary of State for War, met Chamberlain in November 1887 when he was in America to resolve a fishing dispute between the United States and Canada.

*26 April.* [Devonshire House Hotel?]
. . . 'Chamberlain's marriage' placarded all over the city. Engaged to an American girl and shortly to be married. I had heard of the rumour for some time, but I hardly believed it. Now it is an established fact. It is good for me, and good for him – may be the saving of him yet and shows him in a better light. A gasp, as if one had been stabbed, and

then it is over. Fortunately for me, it comes now that I am happy and settled in my own working life. Poor Beatrice Chamberlain, it is hard on her.

'To be or not be.' *Pall Mall* [*Gazette*] 29 April. No one knows. 'Miss Endicott has at last acknowledged, etc.' To be. *Pall Mall* 31 May.

*5 May.* [Devonshire House Hotel?]
The last few days of my active life for some months to come. On the whole I have been very happy, full of interest and blessed with *content.* I have not felt living alone. . . . And I enjoy the life of the people at the East End – the reality of their effort and aims, the simplicity of their sorrows and of their joys. I feel I can *realize* it – see the tragic and the comic side of it.

> Beatrice was called before a committee of the House of Lords which was investigating sweating. She disliked giving evidence and, through nervousness, exaggerated the number of days she had worked as a trouser hand. This figure was widely reported and Beatrice was obliged to amend her remark on the galley proof. She was so conscience-stricken that she almost worried herself into a collapse.

*12 May.* [Devonshire House Hotel?]
Gave evidence yesterday before the Lords Committee. A set of well-meaning men, but not made of stuff fit for investigation. . . . they treated me very kindly, and lunched me in the middle of my examination. A few Peeresses came down to stare at me! . . .

> On 12 May 1888 the *Pall Mall Gazette* published an article entitled 'The Peers and the Sweaters': 'In the morning the only witness was a lady – Miss Potter – dressed in black and wearing a very dainty bonnet, tall, supple, dark, with bright eyes, and quite cool in the witness chair, who was fluent on coats and eloquent on breeches. Unfortunately, though her voice was a little shrill, it was very difficult to hear sentences, which were very sharply delivered.'

*16 May.* [The Argoed?]
Disagreeable consequences of appearing in public; description of my appearance and dress, and an offensive notice in the *Pall Mall* [*Gazette*]. . . .

*25 May.* [The Argoed?]
Detestable mis-statement of my evidence brings down libellous imputations, all the harder to bear as I was pressed into giving evidence and
was unwilling to speak of my personal experience of the workshops.
Perhaps what made it still worse is that Maggie Harkness, taking for
granted that all the newspapers told of my evidence was true, has been
spreading a report that I had been telling stories. A false friend, not
intentionally so, but actually. How differently the Booths have acted!
However, I suppose I shall weather the storm as I have weathered others.
God help me! My intention was to tell the truth and nothing but the
truth and there was as a fact only one small inaccuracy (either on my
side or on that of the shorthand writer) – exclusively instead of inclu-
sively three weeks' work. Both statements would be inaccurate, the one
more than covers, the other does not cover, the length of time I worked
but I altered the proof so that it will now be an understatement.

*28 May.* [The Argoed?]
Foolish to have allowed myself to be so thoroughly upset by false reports
and *Pall Mall* libels. Suffering from attack of nervous exhaustion from
the intensity of my misery. I must have a strain of mania in my nature
which needs all my self-control to overcome.

*31 May.* [The Argoed]
Delightful ride through the country; shaken off distemper and feel more
inclined to work. But cannot forget this time last year! [Beatrice's break
with Chamberlain.] It is hard for a woman to bear. Courage. That is the
one meaningful word of my life; think I have almost a right to adopt it
as an acted-up-to motto.

*1 June.* [The Argoed]
We regret deeply and passionately many things we have done or left
undone, but we fail to rejoice (because of our ignorance) over the evils
we have avoided and the terrible possibilities we have escaped.

*4 June.* [The Argoed]
Why look everlastingly at the past that is irretrievably gone, its facts
engraved on eternity? In the present it is the future that is the living reality, for it is the child we are creating. These last few days, days of
humiliation (haunted by memories) have brought vividly to my mind
the meanness and pettiness of gratified vanity; of the miserable little

excitements in noting one's own tiny successes. Even one's humiliation, the 'Scarlet Letter', is of small significance if one looks at it relatively to the great movements round about one – how much less important therefore the little spasms of admiration in the tiny set one lives in. Now that I am started in public work I must try to avoid the valleys and hills of Egotism – intense depression at failure or loneliness, elation in success.

*6 June.* [The Argoed]
Busy writing my paper on the tailoring trade. It is a horribly stiff bit of work, all the more so as I am not physically strong at present . . . I feel as if I were hammering it out of me, not writing it. . . .

*29 June.* [The Argoed]
These latter days [I] constantly think of Mother: sometimes the feeling of her presence is so strong that I am tempted into a kind of communion with her. We knew each other so little in life-time, and, strangely, I love her better now. I understand her more completely. I feel that she at last knows me, tries to cheer my loneliness and to encourage my effort, now that her outward form lies decaying in the earth. She seems now to belong more to me than to the others; the others have their husbands and their children; I have nothing but my work with the fitful warmth of friendship. So Mother seems to stand by my side, to be watching me, anxious to reach out to me a helping hand, at any rate to bless me. I have been wounded, horribly wounded, and the scar can never leave me, but I can fight through the rest of the bullets of life with courage. And perhaps, when it is over, I shall know that she has been by my side.

> Arabella Fisher had been secretary to the eminent geologist Sir Charles Lyell (1797–1875) and was now married to an elderly retired doctor.

*15 July. Gracedieu*
The charming home of my best friends. The Booths are satisfied with my paper and are, as usual, full of wise and temperate encouragement. Charlie likes me as a fellow-worker, Mary regrets me as a possible married woman, but both alike are constant and warm in their friendship . . .

Bella Fisher staying here for two or three days. She and I have perhaps more in common than I and Mary Booth, for she is essentially the *unmarried* woman, though she happens to have married late in life. But the struggle, work and success of her existence have all belonged to spinsterhood. Her marriage, as she once quaintly put it, was a 'provision for old age', entered into after she felt that the best part of her work was over. . . . I am not quite certain that now and again she does not regret her freedom. Her marriage is one of deep affection but with no intellectual companionship and at times her life is lonely and needs the stimulus of other minds. . . .

*29 July.* [The Argoed]
This day last year I spent with J.C. Now we have each gone on our way – parted for all Eternity (?)

> John Burnett (1842–1914) was the general secretary of the Amalgamated Society of Engineers. Dr Mandell Creighton (1843–1910) was professor of ecclesiastical history at Cambridge, Canon of Worcester, and later Bishop of London.

*6 August.* [The Argoed]
Burnett thoroughly approves of my paper. 'Tone admirable' . . . The *Spectator* is kinder to me this time than last and I should think expresses the general opinion of those who take the trouble to wade through it. 'Heavy reading but full of sound and valuable information.' . . . I *am* so glad that the general opinion is that it *is sound work*. To be thought a sound and conscientious worker, with ability guided by conscience, is my one ambition. I do not care to be thought 'talented' or brilliant. . . .

*15 August.* [The Argoed]
Pleasant stay with the Creightons at Worcester. . . . Canon Creighton is a scholar and a priest with wise and tolerant social sympathies. . . . He is a bit of a flirt, at least I think so, but quite a harmless one. On the other hand he despises feminine efforts, and tacitly insists that woman's mission is to charm and not to instruct. . . . His wife is an attractive woman with a sound intellect whenever she chooses to use it. She has seven children and is preparing for another. She is a devoted wife and an equally devoted mother – somewhat after the Mary Booth type. . . . She has, I think, a warmer heart and a larger mind than her husband's but naturally enough she has not the faculty of acquisition so fully developed. . . .

*17 August.* [The Argoed]
Tomorrow our Monmouthshire farmhouse fills with wedding guests. Rosy and Dyson on Monday to be made man and wife. The last marriage of the Potter girls – 'for you know the other Miss Potter is a confirmed old maid and has taken to writing and statistics, etc.; you would have hardly thought it, would you, from looking at her ten years ago. Some say she was the prettiest of the lot, but then she took to queer ways and that never pays.' 'Ah, but it wasn't that,' says a spiteful mother of unmarried daughters. 'She wanted to make a great marriage and failed.' So thinks the world. . . .

*21 August.* [The Argoed]
The wedding passed off very happily. Old Miss Williams . . . the fairy godmother endowing the young people with [a] means of livelihood, is a pleasant sociable old lady who has seen a good deal of the life of her own class. She is rich and loves to be acquainted with *interesting* men and women (Ah! how well I remember that dinner at her house – the introduction before dinner – the sudden attraction on both sides – the first beginning of years of misery!) . . .

. . . The Courtneys and Mary Playne, Kitty [Holt] and Bill [Mary Playne's son] are here. . . . Miss Kitty is a slim, graceful girl. . . . She longs for a Career (with a big C) . . . Evidently just at present she envies me! Poor child! . . . Mary and Kate talk personalities all day. The more I see of other people the more I realize how utterly unintellectual we are as a family, considering of course our (great!) ability. Mary, though strikingly clever in all she does and says . . . worships *success* . . . And her success and failure are the success and failure of today – the floating on the surface of public opinion . . . 'I like to be *de mon temps*' is her characteristic phrase.

And now I am left alone – the last and only Potter! I am well started in work. My beginning is not brilliant, but it is sound. . . . The next paper is of a different sort and will probably attract more attention – possibly too much attention for my comfort! There is nothing in it but bright description of an audacious adventure. Unhappily it is connected in my mind with a false step: the inaccuracy of my evidence before the 'Lords'. The fear that this may be dwelt on by my enemies in the Press haunts me vaguely. . . .

*27 August.* [The Argoed]
The clouds look as if they were gathering. God help me!

*28 August.* [The Argoed]

Early morning. One of those horrible nights of self-torture: heart palpitating the night through, the mind one mass of whirling possibilities all of them of the nightmare type, the mouth parched. And then, unless I conquer it by turning my mind vigorously to other things, a day of restlessness haunted by the fears born in the morbid hours of the night. I shall not easily forget that time at Dewsbury after I had realized my 'false step' (for at first I thought it a slight inaccuracy of no consequence). All day I rushed from my own thoughts only to meet them at every corner. At last, on that journey down to Monmouth I had become a prey to mania. I lost all control and the laudanum bottle loomed large as the dominant figure. Then there was a reaction: and in a few days my work and the effort it needed had turned aside the current of self-torturing energy. And yet there is no outward sign of this inward misery. I seem to others calm, collected and usually in the highest spirits. In the end of course I bear the signs of extreme physical strain written on my face, but no one could tell that the physical strain arose from mental misery.

As a child I had it – once during my girlhood – and then for four years I was simply a prey to it. Twice it has led me into deep waters of humiliation which will be an everlasting memory to me. It is my nethermost being of despairing self-consciousness. There is only one spirit that quells it – religion, the consciousness of a great Father, the judge of all things, the consciousness of an immortal soul chastened by suffering, strengthened by repentance. . . .

It is strange that the spirit of religion always dwells on an unmarried life devoted to work rather than on the restful usefulness of wifehood and motherhood. Sometimes I wonder whether it is inflation, but the consciousness of a special mission, of duty to society at large rather than to individuals, is constantly present with me in my better moments . . . And it is partly the consciousness of a special mission . . . that brings a strained feeling into many of my relationships, even to my nearest and dearest friends. To them, whenever I hint at it, the whole idea seems ridiculously out of proportion with what they know of my abilities. And their perception of the incongruity is reflected in my mind, and I wake up to moments of self-dissatisfaction and cynicism which are keenly painful. But for the most part I hide this faith away . . . It needs to be chastened, to be freed from ambition and vanity, but it must still remain the central motive of my life.

*30 August.* [The Argoed]
I feel as if I could not set to work until the suspense is over. Oh, how hard any kind of publicity is to a woman, and yet how can one avoid it? It is a sort of fact that follows me in my work, in my friendships, even in the depth of passion.

An unsigned article entitled 'The Glorified Spinster' appeared in *Macmillan's Magazine* in September 1888.

*3 September.* [The Argoed]
. . . Just parted with Ella Pycroft at Tintern [railway station in the Wye valley near The Argoed] and a bitter, cold drive back. She and I have read with amusement a cleverish paper on 'glorified spinsters' in *Macmillan's*. 'A new race of women not looking for or expecting marriage.' 'Self-dependent, courageous, and cool-headed.' Ah, poor things.

*14 September.* [The Argoed]
My 'Pages of a Workgirl's Diary' has been very successful, and no unpleasant consequence has resulted from the publication of it. The success, indeed, has been out of all proportion to the literary merit. It was the originality of the 'deed' that has taken the public, more than the expression of it. However, it seems clear that the little literary faculty I have is of the narrative and picture-making form. . . .

'Glorified spinsterhood' is at present gilded, gilded by the charm of novelty and youth. Dark times will come again . . . Then both happiness and usefulness will depend on the consciousness of good work done and good work doing. I need the prayer more in success than I did in failure: God help and guide me!

Robert Holt was Beatrice's brother-in-law. Lord Granville (1815–91), an eminent lawyer and judge, was leader of the Liberal Party in the House of Lords. Arthur Hobhouse Q.C. had received a peerage in 1885.

*21 October.* [Liverpool]
Three days at Liverpool. Robert as chairman of the Liberal Association entertaining Lord Granville, Lord Hobhouse and a Mr Cross. Liverpool worthies in and out all day. . . . [Lord Granville], like most 'Society men', doesn't care for the likes of me, and until last night he had not addressed me. But he came up (I having appeared in a pretty black gown) while I was discussing vehemently labour questions with Mr Cross, with whom

I had struck up a friendship. Lord Granville listened with a sort of puzzled air, and when I, out of politeness, tried to bring him in . . . he looked still more utterly at sea, as if I had asked him to join us in conversing on Chinese metaphysics. What could a woman, who really by night light looked quite pretty, want with such questions! Still less, how could she expect a polished man of the world to know what she was talking about? So the noble Earl stood silently gazing in mild surprise. . . .

*25 October.* [The Argoed]
Two friends soon to be married, both of whom I looked on as settled in 'glorified spinsterhood' – Ella to Maurice Paul, and Carrie Darling to her old love, Mr Murdoch, each marrying a man many years younger than herself. Ah, women!

> Chamberlain's marriage to Mary Endicott was to take place in Washington on 15 November.

*7 November.* [London, Stratford Place?]
The blow has come. I thought the nerve was killed: it was only deadened, deadened and dying, dying in the life of new and growing interests. Another fortnight or three weeks and it will be dead. And instead of pain slight contempt and good wishes for their happiness.

*8 November.* [Oxford]
The *reading* of my paper was successful and I have broken the ice . . . If I have something to say I now know that I can say it and say it well.

*10 November.* [Oxford]
Delightful two days at Oxford. Far more beautiful than I expected. . . . Still, the whole time I walked about with a bit of cold steel in my heart and at nights I tossed about with the heat and discomfort of feverishness from a festering sore. Oh, it is hard to bear.

And yet when one looks at it, it is better for me. My work will be the better for it. And it is better for him. Surely it is pure egotism to suffer so intensely. . . .

*14 November.* [Stratford Place?]
The eve of his marriage. This afternoon I spent in Westminster Abbey listening half-dazed to the solemnly intoned prayers, and to the heights and depths of the anthem. . . . I prayed for their happiness, that the love

of a good woman might soften and comfort him, inspire him with pure motive in the days of success and tenderly protect him in the hours of gloom and depression. And that she, poor child, might resist all temptation to become hardened with the glare and glamour of great position and great possessions. It is almost happiness to think that he is happy after these long years of hard suffering and hardening ambition. The pain to me – for alas we are all human – seems at times melted into a glow of satisfaction in his softened feeling. If he could only *feel* my sympathy and *understand* it. God bless them.

*15 November.* [Stratford Place?]
2 a.m. Awake – thinking of their future. This marriage will, I think, decide his fate as a politician. He must become a Tory. The tendencies of his life are already set in that direction. . . . She will see entirely through his eyes; by her sympathy with his injured feelings against his old party she will intensify the breach; by her attraction to the 'good society' she will draw him closer to the aristocratic party. She is, besides, an American aristocrat, and like the aristocrats of a new country is probably more aristocratic in her tastes and prejudices than the aristocrats of the old country. Her ambition, too, will be social rather than political. Politics are at a discount in America. Society is everything. All this if the marriage is happy, as I think it will be as far as they two are concerned. If it is unhappy, if it means friction, God only knows where he will go to. Morally he would be utterly ruined. In despair and bitterness of heart, he might become the reddest radical, and sit again as an 'English Robespierre'; politically this would mean hopeless discredit. Unless she be a woman of real genius the middle course, the quiet re-adoption of the old [friends?], will be impossible to him.
    5 p.m. It must be over: and they are man and wife. . . .

*18 November.* [Stratford Place?]
A long morning at St Paul's: the Holy Communion afterwards. Lunched at the Cathedral Tavern and walked from the city to visit Maggie Harkness alone in her little bedroom in Gower Street. Tomorrow intend to 'pull myself together' and begin work in good earnest.

*Epitaph* [on Chamberlain]
Courage: masculine strength: ability to execute and manipulate: intense egotism, showing itself on one side by a strong desire for personal power, on the other by a love of ease, luxury and splendour. Bitterly

resentful of personal slight or personal injury. Originally religious and enthusiastic. The loss of his dearly loved wife seemed to him a death warrant to his faith in a personal God: a clear and sufficient proof that no God, who treated him so badly, could exist, or if he existed, deserved worship. A second loss matured his bitterness. From lost happiness he turned to love of power. . . . Right and left, as he ascended the ladder of political life, he kicked at those beneath him and flung those above him to the ground if they interfered with his progress. . . . his personal charm won him a few friends . . . But he made secret enemies on all sides. The working-class leaders saw in him an instrument of great power, and for a time they looked upon him as their future leader; but they never trusted his single-mindedness, they always suspected his ambition. The time came when he thought himself strong enough to try on the Crown. He over-rated his position – the democracy remained faithful to the old leader. Hisses and groans now greeted the name of Chamberlain. He turned with wounded feelings from his love of power and pursued pleasure. . . . Will he rest in it? . . . His whole life has been a grasping after personal power and personal pleasure: he has seemed to *attain*, but in each instance he has won, not to possess, but to lose.

One great quality, warm devotedness to those who devote themselves body and soul to him. *This* is the secret of his family's devotion: this may secure to him married happiness.

*24 November.* [Stratford Place?]
A week of utter nervous collapse. It is strange that a being who will henceforth be an utter stranger to my life should be able to inflict such intense pain – pain which cannot be controlled but only silently borne with. . . .

*1 December. Devonshire House Hotel*
A whole month of my free time gone, and only just begun work in good earnest. It is refreshing to be back again at the old quarters, with purely working associations. November is always a bad month for me. I suffer from the depths of physical depression, and this November the most exquisite mental torture has been added to it. However, it is over. Onward!

*Xmas.* [The Argoed]
Alone! At the Argoed: Spending my Christmas Day with Don [her dog].

*29 December.* [The Argoed]
In bed with tooth-ache and neuralgia, after a somewhat melancholy attempt to write the first page of my Jewish Community. Obliged to go to London to have the tooth attended to before I can hope for peace. . . .

Well! my dear, if notoriety be desirable as a preliminary step in a literary career, you have achieved it! Enough and to spare of mention of you in the daily papers: why, even a bogus interview with you telegraphed to America and Australia. But how much of that is the frothy foam raised by your plunge into an original adventure? . . . anyway you have learnt one lesson: personal notoriety with its attendant social distinction, with its little train of would-be friends and acquaintances, proves to be as much an 'illusion' as the charming house in London turned out to be in 1884, for a slightly different reason. A working life means to a woman with little strength seclusion from society; you cannot enjoy what you have won in the way of social position, even if you cared to. On the other hand, there remains the solid satisfaction in the *doing of the work* . . .

### ～ 1889 ～

On 9 January Beatrice inserted a cutting from an unnamed newspaper about the new Mrs Chamberlain, and wrote: 'Every Romance has a conclusion. This is the end to the romance of four volumes of my life!'

*14 January.* [Longfords]
Invalided: brain sickness, cold, loneliness, and the horrible stench of a dead rat have driven me from my mountain home into the comfortable house of my 'Playne' sister. Arthur and Bill rescued me, cheered me with their companionship and brought me back with them. Ah me! The wound will heal, time only is needed; the scar will remain there.

Alice Green (1847–1929) was the widow of the historian John Richard Green (1837–83). Irish-born, and a keen Home Ruler, in 1921 she became a senator of the new Irish Free State.

*11 February.* [London]
56 George Street, Portman Square. Pleasant little lodgings with the faithful Neale [her maid] to look after me. . . . Mrs Johnny Green, the historian's widow (and a lady of intellectual as well as social distinction)

is courting me! poor little me! She has called twice in one week and seems to wish to see me every day – suggests I should live with her. She has a wizened face – ugly usually, attractive at times – reminds me of a mediaeval picture; only, unfortunately, one knows it is not only 'bad drawing' that distorts her features. Colourless hair and an acid expression, perpetual discontent written on her face, the rest of her nature an enigma. . . .

### 21 February. [London]

Sad the drifting away of friends. Maggie [Harkness] who is offended that I am offended at her publication of a silly story about me and Herbert Spencer. It was an unpardonable act, but still I have forgiven her and she might forgive me. . . . Then the Booths. It would be strange if the close personal friendship between me and the husband had not ended. Mary has been generous, thoroughly generous, but for the last year the warm affection between us has been cooling. She has discouraged me from coming to them when they are alone, and I, sensitive to the least feeling on her side, have kept away. We have both been in London for some months and I have seen Charlie once. Mary and I have seen each other but I feel it is *forced* on her side . . . I went yesterday by appointment for a chat with her, but she had filled the room with other friends, probably she forgot that she promised me a free afternoon. I felt it the more as I wanted to ask her advice and needed comfort, but she was absorbed in a new friend for whom she has the same feeling as she used to have for me. So after an hour's desultory talk I left, choking with disappointed and wounded feeling, for I am very fond of her and hate breaking ties. Charlie I could have given up but *she* has been so much to me. . . . it is doubtful whether warm sentimental friendships even with women are desirable. When you must face life alone . . . there is no real communion of interests and therefore there can be no permanent tie. With another unmarried or childless woman the circumstances of life are much the same as yours . . . But in the nature of things it cannot be secure, and when the breach comes it is all the more painful. Religious feeling, communion with unknown spirits, beings without ties, creatures of your own imagination . . . are the only safe companions to the lonely mind.

Beatrice Chamberlain had written to Beatrice in November 1888 asking to see her, but Beatrice had put her off. Arabella Fisher wrote to Beatrice on 21 February advising her to see Chamberlain's daughter – 'but do not draw the tie too close'; to ask the Rylands to visit The Argoed late in the year; and to allow the new Mrs Chamberlain to call if she wished. 'The mere fact that you hate seeing any of them is a proof that you should do so in its proper time and place and live it down,' she added; and she gave Beatrice stern advice. 'You have something to *kill.* Kill it deliberately, and you will gain strength for future work and happiness.'

*28 February.* [London]
I have acted on her advice and written to ask Beatrice to come and see me. I wonder whether she would have said the same had she known all. I think so. Anyway I will obey her instructions as if they were words from on high. In the great crisis of life one willingly accepts the judgement of another: if I had only been guided by some strong perceiving woman. If I had had a mother or a sister to whom I could have confessed all! As it is I will struggle through as a self-enforced penance, as an atonement for the vanity, vulgar ambition and want of womanly reticence and self-control. God help me, and make it not *too* hard for me.

Alfred Marshall (1842–1924), professor of political economy at Cambridge, became a leading authority on labour economics.

*8 March.* [London]
Delightful visit to the Creightons at Cambridge. The interesting part of my visit was a long talk with Professor Marshall. . . . He said that he had heard that I was about to undertake a history of Co-operation. 'Did he think I was equal to it?' 'Now, Miss Potter, I am going to be perfectly frank. Of course I think you are *equal* to a history of Co-operation, but it is not what you can do best. There is one thing that *you*, and only *you* can do – an inquiry into that unknown field of female labour. You have (unlike most women) a fairly trained intellect, and the courage and capacity for original work, and yet you have the woman's insight into a woman's life. There is no man in England who could undertake with any prospect of success an inquiry into female labour. . . . if you devote yourself to the study of your own sex as an industrial factor, your name will be a household word two hundred years hence; if you write a history of Co-operation, it will be superseded or ignored in a few years. . . .'
Of course I disputed the point, and tried to make him realize that I wanted this study of industrial administration as an education for economic science. The little man with bright eye shrugged his shoulders and became satirical on the subject of a woman dealing with scientific generalizations – not unkindly satirical but gently so. . . . Still, with that

disagreeable masculine characteristic of a persistent and well defined purpose, I shall stick to my own way of climbing my own little tree. . . .

*7 March.* [The Argoed?]
Ran down to see Father, who has had a slight apoplectic attack. He lies in his bed in a state of complete apathy. His life can no longer be a pleasure to him or to those around him; it would be merciful if he should be taken. But the breaking of the tie would be sad, inexpressibly sad to a lonely life like mine. Still, I long for a complete holiday which his death would enable me to take. . . . At present my strength seems worked out. It is with painful effort that I begin on Co-operation. I look at the detail to be mastered with positive repulsion, and I long every day more for the restfulness of an abiding love. And yet I cannot sacrifice work for which all the horrible suffering of six years has fitted me, and cannot forget the past. But I must not let myself get morbid over it. I must check those feelings which are the expression of physical instinct craving for satisfaction; but God knows celibacy is as painful to a woman (even from the physical standpoint) as it is to a man. It could not be more painful than it is to a woman.

*8 March.* [Devonshire House Hotel]
It is all right with the Booths. Mary and I had a long talk over the keeping and repair of friendship . . . My friendship or, rather, my companionship with Charlie is for the time dropped – our common work is ended. His brave vigorous life with its varied interests and unselfconscious and disinterested pursuit of them will always be an encouraging thought; his thoughtful kindness and true affection will always be one of the comforting memories of my life. But my friendship with him had run in advance of my friendship with his wife and it is good now it should drop behind, for a time at least, and possibly take a permanent 'back place' in his mind.

> J.J. Dent (1856–1936), a bricklayer, became secretary of the Workingmen's Club and Institute Union. He was closely connected with the Co-operative Movement.

*10 March.* [Devonshire House Hotel]
. . . Seen something during my London stay of Burnett, Benjamin Jones and Dent – the three most distinguished of my working-men friends. My friendship with the two former is becoming a close one, and likely to endure as future work will bring us together. . . .

Beautiful communion service at St Paul's. While I knelt before the altar I felt that I had at length made my peace with my own past, that the struggle with bitter resentfulness which began as I knelt at the same altar the Sunday after his marriage had at last ended. . . .

After a visit from Beatrice Chamberlain who, Beatrice said, 'tried her best to start intimate relations' and 'found a perfectly cordial determination to keep to the *status quo*', Beatrice mused about the new Mrs Chamberlain.

*13 March.* [London]

Society is full of talk about the bride. Maggie Hobhouse describes her as a perfectly dressed woman, with quiet, dignified manners, frank blue eyes, retroussé nose, lovely skin, pleasant smile, but with not much behind – in fact, insignificant. If she were not Mrs C., says Kate (who invited her to meet the nobs of the Unionist world) she would be a pleasant nobody, and even in her present position she will never become somebody. 'A little Puritan' the world dubs her; 'charming but not pretty', 'might have come out of a country Rectory', 'a strange choice for Chamberlain to make, looks a mere child' – these are the remarks that fly to and fro. Everywhere she goes the world flocks round her, finds nothing to criticize, but nothing especially to remark about except the absence of anything striking and a certain charm of modesty and simple goodness. 'He is so happy that he cares no longer for Society'; 'I congratulated him but he did not seem "hearty" over it'; 'the affection is most on her side' – these are the contradictory statements as to his view of his charming bride. 'Have *you* seen her?' asks everyone I meet, with a quick glance at my expression. 'No, I have not seen her, but I hear she is charming,' I answer with placid indifference. But if I am taken unawares my feeling is one of sick faintness. . . .

Beatrice was attending a Conference of the Hebden Bridge Fustian Society, then the most successful of the Co-operative production societies. John Mitchell (1828–95), a textile worker, strong temperance man and lay preacher, served for more than twenty years as president of the Co-operative Wholesale Society, receiving a salary of £150 a year for running what may have been the largest business enterprise in the country.

*25 March.* [Hebden Bridge, Yorkshire]

Three days at Hebden Bridge staying with the widow of an iron founder. . . . Hebden Bridge resembles Bacup in its fusion of the working and lower middle class. Upper class it has none. My interest was in the vigorous Co-operative life, and I saw much of Co-operation. . . . Back to Manchester by afternoon train and ran up to see Maggie Harkness in her lodgings. Poor Maggie gets bitterer and bitterer with the whole world – does foolish and inconsiderate things and then is vexed that she loses friends. . . . If only she had religion, that haven of rest and peace for the lonesome worker, the one anchor in this life of strange dreams and feverish feelings. . . .

Boddington a small manufacturing village . . . is the direct opposite to Hebden Bridge and Bacup. Here is practically an aristocracy of manufacture. . . . It is a sort of patriarchal establishment. . . . People are contented and are fond of their masters. It was with one of these that I spent today. A bachelor of some forty years' standing, a good-natured dutiful man, with that sort of unsatisfactory cheerfulness peculiar to elderly bachelors. . . . Poor fellow! He evidently thought that I might be in the same plight, for our eight-hour interview ended up by a suggestion that I should consider partnership, that a life of investigation might well end in an active participation in the business I investigated. There ought to be a trade [union?] for the new celibate order of working women: otherwise with the best intentions one repays kindness by causing 'emotional perturbation' as the old philosopher calls it. This is the second one this year! About two a year who develop *serious* intentions. One consolation, a few years more and that sort of thing will cease. . . .

Mitchell, chairman of the Wholesale, is one of the leading personalities in the Co-operative movement. . . . Three or four times have I dined with the Central Board. . . . Occasionally I am chaffed in a not agreeable way about matrimony and husbands, and pointed allusions are made to the propriety of a match between me and Mitchell! But it is all good-natured, and I take it kindly. . . . I am a general favourite with these stout, hard-headed but true-hearted men and they look upon me as a strange apparition in their midst, the why and wherefore they have not fathomed. . . . The working man has still the eighteenth-century idea of a wife for the relief of physical nature, for the bearing of children, and the ministering to his personal comforts. Suddenly he is introduced to the nineteenth-century woman with her masculine interests and her womanly charm, a womanly charm cultivated by her as an instrument of power in public life, in the movement of the masses, not as a means of satisfying personal vanity and love of admiration. To the woman who unites charm, ability and religious enthusiasm there will someday open out a great future in power for good. Possibly future generations may see a woman step out of the ranks as a saviour of humanity, a supreme incarnation of the Mother's instinctive wisdom for the welfare of her children and their descendants.

*13 April.* [Manchester]
. . . There is now only one thing I need to make my life satisfactory – to rule out of my consciousness two personalities, *Beatrice Potter and the man she cared for.*

*17 April.* [Manchester]
I come back dead tired. As I sink into the armchair in my little lodging the old maid lodging-house keeper says exultantly: 'See, you are completely knocked up. You're only a woman: in spite of your *manly* brain, you're just as much of a woman as I am.' Poor genteel celibate! For days back you have been envying me my energy, and peering into *Life and Labour* on my table with my name standing out as a contributor. Still more, you have been reading the leaders in two London papers sent me by friends and you have been hardly able to contain yourself with silent envy. Now you have your revenge as I roll, tipsy with fatigue, up to bed. 'You're only a woman after all,' I hear her muttering as she collars my bag to save me exertion, feeling herself for once a superior. '*Poor weak woman with a man's brain,*' adds the old maid, trying to define the exact nature of her distinguished lodger.

> While Beatrice was in Manchester the first volume of Booth's survey was published. It included Beatrice's papers on the docks, tailoring and the Jewish community. *The Times* called it the 'grimmest' book of the day.

*21 April. Gracedieu*
'The book' a great success and Charles Booth delighted. Leaders in all the principal papers, and C.B. quite the head of the statistical tree!

*25 May.* [The Argoed]
Began my early-morning readings. This is my day: tea at 8 o'clock, study from 6 to 8 o'clock. Notes and chat till 11; Father till lunch. Cigarettes and bask in the sun, and a siesta after lunch. 3.30 to 5.30 study. Then a delightful walk or ride: supper, cigarette with Father; saunter in the moonlight or

starlight; to bed at 10 o'clock. . . . the one inspiring influence is Faith – faith in the worthwhile of individual effort for the common good.

Francis Ysidro Edgeworth (1845–1926) became Drummond professor of political economy at Oxford in 1891, and editor of the *Economic Journal.*

*4 June.* [Devonshire House Hotel]
Francis Edgeworth (nephew to Maria Edgeworth) Professor of Political Economy at King's College, London: eminent statistician of the mathematical type . . . an old admirer and a present lover! Even if I had not my work, the prospect of a matrimonial engagement, and the preliminary receipt of addresses, bores me intolerably . . . This man is pathetic: his somewhat pedantic and thoroughly conventional conversation, his starved affections, the furtive glance of unsatisfied desire peering through the old bachelor habits and appearance of forty-four years of celibate continence . . . Poor fellow! He bores me. And those relations with men stimulate and excite one's lower nature, for where one can give no real sympathy strong feelings in another seem to debase one and drag one down to a lower level of animal self-consciousness. How one despises oneself, giving way to those feelings (and over thirty too, – it would be excusable in a woman of twenty-five), but that part of a woman's nature dies hard. It is many variations of one chord – *the supreme and instinctive longing to be a mother.*

Beatrice went to the annual Co-operative Congress. Mrs Marshall was Mary Paley (1850–1944), one of the first students at Newnham College. A noted scholar, she was self-effacing in the interests of her husband's career. In what she later described as a 'false step', Beatrice had signed an anti-suffrage manifesto drafted by the novelist Mrs Humphry Ward and published in the *Nineteenth Century.* See 5 November 1906 for her explanation and recantation.

*7 June.* [Ipswich]
A whirl down to Ipswich in a crowded excursion train. Arrived at the White Horse Inn with Burnett and Fielding (manager of the tea department). At the door my old friends of the Wholesale, with Mitchell at their head, welcomed me warmly. In the commercial room I find other Co-operators . . . and the unfortunate lover [Edgeworth] who has followed me hither. . . . Forty of us were installed in this romantic Pickwick inn with its rambling passages and covered courtyard, and here other

leading Co-operators congregated, drank whisky and smoked tobacco. . . . In one of these parties, behold the hero of this year's Congress, the distinguished man whom working-men Co-operators have elected to give the inaugural address – Professor Marshall of Cambridge. . . . In spite of the intellectuality of his face there is a lack of the human experience of everyday life which begets the full maturity of man. Not that the professor is a lonely celibate. That gentle unassuming lady, badly dressed with protruding teeth, weak eyes and quickly changing colour – a former student of Newnham and present lecturer – who sits by his side, selects his food and guards him from obtrusions, is his wife. . . . Tonight his desire to gain information outweighs his nervous fear of a sleepless night, and he is listening with mingled interest and impatience to the modicum of facts dealt out in the inflated and involved phrases of the chairman of the Manchester Wholesale – Mitchell.

As I approach I am greeted by my old friend. 'Now, Miss Potter, come and join me in a cup of tea. I haven't seen anything of you this time. I was just telling the Professor my view of the true nature and real use of the great Co-operative movement'. . . . I turned to the group on the other side, including Benjamin Jones, astride a chair . . . 'Come, Miss Potter, leave Mitchell to his tea, and come and help me to make Dent understand our view of the question.'

'There is another question Miss Potter has to explain to us, one for which she is far more responsible,' Dent remarks in a gruff tone but with a kindly light in his grey eye. 'Why she lent her influence to that appeal against the suffrage. I believe it is just this: she is satisfied with her own position, because she is rich and strong. She does not see that other women need the power to help themselves which would be given by the vote.' This I feel to be an unpleasant accusation especially as Dent and I are old friends and he speaks seriously. But before I have time to advance in sober procession my arguments the little Professor in tones of nervous irritability intervenes:

'Miss Potter sees what the women's suffrage people don't see: that if women attempt to equal men and be independent of their guidance and control, the strong women will soon be ignored and the weak women simply starved. It is not likely that men will go on marrying, if they are to have competitors as wives. Contrast is the only basis to marriage and if that is destroyed we shall not think it worth while to shackle ourselves in life with a companion whom we must support and must consider.'

There are two sides to that question, think I, and the celibate condition of the human race can be begun by either party to the matrimonial contract. However, catching sight of the poor little wife's agonized look, (for female suffrage is a red rag to the Professor's somewhat feminine nerves and shrewish temper), I laughingly reply: 'Mr Marshall, I pity you deeply. You are obliged to come to the rescue of a woman who is the personification of emancipation in all ways, who clings to her cigarette if she does not clutch at her vote. Why do not you leave me to my fate? Convicted of hopeless inconsistency, I might even give up smoking in the hope of protecting myself against my rights.'

'That's just it,' whispers Jones, 'that's why these women are so bitter against you. It is pure perversity on your side, to say one thing and act another.' 'Surely, Mr Jones, I am simply taking a hint from your admirable method of controlling the Co-operative body, signing resolutions in favour of one policy, and acting according to another.' 'She's got you there, Jones', but the smile which plays across Dent's face gives way to the perplexed expression as he adds: 'I believe you are in earnest with your views. I should like some day to have it out with you; a clever strong woman like you must have some reasons to give, and I can't say I think much of those in the protest. Will you come down into the courtyard? . . .'

'I will go anywhere for a cigarette', and the company disperses, the Marshalls retire to bed, we to the smoking-room where I spend the rest of a late evening in telling fortunes from hands, and in a stray search after facts in the chaff of a smoking-room conversation.

On the whole the Ipswich Congress is to me personally unsatisfactory. There is the queer, pedantic, unhappy statistician [Edgeworth] who dogs my steps, makes elaborate speeches on formal matters, and jerks out, every now and again, agonized expressions of romantic regard. I hesitate to dismiss the man with rude coldness . . . But a lover has an evil effect and makes me self-conscious. The little clique of 'exceptional women' with their correct behaviour and political aspirations give me most decidedly the cold shoulder; this in a company of men annoys me more than it should do. But the supreme discouragement of the Congress is in the growing consciousness that I am unfit for the work I have undertaken . . . The little Professor frightens me with asking in sinister tones whether I have considered the effect of 'the appreciation of gold in the years '71–'74 on the Production Societies then started', and tells me quite frankly that I have got the wrong end of the stick. . . .

*29 June.* [The Argoed]

. . . Extract from letter of a lady: 'I pay rent and taxes – £130. I have nothing but what I earn by painting, teaching and writing: and naturally

I have to work exceedingly hard. My stepmother and I let the ground floor to reduce our rent. Now here is the absurdity. Our lodger, a young man doing absolutely nothing but amuse himself has a vote. The owner of the house, working early and late (somewhat useful I hope in her generation, at all events not useless), because she is a woman is not allowed to vote. Again I may vote for parish guardians of whom I know nothing, but for an M.P. of whose opinions I can judge, I may not vote.'

Mrs Fawcett's indignant reply to the 'Appeal' does not convince me: but the above extract contains the pith of the argument in favour of women's suffrage, and as such is valuable. One must realize the strongest argument of one's opponent before one is fit to controvert the whole position. But at present I am anxious to keep out of the lists. I have as yet accomplished no work which gives me a right to speak as representative of the class Mrs Fawcett would enfranchise: celibate women. And, to confess it frankly, I am not sure of my ground. I am not certain whether the strong prejudice I have against political life and political methods has not influenced my judgement on the question of introducing women into politics.

*29 July.* [The Argoed]
Shall always consider this day as sacred [anniversary of Chamberlain's last visit], a sacrament of pain fitting me for a life of loneliness and work, a memory of deep humiliation, and a spur to unremitting effort to gain for others the peaceful joy which I have lost myself. [The next eight pages were torn from the diary and have not survived.]

*4 August.* [The Argoed]
Mrs Johnny [Alice] Green has been here for the last fortnight. . . . She has the originality which springs from a lonely, unhappy and self-absorbed youth, from the enforced independence of a friendless womanhood. Bred up in a remote part of Ireland in a poverty-stricken home, she struggled at self-culture against every imaginable adverse circumstance. A brief married life with a man of talent and she was left without a friend but with a distinguished name. Now she has climbed up the social ladder, social success based on her husband's achievements does not satisfy her. She aims at the position to be gained by personal merit. . . . Such is the woman who has chosen me as her friend, and to whom I am attracted by interest and pity, and by a willingness (bred from indifference) to enter into relations desired by others. . . .

*20 August. The Argoed*
A grind and no mistake! Six hours a day reading and note-taking from those endless volumes of the *Co-operative News*, a treadmill of disjointed facts, in themselves utterly uninteresting, appallingly dry, and not even complete enough to be satisfactory. . . .

The movement to organize the unskilled and casual workers of London had been gathering momentum since the successful 1888 match girls' strike at the Bryant & May factory, led by Annie Besant. The London dock strike was led by socialists who had been agitating in the East End for several years. The demand for 'the docker's tanner' – a rate of sixpence an hour – attracted much public support.

*29 August. The Argoed*
The dock strike becoming more and more exciting – even watched at a distance. Originally 500 casuals marched out of the West and East India Docks – in another day the strike spread to the neighbouring docks – in a week half East London was out. For the first time a *general* strike of labour, not on account of the vast majority of strikers, but to enforce the claims to a decent livelihood of some 3,000 men. The hero of the scene is John Burns the socialist, who seems for the time to have the East London working man at his feet . . . The strike is intensely interesting to me . . . East End society has suddenly proved itself more capable of concerted action than any other district in England.

Beatrice left for Dundee on 30 August to attend the Trades Union Congress. Henry Broadhurst (1840–1911), Liberal M.P., was the leading figure on the parliamentary committee of the T.U.C. *Looking Backward* (1888) was a socialist utopia written by the American Edward Bellamy (1850–98).

*3 September. Dundee*
A battle royal at Congress between the supporters of Broadhurst and old-fashioned methods, and the socialists led by Burns and Mrs Besant. . . . With Broadhurst I lunched and afterwards smoked a cigarette. His suspicions of my intentions were completely dissipated when he heard I was an anti-suffrage woman. He immediately thought me sensible and sound. . . . His view of women is typical of all his other views: he lives in platitudes and commonplaces. . . . in spite of the prejudice and exclusiveness of the leading trade unionists, the frank

fellowship, the absence of personal animus and personal rivalry, the general loyalty to leaders and appreciation of real work as distinguished from talk is refreshing.

*18 September.* [The Argoed]
. . . It was a hard week, scarcely a holiday. When I arrived early on Sunday morning at Auberon Herbert's little cottage on the banks of Loch Awe [north-west of Glasgow] I was thoroughly exhausted, with a bad cold in the head into the bargain. A somewhat dreary little plastered cottage, with none of the charm of 'Old House' . . . The elderly idealist interesting and becoming an intimate friend. But with his nature, distance lent enchantment to the view! . . . between vegetarianism and valetudinarianism he is rapidly sinking into old age, though he is a healthy man of 50.

I enjoyed my days there. Between us we started a novel, *Looking Forward* – an answer to *Looking Backward* – for which I supplied the plot and the characters, while he is to work out a reformed world on individualist lines. He told me during the long evenings, looking on to the moonlit lake, the story of his life and we drifted into discussion on marriage, and I suddenly perceived with intense amusement that he was considering, with much doubting, 'possibilities'. He will doubt too much to make the offer, so the friendship is safe. But as we pushed off from the landing-stage to join the steamer on Saturday and I watched the self-conscious expression of slight sentimentality . . . did I laugh or did I shudder? . . .

*22 September.* [The Argoed]
The dock strike has ended in a brilliant victory to the men . . . Burns' parting words 'Be good to your wives and your children and remember what a man who drinks water can do.' . . .

*30 September. The Argoed*
This last month or so I have been haunted by a longing to create characters and to move them to and fro among fictitious circumstances – to put the matter plainly, by the vulgar wish to write a novel! In those early-morning hours when one's half-awakened brain seems so strangely fruitful, I see before me persons and scenes; I weave plots, and clothe persons, scenes and plots with my own philosophy of all things, human and divine. There is intense attractiveness in the comparative ease of descriptive writing. Compare it with work in which movements of commodities, percentages, depreciations, averages and all the ugly horrors of commercial facts are in

the dominant place, and *must remain so* if the work is to be worthful. . . . in my work Science must precede Art; Art must be the perfect representation of *facts and of their proportionate values*. Science and Art should be One, an Ideal towards which we creep blindly. Poor weak woman – comedy and pathos are in the chasm which lies between you and your goal.

Dear sweet Carrie [Darling]: seven years since we parted on the Victoria platform. A true woman though for many years she was an enthusiast for celibacy in her profession. A strange career. The child of the illegitimate son of a squire married to a woman of refinement and education, her breeding was somewhat mixed. Early in life she had to seek her own livelihood. But that necessity did not keep her from love-making. Twice or three times she was engaged or 'kept company', for her lower-middle-class origin showed itself in her love affairs if nowhere else. . . . At twenty-eight she was helped by friends to spend two years at Newnham: there made friends with the knot of distinguished women who were the first students at the University. From that time for some eight years her thoughts were absorbed by culture and by an immense desire to impart it, her feelings in friendship with women. Just in the middle of this period I first knew her . . . Six months together in Germany confirmed our friendship. At Wiesbaden our rooms opened into each other: in her room we used to sit late into the night with our feet cocked high on the china stove . . . smoking cigarettes and talking philosophy, for we were then both in the metaphysical stage, or poring over some bit of puzzling German, or delighting in some verse of *Faust* or prose epigram of Goethe. It was my first friendship outside my own family, for my feeling for Margaret Harkness was one of pity not of liking in those days. . . . In those days she enjoyed life immensely.

Then came the great crisis. One sister was supposed to be in consumption, three other sisters were doing poorly as governesses. She was offered a headmistress-ship in Australia with a good salary. . . . With a terrible wrench she threw up her position in England. . . . Then came letters from her: her sisters were satisfactorily settled, she was working up the school successfully. But she was living in a society she hated. A year after began the story of the passionate attachment to a married man, the young English master of the boys' grammar school, probably the first really cultivated and attractive man she had come across . . . Four years of struggle and misery, then he left. . . . Suddenly last autumn we heard with dismay she had thrown up her school, her lover had got a divorce or was getting one . . . and, poor and ill, appealed to her tenderness to come to him in Japan. . . . On the way out she falls in with a bluff sea captain, apparently a man of sense and decision. In a few days he is desperately in love; in a few hours she has confided in him her whole story. . . . Meanwhile Robert (the old lover) seems queerly half-hearted and does not meet her as he promised. Then all becomes enveloped in mystery. The captain interviews Robert, extracts a promise from Carrie she will not correspond with him, and seemingly persuades her to become engaged in a sort of queer way to him. . . . Oh, woman, you are passing strange. God preserve me from a lover between thirty-five and forty-five. No woman can resist a man's importunity during the last years of an unrealized womanhood. That to me is the moral of Carrie's story.

### 11 October. Box House

Our new, and our last home. A pleasant little house with wide verandah giving it a comfortable, homely look; small rooms but with large windows and with a general air of dignity and self-respect in the passages and the staircase, the whole compactly built and well designed. Immediately behind Minchinhampton Common; from our front windows a wide view across the valley of beech trees to the Cotswold hills beyond, the delicate outlines losing themselves in the fields and woods of the middle distance. One great attraction: an expanse of western sky. From my bedroom windows I can watch the sunsets of each season of the year. Five minutes' walk and I am in the hall of Longfords listening to Mary's bright personality . . . or I am wandering on the common with its glorious sky and distant hills. . . . This is to be our home until I lose the last tie of duty to another life and become an outcast from domesticity, a worker following her work whither it leads, like an animal following its food.

### 25 October. [Box House]

The Rylands came this evening; morally a *tour de force* on my part . . . I want by my continued friendliness to that woman to put behind me all unworthy thoughts and feelings, to clear my mind of dross, and to work, so far as God gives me strength, in pure gold. God help me.

### 27 October. [Box House]

The strain is over and the task is done. Alice Green, with her extraordinary vivacity of intellect and brilliant powers of expression helped me over it, unknowing of the service she was rendering. . . .

James Keir Hardie (1856–1915), a Scottish miner and trade union organizer who became a leading advocate of independent labour representation in

Parliament, fought a notable by-election in Mid-Lanark in 1888. The Liberals were angry because he split the vote, and it was rumoured that he had received a large Tory contribution towards his election expenses. When H. H. Champion was suspected of being the intermediary for 'Tory gold', Margaret Harkness tried to throw his critics off the scent by claiming that she had given Hardie a hundred pounds, though this was only a third of the sum involved (*North British Daily Mail,* 28 June 1888). Her letter in the *Star* on 16 September 1889 was an excited defence of Champion's political virtue and a flat denial of any complicity with the Tories. Tom Mann (1856–1941), a member of the Amalgamated Society of Engineers, became a leader of the 'New' unions. He had been a key figure in the dock strike.

[14 November?]. *Devonshire House Hotel*
Arrived for a fortnight's holiday in London. Maggie Harkness came in to supper. Sad to feel that I more and more distrust her. The last blow to my confidence, a letter appearing in the *Star* at the time of the victory of the dockers, a letter mad with vanity, claiming to have paid Keir Hardie's electioneering expenses. . . . she tells me that the money was hers 'for that purpose and that purpose alone' which simply means that she served as go-between. The last year she has been hand in glove with the under-ground labour party, with Champion, Burns, Mann, etc. 'The only way to observe them is to pretend to be immensely interested, but aren't they suspicious; mind you don't mention me if you meet any of them', and then she throws out hints of all kinds of mysterious intrigues. . . . I look at her with blank amazement: in face of such utter deficiency of sense of honour there is nothing to be said, for there is nothing to appeal to. . . . At times I feel that the pretence of the old feeling is a hollow sham, that a relationship in which one is perpetually trying to guard oneself against betrayal cannot be healthy or lasting and must end in death. But pity will keep me her friend until I cease to interest her and she slips from me, not I from her. She is typical of the emancipated woman who has broken ties and struggled against the prejudice and oppression of bigoted and con-ventional relations to gain her freedom but who has never been disciplined by a public opinion which expects a woman to work with the masculine standard of honour and integrity. . . .

*17 November.* [Devonshire House Hotel]
This Sunday last year I took the communion at St Paul's and prayed earnestly against bitterness and evil feelings. This day I take it again. Many of my thoughts during the last year have been unworthy. Can it be

otherwise this coming year? I have work before me . . . Without help from the great spirit of Truth and Love I cannot do it. I pray earnestly . . . that my life may be a 'living sacrifice' to the work that lies before me. . . . Let me suffer if by suffering my nature be purified and strengthened. . . .

*Laura Gay* was the title of the novel written by Beatrice's mother.

*26 November. Box House*

Hastily summoned from London. Father sinking – he may linger a few days, a few months, but death is waiting for the body struck down this day four years ago. . . . He was in middle age when I was born. I can remember little of his life in its prime . . . But stories of his childhood and youth, told but yesterday, are fresh in my memory. . . . The pitiful glimpse into that early home . . . the London life of the radical politician's eldest son . . .

His mother was a beautiful woman of gentle family – a Hebrew prophetess to look at – married against her will to the wealthy Manchester warehouseman some 20 years older than herself. . . . [The] Potter brothers live still in the hearts of Manchester folk as the energetic pioneers of Manchester radical politics, as the founders of the civic life of the town. But to the dark-eyed fiery-natured woman, with her fastidious tastes and highly strung feelings, the bourgeois conventions, the gross ideals of the *parvenu* were intolerable. . . . [She] went mad from sheer hatred. After the birth of her youngest child she was removed to an asylum: some years afterwards she recovered sufficiently to live with her mother – to her husband and children she never returned. She became sane on all but one subject – her special mission to lead the Jews back to Jerusalem. . . . This weird figure of the beautiful mad mother loomed large in our father's childhood and youth: it darkened with tragic helpless sorrow the closing years of the active radical politician. . . . Before young Richard was 21 years old, his father became a hopeless invalid; for some years he lingered, dying slowly of tumour on the brain, his son nursing him like a daughter, standing in his stead towards the three young girls . . . At 26 he was left with many friends, a fair fortune, and life before him. . . .

By nature the Potters were Radicals, Dissenting and individualist, believing instinctively that success always meant merit, unconscious of their own and others' feelings so long as they reached their aim. . . . With these qualities the younger Richard began life. He had matriculated at London University, he had been called to the Bar, he had mixed freely in political society at a time when being an M.P.'s son carried prestige. . . . Before settling down to the Bar he decided on taking the 'grand tour' with his pretty sister Kitty. At Rome he met Lawrencina Heyworth. In 1844 they married. Their love story idealized with Mother's conception of her own and Father's character we have in *Laura Gay* . . .

Through Mother's precepts and prejudices Father became after their marriage isolated from his old friends (many of whom were 'irregular' in their views and actions). Discouraged from any serious attempt to succeed at the Bar, and after a year's wandering he settled down with his young wife to live on their income at a country place in Hertfordshire. Four years afterwards, in the French Revolution of '48 he lost the greater part of his capital and at 32 years of age he had to cast around him for means to support the quick-coming family.

This loss of fortune became the great turning-point of his life. . . . Once engaged in business his life became one long series of varied enterprise, Mother's fertile imagination and ingenuity of intellect prompting him, her restless ambition spurring him on. Truly the little woman had both spurs and a bit – and kept a whip in reserve. She was dutiful, ambitious, ascetic, and restrained the natural self-indulgence, easy-going and undisciplined impulses of the far nobler nature she guided and governed. . . .

On all general questions he had a largeness of view, a certain noble philosophy, a childlike reverence for the Good, the Beautiful and the True – and yet in the aims of life he was a materialist. . . . The elder sisters say the railway world with its jobbery, loose commercial views, with its guzzling and low ideals of enjoyment, injured his morale. I do not know as I did not see. When first I knew him he was already in the thick of it, an eminent man in his day. He took his wife and all his children into his confidence: to each and all he showed the cards he held in his hand, described to you exactly the reason for each move, for his suspicions and calculations as to the cards of his opponents. And yet to see him with these men . . . one felt one was in the presence of a born diplomatist. Darling Father, how your children have loved you. . . .

And now that he lies helpless . . . he still brightens up to welcome his 'bright-eyed daughter' . . . In the long hours of restlessness he broods over the success of his children and finds reason for peace and satisfaction. 'I want one more son-in-law', (a proof that he frets near his end, as he has discouraged the idea of matrimony for me, put it off as something I could easily attain). 'A woman is happier married. I should like to see my little Bee married to a good strong fellow', and the darling old father dreams of the 'little Bee' of long ago; he does not realize that she has passed away, leaving the strong form and determination of the 'glorified spinster' bending over him as a mother bends over her sick child. . . .

# A Frank Friendship

## January 1890–July 1892

*1 February.* [Devonshire House Hotel]
Already one month of the new year past. Father lying in a half-conscious motionless state, recognizing his children but not realizing ideas or feelings . . . I am, in the meantime, so long as life lasts, chained to his side. . . . Sometimes I feel discouraged. Not only am I baulked in carrying out my work, but with the lack of all accomplishment I begin to doubt my ability to do so. Continuous reading makes me feel a mere learner, entangled in my own growth, helpless before this ever-accumulating mass of facts. . . .

I feel, too, exiled from the world of thought and action of other men and women. London is in a ferment: strikes are the order of the day, the new trade unionism with its magnificent conquest of the docks is striding along with an arrogance rousing employers to a keen sense of danger, and to a determination to strike against strikes. The socialists, led by a small set of able young men (Fabian Society) are manipulating London Radicals, ready at the first check-mate of trade unionism to voice a growing desire for state action. And I, from the peculiarity of my social position, should be in the midst of all parties, sympathetic with all, allied with none, in a true vantage-ground for impartial observation of the forces at work. Burnett and the older trade unionists on one side, Margaret Harkness with Tom Mann, Tillett, Burns on the other, round about me Co-operators of all schools, a new acquaintance with leading socialists, and as a background, all those respectable and highly successful men – my brothers-in-law, typical of the old reign of private property and self-interested action. There is Daniel Meinertzhagen, a great City financier, earning his tens of thousands each year, upright and honourable but cordially hating 'the social question', describing frankly his ideal: English capitalists retired from business living on an income of foreign investments, the land given over to sport, the people emigrated or starved out, no inhabitants except a few dependants to serve in one way or another the fortunate capitalists. Willie Cripps would add a pauper's hospital as a school for surgical experiment and observation and a limited number of surgeons and doctors to bleed an income out of the capitalists. Alfred Cripps (the youngest Queen's Counsel at the Bar) would maintain the need for legal advice, and the charm of a well-cared-for peasantry dependent on benevolent and wealthy barristers who might choose to spend the recess in the country. And then I turn from the luxurious homes of these picked men of the individualist system and struggle through an East End crowd of the wrecks, the waifs and strays, or I enter a debating society of working men and listen to the ever increasing cry of active brains doomed to the treadmill of manual labour – *for a career in which ability tells* – the bitter cry of the nineteenth-century working man and the nineteenth-century woman alike. And the whole seems a whirl of contending actions, aspirations and aims out of which I dimly see the tendency towards a socialist community in which there will be individual freedom and public property in the stead of class slavery and private possession of the means of subsistence of the whole people. At last I am a socialist!

And this is where observation and study have led me, in spite of training, class bias, etc.

Lord Thring (1818–1907) was a distinguished parliamentary lawyer; Lord Monkswell was a Liberal much interested in London municipal politics; Lord Dunraven (1841–1926), an Irish politician and prominent Liberal, was chairman of the Committee on Sweating, 1889–90.

*9 February. Devonshire House Hotel*
Up here for a fortnight's change. Dined with Lord Thring to meet Lord Monkswell and discuss Lord Dunraven's draft report, and help to draft an opposition. . . . If I can make them retain my suggestions . . . I shall have laid the foundation for a thoroughly efficient Labour Bureau. . . . Though I am suspected of socialism, my anti-sensationalism gives me a footing among the sternest school of *laissez-faire* economists, and this position I must guard jealously if I am to be of even little use as a reforming agency.

[12?] *February* [Devonshire House Hotel]
Margaret Harkness spent two nights here. She is in a much more satisfactory state. Her position with the new trade unionists, and the genuine
affection the leaders have for her, has softened and enlarged her
life. . . . As usual she represents the society she lives in as a huge
whirlpool and her friends seem like monsters (of virtue or wickedness)
in a nightmare, but this time they are lovable.

*14 February.* [Devonshire House Hotel]
Sidney Webb, the socialist, dined here to meet the Booths. A remarkable little man with a huge head on a very tiny body, a breadth of
forehead quite sufficient to account for the encyclopaedic character of
his knowledge, a Jewish nose, prominent eyes and mouth, black hair,
somewhat unkempt, spectacles and a most bourgeois black coat shiny
with wear; regarded as a whole, somewhat between a London card and
a German professor. To keep to essentials: his pronunciation is
Cockney, his H's are shaky, his attitudes by no means eloquent, with his
thumbs fixed pugnaciously in a far from immaculate waistcoat, with his
bulky head thrown back and his little body forward he struts even
when he stands, delivering himself with extraordinary rapidity of
thought and utterance and with an expression of inexhaustible self-
complacency. But I like the man. There is a directness of speech, an
open-mindedness, an imaginative warm-heartedness which should
carry him far. He has the self-complacency of one who is always thinking faster than his neighbours, who is untroubled by doubts, and to
whom the acquisition of facts is as easy as the grasping of matter; but he
has no vanity and is totally unself-conscious. Hence his absence of
consciousness as to his neighbour's corns. [Last words torn and
scratched out.] . . .

[15] *February.* [Devonshire House Hotel?]
Delightful evening with the Booths – an evening of the old sort of triangular discussions.
   'I have found a new definition of socialism' said Charlie, after we had
dismissed the 'Sweating Report', Sidney Webb and various other subjects. 'The prevention by a paternal state of the consequences of a man's
action: *the substitution of a new set of consequences for the natural set of
consequences* following upon a man's action.'
   Mary looked doubtful and critical and I burst forth with indignant
positiveness. 'I don't agree with you one little bit, Charlie. Quite the

contrary, under state socialism, supposing it be possible, which I do not assert; but supposing it were to take place, every man would suffer the exact consequences of his action; he could not protect himself with private property as he does now. Instead of the great class of property holders who need not use their faculties, and who may yet receive the product of other persons' faculties, this class of persons would, under a socialist system, suffer the consequences of their action or their inaction. There would be only one exception – the individual or individuals who were incapable of serving the community in any way whatsoever. Those persons would, I suppose, be dealt with as they are now, by a Poor Law: that is to say they would be protected as they are now from the consequences of their absence of ability, which in a perfectly barbarous and natural state would mean starvation. But with the exception of this one class of paupers – or of incapables – all other men and women will be drawn into the most perfect form of competition. Socialism, as I understand it, instead of destroying competition, will bring about the most perfect and universal form of it, for the simple reason that no class will be able to protect themselves from communal service by the possession of private property.

'But surely, Beatrice, you take a very peculiar view,' said Mary (with the doubtful critical way in which she handles her husband and her friend alike), 'that is not the view of Marx, of Bax, of Morris. To them socialism means the giving according to the needs, the equalizing of conditions, the levelling of all classes to one standard of comfort.'

'And the substitution of the will of the State for the wishes of the individual,' added Charlie. 'For instance, instead of becoming a barrister, a doctor, a merchant as I felt inclined, I should be allotted a place by a state official in return for my food and lodging, and be forced to remain in that place until Death or the State Official removed me. And if I refused to do good work, I should be still given board and lodging, and whether I did excellently, well, middling or badly, the same food and lodging would be assigned me – that's why I define socialism as the substitution by a paternal government of artificial consequences for the natural consequences of a man's action: defining "natural consequences" as the reward a man would get under a strict competitive system.'

'I think you misunderstand socialism altogether,' say I (with, I fear, an increased positiveness of tone as I feel my ground firm under me). 'First, let us define socialism; for we may be talking about entirely different things. *I* mean by socialism, not a vague and sentimental desire to "ameliorate the condition of the masses", but a definite economic form; a peculiar industrial organization – *the communal or state ownership of Capital and Land.* This stands in the front place of the programme of all socialists: Morris, Bax, Webb, Marx, Schaeffner, Schaffle, down to the author of *Looking Backward.* These men would all agree what they mean primarily by socialism, whatever else they may mean besides, is the transference to the community of the *means* of production as distinguished from the *faculty* to produce. They assert that owing to the monopoly of these means of production (land and capital) it lies within the power of a certain class to dictate whether the rest of the nation shall use their faculties or not, whether they shall be worked day and night or be unemployed. I am not for a moment endorsing their assertion. I only give their view of the present individualist system as a proof that the one thing upon which they all agree is state ownership of capital and land. I say that under this system there would be absolute freedom of individual action. . . . I have become a socialist not because I believe it would ameliorate the conditions of the masses (though I think it would do so) but because I believe that only under communal ownership of the means of production can you arrive at the most perfect form of individual development, at the greatest stimulus to individual effort; in other words complete socialism is only consistent with absolute individualism. As such, some day, I shall stand on a barrel and preach it.'

[22 or 23] *February.* [Devonshire House Hotel]
. . . The *Fabian Essays on Socialism* are making way: it is curious how many persons wake up to the fact that they have always been 'socialists'. The delicious *positivism* of the authors, their optimistic conclusion that the world is most assuredly going their way, the plausible proof they bring in favour of their confidence, the good temper and the moderation, all impress the ordinary English reader. . . .

*29 March.* [Box House]
Am labouring with my paper on the Lords' Report, have been for the last three weeks. Stuck in the middle; oppressed with a constant headache and sick to death with grappling with my subject. Was I made for brain work? Is any woman made for a purely intellectual life? Then the background to my life is inexpressibly depressing – Father lying like a log in his bed, a child, an animal, with less capacity for thought and feeling than my old pet, Don . . . One longs for release and yet sickens at the thought of this weary desire for the death of one's father.

*22 April.* [Box House]

Finished my paper and sent it off. Spent a week in London, and dawdled a week away here with Alice Green. . . . In this household [there are] ten persons living on the fat of the land in order to minister to the supposed comfort of one poor imbecile old man . . . The whole thing is a vicious circle, as irrational as it is sorrowful. We feed our servants well, keep them in luxurious slavery, because we hate to see discomfort around us. But they are consuming the labour of others, and giving nothing in return, except useless service to a dying life, past serving. Here are 13 dependants consuming riches and making none, and no one the better for it. . . . It is wrong, wrong, wrong.

> Though Sidney Webb won a Whewell law scholarship to Cambridge, he did not take it up.

*26 April.* [Box House]

Sidney Webb, the socialist, spent Sunday here. The son of a small London shopkeeper. Father isolated from his own class by his superior tastes: disciple and political supporter of J. S. Mill. Scrimped his own expenditure to educate his two sons and one daughter, the two former sent to Germany and allowed to run wild at a pastor's. Here the elder boy took to novels, Sidney to history, metaphysics and German economics. At 16 and 17 respectively they went 'into the City'; Sidney into a colonial broker's. Disgusted with the petty cheating of a low-class broker, the boy worked [in] his spare hours for the Civil Service examination, passed into the second division, spent 16 months in the Inland Revenue, passed into the first division, second, abided his time until a good position was open, passed second again through the first class into a good position at the Colonial Office; became a barrister, took his London degree, won the second Whewell scholarship – all in his leisure hours at the Colonial Office. 'I have done everything I intended to do,' said the little man. 'I have a belief in my own star.' 'Take care, Mr Webb,' say I in a motherly tone, 'don't be complacent about small successes.' Poor Sidney Webb. I surprised him by my sympathy and 'unholy knowledge' (as he termed it) of men's feelings into a whole history of his life, his thought, feeling, and action. 'You reduced me to a pulp by your sympathy, and then impressed your own view on me; you have made me feel horribly small – you have given me an altogether different sense of proportion – and yet I don't believe that I looked at things in a disproportionate way,' says the little man defiantly. 'Come,

Mr Webb, you can feel you have humbled me – by making me a socialist.'

I am not sure as to the future of that man. His tiny tadpole body, unhealthy skin, lack of manner, Cockney pronunciation, poverty, are all against him. He has the conceit of a man who has raised himself out of the most insignificant surroundings into a position of power – how much power no one quite knows. This self-complacent egotism, this disproportionate view of his own position, is at once repulsive and ludicrous. On the other hand, looked at by the light of his personal history, it was inevitable. And he can learn: he is quick and sensitive and ready to adapt himself. This sensitiveness, combined as it undoubtedly is with great power, may carry him far. If the opportunity comes, I think the man will appear. In the meantime he is an interesting study. A London retail tradesman with the aims of a Napoleon! a queer monstrosity to be justified only by success. And above all a loop-hole into the socialist party; one of the small body of men with whom I may sooner or later throw in my lot for good and all.

*5 May.* [Box House]
About my work: suddenly started on a new idea. That I will spend this winter in elaborating my old theory of economics. It seems to me that it is needed, some new view, that now is my time to work it, since I am thwarted in practical work. . . .

It is strange how absolutely *alone* and *independent* my life has become: not *lonely*, for I have many friends and fellow-workers and do not feel the need for more sympathy than I get; quite the contrary, in most of the relationships I willingly give more than I receive. But that terrible time of agonizing suffering seems to have turned my whole nature into steel – not the steel that kills, but the surgeon's instrument that would save. My whole thought and feeling has drifted far out into the future – present persons seem to me so many shadows. It is for future generations, for their *noble* happiness, that I live and pray. . . .

The spring months, since I returned early in March, have passed happily. Those delightful early mornings, my window wide open, reading in bed, looking from time to time out on the glorious wooded valley, with the calm lines of hill behind, the walks on the common, the rides on the highland, the hours of reading and meditation with the bright soft colours and glad sounds of spring – the spirit of peaceful energy within and without.

Beatrice had been sympathetically encouraging to Sidney in the first months of their acquaintance, and at the end of April she invited him to Box for a day. The visit, he wrote to her on 30 April, made 'a very deep impression', and the 'frank friendliness' of his reception made him tell her that 'I really must have a mentor outside of the working circle, a looker-on who sees most of the game, and I hope you will not refuse to repeat the experiment (as opportunity serves)'. Beatrice responded that 'this desire to be helpful' was 'part of the mother's instinct' and that when it was joined to intellectual dependence ('a curious trait in even the most intellectual women') it lends to friendship between men and women that subtle usefulness which will always make such friendships one of the greatest factors in life – so long as it is not blurred by the predominance of lower feeling, when I think it becomes a source of pure evil'. The antithesis between 'intellectual dependence' and 'lower feeling' was to be the source of much difficulty in the relationship between Beatrice and Sidney over the next twelve months, for she saw him essentially as a fellow-worker, while he was in love with her from their first meeting, though any attempt to say so brought a stern rebuke. They travelled together to the Co-operative Congress in Glasgow, and what Beatrice called 'a critical twenty-four hours' began with a letter from Sidney which she inserted in the diary.

You tortured me horribly last night by your intolerable 'superiority'. Surely an affectation of heartlessness is as objectionable as an affectation of conceit. And you blasphemed horribly against what is highest and holiest in human relations.

I *could* not speak my mind last night, but this agony is unendurable. You will at any rate not be indifferent to my suffering. I do not know how to face another night such as I have passed. I believe you are free in the morning: come off somewhere and let us clear up what is more important than all congresses.

Now you know why I could not confess to frank speaking. Even with you.

### 23 May. Glasgow

Exquisite Whitsun weather. A long journey up in third-class saloon, I in one of the two comfortable seats of the carriage, with S.W. squatted on a portmanteau by my side, and relays of working-men friends lying a full length at my feet, discussing earnestly trade unions, co-operation, and socialism. S.W.'s appearance among them surprises, and, on the whole, pleases them. . . .

In the evening S.W. and I wandered out through the Glasgow streets. A critical twenty-four hours followed, and another long walk by glorious sunset through the crowded streets, knocking up against drunken Scots. With glory in the sky and hideous bestiality on the earth, the two social-ists came to a working compact. 'You understand you promise me to realize that the chances are a hundred to one that nothing follows but friendship. If you feel that it is weakening your life, that your work is less efficient for it, you will promise me to give it all up?'

'I promise you. However it ends I will make it serve my life – my work shall be both more vigorous and higher in tone for it. I will *make you* help me, and I will insist on helping you – our relationship shall be judged solely by the helpfulness to each other's work. Forgive me, if I say that I believe that if we were united we could do great things together. I will not bother you with that; but I will vow solemnly that, even if after a time we part, I will do better things for our friendship than I could have done without it.'

'One word more,' say I. 'Promise me not to let your mind dwell on the purely personal part of your feeling. I know how that feeling unful-filled saps all the vigour out of a man's life. Promise me to deliberately turn your mind away from it – to think of me as a married woman, as the wife of your friend.'

'That I can hardly promise. But I will look at the whole question from the point of view of health: as you say, I will not allow myself to dwell on it. I will suppress the purely personal feeling. I will divert my imagi-nation to strengthening the working tie between us.'

One grasp of the hand, and we were soon in a warm discussion on some question of economics. Finis. . . .

On 29 May, Beatrice wrote to tell Sidney that she had been reflecting uneasily 'about all that had passed at Glasgow' and telling him not 'to build up a hope'. 'Personal happiness to me is an utterly remote thing; and I am to that extent "heartless" that I regard everything from the point of view of making my own and another's life serve the community more effectively.' Sidney replied next day with the first of many letters urging her not to commit 'emotional suicide' by sacrificing everything to her vocation. 'Whether we are ever destined to be united or not, you are a source of life and work and happiness to me. . . . Will you simply let things alone and see what happens?' Beatrice wrote back at once. 'I will not withdraw my friendship unless you *force* me to do so, by treating me otherwise than as a friend. . . . Your letter has touched me deeply but it must be the last word of *personal feeling*.'

After these events Beatrice unsealed the letters from Chamberlain which she had put away in the summer of 1887 and re-read them. She added the following note to her diary.

I sealed this parcel up nearly three years ago. I have opened it to try and rid my mind of the whole story by seeing the actual facts. I succeeded in my effort to rise out of the agony of that relationship into a life of vigorous work – may it not be possible to cast even the memory of it from me? It has haunted me day and night. I watch his life with feverish interest, tracing with a horrible ingenuity those qualities that pained me, undermining the public usefulness of his life. I observe narrowly from all the tiny details I can gather from newspaper paragraphs and personal gossip the effect of his marriage on his character. . . . The stern enthusiast with his uncompromising policy who dictated his views to me in the Standish garden has been transformed by circumstances into the man of pleasure, the darling of fine ladies, the centre of half a dozen London drawing-rooms. And this in spite of an overpoweringly strong will which would dictate to the world the manner of its government.

But all this is unworthy of me, this brooding over his ill-success is a heaven-sent vengeance on my deep humiliation, on the humiliation which he seemed to glory in and wish to prolong. After all there may have been misunderstanding on his side – on mine there was eccentricity bordering on madness – the pride and independence of a strong man, the simplicity of a child, and a total absence of the reserve and dignity which should characterize a woman. I was willing to offend him by refusing to yield to his opinions on questions of common weal. I was ready to humble myself by telling frankly of my deep and abiding feeling, how was it possible for a man, bred up in conventions, to see me as I was and to realize all the horrible suffering I was passing through. First I appeared to him as a self-opinionated person, too full of her own ideas to sympathize with his, at other times as an uncontrolled emotional woman, now refusing to see him, then expressing in naked written language the depth of her feeling. Naturally enough he was puzzled – dreading to be refused – frightened of being caught – and amazed with my perfect self-possession in conversation and argument. In short, whatever may have been his faults towards me, there were ample in myself to account for all the sufferings I passed through. Can I be brave and sensible and once for all vow that I will forgive and forget?

*31 May.* [Devonshire House Hotel?]
It is a very solemn thought to feel you have a man's soul in your keeping. This afternoon at Westminster Abbey I prayed I might be worthy of the trust, that it might raise my life and his to a higher level of 'service'.

Beatrice now left with Alice Green for a holiday in Bavaria and the Dolomites. While she was away she and Sidney corresponded with high-minded intimacy. 'A very fearful responsibility has been laid upon us both – unexpectedly, undesirably,' Sidney wrote on 16 June. 'We have the ideas which can deliver the world. . . . You have it in your hands to make me, in the noblest sense, great. I, even I, have it in my power to help your own particular work. . . . Between us two let there be at any rate perfect soul union.' Beatrice wrote back a cautionary letter from Trento on 22 June. 'You are expecting too much from me – if you do not take care – you will frighten me back into acquaintanceship,' she reminded him, and though Sidney accepted the reproof he persisted. 'Our ends are the same, our views are the same; surely out of so much identity there must come harmony,' he wrote on 24 June. In the next entry, Beatrice refers to a holiday taken shortly after her mother's death.

*1 June. Cologne*
A long afternoon spent in prayer, kneeling alone in the Minster. Eight years ago, about this time of year, we passed through here – Mr Spencer, Father, Rosy and I. Then I was in the pride of life, in a whirlwind of striving after personal happiness and personal success. I prayed – but with only half my heart. . . . Six years ago, I passed through again, alone and broken-hearted. . . . I remember well, that in an ecstasy of devotion, I prayed I might pass through the fire, that the evil might be burned out of me, slowly if need be, inch by inch. . . . But am I chastened? I prayed. I implored help and guidance to be humble and pure, to be worthy of the position of influence I have gained. . . . And thus I thought of the worship a man is giving me – not me – but Woman through me – and I prayed again that I might make my life a temple of purity wherein to receive it. And I, so vain, so impure – God help me.

Beatrice gave Sidney a present on his thirty-first birthday on 13 July, and they spent Saturday, 26 July, together. The crusading liberal journalist Henry William Massingham (1860–1924), was then editor of the *Star*, an evening paper with Radical sympathies.

*27 July.* [Devonshire House Hotel?]

I go this morning to take the sacrament at St Paul's. Two months of enjoyment and rest, of friendship and beauty, must now be followed by nine months of sober strenuous work. . . .

Lunched at St Paul's Tavern with Sidney Webb and spent the afternoon in Epping Forest.

'When I left you yesterday [said he] (we had travelled up from Haslemere, where I had stayed at the Frederic Harrisons' and he with a neighbour) I went straight home; found two urgent letters, one from O'Brien begging me to write the London articles for the *Speaker*, the other from Massingham, telling me I must review Marshall's book [*Principles of Economics*] for the *Star*. I went straight to the Club and read right through Marshall's six hundred pages – got up, staggering under it. It is a great book . . . but it will not make an epoch in economics. Economics has still to be re-made. Who is to do it? Either you must help me to do it, or I must help you!'

In the meantime he has arranged for me to contribute a volume on the Co-operative movement to Sonnenschein's Social Science series, a short, slight work, but which I think will be of some avail. We talked economics, politics, the possibility of inspiring socialism with faith leading to works. He read me poetry as we lay in the Forest – Keats and Rossetti – and we parted.

'I give you leave to think of me, when you would be thinking of yourself, but not when you have sufficient power to work. I am willing to replace self in your consciousness, but never, never would I oust work or others. I have promised you – that you know is our compact.'

Those the last words – the answer to the only words of personal feeling which burst from him as we parted.

Beatrice's diary made no reference to the ensuing contretemps. 'You were so *ravissante* yesterday, and so angel-good,' Sidney wrote after their day in Epping Forest, 'that I had all I could do not to say goodbye in a way which would have broken our Concordat. I had to rush away from you speechless to hold my own.' He added that he had not hitherto realized that Richard Potter was rich. 'This is one more barrier between us – one more step in that noble self-sacrifice you must make to pick me up.' All the same, he said, 'I do not see how I can go on without you.' This 'abominable letter' brought a 'hurt and offended' reply from Beatrice on 9 July, insisting that he show more self-control. 'Do not be always brooding on my effect on your own life and feelings. It is truly masculine! I do not quite know what the word Love conveys to a man's mind; but *that* is not what we women understand by Love – Love to us has in it some element of self-control and self-sacrifice.' Sidney replied on 11 August: 'I fully admit that I was wrong to pester you with the expression of my feeling. . . . You shall not need to write me another such letter: a terrible letter.' After this exchange they reverted to a discussion of Marshall's economic theories, and Sidney was content to press his case in terms of intellectual companionship and mutual concern with social problems. Beatrice was happier and their letters soon reverted to their earlier intimate tone. They met several times in the course of the summer, for Beatrice had no concern for the conventions of middle-class courtship and she was willing to meet Sidney and even travel with him unchaperoned: an emotional rather than a physical distance separated them. Graham Wallas (1858–1932), a schoolteacher, was to become a noted professor at the London School of Economics. Hubert Llewellyn Smith (1864–1945), an Oxford statistician and one of Charles Booth's collaborators, was to become an eminent civil servant at the Board of Trade.

*26 August.* [Box House]
Begun my book. Three weeks of reading and receiving friends, mostly men – journalists, socialists and incipient socialists. Graham Wallas, my last visitor, one of the knot of Fabians who would 'run the world'. . . . the charm is in the relations between these men, the genuine care for each other, the trustfulness and practical communism of property and ideas. In the meantime I am very happy, hard at work, enjoying health, the lovely country, friendship.

*7 September. Devonshire House Hotel*
A break to attend the British Association or, rather, the economic section of it, of which Marshall was president and Charles Booth vice-president. Charles Booth, who had promised to stay with me at an hotel at Bradford, accepted a room at Leeds, so that S.W. and I were left in solitary glory at the Midland Hotel! One funny scene – S.W., Llewellyn Smith and I journey back in third-class carriage 11.30 at night. A variety artist jumps in – a pretty smart foreign Jewess decidedly the worse for liquor . . . Tells us the details of her life, becoming more and more 'racy'. L. Smith collapses in the corner, looking alternatively severe and unalterably amused. S.W., by whom she sits, tries to keep her in order by inquiring in the most fatherly manner into her earnings and into the statistical side of her profession. Whereupon I get interested and show

signs of listening. She immediately brightens up and leaning across S.W. tells me in a loud whisper about her latest tights and the sensation they created, remarking that she did not mind speaking of such a subject to a husband and wife. I bury myself in the corner, L. Smith shakes with laughing and S.W. begins hurriedly another statistical inquiry. And it ends by the young lady offering to introduce him as a performer on the variety stage, looking doubtfully the while at his big head and little body!

. . . a great deal of conversation with my fixed companion and back to London (after 3 days) by the late express, indulging in the unwonted luxury of a first-class, S.W. telling me the story of his examination triumphs and reading me to sleep with *John Ball's Dream*. The tie stiffening!

Lying in bed in this quiet back room . . . listening to the City church bells for morning service. Tired but happy.

Beatrice spent the rest of September at Box, working on her book. She sent Sidney a warm letter: 'Let us go forward with this fellowship without thought for the morrow – the form it will take is not in our hands, it will grow up as the joint creation of two natures,' she wrote; and he took this 'beautiful letter' as an encouragement. 'You will do the right thing at the right time and I am content to wait,' he replied on 17 September. 'No one shall say of me that politicians must not be allowed to fall in love for it destroys all their effectiveness. I am quite sure I have never done so much work or been so efficient as this glorious summer. After all, happiness, like champagne, is of some use in the world. . . .' He sent Beatrice a book of Rossetti's poems as 'the first gift I have ventured to make to you' and, since he was giving up part of his annual leave to a Fabian speaking tour in Lancashire, began to keep a daily account of his activities in penny notebooks which he despatched to her as letters as he filled them.

*9 September.* [Box House]
A curt letter from Maggie Harkness telling me she leaves England for 'always' and refusing my offer to come and see her. . . . It is sad. One always feels the worse for a broken tie – feels to some extent a traitor. And she was as tender to one in one's trouble as she has been traitorous to me in success. A strange nature – the two dominant impulses, pity and envy, helpfulness and treachery.

A newspaper description of Sidney Webb. Might have been written of Joseph Chamberlain of ten years ago. Strange fate!

2 *October.* [Box House]

Began my second chapter after four days' rest, chatting with Sidney Webb and Alice Green who were here. . . . 'A dear little man, one would get quite fond of him, so wonderfully clear and kindly in telling you all he knows.' 'A bright woman, clever of course, not a person to whom one would confide one's woes.' – the respective opinions of each other. He is certainly extraordinarily improved and becoming a needful background to my working life and I the same to him. And now to work – the beauty of the friendship is that it stimulates the work of both.

Beatrice's visit to London was the prelude to a second contretemps with Sidney, who was beginning to take her friendliness as a tacit understanding that they would eventually marry. When Beatrice met him in London early in October, before he left for another round of public meetings in the North, she seems to have hinted at her old feelings for Chamberlain, and in this moment of intimacy he clearly misjudged her attitude and presumed to the point where she sharply reproved him. He sent an abject apology, and she replied with a letter that is so relevant to her feelings about him and Chamberlain that the main part of it is included here.

Your letter made me feel very miserable; indeed I sat down and cried. But I will tell you with absolute frankness what I felt and have felt. When you spoke to me in Glasgow I did not say, as I have said to others, a distinct 'no' because I felt that your character and circumstances and your work offered me a sphere of usefulness and fellowship which I had no right to refuse offhand. I felt, too, how hard it would be for me to lead a lonely life without becoming hard and nervous and self-willed. On the other hand you were personally unattractive to me and I doubted whether I *could* bring myself to submit to a close relationship. Remember that I was desperately in love and for six years with another man – and that even now the wound is open.

Since then I have been trying hard to bring myself to care for you – some days I have felt the strength and calm which your affection has brought into my life. . . . I have now a warm regard for you but I do not love you and until I do I will not be in any way bound. . . . The question of marriage is not a practical one at present and may not be so for two or three years. My regard for you is not strong enough to face the terrible self-questionings of an engagement – the immediate pressure of the whole family. If I were in

love it would be different – but I am not in love. . . . Altogether I feel
very very miserable. Try to forgive any pain I have given you, by the
thought of my misery and also in gratitude for my honest effort to
return your feeling. I cannot and *will* not be engaged to you. . . . I
should meet you, feel bound, feel it impossible and cut it once for
all. . . . Dear Sidney, I will try to love you, but do not be
impatient. . . . What can I do more? I am doing more than I would
for any other man, simply because you are a socialist and I am a
socialist. That other man I loved but did not believe in; you I believe
in but do not love. Will it end equally unhappily?

In Sidney's letters he continued to stress her belief that 'personal defects'
would eventually 'sink into insignificance before our common aims and
mutual sympathy', and though Beatrice was very reserved she agreed to
meet his Fabian friends at a party in London. While in London Beatrice
discussed Sidney with the Booths, with whom he had dined a few days
earlier: 'I failed to ingratiate myself,' Sidney wrote afterwards. Arabella
Fisher had already written to Beatrice in June urging her to break off the
relationship. She now wrote more firmly. 'I am afraid of your becoming
entangled in a web of socialism. I should not be afraid if the sphere of the
man were of wider culture and a calmer, more statesmanlike mind.'

*6 November. Manchester*
. . . This is the first November which I have spent without terrible
despondency, gloom overtaking the greyness of my life throughout the
year. And now I am no longer on the bank watching with cold but
intense curiosity the surface currents. I am swimming in mid-water
with another by my side and a host to the fore and the rear of me. . . .

*15 November. [Box House]*
*The day*: and now all that terrible pain is like a passed dream, and even
the scar is well nigh imperceptible: has the whole skin hardened?

At the end of November, Sidney contracted scarlet fever; his illness was
compounded by the effects of years of unremitting work and depression.
On 4 December, as soon as he could send 'fumigated' letters, he complained that Beatrice had sent him 'hard', 'uncomfortable' ones. He said he
was now resigned to the fact that she would not resist her 'whole family and
connection' to marry him, but made a last plea – 'let me wait under
whatever conditions you please' – he asked her to tell him the truth: 'if you

are *quite* sure that no advantage to your own life or mine, or to the socialist cause, could ever induce you to marry me – then it is your duty to tell me so . . . and I must bear it how I can'. Beatrice's reply was touching but firm:

> I cried very bitterly over your letter and tossed about the night through feeling how wrong it had been of me to have been led away from my better judgement last spring and to have granted your request for friendship. But that is now done – and cannot be undone – the question is what is the present position?
>
> First, all you write about your career does not affect the one question. It would suit my work – and therefore me – far better to marry a clerk in the Colonial Office than a leading politician to whose career I should have in the end to sacrifice my own. It was exactly your position which made me hesitate – it was this with your views and your moral refinement which made me try to love you.
>
> But I do not love you. All the misery of this relationship arises from this . . . there is no change in my feeling except a growing certainty that I cannot love you.
>
> To be perfectly frank I did at one time *fancy* I was beginning to care for you – but I was awakened to the truth by your claiming me as your future wife – then I felt – that what I cared for was not *you* but simply the fact of being loved. . . .
>
> Frankly, I do not believe my nature is capable of love. I came out of that six years agony . . . like a bit of steel. I was not broken but hardened – the fire must do one or the other. And this being the case – the fact that I do not love you – I cannot, and will never, make the stupendous sacrifice of marriage. . . .

In a further note she laid down her conditions of remaining on 'friendly' terms.

> 1. That any correspondence between us should be so worded that it might be read by anybody. . . .
> 2. That all the letters written by either to the other up to the end of this year should be returned to the writer thereof in a sealed packet; and that the sender should declare that none have been retained.
> 3. That I should receive from you, with my letters, a solemn promise that you will break off the friendship if you find it is leading again to hopes and that on no possible contingency will you reproach me . . . for having misled you. . . .

Richard Burdon Haldane (1856–1928), an able Scots barrister, amateur philosopher and politician, was one of the coming men on the Radical wing of the Liberal Party. Herbert Henry Asquith (1852–1928), a lawyer, became a liberal M.P. in 1886, Home Secretary in 1892, Chancellor of The Exchequer in 1906 and Prime Minister 1908–16. Sir Edward Grey (1862–1933) later became Foreign Secretary. Sir Arthur Acland (1847–1926) sat in the 1892 cabinet as Vice-President of the Committee of the Council of Education. These men later formed part of the nucleus of the Liberal Imperialist or 'limp' faction.

*1 December.* [Box House]
Mr Haldane, Q.C., M.P., a lieutenant of John Morley's, spent the Sunday here. A successful lawyer, tinged with socialism. Came down to arrange an alliance between the progressive liberals – Asquith, Sir Edward Grey, Arthur Acland and himself, and the Fabian socialists – with an *arrière pensée* of a suitable wife! to give piquancy to the visit. . . . At least 7 hours we spent over the details of a radical socialist pro-gramme, about 3 hours we devoted to skirmishing over the minor business of the 'wife'; he sending out scouts in all directions, I throwing up earthworks in the form of abstract propositions of the suitability of celibacy for the Apostles of the new creed! 'Ah, Mr Haldane: I will let you into a secret of woman's unmarried life. In my days of deep depres-sion I brood over matrimony – but it is as an alternative to suicide.' At which he threw up his hands with an uncomfortable laugh.

*That is exactly it*: marriage is to me another word for suicide. I cannot bring myself to face an act of *felo de se* for a speculation in personal hap-piness. I am not prepared to make the minutest sacrifice of efficiency for the simple reason that though I am susceptible to the charm of being loved I am not capable of loving. Personal passion has burnt itself out, and what little personal feeling still exists haunts the memory of that other man. Why did I watch for hours at the entrance of the South Kensington Museum for two days last summer unless in the hope of seeing him – a deplorable weakness for which I despised myself too much to repeat the third time? But it showed clearly the way of the wind. And the feeling of growing power, the almost passionate desire that not a drop of my bitter suffering shall be wasted . . . and yet over-riding all, the mother's desires to be silently helpful overwhelm me with self-contempt for those moments of womanly weakness when I would throw myself into the arms of any true lover to gain the protecting warmth of a man's love.

In the meantime poor Sidney Webb writes me despairing letters from his sick-room, letters which pain me deeply with their strong emotions. I am surrounded by men, am constantly meeting others to most of whom I am more or less attractive, partly no doubt because I am the first cultivated woman with whom they have been frankly intimate. I have that fatal gift of intimacy and as yet in spite of middle age (!) it is united to personal attraction. All this is egotistical, but what of that, it is true, and becoming moreover an uncommonly awkward factor in my life. It is hateful to feel the ground rotten beneath you, to be ignorant of the *real nature* of your influence. 'Some women mistake the power of beauty for the result of capacity,' said Mr Haldane significantly. Are all women 'nailed to their sex'?

*12 December.* [Bell Hotel, Leicester]
Members' meeting at Leicester. . . . Was called upon to speak, and failed to give satisfaction. Was nervous and thought more of what I wanted to say than what they would like to hear. It will be a long time before I am fit for much in public speaking. I have no ease at present.

Cold week; and cold at heart after my miserable correspondence with S.W. Every now and then I am haunted by a fear lest my new faith should be a delusion and the world destined to go on in its own selfish anarchic way.

*31 December.* [Box House]
The last day. . . . a year of growing convictions, a year of love, accepted but not given. The tie that was tightening between me and another I have snapped asunder and I am alone again, facing work and the world. . . . *He has behaved nobly*: but he insists that we have no right, even if it were better for us individually, to become strangers. I have consented to this provisionally on all intimacy being discontinued. And so the year ends.

From the political point of view, the year has closed dramatically. . . . There has been infinite pathos in the agonizing struggle of the Irish people with their . . . misery at the thought of an indefinite postponement of the cherished visions of Home Rule. In spite of my innate dislike and distrust of the Irish people it was impossible to avoid a real feeling of compassion and admiration. And yet the majority of English look on with a cynical amusement . . . In the meantime, minus Home Rule, the Liberals have no policy. . . . As for leaders in thought and action, we have none. . . . Neither have we a thinker . . . No light anywhere on the one absorbing question of the Haves and the Have-nots.

All of us groping, and no clue, except the attenuated and broken threads of Fabian socialism which valiantly tries to supplement want of substance with self-assurance. They, the only men I know who *feel* themselves leaders, and not merely astute observers of the way of the wind, or obstinate obstructors cloaked in cant or mere cynical *après moi le déluge*. *Of truth the Hour is Here but the Man tarryeth.*

~ 1891 ~

On 30 December, with a sad but gentle covering note, Sidney returned Beatrice's letters. 'Two things support, and will support me,' he wrote. 'I feel absolutely sure of your perfect honesty, to me and to your own self, and that I may count on an unconventional frankness.' Beatrice acknowledged the package next day, regretting 'the misunderstanding and mistakes which have led to your pain and, to a lesser degree, to my own'. This reply was followed . . . by another letter, noting that Sidney had 'fully and unreservedly' agreed 'with the conditions laid down' for the continuation of their relationship. 'Your letter is very noble in tone,' she wrote, 'but you will of course remember that in future you must write as a friend, as a friend only.'

*4 January.* [Devonshire House Hotel]
Up to London to get material for my fifth chapter. Sidney Webb and Graham Wallas dined with me last night. S.W. is in a thoroughly weak, miserable state: not strong enough to work, and excited and jealous, more deeply involved than ever, perhaps it is only his weakness. Conversation unsatisfactory: Graham Wallas beneficently kind to him, but perplexed at the whole thing. Both pressed me to join the Fabians: refused lest it should injure my chances as an investigator, and with a hidden feeling that perhaps it will be impossible for me to continue honourably as S.W.'s friend.

After a meeting in London Beatrice changed her mind about the Fabian Society and sent an anonymous subscription to its funds. 'I wish I were *absolutely* convinced,' she wrote to Sidney on 13 January. 'I am not yet. Every now and then I am haunted by a fear of waking up from a dream: my individualist antecedents have still a hold on me.'

Vaughan Nash (1861–1932), journalist and author, became Secretary to two Liberal Prime Ministers.

Florence Nightingale (1820–1910) was the founder of modern nursing and an influential figure in British social policy.

*13 January.* [Devonshire House Hotel]
Vaughan Nash escorted me through the small production Co-op at the East End. Afterwards dined here and went to big meeting at Charringtons of dockers. . . . Tom Mann urged the men to stick to their union and use it for political purposes, such as the creation of municipal workshops, etc.

Afterwards I spoke to him (Vaughan Nash is his greatest friend) and we arranged to meet at some future time – he was courteous but distant. As V. Nash and I walked back together: 'Tom Mann is prejudiced against me.' 'Yes,' answered V. Nash. 'He looks upon you as a schemer, a person with tin-pot schemes as he calls them, possibly it is your cousin Miss Harkness who has given him that idea.' 'Probably,' say I. . . . This atmosphere of suspicion is hateful; God grant that I may never use my influence to create or intensify it.

And let me bear well in mind when I feel inflated by the affection or approval of others that there are many persons, able and good men and women, whom I inspire with repulsion and distrust. Octavia Hill objected to my being asked to preside at a meeting because I tried to float myself and my work through my personal influence on men: and the same impression had reached Florence Nightingale. Mrs Besant has always distrusted me: and Tom Mann and doubtless John Burns regard me as a schemer! And this is the crown I have won. *There is always some foundation for a deeply graven impression* – despite traitors like Margaret Harkness.

*22 January.* [Box House]
My thirty-third birthday! Just sent off the first instalment of my first book. Working hard and working well – one day goes like another. Breakfast at 8, work from 8.30 to 11.30, a few minutes' turn, then read to Father for one hour. Lunch, cigarette, one hour or so walk, a sleep, read 4.30, work till 7.30. Supper, cigarette, letter-writing or dictating (if I am not too tired) and then to bed at 10 o'clock. . . . Mrs Thompson, little Miss Darling, Neale, Don and the cat – occasional letters from men friends – and my own thoughts fill up the intervals of work. But in spite of my 33 years I feel younger than I have ever done before, except that I feel horribly 'independent', absolute mistress of myself and my circumstances – uncannily so. 'Men may come and men may go, but I go on for ever!'

*7 March.* [Box House]
Ghastly report that I am to be appointed a member of the Royal Commission on the Capital and Labour questions, and that Charles

Booth would be chairman. Gave myself a racking headache worrying over it. I should have to accept, and yet what an ordeal . . . I feel as I should like to throw down my work and cry. But it is all miserable weakness, arising from self-consciousness, instead of forgetting about myself and going bravely on my way; I can but fail and heaven knows that the world is kind to me, too kind and too curious and too determined to push me forward. Oh, how detestable public life is to a woman! And yet a sort of fate drags one into it.

*28 March. Easter Sunday* [Box House]
My book practically finished, just 7 months, written about 250 pages. 'You have taken too long over it,' says my friend (Sidney Webb). I say, 'Not long enough.' What is it, clever political pamphlet or a sound contribution? My former self doubts my present self: which, I wonder, will prove the wisest – the cold-blooded investigator or the would-be reformer, intellect or heart? . . .

Throughout the first months of 1891 Beatrice and Sidney kept up a stilted correspondence, with Sidney reporting his interests, activities and intentions. He was eager to leave the Colonial Office and become a full-time Radical politician, running for the L.C.C. Beatrice, for her part, sent him two chapters of her book and when he wrote rather critically about it, felt dispirited. They were both evidently depressed at their estrangement, uneasy about their respective professional futures, and held back by pride from resuming their relationship. Sidney decided that he must in any case resign from the Civil Service; on 6 April he wrote frankly about his 'cramped and joyless life' saying that he had no time for reading or theatres or concerts, and that he felt 'like the London cabhorse who could not be taken out of the shafts lest he should fall down'. It was a touching letter. 'I am prepared to serve your life, and to ask nothing whatever in return,' Sidney wrote at the end, 'save only your work for socialism and such share of friendship as you choose to give. . . .' Beatrice, too, was troubled. She was anxious about her book, and worried about a series of lectures on Co-operation which she was to deliver at University Hall. She stayed with Alice Green, who brought in Sidney to help her prepare a press release on her lectures for *The Times* – and thus eased the estranged pair over the embarrassment of meeting.

Back on easy terms again, they travelled to Lincoln at Whitsun for the Co-operative Congress. A year before, at the Glasgow Congress, they had made their 'working compact' and now Beatrice at last gave way; Sidney's persistent devotion to her and to their common concerns had touched her feelings, and her own need for a companion triumphed over her fears and pride. A year later Sidney referred to the decisive moment when Beatrice did not withdraw her hand from his; and she afterwards recalled 'that evening at Devonshire House – in the twilight when we for the first time embraced – how well I remember the happiness tempered by great anxiety'.

'I am still a little in a dream,' Sidney wrote on 21 May. Two days later he sent Beatrice another letter full of happiness, touching on the difficulties as well as the 'enormous advantages' of their partnership. 'One – *la vie intime* – I want to talk to you about very frankly or, rather, I want you very frankly to talk to me, who am more than usually ignorant. One thing is quite certain: I will not have your intellectual and working life spoilt, whatever the cost to me. It would not be a "chattel" marriage and we are neither of us likely to insist on anything that would injure our common usefulness.'

### 22 May. Box House
. . . My lectures have been successful, more successful than I expected, and I have gained facility and ease in public speaking. My book too, on the eve of publication, promises success. But it is wearisome work bringing even a little book out.

Co-operative Congress at Lincoln passed off successfully – Alice, I, S.W. journeying down together. I cannot tell how things will settle themselves, I think probably in his way. His resolute patient affection, his honest care for my welfare, helping and correcting me, a growing distrust of a self-absorbed life and the egotism of successful work (done on easy terms and reaping more admiration than it deserves), all these feelings are making for our eventual union, the joining together of our resources, mental and material, to serve together the 'commonwealth'. Meanwhile Father lingers on: and while he lives nothing can be decided on. But if I marry, though I shall be drawn to it by affection and gratitude, it will be an act of renunciation of self and not of indulgence of self as it would have been in the other case. Perhaps, therefore, it will be blessed to both of us. . . .

### 31 May. Box House
. . . If I had dreamt that those years of dull misery, with flashes of veritable agony, would end in Work and Love, I should not have needed to keep before me as a motto, Watch and Pray. They are but the negative of Labour and Love.

Beatrice was staying at Herbert Spencer's house in St John's Wood, London; she had now settled that Sidney would be her collaborator on a history of trade unionism she proposed to write. Clara Bridgen, a young Fabian, was thought to be a possible match for Graham Wallas.

*6 June.* [64 Avenue Road]
Decidedly another 'beginning' in my life. My first book will be 'out' in a few days, then I to Norway for a three weeks holiday with Graham Wallas, Miss Bridgen and S.W. The beginning of a new life out of which the old loneliness and hardness will be banished.

*20 June.* [Norway]
Beautiful Norwegian scenery. . . . At times I am afraid, and disconsolately ask myself whether from my own point of view I have been wise. But the need for a warmer and more responsible relationship with another human being has made it seem the best even for me. The world will wonder. On the face of it, it seems an extraordinary end to the once brilliant Beatrice Potter (but it is just because it is not an end that she has gone into it) to marry an ugly little man with no social position and less means, whose only recommendation, so some may say, is a certain pushing ability. And I am not 'in love', not as I was. But I see something else in him (the world would say that was proof of my love) – a fine intellect and a warm-heartedness, a power of self-subordination and self-devotion for the 'common good'. And our marriage will be based on fellowship, a common faith and a common work. His feeling is the passionate love of an emotional man, mine the growing tenderness of the mother touched with the dependence of the woman on the help of a strong lover, and in the background there is the affectionate *camaraderie*, the 'fun', the strenuous helpfulness of two young workers in the same cause. . . . He is in a state of happy exaltation, I am beginning to feel at rest and assured. It will not wrench me from my old life, simply raise it to a higher level of usefulness.

The long dreamy days with the beautiful scenery passing by; the mountain fiords, rivers, waterfalls all in rapid succession lend a stillness to one's mind, a lengthened brooding over the past and the future. It is well to have this time of almost religious rest, this Sabbath of emotion, for with both of us there is a long dusty road, with steep inclines, before us. Our life will be strenuous, may it not also be peaceful? We have honestly only *one* desire – the commonweal. Why may not the current of our lives be deep and unruffled by all the surface agitations of personal success and failure?

*7 July.* [Norway]

Our last resting-place – high up in the Highlands of Norway. It is rain-ing and I am lying on my bed, knocked up with climbing the Roppen.

The last two days we have been discussing our future. Last spring Sidney decided to leave the C.O. expecting to make sufficient in journalism to go into politics. Now it is no longer necessary for him to make money, since I shall have enough for both. So we have had to reconsider all the half-arrangements we had made to write 'London Letters' for provincial papers and edit a Fabian Review. Last evening, by the glow of the sunset, we wan-dered over the moorland, hand in hand, and talked somewhat thus:

B.P. I don't want to influence you in the detail of what you do, for everyone must work out his own life; but I think it is time that you deliberately planned what you intend to be – and that you made every-thing else fall in with that.

S.W. You forget that has been impossible hitherto. I have decided that I want to take part in the government of the country according to social-ist principles. I also want to think out the problems of socialist administration before they actually come up for settlement.

B.P. Quite so. That is exactly my view of what you want to be. But writ-ing London Letters and writing Fabian Review won't help you to *that.* You know that I think more highly of your abilities than you do yourself. So I don't mind saying that in order to become a first-rate administrator you want more education in the technique of administration, and that in order to think over the various social problems you want technical knowl-edge of those very questions! The London County Council will help you to the one, helping me will give you the other.

S.W. I agree with you about my deficiencies, but I think there is a danger that in trying for big things we may diminish our usefulness, that is, refusing the smaller influence one gains by casual journalism, one may be neglecting the only work one is capable of doing well. To help you will be one of my principal aims – but for other reasons. What I am undecided about is whether you are not (and I also) too ambitious for me, whether you are not expecting too much from me.

B.P. No; I don't expect anything in particular from you. . . .

We are both of us second-rate minds, but we are curiously com-bined – I am the investigator, and he the executor – and we have a wide and varied experience of men and things between us. I have also an unearned salary. This forms our unique circumstances. A considerable work should be the result, if we use and combine our talents with a deliberate and consistent purpose . . . and so on.

. . . We are both of us in the mid-current of our life's work. We are both of us grave and anxious that our marriage – our happiness in each other's love – shall not interfere with each separate work. More especially am I fearful – and he for me – lest my work should be ended and I absorbed in the details of domestic life. I do not despise these details, but it is no use forging a fine instrument with exceptional effort and then discarding it for a rough tool. It may have been misdirected effort to make the instrument, it may be a mistake to transform the Woman into a Thinker, but if the mistake has been paid for, one may hardly throw away the result.

This next year I shall devote to the trade union book, ad he will help me. He on the other hand will be preparing for the life of an active administrator. And we will both try to keep humble, earnest and pure. For we have a great responsibility laid upon us. Not only has each one of us faculty and the opportunity of using it, but both together – the two united for a true marriage of fellow-workers – a perfect fellowship: it is for us to show that such a marriage may be durable and persisting.

### 15 July. 64 Avenue Road

A rather painful interview with Mary Booth. I felt obliged to tell the Booths, though now I am inclined to think it was a mistake. I hoped that after our long friendship they would have come forward and would have tried to get to know Sidney. But evidently it is supremely distasteful to them. Feeling this, I suggested that they might find it easier, considering that my engagement was not known to my family, to ignore it themselves, and to wait until we were married to be friends with him. And she heartily concurred. That curious little look of veiled determination came over her face, and she said: 'You see, Charlie and I have *nothing* in common with Mr Webb. Charlie would never go to him for help, and he would never go to Charlie, so that it would not be natural for them to see each other. When you are married it will be different. Then there will be the relationship.'

There the subject dropped and for the rest of the interview we talked exclusively about Charles's work and their children. She never mentioned my book though I had given it her before I left for Norway. As I had written a warm letter of appreciation of Charles's book I did feel a little hurt. . . . it was not unnatural that I should sit down and cry, not about their not thinking much of my little book, but of their not really caring to know him. It soon passed over and now I feel strong again and peaceful. She has a narrow and conventional nature, and in spite of a genuine affection for me she cannot take with loyal trust my view of my own life and accept it. But from Charlie I expected something different: he is too big a mind for that and his feeling for me was warm and strong. A shadow has crept between us and has deepened into a darkness.

> Though Mary Booth was 'sorry it is so', she was not so unsympathetic as Beatrice believed, for she told her husband that Beatrice 'looks remarkably well, young, pretty and blooming, like her old self. . . . She is evidently happy and believes in Mr Sidney Webb thoroughly.' Charles Booth wrote with more politeness than warmth to say he hoped 'to become better acquainted with Mr Webb' and hoped to gain much 'from a close and cousinly contact with the school of thought and action of which he is so brilliant a representative'. The engagement was secret. Beatrice did not propose to tell her family while her father lived; only a few close friends were told of it.

*16 July.* [64 Avenue Road]
. . . Alice Green is warmly congratulatory about our engagement; so is Haldane, so is Llewellyn Smith.

*31 July.* [64 Avenue Road]
In spite of kind letter, Charles Booth has not offered to see me; and Mary has expressly begged me not to come on Sunday, the only day he is in London. And yet they can afford time enough to go out to some mere acquaintances such as the Winckworths! Obviously he is vexed or simply indifferent. And she still treats me, when I see her, as an unfortunate misled person who is to be pitied and gently repudiated for the impropriety of her conduct. But I am not going to fash myself over it. . . .

*11 August.* [64 Avenue Road]
Breaking ground in trade unionism. S.W. comes and works with me. Yesterday being Sunday and wet he came at 11 o'clock. We allowed half an hour for confidential talk and 'human nature' and then worked hard at the Iron Founders' records. Then lunch, cigarettes, a little more 'human nature' and then another two hours' work. A cup of tea, walk to the Athenaeum, work at the social science records in the library and dinner. . . . It is very sweet this warm and close companionship in work. The danger is that I shall lean on him too much and get into a chronic state of watching him at work and thinking that I am working too. But our happiness in each other takes naught from the world . . . and it

should exalt our effort, strengthen our capacity to make this happiness possible to other men and women.

*14 August.* [64 Avenue Road]
Working every day at the Home Office. . . . There I sit in that big official apartment, strewn with despatch boxes in solitary glory with the roar of Whitehall below and Big Ben tolling out each quarter-hour and occasionally one or the other of my neighbours, superior clerks, comes in to see how I am getting on. . . . There is the feeling of being inside a big machine – but oh! to control it – to *use* it. . . .

A succession of trade unionists to dine here. (Poor Herbert Spencer! to think that his august drawing-room is nightly the scene of socialistic talk, clouds of tobacco, aided with whisky.)

I see I shall have some trouble to get my information. Most of the trade union officials are hard-headed suspicious men, with an anti-feminine bias. . . .

When Beatrice returned to Box House she wrote to Sidney about her family affairs and told him the photograph he had given her was 'too hideous for anything'. She asked him to supply a new one: 'let me have your *head only* – it is the head only that I am marrying!'

*19 August.* [64 Avenue Road]
The last day in these pleasant rooms: five weeks of happiness which is becoming more complete and inspiring each day. . . . Goodbye, Summer 1891 – you can never come again, but others will come to us like unto you.

Sidney had now resigned from the Colonial Office and during the next twelve months when both were doing research and attending meetings they often arranged to meet at a railway junction where their journeys crossed. 'We are evidently going to have a debt of gratitude to the Midland Railway hotels,' Sidney wrote on 16 September. When apart they wrote frequently and at length. 'We need not love each other the less because with both of us our work stands first and our union second,' Beatrice wrote on 12 September, confessing her continuing doubts about combining marriage with her research and writing. 'Every now and then I feel I have got into a hole out of which I can't struggle. I love you – but I love my work better! It seems to me that unless I give up my work I shall make a bad wife to you. You cannot follow me about the country, and I cannot stay with you. How do you solve this problem?'

On 14 September, Sidney replied in much the same vein. 'We could not love each other so well, loved we not our work and duty more.'

*25 September.* [Bath Hotel, Tynemouth]
Three weeks since I left him on the Leeds station that Sunday afternoon. Certainly we are daring in our unconventionality, mostly meeting at a hotel and spending 24 hours there. That long Sunday journey from Leeds to Newcastle arriving midnight at a second-class 'House' in a noisy street of the north capital. Then the rush of the Congress . . .

Since the hurry-scurry of that week I have drudged in offices on records or trudged to interview after interview. The work is stupendous, and as yet does not shape itself. Certainly I work hard – I do little else – work and sleep and work again. My cramped fingers with hours of note-taking threaten positive revolt. My head whirls with constitutions, executives, general councils, delegate meetings, district delegates, branches, lodges, socials . . . until all the organs of my body and faculties of my mind threaten to form one federated Trade Union and strike against the brain-working despotism of my will! Meanwhile there is one bright moment – the clearly written letter which is 'precipitated' every morning, one half hour of willing obedience of the cramped fingers when I throw my work aside and talk with him. And in four days he will be here working by my side.

*10 October.* [Bath Hotel, Tynemouth]
A blessed time! He found me utterly worked out with the combination of hard clerk's work and the insufficient food of a mining village. . . . He took over all the accumulated work, and while I have been lying on the sofa he has been busily abstracting and extracting, amply rewarded, he says, by a few brief intervals of 'human nature' over the cigarettes or the afternoon cup of tea. With our usual coolness I have taken a private sitting-room (he staying at another hotel) and he spends the day with me in the capacity of 'private secretary'. The queer little knot of the inhabitants of the hotel are so impressed with the bulk of my correspondence and the long hours of work that I do not think that they suspect the intervals of 'human nature', but think no doubt that I keep my amanuensis hard at it all hours of the day! And now that I am fairly well again, we are driving through the mass of reports fast and well, with the 'blessedness' of companionship. . . .

*15 October.* [Bath Hotel, Tynemouth]
. . . Tomorrow I leave this bleak North Country sea-town. Each place I

leave now, when we have worked together, I feel saddened at the thought that a bit of happiness is past and gone.

*21 October.* [Rounton Grange, Northallerton?]
Travelled from Darlington to Durham in the same train as Chamberlain and his wife. Watched them set out to walk to the Sunderland train and standing by the side until we speeded out of the station. He was looking self-complacent and somewhat self-conscious, quick to perceive whether he was recognized by the casual travellers. He has lost that old intent look – the keen striving expression of the enthusiast stimulated by ambition. . . . His wife was a plain little thing, but sweet and good and simply dressed. He was on his way to make a big speech at Sunderland. I was on one of my innumerable journeys 'in search of knowledge'. I shuddered as I imagined the life I had missed. Now, indeed, I can bless him for his clear understanding of my deficiencies for the great role of 'walking gentlewoman' to the play of *Chamberlain.*

> Beatrice found it a strain to conceal her engagement from her family: 'After Xmas, when we begin working together again, I will write and tell my sisters,' she wrote to Sidney on 21 November. 'Then we can begin the New Year openly – and face everything openly and together.' Their letters were now a curious mixture of affectionate confidences with working notes on their research into trade union archives and comments on Fabian politics – on which Beatrice offered sound tactical advice. On 16 December, Sidney was selected as a Progressive Party candidate for the L.C.C. in Deptford. On Christmas Day, noting the 'veritable agony' of recent Christmases, Beatrice sent Sidney a 'happy but serious' letter. 'I will try to repay your love and devotion and to make your home and happiness together – in spite of your "professional" wife. I will try and prove that a woman may be a loving wife and gentle mistress without assuming to be a strenuous public servant. But I shall often stumble and fall – and you must help me up and protect me against self-complacency or lethargy either at home or in our work.' Sidney replied two days later. 'It has been a good year to us, dearest – a heavenly year to me though it opened gloomily enough. . . . We shall be very happy and also very useful, playing private secretary to each other in turn – though I want you to think and invent, rather than to work.'

*27 December. Box House*
Two months here and resting and being the daughter in charge of the poor struggling dying father. His breathing is terribly hard – he has

paroxysms in which he seems like one drowning and then intervals of semi-consciousness. It is horribly depressing and casts a gloom even over a happy consciousness. . . .

The year has been uneventful. My engagement was a very deliberate step, each condition thought out thoroughly; now it is an unconscious happiness. Otherwise my life has little altered. I am still the investigator living the life of a bohemian. My friends are the same with few substitutes and additions. . . . With my family my relations are easy . . . 'We know no more of Beatrice than we should were she a man' expresses the family view. I imagine they will take my marriage with their usual good sense and good temper, slightly contemptuous and with friendly unconcern. . . .

∼ 1892 ∼

*New Year's Day.* [Box House]
Dear Father passed away peacefully this morning. Kate and I had been watching through the night and he had been in a heavy stupor breathing quickly and mechanically. When I came in dressed in the morning I found him in the last deadly gasps, not struggling but simply breathing out the last spark of life. . . . Few men have attracted and given more devoted affection. . . .

> 'Dearest, this is the beginning of a new year for both of us,' Sidney wrote when he heard the news from Box, 'and you, for the first time, are *quite* free to give yourself to your work and to me. I will do all I can to make you gain thereby . . . over your father's death let us cement our agreement again that all we do shall be for "social service" as far as we know how.' Rumours of their engagement appeared in the newspapers. Sidney tried to keep the secret by sending telegrams in German and persuading journalist friends to keep silent, but Beatrice realized that she would have to tell her sisters. She was so uneasy that she wrote almost too frankly, offering them a blunt choice between accepting him and losing touch with her. 'He is very small and ugly,' she told Lawrencina Holt. 'He has none of the *savoir-faire* which comes from a leisurely up-bringing and of course he has none of the social position which springs from great possessions and family connections.' Yet, for all her apprehensions, the family behaved well, both sisters and brothers-in-law sending generous letters and ensuring that suitable dinner-parties were arranged to welcome Sidney. Beatrice, in turn, was invited to the modest home in Park Village

East, near Regent's Park, where Sidney lived with his mother and sister, his father having died the previous July.

*21 January.* [52 Ackers Street, Manchester]
Three weeks of emotion. The gathering for the funeral, the impending declaration weighing me down. The publication of our engagement in the *British Weekly* telegraphed to me in Box in German by Sidney provoking a speedy confession. The family behaved with benevolence and good sense and received Sidney at family dinner in London with grave propriety. The uncomfortable week at Alice Green's – the introduction to his little home, dread of its ugliness, and then settling down in it as a guest, all these emotions crowded thick on each other. The little home in a small street near to Regent's Park – the little mother, frail and shaking with palsy, the energetic warm-hearted plain body of a sister, a stalwart German woman who acted as general servant – have become a new surrounding to my life, a new scene laid in the lower middle class. The dingy and crowded little workroom with gas fire where Sidney and I sit the evening through happy and unconscious in our love one for the other! And gradually the feeling of unwished-for dislike to ugly and small surroundings disappeared in the blessedness of love.

And now the old life is over – or rather the old shell is cast off and a new one adopted. Past are the surroundings of wealth, past the association with the upper middle class, past also the silent reserve and the hidden secret. Now I take my place as a worker and a help-mate of a worker, one of a very modest couple living in a small way. . . . That I shall in the first instance suffer, even in my work, for my step downwards in the social scale is probable, but if it is his gain it will not be my loss.

One relation of my life is closed by my acknowledged engagement – one which I prided myself on – the position of literary executor to Herbert Spencer.

We met yesterday at the Athenaeum by appointment. He was affectionate and cordial to me personally. 'I cannot congratulate you – that would be insincere.' Then there was a short pause. 'My family have taken it benevolently,' I remarked and then observed that there was after all nothing against Mr Webb; he had proved himself to be a man of capacity and determination. 'You see that he has succeeded in marrying me, Mr Spencer – that shows he has a will.' 'Undoubtedly,' groaned out the philosopher, 'that is exactly what I fear – you both have Wills – and they *must* clash.' . . . presently the real source of anxiety was disclosed. '. . . It would not do for my reputation that I should be openly connected with an avowed and prominent socialist – that is impossible. . . .'

'I quite agree with you, Mr Spencer,' I answered sympathetically. 'I fully realized that I should have to give up the literary executorship.'

'But what can I do?' he said plaintively. . . .

'What about Howard Collins? [Spencer's amanuensis] . . . I should be delighted to help him in any way you like to propose, either acknowledged or not.'

The philosopher lay back in his chair with a sigh of relief. 'That arrangement would do admirably; that is exactly what I should desire.' . . .

And so ended the interview, he satisfied about his reputation and I at ease with the dictates of filial piety.

*28 February.* [52 Ackers Street, Manchester]
Two days of utter exhaustion. Last Sunday was delightful – I need him once a week to rest me in the sublime restfulness of love, and he needs me to soothe him and reduce his world of cross-purposes to its proper calm. But alas! our work keeps us apart.

> Beatrice made few entries in her diary at this time. She was travelling extensively, interviewing trade union officials; even her letters were rather short and mainly concerned with research. Sidney wrote more often, and at greater length, but he was too busy, first with the election campaign, then with the L.C.C. where he was immediately appointed chairman of two important committees. They met occasionally: Beatrice came south at Easter to spend a short holiday in Sussex, and he joined her for a few days in Manchester. Beatrice had sufficient private means (about £1500 a year) to enable the Webbs to live comfortably, for Sidney to devote himself to unpaid public service, and for them to employ full-time research assistants. The first of these was Frank W. Galton (1867–1952), a young engraver who abandoned his trade to work for the Webbs at a salary of one hundred pounds a year. He was the secretary of the Fabian Society 1920–39.

*4 May.* [52 Ackers Street, Manchester]
Severe attack of influenza broke into my work – a day or two after the last meeting. A fortnight in bed, just at the time of his triumphant return to the County Council, but the last week he was with me and we both went on to Liverpool. There I rested in the luxurious Holt mansion for one week and then back again to work. I found Galton (our secretary)

working on the piles of material I had left. A good deal of his work had to be redone and the ensuing two weeks I spent in training him, he working all day under my eye. A sharp, attractive boy and assiduous worker and as keen as a razor, a former pupil of Sidney's in economics. . . .

Then a fortnight's holiday, during which I managed to spend £29 and an hour at the dentist. A pleasant four days at Arundel with Graham Wallas and the light-hearted Bernard Shaw, then back again to our cosy little lodging. Here for ten days, it only seemed two! . . . Today he has left me and I feel a bit lonesome. We are certainly supremely fortunate. We love each other devotedly, we are intensely interested in the same work, we have freedom and means to devote our whole lives to the work we believe in. Never did I imagine such happiness open to me. May I deserve it.

Sidney was much occupied with the general election campaign in which John Burns was elected in Battersea and Keir Hardie for West Ham; other progressive candidates did well in a contest which brought the Liberals back into office. Beatrice was winding up her research in the north, and, characteristically, devoting the last entry in her diary before her marriage to a fifteen-hundred-word summary of a trades union conference. They were married at 11.45 a.m. on 23 July at the St Pancras Vestry. Kate Courtney noted that it was 'a prosaic, almost sordid ceremony – our civil marriages are not conducted with much dignity and seem rather to suggest a certain shadiness in the contracting parties'. But she thought that Beatrice 'looked good – serious and handsome' and it all 'went very well'. Graham Wallas was best man, and the other guests were all relatives. 'The only thing I regret is parting with my *name* – I *do* resent that,' Beatrice wrote to Sidney three weeks before the wedding, and though Sidney at once wrote back to say 'one name will soon be as well recognised as the other' this was the only point she thought worth making when she made the final entry in her diary on the morning of the marriage.

*23 July.* [London]
Exit Beatrice Potter. Enter Beatrice Webb, or rather (Mrs) Sidney Webb for I lose alas! both names.

# The Ideal Life

## August 1892–March 1898

Henri Frédéric Amiel (1821–81) was a Swiss writer whose *Fragments d'un Journal Intime* (1883) had been translated by Mrs Humphrey Ward in 1885.

*16 August. Glasgow* [6 Blythwood Square]
The ceremony over, a 'bewildering' time at pretty little Chester – Sunday spent on walls in Cathedral and Eaton Park – reading at intervals Amiel's *Journal* by way of relieving the preoccupation of the first hours of married life. Then Dublin – lodgings, depressing climate, unsuccessful investigation into that ramshackle race and its affairs as regards trade organizations; now remaining only memories of huge, dirty, so-called 'rude' hovels in back streets lined with tenement houses with Irish urchins sprawling in the sun in the hot August weather. . . . Then two delightful days of real honeymoon in the Wicklow Hills, escorted there by a brilliant Irish lawyer and good-natured friend. Hence to Belfast. Here we did some serious work. . . . In little quiet Shaftesbury Hotel received levies of trade unionists every night – Sidney and I interviewing in different corners. Then there was the daily excitement of the papers and the long chats over politics, as at present and to come. Altogether happy there working on our holiday task. Now for Scotland.

'The Souls' were a group of Society men and women interested in literature and art. They met at their country houses for weekend parties, and emphasised their distinction from conventional upper class circles.

*19 September.* [6 Blythwood Square, Glasgow]
Exactly four weeks at Glasgow – the last ten days a rush of work. . . .
Out of the four weeks we have had two holidays – a Sunday on Loch
Awe with Auberon Herbert and a weekend visit to Haldane.

Auberon Herbert was as mad and as delightful as ever. Sidney thought
the whole scene – the rickety little cottage overlooking the lake, the
scrambly meals, handsome girls, and the 'on the spot' talk – a very mad
mixture. . . .

Then back to Glasgow, long drive and tourist steamer. Sunday with
Haldane was more remunerative. . . . a fair bevy of 'Souls' came over to
tea – Haldane priding himself on hovering between a fashionable 'paradise' represented by the 'Souls' and the collectivist state represented by
the Fabians. 'Souls' good to look on and very gushing and anxious to
strike up an acquaintanceship with an unconventional couple. . . . But
to me the 'Souls' would not bring the 'peace that passeth all understanding' but a vain restlessness of tickled vanity. One would become
quickly satiated.

*1 December. 10 Netherhall Gardens* [Hampstead]
Gloomy November weather finds us settled three hundred feet above
the sea in a cosy little flat in South Hampstead. Our life an even tenor
of happiness. In the last two months engaged on indexing and arranging our material or wading through Stonemasons and Compositors
[union records] and writing a brief skeleton of the first volume of our
book. Each morning we begin work about 9.30 (breakfast and reading
papers and letters take an hour), Galton joins us about 10 and we three
drive through material until 1 or 1.30. Then four days out of six Sidney
hurries off to London and gives the remainder of his day to the London
County Council. Meanwhile Galton goes on steadfastly. I spend a
couple of hours either walking on the Heath or travelling into London
on shopping errands. At 4 o'clock Galton and I have a cup of tea and a
chat and again set to work until 6 or 6.30. At 7.30 Sidney returns full
of the doings of the L.C.C. or carrying back news of an interview with
a Cabinet Minister on some proposed reform. A simple meat supper,
cigarettes and then an evening of peaceful happiness, either him reading to me or working at L.C.C. matters, or we entertain working-men
friends and so forth. But we mostly spend our evenings alone. Dinner-
parties we have resolutely eschewed, I finding that I cannot keep a
clear brain for work with talk exciting the evening. But as usual in
November my brain has been half torpid: I have not done my full

measure of work. Perhaps also the calm of married happiness deadens, in the first instance, one's intellectual energies. Why work when one is happy; and when he is working it is a silent excuse for physical torpor.

On the other hand Sidney is working well. I see with satisfaction that every day gives him a more complete grasp of L.C.C. work. He is one of that little circle of a dozen committee [chairmen] who practically run the L.C.C. for the simple reason that they do the work; and he is the trusted confidant and helpmate of the great officials of the Council – the chairman, vice-chairman and deputy chairman. And as chairman of the Technical Education Committee he has his own independent work creating a new organization.

Beyond this he is steadily acquiring influence with the official Liberals, regarded every day more as a man who must be listened to, and, if possible, complied with. I doubt whether he will ever be a 'leader', that is, an acknowledged chief. What he is rapidly becoming is the *chief instigator* of policies, the source of Liberal doctrine. He is a kind of indescribable influence which cannot be measured – sometimes it is denied, at other times grossly overestimated! So far as I can tell our life will be, or rather my life will be, that of a recluse, with Sidney as an open window into the world. The distance from London and preoccupation in work, three-quarters strange opinions – all combine to isolate us from our own class. With my own family I am on friendly terms (except Willie Cripps who has practically cut us!) though, as there is nothing in common, we do not seek to meet. The friendship with the Booths is practically broken, through Mary's covered hostility. . . . and I, having struggled for years against it, refusing to believe that she meant it, have finally succumbed and accepted the situation.

The Royal Commission on Labour, chaired by the Duke of Devonshire (1833–1908), was appointed in 1891 to consider the relations between employer and employed. A Minority Report, signed by the Labour members of the Commission (and drafted by Sidney), created a stir when it was presented on 15 March 1894. Gerald Balfour (1853–1945), brother to A. J. Balfour (1848–1930), Conservative leader in the House of Commons, had been elected as a Tory M.P. in 1885. Mrs Alice Dugdale (1843–1902) was the sister of Sir George Trevelyan.

*24 December.* [Hampstead]
How gloomy other Christmas Eves have been! – always the low-water mark of a year's despair, at the best an arid time of family gossip,

overeating, preparation for heartless winter gaieties. Now I have won a vantage ground of wonderful happiness, and even when physical energy ebbs low, I still feel fundamentally happy. And Sidney also has found a resting-place; no need now to struggle for personal happiness or success; all energy can be given to work. . . . It is still to be proved – the experiment of writing a book together; sometimes our ideas clash and we fall between the rival ideas, but on the whole we get on. My only complaint is that I can work such short hours compared to him that I feel a mere dilettante, but when spring comes I shall feel better.

Have seen something of politicians – Haldane and Asquith to dinner . . . All the young men in the government hard at work introducing administrative reforms, yet uncertain whether the old gang will not dictate a policy of evasion to all legislative proposals. . . . the result is that the political world is simply chaotic at present, at least on the reform side. . . .

Royal Commission on Labour a gigantic fraud. Made up of a little knot of dialecticians, plus a carefully picked parcel of variegated labour men, and the rest landlords and capitalists, pure and simple. . . . Spent a somewhat painful day there – the first day of Sidney's examination. He was aggravated with the bad faith of the Commission, and treated them to a little of their own game. His answers read well and were richly deserved, but his manner was objectionable and pained me. Also the Booths, K. Courtney, Mrs Dugdale and others of that set were sitting listening to him, and, as they agreed with the dialecticians, they showed their disapproval markedly. However, the next day the dear boy made a pretty apology and bore the cross-examination with perfect good humour. It ended in an amicable discussion between him and Gerald Balfour for 1 1/2 hours on abstract economics – pleasant to listen to, but fit for an after-dinner talk, and not the sort of question and answer to be delivered at public expense. Utter waste of time to all concerned. . . .

## ～ 1893 ～

*10 March.* [Hampstead]

. . . There is nothing to tell nowadays! No interesting extracts of gloom and light, no piquant relationships, all warm flat midday sunlight – little excitement and no discomfiture. I tell Sidney laughingly that I miss the exciting relationships with marriageable or marrying men, that I feel 'hemmed in' by matrimony. Truly I am too happy to seek excitement, too satisfied to look for friendship. Fortunately I have a bit of solid work in hand. I doubt more than ever whether I could have been long satisfied with a life in which intellectual effort were not the main or rather the most prominent part. . . .

> Theresa Cripps, the sixth of the Potter sisters, died suddenly after a throat infection on 22 May at the age of forty-one. Theresa was attracted to spiritualism and had published a book with messages she believed had come to her by automatic writing.

*22 May.* [Parmoor, Henley-on-Thames]
We were in the midst of the Bristol Co-operative Congress when the telegram arrived that our dear sister, Theresa, had died after a few hours' illness. The shock was inexpressibly painful . . . Our dear sweet sister – the artist, now the 'spiritualist' (used in its true sense) of the family – gifted with an ardent imagination, extraordinary vivid sympathy with all forms of life. Perhaps the best loved of the sisters, for she was open-minded, more ready to believe, without reserve, in the good intentions and high ideals of others than the rest of the hard-headed, matter-of-fact family. . . . And the marriage was absolutely happy – except that Alfred's companionship, able and warm-hearted man that he be, left unsatisfied the 'spiritual' needs of Theresa's nature. . . . Weariness, possibly physical weariness, was one of the notes of Theresa's married life. It was an *occasional* note, not a continuous one. The burden of her life was love given to, and taken from, husband and children, friendship generously yielded to all unfortunates and all whom the world misunderstood.

It was this quality of friendship in Theresa that was beginning to bring me nearer to her these last months. All my sisters have acted in a sensible and kindly way towards my marriage. They had not, however, attempted to understand it. But the last times I have seen Theresa she has really tried, not simply to be kind, but to understand and realize what we are aiming at. And she has done this with such touching grace that I have wondered whether she and I could become more than sisterly acquaintances. . . . No sister of the nine stands perhaps so friendless as I do. No sister so independent of the opinion and approval of her family. Again it is proved that you cannot gain the advantages of all courses. I chose to live apart, so that while living in the very centre of the family, I might yet live my own life. My sisters no longer know me; they know only the shell with which I covered myself. To me this death is, in some ways, horribly tragic. Tomorrow, after the funeral, I shall come back to my husband and my work. Looking back through the years, I shall not be able to recall *one single word of intimacy* from me to her, the memory of this gifted and precious nature, anxious and willing to be loved, will seem like a far-away dream, a picture and not a reality.

And now that I am talking about relationships, let me tell quite frankly that this tragic death, except as it affects others, seems of slight personal consequence to me beside the loss of an old friendship. The utter breakdown of the friendship between me and Charles and Mary Booth has been an ever-open wound. . . . I can never cease to regret it.

*21 June.* [Hampstead?]
A month after Theresa's death, we all met (except Lallie) at Georgie's house – seven sisters – all of us haunted by the idea of the dismal blank. We talked and laughed with the brothers-in-law as of yore, but all of us felt the empty place. The *irretrievable loss*, the absolute extinction of the dear one. Georgie looked the saddest of the sisters – to her, life has had little charm, though on the surface so prosperous; her marriage a big mistake. Poor little Rosalind with her miserable husband, an egotistical invalid, looked depressed but sweet and loving. Mary, Margaret, Kate, all happy women. Blanche too madly noble and nobly mad to be disturbed by death. All and each of us going on our own way, saddened and softened by the common loss . . . Possibly this death will bring us closer to each other, will close up the ranks, as Georgie says so sweetly. But I doubt it. I doubt whether there can ever be companionship without a common faith. . . . And so we go on in life – eight sisters – bound together yet not combining.

> Beatrice enclosed in her diary a letter dated 17 August 1893 from Kate, who wrote; 'Mr Chamberlain dined here last night – expressed a wish to meet you and your husband. I will ask him when you come back if you like. He stays to the bitter end and no one knows how long that will be. He is villainously full of fight, rather too much so for my more moderate-tempered mind.'

*30 July. The Argoed*
Alone here awaiting Rosy Williams and Sidney. . . . It is strange, I wonder that I, a happy wife, should brood over the thought of this day six years ago. It was Sunday 29 July 1887 that Chamberlain spent here – it was on this day that five long-drawn-out years of passionate feeling reached their climax. Since that day we have not met. But he is always there: year in and year out I watch him struggling in the political prize

fight – for a cause? or for personal supremacy? Only a few days since I saw him speaking in the House . . . Each year brings out in stronger relief his extraordinary personality – every political event gives occasion for a display of his marvellous agility, whilst it uncovers his limitations and defects. As a political prize-fighter he easily throws all his rivals; as a man he becomes steadily more vulgar; as a political thinker more shallow and ill-informed. And yet he loses neither his interest nor his charm, at least not to one of his humbler fellows. How will history sum up this man? A great statesman or a maligned orator? More likely than either, a *pre-eminent parliamentarian, ill-equipped with knowledge, and damaged by an irretrievable vulgarity of method and ideals.* . . .

With Sidney's life I am more than satisfied. He has worked hard and well this spring. . . . With my own effort I am less satisfied. . . . Many times I wonder whether the great want in my life – perhaps in our lives – is not 'spirituality', whether I ought not to cultivate my own soul to keep it perforce holy, tender and impersonal. There is such 'dross' in one's thoughts and feelings, unworthy vanities, useless anxiety, conscious self-congratulations, silly castles in the air.

I need prayer, or the substitute for prayer, whatever that may be – a deliberate tuning of one's thoughts and feelings by the deeper and higher tones of life. To the man, with his fully occupied intellectual faculties (with Sidney these faculties are devoted to the good of others) with his adoration of the Woman – the spiritual life seems unneedful. His nature seems more fully satisfied and absorbed in his work and his human affections. With the woman, her delicacy and her incapacity leaves her consciousness more the prey of irresponsible undirected ideas. Spiritual life alone fills her being with the inspiration needful to keep her thoughts on a high plane. . . . One ought to think and to love, but one ought also to *aspire*. . . .

. . . This spirit of prayer, this yearning for personal holiness, I must again attain. There are other wants, some of a lower character, others apparently inconsistent with our lives. I long sometimes for a wider culture, knowledge of other and higher forms of intellectual effort. All the world of art and literature is closed to me. But I do not see how with such slight and intermittent intellectual energy I could well spare any portion of it from my own work. Here I fear I narrowed Sidney's life. He has sufficient energy to use his few spare minutes for other forms of intellectual activity, but I dare not join him so he gives it up to be with me. Then again the same applies to companionship with men and women of more polished minds or workers in different fields of investigation. Again I have no energy to spare, and here again I fear I limit Sidney. The basic desire for social distinction I gladly note as futile – 'Society', however brilliant and distinguished, seems to eat out the hearts of men and women if it does not sterilize their minds. But it is not pardonable, the longing to be more loved and needed by my relations and my old friends. This *want*, this longing to see old ties strengthened, not this pain to see them rudely snapped asunder, is the one and only sacrifice on the altar of my love for Sidney and my faith in the cause he has at heart. . . .

George Bernard Shaw (1856–1950), who had been a friend and political collaborator of Sidney Webb since they met in 1879, shared the effective leadership of the Fabian Society with him. Shaw had so far earned a precarious living as a music and theatre critic. His first play, *Widowers' Houses*, had been performed at the Royalty Theatre in December 1892; while staying with the Webbs, he was writing *Mrs Warren's Profession*.

*17 September. The Argoed*
Seven weeks here – heavenly weather, delightful holiday just flavoured by a few hours' work a day. The first fortnight, alone with Rosy, we spent finishing the sixth chapter of our book. Then Graham Wallas came on the scene, read our first chapter, severely criticized the form of it. He made me feel rather desperate about its shortcomings, so I took it and wrestled with it . . . This Sidney 'wrote to' with my help.

Bernard Shaw came ten days after, and has stayed with us the remainder of our time, working almost every morning at our book. The form of the first chapter satisfied him, and he altered only words and sentences, the second chapter he took more in hand, and the third he is to a large extent remodelling. Sidney certainly has devoted friends, but then it is a common understanding with all these men that they use each other up where necessary . . .

While Bernard Shaw was working on the book, Sidney and I set about different tasks, I attempting to write a lecture on the Sphere of Trade Unions, he at work on Tom Mann's Minority Report. My attempt proved to be a hopeless fiasco. I struggled in vain among my great mass of information . . . the stuff overwhelming me. After five days' work I read to Sidney what I had written. He looked puzzled, and suggested that he should write it out. Then we had a little bit of a tiff. For when my miserable meanderings appeared in his clear hand it was all obviously out of place for a lecture, and that mortified me. I was in a devil of a temper. Next morning he sat down patiently to recast it, and we worked four days together and made a rough draft. Now I am working it up into lecture form. But my failure made me feel a bit of a parasite. So much for our holiday tasks.

All the afternoons we have spent out of doors, taking long excursions, forced out of our natural indolence by Graham Wallas's and Bernard Shaw's energy. Have I ever described either of these men? . . . Graham Wallas, six foot with a slouching figure, good features and genial open smile, utterly unselfconscious and lacking in vanity or personal ambition. Without convictions he would have lounged through life – with convictions he *grinds* . . . In spite of his moral fervour, he seems incapable of directing his own life and tends to drift into doing anything that other people desire. This tendency is accentuated by his benevolence, kindliness and selflessness . . . To some men and women he appears simply as a kindly dull failure, an impression which is fostered by a slovenliness of dress and general worn-out look. He preaches too, a habit carried over from his life as an usher and teacher of boys. To his disciples he appears a brilliant man, first-rate lecturer, a very genius for teaching, a suggestive thinker and a conscientious writer. . . . A lovable man.

Bernard Shaw I know less well . . . though he is quite as old a friend of Sidney's. Marvellously smart witty fellow with a crank for not making money, except he can make it exactly as he pleases. Persons with no sense of humour regard him as a combined Don Juan and a professional blasphemer of the existing order. An artist to the tips of his fingers and an admirable *craftsman*. I have never known a man use his pen in such a workmanlike fashion or acquire such a thoroughly technical knowledge of any subject upon which he gives an opinion. But his technique in specialism never overpowers him – he always translates it into epigram, sparkling generalization or witty personalities. As to his character, I do not understand it. He has been for twelve years a devoted propagandist, hammering away at the ordinary routine of Fabian Executive work with as much persistence as Wallas or Sidney. He is an excellent friend – at least to men – but beyond this I know nothing. I am inclined to think that he has a 'slight' personality – agile, graceful and even virile, but lacking in *weight*. Adored by many women, he is a born philanderer – a 'Soul', so to speak – disliking to be hampered either by passions or by conventions and therefore always tying himself up into knots which have to be cut before he is free for another adventure. Vain is he? A month ago I should have said that vanity was the bane of his nature. Now I am not so sure that the vanity itself is not part of the *mise en scène* – whether, in fact, it is not part of the character he imagines himself to be playing in the world's comedy. A vegetarian, fastidious but unconventional in his clothes, six foot in height with a lithe, broad-chested figure and laughing blue eyes. Above all a brilliant talker, and, therefore, a delightful companion. To my mind he is not yet a *personality*, he is merely a pleasant, though somewhat incongruous, group of qualities. Some people would call him a cynic – he is really an *Idealist* of the purest water (see his *Quintessence of Ibsenism* and his plays).

These two men with Sidney make up the Fabian Junta. Sidney is the organizer and gives most of the practical initiative, Graham Wallas imparts the morality and scrupulousness, Bernard Shaw gives the sparkle and flavour. Graham Wallas appeals to those of the upper and educated class who have good intentions. . . . Sidney insinuates ideas, arguments, programmes, organizes the organism. Bernard Shaw heads off the men of straw. . . .

> The wallpapers, textile designs and furniture of the socialist writer and artist William Morris (1834–96) were fashionable at this time.

[Early October?] *41 Grosvenor Road*
Three weeks' incessant work at furnishing, though still in a muddle here about furniture buying. Have wearied and excited my poor little brain to get the furniture attractive and the home as beautiful as we can make it with my limited cash and still more limited taste. Have deliberately spent money on it because I do not wish it to be thought that simplicity of daily life means ugliness and lack of order and charm. The ideal to be aimed at is strict economy in weekly expenditure, no self-indulgence and show, but beautiful surroundings – i.e. the best tack and the best workmanship in those things you have. So I have gone to Morris's for papers and furniture and spent days over my curtains and in looking up charming old bits of furniture in second-hand furniture shops. All of which causes the enemy (i.e. my sisters) to blaspheme, saying 'They do not see much socialism in that.' It is, in fact, a hopelessly difficult problem of how much one should spend on one's own house. Efficiency only demands plenty of nourishing food, well-ordered drains, and a certain freedom of petty cares – it is somewhat softening to contend that you *need* beautiful things to work with. It *may* be desirable to have them, but it requires a lot of proving! . . . Altogether, though I have deliberately (I say it again) spent this extra £100 in buying prettier and better things than were absolutely necessary, yet I am not altogether

at rest about it. At any rate, as Sidney says, we must work harder in order to deserve it. Next week I hope to begin.

*12 October.* [41 Grosvenor Road]
Spent the whole morning with John Burns looking over the trade union documents he has.

Our relation to John Burns has never been a cordial one . . . he seemed to me an intriguer who suspected everyone else of intrigue. His unfriendly attitude towards Tom Mann also displeased me. Possibly he heard of my dislike, for he treated me with very marked suspicion. Of Sidney he has, until lately, been jealous and was anxious that he should not come on the L.C.C. But, for one reason or another, this unfriendliness has much lessened. On my part, I have long since seen reason to alter my opinion of him as a public man. His capacity, straightforwardness, and power of reason has given him a permanent position, which poor Mann has forfeited by his light-headed change of fronts on all questions human and divine. Sidney has always had a high opinion of him. Burns, on his side, sees now that Sidney does not seek to play the rival Labour leader, that his influence (Burns's) will not be diminished by Sidney's presence on the L.C.C. If Sidney went into Parliament it might be that old jealousy would revive.

For jealousy and suspicion of rather a mean kind is John Burns's burning sin. . . . He is intensely jealous of other Labour men, acutely suspicious of all middle-class sympathizers, while his hatred of Keir Hardie reaches about the dimensions of mania. . . . All said and done, it is pitiful to see this splendid man a prey to egotism of the most sordid kind . . .

The Fabian manifesto 'To Your Tents, O Israel!', published in the *Fortnightly Review* on 1 November 1893, was a sustained diatribe against the Liberals, prompted in part by their failure to implement reforms, in part by Shaw's belief that unless he and Webb satisfied 'the legitimate aspirations of the ardent spirits' among the Fabians they would be discredited as mere hangers-on to the failing Liberal Party, and in part because independent labour representation was gaining sufficient support for the Fabians to show some interest in it. But this sharp and clever article did not please the enthusiasts of the I.L.P., who rightly suspected that Webb and Shaw were at best lukewarm about their cause, and it greatly annoyed some of their Liberal friends. 'The manifesto is a heavy blow to us,' Haldane wrote to Beatrice. 'It hurts *us* more than the old gang.'

*Christmas Day. The Argoed*

Here with Sidney, Graham and Shaw. Writing the last chapter of the book and just sending part of it to the press.

The autumn has gone quickly. I have worked well in the mornings at the book and recast large portions of it. Our house exactly suits us and as yet there is no chance of our being disturbed by too many acquaintances. We entertain much more than we are entertained, having a constant succession of 'professional' friends to dinner, sometimes to lunch, all for some purpose – either to help us or to be helped into the right line themselves.

The excitement of the autumn has been the issue of the Fabian manifesto (*Fortnightly Review*) which for a week or so loomed large to us. Shaw's manufacturing out of Sidney's facts. It boomed in the press – the Tory Democratic papers quoting it freely, the Radical papers denouncing it, and only such standard respectables as the *Spectator* and the *Standard* refusing to notice it out of sheer perplexity how to treat it. I am not sure whether, after the event, I altogether approve of it. There is some truth in Graham's original objection that we were rushed with it by fear of being thought complacent and apathetic by the Labour Party. Whether it is wise to do anything simply from fear of being left behind? But that was not the whole of the motive. All through the spring Sidney and Shaw have been feeling the need of some strong outspoken words on the lack of faith and will to go forward manifested by the majority of the Cabinet. They could hardly go on supporting the Liberals if these were deliberately fooling the progressives with addled promises. Perhaps the Fabian Junta chose the right time to speak – anyway they said only what they thought. They spoke to the world exactly what they had been saying in private. So far the manifesto was justified. . . .

Sad scenes at the Williams's. Dyson becoming a hopeless morphia and chloroform drunkard, the little boy nervous and ailing, Rosy a slave to her husband, trying to recoup herself by having her own way in the management of her child. Mrs Thompson suited them as nurse to both husband and child. . . . Poor Rosebud, the 'unfortunate' one of the family.

She is the only sister of whom I see much . . . The sisterhood is scattered – many of us are becoming strangers with no interest in common. Of Mary Playne, with whom I used at one time to be intimate, I have seen nought since my marriage; Georgie and Blanche mere formal visits from time to time; Lallie too far off; Kate and Maggie rather more, for Rosy is a common source of anxiety. But none of the brothers-in-law care to see much of Sidney (Alfred is hardly now a brother and will in time cease to be an acquaintance). Willie, Leonard and Arthur positively dislike my husband: Daniel is indifferent; Robert chaffingly affectionate, but as I have never been intimate it makes little difference. The Booths, too, retire more completely into the background; we meet rarely and then only on terms of distant and formal comradeship. . . . I must not break off on this minor key. All said and done I am triumphantly happy. I am getting back my intellectual *zest* which I seemed to lose last autumn. Construction is again a pleasure to me. Now for the next three weeks I have to set to and construct the last chapter of our book – 'The Trade Union World'. Welcome New Year 1894.

## ∾ 1894 ∾

The Royal Commission on the Poor Law was set up in 1892 by the Liberal government as a response to Chamberlain's suggestion of an insurance scheme covering old age and infirmity. The Commission did not examine immediate labour problems and no attempt was made to modify the law to meet the case of the unemployed. James Mawdsley (1848–1902), a Conservative trade unionist, led the Lancashire cotton spinners and was a member of the Royal Commission on Labour, which reported in April 1894.

*2 March.* [41 Grosvenor Road]
Getting our work through the press, dawdling between batches of proofs, considering the form of an article promised to Knowles on the Royal Commission, lecturing casually in London and Oxford. Sidney slaving at proofs, L.C.C., and now writing Broadhurst's Minority Report for the Poor Law Commission. Seen a good deal lately of trade union leaders – Burns, Broadhurst, Mann and Mawdsley. Burns excessively friendly, relying a good deal on the Fabians for advice. . . . he is at present suffering from severe disillusionment with labour and an equally excessive admiration for the brainworking class. That is the worst of these working-men: from the standpoint of thinking every man is as good as another, they jump at one bound to a position of cynical contempt for the common lump of men and an altogether extravagant appreciation of the able man of affairs. They forget that the middle-class brainworker is made to order exactly as the engineer or carpenter, and that the greater part of his superiority is simply knowledge of the tricks of the trade . . .

On 3 March 1894 Gladstone resigned as Prime Minister owing to failing health, political differences with his colleagues and the defeat of Home Rule by the House of Lords. Lord Rosebery (1847–1929), Gladstone's Foreign Secretary, succeeded him as Prime Minister (1894–5).

*12 March.* [41 Grosvenor Road]

Thursday last I was settling to work after breakfast when Haldane was announced. 'I have come to see you and Webb about the political situation,' he began, looking grave and put out. I called Sidney in and we both sat down feeling that we were expected to condole with some grievance but not quite certain which . . . then Haldane unburdened his soul to us. He described how the last ten days had been in reality a pitched battle between the old and the new Radicals. . . . Massingham . . . confirmed his account . . . Asquith and Haldane, he says, are hated by the House of Commons Radical, who feels the ground slipping from under him without knowing why. . . . 'It is war to the knife now,' said Haldane impressively, 'either they or we have to go down!' . . .

Our little plan for writing the Minority Reports of the two Commissions seems to be coming off all right. Tom Mann hands his elaborate manifesto and programme in tomorrow. Broadhurst swallowed the bait quite complacently and Sidney has prepared him an excellent document on old-age pensions and Reform of the Poor Law. But we tremble lest some misadventure should spoil our pretty little game and Sidney's work would be wasted. But these sort of risks one has to run with these labour men. They are not *efficient* . . . This 'behind the scenes' intellectual leadership is, I believe, Sidney's special talent if he can get the opportunity to use it to the full. For a popular leader his personality is not sufficiently striking and attractive for real 'direction' and 'mediation'. His intellectual grasp, his resource, ingenuity, quickness and lucidity of expression, above all his quite extraordinary freedom from personal vanity or the vulgar form of ambition, render him an admirable instrument. It is my business to see that he has the material to work upon in so far as hospitality, discretion and tact can bring it. It will be discretion that I shall lack most!

Michael Austin (1855–1916), an Irish nationalist and trade unionist, was a Liberal M.P. and a member of the Royal Commission on Labour. William Abraham (1842–1922), a Methodist preacher and a pioneer of trade unionism among the Welsh miners, was also a Liberal M.P. and a member of the Commission on Labour.

*13 March.* [41 Grosvenor Road]

Amusing afternoon. Mann came in the morning to say that he was bringing Mawdsley, Austin and Abraham to discuss the Minority Report at 5 o'clock, the excuse being that he had left it with Sidney to look over from a legal point of view. We were both rather taken aback . . . We could not imagine Mawdsley, a staunch Conservative, adopting it 'all of a heap'. When Mawdsley turned up early . . . I was relieved to find that he was supremely discontented with the Majority Report and felt in a fix as to what he should do. Sidney took the matter in hand, and asked leave, as a lawyer, to give the others the gist of Mann's Report. Standing in front of the fire, he began reading out all the parts which would affect Mawdsley most, Mann playing into his hand by suggesting more advanced statements, Sidney supporting Mawdsley in many of his criticisms. As he read on Mawdsley expressed his approval and was apparently delighted with the practical and detailed character of the suggestions. It ended by Mawdsley considering the Report his own! and taking it on himself to announce to the Commission that they were drawing up a Minority Report and would present it in a couple of days. The only alteration he insisted on was the omission of the word 'Socialism', though he agreed to the substitution of the words 'public administration, national and local'. So much in a word.

*30 April. Grosvenor Road*

Our book comes out tomorrow [*The History of Trade Unionism*], the Minority Report of the Labour Commission has been handed in corrected, ditto of P.L.C. [Aged Poor Commission] handed in as memo, the article for the *Nineteenth Century* ['The Failure of the Labour Commission'] . . . has been written, so that now we feel free to go off for a real holiday . . . It is the first complete break in our work that we have had since those happy days in Norway three years ago. . . .

The Richard Stracheys were the parents of the biographer and critic Lytton Strachey.

*21 May. Grosvenor Road*

Back from a delightful three weeks' holiday. Nine days in Venice. Charming rooms overlooking an Alma Tadema court, with canal and bridge between us and it and old marble gateway and well, whither Venetian women with their soft-coloured clothes went to draw water. Our days were spent on the water with an old gondolier whom we engaged by the day, and in St Mark's Piazza and in St Mark's itself – that vision of sumptuous beauty which it is a glory to recall. Very sweet hours of companionship – not thinking, but simply feeling the beauty around us – a true honeymoon of love and common enjoyment. Then to Como (Menaggio) where we met the Richard Stracheys – the General, an old experienced Indian administrator, and Mrs Strachey, a strong, warm-hearted, enthusiastically literary woman. But though our evenings were spent with them, smoking cigarettes and sipping coffee on the terrace, our days were spent together wandering over the hills and in the lovely gardens of the Villas. Then a long journey back, and we are again in our little house, beautifully cleaned up by our two maids, and with Galton keenly anxious to be at the next volume. . . .

*10 July. Grosvenor Road*
. . . It is a horrid grind, this analysis – one sentence is exactly like another, the same words, the same construction, no relief in narrative. . . . I sometimes despair of getting on with the book. I feel horribly vexed with myself for loitering and idling as I do morning after morning, looking on while poor Sidney drudges along. London, too, is beginning to get on my nerves, with the heat and the continual noise and movement and the distraction of seeing one person and another. . . .

I sometimes wonder whether I am right in inclining Sidney *not* to go into Parliament. Hardly a month passes but some constituency or other throws out a fly for him, but so far he resolutely refuses to consider it, and that largely because I discourage him. . . . I do not feel confident that he would be a big success in the House; I do not think the finest part of his mind and character would be called out by the manipulation and intrigues of the lobby. And then a parliamentary career would destroy our united life: would cut at the root of a good deal of our joint effort. Perhaps that is why I distrust my dislike of his going into Parliament – it would take so much away from me personally, would add so many ties and inconveniences. Sooner or later I suppose he will have to make the sacrifice, but better later than sooner.

The Webbs often rented houses for the summer. Borough Farm was near Godalming.

*25 July. Borough Farm, Surrey*
Overlooking a little country lane with heather-covered moorland on one side and a thicket of young trees behind, stands the farmhouse we have

taken for three months. The farmer and his wife, hard-headed, some-what grasping folk, who make us pay more than London prices for all their produce and whom I rather suspect of taking toll on our groceries! and a grim old labourer who serves them and does menial offices for us and whom we meet in the late evening with a coat puffed out with con-cealed rabbits, are our co-occupants of the substantial red brick old-fashioned house. Though only one hour and a few minutes by rail from London, it is too remote for postal delivery and we have to fetch our letters some 1 1/2 miles from a village! But this and other drawbacks are outweighed by the exceeding charm of the country. . . .

Spent two days (while Sidney was in London) alone with Graham Wallas. . . . Poor fellow, he is in a dreary mood just now, overworked with organizing the Progressives for the next School Board election – and himself standing for Hackney – besides making his livelihood by lecturing. . . . We are probably his nearest and dearest friends . . . But friends, however dear, are no substitute for a beloved partner who would share evil and good days with him. . . .

*25 July.* [Borough Farm]
An exquisite still evening, cloudless, each leaf on the tree which grows close to the house standing out, with all its own delicate individuality against the blue green of the twilight sky. During my lonely walk (Sidney is away in London, Graham at Oxford) this afternoon, I have been meditating on womanhood – and the perfection of it – what sort of being a woman should be. First and foremost I should wish a woman I loved to be a mother. To this end I would educate her, preserving her health and vigour at all hazards, training her to self-control and to capacity for sustained intellectual work so far as health permitted and no further. From the first I would impress on her the holiness of mother-hood, its infinite superiority over any other occupation that a woman may take to. But for the sake of that very motherhood I would teach her that she must be an intellectual being, that without a strong deliberate mind she is only capable of the animal office of bearing children, not of rearing them. It pains me to see a fine, intelligent girl, directly she mar-ries, putting aside intellectual things as no longer pertinent to her daily life. And yet the other alternative, so often nowadays chosen by intel-lectual women, of deliberately forgoing motherhood, seems to me to thwart all the purposes of their nature. I myself – or rather we – chose this course on our marriage, but then I had passed the age when it is easy and natural for a woman to become a child-bearer; my physical nature

was to some extent dried up at thirty-five after ten years' stress and strain of a purely brainworking and sexless life. If I were again a young woman and had the choice between a brainworking profession or motherhood, I would not hesitate which life to choose (as it is, I sometimes wonder whether I had better not have risked it and taken my chance).

I do not much believe in the productive power of woman's intellect; strain herself as much as she may, the output is small and the ideas thin and wire-drawn from lack of matter and wide experience. Neither do I believe that mere training will give her that fullness of intellectual life which distinguishes the really able man. The woman's plenitude consists of that wonderful combination of tenderness and judgement which is the genius of motherhood, a plenitude springing from the very sources of her nature, not acquired or attained by outward training. To think of the many hours in each day which I idle and mope away simply because I can only work my tiny intellect for two or three hours at the most, whereas I could be giving forth tenderness and judgement to my children hour after hour and day after day without effort or strain. It is this over-abundance of affection which the woman who is simply a brain-worker, even though she be also a loving comrade to her husband, deliberately wastes by forgoing motherhood. And what is perhaps equally sad, with the sacrifice of the function she sacrifices, to a great extent, the faculty.

But what will be the solution of the woman's question? . . . the time is not ripe to deal with it. . . . We do not believe that the cry for equal opportunities, a fair field and no favour, will bring woman to her goal. If women are to compete with men, to struggle to become wealth producers and energetic citizens, to vie with men in acquisition of riches, power or learning, then I believe they will harden and narrow themselves, degrade the standard of life of the men they try to supplant, and fail to stimulate and inspire their brother workers to a higher level of effort. . . . And what shall we gain? Surely it is enough to have half the human race straining every nerve to outrun their fellows in the race for subsistence or power? Surely we need some human beings who will watch and pray, who will observe and inspire, and, above all, who will guard and love all who are weak, unfit or distressed? Is there not a special service of woman, as there is a special service of man? The man is paid directly or indirectly by the community to create commodities in return for his subsistence . . . Should not women, too, be enrolled as servants of the community, creators of something more precious than commodities, creators of the nation's children? And as man with his unremitting activity and physical restlessness seems fitted to labour, direct and organize, so woman, with her long periods of passive existence and her constantly recurring physical incapacity, seems ordained to watch over the young and guard over the rising generation and preserve for all the community the peaceful and joyful home.

All this points to the endowment of motherhood and raising the 'generation and rearing' of children into an art through the elaboration of science. Sometimes I imagine how the men and women of a hundred years hence will wonder at our spending all our energy and thought on the social organization of adult men and women, and omitting altogether the vastly more important question of the breeding of the generation that is to succeed them. . . . But, for all that, we cannot take up the woman's question. We cannot hope to attack individualism or, as we prefer to call it, anarchy, in its stronghold of the home and the family . . . before we have replaced it by deliberate collective rule in the factory, the mine . . . We can but leave this problem reverently to our children, preparing their way by cutting at the roots of prejudice, superstition and rotten custom. . . . One must be content to work for one's own day.

### 30 July. Borough Farm

Another day alone. Yesterday tropical rain deluged the country, the lane in front of our gate becoming a rushing stream of water. Early this morning the thick clouds gave way, a steaming mist arose from the moor to be dispelled at midday by the sun which blazed out in full summer splendour. Oh, the luxury of these hours alone with nature. . . .

### 21 September. Borough Farm

Cannot say that I have been working well this summer. The task is very difficult. I have been in poor health, and this climate, not at any time invigorating, has been especially depressing this damp summer. For the last fortnight we have had during one day after another dank white mist from early morning to the close of evening, with rain in the night. And until ten days ago I did not discover that I was suffering from a bowel disorder that needed a strict diet and proper treatment. Now I have taken to a rigid diet – discarded fruit, sugar, alcohol and most vegetables – and I feel wonderfully better. . . . What I need is a little intellectual regimen – to take my brain in hand as I have my stomach and absolutely refuse entrance to thoughts that are morbid and worthless. . . .

An odd adventure! A few weeks ago Sidney received a letter from a Derby solicitor informing him that he was left executor to a certain Mr Hutchinson. All he knew of this man (whom he had never seen) was the fact that he was an eccentric old gentleman, member of the Fabian Society, who alternately sent considerable cheques and wrote querulous letters about Shaw's rudeness, or some other fancied grievance he had suffered at the hands of some member of the Fabian Society. 'Old Hutch' had, however, been a financial stay of the Society and the Executive was always deploring his advancing age and infirmity. When Sidney heard he was made executor he, therefore, expected that the old man had left something to the Fabian Society. Now it turns out that he has left nearly £10,000 to five trustees and appointed Sidney chairman and administrator – all the money to be spent in ten years. The poor old man blew his brains out, finding his infirmities grow upon him. He had always lived a penurious life and stinted his wife and by no means spoilt his children, and left his wife only £100 a year (which Sidney proposes should be doubled by the trustees). The children are all provided for and do not seem to resent the will.

But the question is how to spend the money. . . . Sidney has been planning to persuade the other trustees to devote the greater part . . . to encouraging research and economic study. His vision is to found, slowly and quietly, a 'London School of Economics and Political Science' – a centre not only of lectures on special subjects, but an association of students who would be directed and supported in doing original work. Last evening we sat by the fire and jotted down a whole list of subjects which want elucidating – issues of fact which need clearing up. Above all, we want the ordinary citizen to feel that reforming society is no light matter, and must be undertaken by experts specially trained for the purpose.

Bertha Newcombe, a professional artist and Fabian, had an unrequited attachment to Bernard Shaw.

### 9 October. Borough Farm

It is some years since I have watched summer turn into autumn and felt the first breath of winter creeping over the country. . . . Perhaps it is the rich tones of the heath and bracken which recall some of those lovely Rusland autumns, for, as I stand and watch the clouds drifting across the moor and try to fathom the glorious depths of colour of land and sky, memories of old days jostle each other and seem to take me back to the thoughts and feelings and daily life of struggling girlhood – the inevitable melancholy of the autumn months, the brooding over books, the long walks with Father, afternoon tea in the little hall at Rusland after a trudge in the mist, Mother's bright welcome to Father, her keen relish of her cup of tea before she went to her boudoir to study her grammars, or settled herself down to a talk with Father over his business affairs and the family prospects . . . But in chewing the cud of these old memories, I am impressed not with the *past-ness* of the old life but with the perfect continuity of the present and the past . . . After nearly twenty years of adult life, I am still living the same daily life, still using my whole energy in unravelling ideas and attempting to clear issues . . . If one could only have foreseen that this daily intellectual effort would one day be set in a frame of loving companionship and constant sympathy, one would have been less restless and morbidly self-conscious . . . When first I was married, I feared that my happiness would dull my energies and make me intellectually dependent. I no longer feel that; the old fervour for work has returned without the old restlessness. Of course my life in London, with its other claims, leaves me with less physical energy, but this I think is almost counterbalanced by the absence of any waste through mental misery. On the whole, then, I would advise the brain-working woman to marry – if only she can find her Sidney!

Beyond Shaw, Wallas and Bertha Newcombe and Rosy Williams we have seen few people here. Rosy and Noel have stayed some three weeks. Rosy is like a shade from the old family life. . . . She likes being with us; the three men make a pet of Noel and are kind to her, and she is not oppressed with our superiority in wealth and successfulness as with the other sisters. And I am glad to pay off old scores of neglected duty to that poor child – I made an ignominious failure with her, a failure which I now recognize. Mrs Green, attended by her devoted Irish lawyer – Taylor – flew down here for three days on her way to a round of fashionable visits. She is, I fear, disillusioned about us, her disillusionment taking the form of an almost irritable criticism of our ways of life, with our sordid simplicity, lack of culture and general lower-middle-class-ness . . . unless we speedily become 'distinguished', that is, thought well of by London Society (a fate which is not likely to befall us) I fear we shall see little more of Alice Green. . . .

Parish councils had just been established under the Local Government Act of 1894. The vestries, based upon an archaic jigsaw of parishes, were London's traditional form of local government.

*11 October. Borough Farm*

Tomorrow we leave. Sidney has trudged across the moor to meet the few village Radicals to advise them as to the parish councils election, and I turn to my old friend the diary for companionship. First, let me correct the libellous account I gave of our host and hostess. The woman turns out to be a fine, honest creature, working from early morning: the man, honest and genial enough, but abjectly lazy, willing to chat, to smoke, to drive us about the country – to do anything but work. If one were to generalize from the three farms we have had dealings with – the women are the wealth producers, the men do the ornamental and social side of life, varying this with the boozer's torpor. The countryside, in its social aspect, is depressing enough: the labourers a low, dishonest lot, the farmers idle and incapable, except for the wives, mere parasites on the land, the tradesmen servile dependents on the great Tory landlords who dominate the neighbourhood, and a floating 'foreign' summer population of middle-class holiday-makers like ourselves and East End tramps in search of odd harvest jobs. Parish councils will hardly turn the inhabitants of these parts into citizens!

For all that I leave this quaint little home with regret. The last months I have pulled myself together and done some hard thinking. . . . I must . . . resolutely refuse to *worry*. Otherwise I shall not do my share of the labour and shall be a source of fatigue and not rest to Sidney. The next six months, with the vestry and L.C.C. elections added on to all the administrative business, seems likely to be somewhat trying for My Boy.

*1 December, Grosvenor Road*

Galton's little study turned into the central office of the Progressive candidates for the Westminster Vestry elections. Sidney has drafted the address, Galton is acting as election agent, and the working-men candidates are doing the canvassing and even the clerks' work. . . . Altogether we have been living in the atmosphere of elections. Graham's candidature for the School Board gave us a personal interest in the fight. . . . It is very curious that both Sidney and Graham, though very advanced in their views, are better liked by the Moderates on the L.C.C. and the L.S.B. than other members of the Progressive Party. 'Wily Webb', as Sidney is called on the L.C.C., is always colloguing with the more sensible of the Moderates with a view of getting them to agree to things *in detail* which they could hardly accept in bulk. That seems also to be Graham's policy . . . The truth is that *we want the things done* and we don't much care what persons or which party gets the credit. . . . The Fabians are still convinced believers in the policy of permeation.

Meanwhile the book hangs fire. With both Sidney and Galton completely absorbed, I feel helpless. Moreover, as a candidate myself for the Vestry, I have caught a little of the election fever and am growing excited and perturbed. . . . It might be better to give myself up frankly to electioneering and use these weeks as an opportunity for observing how elections are fought and won. It is all part of our subject-matter – democracy. Surely we shall end by constructing the great Webb Chart of the Modern Democratic State!

[?] *December.* [41 Grosvenor Road]
Crushing defeat at Westminster Vestry elections; only five Progressives out of ninety-six! . . . apparently the slums of Westminster are as completely Tory as the palaces. I do not think there has been any lack of energy or even of skill in engineering such forces as we had. But it is obvious that our attempt to collar the constituency with three weeks' work – mostly amateur – was a fiasco which we ought to have expected. . . .

*28 December.* [Parmoor]
Spent our Christmas at Parmoor with Alfred Cripps, the children, the Courtneys and various Cripps nieces.

Alfred's home is strangely attractive, with a dash of sadness in it, especially to Theresa's sisters. A charming house, designed largely by Theresa, the soft luxurious colouring, the quaintness of the furniture, the walls covered with her portraits, all bring back to me the memory of her gracious personality . . . And yet the home seems complete without her – the children revel in high spirits and health, the servants are contented. Alfred himself has regained all the light-heartedness of his charming disposition. . . . He is again the young man, unattached, absolute master of his own life. And he is in the full tide of great prosperity. An enormous professional income (he told Arthur [Playne] that he made £1,000 a week during the session) has enabled him to buy the family estate and sit down in front of a promising constituency. . . . With his skill and charm he will succeed in politics as he has succeeded at the Bar – he will 'make money or its equivalent' and that is all. For all that, he remains an essentially lovable man. And without doubt he will one day find another mate, and then we shall lose sight of him.

It is curious to see the three brothers-in-law together. Each one has, for the opinions of the other two, tolerant contempt. . . . Alfred looks on Sidney as a traitor to the brainworking and propertied class, Sidney looks on Alfred as a 'kept' advocate of the *status quo*, Leonard looks on Alfred as a somewhat selfish, thoughtless and superficial conservative, on Sidney as a shallow-minded self-complacent half-educated democrat, whilst both Sidney and Alfred have much the same opinion of Leonard – an upright but wrong-headed man dominated by a worn-out economic creed and shackled by lack of sympathy and quick intelligence. To some extent all opinions are equally true – as a summing-up of each individual they are all equally false.

## ∼ 1895 ∼

*12 January.* [41 Grosvenor Road]
Both 'Front Benches' are throwing all their strength into the L.C.C. fight. On our side the collectivist Ministers, Asquith, Acland, Grey with Lord Rosebery as a London county councillor, have spoken or are about to speak at great demonstrations. Sidney is in constant request, advising them as to what they are to say . . . On the other hand, the Unionists, stimulated and led by Chamberlain, are laying siege to every constituency. . . . Chamberlain is a nasty enemy and is going to make it a hot fight for us. . . . Odd that he and Sidney should be pitting their brains against each other . . . Wonder whether they will ever become face-to-face opponents!

> Sir Edward Hamilton (1847–1908) was private secretary to Gladstone and became a senior Treasury official. Sir William Harcourt (1827–1904) was Chancellor of the Exchequer. Margot Asquith (1864–1945), the daughter of Sir Charles Tennant (1823–1906), a rich Liberal baronet, was Asquith's second wife and one of the most active members of 'the Souls'.

*20 January.* [41 Grosvenor Road]
Haldane utterly discouraged with condition of Liberal Party, says there is now no hope that the Cabinet will pull themselves through. . . . Rosebury sees no one but Eddy Hamilton, a flashy fast Treasury clerk, his stud-groom and various non-political fashionables. Sir William Harcourt amuses himself at his country place and abroad, determined to do nothing to help Rosebery. Even Asquith, under the dominance of his

brilliant but silly wife, has given up attending to his department and occupies his time by visiting rich country houses and learning to ride! 'Rot has set in,' says Haldane. . . . The same strains from Massingham . . . Urged Sidney to go into Parliament and become one of the leaders of the reconstruction party. But Sidney will bide his time.

*1 February.* [41 Grosvenor Road]
For the last three months an idea has haunted me that after we have ended our stiff work on trade unions I would try my hand at pure 'fiction' in the form of a novel dated 'sixty years hence'. . . . Two main ideas should run through it. The fully-fledged woman engaged in a great career should be pictured just as we should now picture a man, and collectivism should be the orthodox creed . . . The truth is I want to have my 'fling'. I want to imagine anything I damn please without regard to facts as they are. . . . I want to try my hand at an artist's work instead of mechanics. I am sick to death of trying to put hideous facts, multitudinous details, exasperating qualifications, into a readable form. Doubtless when I discover that I have no artistic faculties I shall turn back to my old love and write with equanimity *The History of Municipal Institutions.* But before I can have this debauch I have a grind before me that must be got through, however little I like it.

Though the L.C.C. election on 2 March produced a dead heat, the Progressives maintained overall control of the Council. Sidney's running-mate was beaten.

*5 March. Grosvenor Road*
An anti-climax! After all the heat on both sides, after the blowing of both the big party trumpets, the calling to arms of saints and sinners by their respective champions, the rousing, on the one hand, of all the threatened 'interests', the appeals, on the other hand, to the forces of piety and democracy, London citizens send back an exactly even number of Moderates and Progressives, a bare half of registered electors taking the trouble to vote. In so many words, our constituents laugh in their sleeves and say 'tweedledee, tweedledum'. . . . In a Conservative constituency [Sidney] retains a Progressive majority of 1800. . . .

*19 March.* [41 Grosvenor Road]
Poor dear Leonard diddled out of the Speakership by his own party. A mean and discreditable intrigue of Chamberlain's, who has had an

animus against him ever since I can remember; first because Leonard was too much of a Whig, then because he retained too much of the Radical. Most likely, however, it has been all through a personal animus dating from Leonard's refusal fifteen years ago to enrol himself as Chamberlain's follower. It is only fair to say that Leonard has had a contempt for Chamberlain's intelligence and character, and Leonard is not a man to hide his opinions. Leonard's bad manners . . . have been Chamberlain's opportunity. We are grieved not only for his and Kate's sake but because we really believe we have lost the most democratic Speaker available. . . .

W.A.S. Hewins (1865–1931) was a young economist at Pembroke College, Oxford. He was not the first choice for director of the L.S.E; Graham Wallas had already declined. Temporary premises were found at 9 John Street, Adelphi. The Hutchinson lecturers were supported by the legacy and the L.C.C. lecturers were paid out of T.E.B. funds. David F. Schloss was on the staff of the Labour Department in the Board of Trade. Sir William Acworth (1850–1925) was a barrister and railway economist. H. S. Foxwell (1849–1936) was a conservatively minded professor of political economy at University College, London, who had built up a remarkable collection of books on economics that Sidney hoped to acquire for the L.S.E.

*9 April.* [41 Grosvenor Road]
. . . Have settled down quite comfortably to work again, spending all our mornings over our book and Sidney at the L.C.C. in the afternoon. Re-elected chairman of Technical Education Board, and giving a good deal of time to that and the starting of the 'London School of Economics and Political Science'. Selected Hewins (a young Oxford don) as Director, engaged Wallas and Schloss as Hutchinson lecturers, and Acworth and probably Foxwell as L.C.C. lecturers. Also, in treaty with Chamber of Commerce and Society of Arts for rooms free of charge. Great good luck that Sidney happens to be chairman of the Technical Education Board – able to combine the two 'sources'; promises well just at present but impossible to tell whether the old gang won't wake up and cry out before the institution is fairly started which would delay, possibly balk, our plans. . . .

Sidney and I are both somewhat exhausted and we go tomorrow for a week to Beachy Head with a party of six – Graham Wallas and Bernard Shaw, Albert Ball (an old fellow traveller in the Tyrol), C. P. Trevelyan and Herbert Samuel (a wealthy young Jew with Fabian proclivities), and, as the only other woman beside myself, Bertha Newcombe, the Fabian artist. What fortunate people we are: Love, Work, Friends and Health, given holidays whenever we need it! An Ideal Life!

*25 April.* [41 Grosvenor Road]
A 'jolly' time at Beachy Head, learning the bicycle and sitting out chatting on the cliff. Sidney and I both felt better for the change, but [are] now down again, he with his usual cold in the head, I with my usual bowel trouble. . . . whether it is the constant excitement of London life and the atmosphere of 'news' in which one lives or whether I am simply growing old, I do not find that I am strong enough for much real brainwork. I get a spurt on for two or three days and then I collapse with indigestion or other complaints and have to spend most of my day in open air and exercise and lying down to set me on my feet again. If it were only the book one had to think about! Two mornings a week at least we spend patching up other people's work, writing memoranda for politicians or answering conundrums for foreign and native socialists. Sidney believes in helping all and sundry, in always being ready with advice and suggestions, in giving himself away to the world at large. . . .

*8 May.* [41 Grosvenor Road]
The London School looks promising. Hewins has talked over the principal economists including Marshall and Edgeworth; we have squared Foxwell; the Society of Arts and Chamber of Commerce are giving us their rooms free; the Technical Education Board has voted the £500 a year; the trustees are amenable and apparently there is no hitch of any kind. I myself am anxious that the 'show' lecture side should not be too much developed, and that we should concentrate on getting *research really done.* For that object I should like to gather round us all the able young men and women who are taking to economics, free their minds of prejudices and start them with a high ideal of accuracy and exhaustiveness in work. . . .

*27 May.* [41 Grosvenor Road]
A grey outlook in political situation. A heavy reaction setting in against the Liberal government – the Haves thoroughly frightened, the Havenots unsatisfied. Within the Liberal Party each man complaining of the other, no comradeship or cohesion, all at sixes and sevens with regard to opinions.

Sir Hugh Bell (1844–1931) was a coal and iron master in the Tyne area.

*28 May.* [41 Grosvenor Road]
The other night the Booths dined here to meet Hewins and Hugh Bell, and to be informed as to the London School. It was the first time Charlie had been in my house since our marriage (Mary has called periodically). Charles Booth has not changed one whit – he is still the sincere simple-natured man, with an aloof intellectual interest in human affairs, that I knew so well and cared so deeply for years ago. Of course he is now the acquaintance and not the friend. But surely it is not pure imagination that makes me see a change in Mary, a change so fundamental that even if we would we could not again be intimate. From the curiously unconventional little puritan living in almost eccentric simplicity, spending her whole day teaching her little ones and reading books, she has become the worldly-wise woman living in great style whose main preoccupation for the last year has been to get her eldest son into the smartest possible regiment.

After dinner, when she and I retired, I listened for some twenty minutes to her account of the unsuccessful struggles to get Tom into the Guards and the successful compromise of the Black Watch. She was smartly dressed, her hair twisted into the last new knot, her face and figure looking singularly young, bright and charming, resembling much more her portrait as a girl than the highly-strung, worn, dowdy 'mother, friend and wife' that I knew and loved so well for fifteen years. Is it possible that the husband's influence has been slowly killed by the children's? And that Mary has been 'demoralized' by these polished young persons she has taken so much pains to educate? For the family seems strangely incongruous – Charlie living most of the week in an artisan's house in a back street in Liverpool – not for the purpose of investigation but simply because 'it suits him' – Mary carrying on a great house in London and one in the country entertaining the smart young friends of her children. She told me much of Tom's social triumphs, was always recurring to their 'riding in the Row', to their parties, to this and that semi-fashionable friendship, until I became dazed with my attempts to fit in this Mary with the Mary I knew years ago, and fell into a silent fit of wondering whether it was I or she who had so completely transformed our point of view. She treated me with half-condescending kindness, but was full of her own affairs. Her expression I watched narrowly – she looked exceedingly happy. Compared to her old self, she looked as if some *weight* had been lifted off – as if she were breathing freer and living more according to her own will. . . . I remember hearing of her when she was a girl as a socially ambitious and rather artificial woman and her portrait bore that expression. But I always regarded the portrait and the description as libellous and could not make out how persons could have so misunderstood her. . . . Poor Mary! How irksome my friendship must have been to her for years before she shook me off, how complete and satisfactory the occasion for the final severance – my marriage to an undersized, underbred, and 'unendowed' little socialist! If I only perceived this 'growth' I should have saved myself all the intense misery, I should have spared her all the extreme annoyance of my long and fierce struggle to keep the friendship. Anyway, I will keep the memory of it intact. After all, there remains the big fact that for the fifteen hardest years of my life they were my best and most helpful friends – Mary as well as Charlie.

*12 June. Casthrop Farm, Derbyshire*
Three or four days at a noisy, dirty railway hotel at Huddersfield, attending the Co-operative Congress. Lost much of its interest. I have no longer anything to learn from the Co-operators. . . .

> The Liberal government was defeated on a snap vote on 21 June 1895, and in the election that followed the Conservatives were returned with a majority under Lord Salisbury (1830–1903). The new government launched on a policy of expansive imperialism.

*8 July.* [41 Grosvenor Road]
On the eve of the general election. The Fabians are sitting with their hands in their laps. From our point of view no result can be satisfactory. The Liberals, even on the eve of dissolution, show no signs of grace, they go unabsolved to their grave . . . it looks like a triumphant majority for the Tories. Nor does there seem much hope in the future. . . . For the Liberals have no leaders inspired with a new faith. Asquith has been ruined by marrying a silly ignorant wife, and there is no other man who has at once capacity, character and conviction. The Labour men are mere babies in politics. . . .

Though the situation looks bad for our side of things, it is impossible not to be amused and interested in the political drama. Chamberlain is the Man of the Moment. He has kept the little band of Liberal Unionists separate and compact for ten years, and now, just before they must of necessity melt away, he has deftly used them to ride into power . . . It is a testimony to the marvellous force of Chamberlain's personality that he pervades this election – no one trusts him, no one likes him, no one really believes in him, and yet everyone accepts him as the leader of the united Unionists. . . . But alas! for the poor dear Liberal Unionists . . . To be used as the ladder up which 'Joe' climbs into a Conservative government, waving aloft his banner of shoddy reform, then to be thrown ignominiously aside. A fit ending for a company of prigs! . . .

*4 August. The Argoed*
Settled again for the summer in the old home – Shaw, Sidney and I, awaiting Wallas and Rosy and Noel to join us presently. Brought with us our three bicycles (most absorbing new toys) and endless work . . . Just these first days it is rather a struggle to work – the cold wet weather, the reaction from the rush of London and my monthly trouble all combining to make me sleepy and lazy. But this summer I am quite healthy, have fixed on a diet and found an exercise that suits me. Bicycling has brought some 'fun' or 'sport' into my life, an element that was rather lacking in our workaday and somewhat strained existence. We go plodding on with our book, with a childlike faith that some one will value its detailed and carefully wrought analysis. Most persons will think it 'much to-do about nothing'. We plod on in the faith that it will be a sample of political and economic research, a foretaste of what the 'New School' will do in other departments. . . .

*25 September. Grosvenor Road*
. . . I have seldom been so lazy on a holiday – Sidney, too, for the first time, fully enjoyed the life. Shaw stayed with us the whole of the seven weeks: Graham came for a fortnight but was restless and not quite happy in our company. He is going through a crisis – wants to leave the Fabian Society and be free of all formulas and intellectual ties so as to give himself over, as he thinks, to empirical administration and 'untrammelled' thought. . . . Poor Graham, he is one of those sensitive self-conscious men who will always be in trouble about his soul. . . . and we are inclined to douche him with cold water! . . . I must see whether I cannot show more tact. I am horribly narrow and limited and Sidney and I are obviously self-complacent in our perfectly happy married life. I must rouse myself to more sympathy. . . .

The National Union of Women Workers was established at Nottingham in 1895.

*18 October. Grosvenor Hotel, Manchester*

. . . Three days at the Women's Conference at Nottingham. This National Union of Women Workers sprang out of a sort of federation of philanthropic societies to befriend young girls. Louise Creighton with great energy and considerable capacity has organized it into a somewhat incoherent federation of all societies of women dealing with industrial, philanthropic and educational matters. Its chief function is to hold an annual conference to which all women who work are invited to listen to papers on any conceivable topic and discuss. Hitherto it has been dominated by bishops' wives and deaconesses, is almost flagrantly non-political and distinctly religious in tone. Louise persuaded me last spring to be co-opted on to the Executive and this year to stand for re-election . . . Here I thought was an association which would bring me into touch with women all over the country, the silent good and narrow women who do so much to form the undercurrents of public opinion, women whom in one's secular and revolutionary set one never comes across . . . The conference consisted of about six hundred, mostly middle-aged well-to-do, but a good many hardworking professional philanthropists, guardians of the poor etc. A very fair assembly, well-meaning, with a slight tendency to 'cant' but sober and on the whole open-minded, thoroughly typical of provincial English middle class . . . Altogether the Conference was promising; it opens out virgin soil to Fabians, possibly rather stony!

> Leonard Trelawny Hobhouse (1864–1929), a cousin of Henry Hobhouse, later professor of sociology at the University of London, was currently fellow of Corpus Christi College, Oxford. George Macaulay Trevelyan (1876–1962), who became a distinguished historian and Master of Trinity College, Cambridge, was the younger brother of Charles Trevelyan (1870–1958), who was translating *The Referendum in Switzerland* (1898). Robert Calverley Trevelyan (1872–1951), poet and man of letters, was the third of the three brothers, and a helper in some of the Webb campaigns.

*Christmas. Welcombe*

On the whole a satisfactory autumn. Our own little bit of work, the Book, is slowly progressing . . . We have recovered from our feelings of depression at the widespread [political] reaction – we have turned our hopes from propaganda to education, from the working class to the middle class . . . Having been beaten back in our endeavour to make a London Progressive Party with a permanent majority, we are creating the

London School of Economics and Political Science as a wider foundation than street-corner preaching. Hewins is making a success of the
School – 200 to 300 students attending the difficult classes and lectures. . . . We are to some extent trying to gather the promising students
round us. We are also trying our best to attract the clever men from the
universities – Sidney and Wallas lecturing at Oxford and Cambridge –
and letting it be known that anyone coming up who is interested in economics will have a warm welcome at Grosvenor Road. Leonard
Hobhouse recruits for us at Oxford, the young Trevelyans at Cambridge.
All this means a good deal of expenditure of time, sympathy and alas!
money. One cannot keep open house and live economically.

Now we are spending a peaceful Xmas at Welcombe, the gorgeous
mansion belonging to Lady Trevelyan. Charles Trevelyan asked us down
here for a week – we, his brother George and a friend 'camping out' in one
of the wings with one manservant and a due number of maids. . . . Sidney
is very happy here discussing and arguing with these boys . . . The perfect
happiness of his own life has cured his old defects of manner, he has lost
the aggressive self-assertive tone, the slight touch of insolence which was
only another form of shyness, and has gained immeasurably in persua-
siveness. Partly, no doubt, his administrative work as chairman of the
Technical Education Board has taught him how to manage men and get
them to adopt his views; partly also his standard of knowledge has
undoubtedly risen and he no longer feels so cock-sure of his own position.
But principally his improved manner is due to happiness – to the blessed
fact of loving and being loved with a love without flaw or blemish.

## ∼ 1896 ∼

Joseph Chamberlain, appointed Colonial Secretary when the
Conservatives took office in July, had been encouraging Cecil Rhodes
(1853–1902), Prime Minister of the Cape Colony, in South Africa. The
crisis in the Transvaal was the abortive Jameson Raid, in which Dr Starr
Jameson of the South Africa Company crossed the border into the Boer
republic of the Transvaal with five hundred men on 29 December 1895.
He was captured three days later.

*5 January. Parmoor*
. . . Five days at Hadspen – Sidney's first introduction to the Hobhouse
household. For Henry he has always had an honest liking, admiring his

public spirit and his refined view of life, and his painstaking industry. . . . Perhaps it has weighed with us that alone among my
brothers-in-law he has welcomed Sidney with grave courtesy into the
family, has always treated him with respect and friendliness, has apparently never felt that repulsion which most of my brothers-in-law have
shown to him – either on account of his lack of social status or because
of his opinions.

Maggie of course is the same high-spirited, rather vulgar and sharp-
tongued woman, has cut her nature down to suit her husband's
intellectual limitations without raising it to conform to her husband's
moral standard. There is always therefore a jar in the house, Maggie
protesting against Henry's quixotic principles, Henry silently resenting
her plots and plans for social advancement and pecuniary saving. . . . But
this is only superficial. The two are honestly fond of each other, and
Margaret is a capable and wholly devoted mother. . . .

After five days at Hadspen we came on here . . . Alfred . . . is entering political life with all [the] self-assurance and ambition of the man
who has never failed. . . . Having decided to stand by his class, being
honestly (and no doubt justly) convinced that that class has everything
to lose and nothing to gain by an alteration in the *status quo*, the one
thing needful is to appeal to the popular suspicion, fear, prejudices and
fallacies to keep back any further 'reforms' . . .

The whole mind of the country is at present absorbed in foreign politics. There has been a dramatic interest in the Transvaal events. 'Private
enterprise' in international matters has I think been finally discredited so
far as England is concerned. And the occasion has found the man. Joe
Chamberlain is today the National Hero. Only a small section – the
extreme Tories of the Alfred Cripps type – withhold their admiration for
the swiftness and courage with which he has grappled with the crisis. In
these troubled times, with every nation secretly disliking us, it is a comfortable thought that we have a government of strong resolute men, not
given either to bluster or vacillation, but prompt in taking every measure to keep us out of a war and to make us successful should we be
forced in to it.

[?19 January]. *Brighton*
. . . Agreed some time ago to spend a week with Herbert Spencer. . . . The
old man is still living on his living death. He clings desperately to life,
watches every symptom, seems devoured by an inward rage at his continual feebleness. . . . And yet this old man of seventy-six lives in comfort,

can afford to buy every luxury, has far above the average vitality, eats well, goes for months together to his club, continues to spin out his philosophy in volume after volume – has, so far as human observation goes, very little to complain of. But he is terribly exacting . . . Everybody must yield to him. He lies in his bed or on his sofa, when he is ill-disposed, and broods over his 'rights', exacts hard terms from his tradesmen, his housekeeper, his secretary, not because he grasps at money, but because he is possessed with this almost religious craze of getting his 'rights'. . . . Poor old man. For all that he is a noble wreck.

Meanwhile I have caught up the threads of another friendship. Carrie Darling . . . She was the first 'professional' woman I had come across. Fresh from Newnham and full of the fervour and enthusiasm of those early pioneers . . . she stimulated all that was good in me – my love of learning and intellectual ambition, all my moral enthusiasm, and to some extent checked the vulgar materialism brought about by life in second-rate fashionable sets. Her personality had a certain distinction and charm. . . . All this charm is gone . . . For these thirteen years she has lived exclusively with inferiors. Eight years in a small Australian town with all its vulgarity and petty intrigues, five years in an Indian military station consorting with clergy and Eurasians, and, above all, five years' servitude to a husband who is her inferior in every respect – a mere elementary schoolteacher in training and a narrow evangelical prig by constitution. . . . She has practically fled from him. Poor clever Carrie! The whole week we spent in one long tale of married misery. . . .

*1 March.* [Oxford]

Two days at Somerville College. A charming vision of intellectual girlhood. The large quaint red brick building with its conventional garden, the girls' studies with their window-seats from which you can see the Oxford towers and hear the Oxford bells, the calm and peace, the atmosphere of studious leisure without either worldliness or domestic brawls – surely a delightful modern analogue to the convent. How different from the youth of our generation with its storm and stress of quarrelling households and competitive marriage markets! As I sat in the living-room allotted to me, toasting my feet and preparing my lecture for the evening, I felt almost a longing to retire to such a place and give body and soul to 'pure' learning. It is the complete absorption in the intellectual life that gives this college life its charm – the open and avowed cultivation of your intellect without fear of ridicule or abuse for selfishness. Some attractive types of womanhood among the students. It was pleasant, too, to have these young hearts and intellects clustering round me, eager to gain insight and experience and to get a word of counsel from the experienced and somewhat saddened traveller in life's ways. But I was impressed with the narrowness of the life, except to the quite young mind. The women dons were old maids – the old type of boarding-school mistress. To my mind no woman should be accepted as a tutor who has not lived her life in the outside world. A man don is bad enough but nowadays dons are married, and even in old days they were not presumably 'celibates'.

Even without the excuse of delivering two lectures (one to the Women's Liberal Association, the other to the Somerville girls and their friends) I should have been glad of those two days' experience. It brought back the memory of my old enthusiasm for days spent in study – only instead of the ugly setting of my own girlhood, this beautiful new haven with its stimulating calm now open to the intellectual woman. If I had enjoyed good working health, how I should have revelled in such a life twenty years ago! . . .

> The separation of the Library from the L.S.E. as a teaching institution was a characteristic example of Sidney's ingenuity, for it enabled him to raise funds specifically for the Library; and by making the School its nominal tenant, he was able to secure a reduction in rates. John Passmore Edwards (1823–1911) was editor of the *Echo*, a short-lived halfpenny newspaper for which Sidney wrote, a philanthropist and a pacifist. Shortly afterwards he gave £10,000 to provide the L.S.E. with its first building, on the Clare Market site off Aldwych. Sir Hickman Bacon (1855–1945) was the premier baronet in Britain.

*28 March. Grosvenor Road*
Our time, for the last five weeks, a good deal taken up with writing 'begging letters' for the Political Science Library. This winter the rapid growth of the School of Economics made new premises inevitable. But how to raise the money? . . . A brilliant idea flashed across Sidney's mind. We needed, for the use of the students, books and reports – why not appeal to the public to subscribe to a Library of Political Science? At first we thought we could get a millionaire to subscribe the whole amount on condition that he called it by his own name. In vain I flattered Passmore Edwards, in vain Sidney pressed Sir Hickman Bacon, in vain we wrote 'on spec' to various magnates. The idea did not impress

them. So we decided to scrape money together by small subscriptions. Sidney drafted a circular, Hewins secured the adhesion of the economists and then began a long process of begging letter-writing. Sidney wrote to all the politicians, I raked up all my old ball partners, and between us we have gathered together a most respectable set of contributors, a list which is eloquent testimony to our respectability! Next week the appeal goes out for publication to the press. Even if we collect a comparatively small sum, the issue of the appeal has been a splendid advertisement . . .

All this has interfered with our book. I am fagged out – have no value left in me. And during these last months I have been weak and foolish and allowed myself to brood over old relationships. I am absolutely happy with Sidney – our life is one long and close companionship, a companionship so close that it is almost a joint existence. But I shall never quite free myself from the shadow of past events, or, rather, I shall always be subject to relapses. These broodings are the special curse of a vivid and vigorous imagination . . . I must some day write that novel and work in all these brilliant scenes I am constantly constructing.

James Ramsay MacDonald (1866–1937) was a journalist and lecturer before becoming the leader of the emergent Labour Party. He was Prime Minister in 1924 and 1929 and formed the 'National' Government in 1931.

*18 April.* [High Borrans, Windermere]
Delightful holiday in sister Holt's comfortable house. The Holts absent the greater part of the time – Sidney and I enjoyed the moors alone – rode over to Rusland and up the Grisedale valley, over to Thirlmere by Grasmere and Rydal. It was very sweet. Taking my boy to visit the beautiful Rusland valley, one of the seed places of my youth. And the air and the sights of those sublime little hills swept my mind clear of all its diseased rumblings. Now that one's mind is again free one is amazed at the mania.

Whilst we were at the Lakes, had furious letters from J. R. MacDonald on the 'abuse of the Hutchinson Trust' in the proposal to contribute to the Library of Political Science. J.R.M. is a brilliant young Scot, lately I.L.P. candidate for Southampton, whom we have been employing as Hutchinson Trust lecturer in the provinces. . . . MacDonald is personally discontented because we refused to have him as a lecturer for the London School. He is not good enough for that work; he has never had the time to do any sound original work, or even learn the old stuff well. Moreover he objects altogether to diverting 'socialist funds' to education. . . . The truth is that we and MacDonald are opposed on a radical issue of policy. . . . do we want to organize the *un*thinking persons into socialist societies, or to make the *thinking* persons socialistic? We believe in the latter policy.

Bertrand Russell (1872–1970), philosopher and mathematician, married Alys Pearsall Smith (1867–1951) in 1894 and settled near Friday's Hill. The youth organizer in the British Women's Temperance Association run by Lady Henry Somerset, Alys also spoke on women's suffrage. Robert Charles Phillimore (1871–1919), a judge's son, was an active Fabian who served with Bernard Shaw on the St Pancras Vestry and was Sidney's L.C.C. running mate in Deptford 1898–1910. His wife Lucy, 'Lion', was active in many progressive causes. The Phillimores lived at Radlett in Hertfordshire.

*20 June.* [41 Grosvenor Road]
Spent last Sunday with Bertrand Russells. Rode from Guildford through the Milford country to Millhanger, the little cottage in which they have settled themselves. A workman's cottage with stuffy attic bedrooms, but with the inevitable decent size sitting-room added on to it by the Russells. Found the young Phillimores there. A typical nineteenth-century party – two young aristocrats, married, one to a charming American [Alys Pearsall Smith], the other to [Lucy Fitzpatrick] a bright talented Irish woman (reputed a drunken Belfast carpenter's daughter who worked her way up as a district visitor to Lady Henry Somerset's secretaryship, from that to a seat on the St Pancras Vestry and thence to a marriage with her fellow vestryman – the socialist, philanthropic and eccentric son of Sir Walter Phillimore) – both women a good deal older than their very young husbands, mere boys in age though old in thought and tastes. We six spent the Sunday lounging in the cottage garden talking metaphysics, politics, very slightly interspersed with literature and art. The Bertrand Russells live idyllic lives, devotedly attached to each other, living with somewhat disorderly and extravagant simplicity – the simplest result extravagantly achieved – as might be expected from an anarchic American with means of her own, Russell working some six or seven hours at his metaphysical book [*Principia Mathematica*], Alys rushing up to town at short intervals to girls' clubs and temperance meetings and resting with her beloved the remainder of the week.

The Phillimores vary the life of love in a cottage (on the father's estates) by attendance on vestry meetings and committees and preparing themselves to write a 'textbook on London government'. So far as I can see there is only one serious criticism on the lives of the six persons gathered together in a Surrey cottage on this lovely June day – *no children* – all too intellectual or strenuous to bear children! Whether the omission is 'intentional' or 'inevitable' does not much matter from the community's point of view. There is obviously some flaw in these ideal marriages of pure companionship. Can we afford that these rather picked individuals shall remain childless? Is less highly-wrought material better to breed from? I, at least, can fall back with complacency on the thirty-seven nephews and nieces who are carrying on the 'Potter' stock and so far unperturbed with ideas or enthusiasm.

*8 July.* [41 Grosvenor Road]
Went to say goodbye to the Courtneys who leave for Germany tomorrow. A great calamity has overtaken them. At Whitsun Leonard lost his sight for reading and writing – one eye nearly blind and with the other eye, which is slightly affected, he cannot see near objects. Meanwhile Kate's health has collapsed – she is weak and has lost her nerve. Neither of them show any rebound since the first shock a month ago. Leonard especially is struck dumb. From the melancholy and *humiliation* of his expression I gather that this sudden blindness has made him realize that his career is over and his work done. Outsiders can see that, however terrible the deprivation, he exaggerates the effect on his public life. . . . After the events of last year no one could believe that Leonard had any chance of taking part in a government. . . .

281 students (eighty-seven of them women) had enrolled at the L.S.E. The need to accommodate more led to a move to the nearby 10 Adelphi Terrace.

*14 July.* [41 Grosvenor Road]
Making arrangements to start the London School in its new abode at Adelphi Terrace in October. Engaged a bright girl as housekeeper and accountant. Advertised for political science lecturer – and yesterday interviewed candidates, nondescript set of university men. All hopeless from our point of view. All imagined that political science consisted of a knowledge of Aristotle and 'modern' writers such as de Tocqueville – wanted to put the students through a course of Utopias from More downwards. When Sidney suggested a course of lectures be prepared on the different systems of municipal taxation, when Graham suggested a study of the rival methods of election, from *ad hoc* to proportional representation, the wretched candidates looked aghast and thought evidently that we were

amusing ourselves at their expense. . . . Finally we determined to do without our lecturer – to my mind a blessed consummation. It struck me always as a trifle difficult to teach a science which does not yet exist. . . .

*14 August. Stratford St Andrew Rectory, Saxmundham*
A whole fortnight wasted in illness – a rheumatic cold combined with general collapse. This must excuse the absence of the brilliant account which I looked forward to writing of the International Congress! To us, it was, as we expected it to be, a public humiliation. The rank and file of socialists, especially English socialists, are unusually silly folk – for the most part feather-headed failures – and heaped together in one hall with the consciousness that their every word would be reported by the 'world press', they approached raving inbecility. . . . The Fabians sat silent . . . Sidney writing descriptive accounts for the *Manchester Guardian,* Shaw for the *Star* . . . The Fabians at any rate write history if they do not make it!

But though we were ashamed of the 'British nation' . . . the socialists of other lands were exceptionally enlightening. The German Political Socialists are substantial persons, their intellects somewhat twisted by their authoritarian dogmatism, but with strong sterling character . . . Among the French, Swiss, Dutch and Italians there are individuals who are really 'thinking' . . .

Charlotte Payne-Townshend (1857–1943) was a rich Irishwoman. The Webbs introduced her to Bernard Shaw on 29 January 1896.

*16 September.* [Stratford St Andrew]
Last day of our stay in the Suffolk rectory. For first three weeks I was seedy, mooned and dreamed my life away chatting with our visitors or sitting in the little study watching Sidney work . . . or straining after the party on my bicycle, feeling all the time somewhat miserable and woe-begone. The last four weeks we have worked well together . . . Out of our study of trade unionism we are developing a new view of democracy and I think quite an original set of economic and political hypotheses. For the first time since we began this book I am feeling intellectually keen and absorbed in my work.

Meanwhile a new friend has joined the 'Bo' family. ['Bo' was the Potter family name for Beatrice.] Charlotte Payne-Townshend is a wealthy unmarried woman of about my age. Bred up in second-rate fashionable society without any education or habit of work, she found herself at about thirty-three years of age alone in the world, without ties, without any definite creed, and with a large income. For the last four years she has drifted about – in India, in Italy, in Egypt, in London, seeking occupation and fellow spirits. In person she is attractive – a large graceful woman with masses of chocolate-brown hair, pleasant grey eyes, 'matte' complexion which sometimes looks muddy, at other times forms a picturesquely pale background to her brilliant hair and bright eyes. She dresses well – in her flowing white evening robes she approaches beauty. At moments she is plain. By temperament she is an anarchist – feeling any regulation or rule intolerable – a tendency which has been exaggerated by her irresponsible wealth. She is romantic but thinks herself cynical. She is a socialist and a radical, not because she understands the collectivist standpoint, but because she is by nature a rebel. She has no snobbishness and no convention: she has 'swallowed all formulas' but has not worked out principles of her own. She is fond of men and impatient of most women, bitterly resents her enforced celibacy but thinks she could not tolerate the matter-of-fact side of marriage. Sweet-tempered, sympathetic and genuinely anxious to increase the world's enjoyment and diminish the world's pain.

. . . Last autumn she was introduced to us. We, knowing she was wealthy, and hearing she was socialistic, interested her in the London School of Economics. She subscribed £1,000 to the Library, endowed a woman's scholarship, and has now taken the rooms over the School at Adelphi Terrace, paying us £300 a year for rent and service. It was on account of her generosity to our projects and 'for the good of the cause' that I first made friends with her. To bring her more directly into our little set of comrades, I suggested that we should take a house together in the country and entertain our friends. To me she seemed at that time a pleasant, well-dressed, well-intentioned woman – I thought she should do very well for Graham Wallas! Now she turns out to be an 'original', with considerable personal charm and certain volcanic tendencies. Graham Wallas bored her with his morality and learning. In a few days she and Bernard Shaw were constant companions. For the last fortnight, when the party has been reduced to ourselves and Shaw, and we have been occupied with our work and each other, they have been scouring the country together and sitting up late at night. To all seeming, she is in love with the brilliant philanderer and he is taken, in his cold sort of way, with her. They are, I gather from him, on very confidential terms and have 'explained' their relative positions. Though interested I am somewhat uneasy. These warm-hearted unmarried women of a certain age are audacious and are almost childishly reckless of consequences. I doubt whether Bernard Shaw could be induced to marry: I doubt whether she will be happy without it. It is harder for a woman to remain celibate than a man.

*5 October. Grosvenor Road*
The last fortnight we have been a good deal absorbed in preparing Adelphi Terrace for the opening of the School. Found Hewins in a state of nervous collapse threatening severe illness, sent him away with his wife and child and took over the work of preparing for the coming term. Poor Sidney trudges over there directly after breakfast and spends his mornings with painters, plumbers and locksmiths, would-be students intervening to whom he gives fatherly advice, comes home to lunch and then off to the L.C.C. In the interval of arranging the details of the housekeeping at the School, I am getting on slowly with the book . . .

Had to attend Manchester Conference of Women [National Union of Women Workers]. Usual large gathering of sensible and God-fearing folk, dominated by the Executive of bishops' wives . . . I have resigned from the Executive owing to their persistence in having prayers before all their business meetings which, I suggest, is wanting in courtesy to the Jewesses and infidels whom they wish to serve with them. Some of them agree but say that the Union would lose membership if it were not understood to be deliberately Christian. Very well; then I have no place on its Executive. I remain on sub-committees and will keep the Union straight on industrial questions. . . .

Louise Creighton now becomes – as wife to the Bishop of London – one of the great hostesses of London society. In spite of the fact that she is a fervent Christian and I an avowed agnostic, we have a warm respect for each other. She is an absolutely straight woman, who never swerves from what she believes to be right, is sometimes ugly in her brusque directness. . . . To Alice Green, with her tortuous mind and uncertain ways, Louise is anathema, though possibly now that she is the wife of the Bishop of London Alice Green may see 'quality' in her. . . .

One reason I am so fagged is the growth of the social side of our work. We are perpetually entertaining, and the opening of the School has added a long list of students whom we feel it our duty to see and talk to. . . .

My old friend Carrie becomes an enthusiastic Board School teacher! . . . Sent her to our lawyer who has extracted from the husband £300 and arranged a judicial separation. Now she seems to have really made a new start and likely to have a life of influence before her.

## ∼ 1897 ∼

*18 January.* [The Argoed]
Xmas with Alfred Cripps. Last year he was starting his political life: this
year he is well on the road to office. He is in splendid spirits, talks with
easy critical familiarity of Balfour and other leading Conservatives and
gives one to understand incidentally that he is constantly consulted by
them. He is rapidly becoming a sort of legal adviser . . . He is still
making a large income at the Bar and spending it lavishly on his constituency, home and children. . . . The Playnes were staying there:
Arthur cross and uncivil, Mary extremely affable and uncomfortably
anxious to be pleasant. Refused a half-hearted invitation to take in
Longfords . . .

Came on here for three weeks' work – over two weeks alone, Hewins
with us for one week. The hill enveloped in cold mist. But it has been
a splendid time for work: have written the best part of two chapters.
Have worked both together and apart . . . sometimes we would get at
cross purposes – but our cross purposes would always end in a shower
of kisses. I doubt whether two persons could stand the stress and strain
of this long-drawn-out work, this joint struggle with ideas, a perpetual
hammering at each other's minds, if it were not for the equally perpetual 'honeymoon' of our life together. These three weeks, with the
peaceful grey days and long evenings, the wanderings over the moorland
and up and down dale, the cosy evenings by the log fire, he reading
*Brandt* and *Peer Gynt* to me, have been a delicious holy-day, a relief from
the noise, bustle and news of London. And as if to reward us for being
so happy enshrouded in cold mist, the sun, the last three days, has
come out gloriously shining in red splendour . . . I am so well, and so
blessedly happy. Again those morbid troublings of last autumn seem to
me amazing! . . .

The London School is progressing – Sidney has contrived to edge it
in to any possible London University. It is still a substratum in money,
students, and output but it promises well. And while we have been busy
with our little affairs, the greater world of politics has not been doing so
badly from our point of view. The Conservative government finds itself
paralysed. . . . The Liberal leaders are as feeble and half-hearted as ever.
But neither party are putting forward any alternative policy to collectivism . . . Social reform is becoming far too complicated for the
actor-politician or the accomplished *littérateur*. . . . That fact works our
way . . .

*1 February.* [41 Grosvenor Road]
This extract from Chamberlain's speech interests me unusually.

> Why, gentlemen, I daresay that Mr Morley was thinking chiefly of
> our domestic controversy, and, if I might venture to say so, I would
> add that this is a mistake which the leaders of the Radical party are
> constantly making. They forget in the attention which they give to
> these domestic controversies, which, after all, whichever way they
> are settled, are all of minor importance, they forget the great part
> which this country has played, and is called upon to play, in the
> history of the world. (*Daily Chronicle*, 1 February 1897: 'Joseph
> Chamberlain at Birmingham'.)

It means many things in his development as a politician. First that social
reform is from his standpoint 'no go'. This is partly because he is now
irrecoverably a leader of the reactionary party; partly because he has
found industrial problems, with his insufficient knowledge and
untrained intellect, too difficult to unravel. It also means (by the light of
Balfour's failure these two sessions) a definite and timely bid for the Tory
Party's allegiance as distinguished from the Liberal Unionists. To myself,
who knew him as a man in the prime of life apparently inspired by a passionate desire to better the conditions of 'the common lump of men', it
reads like a pathetic confession of failure, not less pathetic because it is
unselfconscious and is expressed in words of buoyant oratory. . . .

*6 February.* [41 Grosvenor Road]
A great gathering last night in Queen's Hall – nine hundred L.C.C.
scholars receiving their certificates from [Edward] Prince of Wales. Sat
close to H.R.H. and watched him with curiosity. In his performance of
the ceremony, from his incoming to his outgoing, he acted like a well-
oiled automaton . . . But observing him closely you could see that
underneath the Royal automaton there lay the child and the animal, a
simple kindly unmoral temperament which makes him a good fellow.
Not an English gentleman, essentially a foreigner and yet an almost
perfect constitutional sovereign. From a political point of view his vices
and foibles, his lack of intellectual refinement or moral distinction, are
as nothing compared to his complete detachment from all party prejudice and class interests and his genius for political *discretion*. But one
sighs to think that this unutterably commonplace person should set the
tone to London Society. There is something comic in the great British

nation with its infinite variety of talents, having this undistinguished and limited-minded German bourgeois to be its social sovereign. A sovereign of real distinction who would take over as his peculiar province the direction of the *voluntary side of social life*, who could cultivate in rich and leisured society a desire to increase the sum of real intellectual effort and eminence – what might he not do to further our civilization by creating a real aristocracy of character and intellect. As it is, we have our social leader proposing in this morning's papers as a fit commemoration of his august mother's longest reign, the freeing of the hospitals from debt, the sort of proposal one would expect from the rank and file of 'scripture readers' or a committee of village grocers intent on goodwill on earth and saving the rates. . . .

Beatrice here contrasts the Greek landing on Crete to support the current insurrection against Turkish rule with the complicity of Cecil Rhodes in the Jameson Raid in 1895. A select committee had been appointed in August 1896 to look into the British South Africa Company; the examination of Rhodes had begun on 16 February 1897.

*23 February.* [41 Grosvenor Road]
. . . A flying visit to Cambridge to address the Newnham and Girton students – stayed with the Marshalls. Professor Marshall is more footling than ever. . . .

Greece and Rhodes – two political raids – one heroic, the other sordid – absorb the attention of the political public. In both episodes the great English nation shows its meanest characteristics. In our foreign policy we are still guided by no intelligible principle – grab, scuttle or fence – according to the exigencies of the day. So far as there exists a community of nations, it is still in the early stages of barbarism in which force is only alternated by deception. England is more successful but no worse than other nations. . . .

Bertha Newcombe's portrait of Shaw – 'The Platform Spellbinder' – was lost during the Second World War.

*9 March.* [41 Grosvenor Road]
As I mounted the stairs with Shaw's *Unsocial Socialist* to return to Bertha Newcombe I felt somewhat uncomfortable as I knew I should encounter a sad soul full of bitterness and loneliness. I stepped into a small wainscotted studio and was greeted coldly by the little woman. She is *petite*

and dark, about forty years old but looks more like a wizened girl than a fully developed woman. Her jet-black hair heavily fringed, half-smart, half-artistic clothes, pinched aquiline features and thin lips, give you a somewhat unpleasant impression though not wholly inartistic. She is bad style without being vulgar or common or loud – indeed many persons, Kate Courtney for instance, would call her 'lady-like' – but she is insignificant and undistinguished. 'I want to talk to you, Mrs Webb,' she said when I seated myself. And then followed, told with the dignity of devoted feeling, the story of her relationship to Bernard Shaw, her five years of devoted love, his cold philandering, her hopes aroused by repeated advice to him (which he, it appears, had repeated much exaggerated) to marry her, and then her feeling of misery and resentment against me when she discovered that I was encouraging him 'to marry Miss Townshend'. Finally, he had written a month ago to break it off entirely: they were not to meet again. And I had to explain with perfect frankness that so long as there seemed a chance for her I had been willing to act as chaperone, that she had never been a personal friend of mine or Sidney's, that I had regarded her only as Shaw's friend, and that as far as I was concerned I should have welcomed her as his wife. But directly I saw that he meant nothing I backed out of the affair. She took it all quietly, her little face seemed to shrink up and the colour of her skin looked as if it were reflecting the sad lavender of her dress.

'You are well out of it, Miss Newcombe,' I said gently. 'If you had married Shaw he would not have remained faithful to you. You know my opinion of him – as a friend and a colleague, as a critic and literary worker, there are few men for whom I have so warm a liking; but in his relations with women he is vulgar, if not worse; it is a vulgarity that includes cruelty and springs from vanity.'

As I uttered these words my eye caught her portrait of Shaw – full-length, with his red-gold hair and laughing blue eyes and his mouth slightly open as if scoffing at us both, a powerful picture in which the love of the woman had given genius to the artist. Her little face turned to follow my eyes and she also felt the expression of the man, the mockery at her deep-rooted affection. 'It is so horribly lonely,' she muttered. 'I daresay it is more peaceful than being kept on the rack, but it is like the peace of death.'

There seemed nothing more to be said. I rose and with a perfunctory 'Come and see me – someday,' I kissed her on the forehead and escaped down the stairs. And then I thought of that other woman with her loving easygoing nature and anarchic luxurious ways, her well-bred manners and well-made clothes, her leisure, wealth and knowledge of the world. Would she succeed in taming the philanderer?

The Webbs took a pretty house on the North Downs near Dorking as a holiday home. In May, Shaw was elected as a member of the St Pancras Vestry; he divided his time that early summer between London and Surrey.

*1 May.* [Dorking]
Retired for three months into the country to finish our forthcoming work. Our party consists of Charlotte Townshend (who shares the expenses), Bernard Shaw and ourselves, and we are enlisting a succession of visitors for Sundays. Already a month of our time here is past. I have been especially vigorous, completely absorbed in thinking out the last chapter of our book. . . . Now that we have found our theory every previous part of our analysis seems to fit in perfectly, and facts which before puzzled us range themselves in their places as if 'by nature'.

We alternate from thinking that the Work will be as great in its effect on political and economic thought as Adam Smith's *Wealth of Nations*, to wondering whether the whole of it is not an elaborate figment of our imagination . . . One broods at times over the question whether our work is worth all the happiness and well-being we are extracting from the life of the community, and at times one feels uneasy lest we are taking more than our share. . . . Our life at present is like the early summer, growth and the delight in growing, love and the delight in loving. We are getting middle-aged and yet we feel young in our intellectual life, always on the threshold of [a] new discovery. . . .

I am watching with concern and curiosity the development of the Shaw–Townshend friendship. All this winter they have been lovers – of a philandering and harmless kind, always together when Shaw was free. Charlotte insisted on taking a house with us in order that he might be here constantly, and it is obvious that she is deeply attached to him. But I see no sign on his side of the growth of any genuine and steadfast affection. He finds it pleasant to be with her in her luxurious surroundings, he has been studying her and all her little ways and amusing himself by dissecting the rich woman brought up without training and drifting about at the beck of impulse. I think he has now exhausted the study, observed all that there is to observe. He has been flattered by her devotion and absorption in him; he is kindly and has a cat-like preference for those persons to whom he is accustomed. But there are ominous signs that he is tired of watching the effect of little words of gallantry and personal interest with which he plied her in the first months of the friendship. And he is annoyed by her lack of purpose and utter incapacity for work. If she would set to, and do even the smallest and least considerable task of intellectual work, I believe she could retain his interest and perhaps develop his feeling for her. Otherwise he will drift away, for Shaw is too high-minded and too conventionally honourable to marry her for the life of leisure and luxury he could gain for himself as her husband.

Haldane had been jilted by Valerie Munro-Ferguson, the sister of his fellow 'Limp' Ronald Munro-Ferguson (1860–1934); she lampooned him in three novels before she died insane in an asylum in 1897. Haldane never married.

*3 May.* [Dorking]
Haldane here for a Sunday. Difficult to estimate what amount of influence that man exercises in public affairs. He has never held office, but during the last Liberal government he was the chief instigator of their collectivist policy . . . He was also responsible for many of their appointments. In this parliament he is in constant confidential intercourse with Balfour and other Conservatives over the many non-party questions dealt with by a government, and even in some purely political questions his advice is asked. He attracts confidence where he is at all liked; once on friendly terms, you feel absolutely secure that he will never use personal knowledge to advance his own public career to the detriment of any friend. The rank and file of his own party dislike him intensely, partly because he detaches himself from party discipline . . . and partly because he seems dominated by some vague principle which they do not understand and which he does not make intelligible. His bulky awkward form and pompous ways, his absolute lack of masculine vices and 'manly' tastes (beyond a good dinner), his intense superiority and constant attitude of a teacher, his curiously woolly mind would make him an unattractive figure if it were not for the beaming kindliness of his nature, warm appreciation of friends and a certain pawky humour with which he surveys the world. And there is pathos in his personality. In spite of the successful professional life . . . he is a restless lonely man – in his heart still worshipping the woman who jilted him seven years ago. . . . He was made to be husband, father and close comrade. He has to put up with pleasant intercourse with political friends and political foes. . . .

*8 May.* [Dorking]
Silly these philanderings of Shaw's. He imagines that he gets to know women by making them in love with him. Just the contrary. His stupid gallantries bar out from him the friendship of women who are either too sensible, too puritanical or too much 'otherwise engaged' to care to bandy personal flatteries with him. One large section of women, comprising some, at any rate, of the finest types, remains hidden from him. With the women with whom he has '*bonne fortune*' he also fails in his object, or rather in his *avowed* object – vivi-section. He idealizes them for a few days, weeks or years, imagines them to be something utterly different from their true selves, then has a revulsion of feeling and discovers them to be unutterably vulgar, second-rate, rapscallion, or insipidly well-bred. He never fathoms their real worth, nor rightly sees their limitations. But in fact it is not the end he cares for: it is the *process*. . . . Whether I like him, admire him or despise him most I do not know. Just at present I feel annoyed and contemptuous.

For the dancing light has gone out of Charlotte's eyes – there is at times a blank haggard look, a look that I myself felt in my own eyes for long years. But throughout all my misery I had the habit of hard work and an almost religious sense of my intellectual mission. I had always my convent to fly to. Poor Charlotte has nowhere to turn. . . .

*24 May.* [Dorking]
Glorious summer days. In excellent working form. . . . Sidney sits at one table and I at another: the sun streams in through the dancing leaves. As fast as I can plan he criticizes and executes, filling in his time with administrative work, but sacrificing everything to the book. Charlotte sits upstairs typewriting Shaw's plays. Shaw wanders about the garden with writing-book and pencil, writing the *Saturday* article [theatre criticism for the *Saturday Review*], correcting his plays for press or reading through one of our chapters. . . . an astute reader will quickly divine those chapters which Shaw has corrected and those which he has not – there is a conciseness and crispness in parts subjected to his pruning-knife. . . .

. . . Our daily life is an earthly paradise. Absolutely the only ruffle, an uncomfortable feeling that my housekeeping is extravagant . . . Some nights I wake up and worry about it . . . But when the morning comes, my fully awakened mind turns to the book and refuses obstinately to consider the price of vegetables or the pounds of butter or meat. All sorts of sophistries sooth my conscience – that I cannot reform a bad system but must make the best of it, that my brains are better employed in unravelling problems – all the same, at the bottom of my heart I know that I am unnecessarily lazy about it and lacking in moral courage not to control my servants with more vigour. If it were not for this uneasy conscience I and they would probably do worse, and I should make Mary cry with my black looks. Sometimes no doubt she laughs in her sleeve at my *laissez-faire, laissez-aller*. I am fond of my two girls with their smart figures and pretty faces, and they, I think, are fond of us – it is now four years that these two sisters have been with us. But the relation between mistress and servant and private tradesmen is a bad one, thoroughly unsound in its capricious carelessness, lack of knowledge and supervision of buyer over the seller. . . .

. . . Alice Green . . . spent the night . . . A multitude of tragedies in that woman's life – always in the process of being deserted and of deserting – and yet withal a certain faithfulness and persistency of disposition, never daring to let go a friendship lest the friend should turn out after all trumps. So she keeps us up, gazing on us with that weird veiled look, uncertain whether to hold on or let go, but giving us only her leavings. Even the clothes she comes in are always her shabbiest! Poor Alice! She chose me as a friend and not I her, but she was good to me in the early springtide of my good fortune and she was one of the first to appreciate and like Sidney. . . . If it had not been for Alice Green's emphatic opinion that Sidney was essentially distinguished in character and intelligence, who knows whether I should have had the courage to back my own judgement against that of my own little world? For it was reason and not love that won me, a deliberate judgement of the man's worth and [an] almost cold-blooded calculation of the life I could live with him and he with me. Perhaps the final consideration that determined me was the conviction that I should turn out better value to him than to any other man. To a well-trained commercial mind there is charm in making the ideal bargain, the best possible to both parties.

*15 June.* [Dorking]
Our last days here passed quickly. . . . Shall have two-thirds of the book in print by the time we return to London . . . Sometime in the autumn the work will be out of our hands. Already sold our German rights: will appear simultaneously in Germany and England. Then for our seven-month holiday – seeing Anglo-Saxon democracy.

Beatrice is referring to the celebrations for Queen Victoria's Diamond Jubilee. On 14 July she attended the Women's Jubilee Dinner and Soirée, given by one hundred distinguished women to one hundred distinguished men in the Grafton Galleries and organized by Mrs Humphry Ward. 'Seeing that it was difficult to discover one hundred distinguished women, some other ladies, among them myself, were called in to advise,' Beatrice wrote in *Our Partnership*.

*28 June.* [41 Grosvenor Road]
Back in London. Imperialism in the air, all classes drunk with sightseeing and hysterical loyalty. Our morning, hard at work proof-correcting: in the afternoon and evening friends drop in to welcome us back . . .

*16 July.* [41 Grosvenor Road]
Sidney and Haldane rushing about London trying to get all parties to agree to a Bill for London University. If it goes through, it will be due to Haldane's insistence and his friendship with Balfour, but the form of the Bill [is] largely Sidney's. He thinks he has got all he wants as regards the Technical Education Board and the London School of Economics. The Commission appointed to carry the Act out is largely favourable, or at any rate 'susceptible' to right influence.

*26 July.* [41 Grosvenor Road]
Spent Sunday with Alfred Cripps at Parmoor. Obviously disgusted with the ways of Parliament this session. 'Balfour has no principle,' he plaintively repeated. . . . Alfred Cripps is, I think, beginning to discover that a government will be flattering and considerate towards an able young lawyer who is ready to advise them and defend them whenever asked; but that these amenities cease when he begins to oppose them either overtly or privately . . .

On 26 July the House of Commons debated the report of the Parliamentary Committee set up to enquire into the Jameson Raid. When the Majority Report condemned Cecil Rhodes, but declared that neither the Colonial Secretary nor any of his officials had any advance knowledge of the venture, cynical critics spoke of the 'Lying-in-State' at Westminster. The minority wanted a more searching examination of the alleged complicity of the Colonial Office, claiming that there had been no proper investigation of this aspect of the incident. Mr Hawksley, the solicitor to the Chartered Company which employed Jameson, possessed some telegrams which he refused to produce to the Enquiry. In the debate Chamberlain was at pains to exonerate Rhodes.

*30 July.* [41 Grosvenor Road]

Massingham dined here last night. Greatly excited about South African debate. 'Superb rope-dancing, Chamberlain's speech.' 'Hawksley in the House ready to produce telegrams and letters unless Chamberlain repudiated condemnation of Rhodes. Harcourt completely taken in: consented to back up government if they condemned Rhodes, and now Chamberlain declares that he accepted condemnation as a compromise and as far as he was concerned he always thought Rhodes a fine fellow. It is superb: it is a delight to watch such a man,' and Massingham bubbled over with the joy of the political dramatic critic. 'Chamberlain's career is extraordinarily interesting – every day brings its own trick.' 'The career is more interesting than the man,' added Massingham more gravely. 'He has neither the knowledge nor the convictions to make him more than a great political artist.' 'Surely', I rejoined, 'we shall look back on the last fifty years of the nineteenth century as the peculiar period of political artists: we have no statesmen – all our successful politicians, the men who lead the parties, are artists and nothing else: Gladstone, Disraeli, Randolph Churchill, Chamberlain, and the unsuccessful Rosebery, all these men have the characters of actors – personal charm, extraordinary pliability and quick-wittedness.'

*10 September.* [The Argoed]

. . . A Sunday spent at Standish where Blanche Cripps has a houseful of children and friends, entertaining among others the two Ravoglis, charming singers and one of them a patient of Willie's. Willie has developed into the fashionable surgeon whose patients adore him. The charming Julia Ravogli sang all day to us to show her gratitude for his skilful operation on her sister Sophia. Blanche, too, is a thoroughly happy satisfactory woman, her large income giving her full scope for her generous instincts. In spite of her mental deficiencies – absence of memory and inconsequence and extremely limited power of reasoning, her noble instincts make her into a fine woman with a good influence. To contrast her with poor little Rosy who is more *morally* deficient than intellectually wanting!

*27 September.* [Moorcroft]

Brain-fag and headache; for a good week enforced idleness, wandering alone over the moorland . . . These two months we have overworked for enjoyment; constantly too exhausted to care for exercise, and days when extreme exasperation from over-brainwork has made me quite incapable of enjoying the country. Also Shaw and Charlotte's relationship is disturbing. Shaw goes on untroubled, working hard at his plays and then going long rides with her on a tandem cycle. But she is always restless and sometimes unhappy, too anxious to be with him. . . . If it were not for the fact that he is Shaw I should say that he was dishonourable. But as he has always advertised his views of marriage and philandering from the house-tops, every woman ought to be prepared for his logical carrying out of these principles.

*18 October. Grosvenor Road*
Worked hard since we came back, finished the last chapter. . . .

Beatrice here included an extract from *The Times* of 29 October 1897 giving a report of the conference of the National Union of Women Workers at which she moved a resolution suggesting that the meeting should not start with prayers. An amendment was carried proposing 'that persons who are unwilling from conscientious scruples to be present during prayers may ask the secretaries to keep places for them'. The Webbs were planning what Beatrice called a 'busman's holiday' to America, Australia and New Zealand, to discover how the English municipal tradition had been transplanted overseas. The record of this narrowly focused tour, to which Sidney contributed about a third of the entries, is summarized in the four-volume edition of *The Diary of Beatrice Webb*.

*30 October.* [41 Grosvenor Road]
So ended my official connection with the bishops' wives. I felt, rightly or wrongly, that it was necessary to clear up the situation: either the Association was distinctively Christian or not. . . . It is strange how a meeting is influenced by the *way of putting it.* My resolution had given great offence, and when I rose to move it I felt hostile feeling all around. But with a few frank and gentle words all the hostility vanished, and though the meeting supported the Executive I had won their sympathy and respect, which again reacted on me and I felt rather a brute to object to their prayers! The association otherwise strikes me as doing good work. Louise Creighton has distinctly a statesmanlike mind, and the group of women who now control the policy are a good sort – large-minded and pleasant-mannered. The 'screeching sisterhood' are trying to invade them but Louise's battalions of hardworking, religious and somewhat stupid women will, I think, resist the attack.

*8 November.* [41 Grosvenor Road]
The last pages of our revise gone back to the printer. For the last ten days
'no settled occupation': it is wearisome to get up in the morning and feel
that there is no more reason for doing one thing than another. If the
elections were not upon us and our journey imminent, I should begin
straight away on another bit of work.

*10 December.* [41 Grosvenor Road]
A chaotic month since I last wrote! Began a course of reading on
Australia and New Zealand, waded through blue-books on Federation,
etc., read page after page of unreadable history, ugly facts told in an ugly
manner. But this sedative occupation was soon broken into by odd jobs,
little bits of journalism that were long due, and three or four days' hard
work revising the work of the scholars of the London School. . . .
Perhaps part of my chaotic frame of mind [is] due to dabbling in society: thought it good opportunity to invite some people to dinner since
it did not much matter whether I felt seedy or not the next day. My little
parties are said to be successful but they don't please me. Directly you
entertain for entertaining's sake, then they become hollow and unpleasant, an element of vanity enters in and you begin to wonder what
impression you make, what your friends think of each other, and so
on. . . . the dross in my nature is not yet eliminated! There is a good
strong strain of the vain worldling left. Thank the gods, there is no
trace of such feeling in Sidney. Work and love are the only gods he lives
for. Oh, my boy, how I love you – past understanding!

*Xmas. Parmoor*
Another pleasant Xmas with Alfred and his children. . . . Long walks,
talking chiefly of the contents of our book, of which we brought him an
'advance copy'. Rosy Williams here, a changed mortal, well in health,
handsome to look at and thoroughly enjoying her life with troops of
young and old men 'after her'. How long this amiable mood will last
remains to be seen!

## ～ 1898 ～

*11 January.* [41 Grosvenor Road]
Our big book [*Industrial Democracy*] has had a brilliant reception. *The
Times* gave us two columns on the day of publication, the *Standard* an

abusive leader, the *Daily Chronicle* and the *Daily News* and half a dozen big provincials were all properly enthusiastic. Other papers followed suit and produced their reviews the next day – the weeklies treated us quite as handsomely. Altogether a small triumph in its way. . . .

The old Eve in me is delighted with buying a trousseau for our nine months' journey. It is a long time since I have really had a good 'go' at clothes and I am revelling in buying silks and satins, gloves, underclothing, furs and everything that a sober-minded woman of forty can want to inspire Americans and Colonials with a due respect for the refinements of attractiveness! It is a pleasure to clothe myself charmingly! For the last ten years I have not had either the time or the will to think of it. For this tour, I harmonize some extravagance with my conscience by making myself believe that I must have everything new and that I must look nice! I believe that it is a deliberate expenditure because six months ago I determined that I would do myself handsomely as part of a policy, but I daresay one or two of the specially becoming blouses are the expression of concrete vanity. My childish delight in watching these bright clothes being made is a sort of rebound from the hard drudgery of the last two years. But it is rather comical in a woman of 40! – 40 all but two weeks – forty, forty, FORTY – what an age, almost elderly! I don't feel a bit old.

*14 January.* [41 Grosvenor Road]
Poor Alice Green! . . . the other evening when I was alone with her she broke down and wept bitterly in my arms. Arthur Strong, after using her money and her influence to climb into the position of Librarian to the House of Lords, marries a brilliant and beautiful Greek scholar – Eugenie Sellers. For eighteen months the poor woman has been eaten into with bitterness; when at times I have watched her unawares she has looked like a lost soul. And a certain lack of dignity and the extreme unhappiness of her expression has alienated some of her old friends, and even Society is becoming cold to her. The world gets impatient at her restless unhappiness: at fifty years of age, with a good income, distinguished position, a woman ought to settle down contentedly. But some women never grow too old to be in love, or at least to require love. And why should they? With intellectual persons love is the passion for warm enduring affection and intimate mental companionship. Only religion can take its place. And Alice Green has no religion, no conviction, not even a cause she believes in.

Audrey (Ada) Radford (1859–1934) was the sister of Ernest Radford, poet and barrister and a friend of Marx and Engels. The *Yellow Book* was at the forefront of *avant-garde* culture. Daniel Meinertzhagen (1875–98), Georgina's son, died of peritonitis in Bremen.

*21 January.* [41 Grosvenor Road]
. . . our old friend Graham Wallas has married – Ada Radford, a woman of forty or thereabouts and one of a cultivated, public-spirited, somewhat aesthetic middle-class family. She was educated at Girton, became assistant mistress of High School, then secretary to a Working Women's College, then a writer for the *Yellow Book*. A woman of a certain originality of life and with a pretty little literary gift for writing short stories. I do not take to her. She is obviously a good woman – sweet-natured (Graham says humorous) with decision and capacity. Her ideas are the old-fashioned aesthetic, secularist, equal rights sort. She is a woman who carries rigid principles into the smallest concerns of life. With Madonna-like features, good complexion and soft golden hair, she ought to be pleasant to look at: but as a matter of principle she dresses in yellow-green sloppy garments, large garden hat with bows of green silk – her hair is always coming down – and generally speaking, she looks as if she had tumbled up out of an armchair in which she had slept the night, and her movements are aggressively ugly. But as Graham sees none of this, what does it matter! They are devotedly attached: she has just enough money to make marriage – with no prospect of children – prudent if not actually desirable for Graham. I doubt whether we shall be much of friends. We are both too set in our own mould, too completely filled up with work and comrades to have time to discover the 'deeper affinities' which doubtless exist between two women who have both struggled with life and work. If we are ever thrown together we might get to like each other – for the differences are superficial and my distaste is really to her clothes. I could forgive them if they were not worn *on principle*. But principle without a deal of intelligence or some personal charm *tires* one!

*16 February. Herbert Spencer's. Brighton*
Second visit this year to this poor old man. . . . The last month filled up with miscellaneous work . . . meanwhile a constant stream of individuals passing through our house . . . their one common feature being that they all ask questions which have to be answered.

Dan Meinertzhagen dead: Georgie's best-loved child, a terrible tragedy in our sister's life.

[?] *March.* [41 Grosvenor Road]

The L.C.C. election. We sallied forth about 8.30 a.m. (Sidney having voted first in Westminster) laden with sandwiches, teapots and oranges, to fit up the committee rooms. It was a glorious morning, the Westminster buildings rising out of the blue atmosphere and the river dancing in the brilliant morning sun. At 9.30 I had settled down at one of the six committee rooms. . . . About 3.30 the 'bringers-up' trooped in – at 5 it was a crowd in the little room, each awaiting to report progress. Then came on a heavy fall of snow, but the feeling of the Progressives was so hot that they trudged on through the sleet and the slush, not one of my fifteen workers gave up working. . . . Then the hurried dinner . . . then the exciting hours of the count, then the midnight visit to the National Liberal Club all aglow with Progressive victories – and then to bed – oh! so tired – far too tired to sleep. . . . just as the L.C.C. election of 1895 was a defeat for us, so this election has been our victory. Fabianism, in one form or another, is again triumphant.

We therefore close this portion of our life with considerable complacency and start on our long journey with a light heart. . . . We can now feel assured that with the School as a teaching body, the Fabian Society as a propagandist organization, the L.C.C. Progressives as an object lesson of electoral success, our books as the only elaborate and original work in economic fact and theory, no young man or woman who is anxious to study or to work in public affairs can fail to come under our influence. . . .

Our journey will be a complete break in our life. We have finished with trade unionism, we have even carted all our material round to the Library of the School. Galton leaves us finally and pushes forward in his own career as election agent and journalist; our two girls, to whom we have grown attached, leave us also and 'better themselves' by going to Maggie's larger and richer household. In most ways I shall regret them; they are attractive natures, first-rate servants and saved me much trouble. If it had not been for poor virtue's lapse last autumn into the habit of taking small doses of our whisky, a habit which I felt I had not time or inclination to root out by constant strict supervision, and Mary's slight extravagance, I should have been ready to sacrifice almost anything to keep them. It is so difficult to find servants whom you care for and who care for you! But probably it is better for them to move on to better wages and under a more careful and watchful mistress. Even our cats – two brothers who have prowled about this house for four years –

are leaving us for new homes! All will have to be new and strange and perhaps difficult when we return – work, secretary, servants. We may easily, on all points, change for the worse. Meanwhile we intend to enjoy ourselves and let the future look out for itself.

# Cliques of Friends
# and Acquaintances

## February 1899–December 1901

The Webbs returned to a Britain alive with optimism and prosperity. The great trade boom of 1898–99 brought wealth beyond all precedence and the whole country was affected by it. There were also personal adjustments to make. As the Webbs were preparing to leave England, Charlotte Payne-Townshend, exasperated by her relationship with Shaw, took her friend Lion Phillimore to Rome. While she was away, Shaw became ill with an inflamed toe joint and, realizing how much he missed her, encouraged her to return. Charlotte returned in May to find Shaw seriously ill and in a neglected state, and took a house at Haslemere in Surrey where, with servants and nurses, he could be restored to health. She 'was the inevitable and predestined angel, appointed by Destiny,' Shaw wrote to Beatrice. Charlotte also arranged for them to marry. The ceremony took place, with Shaw on crutches, on 1 June, at the registry office in Henrietta Street, London. On their return, the Webbs began to research the history of local government. Frederick Spencer (d. 1946) was their assistant.

*5 February. 41 Grosvenor Road*
Since we returned to England I have been disinclined to write in my diary, having nothing to relate and having lost the habit of intimate confidences, impossible in a joint diary such as we have kept together during our journey round the world. One cannot run on into self-analysis, family gossip, or indiscreet and hasty descriptions of current

happenings, if someone else, however dear, is solemnly to read one's chatter then and there. I foresee the sort of kindly indulgence or tolerant boredom with which Sidney would decipher the last entry and this feeling would, in itself, make it possible to write whatever came into my head . . .

With regard to our friends and relations, we found only two persons whose lives had been completely changed during our absence – our two friends GBS and Charlotte have married each other, Shaw has become a chronic invalid, Charlotte a devoted nurse. They live in an attractive house up at Hindhead. He still writes but his work seems to be getting unreal: he leads a hothouse life, he cannot walk or get among his equals. He is as witty and as cheery as of old. But now and again a flush of fatigue or a sign of brain irritation passes over him. Charlotte, under pressure of anxiety for the man she loves, has broadened out into a motherly woman and lost her anarchic determination to live according to her momentary desires. There are some compensations for the sadness of the sudden cutting-off of his activity.

*7 March.* [41 Grosvenor Road]
. . . Sidney has been principally engaged in engineering the School of Economics into its proper place in the new University, bargaining alternatively with the Royal Commission to recognize it as a School of the University and to create a separate Faculty of Economics and Political Science, with the Technical Education Board to endow the proposed Faculty with an income, and with Passmore Edwards to present a new building. Everything seems to be going excellently. Meanwhile we are well into our new enquiry and have elaborated a syllabus for the use of investigators. We have engaged as secretary a clever, ambitious elementary schoolteacher – F. H. Spencer – about twenty-eight years old. We tried a nice young man straight from Oxford but he was a dead failure, not realizing what constituted a day's work, and presenting us with little essays instead of research notes. . . . I am aiming at living a student's life, withdrawing from any social excitement [that is] inconsistent with regular work, regular exercise, plain food and abundance of sleep.

*28 April. Bradford*
Sidney and I left London on our first investigation tour into local government . . . Between this diary and myself, I get on better at the actual investigation when Sidney is not there: he is shy in cross-examining officials, who generally begin by being unwilling witnesses and need gentle but

firm handling: he hates life in provincial lodgings and seeing each day new people, and this repugnance reacts on me and I get disheartened and wonder whether I have not led him into a useless adventure. In dealing with documents he is far more efficient than I, but in the manipulation of witnesses with a view of extracting confidential information his shyness and scepticism of the use of it gives me the advantage. And I am more ruthless in the exercise of my craft when he is not there to observe and perchance disapprove of my little tricks of the trade. . . .

Herbert Gladstone (1854–1930) had held office under his father: he was currently Chief Whip of the Liberal Party.

*16 May.* [41 Grosvenor Road]
. . . Whilst I am mainly occupied in this enquiry, Sidney engineers the School and to a lesser extent the University. He is in the background on the County Council, partly because he has been so long away, partly because he is considered a specialist in education. On educational matters he leads without dispute . . . No doubt this is due to his growing disinclination to push himself forward for any position desired by anyone else, his refusal to take any steps to start a career of political advancement. His dislike of the personal struggle for leadership becomes in fact greater and greater. He is as energetic and persistent as ever, but his energy is perpetually seeking the line of least resistance for the cause he believes in, and the line of least resistance for his cause is the line of least advancement for himself.
. . . Haldane brought a cordial invitation from Herbert Gladstone to Sidney to stand for Deptford or any other London constituency, all expenses to be paid by the party, a sign not of grace but of dire necessity. 'They think your standing would do them good,' said Haldane. 'But I told them,' he added in a half-bitter, half-playful tone, 'that, like Rosebery, you would neither come in nor go out.' 'Until we know who is to be the company,' I retorted, 'we shall stand in the doorway and help to block the door by standing there.'

*15 June. Manchester*
The third week here: Sidney stayed for a fortnight, and has now returned to his L.C.C. work. . . . At times we get discouraged at the bigness of our task; then we console each other by repeating, 'Well, if we cannot do it no one else can' – a conceited reflection. Today I am feeling somewhat lonely in the little lodging, a whole fortnight away from him.

When I am at work I do not feel otherwise than happy and fortunately I am well and can work my six hours. But after dinner when the cigarette is done I either feel depressed or my cursed habit of sentimental castle-building leads me to harp back to the past. Scenes, the vividness of which seem to make them real, dominate my mind and I lose my self-control. And then is the inevitable reaction. Oh, the mysteries of human feeling.

[*Beatrice later added this note.* This extract which I have typed myself, rather than give to be copied by my secretary, evokes no memory in my mind. But I assume from other entries of this and the following year that it related to my past relations with Joseph Chamberlain. This dramatizing of relationships or rather of prospective relationships has always been one of my bad habits – sometimes of quite casual and temporary relations, imaginary letters or encounters. Usually I have had some relationship 'on the stocks' – to use a vulgar expression. But these imaginary relationships have not interfered in any way with the main purpose of my life, at any rate not when I have been in normal health.]

*25 June. Baskerville House*
An act of piety. Some two months ago Clara Ryland lost her husband after a terrible illness, reaching over three years. Her letter revealing a dull despair, I offered to spend this Sunday with her. Here in a luxurious house live the two widowed sisters with no occupation except the routine of house and family, endowed with ample means, with no outside interests other than the circulating library and the talk about current politics and London Society brought them by the Great Man's family. . . . Clara, it is true, has her four little girls. But the home is empty of all but wealth; there is nothing to exhaust energy or stimulate thought – no brightness, no grace, no vigorous activity for others. There is nothing but a meaningless luxury.

This Congress was the first held by the International Council of Women. Its president, Lady Aberdeen (1857–1939), devoted herself to humanitarian causes. Mary Eliza Wright Sewall (1844–1920), a well-known educator and suffragist in America, was the vice-president.

*3 July.* [41 Grosvenor Road]
Back in London in time for the International Women's Congress. The American and Continental women took it quite seriously: but the more

experienced English women, whilst organizing it admirably, mocked at it in private. The press sneered at it, and the public generally ignored it – always excepting the entertainments of the duchesses and countesses who had been drawn in to patronize the Congress. It was not a failure, but hardly a success. The council meetings were stormy and unbusinesslike (I represented New Zealand owing to our recent visit to that land), resolving themselves into a duel between Mrs Creighton, backed up by the National Union of Women Workers set of English women, on the one hand, and on the other Mrs Wright Sewall (an autocratic and self-assertive American), supported by Lady Aberdeen and the American and Continental delegates. Great Britain and her faithful colonies were routed, which is what Mrs Creighton desired, as she wished the National Council [of Women] of Great Britain to withdraw from the International. It would have been better if the N.U.W.W. had refused to let itself be drawn into this adventure: it believed neither in Woman with a big 'W', nor in Internationalism with a big 'I'; it is distinctly parochial and religious – most emphatically insular. To the well-bred and conventional ladies who dominate it, the 'screeching sisterhood' demanding their rights represents all that is detestable. . . .

*24 July.* [41 Grosvenor Road]
. . . Our small circle of acquaintances is pleasant enough, easygoing, unconventional and somewhat distinguished. We are sought, we do not seek – the most agreeable way of seeing people. Not that Society pays us continuous attention: we are only casually found out by persons belonging to the great world. We live in a pleasant backwater of our own but our social status, such as it is, is distinctly advantageous to the local government enquiry: it enables us to see any official from whom we want information. . . .

> Beatrice enclosed a letter from Charles Booth written on 19 August in which he congratulates the Webbs on their 'last great book' which he had recently been reading, and adds his encouragement for their project on municipal institutions.

*10 September. High Borrans*
I was peculiarly glad to get this note from Charles Booth. It is on his part an unconscious testimony to the rightness of our marriage. . . . It is now two years since I have seen him – we have all of us acquiesced in not

meeting. But the bitterness of a broken friendship is past, and any day we might renew friendliness if not friendship.

Five weeks in Manchester in a little rented house, with our own maids to look after us and our secretary to help us – a peaceful, happy time, collecting material and, by a well-regulated life, keeping fit for persistent work. We are more interested in this enquiry than in trade unionism; the problems are multitudinous and the machinery intricate. . . .

> Captain Dreyfus (1859–1935), a French staff officer, was convicted of treason in 1894. The case was reopened when it was discovered that the evidence against him had been forged, but at a new court martial in 1899 he was again found guilty. There was world-wide indignation at the verdict. The war in the Transvaal began on 11 October after an ultimatum from President Kruger demanding the withdrawal of British troops from the frontiers of the Transvaal and the Orange Free State. Boer forces struck quickly and successfully at the ill-disposed British army. As Colonial Secretary, and the dominant imperialist in the Cabinet, Chamberlain was so plainly responsible for the breakdown of negotiations that the fighting was widely called 'Joe's War'. Sir Alfred Milner (1854–1925), High Commissioner for South Africa, was the dominant political figure in the Boer War campaign. F. J. Wheelan (1867–1955), a Bank of England clerk, was an active Fabian. Sydney Olivier (1859–1943), a civil servant who became Secretary of State for India, was a key member of the Fabian Society.

*10 October.* [41 Grosvenor Road]
Back in London after one week in Preston and two in Liverpool, staying with sister Holt. She is a dear old thing, as ugly, voluble, and warm-hearted as a woman could well be, exuberant in her vitality and desire to make everyone happy, somewhat disillusioned with domestic life . . . Our brother-in-law is not improving with age: his small-mindedness and secretiveness has degenerated into a restless kind of vanity, an undignified love of social esteem. It is pathetic to see his little mind always reverting to the glory of having refused a baronetcy. Oddly enough it was his position of mayor which fostered his instinct of self-importance: one would have thought that his social position was too big for that. . . . Lallie, divorced in feeling and interests from her husband, finds little companionship in her children and seeks recreation in lonely theological studies. Perhaps this trend towards the immaterial

and intellectual aspect of life has made her sympathetic to our work. She certainly has taken strongly to Sidney and begins to believe in his usefulness. . . .

This past summer, so far as personal life is concerned, has been full of enjoyment of work, health and love. But it has been marred by the nightmare of the Dreyfus case and the Transvaal crisis. I took a feverish interest in the Dreyfus trial, Sidney grew impatient and would not read it, but to me it had a horrible fascination, became a morbid background to my conscious activities. Equally unsavoury have been the doings of our own people in the Transvaal – an underbred business, from the Jameson Raid to the South African Committee of Enquiry, from the hushing-up of the Enquiry and the whitewashing of Rhodes to the flashy despatches of Milner and the vulgarly provocative talk of Chamberlain resulting in war with the Transvaal republic, that remnant of seventeenth-century puritanism.

I have been mortified that I could not think well of Chamberlain, puzzled to try and resist the atmosphere of hostile criticism of his action in Sidney's and Leonard's minds. . . . I feel the conviction growing that whatever may be the rights and wrongs of his policy in its broader issues, the methods have been vulgar and tricky, a conviction which may not be wholly impartial since I myself suffered years of pain, perhaps from the same coarse-grained indifference to other people's feelings which his critics say he has shown towards the Transvaal republic. I am a prey to an involved combination of bias and counter-bias. So I try to turn away my thoughts and refuse to pass judgement. Fortunately we are so far removed from political influence that it is not necessary for Sidney to express any opinion. We have a constant delight in our daily life of search after truth and loving companionship, far away from personal ambition, competitive struggle and notoriety. I should have hardened and coarsened if I had been subject to the strain of a big flashy social position. The sweet little person that he chose is far better suited to be his wife, a fact which may be taken to justify his action. . . .

*30 October.* [41 Grosvenor Road]
Haldane spent an hour or so with us this evening. Significant is the transformation in his attitude from a discreet upholder of Liberal solidarity to that of a rebel against the views of the majority, determined to assert himself. 'The Liberal Party is completely smashed, Mrs Webb,' and he beamed defiance. He had spent a month reading Transvaal blue-

books and was convinced that Milner was right and that war was from the first inevitable. The cleavage goes right through the Liberal Party into the Fabian Society. Shaw, Wallas and Whelen being almost in favour of the war, J. R. MacDonald and Sydney Olivier desperately against it, while Sidney occupies a middle position, thinks that better management might have prevented it but that now that it has begun recrimination is useless and that we must face the fact that henceforth the Transvaal and the Orange Free State must be within the British Empire.

Sidney lecturing at Oxford: I stayed here for my usual Wednesday afternoon at home. This is rapidly becoming a series of interviews with members of my class at the School of Economics. I enjoy lecturing every Thursday . . . The weekly class brings me into close connection with the work of the School: I see some half-dozen students every week and talk over their work with them. . . .

The Shaws have taken up their residence in Charlotte's attractive flat over the School of Economics, and Sidney and I meet there on Thursdays to dine sumptuously between our respective lectures. Charlotte and Shaw have settled down into the most devoted married couple, she gentle and refined, with happiness added thereto, and he showing no sign of breaking loose from her dominion. What the intellectual product of the marriage will be I do not feel so sure: at any rate he will not become a dilettante, the habit of work is too deeply engrained. It is interesting to watch his fitful struggles out of the social complacency natural to an environment of charm and plenty. How can atmosphere be resisted?

John Burns dined here last night. He is mellowed in temperament, he has lost his restless egotism and personal hatreds and something of his force . . . Of course he will go on being 'progressive', and will back up anything that can be put into an Act of Parliament. But like most untrained enthusiasts, experience of affairs has unhinged his faith and dulled his enthusiasm.

[?] *December.* [41 Grosvenor Road]
. . . The dismissal of Massingham from the editorship, and of the others from the staff of the *Daily Chronicle* reflects the strong patriotic sentiment of its readers, any criticism of the war at present is hopelessly unpopular. The cleavage of opinion about the war separates persons hitherto united and unites those who by temperament and training have hitherto been divorced. No one knows who is friend and who is enemy. Sidney does not take either side and is therefore suspected by

both. He is against the policy of thoroughness in dealing with the Boers. And who can fail to be depressed at the hatred of England on the Continent . . . Chamberlain has injured himself with the thinking men of all parties by his lack of kindliness, courtesy and discretion, but he is still the 'strong man' of politics: and the political 'pit' of men from the street likes the strong man and has no desire that he should mend his manners. Besides, he has convictions and he expresses them honestly and forcibly, qualities at present rare in the political world. I should gather from the growing irritability of his speeches that his splendid physique is giving way.

∾ 1900 ∾

Dissatisfaction with the government over the conduct of the war came to a head in January. There was a series of military reverses from 11 to 16 December – known as 'Black Week' – in which over two thousand men were killed. Parliament met on 30 January and the government faced charges of incompetence and mismanagement of ammunition and supplies.

*31 January. Torquay*
. . . A month at Plymouth at work together, with Spencer to help us, at the Plymouth records. For recreation we had two days' wandering on bicycles over Dartmoor in mist and rain, one or two walks with Sidney on Mount Batten, and pacing along on the Hoe watching the setting sun after the day's work was done. . . . The enquiry has been unexpectedly interesting; my health excellent; and the occasional forty-eight hours' cycling in country lanes round about the towns a joy and a delight, making up in intensity of pleasure for the longer holidays in the country. . . .

But the last six months, and especially the last days at Plymouth, have been darkened by the nightmare of war. The horrible consciousness that we have, at the best, shown ourselves to be unscrupulous in methods, vulgar in manners and inefficient to the last degree, is an unpleasant background to all one's personal life – this thought is always present when one wakes in the night and returns to it every hour of the day. The Boers are, man for man, our superiors in dignity, devotion and capacity – yes, *in capacity*. That is the hardest of these admissions. It may be that conflict was inevitable. I incline to think it was. But that it should come about through muddy intrigues and capitalist pressure and that we should have shown ourselves incapable both in statesmanship and in generalship is humiliating.

I wonder whether we could take a beating and benefit by it. This would be the *real* test of the heart and brain of the English race; much more so than eventual success in a long and costly conflict. If we ultimately win, we shall forget the lessons. We shall say once again, 'We muddled through all right!' . . .

To us, public affairs look gloomy, government is in the hands of small cliques; the middle class is definitely materialistic, the working class stupid and in large sections selfish, with no thought but the 'latest odds'. The social enthusiasm that inspired the intellectual proletariat of ten years ago has died down and given place to scepticism about the desirability, or possibility, of any substantial change in society . . . meanwhile we are rolling in wealth. Almost every class, except the miserable sweated worker, has more than they are accustomed to. Pleasure and ease, ease and pleasure, are now what is chiefly desired by men and women: science, literature and art, even social ambition and party feeling, seem to have been ousted by the desire for mental excitement and physical enjoyment. If we found ourselves face to face with real disaster, should we still have the nerve and persistency to stand upright before it? That is the question that haunts me.

Sir Henry Campbell-Bannerman (1836–1908), a Scots businessman, was an active member of Gladstone's governments. In January 1899 he became leader of the Liberal Party and led the opposition to Chamberlain's South Africa policy. Consistently underrated by the Webbs, he became an effective Prime Minister in 1906.

*20 February. Grosvenor Road*
From all accounts matters are going from bad to worse with the Liberal Party. Rosebery, Haldane says, has decided that the Liberal Party is no good as an instrument for him, and the bulk of the Liberals are angry at his aloofness and upsetting interventions. Campbell-Bannerman, nominally a 'sane' Imperialist, is at heart a 'Peace man' with all the old Liberal principles and prejudices writ large on his mind – retrenchment in public expenditure and no compulsion either at home or abroad. The little clique of Imperialists – Asquith, Grey and Haldane – have been forced to sit tight on the fence, openly condemning the methods whilst they secretly approve of the policy of the government . . . wherever two or three Liberals are gathered together there is a wrangle which ends in a black ball or a motion for expulsion in a Liberal club . . . Meanwhile,

our schemes for London University prosper. The School is recognized as the Faculty of Economics. We have secured a site and money for a building and an income of £2,500 from the T.E.B. to be spent on economics and commercial subjects. Sidney will be a member of the Faculty and represent the Faculty on the Senate. Best of all, he has persuaded the Commission to recognize economics as a science and not merely as a subject in the Arts Faculty. . . . We have always claimed that the study of the structure and function of society was as much a science as the study of any other form of life and ought to be pursued by the scientific methods used in other organic sciences. . . . Of course the School is at present extremely imperfect: its reputation is better than its performance. But we have no illusions and we see clearly what we intend the School to become and we are convinced that we shall succeed.

On 20 February D. A. Thomas, later Lord Rhondda (1856–1918), a Liberal M.P., moved for a fresh enquiry into the Jameson Raid of 1895. This attack by the anti-war group revived old arguments about the white-washing of Rhodes and the crucial telegrams which were not produced at the original enquiry. Chamberlain's reply was called 'a brilliant rhetorical feat'. Martinus Steyn (1857–1916) was President of the Orange Free State 1896–1900. William Schreiner (1857–1919) was Premier of the Cape 1898–1900; his sister was the novelist Olive Schreiner.

*23 February.* [41 Grosvenor Road]
Beatrice Chamberlain came to lunch on Wednesday, ostensibly to tell me about poor Clara Ryland, but really to find out what we felt about the Transvaal. She was as vigorous and attractive as is her wont, a fine generous nature, reflecting the best side of her father. Her tone about the Transvaal was far more moderate and magnanimous than I expected, not nearly so partisan as some of my sisters. Against Steyn of the Free State she was distinctly venomous and she was deprecatory of Schreiner and the Cape government. 'They have been deplorably weak, they have run from one side to the other, imploring each alternately to climb down. And though Schreiner eventually slipped down on our side he did so not out of loyalty but merely to save himself.' All this I disputed with some warmth. When her carriage was announced, I noticed a look of nervous dissatisfaction on her face and she ran upstairs to put on her veil, I following. With an effort she broke out: 'You will congratulate Papa on having smashed his detractors last night?'

'We never attached much importance to the telegram,' I answered affectionately. 'What other people say Mr Chamberlain said is not evidence,' I added. Her face brightened and she said something about misunderstandings of conversations when two persons were referring to different things, from which I gather that we are right in assuming that the telegrams are similar in character to those already published. If only Chamberlain had not whitewashed Rhodes! Though I am inclined to believe that his defence of Rhodes sprang from a defiant loyalty to a man in whose devotion to the Empire he has complete confidence, this explanation is not quite convincing.

*8 March.* [Brighton]
A week with Herbert Spencer at Brighton . . . The old man is better and more benign than I have seen him for years. But about the world in general and England in particular he is terribly pessimistic. . . . He still retains his personal affection for me – more out of habit, I think, for every year he becomes more suspicious of our aims and of our power of reaching these aims. His housekeeping has become quite comfortable: two bright young persons as housekeeper and pianist respectively, three maids, a houseboy, coachman and a secretary, all dancing attendance on the old man. His secretary has not had a holiday for ten years and his two young ladies are kept close at it all day and every day 'making a pleasant circle for me', he calls it . . . Poor old man, it is pathetic to see a nature so transparently sincere, warped by long-continued flattery and subordination of others to his whims and fancies into the character of a complete egotist, pedantic and narrow-minded – a true Casaubon.

> Edward Henry Carson Q.C. (1854–1935) was a prominent Ulsterman and one of the leading advocates of his day. Sir William Ramsay (1852–1916), research chemist and Nobel prizewinner, was professor of chemistry at University College, London.

*16 March. Grosvenor Road.*
Utterly done up with a week of dissipation. The day I came back I dined with Alfred (Cripps) at the House of Commons in a private room without ventilation – a veritable hole of Calcutta. Margaret Hobhouse had to leave, finding it unbearable. I struggled on, chatting with Carson, a clever, cynical and superficial Irishman, an ultra-Tory on all questions. 'Gerald Balfour, the worst Irish Secretary we have had: he and his brother have done more to make Home Rule possible than all the preceding governments put together.' . . .

On Friday we had a little dinner of friends here. On Sunday we supped with Willie Cripps. On Monday I debated in the Chelsea Town Hall with an anti-regulationist, on Tuesday we had to dine with us the Creightons and Professor Ramsay to talk London University, and on Wednesday we dined with Haldane to meet a select party of Roseberyites, including the man himself. Haldane sat me down next Lord Rosebery against the will of the latter, who tried his best to avoid me . . . But feeling that our host would be mortified if his little scheme failed utterly, I laid myself out to be pleasant to my neighbour, though he aggravated and annoyed me by his ridiculous airs: he might be a great statesman, a royal Prince, a beautiful woman and an artistic star all rolled into one. 'Edward,' called out Lord Rosebery to Sir Edward Grey as the latter, arrayed in Court dress, hurried away to the Speaker's party, 'don't tell the world of this new intrigue of Haldane's.' And I believe Lord Rosebery winked as he glanced at me sitting by him. Which showed that he had at least a sense of humour. For the party *was* an intrigue of Haldane's, an attempt to piece together an anti-little-England combination out of the most miscellaneous morsels of political influence. 'I feel deeply honoured at the place you gave me, Mr Haldane,' I said as he saw me out of his luxurious flat, 'but if I were four and twenty hours in the same house with that man I should be rude to him.' Haldane is now amusing himself by weaving, from his gossiping imagination, a Rosebery-Webb myth.

Consequent on all this dissipation . . . My brain is all wool and my thoughts, are wool-gathering.

### 22 May. Marlborough

The last three months have not been satisfactory. My work has not had my best thought and feeling, foolish day-dreams based on self-consciousness and personal vanity . . . a certain physical reluctance to intellectual effort – have all combined to make my work half-hearted and unreal. Sidney is free from all these defects and every day I live with him the more I love and honour the single-mindedness of his public career and his single-hearted devotion to his wife. And every year I appreciate more fully the extraordinary good luck which led me to throw in my lot with him. Just as it was the worst part of my nature that led me into my passionate feeling for Chamberlain so it was the best part of my nature which led me to accept Sidney after so much doubt and delay. And certainly, just as I was well punished for the one, I have been richly rewarded for the other course of feeling and conduct. And yet, notwithstanding this conviction, I find my thoughts constantly wandering to the great man and his family, watching his career with sympathy and interest and desiring his welfare. Sometimes I think I should like to meet him again. At other times I reject the thought as a needless expenditure of feeling. But all this is sentimentalism; it has little to do with any deep emotion. I am at most times buoyantly happy in my love for my boy and in my interest in my work. My sentimentalism is a mere plaything but playthings take time and thought. . . .

*23 May.* [41 Grosvenor Road]
. . . if we are to think out the development of local government in all its different phases, from our chaotic notes, it is clear that I must be free from the distractions of London life. Relations, old friends, Continental and American admirers, students and persons who can help us in our investigations, all have to receive their due amount of attention. I am on excellent terms with the family – the sisters have taken to us and are beginning to wish that we should see much of them and their children. This means the giving and taking of dinners, chaperoning girls on bicycling parties, putting up public schoolboys on their trips to London. The old friends seem to look reproachful when one evades their offers to call or refuses point blank to lunch or dine with them. . . . Lastly there are a multitude of persons one ought to see in connection with local government. And as a penalty for possessing a social conscience, in the background of all the other, the ghostly forms of all sorts and conditions of men, who have helped me in the past to get information on the subjects I was investigating – employers, philanthropists, trade unionists, Co-operators. The only way out of the whole tangle is to get out of London. This we will do next spring.

In February 1899 Rosy married George Dobbs (1869–1946), who worked for the publishing house of Dent. After the marriage he and a colleague started their own publishing firm, but soon went bankrupt and the partner disappeared. The Potter sisters, who had disapproved of the marriage, offered to pay the debts provided that the couple went to live abroad. They settled in Switzerland and Dobbs worked for a travel business. But there was continuing trouble. On 20 May Beatrice wrote that Rosy was 'mad, bad or worse', and complained of the 'insane desire for flattery and for physical indulgence' that led her to 'torture' Dobbs with jealousy. Twenty years later, reading this critical note, Beatrice remarked that she was ashamed of her own 'uncharitableness and lack of reasoning sympathy' and added that Rosy had become 'one of the best and most selfless of women'. Carrie Darling had died of peritonitis.

### 12 June. Leicester

Staying at a rough boarding-house, best in Leicester, for a fortnight's investigation . . . house dirty, meals rough and monotonous and service inefficient but willing. We pay two guineas a week each, for which we get a good bedroom, a small sitting-room and our meals with some half a dozen other boarders. . . . Sidney feels the discomfort more than I do: the greater fastidiousness of the man, I suppose. . . . This Whitsun has been a melancholy time. The Dobbs crisis has cast a deep shadow over the whole family. . . .

Then there was the blow of Carrie Darling's death, that brave, spirited, devoted nature, thinking only of others as she lay dying; and the fact that she desired to see me, the message reaching me too late, oppressed me with a heavy melancholy. While she lay dying I was idling at Bernard Shaw's pretty little place in Surrey. A minor element in my unhappiness was the discomfort that we had more or less imposed ourselves on the Shaws and that Charlotte Shaw did not want to have us. Perhaps this was a morbid impression. But it is clear that now she is happily married we must not presume upon her impulsive hospitality and kindly acquiescence in our proposals. All this made me glad to get to work again . . . I need hard work and obscurity to keep me in good moral condition. The one happiness which never seems to injure me is Sidney's adoring love. . . .

### 4 July. Grosvenor Road

It was on the terrace of the House of Commons that we met again – after an interval of thirteen years – one of Haldane's large dinner-parties of London Society folk. We were awaiting the last comers. Suddenly Mr Chamberlain appeared, apparently seeking some friends he expected to dine with him. We looked at each other and I stepped forward and we shook hands. 'I should like to introduce my husband to you,' I said after we had exchanged a few words. Then I left him and Sidney talking together and turned to fellow guests and tried hard to make conversation. In a few minutes he came and shook hands with me again and disappeared. The assembled company, who had watched us keenly, closed in and in five minutes we were dining in a private room, I talking vigorously to Lord Battersea and Mr Haldane.

We sat out after dinner on the terrace and just as I was explaining to

George Wyndham that 'a Tory was a man without prejudices compared to a Liberal' I became aware that Mr Chamberlain had joined us. He sat by me and we talked – America, Birmingham University, economics. He looked wan and tired; he was uncertain of himself and obviously anxious to be gentle and kindly towards me. It may have been an hour that we chatted on together till I felt that this somewhat hollow talk, all the while under the close and amused observation of this little set of London Society folk, was becoming oppressive, and I rose with the words: 'I think we must be going.' 'Mrs Webb is terminating the interview,' said Mrs Paul to Sidney, as the great man grasped my hand and hurriedly departed. Then I felt conscious that all the company became exceptionally polite and I cursed the fate that brought the casual reopening of the relationship again under the eye of London Society. After I was back in my own home I had time to reflect that on the whole it is better that we have met and been friendly with one another, and that I have shown him that I have no grudge against him and that I am happy in my own life. The lines of our lives cannot bring us together. He is old, I am elderly, we are both of us absorbed in work and interests, he is in the great world currents, I in a backwater of specialism. It may be that our efforts are to some extent antagonistic. Still for all that there is a bond of sentiment between us, I for the man I loved, loved but could not follow.

One humorous incident in this melodrama. On my introducing Sidney the great man said in a tone of kindly condescension: 'I think you were in MY office, Mr Webb.' Sidney replied quickly, 'That is hardly quite correct: when I was there YOU were not.' Sidney told me afterwards that he was conscious of a gaucherie. He meant to say that he had not had the honour of serving under him. But that was not the effect.

*19 July.* [41 Grosvenor Road]
A month in London entertaining, shopping and seeing sisters, snatching from this waste of energy two or three mornings at the B.M. over local newspapers. Longing to get back to quiet days of absorption in our subject. Sidney struggles on, engineering the School, its site, its building, its status as a university institution. Breakfast at 8 sharp; from 9.15 to 1 o'clock we read at the B.M., then back to lunch, he off to his committees and I to anything that turns up. Nearly every day we entertain at lunch or dinner or dine out ourselves. . . .

We have seen much of the Leonard Courtneys this spring. Leonard's determined support of the Boers' plea for independence, even more his denunciation of the war, has alienated him from both political parties. . . . What hurts him most, oddly enough, is the social boycott. Leonard has always enjoyed the leisurely society of persons of culture and position, and today he and Kate find themselves without the accustomed invitations . . . Dear Kate is an incurable sentimentalist and has no sense of humour. She gives happiness and increased self-assurance to Leonard but she aggravates his one big fault – his inveterate mental habit of thinking everyone who disagrees with him immoral or unenlightened. All the same there are few mortals for whom I have so continuous an affection and respect as I have for Leonard Courtney and his worshipful mate.

Political parties become daily more chaotic. The Tories are, as a party, complete cynics, bound together by a rampant imperialism . . . The great Liberal Party – 'the engine of progress' – has lost its old faith and has no notion in which direction progress lies. . . . The Fabian Society, it must be admitted, is completely out of the running. The majority believe in the inevitability of the war whilst the minority accuse the majority of being the worst kind of traitors to the socialist cause.

*31 July.* [41 Grosvenor Road]
Spent Sunday with Alfred at Parmoor. This spring has been a bad time for him. An attack of influenza left him a hypochondriacal wreck. Following on this illness one of his boys got into trouble at school which upset him quite unnecessarily. On the top of it all came the appointment of Carson as Solicitor-General and the spiteful comments in the press of the relative advantage of being a 'bad' and a 'good' boy. Whether Alfred would have cared to give up his large income at the Bar for the Solicitor-Generalship is a question, but he would certainly have liked the refusal of it. . . .

The Webbs spent much of the summer on Tyneside, with a three-week rest at Bamburgh on the coast. The general election of October 1900, known as the 'khaki election' because the Conservatives capitalized on the recent victories in South Africa, resulted in an increase in the Tory majority. The newly formed Labour Representation Committee, which linked the I.L.P. and the trade unions, managed only to return Keir Hardie and one other candidate. Haldane and the other Liberal Imperialists were putting pressure on Rosebery at this time to lead the anti-Campbell-Bannerman forces within the Liberal Party.

*5 August. St Philip's Vicarage, Newcastle*
In the intervals of reading the proceedings of the Newcastle Town Council I study the works of theologians, Protestant and Catholic, stowed away in this house. Impressed with the egotism and narrow-mindedness of Evangelical divines. . . .

*7 October. Grosvenor Road*
The Liberal Party, divided against itself, uncertain as to its policy, is being badly routed at the polls. 'The strong man' of the government [Chamberlain] has played it down low to the man in the street: the street has answered back with emphatic approval. And in doing so the electors have shown common sense. Who would trust a party with a lay figure as ostensible leader, and as the real leaders of its sections men who hate each other and each other's ideas, more than they do the persons or the views of the enemy. . . . Meanwhile we go on, little concerned with the stress and storm . . . We realize every day more strongly that we can never hope to get hold of the 'man in the street'; we are too 'damned intellectual', as a shrewd journalist remarked. . . . Our business is to be friendly to men of all parties, to *try* to be charitable and unassuming, and to go on with our work persistently and loyally. . . .

*19 October.* [41 Grosvenor Road]
Massingham came in last Sunday week and found me alone. . . . He led the conversation on to Chamberlain. 'I hear he has trouble at home: his wife has left him; at least,' he said slowly, 'she took no part in the elections and is travelling on the Continent.' I was so taken aback that I was silent for a few seconds and I felt Massingham looking at me. 'How very terrible,' escaped from me. 'I thought they were so fond of each other.' And then I began to talk of other matters.

Since then I have been struggling with a terrible depression. It may be that I am not physically well. But the thought of the misery of the man I loved haunts me and disables me. I find myself wondering in a useless sort of way why there has been a breach in what from all reports was the most fortunate marriage for him, whether she has repudiated him on account of the 'contract scandal' in which his name has figured. Anyway, if it is true, it is horribly cruel, equal misery to each of them, for what can one of them do without the other? Then I console myself: the whole story may be a libel, invented by hostile journalists. I am allowing myself to be a victim to a foolish and exaggerated sentiment. For after all, what have I to do with it? I have my own life, and my own love, and my own work and I am fully absolved by the past from any responsibility for his happiness. But oh! the pity of it!

*16 November.* [41 Grosvenor Road]
A month of miserable suspense, watching the newspapers to see if Chamberlain was travelling with his wife, a horrible suspicion that he may be acting brutally to her, and yet suffering himself and laying up for both a store of pain in the future. Oh, my cursed imagination. And then a morbid consciousness that owing to that most unfortunate meeting on the terrace in the summer there are some persons who are going about attributing to me the separation, I who have never met her and I who have only seen him once in thirteen years. Of course at the base of this morbid feeling there is a strain of self-conscious remorse. If I had not felt assured that these two were absolutely devoted to each other, that they had as ideal relation to one another as I and Sidney, I would not have remained friends with Clara Ryland and Beatrice. But I desired to be friends with him and his wife and was anxious to intimate that I bore no grudge to either of them. However all this is morbid and exaggerated. I must turn my thoughts away. All I want to feel certain of, in my own conduct, is that if ever I meet him again my whole influence, if I have any, shall be devoted towards their reconciliation.

And to think that I am over forty, and he is over sixty! What an absurdity!

*9 December.* [41 Grosvenor Road]
. . . Charles Booth called one afternoon last week. I was pleased though surprised until I discovered that he had come to canvass Sidney with regard to the post of L.C.C. statistician on behalf of one of his research secretaries. . . .

My relationship to the Booths seems now permanently broken. Last winter there was a flicker of friendliness but when I offered to cycle over with Sidney to Gracedieu from Leicester, last Whitsun, I was peremptorily put off, I think with some incivility, for they knew we were in lodgings for over a fortnight in broiling hot weather a few miles from their gates and they did not ask us even to lunch! That I think was a conclusive intimation that all relations were at an end and Charlie's formal call to canvass Sidney for a good situation for one of his cast-off workers was hardly a tactful act, or likely to accomplish its end, even if the end has been a legitimate one. I often wonder what has caused this breach, and why Mary at any rate has never been willing to bridge it over. I still hate the thought of it, but as each effort of mine is a repulse and fresh pain, there seems no other way than to look on those two friends – for I care for them still – as to me dead. But it hurts one to see their ghosts.

Our autumn has been dissipated with odds and ends. Sidney has been absorbed in his administrative work. London University proves to be the most formidable addition to the L.C.C. and the Technical Education Board . . . And I have been wasting my time as far as our work is concerned, in rather bad health, nursing Alfred, lecturing at the School – and dreaming. I often wonder how much I lose by my persistent habit of 'romancing' – perhaps, after all, it fills up time when energy is at a low ebb. But it is not wholesome and leaves a bad frame of mind. We need an authoritative mental hygiene.

*15 December.* [41 Grosvenor Road]
Met Campbell-Bannerman at Lord Reay's last night. A quite stupid person, for a leader, well suited to a position of a wealthy squire or a sleeping partner in an inherited business. Vain.

～ 1901 ～

*New Year's Day.* [41 Grosvenor Road?]
Every newspaper is national stocktaking, reviewing the new year and forecasting the future in jerky epigrams. Back from ten days' holiday I feel vigorous and active-minded and inclined to give way to the prevailing epidemic. . . .

And looking back on my life as a whole how does it read? Difficult to express in its complications. Three strands of consciousness, intertwined with each other and yet distinct – the body, the emotions and the intellect. Chronic bad health and constant physical pain made me, as a child and a girl, detestably aware of my body – spells of over-exertion and over-eating were followed by exhaustion and under-nourishment. Such mental life as I enjoyed was almost exclusively intellectual. My emotions were not roused. . . . Such was my soul's existence until Mother's death in 1882.

Then came the spring of my nature into health and vigour and a rich seed-time of intellectual life. . . . Then came the catastrophe . . . At a London dinner-party I met Joseph Chamberlain. At once, and I think on both sides, there arose the question of marriage. He was seeking a wife, attractive, docile and capable. I was ripe for love, revelling in newly acquired health and freedom, my intelligence wide awake, my heart unclaimed. I was ambitious, more ambitious than perhaps I knew, to play a part in the world. He had energy and personal magnetism, in a word masculine force to an almost superlative degree. Instantaneously he dominated my emotional nature and aroused my latent passion. But my intellect not only remained free but positively hostile to his influence. . . . And so it came to pass that in spite of great personal attraction on both sides we did not marry one another and that after four years' storm and stress I was left bleeding and wounded . . . What happened to him throughout this long adventure I do not know. Probably the whole episode was comparatively unimportant. Undoubtedly his pride was wounded in the early stages; he felt that he had been snubbed by my family and possibly by myself; afterwards his taste was unsatisfied. That last visit in 1887 he saw a woman, no longer young, living without the surroundings of wealth and social position, badly dressed and without any apparent distinction. And in spite of knowing that I loved him desperately, he turned away and left me. At the time I was ready to condemn him. But that condemnation has long passed away. A riper experience of life has taught me that the one mortal sin towards another is to enter into the intimacy of married life (with or without the marriage ceremony) without love, without faith in your enduring love. So after a period of fourteen years there remains only a tenderness for the man I loved, taking the form of an almost exaggerated desire for his success and happiness.

Meanwhile . . . my intellect had been leading a quite separate life. . . . Indeed my pain and humiliation seemed to intensify my desire to push forward on my own lines. . . . Possibly I owe a debt to Chamberlain. He absorbed the whole of my sexual feeling, but I saw him at rare intervals and loved him through the imagination, in his absence more than in his presence. This emotional preoccupation made my companionship with other men free from personal preferences and deliberately controlled with a view to ends. . . . Passion burnt itself out . . . Intellectual interest grew year by year. . . .

In this state of mind I met Sidney . . . Nearly nine years of married life leads me to bless the institution and my good fortune in entering it with such a partner. We are still on our honeymoon and every year makes our relationship more tender and complete. . . . For the first six years of our married life we . . . lived little in the world . . . This last year we have seemed to drift upward in the strata of society . . . It may be that the circumstances of our work will drift us more into the stream of the big world; it may be that we shall remain pretty well where we are today.

It is a toss-up which course will best promote our plans. One cannot associate with great personages without considerable expenditure of nerves and means, and all this expenditure must come off our efforts in administration and investigation. On the other hand England is governed by cliques of friends and acquaintances. If you are inside the clique you help to rule: if you are outside you cry in the wilderness. . . .

*2 January.* [41 Grosvenor Road]
Back in London after a few days with the Playnes and Hobhouses. The sisters do not grow apart as years roll on: indeed the last few years have seemed to bring us all nearer together. Blood relationship is a very tenacious tie. It outlasts many relationships of choice . . . Old friends die, or marry, or become estranged or indifferent. Of my early friendships few remain . . . the two dear comrades and friends who for some half-dozen years regularly spent their holidays with us – Wallas and Shaw – are both of them married, and though when we meet, we meet as old friends, we seldom see each other. With Audrey Wallas I find it difficult to be sympathetic . . . still, my respect for her increases year by year. Charlotte Shaw does not specially like me, and while meaning to be most friendly, arranges her existence so as to exclude most of Shaw's old friends. And possibly they would all of them say that we were too much absorbed in each other to care for others . . . The man we see most of nowadays is Hewins: every Tuesday he lunches with us to discuss the affairs of the School. He is original-minded and full of energy and faith. Shaw always declares he is a fanatic. So he is. But he is also a born manipulator. . . . With such a character it is difficult to be intimate, however much it may excite one's admiration, liking and interest. . . .

I feel sometimes in despair about 'the Book'. . . . The one subject my mind revolts at is local government. But we shall have to set to and do it directly the L.C.C. election is over. . . .

*15 January.* [41 Grosvenor Road]
Mandell Creighton, Bishop of London – dead. One of our best friends.

When we returned to London this autumn we found him invalided. . . . Three or four times I went down to Fulham to see him. The very last time . . . I told him our plan for reforming the Church, our idea of religion as 'mental hygiene' and the way in which we thought the

High Church doctrine more consistent with it, than the Evangelical. To all of which he listened, and half seriously and half playfully agreed. Then I sent him [William] James's *Will to Believe*. . . .

I first knew the Creightons in August 1887. . . . And from the first they liked and trusted me, liked me for my best side. When I engaged myself to Sidney, they accepted him as their friend without hesitation, saw him through my eyes, and trusted him as they had trusted me. . . .

Our intimacy with Dr Creighton . . . has brought constantly before us the Church, its present difficulties and its future. . . . Of course, our object is to enable the Church to grow out of its present superstitious doctrine and obsolete forms. We have faith that the development would be along the right lines. No doubt at first the direction would be sacerdotal and ritualistic. Personally I do not altogether object to this. The more ritual, the more mystery, the more indefiniteness of thought, the greater the play for emotional purposes. . . . And though there are aspects of the priest which are distasteful . . . We need the expert here as elsewhere. Religion, to my mind, should consist in the highest metaphysic, music and ritual and mental hygiene.

And I desire that the national life should have its *consciously* religious side. . . . I should desire the Church to become the home of national communal aspirations as well as of the endeavour of the individual towards a better personal life. . . .

Queen Victoria died on 22 January, but Beatrice does not mention this.

*9 February.* [41 Grosvenor Road]
Met Lord Rosebery at Haldane's again. . . . I sat next to the great man, who was gracious and less self-conscious than last time. But the entertainment was a futile business. We talked and laughed, 'showed off': we never got anywhere near a useful discussion . . . I was angry with myself afterwards, and was strangely enough, a bit vexed at being the only lady! That would not have mattered had we talked seriously, but in mere light banter 'the eternal feminine' will intrude and in that case one likes companionship.

But undoubtedly our excursions into Society advance the interests of the School. We are to have a meeting at the Mansion House with the Lord Mayor in the chair; Lord Rosebery to make a great pronouncement in favour of commercial education in the abstract and the School in the concrete, Lord Rothschild to act as Treasurer and other great persons to play up, the whole intended to raise a Building and Endowment fund for the School. All this is Haldane's doing . . . 'My dear Hewins,' says Haldane, 'you ignore the personal factor in politics.' For Hewins, though he willingly accepts the result, does not wholly like this 'Society' development.

And, in truth, it has its unpleasant side. It is much wholesomer to win by hard work than by these capricious gusts of fancy in great folk. I feel that I am skating on rotten ice which might suddenly give way under me. I am not afraid of losing the support of the 'Personages' because one does not count on its continuance . . . What I do fear is weakness in my own nature, incapacity to keep my intellect and heart set on our own work . . . Fortunately Sidney is absolutely single-minded. But like Hewins he does not *quite* like it.

*8 March.* [41 Grosvenor Road]
Brilliant victory at the L.C.C. election. . . . we can at last turn back to the Book. . . . London life, with its constant clash of personalities, its attractions and repulsions, its manipulations and wire-pulling, is distracting and somewhat unwholesome. And this last year I seem to have passed into an emotional and imaginative phase, which, while it gives me a certain magnetic effect on others, knocks me to pieces myself. Indeed, I feel [that I am] becoming mediumistic. Country life and intellectual concentration will, I trust, bring back a saner frame of mind. Brainwork is a wonderful specific against the manifold forms of hysteria.

*22 March.* [41 Grosvenor Road]
Our long-planned meeting at the Mansion House came off yesterday. . . . I feel now that we have done our utmost to give the School an independent life . . . Sidney is now turning his mind to the University and has drafted a scheme for the complete reorganization of the University as a great centre of applied science. . . . Meanwhile my boy is exceptionally well and happy. . . . And I think the 'setting' I have given him of simple fare and distinguished friends suits him, both in reputation and taste. It satisfies his sense of consistency to adhere to a democratic standard of expenditure, and yet he reaps many of the advantages, in the scope and variety of social intercourse, of belonging to the inner circle of the political and scientific world. . . .

Beatrice spent Easter with Sidney at Lulworth Cove and for much of the summer stayed with the Russells at Friday's Hill.

*24 April. Churchfield, West Lulworth, Dorset*

A large thatched cottage with low straggling rooms, plain, clean but not too comfortably furnished, has been our living place for the last three weeks. The village is in a hollow of the chalk downs, without trees and cut off from the sight of the sea. . . . But once on the downs, there are glorious stretches of well-shaped hill and abrupt chalk cliff, expanses of sea and sky, and on the other side the most beautiful plain of heath and moor and wooded promontory with bright little rivers running in all directions except seaward. The colouring these last days has been exquisite, the sea – sapphire, amethyst, emerald, moonstone – the white chalk cliff rising out of it in mysterious lines of white, pink, grey. . . .

The first fortnight was wet and cold and, beyond our regulation two hours' walk in the afternoon, we stayed in and worked . . . The last week has been glorious summer weather and we have taken lovely rides inland or long walks along the cliffs on either side. Other times I have blissfully brooded and prayed for guidance and strength. A great peace has come over me. I am again completely absorbed in my subject and completely satisfied with the companionship of nature and the comradeship of my partner, lover, husband. . . .

Sidney away and I play. . . . The day is gloriously hot and I find myself cradled on the rocks . . . Heat and coolness, motion and rest, sun and water, tide and rock – is it the contrasts that are so enchanting? . . . On the horizon the stern outline of Portland and visions of convicts working under the midday sun on the [prison] quarries, squalid lives behind them – mean streets, hot, crowded, one-roomed homes, lack of nourishment, drink, intolerable vacant-mindedness, gambling, monotonous labour, adventurous crime, darkness and dirt, glaring lights and debauch – contrasted evils! I watch the sun's rays dancing on the sea . . . And then I drift on to the personal question. Are the books we have written together worth (to the community) the babies we might have had? Then again, I dream over the problem of whether one would marry the same man, in order to have babies, that one would select as joint author? The old, old question, always being put afresh to our civilization. Ought a man or a woman to have many relations with the other sex or only one? I think of the peace and happiness of these last weeks – the strenuous thought, the long hours of joyful enjoyment of light, colour, form, the physical relief of exercise and the equal relief of rest. I see my boy's blue eyes resting on me with love as he grasps my bicycle to push it up a hard bit of hill, I hear his voice praising me for some rearrangement of our chapter, I see him writing page after page, hour after hour, while I am mooning over a fire or wandering up and down a lane, 'cried off' because I am tired! I think what a fraud I am apart from him, how little I really contribute to the joint work, merely a 'fly-wheel' to get him over 'dead points'.

I decide that the answer is: one lover, not only in the letter but in the spirit. And this is all noonday dreaming, another contrast, a purely fanciful contrast, with no bearing on my personal life. . . .

*1 July. Friday's Hill*
A pleasant, comfortable house – with no special distinction, surrounded by tall spreading trees, a terraced lawn, with meadows sloping in curved lines towards the Fernhurst Valley behind wooded hills; beyond them again, the bare South Downs . . . The Russells are the most attractive married couple I know. Young and virtuous, they combine in the pair personal charm, unique intelligence, the woman having the one, the man the other, in the superlative degree. . . . As individuals they are remarkable. Alys comes of an American Quaker family. She is charming to look at – tall, graceful . . . If she has a defect it is a certain colourlessness of intellect and a certain lack of 'temperament'. But in a woman are these defects?

Bertrand is a slight, dark-haired man, with prominent forehead, bright eyes, strong features except for a retreating chin, nervous hands and alert quick movements. In manner and dress and outward bearing he is most carefully trimmed . . . In morals he is a puritan; in personal habits almost an ascetic, except that he lives for efficiency and therefore expects to be kept in the best physical condition. But intellectually he is audacious – an iconoclast, detesting religions or social convention, suspecting sentiment, believing only in the 'order of thought' and the order of things, in logic and in science. He indulges in the wildest paradox and in the broadest jokes, the latter always too abstrusely intellectual in their form to be vulgarly coarse. He is a delightful talker, especially in general conversation, when the intervention of other minds prevents him from tearing his subject to pieces with fine chopping logic. . . . He looks at the world from a pinnacle of detachment, dissects persons and demolishes causes. And yet he recognizes that as a citizen you must be a member of a party, therefore he has joined the Fabian Society! And more or less accepts Sidney as his 'representative' man. But the kernel of his life is research into the processes of reasoning. . . . What he lacks is sympathy and tolerance for other people's emotions, and, if you regard it as a virtue, Christian humility. The outline of both his intellect and his feelings are sharp, hard and permanent. He is a good hater.

I observe in Bertrand a curious parallel between his intellectual and his moral nature. He is intolerant of blemishes and faults in himself and others, he dreams of Perfection in man. . . . I analyse and describe my own and others' faults. But these faults seldom offend me in themselves . . . I have no 'sense of sin' and no desire to see it punished. Bertrand, on the other hand, is almost cruel in his desire to see cruelty revenged. . . .

A. C. F. Rabagliati (b. 1843), a notable food reformer, wrote *Air, Food and Exercise* (1897). The Boer War had reached a stage of guerrilla warfare: the British army was trying to complete its victories in the field by burning farms and driving civilians into concentration camps. At a dinner of the National Reform Union on 14 June Campbell-Bannerman condemned this policy as 'the methods of barbarism'. Many of his supporters thought he had gone too far; some fifty Liberals showed their disapproval by abstaining in a vote against the government. Asquith led the attack and the Liberal Imperialists arranged a dinner in his honour. There were so many political dinners and counter-dinners that it was said there was 'war to the knife and fork' among the Liberals. Shaw urged Sidney to support Rosebery as the politician most susceptible to permeation, and as the potential leader of a new political group which might lead to a government of national efficiency. Sidney drafted a forceful article, polished by Shaw, which was published as 'Lord Rosebery's Escape from Houndsditch' in the September issue of the *Nineteenth Century*.

### 1 October, Grosvenor Road

A most unsatisfactory vacation. Four weeks spent high up in a Yorkshire dale with mountain pasture and moorland stretching upwards some 1500 feet above us, and one bad road up and down the vale. For a long-distance walker [Sunniside?] would be a delightful spot, but for Sidney and I who depend on bicycles and can only walk some six or seven miles, it was monotonous and tiring. We never seemed to get out of sight of the village. Then our quarters at the inn were noisy – children, clogged, playing on stone sets, herds of cows coming home to be milked and the whole village turning out to talk, laugh and smoke in the summer evenings. Our hostess was always in a slatternly condition, and her kitchen combined the cooking of food with a village bar. There was a miserable little boy about the place . . . Perhaps it was because I was not well that 'Tommy' got on my nerves – the thought of this little, unhappy wretch, underfed, untrained, picking up vices and virtues, kept on there because it was less expensive than apprenticing him to a trade, became intolerable. And my personal sensations throughout the time were the reverse of pleasant: a constant feeling of fatigue and nausea, a total incapacity to concentrate my thoughts or control my feelings. Sometimes I felt that I despaired of myself, that I had drifted into a morass of ill health, idleness and unwholesomeness of thought. . . . My mind was a prey to idle chatterings of personal vanity, to childish castles in the air which left me with mental indigestion of an acute kind.

Then we moved to Saltburn. Here my mental health improved, but physically I remained ill-at-ease and constantly fatigued. . . . Then the morbidness took another turn. I was overtaken with a presentiment of disease and death: I had some mortal complaint, the heart, the kidneys, were probably diseased. I cried myself to sleep and woke up in the morning bemoaning poor Sidney's future loneliness, romanced copiously. . . . and generally played the sentimental fool. But I had settled in the back of my mind that when I got home I would at once go to a good London doctor and be thoroughly overhauled.

But I was to get my advice without a professional fee. We stopped on our way south at the Byles at Bradford. There at dinner we met a certain Dr Rabagliati, author of various books on the subject of diet. By chance the conversation drifted on to public health. Suddenly the little man fired up and gave us a discourse on the one cause of disease – eating too much and at too frequent intervals. He was an enthusiast and described in convincing detail how cancer, influenza, pneumonia and almost all modern diseases arose from the one incontrovertible tendency to eat more than was necessary! Even the working class and the slum-dwellers were going to perdition by overfeeding! Bad air, drink, dissipation were as nothing to this terrible and accursed habit of the human animal. But apart from rhetoric he gave so many instances of recovery from chronic complaints by systematic abstemiousness that I was persuaded. 'How much ought a women to eat who is over forty years of age, weighs 8 stone 11 lbs, height 5ft 7ins, and who is a brainworker?' 'Three-quarters of a pound or at most one pound in the twenty-four hours: but taken twice a day, but at most three times a day. If she is over forty, best food containing starch once a day only.' 'Thanks for the prescription,' I laughingly replied. 'I have had bad health for some months, and I will give the treatment a trial. No wonder the medical men hate you: for if the experiment succeeds with me, you will have done a London doctor out of at least two guineas, probably four.'

Now I have begun the experiment which I propose to note carefully.

I limit myself to one pound of food daily, four ounces at 8 o'clock breakfast, six at 1.30 lunch, and six at 7.30 dinner. I have one small cup of tea without milk or sugar at 7 o'clock in the morning, another at 4.30 in the afternoon and a cup of black coffee after dinner. I take very little water with my meals, having a breakfast cup of hot water at noon and another at night. I take no starchy food after breakfast, taking out my quantity in meat, green vegetables and fruit, sometimes a little cheese and butter.

The first days I have felt queer though on the whole better. All flatulence and indigestion has disappeared, my brain seems stronger, I feel much more inclined to read, but my heart is somewhat uncomfortable and I have uneasy feelings in my stomach! Moreover I slept badly for the first two nights. The most troublesome complaint from which I suffer – acute eczema of the ears and all over the body – is neither better nor worse. But this, the fourth day, is still early to see results of the treatment. Meanwhile my spirits have risen . . . If only I can have a steadfast mind in a healthy body my life will approach the ideal. Abstinence and prayer may prove to be the narrow way to salvation in this world – at least for such as me.

Sidney's article in the *Nineteenth Century* has been a brilliant success. . . . The Asquith, Haldane, Grey lot are delighted with it: Rosebery evidently pleased. The newspapers have taken it seriously and it has improved his standing I think and made people feel that he is to be reckoned with. . . . But national affairs are not invigorating. The wretched war drags on, the newspapers nag and scold and the government seems helpless and the opposition are more and more divided. . . .

*13 October.* [41 Grosvenor Road]
It is over a fortnight since I began the treatment. I weighed myself Monday 6th at Charing Cross: 8 stone 10 1/2 lbs; today I weigh 8 stone 10 1/4 lbs, practically no change. All flatulence and indigestion has disappeared, and my 'monthly period' was passed over with great comfort. On the other hand the eczema is no better: water clear, bowels absolutely regular. I do not sleep well. Somewhat depressed too by feeling muddle-headed and weary: work still wretched in quality and quantity. But perhaps a thirty-mile ride on Saturday was rather a strain to put on my powers. . . . On the whole I am better, but not yet 'fit'.

Sidney and Hewins in first-rate spirits about the School: building nearly complete and paid for, equipment provided . . . and plenty of students. . . . Again one realizes how, in a large and complicated society like the London education world, the whole power of moulding events falls into the hands of the little clique who happen to be in the centre of things. Ten years ago Sidney could no more have influenced the teaching of economics and political science in London than he could have directed the policy of the Cabinet. But now no one can resist him . . . .

*21 October.* [41 Grosvenor Road]
Weighing machine at Charing Cross station (which I patronize every Monday morning) registers 8.8 – a drop which we will hope is due to a readjustment of the machine. That possible loss of weight and the continued presence of eczema are the only unsatisfactory symptoms. Otherwise I feel extraordinarily better. My brain is now working well and I feel free from discomfort. And I have complete control over my thoughts and feelings, a delightful change from the last nine months' mental indigestion.

Treatment slightly altered: hot water instead of tea at 7 o'clock, no hot water in the evening. (Note: changed back again as I find it indigestible.) Breakfast of toast and butter, without egg. And the last two days an arsenical mixture to help to clear away the eczema.

It is as difficult to clear one's mind of all 'waste' matters as to clear one's blood! And the simple plan of starvation does not answer. Quite the contrary; in no place does nature so abhor a vacuum as in the realm of thought and feeling. Since I have taken to my 'diet' I can read much more and so fill up my spare time. . . .

*1 November.* [41 Grosvenor Road]
I am prospering though somewhat erratically. Mercury ointment effectually killed the eczema, leaving me with oh! such a sore mouth. This is yielding to treatment but I am an emaciated white creature, unfit for play or work. So off I go to Freshwater with the Playnes to see whether little food and perfect air will re-establish me. But I mean to persevere and see the experiment out, short of ceasing to exist. The hypothesis is too interesting to be left untested: it promises to solve so many problems. . . .

*10 November.* [Freshwater]
Ten days at Freshwater. The eczema has practically disappeared, mouth is now cured. But I am overcome with apathy, mental and physical and the urine is muddy which means there are still waste products, I suppose. Clearly I shall not be able to do any work for some time. No trouble with thoughts now: I have none. My mind is a blank! . . .

*14 November.* [41 Grosvenor Road]
Dashed to find my weight had gone down in the fortnight three pounds in spite of absolute rest at Freshwater. Began to eat a trifle more but produced attacks of flatulence. . . . Cure is evidently going to be a somewhat long business and will need patience and persistence. But life in London is not favourable: had visitors all Wednesday afternoon, Passmore Edwards and pro-Boer party to dine in evening. Friday lectured to Anglican young ladies, Saturday gathering of students here in the evening with all the consequent arrangements. Tomorrow go to Longfords for a week or ten days rest. If I am not stronger when I return I shall begin to despair . . .

Lost 2 lbs during the six days in London. Now weigh 8 stone 1/4 lb.

*28 November.* [Longfords]
Twelve days at Longfords, keeping to diet and living ideally restful and healthy life. Result: gain of 1/2 lb in weight, eczema entirely disappeared, no aches or pains. Digestion, bowels and kidneys in good order, monthly period somewhat delayed (usually it is the other way with me), weak in body and mind, and suffering from lack of sleep. The amount of sleep I get varies from three to six hours . . .

. . . The comfort of Longfords, Mary's cheery good sense, the very impossibility of settling to anything for more than half an hour without interruption, exactly suited my state of body and mind. And it was interesting to get a vision of the Playnes at home now that they have both become distinctly elderly. One change is remarkable: there is no bad temper in the house. When I think of Arthur's detestable temper in early life and his very infirm one in middle life, this change excites wonderment. Now he is a light-hearted hale elderly man, hunting and shooting two or three times a week, spending two days on 'county business' and the remainder of his time poking about his estate. . . . Mary, on the other hand, is always full of plans and though she works only casually yet she achieves a good deal owing to her excellent abilities. Helping her is a pleasant and capable little woman, half-secretary, half-companion, who assumes the position of a daughter in the house.

. . . Ever since I have known the Playnes there has always been someone . . . with whom they are on the worst of terms, first his old father, then our mother . . . and now Mannie, their daughter-in-law. They got wrong with me when I lived at Box, though owing to my resolute refusal to be a party to the quarrel it never came to open estrangement. This time, I believe, they are more sinned against than sinning, but they have aggravated it by their inveterate habit of talking themselves into an exaggerated frame of mind. The war is the other occasion for thought, talk and feeling and here they can only discuss with persons who hold more or less their opinions. Hence the *rapprochement* between us and them – all the more so as Mary's special 'chums' in the family happen to be pro-Boer. With Kate and Lallie she feels that she must abstain from intercourse and even with the milder Georgie Meinertzhagen she is under constraint. Perhaps if one's only child [Bill Playne] were continuously fighting one would feel equal bitterness.

In the autumn Rosebery made an equivocal bid for leadership. In a speech at Chesterfield, Derbyshire, on 16 December – a much anticipated occasion for which special trains were run from London – he came out for a negotiated peace in South Africa and repudiated the traditional Liberal domestic policies, particularly Home Rule for Ireland: he called, he said, for 'a clean slate', and a new policy based on 'efficiency'.

*7 December.* [41 Grosvenor Road]
Slightly modified my diet . . . Feel very much stronger in body and mind, weight remains stationary. Hope to get to work again about the beginning of the new year.

Haldane called in twice the last week to discuss affairs . . . It is clear that Rosebery whipped them to heel and has reversed the position of a year ago when he was, more or less, their appendage. He is now master of the 'Limps', but he is not yet master of the Liberal Party. . . .

*9 December.* [41 Grosvenor Road]
. . . This year has been the most unsatisfactory year of my life since I married. How far I must apportion the blame between a bad state of physical health and a rotten state of mind, I cannot tell. But for egotism, self-conscious vanity, and for total incapacity for a really good day's work I have excelled all previous record. No one has been aware of this but myself. I have kept a brave face, have seemed to be fully occupied by other thoughts, and my relations to other persons have even been softened and improved by my own intense humiliation at the condition of my mind. I have become infinitely more charitable to Rosy Dobbs for instance (who, by the way, has recovered herself almost miraculously) on the score of character, far more appreciative of other people's small abilities. This is, indeed, the only asset against the deterioration of my own effort. And all this weakness and foolishness has not interfered with my

tenderness for my own darling boy. It has intensified my feeling of his superiority to myself alike in moral and intellectual qualities. The bad result has been confined, in fact, to a much smaller and worse intellectual output and with possibly a weakening of the fibre of character and intelligence. And to what has this state of things been due? Doubtless the 'waste products' accumulated by wrong feeding have had largely to do with it, stimulating activity in some organs and clouding the brain. Until I took to the rigid diet, the sensual side of my nature seemed to be growing at the expense of the intellectual. . . . This year has found me far more emotional than I have ever been. I longed for music, was inclined to be religious, and allowed my mind to dwell on all sorts of sentimental relations. This was the subjective state. Acting on this state was a real or imaginary (I really don't know which) increased personal attractiveness, typified by the admiration – which I thought I had, or actually had – excited in the minds of some prominent personages . . . I spoke to no one, not even to Sidney, about this ridiculous business. Fortunately besides a sense of conduct I have also a sense of humour and the wholesome fact of 'grizzled, wrinkled and over forty' was constantly intervening to check morbid growth. But, thank the Lord, I am now recovering . . .

H. G. Wells (1866–1946) had made his reputation as a writer of scientific romances, beginning with *The Time Machine* (1895), and was now writing naturalistic novels and utopian predictions.

[?] *December.* [41 Grosvenor Road]
Wells's *Anticipations.* The most remarkable book of the year: a powerful imagination furnished with the data and methods of physical science working on social problems. . . . Clever phrases abound, and by-the-way proposals on all sorts of questions – from the future direction of religious thought to the exact curve of the skirting round the wall of middle-class abodes.

# A Slump in the Webbs

## January 1902–October 1905

*30 January.* [41 Grosvenor Road]
I have been so hard at work on the book that I have had no energy left
over for diary-writing.

We spent Christmas with Alfred [Cripps] and the Courtneys. Our
host was in splendid form . . . I fancy that Alfred feels his feet again in
politics, and sees office near at hand should the opportunity for a new
man arise. We laughingly decided that, if the three brothers-in-law were
in leading positions in the House, it would end in Sidney and Alfred
arranging compromises between the two Front Benches with Leonard
always in opposition! The Courtneys were as self-righteously pro-Boer as
ever, but more subdued. . . . Then we went to Margate into lodgings
taking the devoted Emily [the maid] with us . . . We worked well
together and almost ended the difficult chapter on 'Municipal
Corporations'. The number of times Sidney and I have laboured
through these four volumes of Royal Commission reports of 1835 is tiresome even to think about . . .

The regime of restricted diet is beginning to tell most satisfactorily on
my health. I have ceased to lose weight and am working better than I
have done for many months. . . . Physically the cure is not complete. I
am far too thin (only 8 stone), the eczema lingers on, and every now and
again it flares up in the ears or on the back. The regime now is breakfast,
2 oz of toast, egg, butter, cup of cocoa (mostly milk); dinner, meat 3 oz,
green vegetables and fruit; supper, glass of hot milk and 5 or 6 oz of milk

pudding or two poached eggs and 2 oz of toast. Beyond the eczema I have no ailments except occasional flatulence and a certain lack of robustness.

*15 February.* [41 Grosvenor Road]
Met Clara Ryland at Margate and asked her and her little girl to stay here. A strange explanation by which I believe I 'builded better than I knew' for the happiness of others. It was late in the evening (Sidney was out lecturing) and Clara and I had grown somewhat sentimental, sitting close to each other, she with her arm round my waist, talking over her great sorrow and my happiness. 'You deserve your happiness, Beatrice. I always believed that with your strength and devotedness you would end by being happy and it is a joy to me to feel that my thought has come true.'

'*Luck*, my dear Clara,' I retorted, '*extraordinary luck*! If I had married when I was young I might have been swept by passion into a life that would not have suited me.' Clara started and coloured and I saw at once that I had seemed to her to refer to my relations with her brother. 'You would have suited another life perfectly,' she replied warmly. 'No, I shouldn't,' I urged with growing emphasis, 'or rather, the life would not have suited me. I was made for a working comradeship with a man who was no more than my equal in age, capacity and position; only work and work *on equal terms* would have called out my strongest qualities. I need to be leader in some respects and servant in others to be perfectly happy in marriage: for an ornamental position I am not suited. To put it bluntly, I am not sufficient of a lady. I should have hardened and coarsened in a Society life and as the wife of some great personage,' I added defiantly.

Clara rose from her seat with an expression of half offence and half amusement. 'I don't agree with you at all,' she said calmly after a moment's silence. 'However, it is sufficient for me that you are happy. And now I must go to bed and leave you to wait up for Mr Webb.'

I have done that little woman in Prince's Gardens [Chamberlain's London home] a good turn and gratified my frankness and my pride – all in a few words.

Harold John Tennant (1865–1935), a Liberal M.P., was Asquith's private secretary and brother-in-law; he was married to Mary Abraham, the first woman factory inspector.

*28 February.* [41 Grosvenor Road]

We are at present very thick with the 'Limps'. Asquith, Haldane, Grey, Munro-Ferguson, the Tennants, form a little family group into which they have temporarily attracted Sidney by asking him to their little dinners and informal meetings. Close acquaintance with them does not make one more hopeful. Asquith is wooden, he lacks every kind of enthusiasm and his hard-headed cold capacity seems to be given, not to politics, but to his legal cases. His brother-in-law, Jack Tennant, and Haldane both assure us that he could retire tomorrow from the Bar if he chose and that he only stays at it 'for an occupation'. Strange lack of imagination not to see that there is an over-abundance of hard persistent work ready to his hand in politics . . . That lack of imagination and sensitiveness to needs lies at the root of Asquith's failure as a leader of men. For the rest, he has no charm or personal magnetism. . . . Grey is a 'slight' person. He has charm of appearance, of manner and even of character, but he is, I fear, essentially a 'stick' to be used by someone else! . . . Politics is merely, with him, an episode in his daily life, like his enjoyment of nature, books, society, sport (mostly nature and sport be it said).

Neither Asquith nor Grey are, as politicians, well served by their respective wives. Margot is, I believe, a kindly soul, but, though she has intelligence and wit, she has neither intellect nor wisdom. She is incurably reactionary in her prejudices. Her two delights are hunting and other outdoor exercises, and fashionable society. She is said to be ambitious for her husband; but if so, her method of carrying out her ambition lacks intelligence as well as intellect.

Lady Grey is a fastidious aristocrat, intensely critical of anyone to whom work is the principal part of life. She is clever enough to see that work alone counts and yet knows in her heart of hearts that neither she nor her husband are capable of it.

As for Haldane, to whom we are both really attached, he is a large and generous-hearted man . . . But his ideal has no connection with the ugly rough and tumble workaday world of the average sensual man, who is compelled to earn his livelihood by routine work and bring up a family of children on narrow means. . . .

Munro-Ferguson is merely a pleasant young aristocrat. Perhaps the most keen of the lot are the Jack Tennants. Mrs Jack, formerly an inspectress of factories, is a fine-natured woman, with real knowledge and enthusiasm. . . . But 'Jack' is a *little* man, physically and mentally, and the notion of his being a 'force' approaches the ridiculous.

There remains the mysterious Rosebery. . . . Whether on account of his social position, or of his brilliancy, or because of his streaks of wit and original thought, he can make all the world listen. . . . He is first rate at 'appearances'. Moreover he seems to be developing persistency and courage. But . . . All he has yet done is to *strike attitudes* . . .

And why are we in this galley? Partly because we have drifted into it. These men have helped us with our undertakings, they have been appreciative of our ideas, and socially pleasant to us. They have no prejudice against our views of social reform, whilst their general attitude towards the Empire as a powerful and self-conscious force is one with which we are in agreement. . . . And, if Sidney is inside the clique, he will have a better chance of permeating its activities than by standing aloof as a 'superior' person and scolding at them. . . .

We have seen something lately of H. G. Wells and his wife. Wells is an interesting, though somewhat unattractive personality except for his agreeable disposition and intellectual vivacity. His mother was the housekeeper to a great establishment of forty servants, his father the professional cricketer attached to the place. The early associations with the menial side of the great man's establishment has left Wells with a hatred of that class and of its attitude towards the 'lower orders'. His apprenticeship to a draper, his subsequent career as an assistant master at a private venture school, as a 'government student' at South Kensington living on £1 a week, as an 'army' crammer, as a journalist and, in these last years, as a most successful writer of fiction, has given him a great knowledge of the lower-middle class and their habits and thoughts, and an immense respect for science and its methods. But he is totally ignorant of the manual worker, on the one hand, and of the big administrator and aristocrat on the other. This ignorance is betrayed in certain crudities of criticism in his *Anticipations*. . . . A world run by the physical-science-man straight from his laboratory is his ideal; he does not see that specialized faculty and knowledge are needed for administration exactly as they are needed for the manipulation of machinery or [natural] forces. But he is extraordinarily quick in his apprehensions, and took in all the points we gave him in our forty-eight hours' talk with him, first at his own house and then here. He is a good instrument for popularizing ideas, and he gives as many ideas as he receives. . . . Altogether, it is refreshing to talk to a man who has shaken himself loose from so many of the current assumptions, and is looking at life as an explorer of a new world. . . .

His wife is a pretty little person with a strong will, mediocre intelligence and somewhat small nature. She has carefully moulded herself in dress, manners and even accent to take her place in any society her husband's talents may lead them into. But it is all rather artificial, from the sweetness of her smile to her interest in public affairs. . . . I should imagine her constant companionship was somewhat stifling. They are both of them well-bred in their pleasant tempers, careful considera-tion of the feelings of others, quick apprehension of new conventions and requirements, but they both of them lack ease and repose, and she has an ugly absence of spontaneity of thought and feeling.

> Dissension within the Liberal Party grew more acute during the winter. Although the Liberal Imperialists set up the Liberal League to promote their ideas, it lacked the resolution to present a serious challenge to the party leadership. Rosebery was its president and Sidney a member.

*19 March.* [41 Grosvenor Road]
. . . Two months 'sampling' of the Liberal Imperialists has not heightened our estimate of them. . . . the Liberal Party seems cleaved into two equally unpromising sections – Rosebery appealing to the grey mass of convic-tionless voters on the broad and shallow ground of Empire and Efficiency, Campbell-Bannerman relying on every description of 'separatist' interest – on all the 'anti's': anti-war, anti-United Kingdom, anti-Church, anti-Capitalist, anti-Empire. Both combinations seem to me equally temporary and equally lacking in healthy and vigorous root principles.

Having done our little best to stimulate the 'Limps' into some kind of conviction, and having most assuredly failed, we now return to our own work. . . . And between me and this diary, I think the 'Limps' will be glad to be rid of us! Our contempt for their 'Limpness' and our distrust for their reactionary views are too apparent.

> The Webbs were closely involved with the Conservative Education Acts of 1902 and 1903. Though Church and voluntary schools were badly in need of reform, the Acts were difficult to draft and implement owing to divisions within the government, the religious issues raised, and the reluctance of many local councillors to accept changes that appeared to favour the Anglican and Catholic Churches. Sidney was prepared to compromise in order to get critics of the Acts to work them, but in ral-lying support, the Webbs acquired a taste for intrigue, to which Beatrice was especially prone, and this damaged their reputation. Robert Morant (1862–1920), civil servant, worked with Sidney on the 1902 Act and was permanent secretary at the Board of Education from 1903.

*25 April. Crowborough Beacon, Sussex*

A pleasant four weeks, camping out in the large rooms of a girls' school on Crowborough Beacon. For the first ten days the Bobby Phillimores were here. Poor dears. I have rarely seen two mortals incapable of guiding their own lives into health and successful endeavour, largely due to a most consummate conceit of their own abilities, not offensive because Lion is brilliant and sympathetic and Bobby is admirably well-bred, but pitiful in its results. They both suffer physically from the eating craze, Lion having been ordered to 'stuff' and Bobby having a quite morbid appetite. They have too large a fortune to become poor through Bobby's foolish desire to play at business; but they seem not unlikely to eat themselves into disease. Meanwhile, they take up one question after another, fully persuaded that they are going to solve it: local government, housing, the army, the Irish question. . . .

Poor Sidney is somewhat distracted with anxiety . . . His principal concern is the exact constitution of the educational authority for London to be proposed next year. . . . It is perhaps fortunate that Sidney is known to approve the lines of the present Bill applying to the country outside London. Indeed our Radical School Board friends scoff about 'Webbs' Bill', which of course is an absurdity. They will scoff the more if next year we are hoist by our own petard! Meanwhile he is writing an article for the *Nineteenth Century* for June on the London University in the hope of catching a millionaire! . . .

A few days absolutely alone in the country pass happily now that I have my health. . . . I am no longer plagued by foolish fancies and absurd day-dreams. At times my imagination strays to the lives of greater ones; but it is only to wish them well and the desire that some day, when both the struggle and the fame of life has past, I might be of some service. That is hardly possible.

The reading in which I find most relaxation is religion. It seems to rest my brain and refresh my spirit. . . . And yet . . . directly I hear the words in which Christians clothe their religious aspirations my intellectual sincerity takes alarm. I do not believe in their doctrine. I am not even attracted by their God, whether in the Jewish or in the Christian version. My faith is more in spiritual influence. . . .

*4 May. Friday's Hill*

Settled again for our nine weeks' sojourn with the Russells. Hard at work on Poor Law Report of 1834. I had to break into this work to help Sidney through with his University of London article. . . . Alys Russell is away undergoing a 'rest cure'. Bertrand is working as usual – well and hard in health, eager to find someone with whom to talk philosophy but despairing of companionship in his higher mathematics. He and I see much of each other, as Sidney is away for a day or two each week. . . . Sidney is somewhat distracted with his undertakings and feels himself at times unequal to them. 'I am not a big man,' he says plaintively to me. 'I could not manage any larger undertakings.' But as I tell him it is exactly this consciousness of imperfection, whilst others find him competent, that shows that he is more than equal to his task. . . . Enjoyed my week's work on the University article, a relief from the grind of facts, a chance for 'scheming', an intellectual occupation I dearly love.

Sidney had Morant to stay . . . Morant gives strange glimpses into the working of one department of English government. The Duke of Devonshire, the nominal Education Minister, failing through inertia and stupidity to grasp any complicated detail half an hour after he has listened to the clearest exposition of it, preoccupied with Newmarket [horse-racing] and in bed till 12 o'clock . . . the Cabinet absorbed in other affairs and impatient and bored with the whole question of education. 'Impossible to find out after a Cabinet meeting', Morant tells us, 'what has actually been the decision. . .' Sidney and he discussed for many hours the best way of so influencing the Cabinet and its advisers that we get a good authority for London. . . . Sidney has written a short note to Chamberlain . . . Also to Balfour; in fact I think he has written to every prominent personage, to each according to his views and degree of influence.

A peace treaty was signed with the Boers at Vereeniging on Saturday, 31 May.

*30 May.* [41 Grosvenor Road]
Yesterday the formal opening of the new building of the School of Economics, a day of satisfaction for Sidney, Hewins and myself. Our child, born only seven years ago . . . despised by the learned folk as a 'young man's' fad, is now fully grown and ready to start in the world on its own account. There is the building and equipment, all admirably planned to suit the sort of work and life we have built up; there are the staff of teachers modestly but permanently endowed; there are the formidable list of 'governors' over which Sidney presides; and last but not least the School has attained university status with its own curriculum, its own degrees, and with even a prospect of its own 'gown'. Meanwhile

Sidney's personal work has broadened out into the administration of University affairs as a whole; his position on the Senate is strong and seems destined to become stronger, since he is always mentally on the spot long before the others have arrived there. . . .

Peace with the Transvaal; political burial of the pro-Boers. Immediate increase in popularity of government: rise of Rosebery 'futures'. . . .

*7 June. Friday's Hill*
The last days of our stay . . . I have worked well but with small result in actual stuff written. . . . Sidney has only been able to write out (he always elucidates and completes my rough draft) what I have done . . . It has been a broken time for him, absorbed in University and T.E.B. Committees, consultations, redrafting of Garnett's and Hewins's reports, writing memoranda for Haldane on University matters, for Conservative M.P.s and bishops on 'The New Education Authority for London' and keeping an eye on the Fabian Society and the Liberal League . . . But he is very happy in his activity, feels ways opening out before him of getting at least some things done in the direction he believes right. Sometimes he is weary and longs to retire to 'a cottage' with me and 'write books' but more often he is happily active, unconscious of anything but his desire to transact the business in hand successfully. He has a delightful unselfconscious nature. He has (thank the Lord!) no 'subconscious self'. When not at work, or asleep, or talking, he reads, reads, reads – always ready for a kiss or a loving word, given or taken. 'I am frightened at my own happiness,' he often says.

. . . For about three weeks out of the eight Bertrand Russell has been away . . . and poor Alys has been too unwell to be here. A consciousness that something is wrong between them has to some extent spoilt our sojourn here, both Sidney and I being completely mystified. We became so concerned about the situation that I suggested that I should take Alys off to Switzerland to complete her cure, and Sidney acquiesced out of affection for her and genuine admiration for Bertrand. It would be a sin and a shame if these two should become separated, and altogether wanton misery for both. . . . It is quite clear to me that Bertrand is going through some kind of tragedy of feeling; what is happening to her, I suppose I shall discover in the next three or four weeks. It is the wantonness of this unhappiness which appals me, saddens and irritates both of us. . . .

The first thing to be done is to get Alys well. I am myself looking forward to the complete change and rest. My cure is not complete; still suffer from eczema in one of my ears, due, I believe, to my greedy persistence in drinking coffee which I believe is rank poison to me. Also my recent attempts to companionize Bertrand so as to keep him here (which I believe to be Alys's desire) have meant more mental exertion than is consistent with regular work. And I have not always been quite faithful to the regimen: now and again a naughty greedy feeling overtakes me at a meal and I exceed! But I am improving in that respect; keep always before me the scale and the weights. I wanted, having spent yesterday in packing, to get back to the book, but I cannot stand the knocking and cleaning going on in the house – so off I go into the woods with *Mrs Warren's Profession*, just sent me by GBS.

*21 July. Sils, Engadine*
Three weeks in Switzerland – one week at Monte Generosa and the rest of the time here. . . . Alys Russell has turned out a most restful and pleasant companion and I feel that it is I who have been enjoying the rest cure, with her as a bright and sympathetic attendant. All the same, I believe I have done her good. I have given her back a sane perspective of her own and Bertrand's life. . . . The days and nights have been one long dream of pleasant sights, sounds and scents, varied by memories of past events, broodings over present problems and a certain background of sadness at the mysteries of the futility and pain of the great bulk of life . . . a melancholy brought about by absence from my dearest comrade and friend. How terribly lonely life would be without his worshipful love and that joyful combination of helpfulness and dependence.

The coronation of Edward VII took place on 9 August. Beatrice makes no reference to it.

[? *September*]. *41 Grosvenor Road*
Four fruitful weeks at Campden whither we return for another three tomorrow. . . . Odd letter from Rosebery. I sent him a card for my trade union teas, more to let him know what we were doing than expecting him to come. Foolish of him not to have responded to the request from the trade unionists for an entertainment at his house. . . . Asquith, too . . . Why play the game at all if you mean to play so carelessly . . .

*14 October.* [41 Grosvenor Road]
All our Radical friends bitter or sullen with us over Sidney's support of the Education Bill. Certainly if he had political ambitions it would have

been a suicidal policy on his part. Fortunately we enjoy the incomparable luxury of freedom from all care for ourselves. . . .

*10 November.* [41 Grosvenor Road]
The School has opened with éclat. There are now actually at work five hundred students and the staff is hard put to it to meet the new strains. The Railway Companies have at last come into it with a determination to make use of the lecturing both as an educational training and as a test of capacity of their staff of clerks. . . . Hewins of course is a little bit over-confident and elated, but that is his temperament. . . . he and Sidney, and to a lesser extent, I myself, make a good working trio. The whole internal organization of the School is left to him with suggestions from Sidney. The whole financial side is in Sidney's hands, whilst my domain has been roping in influential supporters from among old friends and connections. . . . Almost every week since early in October we have had dinners of eight to ten – of lecturers and governors, likely friends and supporters; and students to lunch. The rest of our social life, which is both lively and interesting, is deliberately designed to help forward the University, the Progressive party on the L.C.C. and to a slight extent to give Haldane and his friends a friendly lift whenever an opportunity comes that way . . . Haldane and Sidney are constantly co-operating in educational matters. Haldane has taken a bold line in supporting the government Bill and breaking from his political friends. . . . It seems likely that the beginning of the twentieth century will be noted as the starting point of the new form of university training and university research . . . In this 'movement' Haldane will have played one of the principal though unseen parts. . . .

Meanwhile we are hammering out our conclusions and throwing them at the head of the public in the form of massive historical analysis. It is a time, we think, for big artillery in the way of books. But hard thinking takes time. . . . It is a curious process, this joint thinking; we throw the ball of thought one to the other, each one of us resting, judging, inventing in turn. And we are not satisfied until the conclusion satisfies completely and finally both minds. I do most of the experimentation and Sidney watches and judges the results, accepting some, rejecting others. It is he who finds the formula that expresses our conclusions.

Lady Horner (1860–1940) was Frances Graham, daughter of a wealthy Liberal M.P. She was married to the barrister Sir John Horner and had two daughters, Cicely, and Katharine, who married Asquith's son

Raymond in 1907. Lady Elcho (1864–1937), who became Countess Wemyss in 1914, was a friend of Arthur Balfour and one of 'The Souls'. The Webbs had met the Elchos while staying in Chipping Campden.

*28 November.* [41 Grosvenor Road]
I took the Prime Minister in to dinner! I say 'took' because he was so obviously delivered over into my hands by my kindly hostess, who wished me to make as much use as possible of the one-and-a-quarter hours he had free from the House. It was a little party of eight at the house of the charming Mrs Horner – high priestess of 'The Souls' in their palmy days, now somewhat elderly and faded but gracious to those she accepts as 'distinguished'. The other guests were Lady Elcho and Haldane, Mr Horner and a handsome daughter.

Balfour has the charm of genuine modesty and unselfconsciousness, and that evening he seemed in earnest about education. He is delightfully responsive intellectually, a man with ever-open mind, too open perhaps . . . His opinions shift uneasily from side to side, the one permanent bias being in favour of personal refinement of thought and feeling. But I doubt whether he has any clear notion of how he would attempt to bring about this refinement . . . he intends to work on the side which at the moment he *thinks right*, not merely on the side that will appear right to other people, which I fear is Lord Rosebery's predicament. All this elaborate analysis based on one hour.

I set myself to amuse and interest him, but seized every opportunity to insinuate sound doctrine and information as to the position of London education. Sidney says I managed skilfully, but then he is a partial judge! We found ourselves in accord on most questions. Perhaps that is only another way of saying that Arthur Balfour is a sympathetic and attractive person who easily tunes his conversation to other minds. I can understand how colleagues in the House of Commons forgive his incapacity for transacting business. The flavour of his personality is delightful.

. . . I am entertaining extensively – a Conservative dinner and evening party on the 20th and a 'Limp' dinner and reception on the 27th. . . . Then there was a dinner to Lady Elcho to acknowledge her kindness to us in Gloucestershire and her introduction to Balfour, an introduction which may have good results. So I asked her to meet John Burns, the Shaws, H. G. Wells and Asquith. John Burns . . . gave us vivid pictures of prison and other episodes, views on the army, Eton and the aristocracy, on working-class and middle-class life, all fresh and interesting with a certain romantic sentiment for what was ancient and distinguished. . . . GBS was jerkily egotistical and paradoxical though he behaved well in encouraging Burns to take the stage. Wells was rather silent; when he spoke he tried too hard to be clever, he never let himself go. Asquith was simply dull. . . . He eats and drinks too much and lives in a too enervating social atmosphere to have either strenuousness or spontaneity. . . . The dinner was successful and 'thrilling' – Lady Elcho on the new sensation of meeting such strange forms of distinction as Burns, Wells, Shaws 'at the house of the Sidney Webbs'. . . .

[?] *December.* [41 Grosvenor Road]
Morant dined here last night alone to talk over chances of London Education Bill – wearied out with the autumn campaign and the prospect of having to superintend the working out of the new Education Act with a rotten staff and a hostile minority in each district determined to wreck the Act. . . . Morant doubts whether anyone wants any particular change sufficiently to get discordant views into line . . . So matters look dark and the present unsatisfactory situation is likely to persist, at least for the forthcoming year.

. . . One of the delights of living with Sidney is his absolute sanity – a sanity and sense of perspective which keeps him free from all elation at his little successes. He errs on the other side. He is perpetually apprehensive. This does not prevent his undertaking ventures but makes him wary and tactful in carrying them out. That is why he finds my audacity and pluck and my familiarity with the risks and chances of big enterprises – the result of being brought up in the midst of capitalist speculation – so comforting and helpful. Father taught me the habit of mind of starting many things and being satisfied if one in ten succeeded, of being 'detached', though persistent in 'trying all things'. . . .

~ 1903 ~

The Webbs were staying on the estate of Lord and Lady Battersea at Overstrand, near Cromer.

*16 January. Overstrand*
. . . For the first time for many years the three old friends – Sidney, Bernard Shaw and Graham Wallas – spent a week together with their wives as chorus, the Shaws at the big hotel near by and the Wallases with

us. Three delightful evenings we spent listening to GBS reading his new work – the *Superman*. To me it seems a great work, quite the biggest thing he has done. He has found his *form*, a play which is not a play but only a combination of essay treaties, interlude, lyric – all the different forms illustrating the same central idea, like a sonata manifests a scheme of melody and harmony. . . . Then I am so genuinely delighted at his choice of subject. . . . it is the most important of all questions, this breeding of the right sort of man. GBS's audacious genius can reach out to it.

Graham was somewhat depressed, physically and mentally, and though affectionate and pleasant to us he has a deeply-rooted suspicion that Sidney is playing false with regard to religious education. He wants all religious teaching abolished. . . . Politically this seems to Sidney impossible, whilst I do not desire it even if it were possible. . . . As Sidney's side is bound to win, though possibly Sidney himself will be sacrificed, it is to be hoped that Graham will retire from educational administration. . . .

. . . We have got on well with the book, though the task grows bigger and more complicated as we toil to complete it. We find ourselves really writing the internal history of the eighteenth century, and for this purpose I am reading eighteenth-century literature, trying to discover what were the good features of the time. . . . But what a lot of the eighteenth century survives in the twentieth! . . .

*25 February.* [41 Grosvenor Road]
A succession of dinners re. Education Bill, mostly Conservative and Church. . . . It is a tiresome fact that, to get things done in what one considers the best way, entails so much – to speak plainly – of intrigue. There is no such thing as spontaneous public opinion: it all has to be manufactured . . . with regard to administrative work, we plunge without hesitation on to the position of an advocate pledged only to display the arguments which tell in favour of the cause we believe in. In our scientific work, however, we honestly seek to tell the truth, the whole truth and nothing but the truth, a distinction in standards that puzzles and perplexes me.

*14 March.* [41 Grosvenor Road]
The L.C.C. Progressives or some of them are playing the fool about the London Education Authority. . . . A little clique headed by J. R. MacDonald are fighting all they know how Sidney's influence on the T.E.B., and some of the weaker of the rank and file, somewhat jealous of Sidney, are playing into their hands. . . . I have been pondering over the question whether I could have done anything to stop the 'slump in

Webbs' on the Progressive side. Of course our attention has been absorbed in getting hold of forces in the enemies' camp and our frequent coming and going has excited suspicion on our own. They have not the wit to see that if a government is in power with an overwhelming majority it is no use fighting it, at least not unless the other way has proved unavailing. . . .

*29 April.* [41 Grosvenor Road]
. . . Happy time at Longfords with dear sister Mary Playne, clouded over by the separation between her and Bill through the determined hostility of his wife. This young woman is a bad example of the self-indulgent, self-willed and self-complacent middle-class woman, who has never been taught to work or think or feel for others . . . She has succeeded in poisoning Bill's mind and he behaves with a strange combination of indifference and insolence to his parents, tempered by anger at their not giving him a larger share of their worldly possessions. . . . Altogether he is not a good product and Mary who has spent the better part of her life planning and scheming for him, is bitterly and finally disappointed. Whether there was good stuff to work on in his nature I somewhat doubt – the shape of his head is not encouraging. . . .

Meanwhile our eldest sister [Lawrencina Holt] has been going through a tragedy of discord. For some time the family life has been one constant wrangle between the two unmarried daughters and the two unmarried sons, the three married pairs and the father – now one combination, now another. . . . A melancholy reflection on their upbringing. Here again there is the note of utter selfishness. Lallie has slaved to make her home one of perfect comfort . . . the children have been flattered and allowed to behave badly to others and to live a life of pleasure. Now they have turned against her and each other. . . . Observing the results of the luxurious bringing-up of children does not make me *less* anxious to redistribute wealth. . . .

The Webbs spent much of the summer at Newlands Farm, Aston Magna, a few miles from Moreton-in-the-Marsh. On 15 May Chamberlain delivered a sensational speech in which he came out strongly for a system of fiscal preferences as a means to Imperial unity. This 'bombshell' split his own party and so divided the Cabinet that Balfour had to declare tariff reform 'an open question' for his government. The talk of a new 'Education' party was a measure of the Webbs' alienation from mainstream politics.

*15 June. Aston Magna, Gloucestershire*

We left London seventeen days ago tired out but with the restful consciousness that our plans had come off. The School gets its grant of £1,100 from the T.E.B. renewed without opposition, J. R. MacDonald not being there. The Education Bill passed through committee the day before we left in almost exactly the same shape Sidney would have given to it: the L.C.C. absolutely supreme . . . The whole controversy between the Progressives and Moderates is stale and has lost its significance. The Progressives, beyond sticking to some old shibboleths, have lost all impetus to further action. . . . the Moderate party has become even more stale . . . Now it is a question which Sidney and I have been mooting between ourselves, whether out of these elements we can produce a new party, formally or informally held together by a broad catholic and progressive educational policy. . . . Can we silently and quietly prepare the ground . . . This is the problem before us. . . . Meanwhile our little schemes have been submerged, even in our own minds, by the new ferment introduced by Chamberlain into Imperial politics. Protection versus Free Trade is going to supersede all other political issues for many years to come. . . . This issue at least will force people to think . . .

Just before leaving London Sidney was appointed on the small expert Royal Commission to enquire into trade union law. This was our friend Haldane's doing, made easy by Mr Balfour's kindly view of us. The job is eminently one for him to do . . .

*3 July.* [41 Grosvenor Road]

Melancholy letter from Herbert Spencer. Ran down to see him . . . Was extremely sensitive as to his reputation and influence, felt that he had dropped out and was no longer of much consideration. 'What you have thought and taught has become part of our mental atmosphere, Mr Spencer,' I said soothingly. 'And like the atmosphere we are not aware of it. When you cease to be our atmosphere, then we shall again become aware of you as a personality.' 'That is a pleasant way of putting it,' and he smiled. . . .

Winston Spencer Churchill (1874–1965) entered Parliament in 1900 as a Tory but broke away on the question of tariff reform and became a member of the Liberal government in 1906. His father was Lord Randolph Churchill.

*8 July.* [41 Grosvenor Road]
Went in to dinner with Winston Churchill [at the Hobhouses']. First impression: restless, almost intolerably so, without capacity for sustained and unexcited labour, egotistical, bumptious, shallow-minded and reactionary, but with a certain personal magnetism, great pluck and some originality, not of intellect but of character. More of the American speculator than the English aristocrat. Talked exclusively about himself and his electioneering plans, wanted me to tell him of someone who would get statistics for him. 'I never do any brainwork that anyone else can do for me,' – an axiom which shows organizing but not thinking capacity. . . . But I dare say he has a better side, which the ordinary cheap cynicism of his position and career covers up to a casual dinner acquaintance.

Bound to be unpopular, too unpleasant a flavour with his restless self-regarding personality and lack of moral or intellectual refinement . . . he is, at heart, a Little Englander. . . . But his pluck, courage, resourcefulness and great tradition may carry him far, unless he knocks himself to pieces like his father.

'We have been living in a veritable whirl – we had twenty-five persons to dinner or lunch last week, having others to see us in the afternoon,' Beatrice wrote to Mary Playne on 9 July, telling her that the 'Charlottenburg' scheme to set up a new science college in Kensington had been successfully launched. Balfour dined at the Webbs' on 21 July. Beatrice implies that he mistook Charles Booth for William Booth, the founder of the Salvation Army.

*23 July.* [41 Grosvenor Road]
Our season ended with a brilliant little dinner here to meet Mr Balfour. Naturally enough I talked almost exclusively at dinner to the guest of the evening. A man of extraordinary 'grace' of mind and body . . . But a strange paradox as Prime Minister of a great empire. I doubt whether even foreign affairs interest him. For all economic and social questions, I gather, he has an utter loathing, whilst the machinery of administration would seem to him a disagreeable irrelevance. Not a strong intellect and deficient in knowledge, but I imagine ambitious in the sense that he feels that being Prime Minister completes the picture of the really charming man . . .

I placed Charles Booth next him – I doubt from his manner whether he knew who Charles Booth was – wondered perhaps that a

'Salvationist' should be so agreeably unsettled in his opinions. Bright talk with paradoxes and subtleties, sentiments and allusions, with the personal note emphasized, is what Mr Balfour likes, and is what I tried to give him! From nineteenth-century schools of philosophy to eighteenth-century street life, from University to Tariff, from Meredith to GBS, we flashed assertions and rejoinders; and 'Bernard Shaw, the finest man of letters of today' was one of his dicta. But he had not read *Mrs Warren's Profession*: 'it is one of the unpleasant plays. I never read unpleasant things,' he added apologetically, and looked confirmed in his intention when I asserted that it was GBS's most 'serious work'. . . .

*24 July.* [41 Grosvenor Road]
One wonders whether all this manipulating activity is worth while, whether one would not do just as much by cutting the whole business of human intercourse and devoting oneself to thinking and writing out one's thoughts. It would certainly be a far pleasanter because a far less complicated life, with fewer liabilities for contraventions against personal dignity, veracity and kindliness. . . . But someone has to do this practical work, and possibly it is just as well that it should be done by those who have 'the other life' to withdraw into . . .

*The Times* was running a quiz competition which Sidney hoped to win.

*4 August. Aston Magna*
Settled in an attractive old farmhouse. With pleasant farmer, wife, son and daughter . . . Only drawback, certain amount of noise from the holidays of the youngsters. But we have a tent out on a piece of unkempt land, where absolute quiet reigns . . .
    . . . I still maintain my regimen of two meals, but today took some meat for the first time for many weeks. I watch myself with interest, not only to secure the greatest efficiency but also to discover whether sustained health is possible on so cheap and easy a fare. My regimen now consists of an early cup of tea 7 o'clock, lunch 1 o'clock, of macaroni or semolina (or occasionally a poached egg and toast), green vegetables with some kind of fruit tart or pudding, a minute bit of cheese, biscuits and a little butter. Afternoon cup of tea. Supper at 7.30 of cereal pudding – grape-nut is my favourite and a little marmalade or sultanas, minute bit of cheese and biscuit and butter, half a small cup of black coffee. I don't think I consume more than about 1 1/2 oz of dry cereal at each meal. I have resumed my monthly periods (rather too frequent I

fear) which stopped for six months last summer. I suffer from no headache or constipation or colds, very little indigestion and very slight eczema. I sleep well and enjoy a placid and unworried state of mind. Today I have a feeling of drag and subconscious headache which disinclines me to exercise – some congestion I should imagine – to be looked for at forty-six years of age. I am lying up to prevent a premature period, and I am stopping off my book.

While I spend four whole mornings in mastering the contents of one little book and rest the whole afternoon and evening in order to work again the next day, Sidney will get through some eight or ten volumes bearing on local government or likely to contain out-of-the-way references to it, besides spending the whole morning finishing up his *Times* questions. . . . The continuous activity of his brain is marvellous. . . . He says that he cannot think without reading or writing, and that he cannot brood, for if he has nothing before him more absorbing he finds himself counting the lines or spots on some object. That is why when he is in a street or a bus he sees and reads and often remembers the advertisements. If I would let him he would read through mealtimes. A woman who wanted a husband to spend hours talking to her or listening to her chit-chat would find him a trying husband. As it is we exactly suit each other's habits. Long hours of solitary brooding is what I am accustomed to and without which I doubt whether I could be productive. . . . Sometimes I am a bit irritated because at some off-time he will not listen to what seems to me a brilliant suggestion – dismisses it with 'that is not new' or with a slight disparaging 'hmm'. But I generally smile at my own irritation . . . Sometimes I flare up and scold, then he is all penitence and we kiss away the misunderstanding. . . .

*5 October. Grosvenor Road*
A refreshing holiday in Normandy and Brittany lasting the best part of three weeks, first a week with the Russells and then two weeks alone together. The Russells we found settled in uncomfortable lodgings in a little Normandy village, riding and reading together but not serenely happy, a tragic austerity and effort in their relations. . . .

We spent last Sunday with Alfred Cripps. . . . He is angry and contemptuous of Balfour and longs to depose him from the position of leadership. . . . He has, I think, made up his mind to become one of Chamberlain's henchmen during the next months. And certainly he will find himself much more sympathetic to J.C.'s signboard painting and vigorous philistine creed than to the slack ways and fastidious culture of Arthur Balfour. . . .

Exactly a month today we returned to London . . . All our little enterprises prosper. The School term has opened successfully, just a slight increase of students and fees on the boom of last year. The Progressive Party is shaping well for the administration of the Act and the agitation against it, as far as London is concerned, is dying down . . . [Sidney] is extraordinarily skilful in producing the impression on all parties that 'he is doing his best' to promote their *real* aims, and he seems to give this impression without in the least concealing his own views as to the next step to be taken or hiding his intention of taking it!

Lord Hugh Cecil (1869–1956) was the youngest son of Lord Salisbury and a Tory M.P. 1895–1906. Victor Bulwer-Lytton, second Earl of Lytton (1876–1947) was strongly in favour of free trade and women's suffrage. His sister Constance became a notable suffragette; his sister Betty married Gerald Balfour. Sir Alfred Lyall (1835–1911), a writer, had been a senior official in the Indian civil service. Augustine Birrell (1850–1933), Liberal politician, lawyer and writer, became president of the Board of Education in 1905.

*3 November.* [41 Grosvenor Road]
Dined at the Asquiths'. Lord Hugh Cecil, the Lyttons, Sir Alfred Lyall and the Birrells. Our host and hostess most gracious . . . Margot certainly has vitality and was full of fervour for the free-trade cause and scepticism of all other aspects of the Progressive programme, told us plentiful gossip about 'Arthur' [Balfour] and called all the élite of High Political Society by their Christian or pet names. It is a strange little clique, in which the bond of union is certainly not common conviction or desire for any kind of reform. (I fancy we are admitted to it, strange to say, not as reformers and experts but as persons with a special kind of chic.) I suggested that why Chamberlain would make headway, in spite of his bad arguments, was because he had a vision, desired to bring about a new state of affairs and was working day and night for a cause, that no one else wished anything but a quiet life and the *status quo*. Whereupon Lord Hugh and Margot exclaimed, 'Why change the present state of things – all is well.' Whereupon I burst out: 'That's all right for you, Lord Hugh, a convinced ultra-Tory, but is that a possible attitude for the leader of the Liberal Party who, one would think was, or

ought to be, "professionally" aware of the mass of misery, vice and distorted human nature of our present state of society?' But conscious of the absurdity of indignation while eating and drinking at the Asquith table I calmed down and tried to make up for my useless and somewhat self-righteous indignation. I suppose it is well to be on good terms with these people, but I come back from their society to our shabby little home and regular hard work with a deep sigh of gratitude that I am an 'outsider' and have not the time or the energy to become one of them even if they opened wide the doors. Probably the door is kept open because we do not try 'to enter in'. . . .

*18 November.* [41 Grosvenor Road]
Hewins sends in his resignation of the Directorship of the School of Economics, having taken service under Chamberlain to work out the details of his tariff proposals. So ends our close relationship with this remarkable man . . . Meanwhile to us falls the task of finding a successor and reorganizing the staff of the London School. . . .

> All through Sidney's courtship he had sought to persuade Beatrice that their combined abilities of 1+1 made 11 not 2. Sir Halford J. Mackinder (1861–1947) replaced Hewins as director of the L.S.E.

*1 December.* [41 Grosvenor Road]
Sidney somewhat disappointed at not getting a prize in *The Times* competition. He had almost persuaded himself that he would win the £1,000 because his number was 4124 which added together makes 11, *our* mystical symbol of partnership. Dear Boy, I love him for his simplicity and his entire lack of 'side' and 'pretension'. It never occurred to him that he was too busy and important to spend spare hours and risk defeat in competing with 16,000 others in answering catch questions. Moreover he made the competition a subject of conversation whenever he was gravelled for lack of matter with relatives and dinner-parties. As Graham Wallas once said when he watched him running to catch a train: 'What I like about you, Webb, is that there is no damned nonsense about style.' . . . Saw Hewins at the School today and had a chat with him. Suffering from a reaction of regret in giving up the School and dread of the difficulties of his task. . . . Warned me to keep a tight hand on Mackinder and to maintain the concrete side of the School. We have [our] work cut out for us as usual.

*8 December.* [41 Grosvenor Road]

My old friend [Herbert Spencer] passed away peacefully this morning. Since I have been back in London this autumn I have been down to Brighton most weeks . . . 'My oldest and dearest friend,' he has called me these last visits. 'Let us break bread together,' he said on Monday and insisted on a plate of grapes being set on the bed and both of us eating them. 'You and I have had the same ends,' he repeated again. 'It is only in methods we have differed.' . . . To me he seemed in these last years to be stumbling in total darkness, hurting himself and then crying aloud in his lonely distress, clinging to his dogmas but without confident faith, with an almost despairing and defiant pride of intellect . . . all these strange shortcomings and defects were like an ugly and distorted setting to a small but brilliant stone. . . . He will be among the elect.

*14 December.* [41 Grosvenor Road]

The last words, honest and noble words, were said by Leonard Courtney to a few friends, and one or two disciples and admirers gathered together in the little brick hall of the Crematorium on the outskirts of London. The ceremony was simple and dignified – with an absence of rite or ostentation – every detail executed according to his instructions, with puritanic spareness, decorum and precision, but with perfect 'consideration towards those who wished to attend'. And here ends a long-drawn-out tie of friendship, extending from my earliest childhood to past middle life – a tie unbroken by growing discordance of opinion, by marriage, or by extreme old age and disease.

∾ 1904 ∾

*17 January.* [41 Grosvenor Road]

. . . Except for four dinners of the staff of the School of Economics, with gatherings of the students afterwards, which I have arranged for February and March, I am keeping myself free from social engagements. It is not the time, but the energy I lack . . . In the afternoons I take exercise, ponder and read – about twice a week I walk along the Embankment to St Paul's and listen to the anthem and join in the beautiful liturgy of the evening prayer. Sidney's news, letters and newspapers, an occasional friend or student to lunch, now and again a few friends to dinner or a 'dinner out' are sufficient from the standpoint of the greatest output. How any sane mortal with resources of their own and a few intelligent friends can exert themselves to get into 'Society' passes my comprehension. And yet I have just expended 21 guineas on an evening dress! I hasten to add that it is four years since I paid the same amount for my present evening garment. Still, I might have done without it, if I had been quite single-minded in my indifference to social glamour. The cold-drawn truth is that though I am honestly indifferent as to whether or not I see the great world, when I do enter in I like to do credit to my reputation – an unworthy desire, I own, unworthy of an ascetic student and a collectivist reformer!

Bernard Shaw had been adopted as Progressive candidate for South St Pancras.

*27 February.* [41 Grosvenor Road]
Sidney and Phillimore returned unopposed for Deptford, a somewhat striking comment on the threats of last summer that 'he shall lose his seat.' He is now turning his attention to getting GBS in for St Pancras. . . . What that erratic genius will do, if he gets on the L.C.C., heaven will know some day, but I am inclined to think that in the main he will back up Sidney. And he will become the *enfant terrible* of the Progressive party and make Sidney look wisely conventional. . . . But he is not likely to get in!

Meanwhile our old friend Graham Wallas is left in the cold, with even a cross against his name so far as our influence with the Church is concerned. . . . One has, in this ruthless world, to accept uncomfortable facts and act on them. . . .

*7 March.* [41 Grosvenor Road]
GBS beaten badly, elsewhere the Progressives romping back with practically undiminished members. As to the first event, we are not wholly grieved. GBS with a small majority might have been useful, with an overwhelming one [he] would simply have been compromising. He certainly showed himself hopelessly intractable . . . Insisted that he was an Atheist, that though a teetotaller he would force every citizen to imbibe a quartern of rum to cure any tendency to intoxication, laughed at the Nonconformist conscience and chaffed the Catholics and Transubstantiation, abused the Liberals and contemptuously patronized the Conservatives – until nearly every section was equally disgruntled. . . . Anyway, we did our best for him, Sidney even puffing

him outrageously in the *Daily Mail*, and he and Charlotte are duly grateful. He will never be selected again by any constituency that any wire-puller thinks can be won. . . .

*19 April.* [41 Grosvenor Road]
We have had a couple of days with H. G. Wells and his wife at Sandgate, and they are returning the visit here. We like him [very] much – he is absolutely genuine and full of inventiveness . . . I asked him to tell me frankly why Wallas and some others were so intensely suspicious of us, and seemed bent on obstructing every proposal of Sidney's. He threw out two suggestions – first that Sidney (and no doubt I) was too fond of 'displaying' his capacity for 'tactics'; that he gave a 'foxy' impression; that he had better fall back on being an enthusiast; secondly that we were always regarded as a 'combination' working into each other's hands but not impelled by *quite* the same motives, or inspired by quite the same purpose; that I was regarded as a 'reactionary' with an anti-radical creed and it was suspected that Sidney would eventually veer round to my side. Of course we have got to be ourselves, whatever may be the drawbacks, but his criticism increases my inclination for a somewhat severe abstinence from trying 'to run the show' . . . Directly the grant for the School is safe we will go into retreat with our papers and books until the October session.

*2 May.* [41 Grosvenor Road]
. . . Have finally given up not only alcohol but coffee and tobacco. Tea remains my one concession to self-indulgence, with occasional overeating of my 'simple food'. In the course of the year I hope that will go too.

[Whitsun?]. *Bramdean*
A fortnight in quiet pleasant rooms in a pretty little Hampshire village by the Meinertzhagens' new place – Brockwood. . . . Before I left London I had been reading theosophy . . . some half-dozen books by Annie Besant . . . I am inclined to believe in some of the extreme positions – in the complete subordination of *Desire*, the rooting out of its hold on thought, feeling and action. The ideal to be aimed at in public education, as in personal culture, is a religious purpose concerned with scientific processes together with the perfect control by the Will of all the faculties of man . . .

In the life of a little village one notes how far happier and more dignified is the existence of the hardworking daughter of the middle-class farmer or shopkeeper than that of the rich young woman who drifts through life in the big upper-middle-class houses dotted about the country. There are seven Miss Legges in the big house next door, there are five Meinertzhagens at Brockwood, there are countless other young ladies all 'awaiting' with more or less self-possession the lot of the marriage market or a useless old maidenhood. Compare these listless young persons to pretty energetic Dolly Hawkins who 'runs' our little lodgings, helps her father, the postmaster, and thoroughly enjoys her casual flirtations, restricted to her few spare hours or afternoons. . . .

I note a certain change in our surroundings. Some of our old comrades of ten or even eight years ago have become indifferent or even hostile to our ideas . . . On the other hand, there is a new group of friendly young men disposed to take our views seriously . . . What is perhaps a less wholesome sign is the accession of Society folk . . . but all of these have a certain usefulness. . . . On the whole it is an extraordinarily varied and stimulating society. The dominant note in our intercourse with these people is *Social Reconstruction* . . . What is utterly lacking is art, literature for its own sake, and music, whilst physical science only creeps up as analogous and illustrative matter; history appears in much the same aspect. The relation of man's mind to the universe is constantly present as a background in my own thought . . . but the subject bores Sidney as leading nowhere . . . exactly as he dislikes discussing what train you will go by before he has got hold of Bradshaw [the timetable]. He prefers reading a statistical abstract or L.C.C. agenda. His relation to the universe – in the spiritual sense, he mockingly suggests – consists in his relation to me!

> Originally the Webbs called for a 'national minimum' of welfare and education as a matter of social justice: they now argued for it as a basis of a more efficient society.

*8 June.* [41 Grosvenor Road]
Turned from 'Roads' to help Sidney to write an article on 'The Policy of a National Minimum'. . . . I thought it better for Sidney to sign the article singly, the double signature overloads so slight a thing and it is too political, in its tone, to warrant the intervention of the female partner. I believe in mere 'wife's politics': only in research do I claim equality of recognition!

Sir William Hill Irvine (1858–1944) was a British-born Australian politician, Attorney-General and later Governor of Victoria. Andrew Bonar Law (1858–1923), a Tory Unionist M.P., was parliamentary secretary to the Board of Trade. He became Prime Minister in 1922. Sir Ernest Bickham Sweet-Escott (1857–1942) was Governor of British Honduras 1904–06.

*10 June.* [41 Grosvenor Road]
In response to a repeated request from Beatrice I called on Mrs Chamberlain on her 'at home' day. A charming little lady, exactly as she is always described – bright, conventional and kindly with a flow of intelligent talk. She looks true and warm-hearted within the limits of her somewhat narrow nature, in spite of her Society equipment. We talked of colonial premiers and I suggested that Mr Chamberlain might like to meet Mr Irvine, ex-Premier of Victoria, a Conservative free-trader who is in favour of the preferential tariff and who is longing to meet the great man. It appears that the ex-Colonial Secretary is keen to do some propaganda in that direction. . . .

*17 June.* [41 Grosvenor Road]
We lunched yesterday with the Chamberlains – to introduce the Irvines – others there were the Bonar Laws and a certain Sweet-Escott, Governor of Honduras. I sat on one side of my old friend and we talked without constraint. He is obsessed with the fiscal question – has lost his judgement over it – refuses to think or talk of anything else. He looks desperately unhealthy, rather than old, a restless look in the eyes, bad colour, and general aspect of 'falling in'. But I should imagine that there is plenty of force in the man yet, an almost mechanically savage persistence in steaming ahead. . . . Then we drifted on to the Education Acts 1902 and 1903 which he quite clearly does *not* favour, afraid of the advent of the bureaucrat. . . . 'If I had been Prime Minister you would not have had the Education Act.' 'The one and only reason for my not regretting that you were *not* Prime Minister,' I answered pleasantly and we passed on to other things.

. . . Upstairs we four ladies had agreeable conversation, drifting from gossip about Rosebery and the future Liberal Cabinet into a serious discussion as to the relative merits of Protestantism and Catholicism. I take to Mrs Chamberlain; there is a look of sincerity and simple feeling in her face, a somewhat pathetic expression of life being too much for her, though she obviously enjoys, to its full, the social side of the position, and I should imagine worships her great man. But there must be times when the great personage, with his irritability, one-idea-dness, physical unhealthiness, egotism and vulgarity is rather a heavy handful for that refined and charming little lady!

As I walked back through the Brompton churchyard I blessed my luck in life and thought with a glow of happiness of the true comradeship with my beloved workmate in my attractively simple little home. Bless him! And I wondered what were Joe's meditations over this second meeting in seventeen years?

Lady Wimborne (1880–1948), the daughter of the Duke of Marlborough, was a prominent hostess. Millicent, Duchess of Sutherland (1867–1955), a distinguished figure in Edwardian society, was such an enthusiast for social charities that she was nicknamed 'Meddlesome Millie'. She was the model for Arnold Bennett's Countess of Chells in the Five Towns novels. Sir Gilbert Parker (1863–1932) was a Conservative M.P. and author, noted for his social ambitions.

[?] *June*. [41 Grosvenor Road]
Sidney's influence on the joint life is wholesome in curbing my 'lower desires'. There have been three separate entertainments that I should like to have gone to – Lady Wimborne's, Mr Balfour's, and the Duchess of Sutherland's evening parties. Feeling secure in the possession of an attractive garment I should like to have paraded myself. But Sidney was obdurate. 'You won't be able to work the next morning. And I don't think it is desirable that we should be seen in the houses of great folk – know them privately if you like, but don't go to their miscellaneous gatherings. If we do, it will be said of us as it is of Sir Gilbert Parker – in the dead silence of the night you hear a distant but monotonous sound – Sir Gilbert Parker, climbing, climbing, climbing.' And I recognized the better voice and tore up the cards. . . .

The last weeks Sidney's days have been over-filled with committees and the work arising from them. Yesterday, for instance, 8.45–11 a.m. drafting a report for a chairman of one of the sub-committees of the E.C. of the L.C.C.; 11 o'clock Royal Commission on Trade Disputes; 12.30 sub-committee at School Board offices; 1.30 p.m. took train to South Kensington, lunching in the train, for 2 o'clock Departmental committee on Royal College of Science; 4.30 took the chair at the London School of Economics at meeting of railway magnates to decide on Railway Department (secured £1,000 a year to start Department); 6 o'clock arrived late at Higher Education Committee at School Board office and transacted, as chairman, remainder of business; 8 o'clock dinner here – Bernard Shaws, Jack Tennants, John Burns, Munro-Fergusons and Stephen Hobhouse; after dinner group of young Progressives to be introduced to John Burns and GBS; to bed 12 o'clock; began work again at book at 8.45 a.m. Very naturally there is not much brain left for the book, and until we get right away from London we shall only muddle on. . . .

*16 October. Grosvenor Road*
. . . When Sidney is with me I cannot talk to the 'Other Self' with whom I commune when I am alone – 'it' ceases to be present and only reappears when he becomes absent. Then the Old Self, who knew me and whom I have known for that long period before Sidney entered into my life, who seems to be that which is permanent in me, sits again in the judgement seat and listens to the tale of the hours and days, acts, thoughts and feelings which the Earthly One has experienced. . . .

*12 November.* [41 Grosvenor Road]
Two days at Gracedieu with Mary Booth and her young folk. Charles Booth being absent I excused Sidney from coming. For the last few years there has been increasing friendliness between the two households; they and their children have dined here and I have once or twice been to their house in the afternoon to see Mary. So I thought I would accept the invitation and close the episode of estrangement.

Gracedieu has grown in magnificence since I was there fifteen years ago! Large reception rooms added to the old structure, three men servants and the rest to match, elegant luxury of a refined type is the note of the establishment. Mary and I slipt into the old intellectual intimacy, exchanged experience of life and opinions and gossip about common relations and friends. But alas! the old affection is, on my side, dead – so dead that it no longer hurts to be with her as it used to. I have a regard for her. . . . She is an excellent wife and mother and a good housewife. But her purpose in life is the advancement of her family, a purpose that does not attract me. Moreover, I cannot help feeling that her return of friendliness to me has been brought about by our rise in the world's estimation. The young folk find my little dinners desirable entertainments and wish to claim me as an old friend and cousin, exactly as they wished to drop me twelve years ago. . . .

The war between Japan and Russia lasted from February 1904 to December 1905.

*22 December.* [41 Grosvenor Road]
. . . Kate Courtney remarked the other day that she always wondered, in reading the published diaries or confidential writings of private persons, why they seemed so little concerned with the great questions of peace and war – so infinitely more important than their own little doings . . . The answer I gave on the spur of the moment, is, I think, the true one – 'The private person has no specialist knowledge' . . . And yet if one looks back on the past year and thinks how much one has brooded over the Far Eastern drama, how eagerly one has read each morning's news . . . it is hardly fair to leave it unnoticed.

For instance, I watch in myself and others a growing national shame-facedness at the superiority of the Japanese over our noble selves in capacity, courage, self-control, in benevolence as well as in all that makes up good manners. . . . They have suddenly raised the standard of international efficiency, in exactly those departments of life that we Western nations imagined ourselves supremely superior to the Eastern races. How far this shock to self-esteem will go in English society, how far it will be neutralized by the vulgar delight of seeing our ally beat our enemy, remains to be seen. But for many a long day the Reformer will be able to quote on his side the innovating collectivism of the Japanese; the Idealist, the self-abnegation of all classes of the community in a common cause. Even in one's own daily life one is inclined towards greater persistency and more self-sacrifice.

So closes 1904 . . .

### ∾ 1905 ∾

Sidney Webb devised two educational 'ladders' for Londoners to climb – the system of scholarship leading from elementary through secondary to higher education and the part-time route of evening classes. His notion was that 'the great bulk of the population' would have access to the kind of schooling 'that their attainments and idiosyncrasies require'.

*29 February.* [41 Grosvenor Road]
Sidney gleeful as to the acceptance of his scholarship scheme, the only piece of constructive work done as yet by the Education Committee of the L.C.C. . . .

*18 March.* [41 Grosvenor Road]
All the news one hears . . . goes to show a stampede out of Chamberlain's camp. He himself is reported ill, much aged and dispirited. . . . It is a pathetic sight, this rapid decline of the once powerful man, but I think it is a decline past retrieving. The end is not far off.

Meanwhile he is bestirring himself about Birmingham University. Mr Haldane dined with him alone and they concluded a sort of alliance to push forward government expenditure in that direction. Birmingham, its municipal organization and the growth of its social and intellectual life, will be his most substantial achievement. In this great work he has had disinterested purpose and accurate knowledge and he has attained what is wholly good.

Henry James published *The Golden Bowl* in England in 1905. The Longfords servants nicknamed Beatrice and Sidney 'The Lovers'.

*17 April.* [41 Grosvenor Road]
. . . H. G. Wells came for the night: he had sent us his *Utopia.* . . . He is full of intellectual courage and initiative, and is now settling down to psychological novels – I fancy somewhat inspired by Henry James's last success.

*11 May.* [41 Grosvenor Road?]
A happy three weeks with the Playnes at Longfords. Wrote about one third of our part on the County, taking the two last days off for long rides in glorious weather – to Malmesbury one day, and then a lovely day in the Standish woods alone with my boy. We hid our cycles in the leaves at the top of the beech woods and wandered down, hand in hand, to the dear old field overlooking the house – the scene of childish sorrow and joy and all the stirrings and strivings of young womanhood. . . . The Playnes are now our intimates in the family. Mary is religious and public-spirited, a gentle and wise elderly woman, the soul of all good effort in the neighbourhood. She is friends with Bill's wife – has won her over by persistent kindness. . . .

A long talk with H. G. Wells at Sandgate. Two articles of our social faith are really repulsive to him: the collective provision of anything bordering on religious or emotional training and the collective regulation of the behaviour of the adult. As to the latter we are not really at variance . . . But he is obdurate as to education . . . We all got hot and exaggerated in our arguments and were no nearer agreement when we parted. Clearly the whole of liberalism in England is swinging into rigid conformity . . . As you cannot have each individual separately provided for according to his needs, therefore you must give identical treatment to all – seems their present dogma.

Julia Faulder (1879–1921) was the second child of Blanche and William Cripps. She married T. J. Faulder in 1904. Abbotsford was Sir Walter Scott's former home.

*2 June.* [41 Grosvenor Road]

The noble-hearted Blanche Cripps gone to her rest. Six months ago, faithful and devoted Fanny Hughes told me that Blanche had tried to strangle herself, that one night Fanny had missed her from bed, had run downstairs and found Blanche wandering about the drawing-room in a half-dazed condition looking for some instrument of death. Latterly she has seemed in good spirits, enjoyed the beauty of their new place in Argyleshire. On Wednesday evening, all the family were assembled at dinner to bid poor Standish Cripps (suffering also from melancholy suicidal mania) 'godspeed' before he left for New Zealand. Blanche seemed excited but said some beautiful words in a little speech. Before going to bed she insisted on ringing up on the telephone Julia Faulder, who had failed to come because of a severe headache, to say 'a sweet goodnight'. She followed Willie into his room and kissed him warmly. In the night, the two boys – Dick and Harry – were conscious that she was in their room bending over them and saying 'goodbye', 'be loyal to your father'. But they were so accustomed to strange words from her that they took no heed.

About four o'clock Willie, who was sleeping opposite Blanche and Fanny's room, possibly awakened by some noise, crossed over to get some water from his dressing-room. The door was locked: he hurried into her room, found her gone and Fanny fast asleep. They broke into the dressing-room by another door, and there was Blanche, robed in white, hanging from the shower-bath – still warm, but dead. The act had been carefully planned and was, in that sense, deliberate. 'God only knows,' she once said to Fanny, 'how I am tempted to kill myself. I feel impelled by a spirit stronger than my own.'

Blanche had a strange mind. She lived with great thoughts and tragic feelings. She was oblivious of the ordinary details of daily existence . . . Whenever she could bring herself down to think of personal matters she was extraordinarily unselfish and generous. But since she was generally brooding on world propositions the net result of her life was not considerate. Her memory was so deficient that for years after father's death she used to ask me whether I was living at York House!

As a girl she was a prey to elemental passions, and as a wife and a mother she was bowed down by periods of world sorrow and religious melancholy. Possibly from an instinct for self-preservation, she incessantly occupied herself in restless fashion during the day, walking, fishing, sewing and lastly painting. 'Sketching' was her one absorbing delight . . . Her pictures showed a weird talent, just wrong both in form and colour, but strangely and powerfully like what she tried to represent. . . . She was a perpetual reader of Shakespeare and had been for years engaged in a futile task of translating Shakespeare into French, a language which she knew only in the schoolgirl way.

She was full of extravagant reverence for certain aspects of life . . . Hard labour and pain raised in her a spirit of exultation. Before she underwent a most dangerous and protracted operation some fifteen years ago, she was in a state of extraordinary happiness. In those fateful hours on Wednesday evening, when she had determined on the act, I can well imagine she was not miserable or even depressed. She was probably enjoying an exalted enthusiasm for death. Her vocation in the world would have been fulfilled by a splendid martyrdom. . . .

She was mated to a man with a nature almost as strange as her own. Willie Cripps has always been at first sight repellent, almost unclean-looking with the manners and conversation of a clever cad. He has no fixed principle: there is no action, however base, of which one would say unhesitatingly that Willie Cripps was incapable. . . . For twenty years he remained Blanche's romantic lover, worshipping her mad beauty and putting up with her innumerable and most aggravating mistakes. The day came when a woman who combined intellect, great artistic talent and considerable physical charm, crossed his path, and since that day he has been an erring husband, persistently inflicting pain on his wife by forcing her to receive this Italian singer [Julia Ravogli]. But throughout it all he has cared for Blanche, and provided in more ways than one for her happiness. Perhaps his worst side has been his persistent carelessness and selfishness towards his children, and his pitiful pursuit of social position . . . A great house in Scotland with fishing, shooting, motors, filled to overflowing with fashionable patients – earls, countesses, smart young men and the Italian singer, mixed up with professional friends and relations, has been his one relaxation from an untiring pursuit of gain. To Blanche it has been protracted pain and discomfort; to the children demoralizing and useless. He has been fully aware of this but has persisted. Will he persist?

When I saw him on Friday he was broken-hearted and grateful for any kind of affection. How long will this impression of her death last?

Sidney and I stayed three nights at Abbotsford last July, with Blanche and Fanny alone. Sir Walter Scott's rococo mansion with its sham towers and turrets, its furbished armour, its pretentious bookcases, and its stream of tourists was not an attractive home. . . . It was a mad life, unconnected with any consistent purpose. Now and again [Blanche] would become ghastly white and be for minutes totally unconscious – a sort of epilepsy – crying in a strange voice, 'Willie, Willie,' as she came to. . . . She spoke little about herself, except to denounce the 'wicked feeling of jealousy'. Poor Blanche. What passed between her and Julia Ravogli when she visited her the afternoon before her death? Did she think that now that Willie had a grand new place he might be better with a new wife? And in her heroic mad way try to bring it about?

22 *June.* [41 Grosvenor Road]
A desolate fortnight in an old farmhouse lodging at Aston Magna. The beautiful countryside . . . was as soothing as I found it two years ago. But the little hamlet in which we lived had become, to my shaken nerves, intolerable with noise . . . The weather was cold and windy: we could neither sit out nor bicycle. We worked and read and read and worked straight on end for the first three days, and then I collapsed into a restless and nervous incapacity. Always my mind reverted to the tragedy, not of Blanche's death – though that was horrible – but of her life . . . Then my thoughts would wander to the family, those young men cursed with sleeplessness and melancholy, that young married woman also trembling on the brink, and those two happy natures – the youngest boy and girl – the only thoroughly sane ones of the family, on whom it had fallen to try to revive this dead mother for a whole hour by artificial respiration! Willie and Fanny called on them because they feared to call the others and tried to keep the facts from the servants. Over and over again my mind rehearsed the scene till I got dizzy with disgust.

Sidney was tender and consoling and now I am back at work on records I am recovering tone. . . .

*26 June.* [Beachy Head Hotel, Eastbourne]
Three delightful sunny days at Beachy Head, spending the whole day
out-of-doors and the whole night in sleep, real good sleep. Now I feel fit
for work again. . . .

*10 July.* [41 Grosvenor Road]
The Progressives have turned Sidney off the party committee. . . .
neither the leaders nor the ordinary members really like his policy and
are vexed to find themselves pursuing it. So they try to keep him down
*personally*, would I think be relieved to get rid of him. Sidney, meanwhile, is in the best of humours – his scholarship scheme is working
admirably and forcing by its mere weight the Council either to subsidize
existing secondary schools or to build and manage new ones. . . .

*30 July.* [41 Grosvenor Road]
. . . We have slipped into a sort of friendliness with Mr Balfour. He
comes in to dinner whenever we ask him, and talks most agreeably.
Perhaps our vanity is flattered by his evident interest in our historical and
philosophical paradoxes, enjoyment of our conversation. . . . The bulk
of men bore him, whether regarded as individuals or as an electorate, or
a Parliament, and all the common thought and feelings of common
folk seem to him ineffably banal, fit only for the subject matter of
Bernard Shaw's derisive wit. . . .
  Fyrish: two months – work, beauty, health. Left my diary, by mistake,
behind.

  Fyrish, on the Cromaty Firth, was the estate of their friend Munro-
  Ferguson. The Webbs had also stayed there in 1904. The Haldane family
  home was at Cloan in Perthshire. Willie Cripps had taken Glendaruel as
  a shooting-lodge. In later years Beatrice thought she had been unfair to
  Julia Ravogli.

*5 October. Grosvenor Road*
On our way from Fyrish we stayed two nights at Mr Haldane's and four
nights at Glendaruel. The pleasant impressions of our stay at Cloan
were rudely swept away by the nightmare of our visit to Glendaruel.
  After a tedious journey of twelve hours we reached our destination to
find a large house-party awaiting us and dinner deferred – Willie determined to show us gushing hospitality. To my intense disgust, there was
the Ravogli woman, flaunted in the face of Willie's children still

mourning for their mother. That was bad enough, but in the next few days I had to watch Willie philandering . . . The business was made almost more revolting by Willie's desire to talk sentimentally to me about Blanche and her 'nobility of nature'.

Puzzled as to what best to do, for the children's sake, I took refuge in cold but pleasant courtesy, withdrawing myself when possible from the general society, either with Rosie and the boys, or alone with Sidney. Poor little Rosie – her slim little figure draped in black, her white agitated face and sad eyes, flitted about uneasily in the background, desperately determined to ignore the Ravoglis but painfully frightened of her father's displeasure. The two boys were gloomy and taciturn and retired to the smoking-room when not shooting, afraid also to offend their father upon whom they are still dependent. . . . Willie . . . was an extraordinarily repulsive figure, a person in a nightmare. . . . It is foolish to make resolutions which events may change. But unless driven to it by some urgent consideration of the children's welfare, never again do Sidney and I enter that man's house or welcome him in our home.

*14 October.* [41 Grosvenor Road]
'Certainly revolting: but you must consider that you were tired and the atmosphere of such a house is wholly uncongenial to you and Sidney,' was Mary Playne's wise remark when I described the visit to her. 'We must consult together and do what is wisest for the children.' So wrote Kate Courtney. 'The more passive we are the better. We cannot influence Willie for good, we had better not drive him into worse conduct by taking any decidedly hostile line,' represents the general feelings of the sisters, to which I suppose, Sidney and I will conform. I had one horrid nightmare of Willie trying to murder me – and then, with the hard work that waited me here, the whole matter passed out of my mind.

A flying visit to Hadspen for the silver wedding of the Hobhouses – that charming home presided over by Henry's dull but honourable spirit and Maggie's exuberant energies and good-humoured but somewhat vulgar sense . . . Then five days' hard grind at the manuscript records of the Bristol Corporation. . . . So we have settled strong and happy into the autumn's work. . . . Meanwhile I have got note after note from the Duchess of Marlborough who apparently has been seized with a whim to hear Sidney lecture and get us to dine with them afterwards. It would have been discourteous to refuse . . . The little Duke is, I should imagine, mildly vicious; the Duchess has charm and I think goodness. I wondered how he came to be dragged by his wife to a technical lecture and into entertaining two dowdy middle-aged middle-class intellectuals, uncomfortably at a restaurant, for quite obviously they had come up to London on purpose. Was it GBS they were after? . . .

The smart world is tumbling over one another in the worship of GBS, and even we have a sort of reflected glory as his intimate friends. What a transformation scene from those first years I knew him: the scathing bitter opponent of wealth and leisure, and now! the adored one of the smartest and most cynical set of English Society. Some might say that we too had travelled in that direction: our good sense preserve us! . . .

# The Crime of Poverty

## November 1905–April 1909

In the last days of his government Arthur Balfour set up a Royal Commission under Lord George Hamilton (1845–1927) to look into the Poor Law of 1834. Its loosely worded brief was an open invitation to arraign the social system as a whole and made difficulties for its members. The principles of 1834 were clear. A man must be destitute before he was offered relief; the level of relief should be lower than the income of the poorest-paid labourer, and a man must submit to a workhouse or 'stone-yard' test by which he earned his relief through degrading labour in near-penal conditions. This rule should be applied across the 600 Poor Law Unions. The severity of the Law had long been criticized. It was no longer universally applied and was open to abuse. It was also losing its deterrent effect: many on relief were too old or young or infirm to work. Above all, as Charles Booth's inquiries and Seebohm Rowntree's pioneering *Poverty: A Study of Town Life* (1901) showed, paupers, strictly defined, were only a fraction of the millions living in grinding poverty and disgraceful conditions.

The first of the Webbs' eleven volumes on English local government, *The Parish and the County*, was published in 1906. Work on the series continued until 1929. The Webbs' numbering of the volumes does not correspond with their order of publication.

*23 November.* [41 Grosvenor Road]
Appointed to the Royal Commission on the Poor Law. Awaiting anxiously the names of my colleagues, Charles Booth being the only one I
know of. . . . the thought of the work on the Royal Commission, added
to the pressure of finishing the book, is not altogether a happy outlook. . . .

*29 November.* [41 Grosvenor Road]
Yesterday A.J.B. lunched with us and went afterwards to GBS's new play
*Major Barbara.* . . . [the] play turned out to be a dance of devils – amazingly clever, grimly powerful in the second act, but ending, as all his
plays end (or at any rate most of them) in an intellectual and moral
morass. . . . It is hell tossed on the stage, with no hope of heaven. GBS
is gambling with ideas and emotions in a way that distresses slow-
minded prigs like Sidney and I, and hurts those with any fastidiousness.
But the stupid public will stand a good deal from one who is acclaimed
as an unrivalled wit by the great ones of the world.

Revolutionary outbreaks in Russia followed Japan's victory in the war.

*2 December.* [41 Grosvenor Road]
. . . Today I called at the Shaws' and found GBS alone in his study. He
was perturbed, indeed upset . . . by a virulent attack on the play in the
*Morning Post.* . . . I spoke quite frankly my opinion . . . He argued
earnestly and cleverly, even persuasively, in favour of what he imagines
to be his central theme – *the need for preliminary good physical environment before anything could be done to raise the intelligence and morality of
the average sensual man.* 'We middle-class people . . . do not realize the
*disaster to character* in being without. We have, therefore, cast a halo
round poverty instead of treating it as the worst of crimes . . . What we
want is for the people to turn round and burn, not the West End, but
their own slums.'. . .
    I found it difficult to answer him, but he did not convince me. There
is something lacking in his presentment of the crime of poverty. But I
could honestly sympathize with his irritation at the suggested intervention of the censor, not on account of the upshot of the play, but because
Barbara in her despair at the end of the second act utters the cry: 'My
God, my God, why hast thou forsaken me?' A wonderful and quite
rational climax to the true tragedy of the scene of the Salvation Army
shelter.

Meanwhile, governments are changing in England and government of any sort is coming to an end in Russia.

A pleasant visit to Gracedieu colloguing in the old way with Charles Booth as to the proper course of the Poor Law Enquiry. I had extracted from Davy, the assistant secretary of the Local Government Board . . . the intention of the L.G.B. officials as to the purpose and procedure they intended to be followed by the Commission. They were going to use us to get certain radical reforms of structure: the boards of guardians were to be swept away, judicial officers appointed and possibly the institutions transferred to the county authorities. With all of which I am inclined to agree. But we were also to recommend reversion to the principles of 1834 as regards policy: to stem the tide of philanthropic impulse that was sweeping away the old embankment of deterrent tests to the receipt of relief. Though I think the exact form in which this impulse has clothed itself is radically wrong and mischievous, yet I believe in the impulse if it takes the right forms. It is just this vital question . . . that I want to discover and this Commission to investigate. Having settled the conclusions to which we are to be led, the L.G.B. officials (on and off the Commission) have predetermined the procedure. We were to be 'spoon-fed' by evidence carefully selected and prepared; they were to draft the circular to the boards of guardians, they were to select the inspectors who were to give evidence, they were virtually to select the guardians to be called in support of this evidence. . . . above all, we were to be given *opinions* and not *facts*. . . . It will need all my self-command to keep myself from developing a foolish hostility and becoming self-conscious in my desire to get sound investigation. Certainly the work of the Commission will be an education in manners as well as in Poor Law. . . .

On 4 December the long run of Conservative government was broken when Arthur Balfour resigned. Sir Henry Campbell-Bannerman took his place as Prime Minister and set about forming his government before dissolving Parliament and preparing for a general election. It had been clear for some time that the pendulum was swinging towards the Liberals. Balfour had been an uncertain leader of the Tories, trying to hold together a party acutely divided on the issue of Protection or free trade. But the sensational scale of the Liberal victory was unexpected, as was the sudden emergence of the Labour Party as a significant force. David Lloyd George (1863–1945), a Liberal M.P. since 1890, was appointed President of the Board of Trade and was the youngest member of the new Cabinet.

Winston Churchill was appointed Under-Secretary at the Colonial Office.

*15 December.* [41 Grosvenor Road]
Certainly the procedure imposed upon us by Lord George [Hamilton] was amazing. There was no agenda. A cut-and-dried scheme was laid before us . . . This was rather intolerable. I wrote a courteous but firm dissent . . . I did not stop there. I went and unburdened my soul to the secretary. . . . 'I don't want to make myself disagreeable,' I ventured to add. 'It is extraordinarily unpleasant for a woman to do so on a commission of men. But I don't, on the other hand, intend to hide my intentions.' . . . I begged Mr Duff to report the gist of the conversation to Lord George. I await the result with some amusement, and a little anxiety. It is a new experience to me to *have* to make myself disagreeable in order to reach my ends. . . .

Whilst I am busy with my little teacup of a royal commission a new ministry has been formed. . . . Our friends the 'Limps' have romped in to the leading posts under Campbell-Bannerman . . . To put Asquith and Lloyd George and Winston Churchill dead in front of 'Joe' [Chamberlain] on the tariff and the colonies, to place John Burns to look to the unemployed, to give Birrell the Education Office, are all apt placements. But the great *coup* is to get Haldane to take the War Office . . . The very day of his introduction to the Cabinet John Burns arrived, childishly delighted with his own post. For one solid hour he paced the room expanding his soul before me, how he had called in the permanent officials, asked them questions. 'That is my decision, gentlemen,' he proudly rehearsed to me once or twice. The story goes that when C.B. offered him the Local Government Board with a seat in the Cabinet he clasped the Premier by the hand. 'I congratulate you, Sir Henry; it will be the most popular appointment that you have made'!

Yesterday afternoon Haldane came in. *He* also was in a state of exuberant delight . . . 'Asquith, Grey and I stood together . . . We were really very indifferent,' he added sublimely. 'Asquith gave up a brief of £10,000 . . . I was throwing away an income of fifteen to twenty thousand a year; and Grey . . . was sacrificing his fishing. But it was a horrid week, one perpetual wrangle. The King signified that he would like me to take the War Office; it is exactly what I myself longed for. I have never been so happy in my life' . . .

~ 1906 ~

*9 January.* [41 Grosvenor Road]

. . . Sidney and I prepared a memorandum on 'Methods of Enquiry' which I have asked to be circulated to the whole Commission. That done, I feel that I have striven to get the enquiry on the right lines and can now rest a bit. . . . up to now I find attendance at the Commission a most disagreeable business – it is extraordinarily unpleasant when one has to force people's hands and make them attend to one by sheer ugly persistency, at the cost, of course, of getting back a certain insolence of attitude on the part of hostile men. (A week after: *This is exaggeration!*) . . .

*5 February. Royal Commission*

. . . Dear Charles Booth is as delightful as ever, but he is losing his intellectual grip . . . Happily, he is unaware of it. Alas! for the pathetic strivings of age – more pitiful to the onlooker than those of youth, because without hope of amendment. . . .

*9 February.* [41 Grosvenor Road]

About 9 o'clock yesterday evening, in walked John Burns. He had an indefinable air of greater dignity – a new and perfectly fitting jacket suit, a quieter manner, and less boisterous vanity in his talk. . . . He had filled in his time with seeing all and sundry – philanthropists, labour representatives, great employers, and asking their advice. 'They are all so kind to me,' he said in glowing appreciation, 'especially the great employers, just the men who might have objected to my appointment.' Oh! the wisdom of England's governing class! . . .

Altogether, Sidney and I are in better spirits as to the course of political affairs than we have been for many years. We do not deceive ourselves by the notion that this wave of Liberalism is wholly progressive in character . . . But it looms as progressive in its direction and all the active factors are collectivist. . . .

*1 March.* [41 Grosvenor Road]

H. G. Wells has broken out in a quite unexpectedly unpleasant manner. The occasion has been a movement to reform the Fabian Society. The details are unimportant, for I doubt whether he has the skill and the persistence and the real desire to carry a new departure. But what is interesting is that he has shown in his dealings with the Executive, and with his close personal friends on it – Shaw, Bland, and Webb – an odd mixture of underhand manoeuvres and insolent bluster . . . The explanation is, I think, that this is absolutely the first time he has tried to co-operate with his fellow men – and he has neither tradition nor training to fit him to do it. It is a case of 'Kipps' in matters more important than table manners. It is strange for so frank a man that his dealings have been far from straight – a series of naïve little lies which were bound to be found out. When at last he forced the Executive to oppose him he became a bully, and remained so until he found they were big enough to knock him down. I tell Sidney not to be too hard upon him, and to remember there was a time when 'the Webbs' were thought not too straight and not too courteous in their dealings (and that after a dozen years of mixing with men and affairs). But we have shown our displeasure by slight coolness; GBS has expressed himself with his usual scathing frankness, and it is more than likely that H.G.W., with his intelligent sensitiveness, will feel he has taken false steps into semi-public affairs and retire into his own world of the artist. . . .

Meanwhile, my Royal Commission grinds slowly on. The three committees that I pressed for . . . have been appointed and have set to work: statistics, documents (on central policy), evidence (on local administration). . . . I no longer find the association with my fellow commissioners disagreeable. But it is a somewhat disastrous interruption of work on the book, which drags on painfully. . . .

The Poplar Board of Guardians had a record of hostility to the constraints of the Poor Law. Early in 1906 a series of inquiries into 'East End scandals' investigated Poplar and four other London boroughs for extravagance, negligence and corruption.

*19 March.* [41 Grosvenor Road]
Attended a meeting of the Poplar Board of Guardians held at 6.30. About thirty were present, a rather low lot of doubtful 'representatives' of labour, with a sprinkling of builders, publicans, insurance and other 'agents'. The meeting was exclusively engaged in allotting the contracts for the year, which meant up to something between £50,000 and £100,000. I did not ascertain the exact amount. The procedure was utterly reckless. The tenders were opened at the meeting, the names and prices read out; and then, without any kind of report of a committee or by officials, straight away voted on. Usually the same person as heretofore was taken, nearly always a local man – it was not always

the lowest tender, and the prices were, in all cases, full, in some cases obviously excessive. Butter at 1s 2d a lb, when the contracts ran into thousands of pounds' worth, was obviously ridiculous! Milk at 9d a gallon, the best and most expensive meat, tea at 2s 8d. . . . If there is no corruption in that Board, English human nature must be more naïvely stupid than any other race would credit. . . .

Count Benckendorff (1849–1917) was the Russian Ambassador in London for many years. George Goschen (1831–1907), a Liberal Unionist, was a strong supporter of higher education. Mary Lowther (d. 1944) was the wife of James Lowther, later Lord Ullswater (1855–1949). Raymond Asquith (1878–1916), Herbert Asquith's brilliant eldest son, was killed in action in France. His sister Violet (1887–1969), who married Maurice Bonham Carter (1880–1960), became a prominent Liberal politician. Anne Dickson-Poynder was the wife of Sir John Dickson-Poynder (1866–1936), a Conservative M.P. who turned Liberal in 1905. Sir Neville Lyttelton (1845–1931) was Chief of the Central Staff 1904–08. Arthur Russell was the brother of the Duke of Bedford. His wife was Laura de Peyrouet (d. 1910). Sir Herbert Jekyll (1846–1932), assistant secretary to the Board of Trade 1901–11, was married to Agnes Graham, whose niece married Raymond Asquith. Sir Francis Mowatt (1837–1919) was permanent head of the Treasury, an Alderman of the L.C.C., and an influential figure in the Senate of the University of London.

*20 March.* [41 Grosvenor Road]
Two dinners that well illustrated a subtle distinction of atmosphere – one at the Asquiths', the other at the George Hamiltons'. The former consisted of the Russian Ambassador, the Desboroughs, Lord Goschen, the Dickson-Poynders, Mrs Lowther (the Speaker's wife), Lord Hugh Cecil, Mrs Lester (Mrs Cornwallis West's sister), one or two aristocratic young men, the Asquiths' daughter and Raymond. The large garish rooms, the flunkeys and the superlatively good dinner gave a sort of 'second Empire' setting to the entertainment. Lady Desborough, Margot, Mrs Lester and Lady Dickson-Poynder were all very *décolletée* and highly adorned with jewels. The conversation aimed at brilliancy – Margot sparkling her little disjointed sayings, kindly and indiscreet, Lady Desborough's somewhat artificial grace, Lady Dickson-Poynder's pretty folly, Mrs Lester's *outré* frankness, lending a sort of 'stagyness' to the talk. We might have all been characters brought on to illustrate the ways of modern society – a twentieth-century Sheridan play. They were

all gushing over GBS and I had to entertain the ladies after dinner with a discourse on his philosophy and personality – mostly the latter. We came away feeling half-flattered that we had been asked, half-contemptuous of ourselves for having gone. And not pleased with the entourage of a democratic Minister.

Very different, the George Hamiltons'. Here the party consisted of the Neville Lytteltons, Lady Arthur Russell, the Herbert Jekylls, Sir Francis Mowatt – persons belonging to much the same set as the Asquith party, though of a dowdier hue. But the reception in the cosy library was homely and the dinner without pretentiousness – the George Hamiltons treating us as if we were part of a family party – no attempt to shine, just talking about the things that interested each of us in a quiet simple way. It would have been almost impossible to 'show off', so absolutely sincere and quiet was the tone. And yet the conversation was full of interest and lingered willingly on each subject. . . . as we drove away, we felt that we had had a restful evening, learnt something and gained stimulus from the refinement and public spirit manifest in our hosts and their guests. The Tory aristocrat [Hamilton] and his wife were, in relation to their class, living the 'simple life'; and the Yorkshire manufacturer's son [Asquith] was obviously 'swelling it', to use the vulgar expression for a vulgar thing. . . .

*15 May.* [41 Grosvenor Road]
. . . The R.C. lumbers along: chaotic and extravagant in its use of time and money, each committee doing as it seems fit in its own sight. There is a lack of method and discipline with which some of us get impatient, and I fear I sometimes offend by my easygoing ways – intervening when I ought to hold my peace. 'You did not behave nicely yesterday,' said Lord George in kindly reproof. 'You should not have referred to current politics.' So I thanked him warmly for the hint, and I promised to be 'seen and not heard' in future. I find it so difficult to be 'official' in manner. However, I really will try. Dignified silence I will set before me, except when the public good requires me to come forward. Ah! how hard it is for a quick-witted and somewhat vain woman to be discreet and accurate. One can manage to be both in the written word – but the 'clash of tongues' drives both discretion and accuracy away.

Beatrice's sister Lallie had been very depressed by family difficulties. She died of cocaine poisoning.

*29 May.* [Bramdean]
Another sister, our eldest, passed away. . . . When I think of our three dear dead ones – Theresa, Blanche and Lallie – the one quality that seems to bind them together in one's memory is impulsive generosity. . . . They each and all *spent themselves* for others – children, husband, dependants and the community at large. Let those of us who have still the day in which to work keep up this family tradition . . .

*15 June.* [Bramdean]
The last days of the Whitsun recess spent in this little country hamlet, close to Brockwood Park . . . A happy peaceful time: good work done, though less of it than we hoped – the 'City of London', with our wealth of material, proving a longer job than we expected. . . . Still, it is important to get on . . . All this while Sidney is giving at least half his time and thought – perhaps more – to the organization of secondary and higher education in London. . . . He is very happy in the success of his unseen work – all his little schemes, or at any rate the most dearly cherished of them, have come off – the scholarship ladder, the innumerable educational institutions, secondary to university, which he has kept alive and under a semi-voluntary management; and, lastly, the London School of Economics has grown in size, significance and 'grace'. . . .

The Meinertzhagen *ménage* at Brockwood is happier than when we were here two years ago. The arrangement by which Dee lives at The Albany, quite apart from Georgie, with occasional visits from his daughters, and week-ends for himself at Brockwood, works most peacefully. Georgie has made Brockwood into a charming home, Dee having relinquished the whole management of it to her. . . . But the atmosphere of Brockwood is still purely materialist – no religion and no public spirit – very little philanthropy. As to religion, the situation is positively comic. Dee, who never goes to Church in London, goes regularly here for 'example's sake' . . . it is the 'country house' attitude – complete indifference tempered by social convention. . . .

During the summer Wells had been writing *The Future in America* and seeking allies against the Old Gang. Franklin Giddings (1855–1931) was a professor at Columbia University. *Frenzied Finance* (1904) by T. W. Lawson (1857–1921) was an attack on the Amalgamated Copper Company. Upton Sinclair (1878–1968) exposed conditions in the Chicago meat industry in *The Jungle* (1906).

*15 July.* [41 Grosvenor Road]

Spent Sunday with the H. G. Wellses at Sandgate. The friendship between them and us is undergoing the strain of a certain disillusionment. He is, we think, grown in self-confidence, if not conceit, as to his capacity to settle all social and economic questions in general, and to run the Fabian Society in particular, with a corresponding contempt for us poor drudgers . . . He dreams of a great movement of opinion which would render all this detailed work unnecessary . . . He distrusts the devious and narrow ways whereby we reach one position after another – minute steps in advance – when, as he thinks, the position could be rushed at one sweep. Hence he is delighted with America and Americans. Two months rushing about from New York to Washington, Philadelphia to Chicago, has convinced him that America is much nearer the promised land of economic equality than we in England are . . . The new sociologists like Giddings and the 'literature of exposure' like *Frenzied Finance* and *The Jungle* are far more likely to force on a complete and right change than our laboured investigations and Sidney's perpetual presence in committee rooms . . . All this is so contrary to our view of the relative state of America and England . . . that there is little room for friendly and hopeful discussion. And the difference of opinion is heightened by his desire to discredit the old methods of the Fabian and supersede them by methods of his own. . . . To all of which we return a puzzled attitude: Sidney and GBS would gladly give up the leadership of the Fabian to younger hands . . . But they cannot yet see what lines Wells is going on . . .

It would be interesting to know what exactly constitutes Wells's disillusionment with regard to 'the Webbs'. But generally, I think he would say that I was not so good and Sidney was not so able as he had previously thought. He suspects me of a kind of worldliness – a suspicion aroused by my association with such reactionaries as A.J.B., smart ladies, bishops. I think he believes I am playing a long deep game of personal advancement into the High Places of the World. He has no such suspicion of Sidney's motives: but he thinks that Sidney is not a strong enough character and intellect to withstand my sophistical and Jesuitical methods of reasoning. Compared to his former estimate of us, Sidney is weak, and I am bad, and we are partially deceiving the world and ourselves as to our motives and methods. All of which attitude on his part interests me. It would require a good deal of self-assurance to feel confident that his suspicion was entirely groundless, though one must forge ahead without bothering too much about the state of one's soul. As for

Sidney's will-power and capacity – that, I think, can take care of itself. . . . I am much more his instrument than he is mine.

*17 July.* [41 Grosvenor Road]
Yesterday we had a field day at the R.C. . . . I confined my effort to keeping open for further consideration questions which [Lord George], or the Commission as a whole, wished to close: old age pensions, the condition of the 200,000 children now receiving outdoor relief, the administration of relief by boards of guardians, and more important than all, the relation of Poor Law medical treatment to public health.

This is a new hare that I have recently started. In listening to the evidence brought by the C.O.S. members in favour of restricting medical relief to the technically destitute, it suddenly flashed across my mind that what we had to do was to adopt the exactly contrary attitude, and make medical inspection and medical treatment compulsory on all sick persons – to treat illness, in fact, as a public nuisance to be suppressed in the interests of the community. . . . I am elaborating an enquiry of my own – with funds supplied by Charlotte Shaw . . . Meanwhile, despairing of any action on the part of the Commission, I have undertaken (unknown to them) an investigation into the administration of boards of guardians. . . .

> Alice Balfour (1850–1936) was the younger, unmarried sister of Arthur Balfour. Eleanor Sidgwick (1845–1936), the older of the sisters and the widow of the Cambridge philosopher Henry Sidgwick (1838–1900), was principal of Newnham College, Cambridge, 1892–1910. Lady Elizabeth, (Betty) Balfour (1867–1945), wife of Gerald Balfour, was a well-known society hostess and a student of social problems. Lady Frances Balfour (1858–1931) was the daughter of the Duke of Argyll and the wife of Eustace Balfour. Henry George Percy, Duke of Northumberland (1846–1918), was one of the greatest landowners in England; Alnwick Castle in Northumberland was his family seat. His wife was Lady Edith Campbell, sister of Frances Balfour. The Balfour home, Whittingehame, was in East Lothian, not far from Edinburgh. The Webbs were touring to study local government archives.

*16 September.* [Whittingehame]
An unattractive mansion with large formal rooms and passages, elaborate furniture and heavy luxury totally without charm, somewhat cold in the fireless September phase. The atmosphere of gracious simplicity, warm

welcome, intellectual interest, is all the more strikingly personal to the family that inhabits it. The four women – sisters and sisters-in-law – are in themselves remarkable: Alice Balfour neither brilliant nor very capable, but singularly loving, direct and refined, with talents both artistic and scientific wholly sacrificed to the endless detail entailed by her brother's political career and patriarchal establishment. Mrs Sidgwick, weirdly silent but also the soul of veracity and moral refinement – openminded, too, in a limited way. Lady Betty (Gerald's wife) a woman of quite unusual delightfulness, good to look at, sweet to listen to, original in purpose and extraordinarily gracious in disposition. Even Lady Frances, whom I expected to dislike, was attractive in her impulsive indiscretions and straightforward friendliness, with her vivid wit and large experience of political affairs. As kind as kind could be were these four women to me on the day of our arrival. In the afternoon 'Prince Arthur' arrived from North Berwick – a veritable prince of the establishment – the medieval and saintly knight (Gerald) and the bore (Eustace) completing the party. Some dozen children hovered around at intervals but did not join us.

What shall I say of our visit? Too self-consciously Arthur's 'latest friend' to be quite pleasant, the party each night becoming a watched tête-à-tête between us two, the rest of the company sitting round, as Sidney said, 'making conversation'. In fact, the great man is naturally enough too completely the centre of the gathering, without perhaps deserving that position of pre-eminence – all the family worshipping him and waiting on his fancies. . . . I learnt little about him on this visit except that he is self-absorbed and lonely, seldom consulting anyone. 'Brother Arthur is independent of human companionship,' sighed Lady Betty, somewhat hurt, perhaps, that even Gerald was not admitted to his complete confidence.

Gerald is really a more attractive nature . . . has none of the self-consciousness and egotism which lies beneath Arthur's perfect manner, has not developed the cunning of the leader, fearing deposition, or the sentimentality of the lifelong philanderer, never thoroughly in love. For philanderer, refined and consummate, is 'Prince Arthur', accustomed always to make others feel what he fails to feel himself. How many women has he inspired with a discontent for their life and life companion, haunted with the perpetual refrain, 'If only it had been so'. Not a good or wholesome record, and demoralizing to the man himself – and not a worthy substitute for some sort of social fervour. But this is a harsh judgement, one aspect only of the man. Deeper down there are other and better things, but they were hidden from me in these hours of philandering!

. . . then on to Alnwick, [where] we found useful material in the records and enjoyed the novelty of lunching with the ducal family [the Percys] – a courtesy we owed to Lady Frances Balfour. This glimpse of 'high life' interested us. Entombed in that magnificent pile exists a family of exceptional worthiness. The present chief is just a commonplace stupid Englishman – all the commoner and stupider because he feels himself to be a Duke. He is 'got up', as Sidney remarked, 'like a stage Englishman of early Victorian time' – red whiskers, clean-shaven upper lip and chin, well-fitting countrified clothes, self-righteous smug expression, formal manners – above all, stiff and silent. The Duchess is a humpy little person with delicate features, powdered and dressed like a stage Duchess . . . Poor little woman, she looks sad and mentally starved . . . Two or three badly mannered and dull girls represent the younger members of the family present on this occasion. An aristocratic old couple (friends of the family) [and] a heavy, bored-looking tutor or private secretary completed the party that sat down to an elaborate luncheon waited upon by six manservants and served in a palatial banqueting chamber.

Of course, I got nothing to eat but peas and apricot tart – the six manservants, finding I did not take the regulation dishes, refused to hand me anything else – denied me the bread sauce and the plain pudding or another piece of bread. His Grace was far too much absorbed in his own dignity to note that I was unprovided with the necessaries of life. The poor man was in fact struggling to keep us at a distance, scared by the assumed attempt of these notable socialists to get access to the records of his manor courts. . . . This determination made him, at first, almost discourteous to me – which I, discovering, turned round and talked to the daughters. At the other end of the table I heard Sidney discoursing most pleasantly with the Duchess. Indeed, if it had not been for ourselves it seems to me the party would have eaten its meal in heavy silence. When the Duke awoke to the fact that we were not otherwise than well-bred people . . . he relaxed a little and after lunch discussed county council business with Sidney – self-important and stupid but not otherwise objectionable . . .

*1 October.* [41 Grosvenor Road]
First meeting of the Poor Law Commission after the recess – all very friendly – to discuss our future plans. . . . Discussion now is premature

and I think a waste of time. But it is pleasant to find that there is no tension between myself and any of the other commissioners. It is generally understood that I am undertaking a good slice of work on documents, exactly as Charles Booth is on statistics. . . . The week before the Commission met we had a most pleasant two days with the George Hamiltons at Deal Castle. . . . I think we and they thoroughly like each other in private life – though the chairman of the Royal Commission finds the 'trusty and well-beloved Beatrice Webb, wife of Sidney Webb' somewhat of a handful. . . . On our way back from the Hamiltons' we called on H. G. Wells and his wife at Sandgate – deliberately, to relieve the strain caused by the Wells revolt in the Fabian Society. We found him in a depressed and rather angered state. His own affairs had not been going well. *In the Days of the Comet* had fallen flat: 'Another failure and I should have to go back to journalism for a maintenance.' . . . He was angry with the Old Gang, partly because he thought they would carry the Society against him, partly because he thought they might retire from it and leave him all the bother – the unremunerative bother – of 'running it' without them. He did not know which eventuality he would dislike most. . . . We tried to smooth him down. 'We must not have another J. R. MacDonald either in or outside the Society,' I suggested to Sidney. 'We must remain good friends with H. G. Wells – properly managed, he will count for righteousness in his own way, and it is no good wasting his and our strength in friction.' . . .

*18 October.* [41 Grosvenor Road]

H. G. Wells gave an address to the Fabian Society on 'Socialism and the Middle Classes', ending up with an attack on 'the family'. Some of the new members welcomed his denunciation, but the meeting, which was crowded, was against him, for the simple reason that he had nothing constructive to suggest. Since then I have read *In the Days of the Comet*, which ends with a glowing anticipation of promiscuity in sexual relations. The argument is one that is familiar to most intellectuals: it has often cropped up in my own mind and has seemed to have some validity. Friendship between particular men and women has an enormous educational value to both (especially to the woman). Such a friendship is practically impossible . . . without physical intimacy. You do not, as a matter of fact, get to know any man thoroughly except as his beloved and his lover – if you could have been the beloved of the dozen ablest men you have known, it would have greatly extended your knowledge of human nature and human affairs. This, I believe, is true of our present rather gross state of body and mind.

But there remains the question whether, with all the perturbation caused by such intimacies, you would have any brain left to think with? I know that I should not, and I fancy that other women would be even worse off in this particular. Moreover, it would mean a great increase in sexual emotion for its own sake and not for the sake of bearing children. And that way madness lies? This is omitting the whole social argument against promiscuity, which is the strongest. Regarding each individual as living in a vacuum with no other obligations than the formation of his or her own character, I still reject 'free love' as a method of development. . . . H. G. Wells is, I believe, merely gambling with the idea . . . throwing it out to see what sort of reception it gets, without responsibility for its effect on the character of hearers. It is this recklessness that makes Sidney dislike him. I think it important *not* to dislike him: he is going through an ugly time and we must stand by him for his own sake and for the good of the cause of collectivism. If he will let us, that is to say. I am not sure he is not getting to dislike us in our well-regulated prosperity. . . .

In 1889 Beatrice had signed an anti-suffrage manifesto drafted by the novelist Mrs Humphry Ward. 'I reacted against the narrow outlook and exasperated tone of some of the pioneers of women's suffrage,' Beatrice explained later in *Our Partnership*. 'Also, my dislike of the current parliamentary politics of the Tory and Whig "ins" and "outs" seemed a sort of argument against the immersion of women in this atmosphere. But the root of my anti-feminism lay in the fact that I had never myself suffered the disabilities assumed to arise from my sex. Quite the contrary; if I had been a man, self-respect, family pressure and the public opinion of my class would have pushed me into a money-making profession; as a mere woman I could carve out a career of disinterested research. Moreover, in the craft I had chosen, a woman was privileged. As an investigator she aroused less suspicion . . . and gained better information. Further, in those days, a competent female writer on economic questions had, to an enterprising editor, actually a scarcity value. Thus she secured immediate publication and, to judge from my own experience, was paid a higher rate than that obtained by male competitors of equal standing.' Her present recantation was related to a new wave of militancy. Frustrated by the failure of the middle-class suffrage societies to make headway and by the refusal of the Liberal government to introduce votes for women, though a majority of M.P.s had pledged their support, Emmeline Pankhurst (1858–1928) broke with the constitutional suffragists led by Millicent Fawcett (1847–1929) and formed the militant Women's Social and Political Union. In October, large bodies of women lobbied M.P.s and several were arrested for riotous behaviour that began a trend towards 'direct action'. On 13 October Christabel Pankhurst (1881–1958) and Annie Kenney (1897–1952) heckled Sir Edward Grey and Winston Churchill at a meeting in Manchester. Beatrice copied her correspondence with Mrs Fawcett into the diary.

*5 November.* [41 Grosvenor Road]
Here is my formal recantation. For some time I have felt the old prejudice evaporating. And as the women suffragists were being battered about rather badly, and coarse-grained men were saying coarse-grained things, I thought I might as well give a friendly pull to get the thing out of the mud, even at the risk of getting a little spattered myself. What is, perhaps, more likely is that I shall be thought, by some, to be a pompous prig. The movement will stand some of that element now!

*The Times*, 5 November 1906

Sir – I have just received the enclosed letter from Mrs Sidney Webb. As she generously allows me to make any use of it I like, may I beg the favour of its insertion in *The Times*?

Those who have been working for many years for women's suffrage naturally regard with extreme satisfaction the adhesion to the movement of two of the ablest women who have hitherto opposed it, Mrs Creighton and Mrs Sidney Webb. Mrs Creighton's change of view was chronicled in your columns about a week ago.

Yours obediently,
MILLICENT GARRETT FAWCETT

41 Grosvenor Road, Westminster Embankment, 2 November [1906]

Dear Mrs Fawcett,
You once asked me to let you know if I ceased to object to the grant of the electoral franchise to women. The time has come when I feel obliged to do so.

My objection was based principally on my disbelief in the validity of any 'abstract rights', whether to votes or to property, or even to 'life, liberty and the pursuit of happiness'. I prefer to regard life as a series of obligations – obligations of the individual to the community and of the community to the individual. I could not see that women, as women, were under any particular obligation to take part in the conduct of government.

I have been told that the more spiritually-minded Eastern readily acquiesces in the material management of his native country by what he regards as the Anglo-Saxon 'man of affairs'. In the same way, I thought that women might well be content to leave the 'rough and tumble' of party politics to their mankind, with the object of concentrating all their own energies on what seemed to me their peculiar social obligations – the bearing of children, the advancement of learning, and the handing on from generation to generation of an appreciation of the spiritual life.

Such a division of labour between men and women is, however, only practicable if there is, among both sections alike, a continuous feeling of consent to what is being done by government as their common agent. This consciousness of consent can hardly avoid being upset if the work of government comes actively to overlap the particular obligations of an excluded class. If our Indian administrators were to interfere with the religious obligations of Hindus or Mohammedans, British rule in India would, I suppose, come to an end. It seems to me that something analogous to this is happening in the Europe of today with regard to the particular obligations of women. The rearing of children, the advancement of learning, and the promotion of the spiritual life – which I regard as the particular obligations of women – are, it is clear, more and more becoming the main preoccupations of the community as a whole. The legislatures of this century are, in one country after another, increasingly devoting themselves to these subjects. Whilst I rejoice in much of this new development of politics, I think it adequately accounts for the increasing restiveness of women. They are, in my opinion, rapidly losing their consciousness of consent in the work of government and are even feeling a positive obligation to take part in directing this new activity. This is, in my view, not a claim to rights or an abandonment of women's particular obligations, but a desire more effectually to fulfil their functions by sharing the control of state action in those directions.

The episodes of the last few weeks complete the demonstration that it is undesirable that this sense of obligation should manifest itself in unconstitutional forms. We may grant that persistent interruption of public business is lowering to the dignity of public life. But it is cruel to put a fellow citizen of strong convictions in the dilemma of political ineffectiveness or unmannerly breaches of the peace. If the consciousness of non-consent is sufficiently strong, we can hardly blame the public-spirited women who by their exclusion from constitutional methods of asserting their views are driven to the latter alternative, at the cost of personal suffering and masculine ridicule. To call such behaviour vulgar is an undistinguished, and I may say an illiterate, use of language. The way out of this unpleasant dilemma, it seems to me, is to permit this growing consciousness among women – that their particular social obligations compel them to claim a share in the conduct of political affairs – to find a constitutional channel.

This reasoning involves, of course, the admission to the franchise of women as women, whether married or single, propertied or wage-earning.

It is, I feel, due to you that I should tell you of my change of attitude, and I thought you would perhaps be interested in my reasons.

Yours very truly,<br>BEATRICE WEBB

*21 November.* [41 Grosvenor Road]
Haldane came in for a quiet talk . . . He is completely absorbed in his office, thinking out the problems of army administration and attempting to adapt the experience of Germany to the character and ways of the English officer. Among other developments there is that connected with the School of Economics . . . We are to have forty officers to instruct in business methods and, in return, to receive about £2,000 a year. It all goes to build up the School as the national institution for administrative science, which is perhaps an aspect of the scheme which appeals to us more than the honour of instructing the army. . . . Meanwhile, it looks like a *débâcle* for the Progressive forces at the March L.C.C. election. . . . But Sidney is really very unconcerned. . . . 'Most of my work they can't undo even if I am turned out,' he chuckles to himself. . . .

*29 November.* [41 Grosvenor Road]
Sidney making up his mind to retire from the L.C.C. in 1910, before we go abroad for our sabbatical year. 'I want to be rid of electioneering and all the devious ways of the elected person. Eighteen years is a fair term of service.' His desires turn more and more to investigation and constructive thinking, and to the organization of the social sciences. . . . 'I am weary of doing harmless things for ulterior motives: it is, after a time, irksome to distribute prizes because an election is at hand.' He feels he has a right to be fastidious in his methods and single-minded in his aims. A luxury I think we elderly folk ought to be allowed.

*30 November.* [41 Grosvenor Road]

H. G. Wells, who was staying here for two nights, first justified the last chapters of *In the Days of the Comet* by asserting that it was a work of art and therefore could not be criticized from the standpoint of morality. However, he afterwards admitted that he thought 'free-er love' would be the future relation of the sexes, when we had got over the sordid stage of the masculine proprietorship of the woman. 'At present, any attempt to realize this free-er love means a network of low intrigue . . . the relations between men and women are so hemmed in by law and convention. To experiment, you must be base: hence to experiment starts with being damned.' There is, of course, truth in this argument . . . But I cling to the thought that man will only evolve upwards by the subordination of his physical desires and appetites to the intellectual and spiritual side of his nature. Unless this evolution be the purpose of the race, I despair . . . It is this purpose, and this purpose only, that gives a meaning to the constantly recurring battles of good and evil within one's own nature – and to one's persistent endeavour to find the ways and means of combating the evil habits of the mass of men. Oh! for a Church that would weld into one living force all who hold this faith, with the discipline and the consolations fitted to sustain their endeavour.

As it is, I find myself once or twice a week in St Paul's, listening to the music of the psalms and repeating, with childlike fervour, the words of the old Elizabethan prayers. It is this recreation that sustains me in these days of murky feeling. . . .

*15 December.* [41 Grosvenor Road]

H. G. Wells made a bad failure of his effort to capture the Fabian Society . . . The odd thing is that if he had pushed his own fervid policy, or rather, enthusiasm for vague and big ideas, without making a personal attack on the Old Gang, he would have succeeded. . . . But his accusations were so preposterous, his innuendoes so unsavoury and his little fibs so transparent, that even his own followers refused to support him . . . GBS, by a scathing analysis of his whole conduct, threw him finally to the ground and trampled on him, somewhat hardly. With a splutter the poor man withdrew . . . An altogether horrid business. . . . However, his nine months' fight in the Fabian will be excellent 'copy' for Wells: that will console him, I think, in the end. . . .

Beatrice with her parents 1865

Herbert Spencer *c.* 1875

ortrait of Sir Charles Booth
y William Rothenstein 1908

Family group 1865. *Left to right*: Georgina,
Mary, Lawrencina Potter, Margaret, Beatrice,
Richard Potter, Theresa, Blanche

Standish House, Vale of Severn, Gloucester

Joseph Chamberlain

Beatrice aged about 27

Sidney Webb 1885

44 Cranbourne Street, London WC2,
Sidney's birthplace

The Argoed

The Potter sisters at Standish, *c.* 1893. *Standing left to right:* Rosy, Blanche, Lawrencina. *Seated left to right:* Margaret, Kate, Beatrice, Mary, Georgina

Beatrice and Sidney Webb photographed by Bernard Shaw

Bernard Shaw

Charlotte Payne Townshend learning to ride a bicycle, *c.* 1896. Pasted into Beatrice Webb's diary for 1898

41 Grosvenor Road

'The Wire Puller', a cartoon published in the *Manchester Evening Chronicle*, 11 March 1908. Described by Beatrice in her diary as 'a disagreeabl[e] infringement of our anonymity'

A.J. Balfour 1898

Adelphi Terrace

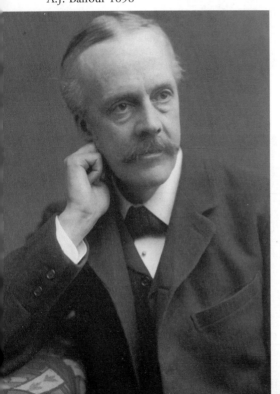

Fabian Summer School, Llanbedr 1909. *Left to right:* James Strachey, unknown, Margery Olivier, unknown, Rupert Brooke, Arthur Colegate, unknown, Rivers Blanco White, Amber Reeves, Clifford Sharp

Winston Churchill 1903

David Lloyd George 1914

H.G. Wells 1920

Sir Oswald and Lady Mosley 1922

Susan Lawrence campaigning

Beatrice and Sidney Webb
at the 1923 Labour
Conference

Labour Government, 1924.
*From left, standing:*
C.P. Trevelyan, Stephen Walsh
Thomson, Chelmsford,
Sidney Webb, Sydney Olivier,
John Wheatley, Noel Buxton,
F.W. Jowett, Josiah Wedgwoo
Vernon Hartshorn, Tom Sha
*seated:* Willie Anderson,
Parmoor, Philip Snowden,
Haldane, Ramsay MacDona
J.R. Clynes, J.H. Thomas,
Arthur Henderson

Virginia Woolf 1926

Lord Passfield at 10 Downing Street, Budget Day, 14 April 1930

Sir Stafford Cripps and his wife, Isobel 1939

Ivan Maisky at the Russian Embassy 1940

The Webbs and Bernard
Shaw at Passfield

Beatrice and her sisters, Kate, *left*, and Rosie

Sir William Nicholson's portrait
of the Webbs, painted in 1928,
which hangs in the Founders'
Room at the L.S.E.

Photographs of Sidney and Beatrice Webb taken in 1941.
The contemporary caption read 'Two Friends of the Soviet Union'

~ 1907 ~

*18 January.* [41 Grosvenor Road]
Three vacation weeks at Bexhill in order to be near Rosy Dobbs, who was having a baby with her husband away. Her state is extraordinarily satisfactory. Here she is with six healthy children, all of whom seem likely to be quite as well gifted by nature and quite as well brought up as the children of her sisters. She is wholly devoted to them, thinks of nothing else but their welfare. The home is almost intolerably uncomfortable for outsiders or servants, and not attractive to her husband, but the only effect on the children is to make them squall at home and be good abroad – all of them starting with a low standard of personal comfort. Apart from her real genius for making an uncomfortable and untidy interior, she is an excellent person, and barring occasional screaming fits, she has lost most of her strange manias. Her children, from Noel downwards, are devoted to her, and George apparently is still very fond of her, though suffering a good deal from the disorderly home. There stands the solid fact that the sum total of her life is good – and to think what she might have been, but for a strong family and means to tide her over a bad strain in her nature!

. . . My paper on Poor Law medical relief and public health has started a ball rolling and it promises, I think, to be a snowball . . . The reports of the assistant commissioners are all pointing away from bad administration as *the* cause of pauperism and towards bad conditions among large classes of the population as the overwhelmingly important fact . . . That is the little lesson the C.O.S. will have to learn from the Commission. But if I am to carry the majority along with me any part of the way, I shall have to be discreet. . . . I am clearly better out of this business: the less I say on abstract questions the better. It only irritates or frightens the bulk of my fellow commissioners. I lack discretion in the 'spoken word': to that extent I lack manners.

*18 February.* [Beachy Head, Eastbourne]
Alone in Beachy Head Hotel with a hurricane roaring around. Came here with Sidney, completely exhausted – so exhausted that he hardly liked to leave me and return to his electioneering, which is imperative. The exhaustion was brought on by two events: a most tiring five days with the Commission in Yorkshire and a tempestuous upset in the Evidence Committee with regard to my special enquiries. . . . I received from the chairman a somewhat curt and crude request to give up

investigating on my own account . . . Whilst gently complaining that my action had been discussed and condemned in my absence, I laid bare all my doings and ended up by saying politely but firmly that I intended to continue, basing myself on the practice of the royal commissions and select committees that I had known. 'Splendid,' said R. B. Haldane (to whom I submitted the correspondence). '*They* won't encounter you in a hurry again.' But all this took a good deal out of me. . . . If it were not for my reliance on Sidney's strength, I should almost retire from business. I tremble to think how utterly dependent I am on him – both on his love and on his unrivalled capacity for 'putting things through'. When he is late, I get into a panic of fear lest some mishap has befallen him. This fear of losing each other is always present – more with me, I think, than with him. 'I don't think about it,' he often says. Sometimes we try to cheer each other in advance, by remembering that we have had a happiness which death cannot take from us.

What has again been troubling me is the question of social engagements. I go out hardly at all; and except for business interviews at lunch and dinner, entertain even less. But such 'society' as we have, apart from professional society, is tending to become of an aristocratic and fastidious character. This is partly because I like brilliant little parties, and interesting folk versed in great affairs, and partly because my reputation of knowing them helps forward the various works we have on hand. But there are grave disadvantages to this 'dallying with fashion'. Least of them, perhaps, is the spiteful things that are said – partly by envious folk, partly by fanatics. More important is the drain on energy, both financial and personal, that any association with the great world involves. Better clothes, fares to country houses, and most of all the exhaustion of living up to a reputation, even of 'letting myself go'. It seems ludicrous to bother about the question – the amount we do is very little – and any day we could give that little up without a pang. For all that, my conscience about it is not quite easy. . . .

Though Sidney held his seat, there was a sharp swing against the Progressives all over London. Beatrice, who never greatly cared for Sidney's L.C.C. colleagues, was not displeased at the defeat of this 'mean lot'.

*3 March.* [41 Grosvenor Road]
Escaped with our bare lives in the general rout. But still here they are, Phillimore and Webb – L.C.C.s again! . . . now it is all over and we see that the Progressives have been completely smashed, I am proud that my

man has survived in spite of his independent attitude. It is a tribute to my boy's personality. How will he find a council run by the Moderates? . . .

*19 March.* [41 Grosvenor Road]
A delightful Saturday and Sunday with the Elchos at Stanway, A.J.B. bringing down his motor. . . . In his courtly devotion to Lady Elcho . . . 'Prince Arthur' is at his best. . . . One can believe that the relation between these two has always been at the same high level of affectionate friendship, without taint of intrigue. With this background, the intellectual camaraderie of the Conservative leader with 'the Webbs' dropped into its right place, as a slight new thing agreeably stimulating to all concerned. . . . Brilliant and pleasant was the talk as we whirled through the countryside in A.J.B.'s motor, or lounged in the famous hall of Stanway. Amused and interested we undoubtedly were (but hardly rested). What was, I think, achieved, was a wholesome settling of our new friendships. The 'sensationalism' apparent at Whittingehame had wholly departed.

But shall we advance matters by our friendship with A.J.B.? . . . we may be playing an elaborate game of cross-purposes . . .

As her inquiries progressed, Beatrice considered leaving the nominal structure of the Poor Law intact, 'and tak[ing] the stuff out drop by drop – the sick first, and plac[ing] them under the sanitary authority; then the children, placed under the education authority; then the aged (pensions), perhaps the unemployed and vagrants.' These ideas were later built into the Minority Report. If they prevailed, Beatrice believed it would be impossible to maintain a separate class of paupers. Without this distinction the 'Principles of 1834' would be irrelevant. A recent government decision to introduce old-age pensions for the poor convinced her that distress beyond the formal limits of pauperism was now being recognized. Beatrice launched a draft report on 15 May and immediately started lobbying for support outside the Commission. She sought Tory backing from Balfour, and made approaches elsewhere. These intrigues infuriated her fellow commissioners and many Liberals, and so upset John Burns, who was in a position to obstruct the Webbs, that their influence diminished inversely to their efforts.

*10 April.* [Bramdean]
. . . What interests me as an observer of human nature is that I have become wholly indifferent to the Royal Commission. I merely work as hard as I know how in my own direction, without caring much what

happens. I find myself perpetually watching my colleagues, dashing in when I see an opening. I sometimes push or squeeze through, sometimes the door is slammed in my face, and I accept either fate (with equal equanimity). . . . I sometimes ponder over whether this aloofness is quite a good quality. But then I recollect that, after all, I am in a minority and that it is my business to be hostile to the government; and if I can be comfortably and good-naturedly hostile, so much the better. With Sidney, this attitude of indifference to his colleagues on public bodies is habitual – perhaps I am merely becoming masculine, losing the 'personal note' which is the characteristic of the woman in human intercourse. What is rather disconcerting is that I catch myself 'playing the personal note' when it suits my purpose, playing it without feeling it. Is that a characteristic of the woman on public bodies? I do try to check myself in this mean little game; but it has the persistency of an inherited or acquired habit.

The failure of Campbell-Bannerman's government to pursue social reform dissatisfied progressive Liberals and an increasingly vocal Labour Party. A desire for change among the enlightened middle classes, in particular, was reflected in the Fabian 'boom', and in support for the Webb campaign for the break-up of the Poor Law a little later. The work of Wells and Shaw helped shape this climate of opinion.

*3 May.* [41 Grosvenor Road]
. . . The little boom in the Fabian Society continues, and Sidney and I, GBS and H.G.W., sometimes ask ourselves and each other whether there is a bare possibility that it represents a larger wave than we think . . . If this pleasant suspicion grows, it will consolidate the Society and draw the leaders nearer together. . . . as a matter of fact, we stand to gain by each other's success, each one introducing the other two to new circles of admirers. With the Shaws our communion becomes ever closer and more thoroughly complementary and stimulating, and I hope and believe it will be so with H.G.W.

Meanwhile Sidney and I are living at the usual high pressure. . . . Just now our usual positions are somewhat reversed: it is he who sits at home and thinks out the common literary work, it is I who am racing around dealing with men and affairs! . . .

The Shaws took a Victorian rectory at Ayot St Lawrence in Hertfordshire in the autumn of 1906; it remained their home until their deaths. Mary Playne was suffering from cancer but an operation proved successful.

*19 July.* [Ayot St Lawrence]
The Bernard Shaws have lent us their little week-end house for two-and-a-half months, they having migrated to a large mansion in Wales, close to the Fabian Summer School. Now we are going to set to work to finish up our volume on *The Manor and the Borough* . . . This somewhat abstruse historical work is restful after the contriving of schemes and the drafting of analyses meant to affect action. And I am convinced that this intimate knowledge of what past generations of one's own race have actually done . . . gives larger scope to one's imagination as a reformer of the present state of things. . . .

*28 September.* [Ayot St Lawrence]
We were working down here, well and happily, when a letter from Mary broke up our peace. For the next week or so, I lived haunted by terror for the life of this dearest sister. Now I have become accustomed to the fear of recurrence – I refuse to think of it – but the fear is there in the background . . . Now and again the fear for Mary seems to extend into fear for Sidney, or even, in my worst moments, for myself, unnerving me for a while. Meanwhile, Mary is full of hope and energy. Now the operation is over, she has returned to her everyday life and work – an example to us all. How hard it is, when one feels life throbbing through one – physical well-being, intellectual interest and love – how horribly hard it is to face death calmly. As a child I had no fear of death: sometimes I longed for it. But with growing strength, with increasing consciousness of capacity, death seems a cruel wasteful destruction of what is good to feel and good to be. . . .

*30 October.* [41 Grosvenor Road]
John Burns has become a monstrosity. . . . He talks incessantly, and never listens to anyone except the officials to whom he *must* listen in order to accomplish the routine work of his office. Hence, he is completely in their hands, and is becoming the most hidebound of departmental chiefs, gulled by an obstructive fact or reactionary argument – taken in by the most naïve commonplaces of middle-class administrative routine. . . . What is the right conduct towards such a man? . . .

*12 November.* [Beachy Head]
The row about my investigations developed: the chairman coming on the track . . . Unfortunately I was, at the moment, in a state of high fever

and there ensued a somewhat angry correspondence between us – he censoring me and I asserting my right to get at facts for myself. All this has meant, on the top of a year's hard work, a bad nervous breakdown, and I am here for ten days' absolute quiet – a truce having been proclaimed in my absence on sick leave. Perhaps when I return it will all have blown over. . . .

But I am low and disheartened. I don't like all this intriguing. I should prefer to play with my cards on the table. . . .

*9 December.* [41 Grosvenor Road]
Lord George scored a great victory today, and I a great success. . . . In their hatred of me, all the C.O.S. members rallied to him . . . Thereupon, I gave them to understand that we considered the issue vital and should have our Minority Report. Short of getting a majority report written by ourselves, this . . . is exactly the position which I prefer . . . a thoroughly Webbian document – in tone, statement of fact and proposals. Meanwhile, our chairman is overjoyed at the victory and received my hearty congratulations most graciously. He and I are excellent friends. With my other colleagues, there is a most distinct consolidation against me – amounting almost to boycott, at any rate to a discourteous coldness. Honestly, I think they are somewhat justified in their dislike of me. I have played with the Commission. I have been justified in doing so, because they began by ignoring me, but it is unpleasant to be played with, especially by a person whom you want to despise. . . .

$\sim$ 1908 $\sim$

The Webbs had turned their thoughts to the able-bodied unemployed. Current remedies included public works, emigration, and land colonization at home.

*13 January.* [41 Grosvenor Road]
A weird Christmas recess at Hollesley Bay Colony, investigating the daily routine of the 300 men's lives, getting particulars about their former occupations and present views, having long talks with the superintendent, the works manager, the farmer and the gangers, with a view to ascertaining the possibilities of the working colony as an element in any scheme for dealing with unemployment. The atmosphere, the impression of the place was mournfully tragic. Half-educated, half-

which every art is used to attract the colonists to the penitent's form. Music, eloquence, the magnetic personality of the trained Salvationist preachers – a personality that combines the spiritual leader with that of the refined variety artist – all these talents are lavished on the work of conversion. And would it be very surprising if the ignorant and child-ishly suspicious men who make up the colonists should imagine that they would be better, even from the worldly point of view, if they accepted the creed of their governors? The Saturday entertainment, though permeated with religious feeling, even the Sunday morning and afternoon services, did not transgress the limits of reasonable influence. But the intensely compelling nature of the appeal to become 'converted' made tonight by Brigadier Jackson and his wife, I confess, somewhat frightened me off recommending that the Salvation Army should be state or rate-aided in this work of proselytizing persons committed to their care for secular reasons! Is it right to submit men, weakened by suf-fering, to this religious pressure exercised by the very persons who command their labour?

*10 February.* [41 Grosvenor Road]
A series of political dinner-parties. . . . The net impression left on our mind is the scramble for new constructive ideas. We happen just now to have a good many to give away, hence the eagerness of our company. Every politician one meets wants to be 'coached'. It is really quite comic. It seems to be quite irrelevant whether they are Conservatives, Liberals, or Labour Party men – all alike have become mendicants for practical proposals. . . .

*24 March.* [41 Grosvenor Road]
Gave A. J. Balfour my Poor Law scheme whilst we were staying at Stanway. Lord Elcho had read it and been captivated by it and begged me to hand it on, in A.J.B.'s presence. 'If he will really read it and remember to return it to me,' I graciously remarked, 'I promise on both counts, Mrs Webb.' So having reported to H.M. Government I report to H.M. Opposition. . . .

Campbell-Bannerman, who died of a heart attack on 22 April, had relinquished the premiership to Asquith on 5 April. With Lloyd George as Chancellor of the Exchequer and Winston Churchill as President of the Board of Trade, the Liberals launched a progressive social policy.

*18/20 April. Kilteragh, Kingston, Co. Dublin*
. . . three days' complete rest before ten days' motoring in West of
Ireland on the pretence of investigating the Irish Poor Law – but really
for a much needed change of scene and idea. . . .

The last days watching the formation of the Asquith ministry have
been exciting. We have not seen any of the principals, so all we have
heard has been mere hearsay. . . .

*3 May.* [Mallaranny]
. . . Feeling the impossibility of getting any kind of knowledge – even the
most casual – from my trip . . . The beauty of the scenery, the freshness
and pathos of Irish life, the complete break in the continual routine
grind of the last two years, have done me a world of good. But this very
enjoyment shows how hopelessly irresponsible I feel with regard to Irish
affairs – no more responsible than if I were travelling in Norway or
Sicily. For the misery is genuine – the men, women and children who
crouch in those filthy huts and toil hour by hour on those boglands in
a listless fashion, are in this their beloved country hopeless and helpless
with regard to this world's affairs. There is heaven and there is America –
and, according to whether they are the children of this world or of the
next, they desire to escape to one or the other. Until this escape opens to
them, they are drearily indifferent to varying degrees of squalor and
want – mechanically day after day they toil, but they do not struggle to
survive the ordeal. In the West of Ireland, one realizes for the first time
the grim fact of the existence of a whole community on the margin of
cultivation. . . .

*19 May.* [41 Grosvenor Road]
. . . we went to lunch alone with R. B. Haldane and found him as
friendly as ever. Clearly his *bête noire* is Lloyd George, and after him
Winston Churchill – the young generation knocking at the door. He is
full of confidence in his Territorial Army and in all the reforms he has
brought about at the War Office. . . .

H. J. Mackinder came to lunch today to discuss who should be his
successor as Director of the School. . . . He has been the best of colleagues during these four years, and has improved both the internal
organization and the external position of the School. Indeed so competent a Director has he been, that he has virtually run the whole business,
Sidney trusting his initiative and executive capacity. We part company
with the highest regard for him, and I think he for us, but with no

particular friendship. It is an instance of the absence of a common creed: our views are not mutually antagonistic, but they never meet and would never meet if we went on working for all eternity. . . .

William Pember Reeves (1857–1932), a Fabian Socialist from New Zealand, came to England in 1896 as Agent General. His wife Maud (d. 1953), also a Fabian, published a widely read book about low incomes: *Round About a Pound a Week* (1913). Amber Reeves (1887–1981), their daughter, a student at Newnham College, was a leading member of the informal Fabian 'Nursery' set up in 1906.

*27 May.* [41 Grosvenor Road]
. . . W. P. Reeves accepted the position [Director of the L.S.E.] at £700, resigning his High Commissionership but retaining a salary of £400 as financial adviser, and another £200 or so as a director of the Bank of New Zealand. We are quite content and he begins with enthusiasm.

*15 September.* [41 Grosvenor Road]
After . . . six weeks at a little house in Hertfordshire and four days at the Fabian summer school, we are again back in London. . . .

The Fabian summer school has become an odd and interesting institution. Two or three houses on the mountainous coast of North Wales are filled to overflowing for seven weeks with some hundred Fabians and sympathizers – a dozen or so young university graduates and undergraduates, another stratum of lower middle-class professionals, a stray member of Parliament or professor, a bevy of fair girls, and the remainder – a too large remainder – elderly and old nondescript females who find the place lively and fairly cheap. The young folk live the most unconventional life . . . stealing out on moor or sand, in stable or under hayricks, without always the requisite chaperone to make it look as wholly innocent as it really is. Then the 'gym' costume which they all affect is startling the Methodist Wales, and the conversation is most surprisingly open. 'Is dancing sexual?', I found three pretty Cambridge girl graduates discussing with half a dozen men. But mostly they talk economics and political science, in the intervals of breaking off the engagements to marry each other they formed a year ago. Meanwhile, there is some really useful intellectual intercourse going on . . .

I had seven of the Cambridge Fabians to stay with me on their way to Wales. . . . I also had the brilliant Amber Reeves, the double first Moral Science Tripos, an amazingly vital person and I suppose very clever, but a terrible little pagan – vain, egotistical, and careless of other people's happiness. . . . A somewhat dangerous friendship is springing up between her and H. G. Wells. I think they are both too soundly self-interested to do more than cause poor Jane Wells some fearful feelings, but if Amber were my child I should be anxious.

*2 October.* [41 Grosvenor Road]
Sidney and I are living at the highest pressure of brainwork. We are working against time on the [Minority] report . . . To enable me to fill my part of the work I am living on the most rigorous hygienic basis – up at 6.30, cold bath and quick walk or ride, work from 7.30 to 1 o'clock, bread and cheese lunch, short rest, another walk, then tea and work until 6 or 6.30 – sometimes as much as seven hours' work in the day. I feel it is too much, and am sleeping badly from brain excitement. But short of breaking down, I must continue at it until Christmas. After the report is done with we *must* and *will* have a complete rest – Egypt or Italy – somewhere where we shall rid our minds of the whole business. . . .

> Winston Churchill had married Clementine Hozier (1885–1977) in September. The meeting with Lloyd George was the last chance for the Webbs to collaborate in drafting the social insurance measures Lloyd George and Churchill were now preparing. The role the Webbs might have played in shaping these reforms then passed to William Beveridge (1879–1963), economist and civil servant, and Hubert Llewellyn Smith.

*16 October.* [41 Grosvenor Road]
. . . On Sunday we lunched with Winston Churchill and his bride – a charming lady, well-bred and pretty, and earnest withal, but not rich, by no means a 'good match', which is to Winston's credit. Winston had made a really eloquent speech on the unemployed the night before and he has mastered the Webb scheme . . . He is brilliantly able – more than a phrase-monger, I think – and is definitely casting in his lot with the [cause of] constructive state action. No doubt he puts that side forward to me, but still he could not do it so well if he did not agree somewhat with it. After lunch Lloyd George came in and asked us to breakfast to discuss his insurance scheme.

On Friday we fulfilled the engagement at 11 Downing Street, meeting Haldane . . . and, after breakfast, Winston. . . . I tried to impress on them that any grant from the community to the individual, beyond what it does for all, ought to be conditional on better conduct; and that any insurance scheme had the fatal defect that the state got nothing for its money . . . Also, if you did all that was requisite for those who were uninsured, there was not much to be gained by being insured, except more freedom. . . . He [Lloyd George] is a clever fellow, but has less intellect than Winston, and not such an attractive personality – more of the preacher, less of the statesman. . . .

29 October. [41 Grosvenor Road]
. . . I was sorry to hear from Kate that the Booth family feel aggrieved – say that somehow or other I 'drove Charles Booth off the Commission'. This is the most annoying story. C.B. from the first gave me the cold shoulder, and even upbraided me for insisting on getting at the documents of the central authority. I took both his rebuke and his coldness with good-natured equanimity – feeling that he had a perfect right to keep clear of me, if he thought I should injure his influence . . . Now it appears that he thinks that I intrigued against him or his scheme, in his absence, and that it was my malign influence which made the Commission so unappreciative when he returned. As a matter of fact, I was surprised at the Commission's rudeness . . . Now Charles Booth, who feels strong enough to join in the Commission's work, is angry with himself for resigning, and puts the blame on me; which chimes in with the anger of the rest of my colleagues. By the time that Commission ends, I shall be a well-hated person. . . . Every reference in the press, every unfavourable speech, every straw that points my way is the result of a Webb intrigue! . . .

15 November. [41 Grosvenor Road]
. . . About a fortnight ago, we were invited to breakfast at the Board of Trade. We found assembled some half-dozen of the Labour M.P.s . . . Winston using us to explain the theory of labour exchanges to the Labour men. . . . The difficulty of solving the question [of the able-bodied unemployed] oppresses me. I dream of it at night, I pray for light in the early morning, I grind, grind, grind, all the hours of the working day to try to get a solution. . . .

15 December. [41 Grosvenor Road]
. . . The poor old Commission – and it is getting more old and weary, if not actually senile, with every week's sitting. It is floundering about in its morass of a report. . . . Are all men quite so imbecile as that lot are? . . .

They play about, altering commas and capitals and changing the names of things, but leaving to mere accident whether or not the vagrants or the mentally defective are to be dealt with under the Poor Law. . . . If I ever sit again on a royal commission, I hope my colleagues will be of a superior calibre, for really it is shockingly bad for one's character to be with such folk. It makes me feel intolerably superior.

## ∾ 1909 ∾

*1 January.* [41 Grosvenor Road]
Our report is finished. . . . On Saturday we are all to attend and be photographed and sign a blank piece of paper. So ends the Commission of 1906–1909. I am in a state of complete exhaustion, made worse by nervous apprehension of more indiscretions in the press in the interests of the dissentient minority. . . . However, my colleagues will now melt back into the world at large and we shall know each other no more. The relation has not been a pleasant one, for either side.

> The Commission had sat for three years. Both the Majority and Minority Reports were enormous. They were divided on one important point – the future of the Poor Law itself. The majority stood for its preservation, much modified; the minority favoured the break-up of the old system.

*18 February.* [41 Grosvenor Road]
. . . We turned out to be quite wrong as to the reception of the Majority Report. . . . Roughly speaking, all the Conservative papers went for the majority proposals, and the London Liberal papers were decidedly for ours. We secured, in fact, belligerent rights, but not more than that! The majority hold the platform. Perhaps we feel a trifle foolish at having 'crabbed' the Majority Report to our family and intimate friends, and exalted our own. That has certainly not proved to be the estimate of public opinion. . . .

*22 February.* [41 Grosvenor Road]
I am recovering my equilibrium slowly. It is always interesting to analyse one's mistakes and successes. In our depreciation of the Majority Report . . . we overlooked the immense step made by the sweeping away of the deterrent Poor Law – *in name, at any rate*, and, to some extent, in

substance – by municipalizing its control. Every now and again, I realized this, but . . . I lost sight of it in my indignation at their attempt to present a new appearance while maintaining the old substance underneath. In a sense, the Majority Report meant success to our cause, but not victory to ourselves. . . . That the Principles of 1834 should die so easily is certainly a thoroughgoing surprise. Even the *Spectator* acquiesces.

Wells always sent copies of his books to a large number of acquaintances. In a letter written on 10 February, Beatrice compared *Tono-Bungay* unfavourably with *The War in the Air*. Wells replied with a characteristically splenetic letter.

*24 February.* [41 Grosvenor Road]
This letter from H. G. Wells is a real gem and I enshrine it with honours in my diary. It is, of course, H.G. at his worst; just now he is at his worst in anything that concerns the Shaws or us or the Fabian Society . . . Will he get over it, I wonder? . . .

His two last books – *War in the Air* and *Tono-Bungay* – are amazingly clever bits of work. I have the bad taste to prefer the former. Both illustrate the same theme – the mean chaos of human affairs. But *War in the Air* is avowedly a sort of allegory, or a parody. In form, an extravagancy; it is, in substance, a realistic description of the lowest and poorest side of social life. *Tono-Bungay*, on the other hand, sets out to be a straightforward description of society as it exists today, a sober estimate of the business world. But it turned out to be a veritable caricature, and a bitter one. Moreover, it bores me because its detail is made up . . . of stray bits he has heard from this or that person. There are quite a lot of things he has picked up from me – anecdotes about businessmen that I have told him are woven into his text, just all wrong, and conveying an absurd impression of meaningless chaos. But he is a useful missionary to whole crowds of persons whom we could never get at. It will be sad if he turns completely sour . . .

*1 March.* [41 Grosvenor Road]
Another letter from H.G., withdrawing the impersonal and emphasizing the personal aspect of his objection to the Webbs. I wrote back a soothing letter . . . he seems obsessed with the notion that we have some scheme to undo his influence. Bless the man! We never think of him now he has resigned from the Fabian Society.

The Webbs went to Naples, Rome and Assisi, and joined the Playnes in Florence.

*20 April.* [41 Grosvenor Road]
Home again, after the most refreshing six weeks' holiday . . . to find our little home cleaned up and re-decorated and our work awaiting us. Above all, I have a completely rested brain . . . Good intention is now dominant, and I have recovered the habit of prayer. What I have to avoid is all silly worry and self-consciousness. We have to go straight for our object – to clean up the base of society, single-mindedly, without thought of ourselves or what people think of us or our work. . . .

# A Plunge into Propaganda

## May 1909–July 1914

Beatrice was confident that the Webb campaign would 'convert the country to a policy of complete communal responsibility for the fact of destitution'. For many years, she concluded, 'that responsibility will be imperfectly fulfilled, but it will never again be repudiated'. In this sense the Minority Report had a lasting influence and paved the way for the modern welfare state.

*15 May.* [41 Grosvenor Road]
Enter the National Committee for the Break-Up of the Poor Law.

Started on our campaign of forming public opinion. My first attempt at organization. . . . We start, with very little money and a good deal of zeal, on a crusade against destitution. It is rather funny to start, at my time of life, on the war-path at the head of a contingent of young men and women. What I have got to aim at is to make these young people do the work, acting as moderator and councillor and occasionally suggesting new departures for them to carry out. I have to teach them how to work, not work myself. All the same it is a horrid nuisance: I long to get back to the quiet life of research, and pleasant friendship, with the long days and weeks in the country we enjoyed before the Royal Commission came in to upset our life.

*18 June.* [41 Grosvenor Road]
A month's grind at preparing forms, letters, membership cards, leaflets, tracts and other literature, for the National Committee. . . . Meanwhile,

we have been quite strangely 'dropped' by the more distinguished of our acquaintances, and by the Liberal Ministers in particular. I have never had so few invitations as this season . . . No doubt this is partly due to our growing reputation for being absorbed in work, but largely, I think, because there is a return of active fear of socialism, or of being assumed to be connected with socialists, though Lord George Hamilton's bad word (and I hear he 'foams at the mouth' whenever I am mentioned) counts. Altogether I am rather in disgrace with the great folk! . . . Unfortunately our estrangement from the Whigs does not mean comradeship with the Radicals: we are in the wrong and likely to become wronger with Lloyd George and Winston Churchill over immediate issues. We do not see our way to support their insurance schemes. . . .

We remain friends with the Balfours. Arthur dined here a day or two ago and was as friendly as ever. Gerald has accepted the presidentship of the Students' Union of the London School of Economics – a very kindly action. But then they are not in office! and any agitation for the Minority Report does not affect them except that it may be an inconvenience to the Liberals and, therefore, welcome – so says the cynic. I am inclined to believe in their genuine friendliness.

*22 June.* [41 Grosvenor Road]
I met Winston on the Embankment this afternoon. 'Well, how do you think we are doing, Mrs Webb?' '*You* are doing very well, Mr Churchill, but I have my doubts about your Cabinet; I don't believe they mean to do anything with the Poor Law.' 'Oh! yes they do,' said Winston. 'You must talk to Haldane about it, he has it in hand. We are going in for a *classified* Poor Law.' . . . We have a formidable fight before us. They are contemplating, not the majority scheme, but a new Poor Law authority of some kind or another. We shall have to fight that hard . . . Meanwhile, the less we see of the Liberal Ministers, the better. We had better not *know* they are against us. . . .

On 4 July the University of Manchester conferred the honorary degree of Doctor of Laws on Beatrice. Earlier in the year 200 Fabians had attended a testimonial dinner to the Webbs.

*6 July.* [41 Grosvenor Road]
A pleasant episode: delighted to get my doctorate, and from Manchester, the birthplace of my family as members of the governing class. Dear old father, how pleased he would have been!

The rumour that Wells and Amber Reeves were having an affair merged with gossip about his earlier involvement with Rosamund Bland, daughter of the pioneer Fabian journalist Hubert Bland and his novelist wife Edith Nesbit. Jane was H. G. Wells' second wife. Sydney Olivier was now Governor of Jamaica. The Webbs were staying in a hotel near the Fabian conference house.

*Early August.* [Brynlerion, Llanfair, Harlech]
The end of our friendship with H. G. Wells. A sordid intrigue with poor little Amber Reeves – the coming of a baby, and the run to cover of marriage with another man, a clever and charming young Fabian (Blanco White), who married her, knowing the facts, out of devoted chivalry. The story got about owing to Amber's own confidence to a Cambridge don's wife, and owing to H. G. Wells's own indiscretions. Moreover, after the hurried marriage, without the Reeveses' knowledge, of Amber and Blanco, Amber and H. G. Wells insist on remaining friends – a sort of *Days of the Comet* affair. We hear of it late in the day and feel ourselves obliged to warn Sydney Olivier, who was over on a holiday, against letting his four handsome daughters run about with H. G. Wells. (Apparently H. G. tried to seduce Rosamund Bland. If the Reeveses had only known of that, they would not have allowed Amber to stay with him [at his Sandgate home] for a month at a time.) So I think we were right to tell Sydney Olivier. But as a matter of fact H. G. had already told him that Amber was going to have a baby, that he was supplying the rent of the house, and that he had been madly in love with Amber and that 'we were much too timid about these things'.

For some reason that we do not understand, Sydney Olivier quoted us as his authority, and so we got these letters from H. G. Wells as well as a pathetic one from Reeves. It is a horrid affair and has cost us much. If Amber will let us, we shall stand by her as Blanco's wife and drop H. G. Wells, once for all, as he no doubt will drop us. He will doubtless drift into other circles – probably the only person of his own *ménage* who will suffer is his patient and all-enduring little wife, who, having entered into that position illicitly herself at the cost of another woman, cannot complain.

But the whole case, and the misery that seems likely to follow, is a striking example of the tangle into which we have got on the sex question. We accepted Wells, in spite of his earlier divorce case, on grounds of tolerance. He and his wife were happy – the other wife had married again, and there seemed no reason, on ordinary enlightened principles, for us to hold back or object. The Reeveses knowing all these facts, and Mrs Reeves claiming to be 'advanced' in her opinions (she did not object to *In the Days of the Comet*), were very intimate with him and allowed him to become Amber's guide, philosopher and friend. Amber being a little heathen, and H. G. being a sensualist, they both let themselves go, and start a surreptitious liaison. At first, both of them think that they will stand it out. But Amber gets into a panic, and marries the first faithful swain who will let himself be married to a lady with a 'past' of an imminent character. But apparently there is no breach; and the household goes on being of a very mixed sort – the Reeves parents looking on in tragic sorrow, and Reeves calling H. G. a 'vile impudent blackguard'.

And all this arises because we none of us know what exactly is the sexual code we believe in, approving of many things on paper which we violently object to when they are practised by those we care about. . . .

Oddly enough, Sidney had long had a settled aversion to H. G. Wells, thought him a purely selfish creature, with no redeeming motive, nothing but his cleverness to recommend him.

The Sassoons were a wealthy dynasty of merchants in the India trade, whose house at Hythe was noted for its lavish entertainment. Edward Sassoon (1856–1912) was the M.P. for Hythe. Taplow Court, near Henley-on-Thames, was the country house where Lady Desborough entertained the fashionable world.

*22 August.* [41 Grosvenor Road]

All is right between us and Reeves, and we have opened friendly relations with Amber. We will make a real, honest effort to get a hold over her and prevent the 'rot' going further. She is a little liar, she is superlatively vain, and she has little or no pity in her nature – but this triad of bad qualities may be but one of her personalities. . . . Whether there is something finer and nobler deep down in her nature, remains to be seen. If there is not, I fear her intelligence will not save her from a 'ruin' that will be apparent to the world.

The rise, grandeur, and decline of H. G. Wells is an interesting study in human nature. When first we made his acquaintance some eight years ago, he was decidedly on the up-grade, not merely in position but, I think, also in character. Now he is most distinctly on the down-grade, and unless he can pull himself up he will soon be little more than a ruined reputation. . . . Exactly when the tide turned towards evil I do not know. Unwittingly I did H. G. a bad turn when I introduced him to the Elcho–Balfour–Desborough set. That whetted his social ambition and upset his growing bourgeois morality. His rise to literary fame and his growing conceit accentuated the irresponsible and wilful side to his nature. He began to fancy himself a Goethe, who was going to experiment in life. His excursion into the affairs of the Fabian Society was also extraordinarily unfortunate. . . . What exactly happened to him after that, I do not know . . . We heard of him at the Sassoons, and at Taplow Court, dining with duchesses and lunching with countesses. I imagine he let himself go, pretty considerably, with women. . . . What he desired to do, and what he evidently thought he could do, was to lead a double life . . . Now he is raging because he is found out and his card castles are tumbling down around about him. . . .

The 'People's Budget' Lloyd George introduced on 29 April had been greeted by a storm of abuse. Opposition resistance to it precipitated a constitutional crisis that was to last until 1911 and force two general elections in 1910. Both produced equivocal Liberal victories and strengthened pressure for Home Rule as the price of Irish support for the Liberals during the crisis.

*27 September.* [41 Grosvenor Road]
The plot thickens round the tragic Wells–Blanco White–Reeves affair; and the Reeveses are coming in their misery to us for counsel and sympathy. The blackguardism of Wells is every day more apparent. He seduced Amber within the very walls of Newnham, having been permitted, as an old friend, to go to her room. He continued the relationship during her visits at his own house, apparently with the connivance of his wife, whilst he was on the most intimate terms of friendship with her parents. He taught her to lie, and to spend, and to grasp every enjoyment and advantage for herself, independently of its effect on other people. He ended by decamping with her to France, writing an impudent letter to Reeves to tell him of his adventures and actually suggesting that Mrs Reeves, by her admiration of *In the Days of the Comet*, had condoned the intimacy! Then, when he discovered that Amber was going to have a baby, he pushed her into a marriage with Blanco, but persuaded the latter to let his young wife carry on 'business relations' with him until the birth of the baby. Here both Reeves and Blanco White seem to have been monuments of folly, shutting their eyes and allowing themselves to be gulled by Amber's audacious lying. Anyway, the position now is that Amber is living in a cottage that has

been taken by Wells, and is receiving frequent visits from him while her husband lives in his chambers in London. And poor Reeves is contributing £300 a year to keep up this extraordinary *ménage*!

Our advice to father and husband is to break off all negotiations with Wells, to employ a solicitor in dealing with him and to insist that Amber returns to her family's home if she refuses to live with her husband. If she insists on staying with Wells, to threaten divorce proceedings and to carry them through directly after the birth of the child. For if they fail to grapple with the situation, they will presently discover that H.G.W. has escaped without punishment and without financial liability, and that poor little Amber is in the gutter, probably consorting, in her despair, with some other man – a ruined woman, doomed to sink deeper in the mire with every fresh adventure. And in the list of co-respondents of the eventual divorce case, H. G. Wells will not be. That is *what he is playing for* – and playing for with impudent audacity.

The whole political world is convulsed with excitement as to whether or not the Lords will throw out the Budget. No one quite knows what will happen to the finances of the country if they do . . . Meanwhile, our agitation booms along in its own way. Our membership rises rapidly . . . We are, in fact, creeping into the public mind much as the School of Economics crept into the University, into the City, into the railway world, into the civil service, into the War Office – before anyone was aware of it.

Our little office, wedged between the Fabian Office close on its right, and the London School of Economics a few yards to its left, is a sort of middle term between avowed socialism and non-partisan research and administrative technique. The staff of the three organizations and the active spirits of their management are all the same persons, and they exchange 'facilities' with the utmost freedom. It is only in London that this triangular activity of the Webbs could occur – London, with its anonymity, with its emphasis on personal likings, and its contempt for intellectual principles – a state of things which favours a rapid but almost unconscious change in the *substance* of the structure of society. . . .

*4 October.* [41 Grosvenor Road]

At her own request I went down to see Amber Blanco White, living in the charming little cottage which H.G.W. has taken for her. She was in a quiet and restrained state of mind, and impressed me far more favourably than ever before. She had lost the deceit and the artificiality of former days and was absorbed in her care for H.G.W. and her affection for his and her coming child. The two are taking up a quite impossible position, according to current morality. Having married Blanco White, she now expresses a loathing of him and refuses to have him near her. And she persists on seeing Wells and living her whole intellectual and moral life with him. And she demands that her father shall go on with the allowance of money, and her husband continue the allowance of his name. When an alternative is presented to them that either they must break off, or be repudiated, they both decide to be repudiated. H.G. is to support her entirely, they are to have a chaperone, and thus avoid a divorce.

Of course, unless they mean to have a divorce, the proposal is lunacy. Meanwhile, GBS has intervened and is trying to persuade the father and the husband to condone everything and accept the situation in order to avoid a public smash! He has even suggested to Reeves that he should entertain all three to dinner every week to show his approval! That merely enrages the poor conventional father, who now takes up an almost melodramatic attitude of furious indignation against the 'blackguard Wells and his paramour'. We go on pressing Reeves to put himself in the hands of an experienced solicitor . . . Meanwhile H.G.W., apparently with Amber's consent, publishes a new novel [*Ann Veronica*] descriptive of his relations to her, or rather of her portrait of him – which adds a roar of insult to his injury of the Reeves family.

I believe he is now engaged in satirizing us in his *New Machiavelli*.

[?] *3 October.* [41 Grosvenor Road]
Winston and his wife dined here the other night to meet a party of young Fabians. He is taking on the look of the mature statesman – *bon vivant* and orator – somewhat in love with his own phrases. He did not altogether like the news of our successful agitation. 'You should leave the work of converting the country to us, Mrs Webb; you ought to convert the Cabinet.'

'That would be all right if we wanted merely a change in the law; but we want', I added, '*really to change* the mind of the people . . .'

*14 November.* [41 Grosvenor Road]
We are carrying on a 'raging tearing propaganda', lecturing or speaking five or six times a week. We had ten days in the North of England and in Scotland – in nearly every place crowded and enthusiastic audiences. . . .

The reception of *Ann Veronica* was affected by the gossip about Wells and Amber Reeves. The novel appeared when a national campaign for moral purity was reaching its peak, and the *Spectator* (whose editor was aware of the scandal) led a hue and cry for the censorship of 'literary filth'. Wells at last agreed to give up the relationship, but the episode was a turning-point in his career. Though he continued to write novels, he became more of a publicist and popular educator. Amber gave birth to a daughter on 31 December. The Shaw play was *Misalliance*.

*27 December.* [41 Grosvenor Road]

The Reeveses dined with us last night, both of them shrivelled up with the pain of their daughter's past(?) relations to Wells. Just at present there is a lull in the episode. Amber and H.G.W. have contrived to make both the Reeveses and Blanco White believe there is a permanent separation between them. After all his insolent bluster, H.G.W. has backed down and agreed to keep away for two or three years, at the same time repudiating all financial liability for Amber's confinement and the infant's keep. He was frightened into better behaviour by the way in which one friend after another was shunning, sheering off, and by the damning review of his book in the *Spectator* – a review which was really an exposé of his conduct under the guise of criticism of a 'poisonous book', written clearly with knowledge and intent. Amber, too, professes to have given up all thought of seeing him. She is now in the nursing home awaiting her baby. It may be that she is seeing H.G.W. every day, unbeknown to her husband or parents. Most likely this repudiation of the financial responsibility by H.G.W. is a mere device to screw every farthing they can out of her parents and to keep his money for more luxury and freedom for her. They wanted to make the Reeveses support an overt relation; they will now make them support a surreptitious one. How long, I wonder, will the deception last? . . .

GBS read his new play to us the other night – a good three hours. It is amazingly brilliant – but the whole 'motive' is erotic, everyone wishing to have sexual intercourse with everyone else – though the proposals are 'matrimonial' for the most part, and therefore, I suppose, will not upset the Censor's mind. I don't see any good in the play except intellectual brilliancy. There is a reflection of the Amber-Wells philosophy of life – I think probably the revelations in the H.G.W. various sexual escapades have largely suggested the play – and the leading woman is Amber, with a rather better excuse than Amber had for pursuing men, since this lady had no other outlet for her energies.

Sidney and I were sorry to see GBS reverting to his studies in anarchic love-making. . . .

*New Year's Eve. Southsea*
. . . Since we took up this propaganda we have had a straightforward job . . . I enjoy it because I have the gift of personal intercourse and it is a gift I have never, until now, made full use of. I genuinely *like* my fellow mortals, whether as individuals or as crowds – I like to interest them, and inspire them, and even to order them, in a motherly sort of way. Also, I enjoy leadership. Everyone has been kind and appreciative; and money has come in when I asked for it, and volunteers have flocked around us. . . .

Sidney has also been thoroughly happy – partly because our comradeship has never been so complete. . . . this year we have organized together, spoken together, as well as written together. And he has been extraordinarily generous in not resenting, in the very least, my having nominally to take the front place, as the leading minority commissioner, and ostensible head of the National Committee. Fortunately, in spite of his modesty, everyone knows that he is the backbone of the Webb firm, even if I do appear, on some occasions, as the figurehead.

~ 1910 ~

*27 January.* [41 Grosvenor Road]
After the elections. The Coalition back with something over one hundred majority – a clear anti-Lords majority and, abstracting the Irish, a majority for the Budget.

What is remarkable is the dividing of England into two distinct halves, each having its own large majority for its own cause: the South Country – the suburban, agricultural, residential England – going Tory and tariff reform, and the North Country and dense industrial populations (excluding Birmingham area) going radical socialist, a self-conscious radical socialist. . . .

*1 March.* [41 Grosvenor Road]
. . . This week Sidney quietly slips out of the L.C.C. to which he has devoted so much time, thought and feeling. The last three years the L.C.C. has been rather dead to him. The Progressive movement which the Fabian Society started in 1889 has spent itself. The machine that has

been created goes grinding on all in the right directions . . . but for the present we can do more in persuading of the country at large than in the administration of London's municipal business.

Harley Granville-Barker (1877–1946) played a significant role in launching Shaw's plays at the Court Theatre and was himself a playwright.

*13 March.* [41 Grosvenor Road]
We met the Prime Minister, Grey and Birrell at dinner the other day. . . . We neither of us spoke to any of them, though it was a small party. Asquith was somewhat marked in his non-recognition of either of us. He is much older, and, in a sense, commoner, in appearance. . . . Grey looked the same charming aristocrat that he has always been . . . Birrell was the same jovial *littérateur* . . . But it was a somewhat odd sensation to see these three ministers for the first time since they were in office, to be conducting an agitation in the country which must eventually affect their policy, and yet not have even a 'good day' from them! . . .

I went to Granville-Barker's *Madras House* this afternoon. After listening to this and to GBS's *Misalliance*, one wonders whether these two supremely clever persons are not obsessed with the rabbit-warren aspect of human society? GBS is brilliant but disgusting; Granville-Barker is intellectual but dull. They both harp on the mere physical attractions of men to women, and women to men, coupled with the insignificance of the female for any other purpose but sex attraction, with tiresome iteration. That world is not the world I live in, or, indeed, think to exist outside a limited circle at the top and at the bottom of the social strata. . . . Where I think GBS, Granville-Barker, H. G. Wells, and many other of the most 'modern' authors go wrong, from the standpoint of realism in its best sense, is their complete ignoring of religion. . . . they don't perceive that there *is* such a thing . . . and that it is a force which moulds many lives and makes the mere rabbit-warren an inconceivable horror.

*20 March.* [41 Grosvenor Road]
Blanco and Amber White came to lunch today. Apparently that bad business is at an end. H.G.W. has been frightened off and has definitely broken off the relationship. Amber is settling down with her husband and is absorbed in her baby. She was shy and subdued, and certainly her expression was both sweet and frank. Blanco watches her with affectionate concern. We are prepared to stand by them and let the past be forgotten. I think the world will do likewise. It is one of those rare cases

where the punishment will fall far more heavily on the man than on the woman. Amber, if she behaves well, will be taken back by her friends. H.G. and his wife will be permanently dropped by most of his old acquaintances. He is too old to live it down. The scandals have revealed the moral rottenness of his life. I am sorry for Jane Wells, but she pandered to him and deceived friends like the Reeveses. I wish we had never known them.

*19 May.* [41 Grosvenor Road]
The King's death has turned politics topsy-turvy . . . London and the country generally is enjoying itself hugely at the Royal Wake, slobbering over the lying-in-state and the formal procession. Any collective thought and feeling is to the good; but the ludicrous false sentiment which is being lavished over the somewhat commonplace virtues of our late King [Edward VII] would turn the stomachs of the most loyal of Fabians. But is it possible for a *crowd* to be anything but exaggerated in its manifestations, with a popular press playing up to it? . . .

*27 May.* [41 Grosvenor Road]
It is just one year since we started the National Committee. . . . We have done what we set out to do. A year ago the Minority Report was one among many official documents: now it is a movement which is obviously spreading . . . And we do seem to be attracting the devoted service of a large body of volunteers. We are moving out of our five little rooms into more spacious offices, and we are developing a highly organized staff out of the salaried workers and some thirty or forty unpaid office helpers and some four hundred lecturers. . . .

Now the question is: can we develop this organization into a really big national movement to do away with destitution as a chronic and wholesale state of millions of our people? Here seems an opportunity. . . . But, at present, the whole organization depends on us, and is limited by the defects of our joint personality and the prejudices which this personality arouses. So long as this is the case, the life of the movement will be precarious, not merely because our strength and means might fail, but because the distrust and dislike of us might blaze out into a powerful hostility to the spread of the philosophy which lies at the base of the minority scheme. . . .

*19 August. Caermeddyg, Llanbedr*
Half through the very exhausting performance of directing the Fabian summer school. . . . What appals me is the fear that we may never be

able to get quit of leadership again. Is our existence going to be one perpetual round of talking and organizing for the rest of our working lives?
It is a terrifying prospect! . . .

*9 October.* [Cloan] Auchterarder
Started on our autumn campaign. After lecturing at Bournemouth and
Southampton, I returned to London for three days and then journeyed
to Hull, Middlesbrough and Darlington, arriving here on Saturday and
leaving again on Monday for Inverness. . . . Now I am spending the
Sunday with the Haldanes before opening the Scottish campaign at
Inverness and Edinburgh. . . . R.B.H. is rapidly ageing . . . He is terribly stout and pasty, and eats enormously and takes no exercise. He is
worried and depressed about his War Office administration – in a very
different state of mind from the buoyant self-confidence and delight
with which he undertook it. . . .

What makes one despair is the atmosphere in which these leaders live.
Their lives are so rounded off by culture and charm, comfort and power,
that the misery of the destitute is as far off as the savagery of central
Africa. . . . They don't realize either the misery itself or the possibility of
preventing it. And the atmosphere of Cloan is practically identical with
that of Whittingehame. There is no difference at all in the consciousness
of the Front Benchers. . . . I don't know from what party we shall get the
most. We may have, in the end, to establish a real socialist party if we
want rapid progress.

> Wells caricatured the Webbs in *The New Machiavelli*. Oscar and Altiora
> Bailey, he wrote, were 'active self-centred people, excessively devoted to
> the public interest': Altiora's soul, he added, was 'bony', and 'at the base
> of her was a vanity gaunt and greedy'. This remains one of the most effec-
> tive (though hostile) descriptions of the Webbs at the peak of their
> careers. The novel first appeared as a serial in the *English Review*.

*5 November.* [41 Grosvenor Road]
. . . H. G. Wells's *New Machiavelli* is now all published in the *English
Review*. We have read the caricatures of ourselves, the Trevelyan brothers and other old acquaintances of H.G.'s with much interest and
amusement. The portraits are really very clever in a malicious way. What
interests us most, however, is the extraordinary revelation of H.G.'s life
and character – idealized, of course, but written with a certain powerful
sincerity. . . . it lays bare the tragedy of H.G.'s life – his aptitude for 'fine

thinking' and even 'good feeling', and yet his total incapacity for decent conduct. . . . One small matter interested us. In his description of acquaintanceship with the 'Oscar Baileys' he shows that he never really liked us – at any rate after the first blush of the intimacy. What annoyed him was our puritan view of life and our insistence on the fulfilment of obligations. There is even a passage in which he distinctly says that he was irritated at our blindness to the fact that he was leading a sexually irregular life – that we *would* assume him to be a conventionally respectable man! Of course, that is absolutely true. He and Jane Wells had all the appearance of a devoted husband and wife, and it never occurred to us to doubt their monogamy. For a little while I think we influenced him, at any rate in thought, and the Samurai of the *Modern Utopia* was the literary expression of this phase. But he passed back again to the theory and practice of sexual dissipation . . . The idealization of the whole proceeding in *The New Machiavelli* is a pretty bit of work and will probably enable him to struggle back into distinguished society. . . . I shall take no steps to prevent this so long as no one expects us to meet him on terms of friendship.

*30 November.* [41 Grosvenor Road]
The autumn lecturing is well nigh over . . . another four in January . . . and we shall have carried out the whole programme of eighty meetings for the two of us in two and a half months. . . .

Meanwhile, we are again in the turmoil of an election. . . . The violent abuse by the Tory press of the Liberals and Lloyd George on the ground of socialism and Irish nationalism is an old game which everyone tires of. . . .

The big thing that has happened in the last two years is that Lloyd George and Winston Churchill have practically taken the *limelight*, not merely from their own colleagues but from the Labour Party. They stand out as the most advanced politicians. And if we get a Liberal majority and payment of members, we shall have any number of young Fabians rushing for Parliament, fully equipped for the fray – better than the Labour men – and enrolling themselves behind these two radical leaders.

*10 December.* [41 Grosvenor Road]
Sidney and I are both feeling weary and somewhat dispirited. In spite of all our work, the National Committee does not seem to be gaining many new members and our friends are beginning to melt away. One

wonders . . . whether our dream of a permanent organization . . . is possible at present? . . .


~ 1911 ~

[?] *January.* [41 Grosvenor Road]
The general election has brought the Liberals back with far greater
power . . . As Lloyd George said to the press interviewers, we are in for a
period of rapid social reconstruction unless foreign complications turn the
nation away from its quarry. . . .

> The Webbs were to spend almost a year on a world tour taking in
> Canada, Japan, Korea, China, the Malay States, Burma, India and Egypt.
> Their composite account of the journey is summarized in the four-
> volume edition of the diary. Luton Hoo was the country home of the
> millionaire businessman Sir Julian Wernher (1850–1912), who had made
> a foundation gift to the Imperial College of Science.

*6 March.* [Eastbourne]
Let our house for one year . . . in order to get it off our hands for our
Eastern tour, and retired first to a little house here for five weeks, then
to Luton Hoo for two-and-a-half months.

It is a relief to get out of London, with its perpetual whirl of talking
and organizing, and occasional lecturing. After two lectures this next
week I am free to turn to the writing of our little book on *The Prevention
of Destitution*, summing up all our lectures of the last two years, to be left
as a legacy to the National Committee for the next session's propaganda.

Since Xmas we have been seeing a good many political personages –
we have had both Haldane and Churchill to dinner; we have breakfasted
with Lloyd George and had A.J.B. to meet various M.O.H.s [Medical
Officers of Health]. The Front Bench Liberals have, in fact, been softening towards us, partly because we are going away, and partly because
we could, if we chose, wreck their schemes of insurance by rousing the
Labour hostility to them. . . .

> Clifford Sharp (1883–1935), the founder of the Fabian Nursery, and the
> most active of the young people who worked in the Poor Law campaign,
> was a natural choice as editor of the *New Statesman* in 1913.

*7 March.* [Eastbourne]

. . . The Fabian Society is going through a crisis, not of dissent, but of indifference. Sidney thought that, as he was leaving England, he had better resign [from the Executive] for a year. Thereupon GBS not only announces his intention of resigning, but persuades some half-a-dozen others of the Old Gang to resign also. All with the view to making room for young men who are not there! Clifford Sharp, who is a loyal and steadfast member of the Executive, is in despair, and Sidney is remaining on if GBS and the others persist in going. . . . It is clear to me that the Fabian Society has to get a new impetus, or gradually dwindle to a mere name. . . .

*8 March, 4 a.m.* [Eastbourne]

. . . Yesterday night I lay right through the long hours twisting every domestic detail or incident of our organization into a giant of evil, a monster of unpleasant things. And it is in the night that I suffer from remorse for lack of consistency between conduct and conviction. All my little self-indulgences – the cup of tea or occasional coffee after a meal, the regular five or six cigarettes consumed daily, the extra expenditure on pretty clothes – all seem sins from which I can never shake myself free. . . . When the morning comes and one returns to the rough and tumble of a hard day's work, or the necessities of human intercourse, these scruples seem mere weaknesses, and one goes forward without thought of justification with the habits and customs of one's daily life. Still, there lies at the back of one's mind a discontent with these compromises, a longing to be completely at peace with one's own ideal even in the smaller details of life.

. . . As for Sidney, he sweeps on one side as irrelevant and foolish all consideration of these trifles! . . . he goes on his way of sane temperance, without temptation or scruple, and with one settled opinion that he wants *me* to indulge myself to the top of my bent! He is the most perfect of lovers, by night and by day, in work and in play, in health and in sickness!

Shaw rebuffed suggestions that the Irish Catholic impresario George Vandeleur Lee (*c.* 1831–86) might be his father. The National Insurance Bill was introduced in May; its acceptance was delayed until the autumn.

*21 April. The Hermitage, Luton Hoo*
In retreat here, toiling at our book on destitution and finding the task a
tediously stale one. . . .

We spent a Sunday with the Bernard Shaws and he read us his last
little play (*Fanny's First Play*). A brilliant but slight and somewhat
futile performance. He and Charlotte are getting every day more luxurious and determined to have everything 'just so' without regard to
cost or fitting in with other people's convenience. But they are neither
of them quite satisfied with their existence. GBS is getting impatient
and rather hopeless of his capacity to produce anything more of value;
Charlotte is beginning to loathe the theatrical set and is even turning
to us to try and interest GBS again in socialism. . . . But GBS is bored
with discussion; he won't give and take; he will orate and go off on to
the sex question, which does not interest Sidney as GBS has nothing
positive to propose. . . . As a matter of fact there does not seem much
reason for meeting – and therefore we seldom meet, and when we do,
the conversation tends to be made-up and not spontaneous. Which is
somewhat sad, as he and Sidney have always cared for one another:
they are perhaps each other's most long-standing friends. Possibly if
we throw ourselves into the work of the Fabian Society I might
increase my intimacy with Charlotte and therefore of the two of us
with Shaw.

About Shaw's parentage. The photograph published in the
[Archibald] Henderson biography makes it quite clear to me that he was
the child of G.J.V. Lee – that vain, witty and distinguished musical
genius who lived with them. The expression on Lee's face is quite amazingly like GBS when I first knew him. One wonders whether GBS
meant this fact to be communicated to the public?

*26 May.* [The Hermitage]
. . . We have written in our new book what is virtually a scathing indictment of insurance in general and the government scheme in
particular . . . we have said our say. By the time we get back from our
holiday, the matter will probably be settled one way or the other – possibly for a generation. . . .

Following their National Conference on Destitution at the Albert Hall,
the Webbs left for their long journey through Asia.

~ 1912 ~

*5 September. Newport Trades Union Congress*
It is now over three months since we got back to England and not a
word have I written. It took me at least two months to get over the effect
of the tropical climate and perpetual journeyings – my nerves were all to
pieces, and waves of depression and panic followed each other. Now I
am all right again and in good working form. . . .

The face of British politics had changed dramatically by the time the
Webbs returned to England. Their friend Arthur Balfour had resigned
the Tory leadership in November 1911 and been replaced by Andrew
Bonar Law. The struggles that led to the Parliament Act of 1911 had
strained the constitutional system almost to breaking point; the period of
'Great Unrest' which followed was marked by a militancy and violence
unknown since the collapse of Chartism seventy years before. Ireland was
drifting into civil war; the failure of the Liberal government to make any
concessions on women's suffrage had driven many of its frustrated supporters to direct action and, during the Webbs' absence, one great strike
had succeeded another. Beatrice could see that new developments
required a new response. The Fabian Society and the I.L.P. started a
joint agitation for a legal minimum wage under the slogan 'War against
Poverty'; it was in some ways a continuation of the Poor Law campaign.
The new weekly was the *New Statesman*. The Webbs were among the
twenty-six original shareholders, who also included Shaw.

*11 October.* [41 Grosvenor Road]
Since we returned to London I have been in a whirl of work – a fine
mix-up of activities – the winding up of the National Committee, the
I.L.P. and Fabian campaign on the National Minimum; our own course
of lectures on the Control of Industry, and the starting of the Fabian
Research Department. In all these enterprises Sidney has been helping
by counsel and drafting, by writing tracts and taking his share of public
speaking. Meanwhile he has been finishing, without help from me, the
book on Roads, one of the innumerable fragments of our unfinished
work. It is annoying not to be able to complete that big task of historical research to which we devoted so much time and money. But there
seems to be a clear call to leadership in the labour and socialist movement to which we feel that we must respond. For that purpose we are
starting a new weekly next spring, and the planning out of this organ of

Fabianism is largely devolving on Sidney. It is by far the most risky of our present enterprises . . . To the experienced journalist it must seem a mad adventure, and we ourselves hardly expect more than a run for other people's money and our own hard work. But then the London School of Economics did not seem much more promising, and today it rolls on majestically . . . Sidney has not even troubled to become chairman again, realizing that the School has now a life of its own. . . .

## ~ 1913 ~

25 May. [41 Grosvenor Road]
I find it increasingly difficult to find time or energy to write in my diary. The *New Statesman* absorbs both. We started with 2,450 postal subscribers. How many of these we shall keep depends on the uniqueness of the paper. There are all sorts of conflicting criticism. The paper is dull: it is mere brilliant writing and there is not enough solid information; the political articles are good but the literature 'rot'; the literary side is excellent, but the political articles not sufficiently constructive.

Our main difficulty is with Bernard Shaw . . . He won't write over his own signature and some of the articles and notes that he sends are hopelessly out of keeping with our tone and our methods. And in order to threaten us, he writes signed letters to the *Nation*, Massingham of course trying to capture him from us. However, we have just to go on making the paper valuable. Sharp is turning out a good man of business, a safe though not distinguished writer. What he lacks is personal magnetism; in some ways he is too doggedly sincere.

5 July. [41 Grosvenor Road]
GBS has in fact injured the *New Statesman* . . . Lots of people will think any article brilliant that they know is by him, whilst dismissing his anonymous contribution as tiresome and of no account, or as purely mischievous. And in all the details of his arrangements he is grossly inconsiderate, refusing to let Sharp know whether or not he was going to write, and what he was going to write about, until, on the day the paper goes to press, there appears on Sharp's table two or three columns – sometimes twice that amount – on any subject that he (Shaw) happens to fancy. Sharp has now decided that if Shaw insists on these terms we are better without him. Meanwhile, persons who subscribed for their weekly portion of Shaw are angry and say they were got

to subscribe on false pretences. The *New Statesman* is in fact the one weekly in which Shaw's name never appears, and it is Shaw's name that draws, not his mind. . . .

Mrs Patrick Campbell (1865–1940) had made her mark in Pinero's *The Second Mrs Tanqueray* in 1892. Shaw wrote the part of Eliza Doolittle in *Pygmalion* for her. His flirtatious letters confirm Beatrice's remark that Shaw was reverting to the philandering manner of his youth. Although the 'affair' reached its climax in August 1913 they continued to correspond.

*13 July.* [41 Grosvenor Road]
Charlotte Shaw asked me to come and see her one day last week. She has been ill, off and on, ever since we returned from India. She was lying on the sofa looking unusually gentle and attractive. She told me, in a singularly gentle and dignified way, that GBS had fallen in love with Mrs Patrick Campbell and that most people knew it, that he was really obsessed by it and had fallen completely under that somewhat elderly witch's spell. (*She* did not call her an 'elderly witch'!) I was not surprised. When he was with us last November he talked incessantly about Mrs Pat and told me a lot of stupid stuff about her past relations with her husband, children and with the stage, as she imagined them to have been, and he repeated her silly and insolent remarks about Charlotte's big waist. I paid little attention to it, one is so accustomed to GBS's vanity and egotism. One used to watch these faults leading to all sorts of rather cruel philanderings with all kinds of odd females. But I had certainly thought he had outgrown this business. . . .

From what I recollect of GBS's chatter about Mrs Pat the relationship is one of gross mutual flattery . . . It is remarkable how long Charlotte has kept his volatile nature attached to her and I am not sure that he won't [will] return to her. The present obsession, reacting on declining vigour, may be more serious. Formerly he was always quite detached and he could pull himself up when he chose. He allowed himself to be adored, I never knew him adore. In this case I gather that he is the fly and the lady the spider. . . .

*4 December.* [41 Grosvenor Road]
GBS is making an effort to keep in with the Fabian Society and ourselves and he has attended every one of our six public lectures, and taken the chair twice. Also he has been most kind in doing things for the Fabian

Society. He no longer writes for the *New Statesman*, though he is quite friendly and asks whether we want more money. Apparently he keeps away from Mrs Pat, and he and Charlotte are outwardly on the best of terms. The two plays he had on the English stage were not a success, but this has been compensated by Continental and American 'big runs' – especially of *Pygmalion*.

[?] *6 December. Midland Hotel* [Burnley?]
On a short lecturing tour, Bradford, Liverpool and Burnley, five lectures in four days. . . .

The labour movement, indeed the whole of the thinking British public, is today the arena of a battle of words, of thoughts and of temperaments. The issue is twofold: are men to be governed by emotion or by reason? Are they to be governed in harmony with the desires of the bulk of the citizens or according to the fervent aspirations of a militant minority . . . Our answer to the first question is that the idealist chooses the purpose of life, whether of the individual or of the community, whilst the man of science thinks out the processes by which this purpose can be fulfilled; our answer to the second is that leaders, idealist or man of science, *propose, but that the ordinary man* (in his collective capacity of being the mass of the people) *disposes, and that it is right that he should dispose.* We uphold the authority of the mass of the people . . .

This philosophy . . . demands patience, discipline and tolerance – characteristics which do not appeal to either the revolutionary or the reactionary. That is why the Webbs are so hated – all the more so because we seem so 'damned sure' of our conclusions. We are extraordinarily unpopular today, more disliked, by a larger body of persons, than ever before. The propertied class look upon us as their most insidious enemies; the revolutionary socialist or fanatical sentimentalist, see in us, and our philosophy, the main obstacle to what they call enthusiasm and we call hysteria. Our one comfort is that both sets of opponents can hardly be right. . . .

~ 1914 ~

On 9 March Asquith moved for the third time the second reading of the Home Rule Bill, first introduced in 1912, which put a time limit on Ulster's right to stay outside the parliament in Dublin. The proposals provoked threats of rebellion and secession from the Ulster Protestants as well as a defiant near-mutiny on 20 March from army officers serving on the Curragh in Ireland. Bonar Law was inciting the Ulster rebels in terms close to a threat of civil war. Asquith now took over the War Office. *Parsifal* was being performed for the first time in England. Mrs Patrick Campbell married the soldier and author George Cornwallis West (1874–1951) on 6 April, six days before the opening night of *Pygmalion*. Philip Snowden (1864–1937) was chairman of the I.L.P. until becoming an M.P. in 1906. He was Chancellor of the Exchequer in 1924. Beatrice later wrote that she did not know Keir Hardie well enough to comment on his personality.

*23 April.* [41 Grosvenor Road]
The turmoil over Ulster and the recalcitrant officers loomed large at Westminster, and in the party papers; and among little cliques of the fashionable and wealthy the talk was of civil war and revolution. For about three days, members of the governing class glared at each other and social entertainments were boycotted by one of the party clans or the other. In the end, Asquith came out on top by his bold bid for confidence as War Minister. . . .

We have resumed relations with two of the Liberal Ministers – Lloyd George and Herbert Samuel. At a performance of *Parsifal* Sidney and I ran up against them during the long interval in the outer hall and presently found ourselves heatedly discussing, surrounded by an ever-widening circle of amused and interested listeners, the excessive sickness of married women under the Insurance Act owing to the humorously ignorant omission by the government actuaries of the 'risk' of pregnancy. As we hurried back to the gloriously dramatized religious service, Lloyd George appealed to us to help him . . . It is certainly to his credit that he bears no malice for our criticism – perhaps it is to our credit that we, also, are willing to let bygones be bygones. . . .

We attended the gala days of the I.L.P. conference (the twenty-first anniversary of its existence) as fraternal delegates from the Fabian Society, and listened to endless self-congratulatory speeches . . . When the conference settled down to business the I.L.P. leaders were painfully at variance. J. R. MacDonald seems almost preparing for his exit . . . Snowden is ill . . . at once bitter and apathetic. Keir Hardie is vain and egotistical, 'used up' . . . The cold truth is that the Labour members have utterly failed to impress the House of Commons and the constituencies as a live force, and have lost confidence in themselves and each other. . . .

We had six days of walking and motoring with GBS after the I.L.P. conference. He was hard hit by Mrs Pat's marriage, but he has taken it in the best possible manner and has been doubtless consoled by the success of *Pygmalion*. He is making piles of money – which is fortunate for the *New Statesman* – and he seems most friendly in his intentions towards Fabianism and all its works.

Meanwhile I am desperately tired. Even the six days walking in glorious weather did not rest me. I have come back more tired than when I left London. Irritable and depressed: a wicked state of mind for one endowed with an extravagant share of all that is fortunate in human relationships and material circumstances. . . .

*3 May.* [41 Grosvenor Road]
. . . I am anxious about the future of the Fabian Society and the Research Department. We do not seem to be securing competent successors . . . The root of the difficulty may be that the Fabian Society has very little to offer to an ambitious young man except unpaid work and a humble type of leadership; there is no career that would be considered a career. To the isolated lower middle-class man of humble faculties and modest needs it offers companionship and intellectual stimulus and a certain contact with men and women whose names are known. But work for it brings neither money nor fame – not even the barest livelihood. . . .

Joseph Chamberlain had died on 2 July but Beatrice made no reference to this.

*31 July. Barrow House*
A fortnight here with two weeks' Research Department conference . . . Meanwhile, Europe has flamed up. All the great powers may be at war in a few days, perhaps in a few hours. A hideous business. Ulsterites, Suffragettes, Guild Socialists and rebels of all sorts and degrees may be swept out of mind and sight in national defence and national subsistence.

[*Beatrice inserted this additional note in August 1918.* All through the last week of the Barrow conferences there had been the rumblings of the approaching earthquake without our awakening to the meaning of it. Sidney had refused to believe in the probability of war among the great European powers: 'It would be too insane.' . . .]

# The Earthquake

## August 1914–November 1918

On 1 August, Germany declared war on Russia and on 2 August, entered Luxembourg and presented a twelve-hour ultimatum to Belgium. On 3 August, Germany declared war on France; Belgium rejected the German ultimatum and Grey spoke to the House of Commons in favour of intervention. On 4 August Germany invaded Belgium and appealed to Britain to allow this violation of an international treaty. The British replied with an ultimatum expiring at midnight. The Bank Holiday was prolonged for three days; the government took over the railways. There was an anti-war demonstration in Trafalgar Square on Sunday 2 August. J. L. Hammond (1872–1949) was a journalist and writer.

*5 August.* [41 Grosvenor Road]
It was a strange London on Sunday: crowded with excursionists to London and balked would-be travellers to the Continent, all in a state of suppressed uneasiness and excitement. We sauntered through the crowd to Trafalgar Square, where Labour, socialist and pacifist demonstrators, with a few trade union flags, were gesticulating from the steps of the monument to a mixed crowd of admirers, hooligan warmongers and merely curious holiday-makers. It was an undignified and futile exhibition, this singing of the 'Red Flag' and passing of well-worn radical resolutions in favour of universal peace. We turned into the National Liberal Club: the lobby was crowded with men, all silent and perturbed. Sidney went up into the smoking-room and brought down Massingham

and Hammond. Both these men were bitter and depressed. We argued with them that if Belgian neutrality was defied we had to go to war – they vehemently denied it. On Monday the public mind was cleared and solidified by Grey's speech. Even staunch Liberals agree that we had to stand by Belgium. But there is no enthusiasm about the war: at present it is, on the part of England, a passionless war, a terrible nightmare sweeping over all classes, no one able to realize how the disaster came about.

The closing of the Bank [of England] for four days and the paralysis of business (no one seems to know whether the closing is limited to banks, and many businesses have stopped because there is no money to pay wages) gives the business quarters of London a dispirited air. Every train that steams out of London, every cart in the street, is assumed to be commandeered by the government for the purposes of war. Omnibuses and taxi-cabs are getting sparse. There is strained solemnity on every face – no one has the remotest idea of what is going to happen now that we are actually at war with Germany. Personally I have an uncomfortable conviction that Germany is terribly efficient, overpoweringly efficient in its army. As for its navy, who knows what will prove to be the winning factor in strategy or arms? And there is complete uncertainty as to what is the ultimate issue before the civilized world. To the Englishman of today it seems the survival of France, Belgium and Holland. To the Englishman of tomorrow it may seem a mistaken backing-up of the Slav against the Teuton. Even if we realize that the mistake was due to the unbearable insolence of the Prussian autocracy, we may live to regret it. . . . There never has been a war in which the issues are so blurred and indistinct. We English, at any rate, are quite uncertain who ought to win from the standpoint of the world's freedom and man's spiritual development. The best result would be that every nation should be soundly beaten and no one victorious. That might bring us all to reason.

A conference supported by the Labour Party, the Trades Union Congress and the Co-operative movement had been called to protest against the drift to war. By the time it met on 5 August the situation had so changed that it set up the War Emergency Workers' National Committee. This body did excellent work on rents, prices, allowances for the families of enlisted men and pensions to war casualties. It also helped to secure representation of the workers on government committees. Sidney drafted many of its documents, and through his membership began to build a new relationship with Labour politicians and trade union officials. Field-Marshal Lord Kitchener (1850–1916) was appointed Secretary of State for War on 5 August and raised a volunteer army of three million men. He was drowned on the way to Russia when the *Hampshire* sank in 1916. The Germans occupied Brussels on 21 August; Namur fell on 24 August.

*10 August.* [41 Grosvenor Road]
. . . We shall do very little the next months but sit on committees – government committees and labour committees. I attended one at the Local Government Board with Burns in the chair, and Sidney went off to another. Every one is excited and perturbed; and most of us are haunted by the horrors that we know are taking place a few hundred miles away.

*25 August.* [41 Grosvenor Road]
Capacity for work destroyed by anxiety and restless searching for more news. We in England are probably the least concerned of all the principal combatants, but even to us the outlook is gloomy and terribly tragic. All those who know the forces engaged believe that the war will last months, perhaps years: that both sides are desperate – the French will fight to a finish and we and the Russians are bound to see them through. . . .

Haldane dined with us last night: serious with the first bad news of the war – the fall of Namur. He was full of his past participation in diplomacy and military organization. He was greatly admiring of Kitchener, and anxious to tell us that it was he who insisted on 'K' going to the War Office. 'K' says we must prepare for a three years' war and is expecting initial disasters. The Germans expect to walk through the French Army 'like butter' and our own Expeditionary Force they consider a mere 'demonstration'. . . .

We are going away for ten days' or a fortnight's holiday to walk ourselves into a quieter state of mind. . . .

Rufus Isaacs (1860–1935), formerly Attorney-General in Asquith's Cabinet, was appointed Lord Chief Justice in 1913. He spent much of the war as a financial envoy and then as Ambassador in Washington. E. S. Montagu (1879–1924), banker and Liberal M.P., was Financial Secretary to the Treasury 1914–16.

*28 August.* [Seaford, Sussex]

Before we left London we dined with Haldane to meet Grey, Lloyd George, Isaacs and Montagu. These men are changed. Grey has lost his conventional aloofness: he was intensely 'human', eager for intimate discussion of practical difficulties and terribly concerned that he had not been able to prevent the war – suffering, I think, from an over-sensitive consciousness of personal responsibility. Haldane has lost his bland self-sufficiency. Lloyd George showed at his best in his lack of self-consciousness, his freedom from pedantry, his alert open-mindedness and his calm cheeriness. Montagu and Isaacs were eager to be helpful. They were all working at their highest efficiency, no dinners and week-ends. . . . All the Ministers grave and fully aware that we were in for the supreme struggle for the life of the British Empire, and that the war would be waged along all frontiers and in every department of life. Whatever else might be the outcome, the war would mean political ruin to one side and financial disaster to all. . . .

There are two perturbing moral paradoxes in this war. There has been a disgusting misuse of religious emotion in the assumption of the Almighty's approval of the aims of each of the conflicting groups of combatants. France, it is true, has kept herself free from this loathsome cant, and our 'religiosity' has been tactfully limited to formal medieval phrases and to an Erastian prayer for the use of the established Church. But the Kaiser and the Tsar have outdone each other in fervent appeals to their tribal Gods: the German vulgar and familiar, the Russian dignified and barbaric. The theologians of Europe have disgraced themselves. No Eastern mystic would be guilty of such vulgar blasphemy. . . .

The other disturbing reflection is that war is a stimulus to service, heroism and all forms of self-devotion. Hosts of men and women are willing to serve the community under this coarse stimulus who, in ordinary times, are dully immune to any other motive but self-interest qualified by self-indulgence. War, in fact, means an increase of corporate feeling and collective action in all directions. An unholy alliance, disconcerting to the collectivist who is also a believer in love as the bond between races as well as between individuals. I am beginning to loathe the newspapers – with their bombast and lies about atrocities, or their delighted gossip about the famine and disease in 'enemy' countries.

With one tiny exception, the whole nation is unanimous for the war. The tiny minority is the I.L.P., with its Executive, and its few admirers among disgruntled Whigs who have quarrelled with the government. . . . The brutal invasion of Belgium has compelled the anti-war propagandists to come out in favour of non-resistance, pure and undefiled . . . I don't believe in non-resistance. Physical force does not differ in morality from mental force: both alike are dependent, for their rightness, on the purpose for which they are exercised – is the purpose consistent with love or not? The act of killing may be a manifestation of love. It is only right to add that it usually is not.

> There are no entries in the diary between 28 August and 21 October. The fall of Antwerp on 9 October resulted in a new flood of Belgian refugees. London was dimmed for reasons of security and energy-saving. The constraints of a Defence of the Realm Act were intensified by a temperance campaign led by Lloyd George.

*3 November.* [41 Grosvenor Road]
Georgie Meinertzhagen died after a fortnight's suffering – not acute pain but the slow ebbing of strength and great discomfort.

I was never intimate with this sister: she married when I was still a school-girl. When, in after years, I was struggling into an intellectual career, she was unsympathetic and somewhat contemptuous. 'All vanity', I remember her remarking, with a tolerant laugh, as she watched me at my somewhat futile attempt to master mathematics. The little intimacy I had with her was over her unhappy relations with her husband. But she was a favourite sister with others of the sisterhood . . . Since her widowhood she had been singularly happy and well; full of new-found enthusiasm for the women's cause . . . It was her misfortune to marry a man of narrow sympathies, of many conventions and more prejudices and with no sense of humour. Her children are devoted to her . . . Barbara Drake is an intellectual and attractive woman, following in my footsteps as an economic writer and a Fabian. The eight other children I barely know. . . .

Work this autumn has gone badly. I have been idle and distracted, mooning over an extravagant expenditure on newspapers for hours during the day, trying to find my bearings in a mass of detail, the technique of which I do not know . . . and suffering from mental and physical depression. And though Georgie's death leaves no gap in my life, it is yet another break with the past – a past which is rapidly becoming the greater part of my personal life. One wonders, which one next? The great war will raise issues which I have no longer the strength and elasticity to understand. The root of my trouble is, of course, a bad conscience: I am neither doing my share of emergency work nor yet carrying forward, with sufficient steadfastness, my own work. Now and again I bolster up my conscience with the plea that I am elderly and past work – the very way to become so.

The darkening of London, now the days are short, adds to the national sobriety but also the national gloom. It is reported that Berlin and its suburbs are blazing with light so as to produce optimism. Our government seems to think that what our people want is increased anxiety and seriousness: they certainly have helped to create a consciousness of personal peril by absence of light and absence of liquor. . . .

## ❧ 1915 ❧

*3 January.* [41 Grosvenor Road?]
Ten days' walking and motoring with GBS – tempestuous weather and heated argument. The terms of settlement [of the war] and his proposals for bringing about equality were the subjects discussed. Sex questions were off, he having put Mrs Pat out of his head. He has been firing off brilliant but ill-digested stuff at the newspapers and in lectures. Yet his aims are straight. . . . And his protest against the self-righteousness of British public opinion about the causes of the war is, in my humble opinion, justified. . . .

G. D. Cole (1889–1957), a Fabian from the Oxford University Society, was a devotee of Guild Socialism.

*14 February.* [41 Grosvenor Road]
Hard at work on professional organizations for the fourth part of our report on the Control of Industry. It is most exhilarating to get back to research, and research into a quite new subject. . . . The Fabian Society and Research Department show signs of healthy development. This autumn I have tried to inspire new work without controlling the direction of it. Cole is now vice-president, with GBS as nominal head. . . .

*18 April.* [41 Grosvenor Road]
For unknown reasons the governing cliques are far more hopeful than heretofore of eventual victory. We dined with Haldane alone the other day: his state of mind was one of quiet confidence . . . By next Xmas he

expects to have peace. The basis of this optimism is the exhaustion of German manpower. There is still very little hatred of Germany among the people we see – far more fear of the growth of bureaucratic and militarist tendencies in our own country. . . . Sidney remains stolidly patriotic; I am still a depressed agnostic. One continues one's work . . . with a background of exasperated misery. Does one over-rate the horror and insanity of the killing and maiming of millions of the best of the human race? I cannot bear to look at the fresh young faces in each week's 'Roll of Honour'. And yet there is moral magnificence in the unsensational dutifulness unto death of the millions now enlisting. The common youth, workman, clerk, or shop assistant, squares his shoulders, spits out his ugly joke; he is obsessed by his thoughts of food, drink and women, but dies game without any particular consciousness of being a hero or a patriot. And the young intellectual, with a privileged life before him, accepts risks and discipline with equal equanimity. . . .

*26 April.* [41 Grosvenor Road]
The war hurricane that is sweeping round our lives is going to uproot many things, great and small, public institutions and private hopes and interests. Among the small things that I am going to lose is the recent friendship with Betty Balfour. . . . With all the others of the Balfour clan, including its greatest representative, I have never had more than a friendly acquaintance . . . But Lady Betty, the wife of Gerald, had insisted on a warm personal friendship and had followed me about with manifestations of almost reverential affection. As she is the most charming of women, quite the most fascinating woman I have ever known, I acquiesced and let my elderly heart be captivated. So we wrote long letters to each other, she came here and I (and sometimes Sidney) went to Fisher's Hill. This spring there has been dead silence on her part. Probably she is absorbed in other interests and attracted to other personalities. Just now I feel sore and hurt. Presently she will fall into her place in the attractive scene of Arthur Balfour and his family which we passed through and enjoyed without claiming or even desiring that it should become part of our world.
. . . I think I understand the meaning of what seems strangely capricious behaviour. . . . Arthur Balfour is as much to the centre of the thought and feeling of his large family as Joseph Chamberlain was at Highbury, and of all his family, Betty is the most devout worshipper. For a few years he had a liking for me – a 'curiosity infatuation' . . . There could be no real friendship between us, since friendship with men based on mutual

attraction, even if I had not been too elderly for it, is barred to me by my perfect marriage . . . Betty Balfour, I think, thought that there would be a lasting friendship between her great man and the Webbs. Directly it became clear that A.J.B. had ceased to be interested in us, she also had a revulsion of feeling. She had no more use for me. She became aware of all my defects, and as she had never cared for me for myself, the disillusionment was complete. . . .

[*Beatrice later wrote three footnotes to this entry. The first was in December 1915.* I add to this entry before putting away this volume the last scene of my friendship with Betty Balfour. She called here in October by appointment and stayed some time talking to Sidney and myself. The poor lady was evidently constrained and perturbed. In fact she was so agitated and unhappy in expression that I thought she had had some mysterious illness. A critical glance at me – a look of unmistakable hostility in her eyes – convinced me that it was not illness but a sort of unpleasant consciousness that she felt herself under some obligation to a person whom she now disliked. I met her the next day, accidentally, at a conference of the National Union of Women Workers. She had recovered her self-possession and lost her look of constraint. Her mind was made up and she greeted me with cold politeness. No suggestion of future meetings – in fact a tentative suggestion by me was decidedly rejected. Since then there has been silence on both sides.

*The second note was added in August 1918.* To finish the story. I met Betty Balfour again this spring, walking with her sister in St James's Park. She accosted me, as if she felt compelled to do so. But when in answer to her remark, 'When shall we meet again, I wonder?' I smilingly invited her to 'come and see us', she unmistakably refused to do so. In fact if she had stopped to speak to me in order to show a defiant unfriendliness, she could hardly have managed better. I was so taken aback that when the two sisters had passed out of sight I sat down on a bench to recover . . . And yet I am convinced that the rudeness was not deliberate but merely the result of a conflict in her mind between two inconsistent impulses, an old affection and a new dislike.

*The third note was written at the same time.* The friendliness between Arthur Balfour and the Webbs died a slow and natural death. The last time he dined with us was in the spring of 1914 . . . I met him once again walking in St James's Park just after the outbreak of war, and tried to interest him in the gross mismanagement of the Prince of Wales Fund [to relieve distress caused by the war]. But it was clear that neither the person approaching him nor the subject interested him, and that his expression of personal but acute boredom – an expression I had noticed before when he was addressed by a Conservative member whom he did not happen to like – was not wholly undeliberate. So I ceased to trouble him.]

*3 May.* [41 Grosvenor Road]

. . . Perhaps the most noted result [of the war] is the consciousness of world failure on the part of the international labour and socialist movement, a consciousness of a certain self-deception – all our fine talk, all our glowing shibboleths are proved to be mere surface froth. . . . And oddly enough, there is, at present, no anger with them. There is no jingo mob. There is a section of the working class who are slacking and drinking, who, like the army contractors, are making the country's need the opportunity for exactions, but there is no popular anti-pacifist feeling. . . . The criminal classes are the only ones to visibly improve in character. They have given up crime and enlisted in large numbers. The women of all classes have emerged into public life – industrial, social and militarist. . . .

*10 May.* [41 Grosvenor Road]

Last night I lay awake thinking over the absence of any recognized ethic of friendship. To most men, friendship does not entail the continuance of the feeling of friendship when the intimacy has ceased to be a pleasure to both sides. . . . A friend is a book which you read and when you have satisfied your curiosity the thing is put on the shelf, in the wastepaper basket or sold. This assumption of lack of permanence, is, to me, tragic . . . But if all friendships are to be permanent then it is unwise to enter into personal intimacy and mutual affection unless you are certain of your own and the other person's faithfulness. . . .

The Coalition government was announced on 19 May. Failures on the Western Front and in the Dardanelles, together with insufficient ammunition for the troops in France, had led to a political crisis. Arthur Henderson (1863–1935), a Labour M.P., entered the Cabinet as President of the Board of Education. Haldane, Lord Chancellor since 1912, had been attacked as 'pro-German' because he had written sympathetically about German philosophy.

*5 June.* [41 Grosvenor Road]

. . . the coalition government threatens to break the Labour Party into warring sections. Rumours as to the meaning of this sudden and unexpected change fly hither and thither. Some say that it has been engineered by Lloyd George and Balfour: others declare that it is the only way round the administrative incompetence of Kitchener; others again hint that the government is expecting a big disaster at the Dardanelles and the break-down of the Russian defence and want to silence criticism; whilst the knowing ones whisper that it means compulsory military service. The Parliamentary Labour Party eventually decided to let Henderson take Cabinet office . . . Personally I think they would have been better advised to keep out of it. But without knowing the seriousness of the sit-uation one is no judge. In fact in almost every department of war politics, one can have no opinion because all the essential facts are hidden from one. The misery of acute restlessness is due to the combi-nation of mortal concern and complete ignorance: we are a prey to rumour, both as to what is happening at the front and what the gov-ernment intends to do. . . .

*14 June.* [41 Grosvenor Road]
We had heard much gossip as to the cause of Haldane's enforced retire-ment. . . . it was interesting to hear his own version. In response to an affectionate letter from me, he dined with us last night and seemed glad to unburden his mind. Asquith had not consulted him about the recon-struction – the first he heard of it was the statement circulated in the Cabinet box that the government was dissolved and that all Ministers were to send in their resignations. He, of course, told Asquith to feel free to dispense with his services, and his old friend accepted his resignation with the excuse that the Unionists demanded it. Churchill fought hard and succeeded in imposing himself and is working with Balfour at the Admiralty. Haldane professed to us to be relieved: except that he regret-ted not being in with Grey at any peace negotiations. . . . He says that he had reported to the Cabinet in 1911 that Germany was preparing for war. His advice was to prepare secretly for war whilst doing all that could be done to keep on friendly relations . . . He believed at that time that there was a chance of avoiding war; now he realized that, given the continuance of the German military caste in power, war had been inevitable. On the whole he was glad that it had come now. . . . He was far more friendly than he has been for many a long year, more friendly than he has been since he became a Cabinet Minister. He states that Grey is seriously incapacitated and very depressed; he is suffering from pigmentation of the eyes – a disease which cannot get better but may get worse. Lloyd George is the one Minister who has scored a popular

success (with emphasis on *popular*). He is the 'man of the hour' with the Tories; he is still trusted by large sections of the Radicals and Labour men.

Jane Addams (1860–1935), an active suffragist and pacifist, was awarded the Nobel Peace Prize in 1931. She was one of a number of American peace workers who visited Europe in 1915 in a vain effort to stop the war.

*22 June.* [41 Grosvenor Road]
Jane Addams, with whom we stayed at Hull House, Chicago, on our first world tour, dined with us last night. Since we knew her seventeen years ago she has become a world celebrity – the most famous woman of the U.S.A., representing the best aspects of the feminist movement and the most distinguished elements in the social reform movement. Some say that she has been too much in the limelight of late, and that she is no longer either so sane or so subtle in her public utterances. But to us she seemed the same gentle, dignified, sympathetic woman, though like the rest of us she has lost in brilliancy and personal charm – the inevitable result of age, personal notoriety and much business. Her late mission to the governments of the world, as the leading representative of the neutral women at the Hague Conference of Women, has brought her into still greater prominence. She and one or two other women of neutral countries were charged with the 'Peace Mission' to the governments of Germany, Austria, Hungary, Italy, France, Belgium and England. She had found Sir Edward Grey politely encouraging, expressing his own personal pacific sentiments, but saying nothing about his government. . . .

Jane Addams herself thinks it inconceivable that the U.S.A. should come into the war and she clearly sees little or no difference between British and German policy, either before or during the war – at least that is the impression she leaves on our minds. Her great thesis to us was 'the neutrality of the seas'.

In April the King had ordered that no intoxicants were to be served in the Royal palaces – as an example to the nation. Balfour was now First Lord of the Admiralty.

*22 July.* [41 Grosvenor Road]
We dined alone with Haldane – a luxurious dinner. He had taken the pledge at the same time as the King and Kitchener: it was a consolation

for loss of office that he chose to think that it was the Lord Chancellor that was bound, not Lord Haldane. So we enjoyed his dry champagne and his super-excellent liqueurs. He was very genial, anxious that we and the *New Statesman* should start a campaign for the reconstruction of our social life after the war. . . . He seemed to be ploughing a lonely furrow. 'The country is being governed by three men: Balfour, Kitchener and Lloyd George, and Balfour is the real Prime Minster.' From which remark we gathered that he had broken with Asquith. I doubt whether our old friend has much initiative left over from his free use of alcohol, tobacco and all delectable food. The same complaint lies at the root of Asquith's slackness. He has become senile from self-indulgence. . . . Slackness has become a national vice. . . .

In October, the Bulgarians came in with Germany; the Austrians attacked Belgrade. By mid-October, Germans, Austrians and Bulgarians were sweeping over Serbia. A British and French force was landed at Salonica.

[?] *October.* [41 Grosvenor Road]
. . . the war itself has become almost suddenly far more serious. If Germany breaks through and connects with Turkey, the British Empire is threatened for the first time: the battleground shifts from Europe, where we are impregnable, to Asia, where we have great dependencies to lose. . . . the horror and terror of the war eats into one's vitality, and I exist in a state of chronic weakness brought about by continuous sleeplessness. . . .

Zeppelin raids became frequent on moonlit nights in the summer of 1915; some reached the Midlands and the east coast. This early-October raid killed forty people in London. The Fabian Society organized a series of autumn lectures by Shaw and the Webbs at the King's Hall.

8 *October.* [41 Grosvenor Road]
The window rattled behind me: then all the windows rattled and we became conscious of the booming of guns getting nearer. 'At last the Zeppelins', Sidney said, with almost boyish glee. From the balcony we could see shrapnel bursting over the river and beyond, somewhat aimlessly. In another few minutes a long sinuous airship appeared high up in the blue black sky, lit up faintly by the searchlights. It seemed to come from over the houses just behind us, we thought along Victoria Street,

but it was actually passing along the Strand. It moved slowly, seemingly across the river, the shells bursting far below it. Then there were two bursts that seemed to nearly hit it and it disappeared. I imagine it bounded upwards. The show was over. It was a gruesome reflection afterwards that while we were being pleasantly excited men, women and children were being killed and maimed. At the time it was impossible not to take it as a 'Sight'. . . .

There was apparently no panic, even in the crowded Strand. The Londoner persists in taking Zeppelin raids as an entertainment – a risky entertainment, but no more risky than some forms of sport. . . .

Pessimism about the war is becoming more pronounced: the optimists are silent, mere passive resisters to the panic-mongers. Even Sidney is getting alarmed about the financial position, and many of us feel doubtful whether our working class would endure any considerable hardships without breaking into industrial disorder. Germany and France ruthlessly suppress their pessimists; our government dare not do so, because, like the Ulster rebels of eighteen months ago, they are in high places. Our newspapers are amazingly free with their exasperated criticism, and certain notables, like poor Haldane, are pursued with venom.

There is a chronic conspiracy to get rid of Asquith and Grey. There is a great deal of screaming, 'You see, I was right,' a great many cries for 'someone's head'. . . .

*14 November.* [41 Grosvenor Road]
In my last lecture on 'The War and the Spirit of Revolt' I had to define my position towards metaphysics. My thesis was that the Spirit of Revolt – the Revolt that looks to violence as its method – was identical with the Spirit of War. . . . There was only one desirable emotion . . . the state of mind, which for lack of a better word, we call love – some call it heavenly love, to distinguish it from animal love. To my dismay, I found myself hailed by some religious papers as a convert to religion, even to Christianity. That makes me feel a hypocrite . . .

Sometimes I try to discover what is the Ideal that moves me. It is not a conception of a rightly organized society; it is not a vision of a perfect man – a Saviour or a Superman. It is far nearer the thought of an Abstract Being divested of all human appetite but combining the quality of an always working intellect with an impersonal love. . . . But it would not be true to say that this faith in love with its attendant practice of prayer is a continuous state of mind. If it were, I should be a consistently happy person, which I am not. I enjoy life after a manner – I seldom want to leave it. . . . But I am haunted with the fear that all my struggles may be in vain; that disease and death are the ends towards which the individual, the race and the whole conceivable universe are moving with relentless certainty. . . .

## ∼ 1916 ∼

*2 January.* [41 Grosvenor Road]
The year opens badly for labour. The Munitions Act and the Defence of the Realm Act, together with the suppression of a free press, has been followed by the Cabinet's decision in favour of compulsory military service. . . . it is obvious that if the war continues, the married men will have to go into the trenches, and directly the Minister of Munitions *dares to do it*, industrial conscription will be introduced into the whole of industry. The 'servile state' will have been established.

Sidney, who is now on the Executive of the Labour Party . . . attended the meeting to decide on the policy of the Labour Party and the trade union movement. He says that though the question of conscription was not discussed . . . it was clear that nearly all the Labour M.P.s and a majority of the other leaders were converted to a minimum measure of conscription. Henderson told them that the alternative was a general election and that if that took place every Labour M.P. would lose his seat – certainly every member who was against military service. . . .

*31 January.* [41 Grosvenor Road]
The cause of national unity and the continued existence in this Parliament of a Labour Party have been furthered by the equivocal resolutions of the Bristol conference. The 900 delegates, representing from two to three million manual workers, administered a good-tempered but effective snub to the I.L.P. pacifists. . . . The British workman, his wife and daughters, are making good money, more than ever before, and they are working long hours and have no time to be discontented. So long as full employment and the bigger income continues there will be nothing more serious than revolutionary talk, and occasional local outbreaks of disorder. And as no one is allowed to report either the talk or the disorder, the world will be assured that there is industrial peace in Great Britain.

*22 February.* [41 Grosvenor Road]

C. M. Lloyd [a Fabian] is back on leave; he is very pessimistic. He does not believe that there is much chance of the British breaking through. He is disgusted with the drinking habits, slackness and want of intelligence of the British officer. The ordinary officer, whether he be a professional or a 'Kitchener Army' man, has no notion of accurate orders or of seeing that these orders are executed exactly and punctually. He muddles everything, and consequently muddles away many lives in every attack. The common soldier obeys orders but with very little intelligence or zeal. His strength lies in his lack of imagination: if he is well led 'he sticks it'. . . .

A British garrison at Kut in Mesopotamia fell to the Turks on 29 April after three months' fighting. The French were desperately trying to halt the massive German attacks on Verdun, begun in February. The No-Conscription Fellowship was founded by Fenner Brockway (1888–1988), editor of the *Labour Leader*. He became general secretary of the I.L.P., and in later life a Labour politician.

*4 April.* [41 Grosvenor Road]

. . . A few weeks ago the rumour was that the W.O. thought that the war would be over in August owing to the exhaustion of Germany attacked on all fronts; that the Admiralty had the submarines well in hand, etc. etc. But today there are new elements of anxiety: the almost certain surrender of the Kut force, diminishing our prestige in the East; the success of the submarine campaign in reducing our already narrow margin of mercantile marine; the belief that the German lines are impregnable, and the fear that France will not hold out during the winter. There is also the steady depreciation, by the war press, of our organizing capacity and technical skill. Whatever else the war is doing, it is not increasing our self-conceit. . . .

The state of my own and other people's mind surprises me. We are becoming callous to the horrors of the war. At first it was a continuous waking nightmare. But with a few months of it one ceases to feel about it. Today one goes on with one's researches, enjoys one's comforts and pleasures and even reads the daily war news with mild interest, exactly as if slaughter and devastation, on a colossal scale, were part of the expected routine of life. This callousness to the horrors of war explains the way in which the wealthy governing class have tolerated the horrors of peace due to the existing social order. Is there no depth of misery and

degradation, endured by other persons, which will not be accepted as
normal and inevitable? . . .

*8 April.* [41 Grosvenor Road]
The Friends Meeting House in Devonshire House Hotel, a large ugly
circular hall with a big gallery running round it, was packed with some
2,000 young men – the National Convention of the No-Conscription
Fellowship. . . . The intellectual pietist, slender in figure, delicate in feature and complexion, benevolent in expression, was the dominant
type. . . . And yet the constant expression, in word and manner, of the
sentiment avowed by one of them: 'We are the people whose eyes are
open,' was unpleasing. There were not a few professional rebels, out to
smash the Military Service Act, because it was the latest and biggest
embodiment of authority hostile to the conduct of their own lives
according to their own desires. Here and there were misguided youths
who had been swept into the movement because 'conscientious objection' had served to excuse their refusal to enlist and possibly might save
them from the terrors and discomforts of fighting – pasty-faced furtive
boys, who looked dazed at the amount of heroism that was being
expected from them. They were obviously scared by the unanimity with
which it was decided 'to refuse alternative service', and they will certainly
take advantage of the resolution declaring that every member of the
Fellowship must follow his own conscience in this matter. On the platform were the sympathizers with the movement – exactly the persons
you would expect to find at such a meeting, older pacifists and older
rebels . . . the pacifist predominating over the rebel element. . . .
     The first argument advanced by all the speakers was: 'I believe war to
be an evil thing: killing our fellow men is expressly forbidden by my religion, and by the religion, by law established, of my country. Under the
Military Service Act *bona fide* conscientious objectors are granted
unconditional exemption: I claim this exemption.' But this plea did not
satisfy the militant majority. They declared their intention to defy the
Act, so that the Act should become inoperative, even if all the conscientious objectors, on religious grounds, should be relieved from service.
They *want* to be martyrs, so as to bring about a revulsion of feeling
against any prosecution of the war. They are as hostile to voluntary
recruiting as they are to conscription. . . . Now it seems clear that organized society could not continue to be organized, if every citizen had the
right to be a conscientious objector to some part of our social order . . .
Moreover, when the conscientious objection is to carrying out an

unpleasant social obligation like defending your country or paying taxes, conscience may become the cover for cowardice, greed or any other form of selfishness. Hence the state, in defence, must make the alternative to fulfilling the common obligation sufficiently irksome to test the conscience of the objectors. . . .

*1 May.* [41 Grosvenor Road]
A series of political crises: the newspapers excited, everyone else indifferent. Ten days ago it looked as if the government would break up on compulsion, and the withdrawal of more men from the army. Asquith was confronted with the pledge he gave to the Labour Party that if the H. of C. determined on extending the principle of conscription to married men, 'someone else would have to take my place.' But as one might have expected, he has broken his pledge. The actual proposal eventually agreed to was the silly and dishonest one of pretending to try voluntary recruiting again for married men, with the proviso that if they did not come in within a month, they were to be conscripted, whilst extending compulsion immediately to all youths reaching eighteen years of age and also to time-expired men. This compromise was accepted by the Labour Party, in spite of Sidney's appeal to stand firm. When the Bill was introduced, everyone saw the absurdity and unfairness of it: so now we have compulsion, *sans phrase.* . . . It is humiliating that the Labour Party has shown, if anything, less resistance than the Liberal Party. On the top of this defeat we have the criminal lunacy of the Irish rebellion, playing into the hands of the reactionaries.

On Easter Day, 25 April 1916, a small band of Irish patriots seized the centre of Dublin as part of an aborted scheme for a nationwide rising. The rebellion was quickly crushed and seventeen of its leaders executed. Sir Roger Casement (1846–1916), an Ulster Protestant and Irish nationalist, sought help for his cause in Germany and, on the eve of the Easter Rising, was landed in Ireland from a German submarine. He was captured and hanged for treason. Intelligence sources circulated his 'Black Diaries' which purported to reveal his homosexuality and may have been forged: they certainly helped to prejudice opinion against him. Shaw published a letter, 'Shall Roger Casement Hang?', on 22 July in the *Manchester Guardian*, after *The Times*, the *Daily News* and the *Nation* rejected it. He did draft a defence speech for Casement, most of which Casement discarded, and drew up a petition to Asquith. He made a final plea in the *Daily News* of 2 August, the day before Casement was hanged.

Sir Charles Russell (1863–1928), a prominent solicitor, held several government appointments. George Gavan Duffy (1881–1951), an Irish barrister, eventually became president of the High Court of Ireland.

*21 May.* [41 Grosvenor Road]

A painful luncheon party: Mrs Green and the Bernard Shaws to consult about the tragic plight of Roger Casement. Alice Green has made herself responsible for the defence of her old friend. He has no money and only two relatives in England – cousins who are school-teachers. On reaching London, with his Scotland Yard escort, he appealed to the only solicitor he knew, Charles Russell (the son of the late Russell of Killowen), who has a large Irish Catholic connection. Russell refused to defend him and sent his clerk to the Tower to tell him so. Meanwhile, Mrs Green had got Gavan Duffy to write and offer to conduct the defence. The letter was not delivered for a fortnight, the unhappy rebel being in solitary confinement with the consciousness of being deserted. Alice declares that throughout this time he was harassed by visits from detectives, examining and cross-examining him. At last Gavan Duffy was permitted to see him and counsel was briefed only four and twenty hours before he had to be defended in the police court. To enable this to be done Mrs Green had to put down £300. But where is the money to come from for the trial in the High Court? Gavan Duffy has already injured himself by taking up the rebels' cause: his partners are said to have repudiated him. . . .

. . . I asked the Bernard Shaws to meet Alice. Charlotte is a wealthy Irish rebel, and I had noticed that when Casement's 'treason' was mentioned, her eyes had flashed defiance and she had defended his action. And GBS had publicly urged clemency and had also defended Casement's action. But GBS as usual had his own plan. Casement was to defend his own case, he was to make a great oration of defiance which would 'bring down the house'. To this Mrs Green retorted tearfully that the man was desperately ill, that he was quite incapable of handling a court full of lawyers, that the most he could do was the final speech after the verdict. 'Then we had better get our suit of mourning,' Shaw remarked with an almost gay laugh. 'I will write him a speech which will thunder down the ages.' 'But his friends want to get him reprieved,' indignantly replied the distracted woman friend.

The meeting turned out to be a useless and painful proceeding. The Shaws were determined not to pay up – not 'to waste our money on lawyers'. GBS went off to write the speech which was 'to thunder down the ages'. Alice Green retired in dismay, and I felt a fool for having intervened to bring Irish together in a common cause. Alice has been heroic: her house has been searched, she herself has been up before Scotland Yard, she is spending her strength and her means in trying to save the life of her unfortunate friend. The Shaws don't care enough about it to spend money; and Shaw wants to compel Casement and Casement's friends to 'produce' the defence as a national dramatic event. 'I know how to do it,' was GBS's one contribution to the tragedy-laden dispute . . . his conceit is monstrous, and he is wholly unaware of the pain he gives by his jeering words and laughing gestures – especially to romantics like Alice Green. He never hurts my feelings because I am as intellectually detached as he is. He sometimes irritates Sidney with his argumentative perversities, but . . . GBS's admiration for Sidney's ability has become part of his own *amour propre*. And there is this to be said: if everyone were as intellectual and unemotional as he is, as free from conventions in thought and feeling, his flashes might alter the direction of opinion. There would remain his instability of purpose. . . . A world made up of Bernard Shaws would be a world in moral dissolution.

*1 June.* [41 Grosvenor Road]
. . . Sometimes I have felt hurt that Sidney has not been called upon by the government to do work of national importance. He has been curiously ignored by the rulers of the world, though constantly consulted by the underlings of government departments and the lesser lights of the Labour movement. Within the Labour Party he has a certain influence and is allowed to draft manifestoes, Bills, questions in Parliament, resolutions for conferences and meetings for other people to gather – like Anderson's Conscription of Wealth Bill and all the reports and circulars of the War Emergency Committee. But the inner ring of pro-war Labour men exclude him from their counsels, whilst his pro-war opinions exclude him from the pacifist movement. He has been exceptionally well and happy, directing the work of the Research Department and writing a book on *How to Pay for the War* and helping with anything I have in hand.

I have been at work on three different jobs. Research for the monograph on the professional organizations of medical men has been my main occupation; but I have attended twice a week at the organizing committee of the Statutory Pensions Committee, and I have been laying the foundation of a new organization, developed out of the Fabian

Research Department: the proposed Labour Research Society. . . . This proposed organization is a device to connect in one working fellowship the Fabian Society, the National Guildsmen and the trade union movement. . . .

On 2 June the Webbs took up six weeks' residence at Wyndham Croft, a substantial house at Turner's Hill, overlooking the South Downs, having exchanged homes with the owner – 'an instance of mutual trust between two strangers brought about by war economy'. Shaw visited Wyndham Croft 6–20 June, while writing *Heartbreak House*; its setting is reflected in the last scene. Leonard Woolf (1880–1969) and his wife, the writer Virginia (1882–1941), were weekend guests, though Beatrice makes no comment on their visit. 'We talked quite incessantly,' Virginia wrote to Vanessa Bell. 'We were taken for brisk walks, still talking hard. Mrs Webb pounces on one, rather like a moulting eagle, with a bald neck and a bloodstained beak. However, I got on with her better than I expected.' Leonard Woolf's *International Government* (1916) had been written at the Webbs' initiative.

*17 June.* [Wyndham Croft]

Charlotte Shaw joined us for the last few days of GBS's visit. Except for the details of daily life, these two have not much common interest. Charlotte detests the stage and is no longer interested in socialism. Pacifist she is – because she is a rebel. Christian Science (or is it Higher Thought?) is her main occupation . . . She is still very proud of her famous man and angry with any criticism of his work. But her thoughts centre in the crude reasoning of the male and female preachers of the new American mysticism. She has in fact become '*dévote*' – the modern *dévote*, who combines a love of personal luxury with intense interest and the happy peacefulness of her own soul. I am, perhaps unjustifiably, irritated at the selfishness of her expenditure. I have never known her ask an overworked person to Ayot. She has never lent the house, in her absence, to poorer friends who need rest and change. Once we took it off her hands because she wanted to take all her servants away (not because we wanted it) and, of course, we can always get a holiday. In old days she was generous, out of her superfluity, to the London School of Economics and the Fabian Society. But she has lost the last remnant of conscience about property. These new cults do not lead to self-sacrifice . . . Faith and not works is the purpose – faith in your own happiness. (I doubt whether I am fair to Charlotte: she and I are not sympathetic.)

*24 June.* [Wyndham Croft]

I have had, in the last few days, a deplorable proof of the lack of Christian Science in myself. Owing to certain physical symptoms showing a steady decline in energy and weight for some months past, I became obsessed by the conviction that I had an internal growth, that this would necessitate an operation and that I should die under it. Each link in the chain of proof was unsound, but to my distempered imagination, each supposition seemed an uncontrovertible fact. And I even infected poor Sidney with my fear. So we journeyed up to London with melancholy expectation, to see a specialist. He dispelled my fears, telling me there was no sign of any organic trouble. I was to eat more and, if sleeplessness continued, I was to take a sleeping draught. I feel humiliated – humiliated alike by my absurd obsession and by the absence of courage, even if it had been justified, in meeting physical pain and death. With millions of young men facing death and dying on the battlefields of Europe, it seems contemptible for an old woman, who has had a full and happy life, to blink miserably at the inevitable end. . . .

Why does one fear death? One does not fear sleep . . . Some part of the fear is for Sidney: leaving him alone in the world . . . But he is brave and has still sufficient vitality to enjoy work and human companionship. His very love for me would help his natural humanity: he would become absorbed in finishing the work we had planned together. And with the wearing out of his energies there would come the wearing out of his sorrow. I should become a holy memory to him, and old people live in their memories. . . .

[*Beatrice added this additional note in 1919.* This illness was the opening phase of a breakdown, which lasted in an acute form for six months and from which I did not recover for over two years. Partly war neurosis, partly too persistent work to keep myself from brooding over the horrors of the war, partly I think general discouragement arising out of our unpopularity with all sections of the political and official world. . . . Oddly enough, the first push upwards came from an article in the Lancet which I read at Margate in October, describing all the symptoms of neurasthenia, which I promptly recognized as my own. Once aware that my disorder was more mental than physical I took myself in hand, did short intervals of regular work and physical exercise, and gradually pulled myself into the normal routine of a working life. But the breakdown proved to be the turning-point from middle to old age. . . .]

The Somme offensive was launched on 1 July. British casualties on the first day alone exceeded 57,000, of whom 19,240 were killed.

*2 July.* [Wyndham Croft]
We hear from overseas the dull noiseless thud beating on the drum of the ear, hour after hour, day by day, telling of the cancelling out of whole populations on the vast battlefield. One sometimes wonders how one can go on, eating and drinking, walking and sleeping, reading and dictating, apparently unmoved by the world's misery.

*6 July.* [Wyndham Croft]
Graham Wallas has been staying here. The oddly slovenly young man of a quarter of a century ago . . . is now a leader of thought, with a settled and sufficient livelihood and a body of devoted disciples. . . . His books are widely read in the U.S.A., his lectures are well attended, he sits on royal commissions, and is often referred to and consulted. . . . One thing is clear. Graham Wallas has a greater consciousness of success than we have. He does not feel as I certainly do, beaten by events. . . . Today I feel like the fly, not on but under the wheel. . . .

The Reconstruction Committee, of which Vaughan Nash (1861–1932) was secretary, was a small group of civil servants. Early in 1917 it was reorganized into a larger, more representative body.

*8 July.* [Wyndham Croft]
Vaughan Nash came down yesterday for the afternoon to consult Sidney about his Reconstruction Committee. . . . V.N. suggested that Sidney should come on the sub-committee on the Relations between Capital and Labour, which Sidney accepted, and that I should be on the Committee on Maternity Provision, which I refused, feeling that I have only just enough strength for the work I have in hand.

*18 October. Longfords*
Here trying to recover strength for work, in this peaceful and comfortable home – an attempt not hitherto successful, in spite of dear sister Mary's overwhelming kindness and consideration. I spend my days in elaborate idleness, sauntering in the garden, learning to knit, reading newspapers and driving with Mary in the pony-cart. I should enjoy it if it were not for the perpetual dizziness and the long restless nights. With Sidney away they become painfully fearsome. I have discovered from the

second medical man that I have consulted that it is the muscle of the heart, that shows slight weakness, which seems to account for some of the symptoms. . . .

The Playne household is transformed by the war. The majority of the rooms are dismantled, the bedrooms locked up, the hall and drawing-room bare for working parties. [There are] only the new sitting-room for the family and Arthur's little office and one spare bedroom and dressing-room. The meals are of the simplest. Mary and Bichy [Mary's companion] are at work most of the day. Large working parties of neighbours gather at Longfords to turn out hospital necessaries and comforts for the troops twice or three times a week. Longfords has become a veritable house of industry . . .

By the end of November British casualties on the Somme exceeded 400,000, with little gained and the 'volunteer' army destroyed in the process. The novelist Arnold Bennett (1867–1931) became a director and financial supporter of the *New Statesman* in 1915. In 1916 he started writing articles under the name of Sardonyx. Beatrice does not mention the death, in November, of Charles Booth.

*3 November. Fort Paragon Hotel, Margate*
. . . GBS has definitely severed his connection with the *New Statesman*. . . . Possibly Shaw's prophecy that Sharp will presently dispense with Sidney may be fulfilled. Arnold Bennett is the one director with whom he seems in complete sympathy, and A.B. is just starting a weekly article of the hard pro–Liberal–Minister type. But if the paper succeeds, we do not grudge Sharp his independence. The new generation must take its own line. It is useless for the older generation 'to cut up rough'. . . .

The gloom of the war deepens. Both sides seem to be hardening; the greater the losses, the more determined are each set of belligerents to get some sort of equivalent gain out of it. . . .

*17 November. Margate*
. . . These last days have been saddened by hearing that our dear sister Mary is again to be operated on for cancer of the breast. She came here out of kindness to me and left last week, alarmed by some symptoms, an alarm which has been justified by the surgeon's diagnosis. She has been very sweet. Sometimes she has irritated me with her fussiness about my health, but I have been lost in wonder at her saintliness.

There is no other word for her attitude towards life. She has continuously grown in grace with advancing old age. The mechanism of her mind is failing: she has lost her memory and her power of understanding many things and she has a strange restlessness, due, I suppose, to weakness. If it were not for Arthur and for the loss of her gracious influence at Longfords, I should wish her not to live much longer, especially if she has to face pain and weariness. 'I should like to see the end of the war and then I would gladly go,' she said to me in our last walk together. All the remaining sisters are saddened old women, except Rosy, still in middle life, but who is, poor woman, much troubled by her sick child. What has saddened us all is the war, and the terror of the world catastrophe.

### 2 December. Grosvenor Road

At work again. The neurasthenia has apparently cleared away, the month's dullness at Margate having sufficiently strengthened my nerves to make mental work a stimulus to bodily health. . . . I find my mind gradually crystalizing as to my own secret desires . . . I want a peace in which none of the great belligerents gain anything whatsoever. I want all of them to feel that the war has been a hideous calamity without any compensating advantages – a gigantic and wicked folly from which no good can come. . . . On this basis of universal loss and humiliation I would build the new League of Nations with the U.S.A. as one of the guarantors.

> Lloyd George, who had taken over the War Office after Kitchener's death on 6 June, now became the leader of a new 'win-the-war' Coalition of 15 Conservatives, 12 Liberals and 6 Labour. Arthur Henderson became a member of the inner War Cabinet.

### 7 December. [41 Grosvenor Road]

The turmoil of the political world of the last few days has been brought about by a series of disasters – the collapse of Rumania, the trouble in Greece, the cessation of the Somme offensive, the revival of the submarine menace, and most important of all the prospect of an actual shortage of food in the U.K. But this turmoil has been sedulously fostered by the Tory press, restive under the presumed pacific tendencies of Grey and the incapacity of the other Ministers to take energetic action. We have expressed our view of the cleavage of policy in an article in the coming issue of the *New Statesman*. Asquith and his lieutenants are mildly against any interference with anyone or anything: the Lloyd George–Curzon group want to mobilize labour whilst retaining for the ruling class property intact and the control of trade and industry. . . . As we personally belong to the ruling class, the outlook is not detrimental to the comfort and freedom of our lives. But it is ruinous to the cause that we have at heart . . . And it means a continuance, to the bitter end, not only of the present war, but of faith in war as the universal solvent. It means the supremacy of all I think evil and the suppression of all I think good. Lloyd George would represent Mammon, though Heaven knows that Asquith and Co. do not represent God. God is unrepresented in the effective political world of today.

*12 December.* [41 Grosvenor Road]
The Lloyd George government, announced today, is a brilliant improvisation, reactionary in composition and undemocratic in form. For the first time (since Cromwell) we have a dictatorship by one, or possibly by three, men; for the first time we see called to high office distinguished experts not in Parliament; for the first time we behold Labour leaders in open alliance with Tory chieftains; for the first time a Cabinet has been created, not by a party political organization or by any combination of party organizations, nor by the will of the House of Commons, but by a powerful combination of newspaper proprietors. The House of Commons in fact almost disappears as the originator and controller of the Cabinet. . . .

Germany and Austria made a peace offer on 12 December.

*18 December.* [41 Grosvenor Road]
The peace overtures of Germany find the country (except for the little sect of pacifists) curiously united in favour of carrying on the war without an attempt to negotiate. . . . Either our public men are perfect masters of bluff or the governing clique believe that the country can and will hold out . . .

~ 1917 ~

For the next six years Beatrice worked intermittently on the manuscript that was to become *My Apprenticeship* (1926). From this point onwards, either she or a secretary made a typed copy of her handwritten diary.

*3 January.* [41 Grosvenor Road]
I have bought a small cheap typewriter and I am using up some of my spare hours in the afternoon in copying out and editing my manuscript diaries so as to make a book of my life. It is no more tiring than endless reading, hardly more so than my desperate attempt at Longfords to knit soldiers' socks. And it is more interesting to me than either, and perhaps more useful. . . .

*19 February.* [41 Grosvenor Road]
. . . Routed out of my secret and pleasurable occupation of typing and editing the 'book of my life' by an invitation to join the new Reconstruction Committee . . . the task of surveying and unravelling the whole tangle of governmental activities introduced by the war . . . is an attractive one. It means the sort of work that Sidney and I are skilled in . . . Moreover, the Reconstruction Committee is . . . made up . . . of young and vigorous persons with the Prime Minister as chairman and the youngest and ablest of the ex-Cabinet Ministers as vice-chairman. Out of the fifteen members there are three Fabians, as well as two Labour men, and one of the two assistant secretaries is a Fabian. . . . Altogether, if I keep my health and mind my manners, I shall find the work far more stimulating than that of the two government committees I have served on since the war. . . .

> The collapse of the Tsarist regime in February 1917 (Russian old-style date for March) was greeted with joy by progressives everywhere, and the advent of a people's government raised hopes of a negotiated and reasonable peace. Woodrow Wilson (1856–1924), President of the United States, had made several attempts to promote such a peace, but the deteriorating American relations with Germany were brought to breaking-point by the resumption of unrestricted submarine warfare at the beginning of February. On 6 April the United States formally declared war on Germany.

*18 March.* [41 Grosvenor Road]
. . . The life I should enjoy, at present, would be a comfortable small country house, noiseless, except for birds and the rustling of water and wind, with my diaries to type. Sidney, meanwhile, might complete those endless volumes of historical material which are almost finished; and the two of us together might write the two books we want to bring out before we die – *What is Socialism?* and *Methods of Investigation.* But the *New Statesman* and this new Reconstruction Committee are going to

keep us in London, with its noise and its dirt and its constant overstrain of nervous strength and consequent sleeplessness. What troubles me is the doubt whether my feelings of old age and weariness are justified physiologically or whether I am giving way to an obsession. I am in my sixtieth year; if it were not for the war I have a right to retire. Until the war is over I suppose that Sidney and I ought to render national service. . . .

The Russian revolution and the entry of the U.S.A. into the war completely alter the situation. The Entente does now represent democracy at war with autocracy. . . .

*18 July.* [41 Grosvenor Road]
Exit the Reconstruction Committee. . . . the machine was too rickety to survive. . . . The specially appointed sub-committees will, I assume, continue to function, and I shall have enough to do on the Local Government Committee and the Machinery of Government Committee. . . . I feel too old and tired for the immense changes that lie in front of us. To Sidney they are exhilarating . . . He refuses to dwell on the horrors of the war and he believes that through the war will come the changes he believes in.

At the end of 1916, Beatrice's nephew Stephen Hobhouse was sentenced to six months' hard labour in solitary confinement at Wormwood Scrubs. In April 1917 he was sentenced to another two years' hard labour at Exeter after a second court martial. In protest Margaret Hobhouse wrote *I Appeal Unto Caesar* in July. It sold 20,000 copies. Her son was released in December 1917.

*22 September.* [41 Grosvenor Road]
A fortnight with the Courtneys at Bude and a week-end with the Hobhouses at Hadspen has proved the most restful holiday we have had for years. The sisters, as they grow old, are more than ever dependent on each other's affection, and the remaining brothers-in-law are more completely included in the strong family feeling. Dear old Leonard, the patriarch of the family and acknowledged as its central figure by the second and third generation, is a marvellous old man . . . in spite of his anti-war bias he remains cheerful, serenely contemptuous of his country's leaders and hopeful that a 'bad peace' will bring the British people to its senses. Kate remains morbidly obsessed with her country's wrongdoing and aggressively disputatious in her reiteration of the pacifist ethical stereos. . . .

376  The Diaries of Beatrice Webb

Margaret Hobhouse is elated over the success of her little book on the woes of the conscientious objectors, and has thoroughly enjoyed pushing it. The war activity of her four sons (three in the army and one in prison for refusing service) has given her a public interest. She retains the qualities she had as a girl: high spirits, restless energy with a background of cynical melancholy. I doubt whether the admirable Henry has had the remotest influence on her; her quixotic son Stephen has had considerable influence. . . .

Arthur Henderson had resigned from the War Cabinet in August, following a serious rift with Lloyd George. His resignation set the Labour Party on an independent and more self-sufficient footing. J. H. Thomas (1874–1947), general secretary of the N.U.R. and labour M.P., became Colonial Secretary in 1924.

### 3 October. [41 Grosvenor Road]

J. H. Thomas, the general secretary of the Railwaymen, dined here last night . . . He and Henderson are running the new party. It is interesting to note that, for the first time, he told Sidney that the responsible T.U. officials would like him to stand for Parliament, and Henderson repeated this request yesterday. . . . As Sidney has not the remotest wish to go into Parliament, and much prefers to remain in the background, I hardly think the request will be pressed.

The British offensive in Flanders, begun on 31 July, continued through the autumn with heavy casualties. Rain and mud made conditions in Passchendaele appalling. The collapse of the Russian army enabled the Bolsheviks to carry out a second, 'October' revolution. Although Beatrice persuaded the Local Government Committee to adopt some of her Poor Law proposals, a thoroughgoing reform was not completed until the election of the 1945 Labour government.

### 5 October. [41 Grosvenor Road]

Six successive air raids have wrecked the nerves of Londoners, with the result of a good deal of discreditable panic even among the well-to-do and the educated. The first two nights I felt myself under the sway of foolish fear. My feet were cold and my heart pattered its protest against physical danger. But the fear wore off, and by Monday night's raid, the nearest to us, I had recovered self-possession and read through the noise of the barrage with the help of an additional cigarette. . . .

*11 December.* [41 Grosvenor Road]
It is a year since the Lloyd George government came in and we seem further off than ever from the end of the war. The collapse of Russia, the invasion of Italy, the checkmate on the French front and the continued menace of the submarine have placed the Central Powers in the ascendant. . . . Sidney still retains his equanimity if not his optimism. I am still a melancholy agnostic. . . .

This autumn's work has been exhilarating. I have piloted the Minority Report proposals through the Local Government Committee . . . This is the crown of those three years' hard propaganda after the three years' hard grind on the Poor Law Commission. My success was mainly due to Lord George Hamilton's generous help, coupled with innumerable argumentative memoranda . . . Also, I have learnt committee manners – an art in itself.

. . . I have put my diaries away again, partly because I felt my attempt to compose 'The Book of my Life' was not successful, but mainly because there is sterner work to do, and work for which I am peculiarly fitted by long experience and training.

∼ 1918 ∼

Maxim Litvinov (1876–1952), married to the English novelist Ivy Low (1889–1977), was the first Soviet plenipotentiary in Britain.

*10 January.* [41 Grosvenor Road]
. . . The new year opens in gloom. Germany is stronger and more successful relatively to the Allies than she has ever been since the first rush to Paris. The governing class of Great Britain is no longer certain of ultimate victory . . . The mass of the population is irritated by the scarcity of food in the shops; the propertied class is getting more and more frightened at the coming taxation in redemption of war debt, and the always swelling demands of the manual workers for equality of circumstances. Both sides are preparing for class war. . . .

Litvinov, the Bolshevik 'ambassador', lunched with us on Wednesday . . . He is pessimistic about the Russian revolution. . . . If European militarism does not destroy it, economic pressure will. When we asked him what was the alternative . . . he replied: 'We shall become a colony of the German empire.'

*31 January.* [41 Grosvenor Road]
I was rung up this morning by Mrs Asquith's secretary. 'Mrs Asquith wanted to see Mrs Webb.' . . . So the little lady appeared, after an interval of twelve years or more since we last met. She greeted me effusively. 'You are more beautiful than ever – let me come where I can look at you.' And then followed two hours of rapid and somewhat incoherent talk about 'Henry' and his political concerns, vivid and entertaining abuse of Lloyd George, Bonar Law, Arthur Balfour, and Winston Churchill – all the great ones who had deserted her husband. . . . Her object in coming was quite clearly to tout for the support of Sidney for a coalition between the Liberal leaders and the Labour Party. 'Would Mr Webb come and see my husband?' 'I am afraid Mr Henderson would not like that, Mrs Asquith,' I replied, in as pleasant a tone as I could muster. 'My husband is merely a friendly outside helper' . . . She ended by embracing me most affectionately. So we parted. She impressed me as she has always impressed me: a scatter-brained and somewhat vulgar but vital little woman acquainted with the mentality of great personages but wholly unversed in great affairs, and with the social creed of the commonplace plutocrat. . . . I think she left feeling that the Webbs were as usual obdurate and that nothing was to be gained by trying to deal with them. . . .

*14 February.* [41 Grosvenor Road]
. . . Sidney is very happy in his new role of adviser-in-chief to the Labour Party, and Henderson, Middleton [assistant secretary] and the trade union leaders quite clearly are grateful to him. His old enemy MacDonald is friendly in manner to him, and if he is not liked by the I.L.P., they have confidence in his essential friendliness. And he is too old to excite jealousy in the young men.

*1 March.* [41 Grosvenor Road]
We dined yesterday with Haldane to meet one other guest, at his own request – the Prime Minister. . . . Prime Ministers usually excite, in all but the most sophisticated minds, a measure of awe and instinctive deference. No such feeling is possible with Lloyd George. The low standard of intellect and conduct of the little Welsh conjurer is so obvious, and withal he is so pleasant and lively, that official deference and personal respect fades into an atmosphere of agreeable low company – but low company of a most stimulating kind, intimate camaraderie with a fellow adventurer. . . . His object in meeting us was, I think, to find out

whether any co-operation with the Labour Party was practicable – or at any rate how the land lay with regard to the Labour Party and the Asquithian Liberals. It was, in fact, a counter-thrust to the Asquith touting . . . He could not approach Henderson, so he approached Sidney. Like many other persons who have known Henderson as a Cabinet Minister, he thinks that all the recent success of the Labour Party must be due to someone else – who else is there but Webb? . . .

*20 March.* [41 Grosvenor Road]
The Labour Party is the most ramshackle institution in its topmost storey. Henderson sits alone in the untidy office at 1 Victoria Street: no member of the Executive or of the Parliamentary Party ever comes near him except Sidney. J. R. MacDonald, the treasurer, supposed to be his fellow Executive officer, is conspicuous by his absence. . . . Snowden, the chairman of the I.L.P., the leading socialist organization . . . never loses an opportunity of sneering at Henderson or denouncing the 'official Labour Party'. . . . it is difficult to imagine that such a crazy piece of machinery . . . will play a big part in the reconstruction of the United Kingdom and the British Empire after the war. . . .

> On 21 March the Germans launched a massive attack on the British Fifth Army south of Arras in the hope of forcing a decision before American troops could sweep them out of France. The desperate fighting continued until the end of April, when the Germans launched a final and unsuccessful offensive against the French. Thomas Jones (1870–1955), a Fabian professor of economics and close friend of the Webbs, was Lloyd George's go-between in discreet policy negotiations.

*31 March.* [41 Grosvenor Road]
A week of miserable anxiety. We first realized the seriousness of the German onslaught last Sunday – a realization further intensified by Tom Jones, who came straight from the Cabinet to supper with us. Not one minute did I sleep that night, and even Sidney has been disturbed in his usual equanimity, though he does not let his anxiety have any influence on his output of work. The success of the Germans when all the authorities thought the Western Front secure is only another instance of their superiority in forethought, in technique and in concentration of purpose. What is the explanation of the paralysis of British brains which shows itself in the War Office, in the Admiralty, in Parliament, and in private enterprise?

The answer is a complicated one. The British governing class, whether aristocratic or bourgeois, has no abiding faith . . . in the scientific method. Science . . . means the objective testing of persons and policies, and this measurement and testing is against all good comradeship in common undertakings. For the Englishman of all classes – peer, shop-keeper and workman – is a kindly creature who hates the thought that anyone who is related to him, who belongs to his own set or class, or with whom he usually consorts, should be made uncomfortable or dis-possessed of that to which he is accustomed, however inefficient he may be. . . .

*1 April.* [41 Grosvenor Road]
I can see Sidney sitting down early last July to draft the memorandum on *War Aims*, and early in October to draft *Labour and the New Social Order* – exactly as he sits down morning after morning . . . quite oblivious of the fact that he was a man of destiny creating 'the most powerful organized political force in the U.K. excepting only the state.' [*New Republic*, 16 February 1918.]

For assuredly this new and, I fear, wholly undeserved reputation of the Labour Party is based on little more than these two publications. He made the reputation of the Progressive Party of the L.C.C. by his ideas and intellectual propaganda. Is he going to do likewise for the Labour Party? The analogy is not comforting. The Progressive Party went to pieces after the leaders of the Progressives quarrelled with and denounced Sidney over the Education Bill of 1902–03. Now he is an elderly man and the Labour Party cannot reckon to have him for more than a few years, even if the leaders are wise enough to continue to make use of him.

Paul Hobhouse (b. 1894), a captain in the Somerset Light Infantry and youngest son of Margaret Hobhouse, was killed near St Quentin on 21 March.

*16 April.* [41 Grosvenor Road]
A fortnight of gloom and anxiety. The absence of any counter-offensive, even in the pauses of the German advance, has made us all sceptical of any power to resist the German army. . . . One goes about the daily task in a sort of dream, exactly as if one had suffered some dreadful personal bereavement. And a great personal sorrow has come to our family. Paul Hobhouse, last seen to fall fighting desperately on the first day of the

great battle in the first trench of the ill-fated 14th Division of the 5th Army, has not since been heard of. All sorts of rumours are flying around about as to the state of mind of our soldiers, and we none of us know what the country is thinking about it. The mass of people are probably as bewildered as one is oneself.

The government now put forward proposals which gave up the idea of a separate Ulster and extended conscription to Ireland. George Lansbury (1859–1940), one of the members of the Poor Law Commission who had signed the Minority Report, was a future leader of the Labour Party.

*25 April.* [41 Grosvenor Road]
We had the first of a series of meetings of Labour leaders at dinner last night to discuss some kind of common policy. The loneliness of Henderson in his tiny office, and his consciousness of isolation, led me to suggest that our house might be used as a meeting-place. He responded gladly . . . The main question raised was what should the Labour Party do if the Lloyd George combination collapsed over Ireland or over the ill success of the war. Henderson put forward the view that if Asquith were asked to form a government and stated that he could not do so without the participation of the Labour Party, the leaders would be obliged to take office 'on terms'. . . . He intimated that leaders not in Parliament would have to be taken in – Webb and Lansbury, he suggested half-jocularly. . . .

[?] *13 May. Bryan's Ground* [near Presteigne, Radnorshire]
Leonard Courtney passed away after a short illness, the day after we left London for our Whitsun holiday. I saw him on Wednesday, weak from one of his recurring attacks of internal haemorrhage, but still vigorous in intellect and emotion. He denounced Wilson, his eyes flashing under his heavy eyebrows as he beat the bed with his closed fist. He had just dictated a letter and sent Kate off with it to *The Times* (*The Times* refused it and it appeared next day in the *Manchester Guardian* – the plea of a noble old man for readiness to negotiate with the Germans when they were so minded. . . . Kate has lost her other and most loved self, but her devotion to his memory and her amazing kindliness will cover her loneliness, and her old age will, I think, be a happy one.

The militant campaign for women's suffrage had been called off during the war, but in June 1918 the vote was given to women over thirty; the same Act established complete male suffrage. A further Act passed in November made women eligible to stand for Parliament. A small number of seats in the House of Commons were still reserved for M.P.s elected by university graduates.

*16 June.* [41 Grosvenor Road]
I note with interest that not once in this diary have I mentioned the outstanding event of the year's home affairs – the passage of the Representation of the People Act, extending the suffrage from eight to about eighteen millions and admitting women to citizenship. This revolution has been on my consciousness the whole time, but it has not risen into expression because I have been a mere spectator. It is only the events that are vital to one's own life that get into so personal a record. I have always assumed political democracy as a necessary part of the machinery of government; I have never exerted myself to get it. It has no glamour for me. I have been, for instance, wholly indifferent to my own political disfranchisement. But I do not ignore the fact that the coming of the Labour Party as a political force has been largely occasioned by this year's extension of the franchise.

Almost accidentally, this great revolution has forced Sidney to enter the political arena . . . Sidney from the first decided that the Labour Party must contest the university seats as part of its pretensions to be a national party, and if these seats were to be contested, he had to stand for London. We are spending money and time on the election – more as a great propagandist attack . . . than as a serious attempt to win a seat. Sidney does not want to be in Parliament unless there proves to be a real 'change of heart', and a change of heart common to brainworkers as well as manual workers. If there is not this revolution in public purpose we are better outside, trying to make it by writing and speaking and researching. . . .

The American novelist Upton Sinclair, who ran a reformist magazine under his own name, had published a letter from H. G. Wells attacking Lenin as a power-hungry 'little beast' and adding: 'He's just a Russian Sidney Webb, a rotten little incessant egotistical intriguer.' 305,000 American troops were now in France.

*12 July.* [41 Grosvenor Road]
Here is H. G. Wells's latest attempt to injure us which is, I assume at his request, being distributed [and] broadcast among journalists and our common acquaintances. It interests me as a strange display of his morbid

obsession about us. . . . The abuse of Sidney is not clever and neither he nor I feel any anger at it.

*23 July.* [41 Grosvenor Road]
The U.S.A. is today in the ascendant. Delegations of Americans, socialist, labour, university or directly governmental (they are all indirectly governmental – no anti's being allowed across the water) look us up in order to assure us in modest, but determined, tones that America means to continue the war . . . Frenchmen who come over here tell us that the Americans are now the rage in France – they have captured the French imagination by their clean mental and physical strength, the simple dogmatism of their faith and the largeness and lavishness of their preparations. . . .

*1 September.* [41 Grosvenor Road]
A month's holiday at Presteigne with GBS and Maggie Hobhouse as successive visitors. Long walks over the hills enlivened by discussions with GBS: mornings spent typing the diary of 1912–16, with Sidney writing articles for the *New Statesman*, pamphlets for the Labour Party and his own election literature – a right happy time. Variety was added to our life by observing the spiritualistic obsession of our two nieces – Betty Russell, a war widow, and her unmarried sister, Molly Holt. These two are kindly, comely women, in the prime of life with one little boy of four years old to dote on, a score of acres to farm and many humble neighbours to be kind to. But with untrained and idle minds and Betty's man 'on the other side' as the occasion, they have fallen a natural prey to . . . a veritable 'Mr Sludge the Medium'. . . . I attended one seance. We sat round a table with hands touching in the gloaming. With shiverings and contortions he came under 'direct control'. He spoke baby English interlarded with a few familiar French terms in a squeaky voice with eyes screwed up and fingers twirled and twisted. He was apparently set on converting me. But all the spirits who claimed to be present in my honour – Father, Mother and others of vague identity – failed to present characteristics which I could recognize. In fact, if they had deliberately tried to make themselves unrecognizable they could hardly have been more successful. . . . The unhappy spirit-monger became impatient and suggested that I was 'resisting' – 'there is too much dust around you through which the spirits cannot penetrate.' With signs of mental exhaustion he broke up the sitting. This man struck me as half dupe of his own hysteria, half deliberately fraudulent. . . . But he made

a bad mistake when he described my mother as 'the most lovable of women'!

The day before I left Presteigne I had a telegram from the Prime Minister asking me, in no uncertain language, to be chairman of a committee on the relation of men's and women's wages. The subject did not attract me, but I was flattered and excited at being offered the chairmanship and forthwith wired a gracious acceptance. Great was my discountenance when the following day I received an apologetic telegram announcing that Mr Justice Atkin [1867–1944] was to be chairman and that I had only been invited to be a common or garden member of yet another committee. It appears that an incompetent typist had repeated the message to the selected chairman of all the members of the committee, and that they each and all accepted the chairmanship. It remains to be added that we all accepted the position with dignified good humour.

German acceptance of President Wilson's peace terms on 12 October was apparently premature. After the torpedoing of the Irish mailboat *Leinster* on the same day, Wilson's terms stiffened; the Germans had to give much more ground before the war ended at 11 a.m. on 11 November. On 4 November the crews of the German fleet mutinied and raised the red flag. Two days later the revolution spread to Munich. The Austro-Hungarian regime had also collapsed in revolution.

*13 October.* [41 Grosvenor Road]
The acceptance by Germany of President Wilson's terms will be welcomed by all the good and cursed by all the bad men among the Allies. The struggle of the next few days will test the relative power of the saints and the sinners among the Allied nations. . . . Revenge and greed die hard when satisfaction seems at hand.

*28 October.* [41 Grosvenor Road]
Apparently the sinners have prevailed, even over President Wilson. There is an unnecessary hardness in his subsequent communication. It may be that the German government will surrender unconditionally; but in that case the terms Germany will have to accept will be past endurance: they will break her or turn her into a secret rebel against the world.

*4 November.* [41 Grosvenor Road]
There is little or no elation among the general body of citizens about the coming peace. . . . The absence of public rejoicing and sombre looks of

private persons arises, I think, from preoccupation as to the kind of world we shall all live in when peace has come. Burdened with a huge public debt, living under the shadow of swollen government departments, with a working class seething with discontent, and a ruling class with all its traditions and standards topsy-turvy, with civil servants suspecting businessmen and businessmen conspiring to protect their profits, and all alike abusing the politician, no citizen knows what is going to happen. . . .

*11 November.* [41 Grosvenor Road]
Peace!

London today is a pandemonium of noise and revelry, soldiers and flappers being most in evidence. Multitudes are making all the row they can, and in spite of depressing fog and steady rain, discords of sound and struggling, rushing beings and vehicles fill the streets. Paris, I imagine, will be more spontaneous and magnificent in its rejoicing. Berlin, also, is reported to be elated having got rid, not only of the war, but also of its oppressors. The people are everywhere rejoicing. Thrones are everywhere crashing and the men of property are everywhere secretly trembling. 'A biting wind is blowing for the cause of property,' writes an Austrian journalist. How soon will the tide of revolution catch up the tide of victory? . . . Will it be six months or a year?

# A Distinct Dash
# of Adventure

## November 1918–January 1924

*17 November.* [41 Grosvenor Road]
. . . The toll of the war for our family is three killed and four others wounded, two seriously injured, out of a total of seventeen nephews and nephews-in-law in khaki. Betty Russell has lost her husband, Maggie Hobhouse has lost her Paul, and now, three weeks before the signing of the Armistice, the dead body of Noel Williams is reported found. Paul and Noel were among our favourite nephews, clean-living gallant youths of intellectual promise. Rosy Dobbs, who loved Noel better and trusted him more than she did all her Dobbs children, is terribly grieved. Margaret, with her exuberant energy, has rallied. Every day one meets saddened women, with haggard faces and lethargic movements, and one dare not ask after husband or son. The revelry of the streets and the flying flags seem a flippant mockery of the desolation caused by the slaughter of tens of millions of the best of the white race.

> The Fabian Society published the minority report as *The Wages of Men and Women – Should They be Equal?* Bruce Lockhart (1887–1970) was a British diplomat and intelligence agent in revolutionary Russia.

*8 December.* [41 Grosvenor Road]
The War Cabinet committee on Women in Industry bores me. I am not in the least interested in the relation of men's and women's wages. My

colleagues do not attract me. And it looks like my being forced to have a minority report, all by myself. . . .

We are watching with painful anxiety the tragedy of Continental Europe . . . In the dark hours of sleepless nights I wonder whether it is the end of western civilization. Sidney comforts me by his stolid faith in human sanity and human kindliness. He sees no reason to believe that the great German people will not pass through the ordeal of defeat and the ordeal of revolution towards an ordered freedom. He is not so optimistic towards Russia: he has no liking for what he imagines to be the Russian temperament. He hates what is called 'temperament'.

*12 December.* [41 Grosvenor Road]
I feel physically sick when I read the frenzied appeals of the Coalition leaders – the Prime Minister, Winston Churchill and Geddes, to hang the Kaiser, ruin and humiliate the German people, even to deprive Germany of her art treasures and libraries. These preliminaries of peace have become almost as disgusting as the war itself. It may be all election talk, but it is mean and brutal talk, degrading to the electorate.

*22 December.* [41 Grosvenor Road]
We leave tomorrow for a fortnight's country holiday. It is the end of a period. For the last three years, such energies as I have had, poor in quantity and quality, have been absorbed in government committees. . . . This coming year I shall devote myself to three tasks: getting our own publications forward, helping with the advisory committees of the Labour Party, and in holiday intervals, typing out the back volumes of my diary. This latter occupation – I can hardly call it work – pleases me most. I am tired of investigating new subjects. I want to brood over the past and reflect on men and their affairs. It amuses me to watch, in these jottings of my diary, the development of my own thought and of Sidney's activities. I want to summarize my life and see what it all amounts to. . . .

Sidney is disappointed that he has not won the university seat. I think he had been looking forward to a spell in Parliament . . . And yet he does not want it sufficiently to get himself adopted for a constituency which he could win, he wants to be pushed into Parliament, he does not want to push himself in. . . .

It seems extraordinarily difficult to get at the truth about Russia. Lockhart, the British consul at Moscow who, after being imprisoned by the Bolsheviks, was allowed to get back to England, could give us no clear account of what was being actually done or even any decided impression for or against the Bolshevik government. . . . About the reality and extent of the 'terror' Lockhart is equally vague.

~ 1919 ~

On 14 December 1918 the new electorate, three times larger than in 1910, returned Lloyd George and his coalition, largely made up of businessmen and opportunists, with a huge majority of 340. The Asquithian Liberals were reduced to thirty. Ten Labour M.P.s supported the coalition, but the party as a whole opted out; it returned sixty M.P.s. William Adamson (1863–1936), Scottish miners' official, was chairman of the Parliamentary Labour Party.

*10 January.* [41 Grosvenor Road]
. . . The Liberal Party, which has for years governed the Empire, has been reduced to an insignificant fraction, with all its leaders without exception at the bottom of the poll. The Labour Party has doubled its numbers and polled one-fourth of the entire voting electorate. It is now 'His Majesty's Opposition', or claims to be in that position. Lloyd George, with his Conservative phalanx, is apparently in complete command of the situation; as the only alternative government there stands the Labour Party, with its completely socialist programme and its utopia of the equalitarian state. But the Parliamentary Labour Party is a very tame lion. All the militants (because they happen to be also pacifists) have been ousted from Parliament. . . .

*14 January.* [41 Grosvenor Road]
I have never seen Adamson, the chairman of the Parliamentary Labour Party, before he lunched with us yesterday, except as a squat figure on the platform of the Albert Hall mass meeting just prior to the election. . . . He is a middle-aged Scottish miner, typical British proletarian in body and mind, with an instinctive suspicion of all intellectuals or enthusiasts. . . . I think he had hesitated before accepting our invitation and he was more at home with me than with Sidney. But we soon got on friendly terms and a good lunch relaxed his cautious temperament.
. . . He had brought with him a typewritten paper and read from it the requirements which he and his pals among the Labour members had decided were necessary to enable the fifty-eight to tackle Lloyd George

and his immense following. 'Two clerks, three typists – we cannot do with less,' he deprecatingly insisted. But what exercised his mind most were the messengers. The Liberals, in the last Parliament, he said, had had three messengers; *he thought* and it was clear from his wrinkled fore-head and slowly emphatic tone that he had thought strenuously on this question – *he thought* that the Parliamentary Labour Party might take over one of these messengers to fetch members to important divisions. He waited anxiously for Sidney's reply. 'There is always the telephone,' I said, to relieve the intense gravity of his suggestion, but he shook his head. No, the messenger was all important. Sidney cheerfully agreed but gently implied that the Parliamentary Labour Party would require something more than three clerks, two typists and one messenger. . . .

The months after the Armistice saw an alarming number of strikes – among shipwrights, engineers, gas and electricity workers – and rioting in Glasgow. Threat of imprisonment under the Defence of the Realm Act calmed the situation. The miners threatened to strike for improved wages and hours, and the nationalization of the mines. A Royal Commission set up to examine these issues under Mr Justice Sankey (1866–1948) appointed Sidney as one of the experts acceptable to the miners.

*8 February.* [41 Grosvenor Road]
Sidney and I watch the chaotic strikes – the most melodramatic being the strike of the London electricians – with complete calm. The men will be beaten, but in being beaten they will undermine this government by unwittingly convincing organized labour that the British citizen will not tolerate the direct action of a minority as a means of gaining its public ends. In order to win, constitutional methods will have to be adopted. The first effect, however, is to disintegrate the trade union movement and to damage the Labour Party in the eyes of the common run of men and women, especially women electors.

*12 March.* [41 Grosvenor Road]
I looked in at the Coal Commission this afternoon. It was a scene of strange contrasts. The robing room of the House of Lords is appropriately decorated with highly ornate frescoes of faded and sentimental pomp. But today it is serving as the crowded stage . . . for a body calling itself a royal commission on the mining industry . . . The ostensible business of the Commission is to examine and report on the miners' claim for a rise of wages and a reduction of hours; but owing to the superior skill of the

miners' representatives it has become a state trial of the coal-owners . . .
Mr Justice Sankey is an urbane lawyer, who treats every commissioner, in
turn, as the most distinguished of the lot and gives almost unlimited
licence to questions and answers . . . But the significance of the proceedings is the precedent set for similar state trials of the organization of each
industry . . . Sidney is enjoying himself hugely. I have never seen him so
keen on any task since the halcyon days of the L.C.C.

Alys Russell now lived in Hampshire with her brother, the man of letters
Logan Pearsall Smith (1865–1946). Sir Ernest Cassel (1852–1921) was a
German-born financier and philanthropist.

*29 April.* [41 Grosvenor Road]
A delightful twelve days with Logan Pearsall Smith and Alys Russell at
Big Chilling. During the eight days that Sidney was there – he had to go
up for three days to the Coal Commission – we wrote Part I (five chapters) of our new book on British Socialism . . . The walks by the sea in
mid-springtide in brilliant sunshine – waves, birds and buds – were
healthful and happy. . . .

In the intervals of other business Sidney has been busy with his old
love – the School of Economics. His position as one of the Cassel
Trustees, dispensing the seven thousand a year to be devoted to a Faculty
of Commerce, has given him a position of vantage for the reorganization
of the work of the School after the arid period of the war. For this purpose he had to undertake the unpleasant task of telling an old friend, W.
Pember Reeves, that the time had come for him to resign . . . It was a
painful interview. Reeves clung to the directorship and argued his fitness.
Sidney was firm and Reeves eventually agreed to resign, remarking,
somewhat bitterly, that Sidney 'was ruthless in the pursuit of his causes
and allowed no personal considerations, either on his own behalf or on
that of his friends, to stand in the way of the success of an institution or
a movement he believed in'. Which is of course true! . . .

The terms of the Treaty of Versailles were known after 7 May when they
were presented to the Germans. It was signed on 28 June – 'in many
respects terrible terms to impose upon a country', said Lloyd George.

*10 May.* [41 Grosvenor Road]
A hard and brutal peace, made more intolerable by the contumely of circumstances deliberately devised, in the method of its delivery to the

representatives of the German people. What disgusts me most is the fact that Great Britain gets the cleanest cut of all out of the possessions of the fallen enemy. France has hurt Germany most, Italy has been the most unreasonable. But it is Great Britain who adds most to her territory, prestige and power. . . .

*20 May.* [41 Grosvenor Road]
Victorious troops, British, Dominion and American, march through London, day by day, with bands playing and colours flying, to be reviewed by the King. What with brilliant sunshine and the consciousness of being a victorious race, the crowds in the streets have lost the look of strain and anxiety and have become smiling and buoyant. The war profiteers with their gains and the officers and men with their 'bonuses' vie with each other in extravagant eating and drinking, extravagant shopping and 'all-night' dancing, with all that that means. . . . But those who realize the financial position have little peace of mind. No political party is prepared for the stern measures of equalization and discipline necessary if we are to avoid embittered class war. . . .

> Three of the Sankey Commission's four reports recommended a measure of nationalization, but the government evaded the issue. The miners felt tricked; the coal owners hardened their stance. All that came of the Commission's high hopes was the Coal Mines Act of 1919 which enacted the seven-hour day.

*23 June.* [41 Grosvenor Road]
The second and final stage of the Coal Commission has not been so exciting as the first, but it has been an equally strenuous time . . . [Sidney] believes that the Coal Commission will be the beginning of a landslide into the communal control of industries and services.

Sidney has also been busy with the affairs of the London School of Economics. . . . Beveridge . . . has been accepted [as director] by the governors. He has his defects – he is not the sweetest-tempered of men and has a certain narrowness of outlook. But he is a good administrator, an initiator of both ideas and plans, and a man who will concentrate his energies on the School. . . . Moreover, there was really no alternative. . . .

*5 July.* [41 Grosvenor Road]
Completed Part I of our new book on Socialism – the indictment of profit-making capitalism. . . . we are back in our old style of partnership. . . .

*14 July.* [41 Grosvenor Road]
The three old wives – Kate, Mary and Beatrice – watched this morning with gladness, tinged with sorrowful memories of our sister Theresa, our dear brother-in-law Alfred married to Marion Ellis, daughter of the late Liberal statesman John Ellis. Alfred . . . chose the most charming of the Potter sisters; . . . he has now won an exceptionally attractive woman . . .

During the war Parmoor has developed into a political idealist. Whatever may have been his reasons for being against the war at the beginning, the horrors of it, and the revengeful spirit of the peace, have turned him into something very like an international socialist. So does evil company corrupt good manners! . . .

Industrial unrest and dissatisfaction continued throughout the autumn. The railway strike, begun on 26 September, brought all the railways to a standstill. It was provoked by the high-handed attitude of Sir Auckland Geddes (1879–1945), President of the Board of Trade, with whom the railwaymen had been negotiating since February for an increase in wages. Troops were called out and wartime emergency regulations brought into force but the strike was settled within a few days.

*28 September.* [41 Grosvenor Road]
The Great Strike – which has been brewing since the close of the war – has happened. Not of the engineers as was expected, nor of the miners as the public has long expected, but of the railwaymen. Never has there been a strike of anything like this in magnitude or social significance which has burst on the world so suddenly . . . We are all at sea as to what will happen . . . There are rumours that the government are preparing heroic measures – for confiscating the railwaymen's funds, for starving the railwaymen's families, for running the railways with soldiers: there are equally rumours that the trade unions are preparing for Soviets to take over the government of the country. We tend to believe that these suppositions are baseless and that in a week or so there will be a compromise arranged . . .

Sporadic outbreaks of violence in Ireland throughout the year, largely organized by Sinn Fein, which had emerged in the 1916 rising, culminated in an attack on Field Marshal French, the Viceroy. To counteract the growing disaffection Lloyd George produced one more scheme for Home Rule – two separate parliaments with a single federal council for the whole of Ireland. The Republican Congress in America refused to ratify the Peace Treaty and Woodrow Wilson refused to compromise over the League of Nations. On 2 October he had suffered a stroke; he never recovered his political influence.

*25 December.* [41 Grosvenor Road]
We have had a happy, healthy, hard-working time since we returned from our country recess the end of September. But I have been haunted, almost more than during the war, with the horrors that are going on in Austria and other Continental countries and with the fact that Europe is on the eve of worse catastrophies than she has yet lived through. The big events of the year: the evil peace, the moral, political and physical fall of Wilson, the savage suppression of Ireland and the success of [the] Bolsheviks – four world tragedies – are horribly perturbing to a benevolent British bourgeois progressive. Where is the freedom broadening down 'from precedent to precedent', either within the British Empire or in the world outside? . . .

~ 1920 ~

George Lansbury made a six-week visit to Russia in February. His wireless message was the first to be made to Britain by any newspaperman since the revolution.

*25 February.* [41 Grosvenor Road]
. . . the big public event is the victory of Soviet Russia over all her enemies and the transformation of the Bolshevik government into a bureaucratic administration exercising far-reaching coercive power over the life and liberty of the individual citizen. George Lansbury's spectacular visit to Russia and his wireless message to the *Daily Herald* have certainly raised his prestige and that of his paper. Lansbury has, in fact, become the 'chartered revolutionary of the world'.

*11 May.* [41 Grosvenor Road]
The last six weeks has been strenuous work, day after day, finishing our book on *A Constitution for the Socialist Commonwealth of Great Britain.* It has been a great lark writing it: I have never enjoyed writing a book so much. . . . Neither of us would have written the book alone – it is the jointest of our joint efforts. No one will like our constitution: we shall offend all sides and sections with some of our proposals. But someone

must begin to think things out, and our task in life is to be pioneers in social engineering.

In the spring of 1920 various miners' lodges within the Seaham division of Durham approached Sidney to stand as their Labour candidate, despite opposition from their Executive who felt that a miner should be nominated for the seat.

*8 June.* [Roker Hotel, Sunderland?]

. . . The Seaham miners persisted in their demand for Sidney as candidate . . . So here we are, speaking in all the miners' villages 'on approval'. There seems little doubt that he will be selected . . . so we are in for the job of winning the constituency.

The division is a long narrow belt of coast with some eighteen pit villages at about two-mile intervals, and the port of Seaham as the centre. The miners themselves are a mixed lot, drawn to new mines from all parts of the United Kingdom – Staffordshire, Lancashire, Scotland and Ireland. They are very well off in the way of wages; their houses are substantially built but terribly overcrowded; their hours short, and they enjoy the priceless advantage of field and wood and coast wherein to roam . . . But there is no centre of intellectual or spiritual life; a mechanically black-leg-proof union is the only corporate life. [Apart from] a dingy and commercialized Co-operative and a vigorous Club movement for the purpose of drinking 'out of hours' [there is] little or no social life, nothing but the 'pictures' in the larger villages or the same pictures on a more sumptuous scale in Sunderland. The women have no leisure and not much sleep with the three, sometimes four, shift system and the perpetual coal-dust to grapple with. Consequence, every woman is short and pale. There is a lot of money flying about and much spent in alcohol and betting. The life seems, in fact, to be completely materialist, though fairly respectable.

There are groups of fervent chapel folk. Here and there is a bookish miner, usually a secularist with quite a large bookcase filled with the well-known poets and classics, a little philosophy and more economics. It is to these 'bookish miners' that is due the pertinacity with which Sidney's candidature has been pursued. How far they represent their rough and stupid fellow miners is doubtful, though probably these will vote in herds when the day comes. . . . we have discovered a pleasant little hotel to live at with a private sitting room at 7s 6d a day, overlooking the sea. So on the whole we are content to proceed with this adventure. But it will mean six weeks' work in the year, organizing and lecturing – £300 a year expenditure or more prior to the election, and probably £800 or £1,000 for the election, whenever it comes. And we are both over sixty! And it is I who am responsible for persuading Sidney to undertake it with the risk, if not the certainty, of getting into Parliament and all the disturbance of our daily life that this would involve. . . .

*11 July.* [41 Grosvenor Road]
Sidney was unanimously chosen yesterday by the Seaham divisional Labour Party to fight the next general election. There is a strange irony in these simple-minded miners, living in a remote backwater, seeking out and persistently pressing into their service the most astute and subtle – and, be it added, the least popular leader of the labour and socialist movement. . . .

In the spring of 1920 the Poles, encouraged by the French, invaded Russia and supported a nationalist government in the Ukraine as a buffer between themselves and the Bolsheviks. When the Bolsheviks counter-attacked, the Poles sought Allied help. Warsaw was saved by a Polish victory at the battle of the Vistula and an agreement reached at the Treaty of Riga. The Bolshevik scare now began to die down. Ernest Bevin (1881–1951), who became the general secretary of the Transport Workers' Union in 1921, was the dominant trade union leader between the wars.

*20 August.* [41 Grosvenor Road]
Our week at the Second International in Geneva, in brilliant sun and seething heat, left on my mind a mixed impression of apparent futility and real usefulness. . . . To all the delegates, even to the one or two British who felt obliged to oppose, because according to English ideas there must be a recognized opposition in every well-conducted assembly, the Russian Communist dictatorship seemed a huge and disastrous fail-ure. . . . Without science, without goodwill, without tolerance, all of us feel that no social democracy is possible. . . .

Now that Poland seems to be beating Russia, the British government has reacted and is backing France in her subsidies to Polish militarism. Never has the European outlook been so gloomy as it is now . . . we seem [to be] sinking into a morass of violence out of which we are not climb-ing and, maybe, cannot climb. It is like a nightmare which one dreams is not a nightmare but an awakened state of mind. On the top of this colossal foreign turmoil comes the ballot for the miners' strike. . . .

L. B. Krassin (1870–1926) was an engineering specialist who became a Bolshevik in 1903. He was in London in 1920 to conclude a commercial treaty with Britain. Leo Kamenev (1883–1936), one of the leaders of the 1917 Bolshevik Revolution, was executed as a Trotskyist in the great purges of 1936–37.

*4 September.* [41 Grosvenor Road]

A week at the Fabian summer school . . . the crowning success was the lightning visit of Kamenev and Krassin on the Thursday afternoon. . . . Sidney and I received our visitors in a private sitting-room . . . Presently it became clear that our Russian comrades were not only willing, but anxious, to address the whole of the guests. So we ushered them into the drawing-room in which some seventy or eighty persons were closely packed on sofa, chair and floor, eager to see and listen to these mysterious visitors from the mythical Bolshevik heaven or the mythical Bolshevik hell.

Kamenev spoke for an hour in ugly but fluent French . . . The address was plausible and diplomatic. It left little impression on my mind because every word of it was devised to produce a given effect, and quite obviously so devised. . . . Directly he had finished I . . . called on Krassin to address us. He spoke in German, with the clear enunciation and the limited vocabulary of an accomplished linguist speaking in a foreign tongue, so that even I could understand every word of it. It was a remarkable address, admirably conceived and delivered with a cold intensity of conviction which made it extraordinarily impressive. . . . The greater part of the speech was a detailed account of the industrial administration he had actually set up or hoped to introduce into Russia. *Working to a plan*, elaborated by scientific experts . . . Russia's needs, external and internal, were to be discovered and measured up and everything was to be sacrificed to fulfilling them. . . . Finally, in a splendid peroration . . . he asserted that Soviet Russia alone among nations had discovered the 'philosopher's stone' of increased productivity in the consciousness, on the part of each individual Communist, that he was serving the whole community of the Russian people – a consciousness which would transform toil into the only true religion – the service of mankind. . . .

In the minds of many of the audience the question arose, 'How would it be possible to depose from power these three castes – the elders, and leaders of the Communist faith, the scientific experts and the town workmen, not to mention the two castes which were not referred to, the

Red Army and the Secret Police – when the need for this autocratic government had disappeared with Russia's enemies?' . . .

*21 October.* [41 Grosvenor Road]
Sidney off to Seaham to talk to miners, who have nothing to do but to listen to the Gospel.

The long-dragged-out negotiations, nearing three months from the miners' initial demand of two shillings a shift increase and a reduction of fourteen shillings on the price of coal, have at last ended in a national strike beginning last Saturday. . . . When Ireland is being treated with savage brutality, when central Europe is slowly dying, both catastrophes being deliberately brought about by the Lloyd George government, it is tragically absurd to be destroying the national wealth for the sake of a two shilling increase per day in the wages of one of the best-paid sections of British labour. And yet the strike is bigger than the occasion for it: the huge vote and hasty temper in the coalfields are, in a sense, a vote against the government on all issues. . . .

Margaret Hobhouse had an operation in February 1919 and another on 21 July 1920.

*23 October.* [41 Grosvenor Road]
. . . Margaret Hobhouse . . . and I had spent three days at Margate a few weeks ago. She had seemed depressed and wanted a change of air, so I agreed to go down with her. We had long talks together about life and death and our old comradeship as girls before the lines of our lives diverged . . . But throughout these intimate talks she had never hinted at the imminence of death. Yesterday she told me that she had undergone two operations for cancer of the breast – the last as recently as July, a bad operation involving the nerves of the neck. She is now suffering from a chronic cough and breathlessness, a bad symptom. She has told her husband, and after the second operation in July she told her children, but no one else knows. . . . Her spiritualistic experiences – her certainty that, at any rate, there is proof of telepathy, of a sort of universal consciousness underlying individual life, are a great comfort to her. Poor human beings! How deep is the craving for extended personality beyond the limits of the thoughts, the feelings, the sensations of a mere lifetime on earth. . . .

Conditions in Ireland had gravely deteriorated and the Sinn Feiners were in open rebellion. The government reinforced the Royal Irish Constabulary by enlisting the 'Black and Tans' who began their own raids and ambushes. The government, engaged in its new Home Rule proposals, failed in its efforts to inhibit reprisals and during the first months of 1921 there was widespread guerrilla war. Terence MacSwiney (1880–1920), Lord Mayor of Cork 1918–20, died of a hunger strike in Brixton prison. Wells published *The Outline of History* in 1920.

*29 November.* [41 Grosvenor Road]
. . . Our absorbing preoccupation during the last few weeks – alas! a symbol of what is happening – have been public funerals! The public pageant of the 'unknown warrior' symbolizing the ten million white men killed in the war, the funeral of the martyred Lord Mayor of Cork, and as a reprisal, the military parade through London of the corpses of the English officers murdered in Dublin. Yesterday Downing Street was barricaded lest there should be yet another and still more impressive public ceremony – the funeral of an assassinated Prime Minister! It is said that he lives in fear of the Green Terror and is looking for a compromise with Sinn Fein.

A trifle to note. We are reconciled to H. G. Wells. He sent me his *History* with an inscription. I wrote a friendly acknowledgement, which he bettered in reply. And after he returned from Russia I asked him and his wife to dinner to meet Haldane and Krassin, Cole and the Shaws. He came: Mrs Wells was otherwise engaged. He is fat and prosperous and immensely self-congratulatory; towards us he was affable, but suspicion lurked in his eye and I doubt whether he is really friendly. Nor do I desire any renewal of friendship. But I am too near to the end of life to care to keep up a vendetta with any human being. Also I have never ceased to respect his work, and his *History* is a gallant achievement. . . .

*21 December. Roker Hotel, Sunderland*
Clearing up papers, packing books and our scanty wardrobe; a last walk on the sands . . . Depressed tiredness is the sensation left by my ten lectures to Durham miners. The campaign has been remarkably successful – Sidney has lectured in every pit village. . . . But it has been an exhausting experience for me. . . . Giving decidedly stiff discourses on difficult subjects to little meetings from 40 to 150 miners in bitterly cold miners' halls – starting off at six o'clock and getting home at ten – is rather an ordeal for a woman over sixty. . . . Part of my nervous exhaustion was, however, due to the shock of hearing from dear sister Maggie that the radiograph showed her lungs covered with cancer spots and that

the end could not long be delayed. She is brave and I try to help her by taking an equally philosophic attitude, treating death as the last adventure in life. All the same, the thought that she also will have gone in a few months, the seventh and best beloved sister, the eldest of my living friends, is gloomy for the survivor. And feeling so near the end, it seems almost absurd to be starting on the new life of having Sidney in Parliament. . . .

∼ 1921 ∼

*1 January. [41 Grosvenor Road]*
The wicked 1920 dead; but judged by British doings in Ireland and French doings in Germany, the child will be as wicked as the parent. . . .

The temporary 'dole' was becoming established as part of the social insurance system.

*8 February. [41 Grosvenor Road]*
The growing unemployment has added to the ferment of rebellious discontent. . . . The wonder is that there is not more outward sign of angry resentment. Perhaps it is due to the fact that [for] the first time some sort of weekly allowance is being received without the stigma of pauperism, and that even the boards of guardians dare not refuse unconditional outdoor relief to those without it. . . .

*9 February. [41 Grosvenor Road]*
Since I returned from Seaham . . . I have walked across the parks to Airlie Gardens to be with my dear sister and old chum in her last days of life. With great courage and cheerful endurance she is experimenting in a possible cure or rather possible arrest of her fatal disease – grimly hanging on to her life, prepared to end it, if it turns out there is no hope. I am the only person with whom she talks freely . . . I tell her all about my work; we talk of old days at Standish and Rusland; of her children and her relations to her husband, of the symptoms of her illness, the course of the copper inoculations (the cure she is undergoing, on the advice of a well-known specialist); we weigh up the desirability of an overdose . . . we hazard guesses as to how long I shall survive her. . . . 'I wish I could do more for you, dear old chum,' I said to her yesterday as I stood by her, watching her gasping for breath, 'but all my love cannot

sweep away the loneliness of death. Paul may help you but I cannot.'
'Paul, Theresa and Mother,' she answered. 'I dare not let myself think
about them. I am too weak for emotion. You are awfully kind to come
here, a true friend to the very end.' 'After Sidney you are the person I
love most, dear one,' and we embraced, remembering the old days of our
girl friendship over forty years ago. Here we are again holding each
other's hands close up to the blank wall of death.

*16 March.* [41 Grosvenor Road]
Margaret Hobhouse died early this morning. . . . The last time we talked
together she suggested that we should go to Eastbourne when she was
better, though she was quite obviously dying. . . . In my young days it
was tuberculosis that was the fearsome thought: now it is cancer. All elderly folk live in terror of it. . . . I take up my work again sorrowing and
with a strange fear of the ordeal through which I like all others must
pass. A fear, not of death, but of the fear of death.

1921 saw a fundamental change in policies and attitudes. Government
intervention in the economy had seemed to offer fresh prospects for the
country after the war, but it was becoming increasingly clear that the pro-
jected betterment schemes were unacceptably expensive. The runaway
inflation in Germany and Austria was a warning of the danger of solving
problems by creating government credit. Subsidies for housing were now
cut; controls were taken off food, the mines, railways and agriculture.
This change of policy meant the abandonment of election promises and
a weakening of the Coalition. The anger of the miners at the abrupt
change of direction resulted in yet another coalfield strike. Within a
week a general strike was threatened. A Special Defence Force was created
and civil war anticipated. At the last minute Lloyd George proposed a
temporary settlement on wages and the other members of the Triple
Alliance (railwaymen and dockers) urged the miners to negotiate. They
refused and J. H. Thomas called off the planned sympathetic railway
strike. This was known as 'Black Friday' and regarded in the labour
movement as a day of betrayal and the ruin of the Triple Alliance which
had been formed in 1914.

*14 April. Roker Hotel, Sunderland*
. . . The Labour storm which has been beating up for the last two years
has at last burst. . . . but though this one is catastrophic in its bigness, I
am merely bored . . . there will be another compromise: one side or the

other will get scared and temporarily give way. But no progress will be made towards a better state of things. . . .

*18 April.* [Roker Hotel]
'The Strike cancelled' was the staggering new line of yesterday's evening paper. A catastrophic anti-climax (if such a term be permissible). My forebodings were justified. . . . The trade union officials are not 'fit to govern' . . . There must be a gay party at Downing Street or Chequers tonight! . . .

> The Half Circle Club was set up by Beatrice as a social centre for the wives of Labour M.P.s. Richard Ellis Roberts (b. 1879) was briefly literary editor of the *New Statesman.* The poetry of the American poet Vachel Lindsay (1879–1931) was particularly effective when read aloud. Susan Lawrence (1871–1947) was a middle-class Labour politician and organizer of the National Federation of Women Workers. Margaret Bondfield (1873–1931) was an organizer of the Shop Assistants' Union and in 1924 became the first woman to hold a government post.

*24 April. 41 Grosvenor Road*
I came away from Roker four days before Sidney could leave in order to be present at a gathering of the Half Circle Club and their male friends. . . . Over a hundred persons turned up and we had a rollicking evening, with friendly chatter and a vivid entertainment by Ellis Roberts, recitals from Vachel Lindsay's Negro poems, the company who could not get seats squatting on the floor, all of us trying to sing the boisterous choruses. Henderson acted as chairman, introduced Ellis Roberts and was in his most beneficent mood and delighted with the entertainment. What interests me is the unusual friendliness, the absence of any constraint between the different sections of women who have joined; the wives of the Labour M.P.s and T.U.C., the professional Labour women like Susan Lawrence and Margaret Bondfield, the wives of the well-to-do Labour candidates like Mrs Noel Buxton and Mrs Trevelyan. . . .

> In the summer of 1921 the idea of keeping Ireland under the London government was finally abandoned. A truce was declared and conversations took place with Sinn Fein, now regarded as a provisional government. It was hoped to keep the country within the Commonwealth by giving it dominion status, with Northern Ireland being left to decide its own

relations to the new dominion. A fatal division among the Irish leaders now appeared. The hard-line Republicans, who had led the 1916 rising and carried the brunt of the guerrilla fighting, believed that the proposals did not provide for the Republic, nor promise the end of partition. Negotiations continued into December, when dominion status – the Free State – was accepted in return for a private undertaking that Ulster's boundaries would be so contracted that it would have to join Southern Ireland in order to survive. A treaty signed in London on 6 December retained the oath of allegiance to the King. Although narrowly accepted by the Irish parliament, dissident resistance led to a civil war between the Free Staters and the Irish Republican Army.

*12 July.* [41 Grosvenor Road]
There is a strange feverishness in London today, a physical feverishness brought on by the amazing light and heat of the drought; a mental feverishness arising from the truce in Ireland and the peace conference at Downing Street. We are all of us restlessly hopeful that there is to be at last an end to the infamous tragedy of a peculiarly bestial civil war, for which we, the British democracy, are responsible. . . . There remains the black fever of unemployment. The Thames Embankment at night is once again the resort of tired and hopeless men and women. This rising tide of destitution is still inarticulate and orderly. But will it remain so? And if the *miserables* of Great Britain take to direct action like the *miserables* of Ireland, will there be yet another civil war, more chaotic and disastrous because it concerns a greater mass of human beings? . . .

*16 July.* [41 Grosvenor Road]
. . . In some ways Sidney and I have never been so happy in our personal lives. Welded by common work and experience into a complete harmony of thought and action, we are also in harmony with those with whom we work and have our being. Our servants and secretary are devoted to us; with our relatives we are on the best of terms. In our inconspicuous way we are successful: our books sell better than ever before, the London School of Economics (Sidney's favourite child) is brilliantly developing under the able direction of Beveridge, whom Sidney selected; the *New Statesman*, though still losing money, is not losing our money and is daily gaining credit. . . . And Sidney's work in the Labour Party . . . brings with it no personal friction and a good deal of pleasurable comradeship with men who respect and trust him. . . .

*28 August.* [41 Grosvenor Road]

. . . For many years I have wanted to give my personal philosophy of life . . . And so for the last fortnight or so I have been attempting to formulate on the one hand my faith in the scientific method as applied to social institutions, and, on the other, my realization that without the religious impulse directing the purpose of life, science is bankrupt, or may lead as well to the decay and death of civilization as to its life and ennoblement. Whether I shall succeed in writing anything that is worthy of publication remains to be seen.

> Blanche Cripps's daughter Julia, unhappily married to the doctor Tom Faulder, had killed herself the week before this entry with an overdose of cocaine. Ethel Bentham (d. 1931) was a doctor and Labour M.P.

*28 September. 41 Grosvenor Road*

Lawrence Cripps and his wife dined alone with me on Saturday, and poor distracted Tom Faulder came to supper on Sunday. It appears that Julia left life with the same quiet and cheerful deliberation shown by her mother. Looking back over the last months, it is now clear to Lawrence and to Tom that she had settled to go, and had been calmly making all her arrangements whilst continuing her normal life . . . She had withdrawn property from the bank and parcelled out all her little bits of jewellery among her nephews and nieces and deposited them all in a dressing-case with Lawrence, on some excuse; she had given away many of her clothes, made presents to old servants; she had, before leaving London, mended all Tom's things and put away articles not required, settled up all her accounts, and even, in the last days of her life, knitted Tom a dark mourning waistcoat. The day before she died she sent a subscription of £1 to the Fabian Society with a notice to withdraw her name so that the *Fabian News* should not be sent to her. . . . Poor Tom; he looks a complete wreck. (He says that he has never done so well in his profession as he has done this year.) I could not do otherwise than be affectionate and uncritical; it is useless to torture him by assuming that her death was brought about by his neglect. With her strange mentality and with the blight of her mother's suicide, it is impossible to say that she might not have done the same even if circumstances had been happier. . . .

Meanwhile, I notice that suicides, like divorces, are on the increase. According to Dr Ethel Bentham, mental misery and mental sickness of every kind and degree is rampant among all classes, in spite of the falling of the death-rate and the better physical health which that is supposed to indicate. The world of man is sick at heart; its old religious faith has gone, and its new science, which seemed to the pioneers of 1870 to be able to solve all problems, has been proved by the great war to be bankrupt in directive force.

*28 October. Roker Hotel* [Sunderland]
The sixteen days at Roker have passed energetically for Sidney and slackly for me. For on only two of Sidney's nineteen meetings have I accompanied him. I came here ill at ease with rheumatism and bad sleeping. I think I shall have to return to the two meals a day and no meat. Certainly some of my secretions have gone wrong. . . . And though I have got through three heavy volumes since I have been here, I have done no more to my book. The plain truth is that I am a little depressed, wondering whether what I have to say is really worth the toil of saying it. . . .

The Washington conference (11 November 1921–6 February 1922) achieved some measure of disarmament and guarantees of the *status quo* in the Pacific. It was considered a great success for Arthur Balfour, who led the British delegation. In an effort to revive the Soviet economy Lenin had introduced some measure of private enterprise under the New Economic Policy.

*7 December.* [41 Grosvenor Road]
The Irish Treaty is the big event since the great war and its warlike peace. The amazing skill with which Lloyd George has carried through the negotiations with his own Cabinet and with Sinn Fein has revolutionized the political situation. Whether or not it be true, few enlightened persons, even among Liberals and Labour men, believe that any other man could have got this peace by understanding; no other leader could have whipped the Tories to heel and compelled them to recognize the inevitability of Irish independence. Moreover, the peace puts us right with the world, at any rate until Indian troubles bring up the same question of racial self-determination in a far larger and more complicated way. The other great event (at any rate in appearance) . . . is the Washington conference. The virtual repudiation of Communism by Lenin – the readiness of the Bolshevik government to come to terms with capitalist governments – is another blow to international socialism and to the revolutionary movements in all countries. On the other hand, the economic disasters brought about by the peace have discredited capitalism. . . .

~ 1922 ~

Dora Russell (1894–1986) was to become a notable campaigner and feminist writer.

*16 February.* [41 Grosvenor Road]
Our old friend Bertrand Russell, with a new life and a son and heir (who just managed to scramble into existence 'in wedlock'), has come back into the outer circle of our friends and acquaintances. For some years he has been travelling and living with a young woman – a secretary, she was styled – a Girton girl, the daughter of an Admiralty official. She went with him to Russia two years ago and has spent the last year with him in China and nursed him through [double pneumonia]. Last year, at his own request, Alys divorced him, and on his arrival last December in London he married Dora Black, within a fortnight of the birth of John Conrad Russell, the future Earl. I had to decide whether I would recognize the marriage and be friends with them, or run the risk of being thrown in their company without recognition, and I decided to call and ask them here. We spent the last week-end with them among a large party of young Labour economists at Dunford . . .

I should be sorry to bet on the permanence of the present marital tie. . . . Possibly the boy may keep them together, for Bertie seems inclined to dote on this son and heir. His bad health may also be a restraining factor preserving his domesticity. But there is a strange excited look in his eye (does he take opium?), and he is not at peace either with himself or the world. His present role of a fallen angel with Mephistophelian wit, and his brilliantly analytic and scoffing intellect makes him stimulating company. All the same, I look back on this vision of an old friend with sadness. He may be successful as a *littérateur*, I doubt whether he will be of value as a thinker . . . When one remembers the Bertrand Russell of twenty years ago . . . it is melancholy to look on this rather frowsy, unhealthy and cynical personage, prematurely old. . . .

Harold Laski (1893–1950), a lecturer in political science at the L.S.E., became a prominent Labour theorist and politician. R. H. Tawney (1880–1962), a Workers' Educational Association lecturer and Christian Socialist, was to become an influential Labour intellectual and distinguished history professor at the L.S.E. C. M. Lloyd (1878–1946) was a Fabian professor of economics at Sheffield. Jessie Mair (1876–1959), who had worked with Beveridge during the war, was the new School secretary.

*14 May. Dunford*

... The two last week-ends the house has been filled with congenial guests ... Last week-end the Laskis brought down Finer and Smellie (the two youngest lecturers, with Labour and socialist sympathies) and we had the Tawneys to meet them. This week-end the Director and Mrs Mair, her husband and daughter ... From all these separate persons we heard a good deal about the School and its internal life. Laski is the most brilliant of the lecturers and his little wife is as restless and critical as he. ... He knows, or says he knows, everyone of importance; his sympathies and likings are volatile; he scoffs at the Labour leaders, dismisses the Asquith-Grey combination with scorn and hates Lloyd George. ...

What interested and perturbed us was the hatred of Mrs Mair ... Mrs Mair is a tall, fine-looking Scottish woman, very much a Scot in manner and speech and in her ambitious and domineering temperament. To us she is as sweet as can be. She is reported to be all-powerful with Beveridge, who brought her as his secretary into the School administration. She is married to Beveridge's cousin, a distinguished and good looking civil servant who is quite clearly suffering mentally from the intimate companionship of his wife and his cousin ... How near the relationship borders on a domestic tragedy I do not know: Sidney pooh-poohs my concern. But Mrs Tawney, Beveridge's sister, burst out with expressions of hot dislike, and the dislike is shared by Tawney, by the Laskis and by Lloyd, by Wallas and apparently by the great majority of the staff. ... [Beveridge] has done wonders in the way of organization. Sidney has the utmost confidence in him and is always congratulating himself at having got him as Director. It would be horribly annoying if there was an upset over his stalwart and handsome colleague and cousin. ...

*25 May. Llandrindod*

... After an interval of five months I am back again at my little book ... I have been reading through my diaries ... It is amazing how one forgets what one thought and felt in the past, and even what one did and with whom one was intimate. Reading of all our intrigues over the Education Bill was a shock to me: not so much the intrigues themselves as our evident pleasure in them! ...

H. G. Wells published *The Secret Places of the Heart* in 1922. His relationship with the writer Rebecca West (1892–1983) was now breaking up. She had given birth to his son in 1914.

*10 July.* [41 Grosvenor Road]

. . . The war wrecked many things, upset the government of races and the self-control of individuals. As for divorces, they are as common as flies in a hot summer. . . . For the richer classes, there is practically free divorce without scandal, so long as the man is ready to go through rather unpleasant and expensive preliminaries so as to dodge the written law. This reputable divorce by consent is by far the most significant change in manners and morals that has taken place in my lifetime, and it has taken place without any change in the law, and without being the subject matter of any public controversy. But over and above these divorces by arrangement, with respectable re-marriages on both sides, there is now an amazing tolerance, on the part of the respectable bourgeoisie, of what would have been thought the last word of wickedness. The various Freudian 'complexes' are joked about, and the character of the emotions of young girls for the father, or of mothers for their sons, and vice versa, is openly discussed without any apparent reprehension. 'Never talk about your dreams in mixed company,' is *Punch's* typical joke. . . . The consequence is that old people like ourselves, who have never thought out social morals, find ourselves more and more troubled as to what line to take in the public interest . . . one sits in judgement with increasing bewilderment.

Such a problem is H. G. Wells, now Labour Party candidate for London University. . . . Wells was approached because he had signified his wish to stand, and to refuse such an obviously eligible candidate, except for his scandalous exploits (none of which, however, have come into the courts), seemed an unjustifiable insult. So Sidney and I acquiesced and he accepted the candidature. Whereupon R. H. Tawney resigns from the chairmanship of the University Labour Party, but before doing so, proposes as the alternative Bertrand Russell! He declares that Bertrand Russell is a gentleman and H.G. a cad, which is hardly relevant if it is sexual morality which is to be the test.

Once a Labour candidate, it seemed desirable to bring Wells under Henderson's and Clynes's influence. So that with some hesitation I ask him and his wife to lunch . . . When he sat by me I could not help feeling that in some ways he is an unclean beast, not so much on account of his various paramours but because he is perpetually making 'copy' out of his love affairs – his last book being a bad example, with its quite obvious portrait of Rebecca West. . . .

*9 August. Bryan's Ground*

About a fortnight ago we started from London, taking in Longfords on our way, with a great kit-bag of work which we proposed to do down here during our six weeks' stay. We find ourselves in the hands of the local doctor: Sidney for severe nervous breakdown and I for equally severe colitis, living the life of invalids, anxious about each other and unpleasantly doubtful about the future of 'the Webbs'. Sidney's breakdown is the most disconcerting. Right through the last year, up to and over the Labour Party conference, he seemed in the best of health, working easily and steadily. One little episode made me anxious. When we were at Hastings in the winter he and I went out immediately after lunch and walked quickly up a steep hill, the sun hot and he with a heavy overcoat. Quite suddenly his face became purple and he became faint, with cold perspiration, and I had to put him on the ground for two or three minutes before he recovered full consciousness. But he was quite well the next day and walked some nine miles in a bitter wind to Winchelsea. The present breakdown started off suddenly with an attack of vertigo in the night, followed by occasional dizziness. When we got here, having to call in the local medical man for my own complaint, I asked him to examine Sidney. Every organ was found to be healthy – no blood pressure and arteries very young for his age – the only apparent cause of the vertigo and dizziness being a pad of wax in the ear, which was removed.

But the dizziness and weakness and uncertainty in walking continued and even got worse, and the doctor became seriously concerned. 'Must stop work for three or four months,' was the verdict. Meanwhile, I was feeling horribly unwell with bowel and backache and losing weight. I am now undergoing treatment and slowly, I think, improving. What troubles me is not my own health. I don't believe my life is a good one and I don't much want to drift into a long senility. But what would Sidney do without me if he became an invalid? I have always contemplated leaving him still vigorous, with Parliament as a new career to interest and absorb him. There is no one to look after him and he is so absurdly dependent on me. However, the Lord will provide! . . .

### 4 September. Southport. Trades Union Congress
Our six weeks at Bryan's Ground sees both of us fairly normal. Except for occasional giddiness when he gets up in the morning or suddenly bends down, Sidney is as vigorous as ever, whilst I have got rid of colitis and gained weight (7 stone 5 oz) and I can walk eight or nine miles without being too exhausted. But we both feel that we are definitely old people; Sidney for the first time. And everyone tells us that we

must slack off, and Sidney certainly *looks* older than he did a year ago. . . .

> At a dramatic meeting of Tory M.P.s, Bonar Law advised the party to leave the Coalition to preserve its own unity. Chamberlain and other ministers resigned; Lloyd George then tendered his resignation. The ensuing election on 15 November produced a Tory victory, but its most significant factor was the large increase in Labour votes. Ramsay MacDonald was elected leader of the Labour Party with J. R. Clynes (1869–1949), leader of the Gasworkers Union, his deputy.

*17 October.* [41 Grosvenor Road]
The political world is tumultuous, but we hear little of its tumult . . . Absorbed in our work, we have only heard the echoes of the battles of Downing Street and the Carlton Club and the fall of Lloyd George . . . Sidney and I are becoming every day more philosophical. We do not want a Labour government before the labour movement has found its soul. At present the mass is dully apathetic, thinking only of the next meal, the next drink, the next smoke, or the next 'odds' – whilst the advance guard lives on hot air. . . .

*28 October.* [41 Grosvenor Road]
. . . Depressed at the prospect of the larger life of Sidney in Parliament. I shall hate him to be beaten: I shall thoroughly enjoy a rattling big majority on the day of the count and a few days after, but if he were beaten, through no fault of our own, there would be a subconscious sigh of relief when I had got over the first shock. . . . The life of learned leisure is what we both best enjoy . . . And especially now that I have this little book of my own . . . I long for leisure and a quiet mind. . . .

*15 November. Polling Day. Seaham Harbour*
Spent this morning touring the miners' villages: received everywhere by a little band of enthusiasts. . . . In Seaham Harbour itself the Bradford cars, scores of them, are whizzing around conveying women to the poll. If we lose, it will be the women who will have done it. Sidney keeps cool: he feels he is doing what he had to do . . .

*17 November.* [Seaham Harbour]
The long day at the count – from ten o'clock to six – was an exciting, tiring but triumphant experience. We knew we were winning after the

first box had been opened, and after the first two hours it became apparent that Sidney would have a great vote and a great majority. . . . Sidney continued his almost boyish pleasure in the adventure to the very end. I really believe he is going to enjoy Parliament. He is amazingly young for his age. The miners from the first treated him as their 'property' . . . I gather [they] had betted heavily on him in Sunderland. . . .

*23 November. 41 Grosvenor Road*
To enter Parliament for the first time at sixty-three years of age is a risky adventure . . . It would be a foolhardy risk if the need within the Parliamentary Labour Party for steady-going intellectuals were not so great . . . MacDonald's chairmanship has much to recommend it. . . . If he is not the best man for the post, he is at any rate, the worst and most dangerous man out of it! . . .

So far as I can foresee, I shall have a quiet time of it. Except for little dinners and lunches of Labour M.P.s during the session and the monthly gatherings of the Half Circle Club, I shall avoid all social functions, excusing myself on grounds of age and health and pressure of work. There will be some preoccupation with Seaham . . . I am planning a monthly letter to the Women's Sections and I shall have to lecture there twice a year and do odds and ends of letter-writing in the intervals between our regular visits in the spring and autumn. I am haunted by the vision of those pit villages and those strained faces of the miners, their wives listening to our words. Can we get into an intimate and sincere relation to them, so that we may understand their lives? . . .

In 1923 the *New Statesman* amalgamated with the *Nation* and the Webbs' links with the magazine were formally severed.

*10 December.* [41 Grosvenor Road]
Our relations with Clifford Sharp and the *New Statesman* practically though not ostensibly severed. For some time Sidney has felt his position as chairman of the *New Statesman* company untenable: in the notes and editorials there were too frequent depreciations of the Labour Party and all its works. So he took the excuse of 'pressure of parliamentary duties' to resign . . . The breach was inevitable and was foretold by GBS before the war. Clifford Sharp had a natural affinity for the Asquiths and their set, and when the door was opened wide to this delectable social abode, and Margot with her wit, flattery and caressing familiarities beckoned to him, he was doomed to enter in . . .

~ 1923 ~

*9 February. Lyme Regis*
We came here a week ago for a spell of rest and walking. Sidney has returned to London today and I follow on Sunday evening. . . . My life will now be divided into quite unconnected strands. My first duty is co-operating with Sidney's parliamentary work . . . The other strand is getting on with my little book. . . . There is a certain morbid tendency in writing this book – it is practically an autobiography with the love affairs left out – the constantly recurring decision of what degree of self-revelation is permissible and desirable. The ideal conduct would be to treat the diaries exactly as I should treat them if they were someone else's. . . . But it is almost impracticable to get into that frame of mind – one's self-esteem is too deeply concerned, also Sidney's feelings have to be considered. . . . But how short is the time before Sidney and I will be nothing more than names on the title-pages of some thirty books! I suppose all old persons are haunted by the nearness of death. . . . We sometimes agree that the ideal ending would be for both of us to be simultaneously shot dead by an anarchist on the day of our golden wedding, 23 July 1942.

*13 February.* [41 Grosvenor Road]
Sidney is like a boy going for his first term to a public school! This light-heartedness, odd for a man of sixty-three, is due to the youthfulness of the party, as individuals and as an organization, and to being elected on the Executive committee of the Parliamentary Party and also to being asked by J. R. MacDonald to sit on the Front Bench. How long this phase of youthful keenness will continue, when exactly it will give way to physical fatigue and mental nausea, it is difficult to foresee. . . .

*6 March. 41 Grosvenor Road*
My old friend Alice Green staying here for a week's respite from a Senator's life in Dublin, with an armed guard always on her house, the armed guard being almost as dangerous as the I.R.A.! She is now an old woman of seventy-six who has been living an heroic existence doing her little best – and alas! it is little she can do to save Ireland . . . She is desperately pessimistic. 'All the idealism is dead; the people have become thoroughly demoralized; they no longer care . . . Every man's hand is against his neighbour either in offence or defence. Religion is dead; Irish tradition is dead; co-operation is dead; decent

methods of trading and agriculture are dead; there are a few heroes and many martyrs, but the bulk of the people have no notion of being citizens.' She is querulous, poor dear, with old age and loneliness, but she has kept her wits and has developed her wisdom. And she is only too grateful for affection. She thinks she sees in her old friends the Webbs an amazingly fortunate couple living an ideal existence of successful citizenship. . . .

. . . I find my life distracted, distressingly distracted. . . . I think I see the source of my *malaise* in the steadily worsening condition of Europe. . . . And on the economic plane within each country class hatred is being intensified. Never before have I been so aware of belonging to an army of persons who will either be oppressed by, or will oppress, their fellow countrymen. As I looked down on the House of Commons last night I seemed to see a system of government in process of dissolution, a dissolution of which our last book is a tiny echo. Has the British race the good conduct or the intellect to pull through this dissolution to a new and better order for themselves and the world? That is the all-absorbing question. . . .

### 9 March. Longfords

Came down here to be with dear old Mary during the first days of her widowhood. Ten days ago I hurried her away, at ten minutes' notice, from Grosvenor Road, where she had spent a week with me, on an urgent telephone message that her old man was dying. He lingered on for another three days and sank peacefully into unconsciousness. . . . She has taken his death with gentle but haunting sorrow; she *would* sit in the room where lay his body with its peaceful smile, and this morning she and I walked up together to the church to see the casket with the ashes. . . .

Lady Warwick (1861–1938) was a celebrated society beauty and intimate of Edward VII. Easton Lodge was her country estate in Essex. H. G. Wells was her neighbour.

### 11 April. [41 Grosvenor Road]

An odd and not altogether pleasing episode in the social life of the Labour Party. Early in the year the notorious Countess of Warwick, who has been a member of the Labour Party for nearly twenty years . . . put at their disposal Easton Lodge as a week-end resort for small conferences and intimate consultations. There would be little more to pay than the railway tickets. . . . The offer was so unexceptional that the

Executive decided to accept it; and a small party . . . were deputed to go over and prospect. Unfortunately, Lady Warwick unwittingly published the fact, and from the beginning to the end of the episode we were pestered with photographers and film producers. As our hostess obviously desired these attentions, the rest of the party had to submit, and we appeared in groups not only in the newspapers but also on the movies. . . . 'Can the party touch the pitch of luxurious living without being defiled?', many of the left ask. And personally, though I agreed to the acceptance of the offer, I am in two minds as to the wisdom of this acquiescence. In principle there is nothing wrong in it. Lady Warwick cannot help being a Countess . . . Of course, H. G. Wells says she is a spoilt child and that she is moved by a desire for notoriety, but I am convinced that there is also an element of genuine conviction and sincere reforming zeal – otherwise she would not have persisted in her good intention. . . .

The Wellses were much in evidence with their two boys. . . . The two sons are devoted to the mother but somewhat critical, I think, of the father and his ways. Probably they resent the atmosphere of scandal that surrounds the establishment. The eldest son, particularly, looks as if he were quite capable of giving his father a bit of his mind. . . .

*11 May.* [41 Grosvenor Road]
Now that I have this autobiographical book on hand I have not the energy to write up current events. And yet Sidney's life in the Parliamentary Labour Party is full of interest. The Parliamentary Labour Party is unlike either of the other political parties as I knew them through my brothers-in-law and friendly M.P.s. It is a closely-knit organization with a vivid internal life of its own. The leaders do not dominate, and in so far as they lead, they lead by perpetual consultation with the rank-and-file members. . . .

This week all my energy has been taken up with political work. On Monday I travelled up to York to the conference of Women's Sections, spent the whole day in conference, entertained the four Seaham delegates to lunch, and left York 6.20 arriving in London 10.30. Yesterday I had an M.P.'s dinner – with Lord Acton thrown in as a possible Labour Peer. Today a lunch of twelve Labour M.P.s to meet Shaw and Henderson. Tomorrow I must draft the monthly letter to the Seaham women; in the evening I have 130 Fabians coming here for a reception. On Saturday I shall have to finish the monthly letter and I have a Half Circle entertainment all the afternoon. Not a stroke of work done at the book! . . . Fortunately I have ideal servants and no friction; if it had not been for the admirable running of my housekeeping it could not have been done.

*30 May.* [41 Grosvenor Road]
We have just spend ten days with the British delegation at Hamburg attending the International Socialist congress. . . . The countryside through which we passed to and from Hamburg looked the picture of prosperity. . . . But Hamburg struck me as strangely empty of traffic. . . . What was painful to see was the pallor and the apathy of the faces, the lack of joy and laughter, the 'oldness' of the quite young children; above all, the suppressed anger in some faces . . . the population was dignified, but there was silence – dark, brooding silence. . . .

During the last week or so, Sidney has much improved his position as a Front Bencher by a brilliant speech . . . the first really successful speech he has made. . . . Now I think he has caught the right tone. . . .

Sir Oswald Mosley (1896–1980), a Tory M.P. since 1918, became an independent in 1920. He joined the Labour Party in 1924 but, critical of its failure to deal effectively with unemployment, broke away to form the New Party in 1931. When the New Party failed to make headway in the general election it fell apart, and in 1932 Mosley launched the British Union of Fascists. His wife Cynthia (1898–1933), the daughter of Lord Curzon, the Tory Foreign Secretary, was herself a Labour M.P. 1929–31.

*8 June.* [41 Grosvenor Road]
We have made the acquaintance of the most brilliant man in the House of Commons – Oswald Mosley. 'Here is the perfect politician who is also a perfect gentleman,' said I to myself as he entered the room (Sidney having asked him to come back to dinner from the House). If there were a word for the direct opposite of a caricature, for something which is almost absurdly a *perfect type*, I should apply it to him. Tall and slim, his features not too handsome to be strikingly peculiar to himself, modest yet dignified in manner, with a pleasant voice and unegotistical conversation, this young person would make his way in the world without his adventitious advantages, which are many – birth, wealth and a beautiful aristocratic wife. He is also an accomplished orator in the old grand style, and an assiduous worker in the modern manner – keeps two secretaries at work supplying him with information but realizes that he himself has to do the thinking! So much perfection argues rottenness

somewhere. I shall not easily forget my desolating experience with the fascinating Betty Balfour. Oswald Mosley reminds me of her in this respect – he seems to combine great personal charm with solid qualities of character, aristocratic refinement with democratic opinions. Is there in him, as there was in the charming Betty, some weak spot which will be revealed . . . ? And what about his wife, the daughter of Lord Curzon? . . .

Sidney is completely absorbed in his parliamentary work and it is clear there will be no time for the writing of books. . . . For four days he is at the House from 2.30 to 11 or 12 o'clock at night, coming home for 1 1/2 or 2 hours' dinner-hour. On Friday he is there from 11 in the morning till 4 in the afternoon. . . . Now he is on the Standing Committee on the Rent Restriction Bill which will meet in the morning. . . . Parliament in fact is not a half-time job as the L.C.C. was: it is a full-time job. . . . I watch his career in Parliament with a sort of motherly interest. He is singularly simple about it; just does what the party tells him to do, to the best of his ability, enjoying the life and interested not only in all questions which come up but also in the ups and downs of party organization. . . . He has lost his will to power, even to hidden and unrecognized power. Here again the disinterestedness of old age comes in. 'I am no longer quite so certain that I am right,' he says; 'in any case, it will be younger men who will settle the matter'. . . .

At this conference Sidney, in his chairman's address, used the phrase 'the inevitability of gradualness' by which he is most remembered.

*28 June.* [41 Grosvenor Road]
. . . It is clear that if I am to finish my book I must provide for a country residence after Whitsuntide each year, as we used to do . . . I cannot stand the noise of the perpetual motor traffic in front of the house and the constant seeing and talking to people. . . .

Sidney is presiding over the Labour Party conference for five days this week and doing it very successfully. His opening address, 'Labour on the Threshold', has been well received and considerably reported. . . .

Bonar Law's health had been failing for some time. He resigned as Prime Minister on 20 May and was replaced by Stanley Baldwin (1867–1947). The *Punch* cartoon showed Sidney walking down the road waving a red flag in front of a steamroller.

*7 July.* [41 Grosvenor Road]
After an interval of a dozen years, like an echo of past relationships – or is it an echo of present prominence? – came Lady Wemyss to see me this afternoon. . . . Much older, somewhat wizened in appearance, but with the pleasant friendly manner she used to have before she began to dislike us (a change of feeling we never understood), she tried in an apologetic tone and in confused words to explain exactly why we had not met for all those years. I helped her out gallantly by suggesting common absorption in the war, and our own retirement, through old age, from general society. Obviously relieved by my unconcern and ease of manner she chattered on, telling me all about her two sons who were killed in the war . . . Then about A. J. Balfour's splendid career during the war, and the King's summons to him during the recent crisis . . . and how Balfour had decided that Baldwin, and not Curzon, ought to be P.M. . . . She asked a few vague questions about the Labour Party – 'I know nothing above movements' – and we parted, after an hour's talk, on the most friendly terms but neither of us suggesting any future meetings. Cynically I reflected that if Sidney had not been returned to Parliament by a triumphant majority and seated on the Front Opposition Bench – not to mention the cartoon in *Punch* – I should not have been 'resumed' by the former Lady Elcho. It is amusing but unpleasing to note that among the complimentary letters to Sidney on his election was one to me from Miss Wedgwood, Lady Wemyss's companion and friend, and dated Stanway, and another to Sidney from the charming Betty Balfour, ending with 'May I send my love to Mrs Webb.' My 'lost friend' got a cordial reply from Sidney . . . but no message from me. 'She cannot send what she has not got,' I said to Sidney. 'You better leave me out of the picture.' . . .

*26 July.* [41 Grosvenor Road]
Our visit to H. G. Wells during the Easton Lodge Half Circle Club week-end was most pleasant and friendly. Sidney had a slight attack of faintness at breakfast on the first morning, which frightened me and led to a great display of considerate concern from H.G.W. and a certain amount of intimacy with both the Wellses. In fact, we are very nearly on the old footing now, our relations being still slightly tainted by mutual suspicion. Mrs Wells shines as a hostess; she is alike more dignified and more natural than she used to be. She has won through a terrible ordeal and come out the mistress of her circumstances. He is the same brilliant talker and pleasant companion, except that he orates more than he used

to do and listens less intelligently to other people. . . . He has become a sort of 'little god' demanding payment in flattery, as well as in gold, for his very marketable goods, and he has grown contemptuous of his customers. Moreover, he has another and even more damaging consciousness – he feels himself to be a chartered libertine. Everyone knows he is a polygamist and everyone puts up with it. He is aware of this acquiescence in his sins – an acquiescence accompanied with contempt. And this contemptuous acquiescence . . . results in Wells having a contempt for all of us, because we disapprove, and yet associate with him. . . .

The Webbs advertised for a retirement home in the *New Statesman* – 'it must be relatively high, with pretty view; and above all completely isolated from houses harbouring cocks or dogs.'

## *11 August. Longfords*

The fortnight here, looking after Mary while the faithful Bice takes her holiday, has passed happily enough, with Sidney down for a week of the time and the old school-room for our sanctum. I have actually written, or rather 'put together' out of my diary some dozen or more pages of the second chapter of my little work, Sidney meanwhile lazing at my side, finishing up parliamentary correspondence, writing an article for the *Labour Magazine* and discussing with me the offers of cottages and sites arriving by every post – owing to the gratuitous repetition of our *New Statesman* advertisement in a dozen papers, some of them with leaderettes on our dislike of dogs and cocks. Such are the pecuniary benefits arising out of a little fame.

Without a private sitting-room it would have been impossible for me to have stood the nervous strain of taking Bice's place. . . .[Mary] is as sweet-tempered and beneficent as ever. . . . But owing to her absent-mindedness, in the literal as well as the metaphorical sense, she has become in everyday life a mental automaton, repeating questions or statements according to particular stimuli in her environment, so that one waits to hear one of the old tags as if one was pressing the button of a speaking doll. But what is even more distracting is her physical restlessness. She must walk many miles a day out of doors; but when she is not walking she is jumping up and down from one momentary occupation to another – knitting, smoking, pianola, playing patience, or glancing at a stray book or newspaper, rarely spending more than five minutes, if so much, doing one thing. . . .

At this point the other of the three old wives, Kate Courtney, arrives – aged seventy-six. She jumps out of the pony-cart like a girl of fifteen and greets me with rapid remarks on foreign affairs, the wickedness of the French and the dull apathy of the English government . . . Well in health and alert in mind . . . this eldest of the remaining sisters is a model of what an old woman ought to be and do. But in spite of continuous kindness, she bores me – she has always bored me – but that may well be my fault, not hers. . . . Blood relationship is a strange tie – so much affection and helpfulness, so little sympathy and understanding. . . . There is perhaps even a subtler and subconscious jealousy – jealousy which disappears when misfortune or pain bears down on the beloved sister but which rises to the surface in calm weather when everyone speaks well of her, when the world insists, as the others think, on over-rating her. Certainly Georgie Meinertzhagen and some of my other sisters had that feeling about me, and Maggie had it about Kate. But for this slight distemper, the relations between the Potter sisters have been almost ideal – no quarrels and loyal helpfulness in all the obvious troubles of life. . . .

*31 August.* [41 Grosvenor Road]
. . . in search of our proposed country home. This was a tiresome but, thank heaven! a quickly successful venture, lasting only four days in all. After seeing two or three other impossible places we plunged on 8 1/2 acres with a habitable cottage two miles from Liphook and four miles from Hindhead, costing £1,750 for the freehold, a sum well within our means. With the addition of a third sitting-room for our sanctum and three more bedrooms it will be a home we can retire to in case either of us breaks down, and it can meanwhile be used as a holiday residence. Enclosed in the estate of a wealthy bachelor . . . It is a sufficiently pretty view and includes a delightful corner of woodland with big forest trees and some acres of hayfield. I mean to plant the garden with heather, broom and gorse and bushes of lavender, sweeping away all the ugly patches of cabbage and potatoes and silly little beds of formal flowers, so as to dispense with a gardener. Happy hours Sidney and I spend in discussing alterations and possible extensions. . . .

*22 September. Longfords*
Watching over the dear old sister dying of cancer of the lung. . . . Again one asks as one watches the painful process of dying – is it necessary that men and women should pass through this long-drawn-out weariness,

discomfort and pain, when there can be only one end to it? Would Mary prefer to be told the truth – that she had to die in a few weeks, probably a few days, and would get gradually or rapidly more weary and miserable?

*12 October.* [41 Grosvenor Road]
After I left her end came quickly, accelerated by morphia. The dear old sister passed into the unknown peacefully sleeping. . . . Kate and I are left alone in the world; the dear old lady clings to me and is as loving and open-handed as ever; whilst poor neurotic Rosy and her neurotic children are a burden on us both. So dwindles out of sight the 'R.P. family'!

> The economic situation had grown worse during the autumn, with more than 11 per cent unemployed. There was talk of a protective tariff to help the British worker and manufacturer. Baldwin made Protection his rallying cry, thus reuniting the Tory Party after the tensions of the Coalition. Parliament was dissolved on 16 November and the election held on 6 December.

*27 October. 41 Grosvenor Road*
Ten days with Sidney at Seaham Harbour in our comfortable lodgings with the peaceful view of the dale and, at night, the twinkling lights of the collieries on the horizon of the hills surrounding us. . . . There is something very touching in these few hundred miners' wives, with here and there a professional woman, gathering round me with a sort of hero worship. . . . The monthly letter I started last spring has been a great success. This time I have begun another experiment – a free circulating library of some 150 or 200 books distributed in dozens among the eleven Women's Sections . . .

Meanwhile, I have to set about furnishing the cottage . . . The book has again to be put on one side . . . Then, in all probability, an election and three weeks of exhausting turmoil at Seaham, with a new Parliamentary Party to cater for . . . Damn it! How I long for a country home and time and strength to finish the work of art(?) I have begun. . . .

*19 November.* [41 Grosvenor Road]
Sidney off this morning for Seaham in first-rate form with no anxiety about his own seat . . . The real and significant issue before the country

is Liberalism v. Labour – there is no other issue of any importance. . . . The Liberals, reunited under the ostensible leadership of Asquith, but really under the leadership of Lloyd George . . . seem to be in a first-rate position to win in the fight with Labour. . . . To read the capitalist press, whether Tory or Liberal, the Labour Party barely exists. . . .

I am moving today into the cottage . . . This day week I go to Seaham for ten days' speaking . . . It is fortunate that I am not otherwise than well for a woman of my age; I still suffer from intestinal trouble and wonder whether I ought to live more ascetically – give up tea, coffee, tobacco, and the whisky at my evening meal, but I don't do it because I am not convinced that it makes any difference, and no medical man will tell me that it will. . . .

*22 November. Passfield Corner*
Entered with furniture and Jessie [a domestic servant] yesterday . . . Impression of our new home not altogether favourable in this dank weather. Silence absolute – no crowing cocks or barking dogs, not even the hoot of the motor. Cottage comfortable with distinct charm; country beautiful for walking and dry under foot on commons. But dankly cold after sundown owing to prevalence of water – near to river, and series of ponds. Also cottage arrangements about water, relying on pump which is tedious to work and troublesome after the modern conveniences. Not a possible all-round-the-year place because of the ground mist. But is this not true of all country places that are below the highest hill in the neighbourhood? . . . We shall come here for a fortnight at Xmas and then see whether we like it sufficiently to plunge into extensive building and expensive upkeep. . . . Certainly the silence is weirdly attractive. . . .

*3 December.* [Seaham Harbour]
The Sunday before an election is always a day of rest in your *own* constituency, as it is bad form for the candidates not to seem to go to church or chapel, or at any rate refrain from speaking to his own electors. . . . So far as we are concerned, we are on velvet in this ideal constituency. There is far more enthusiasm than a year ago, far more voluntary work. The miners have become genuinely attached to their member. . . . And the miners' wives are fond of me. I have raised their status with their husbands and neighbours. They regard me as *their* representative and they are delighted with the monthly letter . . . there is always a group of women, sometimes sixty or seventy, at the

meetings. Last year, if there were two or three women one was agreeably surprised. . . .

The election result was a decisive rejection of Protection, although the
Conservatives remained the largest party, with 258 members. Against
expectations, the Labour Party increased from 142 to 191 seats and the
nominally reunited Liberals could only win 158. This indecisive result
meant either a new Coalition or a minority government. Labour took
office with Liberal support.

*12 December.* [41 Grosvenor Road]
These are the hectic days of victory tempered by the cold feet of the leaders at the consequences of victory! On the Saturday, the day of our
return, Massingham appeared in the evening to implore us *not* to allow
the Labour Party to enter into any relations with the Liberal Party . . .
On Monday we had a dinner here of leaders – J.R.M., Henderson,
Clynes, Thomas and Snowden – to discuss taking office and what
exactly they would do if they did. Sidney reports that they have all,
except Henderson, 'cold feet' at the thought of office, though all of
them believe that J.R.M. ought not to refuse. . . . while I agree that the
Labour Party *must accept* rather than refuse office, it seems absurd, from
a mere commonsense community standpoint, that they should govern
without having a majority . . .

~ 1924 ~

Sidney was to become President of the Board of Trade – the post Joseph
Chamberlain had held at the time of Beatrice's infatuation for him in the
1880s.

*3 January.* [Passfield Corner]
This time last year Sidney was on the threshold of his Parliamentary
career; today he is on the threshold of the Cabinet! . . . but which
office? . . . On New Year's Eve came the letter from J.R.M. offering him
the Ministry of Labour. 'He has learnt the manner,' says Sidney in a con-
templative tone. 'He tells me that it is the post of greatest difficulty!
Anyway, it just suits me – it is an unpretentious office with a low salary
and no social duties.'. . .
'What a joke – what an unexpected and slightly ludicrous adventure,'

said he to me as we smoked the after-lunch cigarette, 'for a man of sixty-four to become, first, a Member of Parliament, and within a year, a Cabinet Minister; and that with colleagues none of whom have held Cabinet office before; whilst only three of them have been in the government – and these three do not include the Premier! If anyone had prophesied ten years ago that J.R.M. would be Prime Minister and would invite me to be in his Cabinet, I should have thought the first extraordinarily unlikely, but the two combined a sheer impossibility.' . . .

*18 January.* [41 Grosvenor Road]
J.R.M. sent for Sidney on Thursday and Friday to consult him . . . Apparently some of the inner circle had objected to Sidney being relegated to so small a post . . . J.R.M. said that he had not realized that the Ministry of Labour was so much the 'Cinderella of the government offices', and pressed Sidney to take the Board of Trade. . . . Sidney left it in his hands, and they discussed other affairs. Sidney came away feeling that the Cabinet would err on the side of *respectability* – too many outsiders and too many peers. . . . If Sidney had had the making of the Cabinet it would have been far more working class and more to the 'left' of the Labour Party. . . . Henderson, we are glad to find, is to be Home Secretary – a post which is sufficiently impressive. . . .

'And what do *you* feel about the change in *your* life?' asked Kate, somewhat perturbed at my detached and unexcited attitude. 'Personally I prefer a quiet student's life, but of course I am glad for Sidney's sake,' I replied. 'Sidney as Cabinet Minister is one job like another. I shall chime in with it,' I concluded.

Here ends the Old Testament.

# A Nine Days' Wonder

## January 1924–March 1929

[28?] *January.* [41 Grosvenor Road]
Enter Labour government, January 1924. Exit November?

Maurice Hankey (1877–1963) was Secretary to the Cabinet 1919–38. John
Wheatley (1869–1930), owner of a prosperous printing business and
Clydeside M.P., was Minister of Health. Ethel Snowden (1880–1951), an
ex-schoolteacher and suffragist, was a socialist lecturer.

[28?] *January.* [41 Grosvenor Road]
. . . On Wednesday the twenty Ministers-designate, in their best suits
(Sidney went in the frock-coat and tall hat he had brought from Japan
and which had not been looked at since we returned in 1912 – fortunately it fitted and was not moth-eaten), went to Buckingham Palace
to be sworn in; having been previously drilled by Hankey. Four of
them came back to our weekly M.P.s' lunch . . . Uncle Arthur was
bursting with childish joy over his Home Office seals in the red leather
box which he handed round the company; Sidney was chuckling over
a hitch in the solemn ceremony in which he had been right and
Hankey wrong; they were all laughing over Wheatley – the revolutionary – going down on both knees and actually kissing the King's
hand . . .

Meanwhile I am living a distracted life which does not please me. I
have taken over Sidney's unofficial correspondence and dictated forty

letters yesterday in twice as many minutes. What is far more troublesome is acting as the 'doyenne' among Ministers' wives . . . My latest job has been to help Mrs Clynes to get her establishment fixed up at 11 Downing Street. I have provided her with housekeeper, cook and butler – no, I forgot, the *very* latest task has been to soothe the feelings of Mrs Snowden, deeply offended at being excluded from occupying the usual residence of the Chancellor of the Exchequer in favour of the wife of the Leader of the House. But the whole of the Labour world would have revolted at the bare idea of 'Ethel' established in an official residence. She is a 'climber' of the worst description, refusing to associate with the rank-and-file and plebeian elements in the Labour Party. Hence every class-conscious Labour man or woman listens for the echoes of Ethel climbing, climbing, climbing, night and day! . . . The only other climbers are Thomas and his wife and daughters; but Thomas drops his 'h's' defiantly; and Mrs Thomas is a retiring and discreet climber . . . the daughters are so far removed from Labour circles that one of them, when asked by a partner at a Half-Circle Club dance whether she was a 'Fabian', retorted indignantly, 'No: I am a "Thomas"'!

One of the minor annoyances of my present existence is the sudden and effusive resurrection of the social acquaintances of former years . . . Every afternoon there appear cards reminding me of one or other 'revenant' of a former episode of 'being fashionable' – 1900–06, for instance. How to combine politeness and recognition of old ties . . . with keeping clear of Society folk is a delicate problem of manners. The plea of old age suffices for the more shadowy of these ghosts, but some bills on the past have to be honoured. When the newness of Labour Cabinet Ministers wears off, the mere lion-hunting will cease. But the persons who want places, mostly males, or the vaguer applicants for a chance 'to work for the Labour Party' – worldly women – means dozens of letters to be answered with courteous discouragement.

*8 February.* [41 Grosvenor Road]
Sidney is liking his work at the Board of Trade – finds his officials polished instruments, waiting on him hand and foot, seemingly acquiescent in any practicable policy. Fabians who are in the office report that after the first meeting of the General Council of the Board of Trade, over which Sidney presided . . . the permanent heads remarked to each other, 'These new men are very good – we have at last a business government – these men have trained minds.' . . . The peculiar characteristic of

this government is, in fact, that every member, except perhaps Wheatley, has been a public servant and not a profiteer. . . .

MacDonald's wife, Margaret, had died in 1911. His eldest daughter, Ishbel, acted as her father's hostess at Downing Street.

*9 February.* [41 Grosvenor Road]
At the suggestion of the Half-Circle Club executive, Ishbel MacDonald summoned a meeting at 10 Downing Street of Ministers' wives (Cabinet and Under-Secretaries), to discuss whether or not there should be any organized effort to get acquainted with the wives of Labour M.P.s and to start a common room for the Parliamentary Party and their womenkind . . . The stately formality of the Prime Minister's residence, with its messengers, menservants and private secretaries moving to and fro with an odd combination of secretiveness and solemnity, with its inhospitable hall where a dozen of us were kept waiting, and grand reception rooms, through which we were ushered like a deputation, is not a homely surrounding! But 10 Downing Street, and respect for the Prime Minister's daughter, attracted some twenty of the wives, including Mrs Snowden and Mrs Patrick Hastings, who are seldom seen in the homes of the humbler members . . . Ishbel is an attractive creature; charming to look at, in a pretty new frock, simple and direct in speech and manner. Today she is a little puritan; how she will develop under the glare and glamour of official splendour and power remains to be seen. She herself is against anything that is 'organized'; she announced her intention of being 'At Home' one day a week, asking the Labour M.P.s' wives to visit her and have a 'homely cup of tea', and suggested that other Ministers' wives might do likewise. Mrs Snowden also thought that the matter could be left to individuals, and that 'tea on the terrace' [of the House of Commons] is what most women liked. The less important Ministers' wives were emphatically in favour of some common place for meeting; and urged that a determined effort to see Labour members' wives should be made, *at times which suited these women*; and that they should not merely be sent cards for 'At Homes' at big houses. . . .

*11 February. Passfield Corner*
Came down here with Sidney and Jessie for two quiet week-ends for him, and nine days for myself; Jessie took to her bed with influenza, so on Sunday I stumbled through household work, and this morning was

up at six o'clock to get Sidney his coffee and a fire before he left by the eight o'clock train. Now, having secured an excellent neighbour to do my work, I am sitting alone by the fire writing in my diary after an afternoon nap and a cup of tea. Cold dank weather, but absolute quiet; just a far-off hint that birds sing in the coldest and wettest February! How I should enjoy retiring here and getting on with my book! How I look forward to the time when I shall be able to do so – when Sidney is once again out of office or when the routine of a Cabinet Minister's wife is sufficiently fixed to permit me to spend half the year here. Clothes, curtsys, parties, dances and dramatic circles, all the detail of cultivating social intercourse within the Labour Party, Rebels versus Front Benchers, salaries and contributions out of salaries for collective purposes, are all absurd matters to trouble about when whole districts of Europe and some of the noblest individuals and promising races are dying of starvation and others are distorted with lust of power and greed of gain. How lacking in perspective seem most of my activities! But on looking back over a fairly intimate knowledge of the two great political parties who have hitherto ruled our national destiny, one remembers the careers of Joseph Chamberlain and Lloyd George, of Balfour and Asquith, not to mention the minor roles of my brothers-in-law. The root of their inefficiency as rulers was more often than not due to their absorption in a too aristocratic and pleasure-loving social intercourse. . . . Unless we can maintain within the Labour Party a far higher standard of manners, unless we can resist the scramble up the ladder, our terms of office and our wielding of power will leave the world no better than we found it. . . .

*3 March.* [41 Grosvenor Road]
Definitely refused to go to Buckingham Palace to an afternoon party, which I imagine is to consist of Ministers' wives. . . . there is not the remotest reason why the *wives* and *daughters* should be dragged into Smart Society, with the inevitable 'dressing up' and extravagant expenditure in returning hospitality. And once the wife has allowed herself to be presented and has made her curtsy she becomes part of the Court Circle and there is no way out of accepting invitations to meet royalties at the houses of the leaders of London Society. So I cut the knot by refusing – in the curiously ungracious accepted formula, 'Mrs Sidney Webb is unavoidably prevented from obeying Their Majesties' Command to, etc. etc.' – to take the first step into the charmed circle, and I shall not be troubled again!

*15 March.* [41 Grosvenor Road]
The Parliamentary Labour Party is drifting badly in the House of
Commons. . . . The P.M. is unapproachable by Henderson, who is
responsible for the Labour Party organization in the country; and apparently by Clynes, the Leader of the House. 'No. 10 and No. 11 see no
more of each other,' said Henderson to me, 'than if they slept and ate a
hundred miles apart'. . . .

What interests me as a student of the British Constitution is the
unlimited autocracy of the British P.M. . . . It was MacDonald who
alone determined who should be in his Cabinet; it is MacDonald who
alone is determining what the Parliamentary Labour Party shall stand for
in the country. . . . And it is clear that the P.M. is playing up – without
any kind of consultation with the majority of his colleagues or scruple or
squeamishness about first pronouncements – towards the formation of
a Centre Party, far less definitely socialist in home affairs, far less distinctly pacifist in foreign affairs, say, than Sidney would be if he were
Prime Minister. MacDonald wants eight million voters behind him and
means to get them even if this entails shedding the I.L.P., the idealisti-
cally revolutionary section who pushed him into power. . . . I do not
accuse him of treachery: for he was never a socialist . . . Where he has
lacked integrity is in *posing* as a socialist, and occasionally using revolutionary jargon. . . . One of the unpleasant features of this government
has been the willingness of convinced and even fanatical pacifists to go
back on their words when once they are on the Treasury Bench as
Under-Secretaries for the War Services. Hot-air propaganda in mean
streets and industrial slums combined with chill moderation on the
Treasury Bench and courtly phrases at Society functions may be the last
word of political efficiency but it is unsavoury, and leads, among the
rank and file, to deep discouragement. Even Sidney is depressed. . . .

*Easter Week. 32 Maureen Terrace.* [Seaham Harbour]
Five days here with Susan Lawrence: she and S. speaking twice a day, and
I only twice during the time. . . . Susan Lawrence is a remarkable
woman. More than 'well-to-do', with a forceful intelligence, presence
and voice, more forceful than attractive, she is one of the best of souls.
Brought up a Conservative and a churchwoman, she championed these
creeds with capacity and courage for twelve years, first on the dying
London School Board, and then on the County Council. 'Trying to
carry social reforms by a Moderate party is like running temperance
reform by a company of licensed victuallers,' said she. Susan and Sidney

have always liked and respected each other. For so able a woman she is strangely emotional about persons and causes; but the way she expresses her love, pity or indignation is oddly irritating. She has read enormously, and gets up a case exactly like a lawyer, but her remarks are not original, and she lacks intellectual perspective. Above all, she is free from all the pettiness of personal vanity or jealousy. Is she lovable? I have never heard of anyone being in love with her; I am inclined to think this lack of the quality of lovableness accounts for a certain recklessness, a certain dare-devil attitude towards life . . . As a speaker she interests women more than men; her very masculinity and clearness of mind attracts women. Clever men appreciate her serviceable talent and lack of egotism, but she tires them. . . . Of her John Morley would certainly have said, as he did of me: 'Charming, no: able but not charming.' . . .

Throughout the Easter recess MacDonald has continued his remarkably successful 'word-spinning' (to use Lansbury's term of abuse). . . . His constant insistence that there is no need for an election, that no one wants it, and that the Labour government is quite prepared to carry on for two or three years, puzzles us. . . . from what his friends say, he is enjoying himself vastly, whether he is week-ending at Windsor Castle or receiving the homages, always paid to attractive persons in great positions . . . It is amazing, the guileless, the stupid *worship of power* by the British people of all classes and all parties. . . .

*17 May.* [41 Grosvenor Road]
. . . I have had two miners' wives from the Seaham Division staying with me for the Women's Conference (a thousand delegates from all parts of Great Britain). What interested me was the moral refinement and perfect manners of these two women, who had never seen London before and never stayed in a house with servants. One of them was a delicate, excitable and intellectual woman – a bundle of nerves – the other a phlegmatic Scot. They were attractively clothed and their talk was mostly about public affairs, the one emotionally stirred by the socialist faith and familiar with all its shibboleths; the other shrewd, cautious and matter-of-fact in her political expectations. They were completely at their ease, and their attitude to their host and hostess was more that towards a class teacher and a minister of religion than to social superiors. I don't think they had any trace of feeling that they belonged to a different class, though they realized that we had greater knowledge and a wider experience of life. The conference was a real success; education, mothers' endowment, and birth control were the questions which really

interested the assembly. And there was a certain impatience at having to listen to Ministers or even to women officials; they wanted to talk themselves and hear from fellow delegates . . . At the Albert Hall meeting, they were of course enthusiastic about the P.M. and Margaret Bondfield and the other ministerial speakers – and with the singing of part-religious and part-revolutionary hymns, the great gathering likened a religious festival more than a political demonstration. What a strange blend of ancient tradition and modern outlook is the British Labour Party!

Bryan's Ground, Presteigne, Radnorshire, was the home of Betty Russell, Lallie's daughter, who was suffering from Graves's disease. Molly was her sister. The former Liberal Minister R. B. Haldane was now Lord Chancellor and chairman of the Committee of Imperial Defence.

### 2 June. Bryan's Ground
Ten days alone in this enchanting countryside: living comfortably according to my own habits in the gardener's cottage, working quietly at the book in the mornings, long lonely rambles – five to eight miles – in the evenings, and little visits to the nieces in between, to cheer up poor Betty in her mysterious illness and devoted Molly in her anxiety. So far as I am concerned, I have thoroughly enjoyed the time – the peace and beauty – the only breaks in the silence being the songs of the birds: robin, finch, blackbird and thrush and the wilder calls of peewit, curlew and the owl. . . .

### 23 June. [41 Grosvenor Road]
Yesterday morning, being Sunday, as I was returning home from the usual walk round St James's Palace, I thought I would look up Haldane, whom I had not seen for many weeks. He was in his dignified study – surrounded by the portraits of philosophers and statesmen – two flights up, and welcomed me warmly. 'Are you more satisfied with the Cabinet than you were when I last saw you?' I asked. 'Yes,' said the beneficent one, who always reminds me more of a French seventeenth-century abbé than of an English politician, 'they are becoming more intelligent'. . . . Haldane was, as usual, busy manipulating civil servants and Ministers to his way of thinking – the only person, he said somewhat sarcastically, he did *not* see was the P.M. But then that is a common complaint . . . What puzzles me – is MacDonald an able statesman as well as a clever parliamentarian and attractive popular preacher? My mind is

literally a blank on this subject . . . He has certainly had good luck, up to now; and persistent good luck usually means a strain of unusual talent, if not genius. . . .

*28 June. Passfield Corner*

One week getting more furniture in, superintending builders and finishing operations, making provision for a drive to the house, seeing the Lady of the Manor about bridging the ditch, and our neighbour Anketell about an exchange of land; and at last I am again at work on the book, Sidney having departed yesterday after a happy week-end together. The cottage, with its comfortable study and delightful loggia, its woods and views and walks, is almost too good to be true! To make a new home when one is nearing seventy seems, in some moods, a melancholy task: one is haunted by a vision of the funeral procession wending its way down the new drive, a few years hence, perhaps a few months hence, of one of us leaving the other one desolate and alone. . . . Also there is present in my mind [the thought] that this new home must mean a certain separation from Sidney – at any rate, while he remains in Parliament. I comfort myself by remembering that for some years I always lived in the country during the spring and summer months whilst he was mostly in London on County Council business. But we were at work on the same book: he came back to me as a workmate; we toiled together all the days he spared from administration; we talked about what we were both keen about. Now when he returns, we love each other, but he has interests about which I know little, and I am absorbed in creative writing in which he has no part but that of a kindly and helpful critic of style.

Aldous Huxley (1894–1963) published his first novel, *Crome Yellow*, in 1921; *Antic Hay* followed in 1923. E. M. Forster (1879–1970) had just published *A Passage to India*. Albert Einstein (1879–1955) received the Nobel Prize for physics in 1921; his *Relativity* was translated into English in 1920.

*10 July.* [Passfield Corner]

Assuredly some of the younger authors can write. Aldous Huxley is a brilliant *littérateur*, but at present a shallow-hearted thinker. E. M. Forster – a much older man, but one who has written fewer books, because he has thought and felt as well as searched after *le mot juste* – appears to me in his latest novel *A Passage to India* as a genius, and not merely a man with an exquisite gift for words. [Beatrice here quotes a passage from the novel about Mrs Moore.]

> She had come to that state where the horror of the universe and its smallness are both visible at the same time – the twilight of the double vision in which so many elderly people are involved. If this world is not to our taste, well, at all events there is Heaven, Hell, Annihilation – one or other of those large things, that huge scenic background of stars, fires, blue or black air. All heroic endeavour, and all that is known as art, assumes that there is such a background, just as all practical endeavour, when the world is to our taste, assumes that the world is all. But in the twilight of the double vision, a spiritual muddledom is set up for which no high-sounding words can be found; we can neither act nor refrain from action, we can neither ignore nor respect Infinity.

In this description of an old woman's mind, what appeals to me are the phrases 'the twilight of the double vision', 'a spiritual muddledom is set up'. Certainly with me there is the strange consciousness of standing on a bare and bleak watershed of thought and feeling . . . the concrete questions which I have investigated – trade unionism, local government, co-operation, political organization, no longer interest me . . . I am conscious of the past and I am conscious of the future; I am wholly indifferent to the present. It is my *duty* to be interested in the Labour Party and the Labour government . . . But I am not really interested, except in so far as Sidney's activity and happiness are concerned. . . . During the last few weeks I have been pressed to serve on two Royal Commissions and one government committee – London University, Lunacy and the Export Trade. The very sound of those words bored and irritated me. I should have loathed having to turn my mind on to all the maze of technical detail, and I am glad enough to plead 'old age' and to suggest some younger woman who would be proud to undertake the task. What rouses thought is: how can the human mind acclimatize itself to the insecurity and uncertainty of this terrible doctrine of relativity, latent in all modern science long before Einstein applied it to the astronomical universe? It is a most disconcerting conclusion, that there is no absolute truth . . . Is morality a question of taste, and truth a question of relative standpoints? And are all tasks and all standpoints equally valid? What, in fact, is my own standpoint from which I survey the world of the past and the future? For it is exactly these questions which

I shall have to answer in the last chapter of my book! And it is this point in space and time – the exact point at which I stand – that seems to me so singularly bleak and bare, so featureless.

*21 July.* [41 Grosvenor Road]
An exhausting forty-eight hours in Edinburgh receiving the LL.D. from the University. On the evening of arrival, a ceremonious dinner with speeches lasting four hours in the great hall of the University; the next day, lengthy process in the crowded MacEwan Hall of being 'capped' with sixteen other honorary graduates. . . . the walk through the town in cap and gown to the Cathedral, listening to an inaudible and dully read sermon by the Moderator; then another ceremonial meal, the lunch given by the Students' Union – at which I was one of the speakers – lasting another three hours; a reception at the Principal's; after that I struck work and refused to attend the evening function. On the following evening I lectured for 1 1/2 hours to the Fabians, and then left by 10.50 night express for London. . . .

*30 August. Passfield Corner*
Already one month of the recess past. In spite of the gloomiest August on record . . . we are more than satisfied with the Home of the Aged Webbs. The peacefulness of the place continues perfect; and the new room 'to work in' is already old in our affections and admired by all who come here . . .

Outwardly the session ended with a blaze of glory for the P.M. . . . But within the charmed circle of the Cabinet there is disintegration going on; within the party disaffection is spreading . . .

*2 September.* [41 Grosvenor Road]
J.R.M. . . . seems latterly to have become even more aloof and autocratic . . . Sidney, however, regards the whole matter of the Labour administration as so short-lived and exceptional that he is not concerned to criticize, except that he hopes it *will* be short-lived, or he fears trouble. . . .

By the autumn, confidence in the Labour government had been undermined by various incidents. One hinted at personal scandal. The head of the McVitie and Price biscuit company, an old friend of MacDonald's, provided him with a Daimler car and an income to run it. Shortly afterwards, the philanthropic biscuit-maker received a baronetcy. The other incidents were more dramatically political – part of the 'Red Scare' that finally brought the government down. Anxiety had arisen over a proposed treaty with Russia. MacDonald had announced Britain's recognition of the Soviet government in February. After difficult negotiations two treaties were signed in August and the government recommended to Parliament the guarantee of a loan to Russia. This proposal was at once attacked by both Liberals and Conservatives. The government seemed to be set on a socialist course and the Liberals threatened to withdraw their support. The *coup de grâce*, however, was the Campbell case. Early in August the acting editor of the Communist *Workers' Weekly*, J. R. Campbell (1894–1969), had been arrested and charged, under the Incitement to Mutiny Act, as the author of a 'don't shoot' article urging soldiers not to fire on their fellow workers. When questions were asked in the House, Sir Patrick Hastings (1880–1952), the Attorney-General, found himself under attack from the left wing of his own party and the prosecution was dropped. When Parliament re-convened, both Tories and Liberals accused the government of having acted improperly and on 8 October a Liberal vote of censure was carried. Since MacDonald had declared that he would treat it as a vote of confidence, Parliament was dissolved the next day. The atmosphere of Bolshevik menace was confirmed towards the end of the election campaign, when the newspapers reported that revolutionary instructions signed by Grigori Zinoviev (1883–1936), the President of the Communist International in Moscow, had been sent to the Central Committee of the Communist Party in Britain. The newspapers also printed a Foreign Office statement protesting against such interference in British affairs – a rash move which gave credibility to the damaging 'Zinoviev Letter', even though the Labour leaders denounced it as a forgery, an election stunt, and an attempt to jeopardize the improvement in Anglo-Soviet relations. Polling took place on 29 October and the Tories won a decisive victory, capturing 419 seats. The Labour Party returned 151, the Liberals came back without Asquith (who now went to the Lords) and with only 40 seats. Winston Churchill now returned to the Conservative Party.

*13 September.* [41 Grosvenor Road]

### The Fall of MacDonald

(I write this heading early in the morning before I see the daily papers commenting on the extraordinary episode reported in the Stop Press in yesterday's *Evening Standard.*)

Has MacDonald killed the Labour Prime Minister by a blunder in personal conduct so grotesque that it almost disarms the criticism of his friends by its innocent crudeness? In March 1924 the P.M. accepts from his old friend Alexander Grant (the principal partner in McVitie's biscuit factory) £30,000 ordinary shares; in May his friend is made a baronet. Those are the bald facts. There are of course extenuating circumstances. Grant was not only a successful self-made man; he was a generous and wise public donor: he had given £100,000 to the public library in Edinburgh. He may be said to have 'deserved a baronetcy'. MacDonald is taking an income, not from a stranger, but from a lifelong friend. Further, other statesmen have done exactly the same thing; but have hidden it up. MacDonald did it in a way which was bound to be discovered, and therefore it may be assumed he saw no objection to it. For all that, the bald facts look as if he had 'sold a baronetcy' . . . The blow is staggering . . . Hitherto we have prided ourselves on being a party of incorruptibles. Shall we be so, even in our own sight, any longer? . . .

*10 October.* [Passfield Corner]
The end of the tale of the Parliament of 1923–24, and of its Cabinet, is soon told. The two oppositions decided to kill the government on the Campbell issue. . . . Before twelve hours had passed away, the P.M. met his colleagues with the King's consent for a dissolution that *very afternoon*! 'The King's Speech must be written and ready for him to see at one o'clock,' said he, looking round the table. 'Webb, you had better go and do it.' So Sidney and Tom Jones summoned the heads of the different departments, and a dozen men sat down at tables and drafted paragraphs, while Sidney strung them together and polished up the whole. At three o'clock the Council was held: and the Dissolution proclaimed.

The following day Sidney was kept hard at it, drafting the manifesto for the party; in the intervals between the MSS's typewritten and printed form, he struggled to get his own Seaham election campaign started. Yesterday he went off to Seaham, and I follow on Wednesday. . . .

[No date. Seaham Harbour]

### The Fall of the Labour Government

Which of course was foreseen; but even we did not forecast the catastrophic character of the rout so far as the parliamentary representation of Labour is concerned, nor did we anticipate a two thousand drop in our majority. . . . A more careful consideration of the response of the huge electorate to the virulent anti-Communist propaganda carried on by Liberals and Conservatives alike makes us almost content with the verdict. . . . The big joke of the general election is that the grave of anti-Communism, which the Liberal leaders dug so energetically for us, swallowed them up instead, whilst the Labour Party was left with a million increase on its total poll. . . .

*6 November.* [41 Grosvenor Road]
This morning Sidney said good-bye to his department. . . . The post has suited Sidney . . . and he was certainly popular with everyone concerned. I doubt whether he will be again in office unless he is compelled sooner or later to go to the Lords in default of other peers, which I trust is not likely as it would diminish our income and raise awkward questions. . . .

*2 December. Passfield*
At last in our dear new home and at the beginning of the last lap of life together – short or long. Surrounded at present with wage-slaves digging, planting, building and path-making, some dozen of them in all. Shocking sight, the aged Webbs adding acre to acre (the original eight has now grown to near twelve!), laying out these acres in park-like avenues, cutting down trees to make vistas, discussing with the expert from Kew (or rather bred at Kew) what trees and shrubs to plant – good to look at. We salve our conscience by assuring each other that we are preparing a country residence for the staff and students of the London School of Economics, but in our heart of hearts we see pictures of two old folk living in comfort, and amid some charm, writing endless works, and receiving the respectable attention of an ever larger public. But my greatest satisfaction is to get back to my particular work . . .

MacDonald returned the shares on which the £1,500 endowment depended and gave up the car on 17 December.

*19 December.* [Passfield Corner]
We lunched with the Snowdens yesterday. Bitter about MacDonald and would have been more bitter if Sidney had encouraged it even to the extent that I did, out of a woman's curiosity! They are obsessed with the danger of Communism . . . The party is certainly in a bad state of mind – the fall of MacDonald from the real leadership, the secret

contempt with which many of his Front Bench colleagues regard him, the anger of the majority of the rank and file, leaves the first place open to any big man, brilliant politician, clever intriguer or log-roller who comes along. . . . Poor MacDonald. What a mess he has made of it: all that is left of the glamour of nine months' premiership is the Daimler and the £1,500 a year clear of income tax. . . .

~ 1925 ~

*12 February.* [Passfield Corner]
It is a testimony to my industry that it is nine weeks since my last entry. It means that I have been too absorbed in the book to have energy left to write in the diary; also Sidney has been here and I never can write in his presence. . . . We have had little political news . . . When I looked down from the Ladies' Gallery last Tuesday it was a shock to see no Liberal on the Front Opposition Bench; and to watch Lloyd George, almost a comic figure, gesticulating from under the gallery. Whatever else has happened, the Liberal Party as a force in the country is dead and gone. . . .

*20 February.* [Passfield Corner]
Ran up to London for two or three days to attend a Labour Party reception and make arrangements with Susan Lawrence to take over two floors of Grosvenor Road – drawing-room with study and two second-floor bedrooms, leaving us with dining-room, two attic bedrooms and box-room – for £200 a year unfurnished, a sum which will cover all our outgoings except service, lighting and heating. Now that we have the cottage with nine acres of grounds, a gardener and his wife, I am making it into my permanent home, and Sidney's too, except for House of Commons days during the six to nine months' session. It seems wasteful to have Grosvenor Road on our hands even if it were wise for us to afford it. But I felt that Sidney had a right to a comfortable abode close to the House . . . When I have to be in London for a few days I would rather have someone else in the house to talk to. I can't work there, so I like to gossip! It seems an ideal arrangement, especially after the solitude of this place. . . .

Meanwhile I have altered the plan of my book. To my surprise I discovered that with Chapter IV finished I have written about 100,000 words and that with the next chapter, which brings the tale up to our marriage, I shall have done as much as can be contained in one volume. Why not publish the volume, say next winter, thought I. At my age the other may never get finished and I am beginning to feel that I need a break and a holiday. . . . I am very very tired; I need a change of thought and scene.

My depression is, I think, probably a reflex of Sidney's lowered interest and lesser participation in the work of Parliament. He has not been well treated by the Tories – the more vulgar of the young bloods jeer at him. He has never got complete control of the House of Commons: he is too modest and feels his own limitations without having the personal ambition needed to put himself right. Also the ruck-up within the Parliamentary Labour Party against the ex-Cabinet and the old junta of MacDonald, Henderson, Clynes, Thomas, Snowden and Sidney has affected him at least as much, perhaps more, than it has the others, as he is a comparative newcomer in the parliamentary arena and has never quite got his footing in the party. He is so unegotistical and unselfconscious that he may not feel it as much as I think he does. . . .

The success of *St Joan* reaffirmed Shaw's position as Britain's foremost playwright.

*19 March.* [41 Grosvenor Road?]
Spent three days, one with Lion at Radlett, two with the Shaws. GBS in excellent spirits . . . His prestige since the publication of *St Joan* has bounded upwards, everywhere he is treated as a 'great man' and his income must be nearer thirty than twenty thousand a year! Charlotte purring audibly: these two are very happy together and both are full of kindness towards old friends and new. . . . At Charlotte's request I am sending them the four chapters . . . I have become rather morbid about the book, far too anxious for its success and counting too much *on its being a success.* I don't think Sidney quite likes it: he does his best to approve, still more to help me, but there is something about it that he not exactly resents, but to which he is unsympathetic. In his heart he fears I am over-valuing it, especially the extracts from the diaries; the whole thing is far too subjective, and all that part which deals with 'my creed' as distinguished from 'my craft' seems to him the sentimental scribblings of a woman, only interesting just because they are feminine. However, I have enjoyed writing it and the book as a whole will have some *value* as a description of 'Victorianism'. Old people ought to be *less* anxious for applause. Poor dears, I am afraid they are

more affected by personal vanity than the young. It is now or never with them!

*31 March.* [Passfield Corner]
In better spirits. Sidney also is enjoying what he calls 'walking through his part' at the House of Commons. He likes the life. I know he would miss it if he settled down here to do nothing but write and read. This house and garden is getting settled . . . I have got a bicycle, and when the weather is warmer I shall go further afield instead of mooning over the common near by. The book gets on apace. . . . If this book is successful I shall go on with another volume: *Our Partnership.* I await with some anxiety the opinion of the Shaws; they are sufficiently true friends to give an honest one.

*9 June. 2 a.m.* [Passfield Corner]
Indigestion and sleeplessness. The book drags on and I sometimes wonder whether I shall end it, or whether it will end me. . . . GBS has been thirty days ill with a nasty attack of influenza. In spite of his amazing success with *St Joan* he is dispirited for he, too, has become involved in a book which he cannot end – a book on socialism, designed to explain matters to a stupid woman. It will be a marvel if it is not a bad book and I think he knows it is, and yet will not let go. . . . Charlotte is intent on his starting another play instead of meandering on with this work on socialism. And I think she is right. He is a magnificent critic of life and consummate literary craftsman. He is absolutely futile as a constructive thinker. . . .

Robert Smillie (1857–1940) was the leader of the Miners' Federation, a pacifist and I.L.P. supporter.

*22 June.* [Passfield Corner]
Completely recovered my sanity about the book. The Shaws and the Laskis pricked the bubble which had blown up in my mind . . . I no longer think that it is going to be a literary success or add to my reputation, and some may say nasty things about it. . . . But today it is almost finished and it would be sheer cowardice to funk publishing it. . . .

Sidney reports that the joint meeting of the General Council of the T.U.C. and the Labour Party executive was most disheartening. Robert Smillie, with his little bodyguard of pseudo-Communists, is trying his level best to damage the P.L.P. and cut off trade union support from MacDonald . . . Certainly the Liberals must be smiling in very broad smiles over [his] revolutionary speeches . . . on the one hand, and, on the other, the vision of J. H. Thomas in frock-coat and top hat at Ascot and J.R.M. taking tea with their Majesties at the Air Force pageant! Poor old Labour movement: you will get the power your leaders deserve, and I fear it will be a minus quantity. . . .

What puzzles me is the gross discrepancy between the alarmist views, held not only by left-wing Labour men but also by competent Conservative and Liberals, about the industrial decadence of Great Britain – confronted by the absence of all *signs* of extreme poverty among the people at large. Compared with the 80s, even the early years of the twentieth century, there is no outward manifestation of extreme destitution: no beggars, few vagrants, no great and spontaneous demonstration of the unemployed, no 'bitter outcries' or sensational description of sweaters' dens and poverty-stricken homes, no Lord Mayor's Fund or soup-kitchens. The Communists are dwindling; socialism is certainly not making headway, and the more revolutionary the utterance of Labour men, the less inclined are the people of England to listen to them. . . . What is the explanation of this curious combination of the permanent unemployment of eleven per cent of the population with a general sense of comparative prosperity on the part of the bulk . . . Are we living in a fool's paradise fostered by the Press, are we living in some abstruse way on credit, running up debts which some day we shall have to pay?

*8 August.* [Passfield Corner]
. . . Sidney came down for good last week, with a heavy cold and considerably exhausted. He has quite made up his mind not to stand at the next election and has told Henderson so. It is clear he can be of little further use to the Labour Party; the turmoil within the party is too great; only a young and vigorous man can swim in those troubled waters . . .

*20 August.* [Passfield Corner]
There is today complete anarchy in opinion about sex relations. So far as I can make out . . . there is no objection to unfaithfulness to the marriage tie; no recognition that either husband or wife has any claim to the continued affection of the other, no insistence that legal marriage shall precede cohabitation. Some taboo is still maintained about homosexuality, as this is a criminal offence. . . . But today men and women can have what relations they like and no sensible person will shun them. . . .

As an instance I take the relation of Beveridge, the Director of the School of Economics, to Mrs Mair, the Secretary. Whether they are, or have been, technically 'lovers' I really don't know. But they are inseparable and have all the appearance of being more than friends. He, at any rate, is obviously infatuated and everyone sees it. What upsets my equanimity is watching the unfortunate husband's reaction . . . Mair is a distinguished civil servant and a cultivated and attractive man. He has accepted the position with benevolence and dignity. But anyone can see his misery . . . We like both Beveridge and Mrs Mair and they have been charming to us; but from the standpoint of a large educational establishment, with three thousand students of both sexes and mostly young, this relationship of the Director and the Secretary is not a desirable 'example'. And yet we all turn away and say, 'It is their affair'. . . .

*19 September.* [Passfield Corner]
. . . Sidney is optimistic in believing that the Conservative government will go forward in our direction; that exactly as the Labour government failed to go rapidly forward, so the Conservative government will find itself prevented from going backward. Public opinion in both cases will insist on the *middle way*, but it will be a collectivist middle way. In his heart of hearts I think he still believes in Fabian permeation of other parties as a more rapid way than the advent of a distinctly socialist government. . . .

*27 September.* [Passfield Corner]
Graham and Audrey Wallas here for two or three days. . . . we three spent the time we were not working in our separate sitting-rooms, in reaching each other's manuscript books and criticizing what we read! Graham brought twelve chapters down, Sidney submitted his great description of the eighteenth-century Poor Law, whilst I contributed my proofs. . . .

In kindliness and honesty Audrey is a fit mate for Graham. I respect her, even admire her; but she irritates and bores me and I could live more easily with many an inferior woman. Her combination of literary pretensions, practical incapacity, and queer self-consciousness – she is always deprecating her lack of personal or social distinction – is tedious and ugly. . . . She revealed a quite unexpected bitterness about Charlotte Shaw who, it appears, had resolutely refused to endorse GBS's invitation to them to stay at Ayot. 'We are summoned to lunch once in two years, but that is all we see of them.' As Graham was, next to Sidney, GBS's nearest friend, it was not very kind of Charlotte to ignore Audrey. Audrey told me that when in the early years of her marriage she asked Shaw (who had come down to see them at their cottage at Radlett) to bring Charlotte next time, he said 'My dear Audrey, Charlotte likes people according to the size of their income,' a saying that remains branded deep in her memory. . . .

*2 October. 2 a.m.* [Passfield Corner]
'The great surprise in the election of the Labour Party executive is the defeat of Mr Sidney Webb,' was announced in a clear tone of pleasant satisfaction over the wireless last night.

It was no surprise to me, though I confess to a slight shock when I heard it broadcast to millions of listeners! . . .

*23 October. 1 a.m.* [Passfield Corner]
Sleepless nights over these last few pages of the book on 'The Other One'. Can I dash in the portrait so as to make it attractive without the absurdity of over-appreciation by a loving wife? It must be lightly and swiftly done, without affectation or self-consciousness, indicated more than described. This last chapter is, I think, distinctly good if only I can give it a good end.

*29 October. 5 a.m.* [Passfield Corner]
Done it! and never before have I been so relieved to see the last words of a book, for never before have I been so utterly and painfully uncertain as to its value. . . . Added to this uncertainty is the unpleasantness of selling your personality as well as your professional skill. You are displaying yourself like an actress or an opera singer – you lose your privacy. But today the book is done and in spite of all opinion to the contrary, I believe it is well done! . . .

> Elizabeth Haldane (1862–1937), Haldane's sister, was a governor of the L.S.E. and the first woman magistrate in Scotland.

*19 November.* [41 Grosvenor Road]
. . . Lunched today with Haldane. I wonder whether it is the last time! The hand of death seemed to be moulding his features. To me it was inexpressibly sad watching him eating, drinking and smoking away his life, though he looks so far gone that what he does matters little. . . . He still goes to the House of Lords and speaks, and his mind seems clear

enough, but there is a look of vacancy in his face which is new. . . . As I watched him, I wondered whether he knows the end is near? Elizabeth, who was there, showed no sign of anxiety. Perhaps we are wrong. 'A death's head,' said Sidney as we left the house. . . .

*22 November.* [Passfield Corner]
The Shaws have been here for three days. Charlotte has taken a fancy to this cottage; or rather, she now dislikes Ayot and is glad to get away for visits. They are both at the top of their form. And they are good enough to be complimentary about the two last chapters of the book, quite unexpectedly so, especially GBS, who declares that my style has become like his and that he finds nothing to alter! . . . Meanwhile he is putting in a great deal of work on *The Intelligent Woman's Guide to Socialism* . . . He is also meditating another play on revolution or the coming of socialism. . . . What has always been disconcerting to me in GBS are the sudden revolutions in his ideas. . . . GBS never tests or finishes his processes of reasoning – it is all brilliantly expressed improvisations to meet new emergencies or carry out sudden impulses, usually dislikes and indignations. Bertrand Russell has the same characteristic.

*5 December.* [Passfield Corner]
. . . the book has exhausted health and strength and upset my state of mind. I have learnt a good deal from it. I have ruminated over my experience of life and the reflections have sometimes been pessimistic. Somewhere in my diary – 1890? – I wrote, 'I have staked all on the essential goodness of human nature.' I thought of putting the entry into the book. I did not do so because it was too near the truth! Looking back I realize how permanent are the evil impulses and instincts in man, how little you can count on changing some of these – for instance the greed of wealth and power – by any change in machinery. We must be continually asking for better things from our own and other persons' human nature. But shall we get sufficient response? . . . One reason for my happiness with Sidney is that *he* does not seem to have any evil impulses; he does not want to get the best of every bargain; he has an instinctive liking for equality and a definite impulse towards inconspicuous and unrewarded service. But then, as he is always saying, he has got my love, and what does he want more? . . .

Problems in the mining industry were continuing and would erupt the following year, as Beatrice predicted. William Graham (1887–1932) was

President of the Board of Trade 1929–31. The British Broadcasting Company was set up in 1922; broadcasting began in London on 14 November. J. F. S. Russell, 2nd Earl (1865–1931), was Parliamentary Under-Secretary, India Office, 1929–31. Arthur Ponsonby (1871–1946), Parliamentary Under-Secretary at the Foreign Office in the 1924, became Under-Secretary for the Dominions in 1929.

*23 December.* [Passfield Corner]
This year ends on a note of happiness and encouragement. Sidney has been re-elected on to the Parliamentary executive and I have my book and all arrangements for publication in the U.K. and U.S.A. finished and done with. . . . We are well established in our new home and like it better and better every day.

The Labour Party itself is in a wholesomer condition than it has been since the Labour government went out of office. . . . The P.M. has recovered his position to a certain extent, sufficient for his leadership in the country, and the saner members of the Front Bench – Henderson, Clynes, Graham – are distinctly in the ascendant. Against this is the mess being made of the miners' case . . . We are going to have an infernal row next summer unless Labour is willing to take the attack on hours and wages – first among the miners – lying down. . . .

To my mind by far the most significant event of the last two years is the spread of wireless and the admirable way in which the B.B.C. is using this stupendous influence over the lives of the people, in some ways greater than the written word because it is so amazingly selective and under deliberate control, and on the whole of an eminently right control. This new power must necessarily be a monopoly and cannot be left to Gresham's law of the bad coin driving out the good. . . . Moreover there is at present no pecuniary self-interest involved; no one is the richer or the poorer because one programme is adopted rather than another. And the result is certainly remarkable. Every item in the day's programme is not to one's taste, but the ensemble is admirable . . . But what a terrible engine of compulsory conformity in opinion and culture wireless *might* become. . . .

Gradually we are making ourselves a neighbourhood round our home. There are a few members of the Labour Party within easy motoring distance – the Snowdens, Ponsonbys and Lord Russell . . . Then there are various schoolteachers, a district nurse, a dissenting minister, friends of my gardener and his wife, more or less Labour in sympathy and with a good deal more to talk about than the ordinary *rentier*. I do not wish to live an isolated life. I accept the obligation of near neighbourhood, especially towards the intellectual proletariat . . . But I see no reason for knowing the gentry . . . even if they cared to know us . . . they would only know us out of curiosity and because we were 'personages'.

## ∽ 1926 ∽

The Webbs went on holiday to Italy at the beginning of January, where they interviewed journalists and politicians about Mussolini's regime. *My Apprenticeship* was published on 25 February.

### 18 February. [Passfield Corner]

Back at Passfield again, refreshed in mind but exhausted in body by our Sicilian tour. . . . Except that I did not find Sicily a health resort, the tour was a success. . . .

The present regime is a ghastly tragedy for all the intellectuals who are definitely non-Fascist, more especially, of course, the politicians and the journalists who find themselves not only robbed of their livelihood and their liberties as citizens but also physically threatened. To the ordinary man, who in Italy is not in the least interested in public affairs, the Mussolini government is a relief from anxiety and bother: there is more efficiency and regularity and honesty in public and private affairs. Also . . . Italy is, or appears to be, in the ascendant. Mussolini's bullying attitude towards Germany, Austria and France is an agreeable change from the old rule of 'poor relation'; and the Duce's bombastic utterances about the inheritance of the Roman Empire etc. are pleasant day-dreams . . .

On the eve of publication I am downcast! Courage, old woman, courage: be game to the end. And don't give way to the egotism of old age; live up to what old age *ought to be*, the impersonal beneficence of the Ancient unmoved by the opinion of a world he or she is about to leave. The book is done and cannot be undone . . .

### 1 March. [Passfield Corner]

Reviews of the book are unexpectedly good and my self-esteem ought to be more than satisfied! I have now . . . to rid my mind of the egotistical brooding over my own personality which has been induced by autobio-graphical writing; to concentrate on the history of the Poor Law . . . and to create a neighbourhood here of kindly sympathy and good will. . . .

*15 March. 2 a.m.* [Passfield Corner]

It is during sleepless hours in the night that I get things down in my diary; during the day I am either at work, or reading newspapers and interesting books, or listening to the wireless or wandering about the country, or merely chatting or brooding – I have no inclination to write. But in the loneliness and silence of the night, impressions and thoughts fly through my brain and if I refuse to express them I begin to worry. Also, to begin to write is an excuse for a cup of tea! . . .

Bertrand Russell and his wife have spent a week-end here this spring. He has settled down to happy domesticity and the agreeable task of earning his livelihood by brilliant thinking, brilliant writing and still more brilliant lectures. . . . His wife suits him. She also has improved since I first saw her, softened by motherhood and admiration of her great man, and refined by intellectual companionship and hard work – for she lectures incessantly during the winter on birth control and maternity clinics. . . .

*30 March. 5 a.m.* [Passfield Corner]

Haldane's imposing review of my book, accorded the pride of place in the *Observer* of the 28th . . . symbolizes by its friendly, critical attitude our longstanding and close association with this remarkable personality.

For more reasons than one, the book has roused some antagonism in his mind. Perhaps he had a right to expect more recognition of his spontaneous and useful friendship to Sidney and me during our engagement and on our marriage. But I doubt whether this slight subconscious grievance did more than release what is and has been a genuine and permanent judgement about us – the sort of judgement which we would give in conversation with an intimate friend. 'The Webbs are very able, whether as writers or organizers; they are honest and public-spirited; they are remarkably hard-working and purposeful. But alike in intellectual gifts, personal culture and social standing, they are restricted in range – they are in fact "little people" who have accomplished a useful but not outstanding important book.'

And of course in one sense he is right; we have, in fact, never claimed to be otherwise than useful citizens. How useful depends on the rightness of our particular scale of values. . . . Haldane and we have worked together without enquiring too curiously about each other's instinctive aims. But now and again our diverse scale of values have obviously clashed, and then we have become for a time antagonistic or indifferent to each other. There has even been not a little mutual contempt. . . .

A second Royal Commission into the mining industry, appointed in 1925 under Herbert Samuel, published its report in March 1926. It called for reduced wages but rejected the mine-owners' request for longer hours. Negotiations between the Miners' Federation and the Mining Association deadlocked, despite T.U.C. and government intervention. On Monday 3 May the public learned that it faced a general strike at midnight. On 12 May the T.U.C. called off the strike on the understanding that talks would be resumed. A second strike began the next day, when men returning to work found themselves refused entry or else accepted only with reduced wages. Those who had gone on strike to help the miners now found the miners abandoned and their own livelihoods threatened. In the next few days settlements were made in these industries, but the coal dispute ran until the end of December with the miners losing on all counts. In the next few years unemployment in the industry reached tragic proportions.

*14 April. Passfield Corner*
Back from our Easter visit to Seaham – a gloomy business, with the dark prospect of an embittered strike hanging over our little meetings of miners and their wives.

The beginning of another long spell of work coincides with the first page of another diary book, and the two together incline me to look inward and tell what I am thinking . . . I am perpetually brooding on my inability to make clear even to myself, let alone to others, why I believe in religious mysticism, why I hanker after a Church with its communion of the faithful, with its religious rites and its religious discipline and above all with its definite code of conduct. . . . Somehow or other we must have the habit of prayer, the opportunity for the confession of sin and for the worship of goodness, if we are to attain personal holiness. . . . I have no home for my religious faculty, I wander about disconsolate – that is the root of my indifference to life. . . . I am not at peace with myself. I have failed to solve the problem of life, of man's relation to the universe and therefore to his fellow man. But I have a growing faith that it will be solved by a combination of truth-seeking and personal holiness, of the scientific mind with the religious life. When will such a leader arise who will unite the intellect of an Aristotle, a Goethe or an Einstein with the moral genius of a Buddha, a Christ or a St Francis d'Assisi?

*3 May. 4 a.m. On the night of the great strike.* [Passfield Corner]
'The Decay of the Capitalist System' has certainly begun in the biggest and most characteristic of British industries . . . Why the capitalists of

the coalfields are so dreary and incompetent a lot is a curious question, but the verdict that they have been and are wholly unable to run their business with decent efficiency has been given over and over again and by all parties in the state. There is not a Conservative politician or journalist of repute that dare advise that the colliery owners be left to go on as they are doing at present. Each successive court of enquiry, whatever its composition, has declared against them. But alas! this conversion of those in power has been more apparent than real. They have not any honest determination to do the job; they want to *seem* to do it but to leave it undone. . . .

The General Strike will fail; the General Council may funk it . . . or the men may slink back to work in a few days. We have always been against a General Strike. But the problem of the collapse of capitalism in the coal industry will remain – and woe to the governing class that refuses to solve it by taking control, in one form or another, of the organization of the industry. . . .

*14 May. General Strike, 1926* [Passfield Corner]
Little more than a nine days' world wonder . . . In the first two or three days there was complete stoppage and paralysis of trade, but hosts of volunteers started skeleton services, and Hyde Park and Regent's Park became great camps of soldiers living in tents, with improvised shelters for the store of milk and other commodities. Not a shot has been fired, not a life is lost. In one town the police and strikers played cricket, and the victory of the strikers is published to ten million listeners by the government-controlled wireless! Slowly buses and trams begin to appear; the London taxi-cab drivers decide to 'come out', but the next morning the buses are seen in the London streets obviously driven by professionals!

On Monday, the seventh day of the strike, Sidney and I travel up by the milk-train to London – it is crowded but not a single remark did we hear about the strike; the third-class passengers at any rate were unusually silent, even for English passengers, more bored than alarmed – and the same silence is in the streets, more like a Sunday with the shops open, but with no one shopping. Just a very slight reminiscence of the first days of the Great War, the parking of innumerable motors in the squares and by-streets and here and there officers in khaki, even one or two armoured cars in attendance on strings of motor buses piled up with food. It is characteristic that government lorries, sometimes driven by army engineers, are labelled 'food only', as if to appeal to the strikers not to interfere with them. No strain or fear on the faces of the citizens male or female, only a sort of amused boredom. Universal condemnation of the General Strike but widespread sympathy with the miners. . . .

. . . On Thursday morning, the very day of the 'call-off' of the strike, I motored with Susan [Lawrence] into her constituency [East Ham]. . . . What will those East End workers think who listened to Susan yesterday, coming straight from the centre of things, to tell them that they were winning hands down, when they heard the news a few hours later: General Strike called off unconditionally? What is the good of having professional brainworkers to represent you, if they refuse to give you the honest message of intelligence but treat you to a florid expression of the emotion which *they* think the working class are feeling or ought to be feeling? . . .

*18 May.* [Passfield Corner]
Churchill's announcement in the House today that the General Strike will have cost the government no more than three-quarters of a million – a sum which the death of a couple of millionaires will pay – puts the cap of ridicule on the heroics of the General Strike. The three million strikers will have spent some three million pounds of trade union money and lost another four or five in wages . . . The General Strike of 1926 is a grotesque tragedy. The Labour leaders and their immediate followers, whether political or individual, live in the atmosphere of alternating day-dreams and nightmares, day-dreams about social transformation brought about in the twinkling of an eye, and visions of treachery in their own ranks and malignancy on the other side – all equally fantastic and without foundation. We are all of us just good-natured stupid folk. The worst of it is that the governing classes are as good-natured and stupid as the labour movement. . . . I have lost my day-dreams, I have only the nightmare left – the same sort of nightmare I had during the Great War: that European civilization is in the course of dissolution. . . .

*31 May.* [Passfield Corner]
There remains over from this sensational episode of the General Strike, the miners' lock-out – a far bigger challenge to capitalist enterprise. The million miners are obdurate and no one can take their place . . . There are only two ways of beating them: sheer starvation, or a sufficient importation of coal to make them feel that the struggle was useless. But dare the government let them and their wives and children starve? . . . If there were to be any sensational stoppage of food in the pit villages or if coal were to be freely imported, a drastic sympathetic strike would burst out again. . . .

Sir Almroth Wright (1861–1947) was a bacteriologist at St Mary's Hospital, London, who introduced anti-typhoid inoculation. The political play Beatrice refers to is *The Apple Cart* (1929), written, Shaw told Beatrice in a letter of 5 September 1939, 'to your order'.

*23 June.* [Passfield Corner]

GBS and Charlotte here for the inside of a week. Since we were with them in April he has been seriously ill with kidney trouble and continuous temperatures – threatenings of organic disease. Now Almroth Wright tells him that he has apparently cured himself. It has been a depressing time; Charlotte says he has lost interest in everything, though he went on working at his book. . . . also he is obsessed with his correspondence. . . . But ill or not ill, he is just the same dear friend and somewhat sobered but still brilliant sprite that used to stay with us at The Argoed over thirty years ago. . . . he is less vain than he used to be – indeed, he is not vain at all; he has lost all the old bitterness, and with it the capacity for invective. But that is perhaps due to his outstanding success. The wonder is, not that he has lost the spirit of revolt, but that he has retained the demand for equality and his consideration for the underdog. He is brooding over a new play – a political play. . . .

*18 July. 2 a.m.* [Passfield Corner]

The last few nights have been so hot and sleepless that I have spent some hours on a portrait of Sidney for use in *Our Partnership* . . . I have honestly tried to describe him as I see him objectively with all his defects, not as I, in my weaker moments, should like my beloved to appear to the world. I know that what is true of other lovers is true of me – it is silly to touch up the photograph, to smooth out all the ugly lines and disproportions; the outcome is a meaningless human being . . . few would like so faultless a person. Pity and loyalty as well as admiration and dependence are among the ingredients of love. And how can one pity or be loyal to an all-perfect being? Meanwhile my share of the Poor Law book does not get done – in the main because I am preoccupied with preparations for the Labour fête on the 31st – an annual undertaking for us; and expensive as well as troublesome. . . .

Perhaps more distracting has been my worrying about Jessie and her influence on the young servant who has been brought in to help her from the village. Jessie Norris has been with me for fourteen years: she is, in many respects, an excellent servant and I have a real liking for her, and I think she was fond of me. But bottles of whisky disappeared at a greater rate than usual. I checked her entries by keeping an account myself and the result was unmistakable! Which raises doubts as to her trustworthiness in other matters, a horrid state of things. For the last two years I have been so absorbed in the book that I have been a careless housekeeper; also I am getting old and my memory fails me when I am working hard. The result has been an unwelcome rise in weekly expenditure which we cannot afford even if we ought to allow it. After consulting Sidney – who also is attached to Jessie as an old servant – we decided 'to wait and see'. . . .

*24 July. 2 a.m.* [Passfield Corner]
Thirty-four years ago, on 23 July, we were married, and yesterday we celebrated it by spending the whole day together like two young lovers, driving in the morning to Petersfield to redeem the land tax on this plot of land and going for a long walk in the afternoon, finishing up by listening to a symphony concert over the wireless in the evening. The Other One is extraordinarily well and happy; perhaps getting a wee bit restive at dissipating so much time at Westminster and thus not getting on with the book. . . . For my part, except for my chronic melancholy – perhaps *indifference to life* is the better phrase – due to declining vitality, I am content with this last year. The labour and worry spent on *My Apprenticeship* has been justified, so far as public appreciation is concerned. 'Original and distinguished' has been the general verdict. It is clear that the book will influence thought, and be read by students and thinkers and quoted by future historians. . . . My literary reputation has gone up considerably . . .

Lord de la Warr (1900–76) was an aristocratic convert to Labour.

*2 August.* [Passfield Corner]
Our gathering of near on two thousand members of the Labour parties of Hampshire, Surrey and Sussex, arriving in eighty charabancs, to listen to MacDonald and Margaret Bondfield, with Ponsonby, Russell, de la Warr and ourselves as minor performers, went off brilliantly . . . The secret is that with charabancs and the increasing habit of jaunts of town workers into the country . . . these garden-parties are bound to attract large numbers . . . There is the risk of bad weather, but even here it can be almost overcome if you provide, as we did, a monster marquee. Our luck was a delightful warm grey day ending in a burst of sunshine when J.R.M. was giving his second speech and final farewell. . . . The leader of the Labour Party was in his best form. . . . But his conversation

is not entertaining or stimulating . . . When he and I walked round the garden together he talked exclusively about his weekly visits to Christie's and the pieces of old furniture he was picking up. Directly you turn the conversation off trivial personalities on to subjects . . . J.R.M. dries up and looks bored. Not once did we *discuss* anything whatsoever, and even the anecdotes led nowhere. . . . Ramsay MacDonald is a magnificent substitute for a leader. . . . Our great one has yet to come. Shall I live to see him? Or will it be *she* who must be obeyed?

*5 August.* [Passfield Corner]
'Look for the man.' In poor Jessie's case a dissolute married man, who has already seduced a well-to-do woman, got married to her and is today living on an allowance she makes him to be rid of his claims. He is the son of our builder and has frequently worked here. This unfortunate affair which, unknown to me, was one of the scandals of the village, ended in the infatuated Jessie outrunning all discretion by letting him sleep with her in the scullery, in sight of the little girl from the village. Here is the explanation of all the rest of her misbehaviour – pilfering whisky and perhaps other things, underhand dealings of all sorts and general untrustfulness. She seemed dumbfounded when I said she must go; apparently she has counted on my affection for an old servant to cover all her sins – not a flattering estimate of my capacity as a mistress. . . .

The break-up of all the conventions about sexual relations makes the relation of mistress and servant far more difficult than it was in the good old times of recognized Christian ethics. How far has the mistress the *right* to demand chastity in the woman servant? In London the question does not necessarily arise. Who knows and who cares? In a village *everything* is known and talked about. . . .

J. M. Keynes (1883–1946), an economist noted for *The Economic Consequences of the Peace* (1919), was married to the ballet dancer Lydia Lopokova (1892–1981) and was one of the central figures in the Bloomsbury Group.

*9 August.* [Passfield Corner]
There must be scarcity of politically constructive minds if J. M. Keynes seems such a treasure! Hitherto he has not attracted me – brilliant, supercilious, and not sufficiently patient for sociological discovery even if he had the heart for it, I should have said. But then I had barely seen him; also I think his love marriage with the fascinating little Russian

dancer has awakened his emotional sympathies with poverty and suffering. For when I look around I see no other man who might discover how to control the wealth of nations in the public interest. . . . He would make a useful member of a Cabinet, but would he ever get there? Certainly not as a member of one of the present Front Benches. I do not know which one – Conservative or Labour – he would despise most. As for the rank and file! Heaven help them. . . .

*21 August.* [Passfield Corner]
The agony of the miners' resistance to the owners' terms has begun; how long and how fierce it may be no one can say . . . Taken with the failure of the General Strike it is a big catastrophe; it is the biggest defeat trade unionism has ever experienced . . . But, as in the Great War, it is very doubtful whether the victors will not lose as much as the vanquished. . . .

The thought of all this needless misery, the burden of debt in the miners' homes, the disheartening unbelief in leaders and causes, is a nightmare made worse by a subconsciousness that Sidney and I, though associated with the miners, have not been able to give a helping hand. We have simply stood on one side. All we could have given is money and to give money has seemed to us at best throwing it away. . . .

All the same I feel horribly mean, living here in comfort and peace, whilst the battle rages and the lines of the workers' army begin to waver before the savage onslaught of the employers. It would have been easier to have sent £100 and – I will not say saved one's conscience – but saved one's reputation! 'We sent £100 to the Miners' Relief Fund,' one could have whispered sympathetically to our Seaham friends. 'We did not see what else we could do,' one could have added . . . Heaven know what we shall say when we get up to Seaham in October. It is clear we can't tell the truth even if the battle is over, which it may not be in Durham. In the first hour of defeat the truth would be far too cruel for human endurance.

G. D. H. Cole had directed the Labour Research Department until 1924, resigning when it came under Communist Party control in 1924. His wife Margaret (1893–1980), a Cambridge graduate, was its secretary before their marriage in 1918.

*5 September.* [Passfield Corner]
G. D. H. Cole and his wife – always attractive because they are at once disinterested and brilliantly intellectual and, be it added, agreeable to

look at – stayed a week-end with us and later came on to the T.U.C. Middle age finds them saner and more charitable in their outlook. Cole still dismisses this man or that with 'I hate him,' but it is the remnant of a mannerism, for he no longer means it. He is still a fanatic but he is a fanatic who has lost his peculiar faith. . . . Despite a desire to be rebels against all conventions, the Coles are the last of the puritans. . . .

*10 September.* [Passfield Corner]
Two days at the Bournemouth Trades Union Congress. The same old crowd (mostly grey-headed, *not* bald-headed, for the British Labour Party keeps its hair on, actually as well as metaphorically!) of heavy solid men meeting punctually at 9.30 in the morning and adjourning five minutes before the time in the afternoon, a habit which amazes our Continental comrades. The same sensible procedure, strictly enforced, the same orderliness and unfailing good nature and, in spite of unemployment and empty trade union chests, the same jokes and laughter. Behind these persistent traits there was a difference . . . There is almost a note of panic in the talk . . . 'Capitalism is not dead – it is not weakening,' was the burden of the speeches. The miners sat silent and depressed . . . We ourselves felt like ghosts – 'Ancients' – coming back from the backwoods of historical research to our old haunts, there to discover other ghosts wandering among a gathering of bewildered and frightened children. . . .

*18 September.* [Passfield Corner]
I imagine one of the refinements of the future hedonistic society will be that whilst the unwanted child will be prevented from coming into life, the Ancient, who is tired of life, will be allowed to leave it in a painless and dignified way. From the standpoint of personal and race happiness I am more doubtful about birth control than I am about the freedom to depart! The memory of poor little Mother's death struggle and of Father's long-drawn-out senility, of Lallie Holt's slow self-poisoning, of Mary Playne's loss of memory, of Maggie's melancholy and neglected ending, of the unnecessary horror of Blanche's suicide – all point to an art of dying which will include a voluntary exist before life has become meaningless or troublesome. Whether this act would be able to adjust the individual's desire to live with the social inexpediency of his being alive is the crux of the question. . . . At present a voluntary departure, a refusal to outstay your welcome, is a slur on your own capacity for a useful and happy existence and a reflection on the kindness and

generosity of your relations and friends. In the case of the voluntary death of an aged person, perhaps even of a person who is hopelessly sick or mentally defective, 'the tragic death of' ought to read 'the happy ending of'!

*20 September.* [Passfield Corner]
Jessie Norris leaves us tomorrow after fifteen years' service. . . . Alys Russell was anxious to have her – she knew and liked her – and though I told her about the scandal she was willing to take her on trust . . . If we were going again to live in London I should certainly risk keeping her – so I suppose I am justified in allowing Alys to risk it. But it has been a horrid business and rather a disreputable one, with a young girl from the village to watch and report on the intrigue to all and sundry. And I, who have always prided myself on having no trouble about servants! . . .

Meanwhile our gardener Oliver and his wife are becoming confidential servants. Oliver I selected from a host of others – gardeners are a drug on the labour market – largely on account of his very respectable-looking wife and on his record. . . . All the same a gardener and a garden – twelve acres of land – is a luxury and costs at least £200 . . . but then without a gardener it would be difficult to provide electricity, water, vegetables and protection for the house and its inmates when Sidney is away. It is the principal extra expense of living in the country . . . If our income from books (about £500 a year) were to fail us we could barely afford to live here. . . .

*2 October.* [Passfield Corner]
The last days of the spell of work on Volume I of English Poor Law History; yesterday we sent the last chapter to the printer and tomorrow we start off on our autumn tour – London, Margate (Labour Party conference) and Seaham. . . . Whether this ponderous tome will get itself read except by a few highly specialized students, is doubtful, but taken with Volume II we shall have written a definitive history of English Poor Law. As the work has proceeded I see that it will really sum up a good deal of our social philosophy. . . .

We go to Seaham with a £100 subscription to the relief fund in our pocket, but what shall we say?

*24 October.* [Passfield Corner]
Back from autumn visit to Seaham. In the six days we had twelve meetings – crowded-out meetings – and we saw many of our leading

supporters. The surface facts show no exceptional distress; indeed the pit villages look clean and prosperous and the inhabitants healthy (death-rate unusually low). Various people told us that the men and boys had benefited by the rest, sun and open air and abstinence from alcohol and tobacco. And the women were freed from coal-dust and enjoying regular hours, whilst the school-children, through the ample supply of first-class food (eleven meals each week at a cost of 3s 6d per child at wholesale prices) were certainly improved in health and happiness. The one want was clothing and boots, and our gift of £100 to the Repair Fund was much appreciated. . . .

The state of mind of the miners and their wives was less easy to discover than the state of their health. I had a lunch of the thirty chairwomen and secretaries of the Women's Sections and a delegate conference of about four hundred representative members. They all seemed in good spirits, hard at work running relief funds and collecting money by whist drives, football matches (women players), dances and socials; they had raised, in the last two months, £1,700 for the central relief fund for pregnant and lying-in women and infants. Some of the lodges were paying a few shillings a week to the unmarried men; the Guardians were paying 12s a week to the wives and 4s a week (3s 6d deducted for school meals) to each child. But to return to the state of mind of the women. There was certainly no sign of strain. As I looked at the gathering of four hundred miners' wives and daughters in their best dresses, and the prettily decorated tea-tables with piles of cake and bread and butter, it might have been a gathering of prosperous lower middle-class women. . . .

The men and boys were more silent and sullen; some of the elder men were anxious and wistful. Sidney's speeches were not encouraging about the future; and though the audiences were respectful, even affectionate in their attitude towards him and his wife, it was clear that they were disappointed with his guarded and deprecatory attitude towards the strike, and some of them said so. . . . We came back gloomy about the future but we can do little or nothing to help to make it better. We gave our £100 not because it would help but out of gratitude to the miners for their generosity towards us – we were paying back some of our election expenses – that was all!

T. E. Lawrence (1888–1935), 'Lawrence of Arabia', wrote *The Seven Pillars of Wisdom*. He was killed on a motorbike the Shaws had given him.

*8 November.* [41 Grosvenor Road]
A hectic seven days in London. . . . Sunday we spent with the Shaws. . . . At lunch Colonel Lawrence came in to bid the Shaws farewell before leaving for India; he was in private's uniform. . . . an attractive and arresting figure, obviously self-centred and self-conscious. He was more interesting to look at than to listen to . . . More than a bit of a poseur . . .

Last night Susan [Lawrence] and I entertained the Parliamentary Labour Party and today Sidney and I lunched with the Oswald Mosleys . . . So ends my week's dissipation. . . . A week in London means talk, endless talk and unaccustomed food and hours, small doses of alcohol and too many cigarettes – consequent unhealthiness. In the country one works too hard. Don't fuss over the last years of life, a voice tells me. . . . The Ancient should fade away from the sight of fellow mortals noiselessly leaving, like the Cheshire Cat, a smile, and then the memory of a smile. There is comedy in the way we old people – Shaws, Haldane, Graham Wallases, etc. etc. – gaze and listen to each other, watching for the signs of senility and wondering whether the symptoms are as apparent in ourselves as they are in all the others!

*15 November.* [Passfield Corner]
The Miners' Federation delegate meeting surrendered yesterday to the government terms – the worst possible terms, barely better than unconditional district surrender . . . No critic or enemy of the trade union movement could have planned or even imagined so catastrophic a defeat. . . . The shock may disintegrate the present industrial order; but I cannot see how it can lay the foundation for a better one. . . .

*2 December.* [Passfield Corner]
. . . The fact that a considerable number of articles have disappeared, under the domestic dispensation of Jessie and Alice during the last months of their service, has left me a prey to doubts about the honesty of everyone, and conscious of my own stupidity and helplessness in not preventing it. And under black skies and perpetual rain, with Sidney away all the week, I connect these personal mishaps with a rising fear of a general decay of morals and manners . . . Meanwhile men and women, each one with his or her peculiar interests and troubles, come and go, claiming my sympathy and asking my advice; and I drudge on day by day with the book, varied these last two days by dictating the Seaham letter – a tiresome task – because what *can* we say to those sick-hearted and downtrodden folk? My brain whirls round quicker and quicker and

I get more and more sleepless, and wonder whether life would be tolerable if Sidney were gone or I were to become incapable of writing books and getting them published. But then am I not supremely fortunate, at nearly seventy years of age, to have devoted mutual love and absorbing work which is recognized as useful? – recognized the other day by the University of Munich sending honorary doctorates to Sidney and Beatrice Webb – the *jointness* being a pleasing touch, a recognition not only of our work but of our love.

~ 1927 ~

*22 January.* [Passfield Corner]
Enter my seventieth year: I am well and happy and hard at work on the second volume of the Poor Law. This book will be our last big piece of research. . . .

> Clive Bell (1881–1964), an art critic, was married to Virginia Woolf's sister Vanessa, a painter. Virginia Woolf attacked Arnold Bennett in her essay 'Mr Bennett and Mrs Brown'. She was just completing *To the Lighthouse* (1927). Beatrice had probably been reading *Mrs Dalloway* (1925).

*6 February.* [Passfield Corner]
The Leonard Woolfs spent the week-end here – we had lost sight of them and were glad to renew relations with this exceptionally gifted pair. A dozen years ago, when we first saw them, they were living under a cloud – she on the borderline of lunacy, he struggling desperately to keep her out of a mental home. For some years it seemed doubtful whether he would succeed. Now the cloud has passed away. Her appearance has altered: instead of a beautiful but loosely knit young woman, constantly flushing and with a queer, uncertain, almost hysterical manner, she is, though still beautiful, a spare, self-contained ascetic-looking creature, startlingly like her father, Leslie Stephen; the same tall, stooping figure, exquisite profile; refined, an almost narrow and hard intellectuality of expression. Woolf also is matured and has lost his nervous shyness. Wholly unconventional in their outlook on life and manners, belonging rather to a decadent set (Clive Bell is her brother-in-law) but themselves puritanical, they are singularly attractive to talk to. In one matter they are not up-to-date, for they are rigid secularists, regarding theology or even mysticism as *l'infâme*. Here his Jewish blood comes in: he quite

clearly is revolted by the Christian myth, the anger of a Jew at an apostate from the Judaic faith. (Considering the persecution of the Jews right up to the nineteenth century by the Christian Church, I wonder why they are not more obsessed by hatred of the author of Christianity.) He is an anti-imperialist fanatic but otherwise a moderate in Labour politics – always an opponent of 'workers' control' and 'proletarianism'. She is uninterested in politics – wholly literary – an accomplished critic of style and a clever artist in personal psychology, disliking the 'environmental' novel of the late Victorian times, especially its latest exponent, Arnold Bennett. Like other works of the new school of novelists, I do not find her work interesting outside its craftsmanship, which is excellent but *précieuse*. Her men and women do not interest me – they don't seem worth describing in such detail; the mental climate in which they live seems strangely lacking in light, heat, visibility and variety; it is a dank mist of insignificant and monotonous thoughts and feelings, no predominant aims, no powerful reactions from their mental environment, a curious impression of automatic existence when one state of mind follows another without any particular reason. To the aged Victorian this soullessness is depressing. Doubtless our insistence on a purpose, whether for the individual or the universe, appears to them a delusion and a pernicious delusion.

The last hours with them were spent in a raging argument about denominational education and the validity of religious mysticism. They were against toleration. What was 'manifestly false' was *not* to be *taught* at the public expense and not to be *thought* by persons above a certain level of intelligence who claimed to be honest with themselves and other people. I pleaded for 'the endowment of error', and threatened them with fundamentalism, or Roman Catholicism, if they insisted on universal and compulsory sectarianism.

*7 February.* [Passfield Corner]
Ellen Wilkinson [(1891–1947)] reached here on Friday for lunch in a state of collapse from over-speaking at great mass meetings . . . I have known her slightly for ten or twelve years; she was one of the Guild Socialists and University Federation group of 1913–19. The daughter of a Lancashire cotton spinner of rebellious temper and religious outlook, she passed from the elementary school to the pupil teacher centre, from thence, on a scholarship, into Manchester University, where she took a good degree. After a year as a suffrage agitator, she became an organizer of the rapidly growing Co-operative Employees' Union [later the Union

of Shop, Distributive and Allied Workers] and finally landed herself in the House of Commons in 1924 as M.P. for Middlesbrough. 'The mighty atom,' she was immediately nicknamed. For the first session she was the darling of the House; in the next session she became a formidable debater, and now, as 'Miss Perky', she is somewhat under a cloud of disparagement, suffering the penalty of immediate popularity and premature success. She is amazingly vital and a first-rate debater. . . . Her opinions do not strike old people like ourselves as wise or particularly relevant . . . 'Ellen Wilkinson, regarded as a practical politician, is a fool,' says Sidney. But the House of Commons, and the amenities of social life it brings with it, are taming her spirit and she is becoming, unknown to herself, moulded for the Front Bench and eventually for office. . . .

*5 March.* [Passfield Corner]
I think of Sidney as an optimist – and so he is . . . But when the other day I asked him whether he would accept another life – beginning afresh in the same sort of circumstances – if it were offered him, he answered that, on balance, he thought he would not care to risk it; the whole business was too meaningless, or rather too uncertain and unknowable in its meaning, to make the risk of personal unhappiness worthwhile. That is *my* predominant feeling. . . .

*27 March. 4 a.m.* [Passfield Corner]
Struck work. For the last month I have been doing little at the book; every morning I have worked as best I could, reading and dictating, getting dizzier and dizzier and seeming to lose not to gain my grip of the subject. At night I cannot sleep and when I do drop off I awake in some sort of nightmare – all of which means that my reserve strength is exhausted. So I have decided to take five weeks' rest from any attempt to work, ending up with a week with Kate at Beachy Head. . . .

*14 April.* [Passfield Corner]
It is seventeen days since I struck work, and I am no better – the whizzing in my right ear and the buzzing in my head gets continuously more troublesome, and my capacity for either walking or reading grows less and less. . . . I have had these nervous breakdowns before. One of the worst was in the summer and autumn of 1900. I used to go out on the Yorkshire moors and cry from depression. This I cured by starvation. Another spell in 1916, perhaps more severe, was accentuated by war neurosis, and our first experience of personal unpopularity and depreciation. Today we

have no reason for discouragement except the coming of old age, which being inevitable and universal it is cowardly to resent. . . .

The Trade Disputes Act was being debated. It declared sympathetic strikes illegal and abolished the political levy.

### 23 April. 41 Grosvenor Road

Back from Seaham. The miners and their wives are deep down in gloomy bewilderment, the responsible ones deploring the mess made by their leaders, despairing about the condition of the industry and furiously angry about the Trade Union Bill, the irresponsible ones talking vaguely about another strike. . . .

### 8 May. [Passfield Corner]

Tom Jones, whom I have not seen to talk to since the Reconstruction Committee time – except for the Sankey Commission episode – spent a week-end here . . . From his account, Baldwin is stupider and weaker than we thought. He lives an isolated life, never reads or talks with experts and has a horror of clever brains 'like Keynes and the Webbs'!!!

. . . The Great Ones – those actually exercising power – have no time to solve the questions submitted to them . . . Their success or failure as governors of men will depend on whether they can acquire this knowledge second-hand . . . Jones says that Lloyd George's great quality was his readiness to get this knowledge and to be intimate with anyone who could help him. Which I think is true. Winston had that gift of accessibility and eagerness to know. Haldane also, and – in a certain but much more limited fashion, because of his indolence and fastidious aloofness – A. J. Balfour. . . . 'He and Haldane are the only statesmen who really care for the advancement of science and learning,' was Jones's opinion. . . .

### 24 May. [Passfield Corner]

GBS and Charlotte staying here; Sidney and I reading proofs of *The Intelligent Woman's Guide to Socialism and Capitalism* and giving him our criticism. . . . In our old age Charlotte and I have become affectionately intimate. . . . However self-centred her activities may be, she has developed admirable manners and a pleasing and cheerful personality. Like a perfectly appointed house there is fascination in an exquisitely clothed and cared-for person, if those artifices are combined with personal dignity and graciousness. Certainly she holds fast GBS's respect and affection; he recognizes her value to him not merely as a devoted wife but as an appropriate complement to his own distinction, restful at home and more than creditable abroad.

*3 June.* [Passfield Corner]
. . . I am no longer fit for the friction of visitors staying in the house – the most I can bear is two nights, and I prefer one! This Whitsun I have Kate Courtney and Maud Keary [Kate's companion] staying ten days or more and various persons coming to tea or lunch during the week; consequently I am sleepless and worried, and long to see the last of my guests. Kate is a dear and generous old lady. The restlessness of old age takes the harmless form of dozens of little walks round the garden, and up and down the drive, in the intervals of ethical thoughts and sayings on public affairs – more especially, foreign affairs, interspersed with proportional representation propaganda. . . .

*20 September.* [Passfield Corner]
. . . For the last eight weeks Sidney has been working continuously, from morning to night, whilst I have been putting in a regular morning's work every day of the week. . . . The book is a monstrous performance – one of the most monstrous, in its bulk and weight and elaborate and meticulous detail, that the Webbs have perpetrated during their thirty-five years of partnership! . . . Where I think we went seriously wrong in the Minority Report was in suggesting that we knew *how to prevent unemployment.* We did not. All we knew was that it was high time to set about getting this knowledge . . .

> Jane Wells, whose marriage to H. G. Wells had survived despite his notorious promiscuity, had died of cancer. Charlotte Shaw was embarrassed by Wells's panegyric: 'It was hideous – terrible and frightful,' she wrote to T. E. Lawrence on 10 October.

*1 October. Passfield*
Our days at Roker were filled in with Sidney's seven meetings, and my usual lunch to the thirty officials of the Women's Sections and the Federation meeting in the afternoon – the mornings being taken up with Poor Law interviews and expeditions. Having settled that Sidney retires at the end of this Parliament, our visit was spiritually perfunctory, our chief interest being who will be his successor . . .

Meanwhile GBS has created a sensation; he has gone out of his way to testify to the excellence of Mussolini's dictatorship . . . His argument seems to be that either the Haves or the Have-Notes must seize power and *compel* all to come under the Fascist or the Communist plough. It is a crude and flippant attempt at reconstruction . . . It will injure GBS's reputation far more than it will the democratic institutions in Great Britain. But it reinforces the Italian tyranny. It is only fair to add that this naive faith in a superman, before whose energy and genius all must bow down, is not a new feature in the Shaw mentality. What is new and deplorable is the absence of any kind of sympathetic appreciation of the agony that the best and wisest Italians are today going through, any appreciation of the mental degradation as implied in the suppression of all liberty of act, of thought and of speech.

He and Charlotte lunched with us the day we passed through London . . . He was very insistent that we should agree with him, and peculiarly exasperating in his dialectic. So we all got rather hot, but presently I turned away and talked to Charlotte about Jane Wells's death and funeral, and Sidney tried to turn the conversation with GBS on to other subjects. . . .

[?24 November 41 Grosvenor Road?]
Out of curiosity I attended the Shaw lecture on 'Democracy and Delusion'. An utter failure . . . He hammered and hammered on absolute equality of income and compulsion to work as the be-all and end-all of social organization. This could only be brought about by a dictatorship. . . .

The audience became more and more bewildered and when he sat down at ten o'clock – in order, as he remarked, to avoid any questions – there was the feeblest clapping I have ever heard at Kingsway Fabian lectures, and a hurried and silent departure of depressed men and women. He himself seemed down-hearted, and observed that he must 'give the lecture a good many times' before he could make his points clear. If he does, he will not add to his reputation! . . .

Waldorf Astor (1879–1952) was Conservative M.P. for Plymouth from 1910 until the death of his father in 1919, when he succeeded to the peerage. His American-born wife, Nancy (1879–1964), was elected to succeed him, becoming the first woman to take her seat in the House of Commons. The Astor home at Cliveden became a notorious political and social centre.

*5 December. A week-end at Ayot*

GBS and Charlotte were in excellent spirits – just a wee bit apologetic and wistful about GBS's escapade. The lecture was a 'dead failure', he cheerily remarked. 'I ought to have rehearsed it. I lost the trend of the argument.' So I gave him a bit of our mind about it, put gently. . . . There seems neither poetry nor reason nor common sense in GBS's state of mind. . . . He no longer subscribes to the Fabian Society; he has never subscribed to the Labour Party. All that he gives is an annual lecture or speech, which is accepted, not on its merits, but because it brings men and money into the hall. . . . The sooner he gets back to his plays the better for all concerned. In his old age he is not fit for the criticism of public affairs. . . . he has lost his pity for suffering. He has become complacent with the world of wealth and leisure he lives in. Does he really want it changed here and now? I doubt it. He and Charlotte are spending Xmas with the Astors! They were recently at the Philip Sassoons. Alas! poor Shaw, you have succumbed to Charlotte!

## ◦∼ 1928 ∼◦

*2 January. Passfield*

A happy new year alone with Sidney (the Tawneys spent Christmas with us), working well at the book . . . But few will buy these ponderous volumes. Who today is interested in the question of 'Poverty in the midst of riches'? The rich seem to be more callous than of old; fear of Communism, of increased taxation and diminished privilege, has become their dominant emotion; pity for the misery of poverty is dead; indeed, there is a certain resentment at the rise in wages, following the rise in prices, and also at the 'dole' . . . Anyway we delight in this continued work together – one perpetual honeymoon – day after day, year after year . . . 'Ridiculous old souls,' we say to one another as I curl up on his knees in the fire-light!

*21 January. 3 a.m.* [Passfield Corner]

The eve of my seventieth birthday! If I thought I were fifty instead of knowing I am seventy should I feel aged, I wonder? I have my eyesight and my hearing intact, perhaps a wee bit hard of hearing when voices are low and words mumbled. I am seldom actually ill. . . . such minor ailments as eczema, sleeplessness and bowel trouble I have always had and have now. I am just as keenly interested in rather a wider range of subjects . . . I have even added a new source of delight – music – mostly wireless, but I go to more concerts than ever before . . . All the same, I am conscious of failing strength; the hours I work, or *could* work, get shorter and shorter like the autumn days; the longer walks we took the first years we were here . . . have been given up. If I let myself worry over anything I feel less able to cope . . . And I think I notice the same slackening in Sidney's energies. There is not much to complain of . . . But it means that we must learn 'the habit of resignation' . . .

In the early hours of Saturday 7 January, a combination of gales, flood water and high tide produced a surge which broke the parapet of the Thames by the Tate Gallery. Fourteen people drowned.

*7 February.* [Passfield Corner]
Raging south-west gales, torrential rain, alternating with days of dull, drizzly mists, have been our lot this winter. Never before have I heard the winds springing up on all sides, wailing and moaning round the cottage and through the trees insistingly, night after night, driving away sleep. An atmosphere of gloom: the disaster of the Thames tidal wave, six persons drowned in the basements of our span of Grosvenor Road, heard one evening over the wireless, seemed but the climax . . . The basement is to be virtually closed, and we are to clear out of the box-room to serve as Emily's bedroom and to give up the pantry as a kitchen for Susan. Emily is to transfer her services to Susan and we are to pay for all the service we have with appropriate arrangements about lighting and heating in proportion to use. That means that we shall seldom go to Grosvenor Road. . . .
. . . I have been working at too high pressure. To which . . . I recently added, accepting an offer to broadcast: a quarter of an hour's talk on Herbert Spencer (for which I get ten guineas) on 27 February. It is absurd that I should put two or three days' work and considerable worry into this little piece of artistry. But it struck me that when I am no longer pressed with writing I might like occasionally to broadcast – *if I prove to have the knack of it.* . . .

*29 February.* [Passfield Corner]
I was in a devil of a funk as I walked along the Embankment to Savoy Hill – in fact my heart and brain were so queerly affected that I wondered whether I was going to be too ailing to get through the job. The extraordinarily restful atmosphere of the B.B.C. mansion set my mind

and body at ease; I was comforted by a sense of my own unimpor-
tance. . . . I waited in the 'Artists Room' – one or two men with
instruments and another with a photographic apparatus wandered
through this passage apartment. About nine o'clock there entered a tall,
fair-haired, clean-shaven gentleman, in evening dress . . . and he led the
way along the silent passages. I tried to enter into some sort of relation
with him, but he barely answered me. We entered the padded chamber . . . The announcer, without even looking at me, sat down at the
table over which hung the microphone, and in a mechanical voice, read
out the news, pausing between each item and keeping his eye on the
clock. At 9.15 sharp he rose slowly out of his chair, remarked in the same
impersonal tone to the microphone that 'this evening Mrs Sidney Webb,
economist and social historian, will give the talk on Herbert Spencer,'
made way for me, again without looking at me, and left the room.
Once seated at the table and thinking myself alone I started off with
little or no nervousness – indeed I rather enjoyed myself – it was like
rehearsing in one's bedroom. I had hardly any consciousness of being listened to, so private and quiet was the place one was in. As I came to the
last page of the MSS I was conscious of someone just behind me getting
restless. I looked at the clock and saw that I was two minutes over my
time. I refused to hasten and finished off on a good round note, with a
pleasant sense of successful achievement. When the red light went out,
I made some harmless observation to the attendant youth. 'Anyone
could hear *you*; but what a terrible life the poor man must have had,' was
his informal retort. The red light flared on again: 'London will take a
little music while Daventry takes the shipping news.' Then he hurried
out of the room, and I made my way through silent empty passages to
the entrance and out into the Strand. . . .

The portrait of the Webbs was painted by Sir William Nicholson
(1872–1949).

*5 March.* [Passfield Corner]
This morning Sidney and I started on the last lap of our English Poor
Law history. I doubt whether it will be a well-finished book. Sidney is
preoccupied with Parliament and I am not strong enough for sustained
day-by-day drudgery. The most I can do is to add architectonics to his
more massive knowledge. And to interrupt our few mornings' work
together there comes a fashionable portrait painter to construct a picture
of the Webbs for the Founders' Room at the L.S.E. Though flattered by

Beveridge's insistence that we must be staged as the recognized Founders, I disliked the procedure of his 'dunning' people for their names and their guineas. . . .

*18 April.* [Passfield Corner]
A gathering of nephews and nieces at 'Aunt Kate's'. A sort of gathering the dear old lady delights in. The hundred and fifty odd nephews and nieces, grand-nephews and nieces and now great-grand nephews and nieces are a mixed lot, of whom I only know, at all well, about a score . . . Very representative of English society, the older generation pre-eminently a company of businessmen and their wives, the younger generation being more professional – lawyers, medical men, civil servants, university dons. But among the lot there is an ex-chorus girl, an ex-duchess, half a dozen peers' sons, a baronet, an out-of-work actor, a shorthand typist, an old curiosity dealer. In so large a group, in which males predominate, it is odd that there should be only one minister of religion, and he only a Unitarian who gave up his ministry when he married our niece and who was killed in the war. There is one suicide and one lunatic in the first generation and one suicide and two mental defectives in the second. Otherwise the family group is distinctly above the average in health and capacity. But there is no great personal distinction – not so much as in the group of parents, the nine Potter girls and their ten mates. Among the great-nephews and nieces there are one or two who *promise* distinction . . . The only *friend* we have is Barbara Drake – a Fabian, a writer on economic questions, a member of the Education Committee of the L.C.C., a lover of music and a charming woman. . . . My relation to all of them is 'dutiful', not affectionate, and unless they want to see us, or I think they do, I certainly don't want to see them. Kate is the real centre of the Richard Potter family life, in so far as it has a centre. . . . Kate is loved, I am liked and Rosy is tolerated. So fare the remnant of the Richard Potter sisters in the minds of their descendants.

*5 May.* [Passfield Corner]
Nicholson, the agreeable portrait painter, has been here three weekends doing studies of us to be translated on to the large canvas, a pleasant waste of Sidney's time and my strength and other people's money. I doubt the result. It may be a clever picture ('especially of the brickwork,' GBS suggests), but it will be an insignificant portrait, the figures being too small relatively to the background and too insignificant for the Founders' Room. If it be desirable that the L.S.E.

should have a Webb seal, this particular seal will do as well as any other. . . .

Ada Webb (1864–1946) and Charles Webb (1857–1954) were Sidney's sister and brother. Beatrice knew them for over half a century but they are scarcely mentioned in the diary.

*28 May. 3 a.m.* [Passfield Corner]
*To the Lighthouse* by Virginia Woolf represents the latest fashion in the technique of novel-writing. The story, so far as there is a story, is told by a running description of the 'stream of consciousness' in the principal person's mind. When this person dies, then another mind is taken as the medium; in this book both are women. To me this method is objectionable because it assumes that the author can see into and describe another's mind . . . What one suspects is that Virginia is telling you of her *own* stream of consciousness, the only one she knows 'of her own view and knowledge'. And that brings me to the question: could I record my own consciousness? So often it seems too vague and diverse and disconnected . . . even one's own consciousness defies description.

For the last few days I have been haunted by the shocking appearance of Ada Webb – she came here with the Charles Webbs for lunch and tea. She has always been plain, but this time she looked repulsive and Sidney perceived it as quickly as I did. 'Some drug on the top of loneliness, no occupation and the lack of any creed or purpose in life,' I ventured as an explanation. She has become immensely fat, especially the lower part of her face relatively to her forehead; and her body seemed swollen. She said she was 'quite well'. I remembered that poor old Lallie said the same when she was obviously dying of cocaine poisoning. Ada was sucking tablets, she said, for her cough. . . . It is the tragedy of a vacant heart and an unoccupied mind. Her condition raises the question, and Charlie writes anxiously to Sidney: can anything be done? Neither of her brothers are in a position to take charge of her, even if *she* would allow herself to be controlled; they have done all they can do in giving her a sufficient income to live in ease and comfort. And at sixty-five years of age, there is little chance of a change of conduct . . . But the thought of her sinking into a self-drugged senility (Charles says it is overeating without exercise) is painful. One feels guilty of neglect without exactly knowing why one should feel guilty, and without the remotest intention of accepting further responsibility. So that's that. . . .

The Aberavon constituency, for which MacDonald had sat since 1922, required too much of his time and money.

*28 May. Whit Sunday.* [Passfield Corner]
The Snowdens lunched here to meet the Hendersons, who are staying a long week-end with us. Snowden was remarkably fit and self-complacent. Mrs Snowden looked out of sorts. I took her round the garden and she insisted on confiding to me, very deliberately I thought, that she *might* be suffering from an internal complaint. She is at the turn of life and obviously feared cancer, like nearly all women do at her age. And she added 'very confidentially' that she had never 'lived with' Philip and that as she was a 'normal woman' her lot had been very hard. Which I can well believe; it excuses a good deal of her search after social prestige and the agreeable excitements of the smart set. . . .

Henderson is convinced that Baldwin will lose his majority and that the Labour Party will be called to office, however short may be their tenure. Sidney still believes in, or hopes for, a small Conservative majority . . . Henderson, I was interested to note, assumed that if the Labour Party took office Sidney would go to the House of Lords. 'I shall obey orders,' Sidney remarked, 'but quite sincerely I should prefer not.' To which I added 'Amen'. . . .

Meanwhile Henderson and Sidney are conspiring to hand over the safe and cheap seat of Seaham Harbour to 'our leader'. Who would have thought that the embittered vendetta of former years would have terminated in such a model manner!

*9 June.* [Passfield Corner]
GBS has had a good Press for his five-hundred-page socialist tract. . . . To me the book is boresome. Perhaps any other work on abstract capitalism or abstract socialism would be, to me, unreadable; only Shaw's amazing cleverness can make such a subject, here and there, entertaining and thought-provoking. . . .

*15 June.* [Passfield Corner]
Watching a well-known portrait painter at work has been instructive. He has taken an incredible time over me, owing to the wrong scheming of the picture in the first instance. I have been painted in and painted out half a dozen times. Now at last the figure satisfies him and is quite good enough for me – rather too young and good-looking, but that fault is inevitable in a woman's portrait.

*5 July. Val d'Isère, Savoy*
Not for years have I enjoyed a holiday as I have this fortnight here; the long-houred walks up the villages by rushing glacier streams, resting among the rocks, larch and flowers, watching the glorious intimacy of mountain, cloud and sun – all the time honeymooning with my beloved! Also I am glad to discover that I can still walk for five hours or more and even climb three thousand feet in broiling heat without serious strain. . . .

> Richard Meinertzhagen (1878–1967), soldier and anthropologist, was Georgina's son. He was married to Annie Jackson. Robert Holt (1872–1952) was the son of Lallie. His son, Oliver (1907–60), was suffering from polio, not sleeping sickness.

*19 July.* [Passfield Corner]
. . . An evening with dear old Kate, who has failed to find comfortable summer quarters and comes here for August. Two family tragedies – Dick Meinertzhagen's wife, an attractive and wholly desirable person, shot herself accidentally whilst revolver practising, and Bob Holt's boy down with the most ghastly of ills, sleeping sickness. That about sums up the situation – at least the foreground of our consciousness. The background is menacing: growing unemployment, the desperate condition of the miners, the terrible dilemma of demoralizing outdoor relief on the one hand, and, as the alternative, semi-starvation and slow demoralization, a hell of a mess which we have got to describe, if not prescribe for, during the next six months. Fortunately I *do* feel stronger in body and mind and the memories of that Val d'Isère are wonderfully refreshing.

> R. B. Haldane died on 19 August 1928. Beatrice spent ten days at the end of August touring the mining districts of South Wales, collecting material for the Poor Law history.

*21 August.* [Passfield Corner]
Haldane's death was no shock. We saw it coming and no friend could regret it. He was not only powerless; he was wretched. But it is a sorrow to think that our oldest and most constant friend has passed away. It was Haldane who created and fostered the flattering 'Webb myth' that flowered so agreeably and advantageously for us and our schemes in the first decade of the twentieth century. Even when the idealized myth

withered and was replaced by a caricature, Haldane was one of the few who, in spite of a certain disillusionment, remained faithful to an old friendship . . . If I had to write his epitaph it would be 'a powerful and beneficent personality, a great citizen, above all a loyal and generous friend.'

*1 September.* [Passfield Corner]
. . . My general impression is that the Welsh miners, though not starving – there are no soup kitchens and the homes look clean and the people respectable – feel themselves to be 'down and out'. There is a grim silence in the streets, and the little knots of boys and men look apathetic and slink about as if ashamed of the shabbiness of their garments. The homes are getting barer and barer and the food deteriorating in quality – there is little drinking and smoking. . . . In fact the Rhondda valley reminded me of the streets of Hamburg when we were there in 1923; the people were respectable and quiet but they looked terribly depressed physically and mentally . . .

*28 September.* [Passfield Corner]
Sidney works steadily on at the book; for the last fortnight I have done little or nothing to help him . . . Not exactly ill, but hopelessly unfit – insomnia, bowel trouble, intermittent rheumatism and headache. And Mr Nicholson appears again on the scene and requires more sittings. He is a most agreeable and sympathetic person. But the long-drawn-out process annoys and irritates me . . . Neither the artist nor anyone else likes the result of all this effort. It seems all right to me. If only he would leave it alone and finish the picture and be gone! . . .

Aldous Huxley's *Point Counter Point* appeared in 1928. *The Magic Mountain* by Thomas Mann (1875–1955) was published in 1924 and translated in 1927. D. H. Lawrence had just completed, but not published, *Lady Chatterley's Lover*. Norman Douglas (1868–1932) made his reputation with *South Wind* (1917) and wrote *In the Beginning* (1927). David Garnett (1892–1981), Bloomsbury novelist and critic, wrote the prize-winning *Lady into Fox* (1922). Compton MacKenzie (1883–1972) began his career as a novelist with *Carnival* (1912) and *Sinister Street* (1913).

*26 October. Roker*
Our last visit to this little seaside suburb of Sunderland – my last meeting with the miners' wives, daughters and menfolk, saying farewell and

introducing Ishbel MacDonald. . . . We did not interest each other, but we made pleasant conversation on our drives to and from the meetings, and in our walks along the sea front . . . It is good to feel that our relations to Sidney's constituency have been wholly friendly; we leave no enemies and many good friends.

While Sidney has been out at six meetings I have been reading Aldous Huxley's *Point Counter Point*, and pondering over this strangely pathological writing, pathological without knowing it. The febrile futility of the particular clique he describes reminds me of that far more powerful book *The Magic Mountain*, by Thomas Mann. Far more powerful because Mann is describing a society of sick people . . . Huxley's group do not know that they are sick and are presented as a sample of normal human life. What with their continuous and promiscuous copulations, their shallow talk and chronic idleness, the impression left is one of simple disgust at their bodies and minds. . . . And the book, apart from arousing a morbid interest in morbidity, is dull, dull, dull. In a few years' time it will be unreadable – it represents a fashion. In this characteristic of fashionableness Aldous Huxley is like his maternal aunt, Mrs Humphry Ward; also in his tendency to preach.

'Your generation,' said a Cambridge undergraduate to his mother, 'lost faith in God. Our generation has lost faith in man.' The 'Religion of Humanity' and its successor, 'The coming of the Superman', alike mild reflections of the consciousness of God, have vanished from the public eye in my lifetime. The Great War disgusted everyman with its manifestation of human power, which appeared as the Will to Murder. Today there is a demand for the sub-human in art and literature and music. Clever novelists – Huxley, D. H. Lawrence, Norman Douglas, David Garnett, Compton MacKenzie – are all depicting men and women as mere animals, and morbid at that. Except always that these bipeds practise birth control and commit suicide. So it looks as if the species would happily die out! It is an ugly and tiresome idol of the mind, but it lends itself to a certain type of fantastic wit and stylish irony.

*21 November.* [Passfield Corner]
Graham Wallas here for four nights . . . I enjoyed his visit . . . we old Fabians – GBS, Wallas and the Webbs, and for that matter many of our other Fabian contemporaries – are pleasantly self-complacent. We are a lot of happy old people, who think they have done well by the world and also had a good time of it.

. . . Poor Audrey has had an operation for cancer and is in a depressed and nervous state. . . . Audrey is a virtuous woman . . . Why is it that the good is so seldom combined with the beautiful? . . . It is so easy to win applause, luxury, power, by personal charm, whether of body or mind, but the ways of virtue are dull and the toil of thought is hard. Audrey has certainly had a duller life than she would have had if she had had less goodness and more charm.

Tom Shaw (1872–1938), a textile trade union official, had been Minister of Labour in 1924.

*24 December.* [Passfield Corner]
Oswald Mosleys stayed here. We had seen little of them since a week-end at Lion's in the autumn of 1922, when he had just come over to the Labour Party and was about to lose his seat therefore. It struck us both that he and she had changed – partly from his long illness last autumn and winter, partly from the ups and downs of electoral failure and success; also from social boycott by their own set and an uneasy position in the Labour Party. He is disillusioned. Labour politics for an aristocrat are not attractive – current and cross-current from left and right and very little real comradeship. 'Labour people,' said Cynthia, 'especially the better sort and the intellectuals, are shy of us, except the few snobs among them who are subservient.' Sidney and I are recognized as genuine 'Ancients' in the labour movement, but even with us there has been the difficulty of becoming *intimate*, the sort of intimacy we have had with Haldane, with Beveridge, Wallas and GBS, with the professors and lecturers of the School of Economics. There is no *intimate* inner circle in the labour movement; every Labour leader (except perhaps Uncle Arthur) is a lonely figure, neither friendly nor unfriendly towards other leaders but merely unconcerned . . .

Mosley has his political career before him, and with his money, his personal charm and political gifts, his good-looking and agreeable wife, he is dead certain of Cabinet office, and possibly has a chance of eventual premiership. . . . Sidney is good friends with all the party; constantly consulted, always willing to help or to stand on one side, as is most convenient. He, Willie Graham and Tom Shaw, at the request of the Parliamentary executive, are to meet at Philip Snowden's to draw up a programme of immediate legislation and administration, should the Labour Party find itself bound to take office after the June election. . . .

## ∽ 1929 ∽

Neville Chamberlain (1869–1940), the Minister of Health, had introduced a Local Government Bill. The Poor Law guardians were abolished and their powers transferred to the counties and county boroughs.

*4 January.* [Passfield Corner]
Exactly twenty years ago – 1908 – we were putting the finishing touches to the Minority Report, I in a state of abject exhaustion. On New Year's Eve 1928, we were writing the last words of the epilogue of our lengthy history of the English Poor Law, recording the sentence of death passed by Parliament on the boards of guardians and the opening of a new era in the legal relations between the rich and poor. . . .

There has been a certain exhilaration and self-complacency in the writing of the epilogue because it is clear that so far as the Chamberlain Bill goes it does *break up the Poor Law* in respect of the non-able-bodied. Further, it leaves the whole problem of unemployment in such a hopeless tangle that it is safe to predict that the second part of the Minority Report – a national authority for the able-bodied – is almost certain to be carried out. It is in fact in process of being formed in the Ministry of Labour. To be able to *make* history as well as to write it – or, to be modest, to have foreseen, twenty years ago, the exact stream of tendencies which would bring your proposal to fruition, is a pleasurable thought! So the old Webbs are chuckling over their chickens!

*16 January.* [Passfield Corner]
In the beautiful Founders' Room at the L.S.E. there was a reception to see the Webb portrait hung over the mantelpiece – a really lovely picture, as a picture, whatever criticism my friends may make about my portrait. And a most friendly little gathering – mostly Fabian – the other subscribers not turning up. Beveridge made a gracious little speech, far too impressive about us. . . . Altogether our stock is up, or rather, we have, through old age, ceased to have detractors . . . Which adds to the pleasantness of life, though possibly also to its illusions. . . .

*6 March.* [Passfield Corner]
On the morning of Saturday 24 February Mary Anne, Kate's old servant, telephoned me that Kate was dangerously ill and begged me to come at once. I had just time to phone Sidney that I would join him in London and to catch the early train. When I reached Cheyne Walk it was clear

that she was not dying, but near to death. She was glad to see me, and as the only nurse who could be got in this epidemic of influenza had been with her two nights and one day, I took her place for the rest of the day. Her medical man assured me that we would pull her through; it was influenza poison, there was no pneumonia and the bronchitis was not severe. The poor dear did not like her nurses and there were three in succession during her week of illness. But she was happy in her mind and in no pain and would have liked to talk to me more than I dared let her. Reassured, I dashed down to Passfield on Sunday afternoon to finish packing, planning to return on Tuesday. But on Monday morning Mary Anne again telephoned for me and from that afternoon I stayed with her until she passed peacefully away on Tuesday the 27th at about three o'clock in the afternoon, choked by an accumulation of phlegm which she could not cough up. Apart from weariness and restlessness and all the discomfort of laboured breathing, I don't think she suffered. . . .

. . . I do not think [Kate] was really intimate with any of her sisters; the rest of us had a certain hardness or cynicism which was intensely repellent to her nature. . . . And perhaps I was the least intimate, and so was most to blame for this lack of tenderness. For Margaret I had a real affection and her death was a direct sorrow. For Mary too I had a tender heart. Kate's death, now that it has come, is also a sorrow, but the sorrow is more because I feel I *ought* to feel her loss more than I do, than because I *do* feel it. I sorrow because her beneficent presence meant so little in my life. . . .

> After her first broadcast Beatrice was asked to read poetry; she declined but suggested a series on 'How to study social facts', for which she asked £50 – 'a good deal more than the ordinary fee'. Her terms were agreed, but Sidney had to deliver the first talk, as it coincided with Kate's death.

*28 March.* [41 Grosvenor Road?]
I struggled through the three BBC talks, without failure but on a low level of achievement . . . Meanwhile Sidney has been slaving at the last stages of getting the book through the Press . . . Altogether we are rather depressed and glad to get away. We need a complete change of scene before we start on the eighth decade of our lives, the fifth of our married life and in all probability the last of our partnership. When I was down at Passfield the other day surveying the building alterations I longed to be back in the quietude and peace of our little home. 'But we shall want a book to write,' Sidney observes.

# A Drift to Disaster

## April 1929–December 1931

In April the Webbs took a six-week holiday to Greece, Turkey, Germany and Austria. The outstanding episode of their stay in Constantinople, Beatrice said, was their 'romantic' interview with the exiled Soviet leader Leon Trotsky on the island of Prinkipo. Sidney had written a letter suggesting a meeting and it was quickly arranged.

*April*
In a ramshackle villa, with a secret service officer sitting in the garden, we found Trotsky and his wife and son. We were alone with the great revolutionary for a couple of hours. He is a charming and accomplished man; looks more like an intellectual musician than an organizer of war and revolution. He opened in polished French with a suave and deferential claim to being one of our disciples who had strayed away from our teaching! He refused to talk himself either about Russia or to let us talk about England; he led the conversation exclusively on to the inevitability of a world revolution – perhaps not the inevitability but the desirability? He admitted eventually that it might be that capitalism was finding a new equilibrium in the U.S.A. and Europe. In that case Soviet Communism would fail in Russia; that system could not stand against a hostile and vigorously successful capitalist organization in the rest of the world. He intimated that the only chance for Russian Communism was the approaching great war between the U.S.A. and Great Britain, which would wreck the *status quo* in both countries. We

476 The Diaries of Beatrice Webb

tried to explain that this war would not happen, that revolutionary propaganda of the kind carried on by Communists was doomed to ignominious failure in the U.S.A. and Great Britain. We suggested that if the Russians could make Soviet Communism successful so that the worker would gain a higher standard of life and more freedom and dignity in Russia than elsewhere, then an enormous stride would have been made in converting other countries to Communism. And why should not this success be possible?

I don't think we impressed each other with our respective arguments – partly [because] we could not speak much French and he could not understand English well enough to come to grips with each other's outlook. Also I think beneath all his polished intellectualism he has the closed mind of a fanatic who refuses to face the fact of Western democratic organization.

> Beatrice was staying at the house of her late sister Kate. Polling took place on 30 May. For the first time Labour emerged as the largest party in the House of Commons, winning 287 seats against 261 for the Tories and 59 for the Liberals.

*1 June.* [15 Cheyne Walk]
Sidney and I sat up with the Laskis till 2.30, listening to the flowing tide of Labour victories – almost hysterical at the prospect of Labour being in a majority in the House. . . . What has been accomplished is the final collapse of the Liberal Party. Considering their money, their Press, their brilliant demagogic leader with his pledge 'to cure unemployment in one year', the failure to add even a score to their numbers is decisive. They will never again reach their present number in the House of Commons. . . . Baldwin will be smoking his pipe philosophically . . . J.R.M. will be enjoying the sensation of inflated prestige . . . But for Lloyd George the future is blank. . . .

*4 June.* [15 Cheyne Walk]
Baldwin resigns. Informed public opinion – *The Times,* the *Evening Standard* – insisted that the wisest course was dignified resignation and acquiescence in the advent of a Labour government. . . . So Baldwin makes way for MacDonald . . .

*5 June. 10 a.m. 15 Cheyne Walk*
Over the wireless we heard that the P.M. had submitted a list of his

Cabinet to the King this morning, so that finished the uncertainties of these last few days. . . .

Midnight. A violent ringing of the front door bell. I thought it was Maud Keary locked out, but found her coming down to answer it. 'Must be a telegram,' she said. I followed on, opened the telegram – 'Phone me tonight, MacDonald.' I woke Sidney who came near swearing, trying to discover, still dazed with sleep, J.R.M.'s telephone number. He is to be up at Hampstead by nine. 'Wants to persuade you to accept a peerage without office,' said I. 'I shall not do it,' said he, and returned to his bed. . . .

MacDonald's 1929 Cabinet was dominated by the same five men – himself, Snowden at the Treasury, Henderson at the Foreign Office, Clynes at the Home Office, and Thomas as Lord Privy Seal with a special responsibility for tackling the chronic unemployment. Margaret Bondfield at the Ministry of Labour became the first woman to enter the Cabinet.

*6 June.* [15 Cheyne Walk]
The interview ended in Sidney accepting a peerage in order to take over the Colonial Office. . . . Sidney was delighted . . . it is his old office as a civil servant . . . Meanwhile I was at Passfield awaiting the news by telephone – amply disguised by code. An odd compound of satisfaction for him, of tiredness on my part and of a rather morbid awareness of old age in both of us, came over me for the rest of the day. When poor old [Sidney] Olivier called (quite obviously unfit in body and mind), quivering with anxiety and indignation at not having 'heard from MacDonald', I wondered whether there ought not to be a hard and fast retiring age for Cabinet office? Parmoor, for instance, is too aged and infirm for leadership of the House of Lords. What are other people saying of the old Webbs? . . .

*20 June. 41 Grosvenor Road*
When first it was mooted that Sidney should go to the Lords the question of becoming 'Lord' and 'Lady' was discussed between us. My instinct was against the use of a title, and Sidney, though feeling less strongly, acquiesced. But breaking a convention, which all accept, needs something more than mere dislike. . . . The British Constitution being what it is . . . there have to be Labour peers in order to form and maintain a government. . . . So far as Sidney is concerned, assuming

that he thought himself fit to be in the Cabinet, he was in duty bound to go to the House of Lords. . . . It is clear that Sidney himself, having accepted a peerage, is bound to use the title in his official acts . . . But this obligation does not extend to his wife . . . By refusing to become one of a social caste – honoured because it is a caste – I make it slightly more difficult for other Labour men to succumb to the temptation. . . . An honour ignored is an honour deflated. What amuses me is that the only possible retort, as far as I am concerned, on the part of the Court and London society generally, is social ostracism, and that, of course, is the one that will best suit me. . . . I respect our King and Queen and I acquiesce in a constitutional monarchy – the British monarchy is an anachronism but it is a useful anachronism, an institution for which it would be precious difficult to find an equally good substitute. But its social environment of aristocracy and plutocracy is wholly bad . . . I shan't be fussy or pedantic about it; if I find myself called 'Lady Passfield' on official occasions I shall not protest. Obviously anyone has a right to call me by that name. But I shall persistently call myself Mrs Sidney Webb and when once Sidney is out of office my intention will prevail . . .

*21 June.* [Passfield Corner]
Sidney is of course enjoying himself. It is agreeable to be treated with deference by a long procession of persons of importance, to have skilled assistance in every task and to give what seem to be your own decisions on innumerable questions, especially when you happen to have an out-standing capacity for swiftly mastering new issues and intricate situations. . . . I dislike the inevitable separation which this office work will entail. Which means that we must have a comfortable abode in London – the getting of which will be my next job – and a full-time sec-retary. Fortunately the singularly helpful and attractive little woman I had at Passfield for a year, Miss Burr . . . is willing to come for the period of Sidney's office, short or long. If I have not sufficient work for her I can lend her to one of the women Labour M.P.s. So that's that.

Sidney, in fact, continued to use the title until his death.

*29 June. Ayot St Lawrence*
The episode of 'Mrs Sidney Webb', wife of Lord Passfield, has passed off quite happily. The Press have been quite pleasant about it . . . To get it published was not my intention. But the publication has been fortunate

as everyone now calls me Mrs Webb. The Labour people I have seen are quite pleased. By the general public it has been accepted as 'an extreme feminist gesture'; not as a depreciation of titles, which might have caused resentment. No one has yet tumbled to the reason for Sidney's assumption of 'Passfield' instead of Webb as his ennobled name. But now that I have got my name accepted, he will gradually drop the title in private life . . . And when he retires from office we shall manage to get the second step accepted – his resumption of the name and status of plain 'Sidney Webb'.

. . . I walked with Sidney to the Colonial Office yesterday morning. . . . When the Secretary of State passes through the door, a bell rings throughout the passages and silent and attentive messengers spring up at intervals, ushering him into the large ugly room in which he sits. . . . It is all very funny, very unlike the informal camaraderie of the labour movement. At the National Labour Club where I usually lunch there are to be found, sitting side by side, short-haired typists from the trade union offices, M.P.s, Cabinet Ministers, all being served in strict order of their coming, and all chatting together indiscriminately. 'Well, Mrs Webb,' said a porter to me at King's Cross, 'I really don't think a live Lord ought to travel third-class. I see you are not using the title,' he added in a tone of approval. So we stood and chatted, one or two other porters joining in. A taxi-driver jumped down from his seat in Downing Street and grasped Sidney's hand. . . .

The Duke of Connaught (1850–1942) was the brother of Edward VII and uncle of the reigning George V.

*6 July.* [41 Grosvenor Road]
I have won on the name and lost on the curtsy! At the Colonial Office there is a cleverly tactful official, Colonel de Satge, who acts as Master of Ceremonies and organizer of social gatherings . . . 'Could Mrs Webb be induced to present some dozen colonial ladies at the forthcoming Court?' 'No,' said Sidney. 'A woman of over seventy ought not to be expected to attend evening Courts. But my wife will gladly meet any colonial ladies who wish to see her,' he added. 'Then Mrs Webb will no doubt be present at your reception of the Canadian Clubs on July 3rd' . . . Of course I agreed . . . What de Satge had not told us was that the Duke of Connaught and Princess Patricia would be present . . . Without a grave breach of courtesy there was no way out of the curtsy. The Duke is a kindly old man and as he hobbled up to me I had not the

heart to disappoint him. 'She curtsyed,' recorded the Press correspondents in some of next morning's papers. I am told that this world-moving event was duly broadcasted that very evening. So that's that, and curtsy I must on all future occasions. . . .

An odd parallel between two careers in which I have been specially interested. Joseph Chamberlain first entered the Cabinet in 1880 as President of the Board of Trade; he finally retired from Cabinet rank in 1903 as Secretary of State for the Colonies. Sidney Webb first entered the Cabinet in 1924 as President of the Board of Trade; he is again a member of the Cabinet in 1929 as Secretary of State for the Dominions and Colonies. When Mary Booth came to congratulate me yesterday and embraced me with emotional enthusiasm I could not help suspecting that this dramatic coincidence, with the long time-lag between the twin events, was in her mind as it had been in mine. A few days ago, Sidney met Austen Chamberlain at a dinner to the Prime Minister of Egypt. After compliments to the new Secretary of State Austen lent over the table and observed in a confidential tone: 'I wonder whether Mrs Webb remembers my coming with my father to stay with Mr Potter when she was acting as hostess? I was a boy at Cambridge. I fell desperately in love with one of her nieces,' he added, by way of explaining this reminiscence. It was during the winter of 1883 that Austen narrowly missed becoming the stepson of the lady who is today the wife of one who has succeeded his father at two Cabinet offices. A curio in the play of destiny.

We attended the Thanksgiving Service in Westminster Abbey . . . a survival of a dead ritual, meaningless to the majority of those present. The King and Queen were formal figures, not impressive or attractive. The last touch of ugliness and unrest was given by the figure and expression of the Countess of Oxford in a prominent corner seat of the front row – over-dressed, haggard, rouged and seemingly desperately miserable. As we filed out behind the Royal cortège Margot [Asquith], followed by a child, pushed past me, fighting her way out with the ugly intentness of a spirit escaping out of Hell. The fall from prestige, power, meant to her boredom tempered by misery. . . .

*12 July. Passfield Corner*

My first night spent in our little home since I left it to hurry back to Kate's deathbed – over four months ago.

. . . I look forward with a certain nervous dislike to this spell of official life. Our plan to write a Manual of Social Study is clearly impracticable. It may be that after six months of social life, mainly in

London, I shall begin to collect the material for *Our Partnership*. Whether I could be as frank about our married life and joint career as I was about my girlhood is doubtful; the narrative might have to be far more objective and less personal. It would depend on whether I write for publication during our lifetime or merely prepare the separate episodes for our editors' use. Also I should have to consider Sidney's susceptibilities. What I yearn to do is to sum up my experience of life. Have I come to any conclusions? What troubles me is our own good fortune – a superlative good luck, a good luck which is almost ridiculous in its completeness, contrasted with the daily grind of human life, as it is lived by the vast majority of men. . . .

If we were really single-minded about the equalitarian state, ought we to be living a life of relative luxury and social prestige? Ought we to have a flat in Whitehall Court? Ought we to buy expensive clothes? and participate in extravagant entertainments? . . . Or is it a question of compromise? . . . We have tried to compromise, leaning heavily towards the simple life, and since Sidney has been in politics, refusing to associate with the other camp. But then we are old and blasé – it is easy to resist temptation with these disabilities. . . .

*27 July.* [Passfield Corner]
I am quits with the Court! Ethel Snowden told me that the King and Queen were seriously annoyed – she said 'hurt', which was meant to be appealing – at my refusal, in spite of seven years of invitations, to present myself at Buckingham Palace. I replied that it never occurred to me that my absence would be noticed. But that if it were resented I would, of course, go whenever I received another command. I had already settled in my own mind that a Secretary of State's wife had Court obligations unknown to an M.P.'s wife, or even to the wife of a President of the Board of Trade. The invitation came to 'Lord and Lady Passfield' and we attended the Garden Party. The organization of this super-fête seemed defective. The refreshments for the ten thousand were heaped up in one marquee and no one without an active person in attendance ready to push through the crowd could get service. The dense semi-circle of gazers at Royalty, seated or standing round the Royal enclosure as if it were a show, was ugly. The manners of the crowd, mostly upper-class, were not kindly, leave alone courtly . . . Sidney had to present colonials, whilst I wandered about in the crowd, quite amused by this private view of Buckingham Palace gardens, chatting with old and new acquaintances. At the end of Sidney's presentations the Queen asked, 'Is

your wife here?' 'Yes, Ma'am, she is in the crowd out there. I am afraid I could not easily find her,' he added. 'That's a pity,' said the Queen, 'I should like to talk to her.' 'Thank you, Ma'am,' said Sidney, and retired. It was past six o'clock and the Queen and her cortège passed into the Palace. Seeing that I was not told that I was to be . . . invited into the Royal enclosure it was not my fault that I came away from Buckingham Palace without being presented to Her Majesty. But in deliberately going there I have done my duty and need do no more!

*2 August.* [Passfield Corner]
One reason for liking the student's and author's life . . . is that the content of one's consciousness becomes so far more agreeable and wholesome . . . Leonard and Kate Courtney could always fall back on reciting to themselves their favourite poetry; other people enjoy re-reading classics. . . . I must have something new to discover or digest, or I must myself be engaged in the art of expression. That is why I write a diary. Without this invigorating food, I go on chewing the cud of some past episode or imaginary happening . . . On the other hand, by merely describing my pleasant or unpleasant adventures I can often rid my mind of them . . . All of which points to getting, as soon as I have the strength, something outside the daily life to think about, some state of being to be discovered, described, analysed or summed up. . . .

> In a letter of 31 July MacDonald told Sidney that 'you are getting me into hot water'. The King had apparently objected to an official invitation which read: 'Lord Passfield and Mrs Webb will receive . . .' MacDonald plaintively suggested that 'no principle is involved. In this matter poor Mrs W. is pinned on to you and you drag her up automatically.'

*4 August.* [Passfield Corner]
In response to J.R.M.'s very courteous remonstrance Sidney instructed de Satge to omit my name from the card of invitation to the Canadian and American undergraduates next Thursday, and it will be so in all future invitations. . . . The only way out of defiance or surrender is for me to efface myself as the wife of the Secretary of State for the Dominions and Colonies – which means, in effect, limiting my entertainments to the Labour world plus old friends, and such of the colonials as I can ask privately to come and see 'the Webbs'. All of which looks promising for literary work next spring.

I love this little house in sunshine and rain: the absolute quietude during the night, the distant sounds now and again in the day, the long rambles in Woolmer Forest and Ludshott Common, honeymooning with my beloved or brooding alone with Sandy [her dog] as my companion. And I enjoy the visits of friends. . . . On the other hand, social functions in London weary me past endurance . . . The one pleasure of this episode is watching Sidney . . . What troubles me is the offchance that my recalcitrance might make matters less easy for him, might prejudice the smooth working of his official life. . . .

Sir Horace Plunkett (1854–1932) was an Irish statesman who had done much to promote rural co-operatives.

*30 August.* [Passfield Corner]
The day of unusual excitement: our first flight in the air, and a visit of reconciliation to the Gerald Balfours.

The flight, each one alone, in a Moth, off the Brooklands aerodrome, was arranged and provided by our old friend Horace Plunkett, at whose house we stayed last night. This fragile and, we always thought, hypochondriacal old man, four years my senior, has suddenly found salvation from insomnia in becoming a pilot of his own machine. He is actually applying for his certificate, which he will not get. Having failed to persuade the Shaws to fly, he tried it with us. I did not need any pressing . . . Sidney, with some reluctance, agreed to follow suit. A very delightful jaunt it was. . . .

The other ordeal was less welcome, though I am glad to be through with it. The strange breach of my friendship with Betty Balfour . . . I have never understood and always regretted. This spring, when I heard that Arthur Balfour had retired to Fisher's Hill – it was thought, to die – and that my old friend was leading a troubled life with three or four aged relatives of the Balfour clan, my heart softened. The publication of our Poor Law book with the chapters on the Royal Commission of 1905–09 – an episode so closely connected with our friendship with the Balfours – seemed to offer an occasion for some sort of reconciliation. So I sent them an initialled copy of the special edition. The warmth of her reply drew from me a letter in the old style of intimacy . . . Last night Horace Plunkett . . . told me that Betty Balfour wanted me to lunch there on my way back from Brooklands . . . So I found myself once more at Fisher's Hill after an interval of fifteen years. At sixty years of age Betty Balfour has become an old woman, though she retains much of her charm of voice and manner. She embraced me, but in

what she said and in the way she said it, there was not the ring of friendship. . . . it was, I think, an attitude rather than a feeling. 'In her cold
effusiveness she reminded me of Mary Booth,' I told Sidney. A.J.B., she
told me, was slightly better; he kept to his room. She implied that he
would never again be able to move out of his present abode. . . .
Altogether I am inclined to agree with Horace Plunkett's verdict that
poor Betty Balfour has a heavy load to bear and has borne it with singular courage and self-devotedness. So if my visit interested or pleased
her I am glad I paid it. But whether she likes me . . . today, I really don't
know! . . .

*29 September.* [41 Grosvenor Road]
Our last twenty-four hours in the little house overlooking the
Thames . . . I, certainly, feel relieved to be rid of it, or rather of the small
part of the house which was still our possession. The untidy, dingy
dining-room, the long tramp up three flights of stairs – fifty-nine in all –
to the two little garret bedrooms, and the dreadful noise, back and
front, made the old home an unpleasant lodging for me on my occasional visits to London. For Sidney, with his preference for the habitual,
it has served well. Incidentally we part company with Susan Lawrence on
the best of friendly terms, but without intimacy, given or taken. I respect
and admire her, but I do not like her – a mixed reaction which I recognize that not a few persons have towards me! . . . More regretful am I in
parting from my old servant Emily Wordley, who transfers her allegiance to Susan rather than follow me into the country.

Good-bye little house . . . I doubt whether you will outlive the Webbs!

*2 October.* [2 Whitehall Court]
Settled in our costly furnished flat in Whitehall Court (fourteen guineas
a week including service!), which we have taken for six months to enable
us to entertain (in return for our salary) the Parliamentary Labour Party
and colonials. . . . whilst Sidney will spend five days a week in London,
I shall still live mainly in the country.

We spent the week-end at Brighton at the headquarters of the Labour
executive and attended one day of the conference. The Parliamentary
Labour Party has the air of being thoroughly established; all the
Ministers are self-possessed and self-confident and just at present purring
over the popularity of their government . . . The left was not in evidence.
The Communists have been effectually excluded and the I.L.P. discredited as an impracticable faction without constructive force. . . .

The evening before our Brighton visit we saw *The Apple Cart*, that amusing and annoying satire on democracy . . . What struck me as odd was the very minor note of sex, even in the interlude. . . . No wonder our brilliant nephew Malcolm [Muggeridge] dismisses GBS as 'early Victorian'.

The smugly bourgeois audience received the new tidings of loyalty to the royal family with fat satisfaction and swarmed out with beaming smiles to the strains of 'God Save the King'. The wonder is that GBS and Charlotte have not been invited to Sandringham, but Baldwin refused to recommend him for the 'O.M.' on the ground (so Tom Jones told us) that GBS might 'guy' this still revered honour. So little do we now know about GBS's mind that we have not the remotest idea of what line he would take . . . We have never liked to discuss these delicate questions of personal behaviour with him – for the very good reason that Sidney thinks his presence in the House of Lords would be bad for the Parliamentary Labour Party but does not wish to say so, either to GBS himself or to anyone else. . . .

Meanwhile I am suffering from cold feet physical and mental – sleeplessness by night and dizziness by day, and I wonder whether I shall escape without some severe breakdown during Sidney's period of office. I have got to concentrate my strength on helping him – his health and peace of mind are all important; everything else is relatively of no consequence. Amen.

*5 October.* [Passfield Corner]
Rosy here for a week. Whether because we are the only sisters left or because she is particularly well and pleasant, I have really enjoyed her stay, and the gossips, mostly about her own family affairs. Her five children are all now settled in the world, two married with babies, and all rather impecunious. She has the disposal of £1,500 a year – certainly she does not spend it on herself – her husband makes his own small salary of £500 and keep in the hotel, so she is free to subsidize her children's earnings . . . She loves them all and is perpetually thinking about them and slaving for them. . . . As her recreation she travels adventurously, far and wide, at an incredibly cheap rate. She has decided artistic talent, but not enough to be a professional. Altogether, at sixty-five years of age, Rosy Dobbs is a remarkable woman who has weathered well . . . She shocked us with her free ways during her widowhood. Today her free ways are *à la mode*. . . . Meanwhile I have been compelled to shift my position and to tolerate and accept conduct in the younger generation which twenty years ago I should

have boycotted. The decay of religion, whilst not affecting the current code on many matters, has completely undermined sexual morality. . . .

Herbert Hoover (1874–1964) was Republican President of the United States 1928–32. The Wall Street crash had taken place in October, but Beatrice does not refer to it. At the time its repercussions were not fully appreciated. Unemployment was then about 1,300,000. Ramsay MacDonald left England on 28 September for America – it was the first visit of a British Prime Minister – to discuss naval disarmament. His visit was a milestone in British foreign policy, marking the end of Britain's supremacy at sea and America's emergence as a naval power.

*2 November.* [Passfield Corner]
Sidney reports J.R.M., who summoned his Cabinet Ministers to meet him on his arrival at 10 Downing Street yesterday, is immensely pleased with himself and says that he has done more for Hoover than for Great Britain. The Labour Cabinet is still in its honeymoon. But dark, thunderous clouds are arising among our own people – coal and unemployment; for the public at large, increased expenditure. Mosley, whom I met at lunch, is contemptuous of Thomas's incapacity, of the infirmity of manual working Cabinet Ministers generally and very complacent about his own qualification for the leadership of the Labour Party. That young man has too much aristocratic insolence in his make-up. Meanwhile . . . Cynthia has charmed the house. . . . When Neville Chamberlain objected to increased pensions and allowances as 'giving something for nothing' and therefore demoralizing to character, the charming Cynthia retorted, in her maiden speech, that she herself and most of the Honourable Members opposite had been brought up 'on something for nothing'; were they all demoralized? There was no answer. . . .

*10 December.* [Passfield Corner]
GBS and Charlotte staying here . . . As I watched the handsome 'Ancient' talking and laughing . . . I realized that I should miss him more than anyone else in our intimate circle: he is the most closely associated with our long married life, most continuously our friend. And Charlotte is a fit mate. Enthroned in the world's esteem and enrobed in wealth, they smile at each other and gaze with an amused good nature on the rest of the world. It is a pleasant sight to look on! 'We never think or talk of old age, we try to forget we are old,' said Charlotte; and GBS acquiesced.

*27 December.* [Passfield Corner]

Preparing a broadcast on 'Changes in the World of Politics' during the half-century I look back on, and cursing myself for having engaged to do it. I am no longer fit for any public engagements! . . .

Why, I do not know, but my mind goes back forty years to the Xmas of 1889 . . . The weather was dark and gloomy, as it is this week, and I was feeling discouraged by not having the material I wanted and living without companionship, struggling on day by day alone in the world. . . . Sidney and I met in that first week of January 1890. And now, at the very tag-end of our joint life together, he is again at work in the Colonial Office, not as a clerk but as Secretary of State and a peer. So far as we are concerned it has certainly been a topsy-turvy world, but the top has come last. Yet just because it has come last, it does not seem a top at all, only a step on one side from our own way in life . . . But personal content is not the sum total of consciousness. And 1929 ends in gloom, so far as I realize the condition of my country. Is Great Britain suffering from a sort of sleepy sickness? Sidney says so.

~ 1930 ~

*23 January.* [Passfield Corner]

The broadcast went off happily on the eve of my seventy-second birthday. The B.B.C. young man cheered an old woman's heart by telling her she has a perfect voice and is a born broadcaster. But in spite of these blandishments, broadcasting is a doubtful venture compared with the effort I put into composing the talk and the nervous strain of these infrequent interviews with the microphone . . .

*25 February.* [2 Whitehall Court?]

The life I lead is displeasing in its restlessness. Always week-end visitors chosen for political reasons, which means talk, talk and again talk – often interesting, but always exhausting. Then two or three nights in London: lunches, dinners, afternoon parties, Press interviews and occasional social functions of a more pretentious sort. These I avoid like the devil; they have to me a ghostly flavour. Last night at the Foreign Office reception, where I went from a dinner at 10 Downing Street, as the wife of the Secretary of State for the Colonies, there arose a memory of my first Foreign Office reception. I had come from the dinner at which I first met Joseph Chamberlain – forty-seven years ago! At Admiralty House a funny picture emerged of a flirtation in a corner of the great reception room with an Admiralty clerk in 1876 – the year I 'came out' – over half a century ago. It is uncanny, this looking backwards through vistas of bygone figures, great personages or interesting but little-known individuals, all dead and gone. . . .

*30 March.* [Passfield Corner]
For the second time Sidney has found crucial questions referred, not to the Cabinet for consultation and decision, but to a suddenly called meeting of the two ex-Prime Ministers, the P.M. and himself. . . . As for the Parliamentary Party and the House of Commons as a whole, neither one nor the other comes into the picture. . . . Of course, there is a Cabinet meeting every week . . . but the main business of these meetings seems to be telling the Ministers, as a body, decisions already arrived at by other means . . .

*3 April.* [Whitehall Court]
The last evening at 2 Whitehall Court. 'A rich man's slum,' as it has been nicknamed by contemptuous millionaires. Our little furnished flat . . . has served us well . . . But it is unpleasant living economically in an expensive establishment and we shall be glad to get into Artillery Mansions, where everyone has modest means or wishes to live modestly.

I have finished up entertaining the Parliamentary Labour Party for this first year of salaried office. I have invited all the 292 M.P.s to lunch (over 200 came) and given a reception to them and their wives, and Dominion and Colonial personages, at Admiralty House, all being successful. . . .

Churt was Lloyd George's country home in Surrey. The writer G. K. Chesteron (1874–1936) was notably rotund.

*5 April.* [Passfield Corner]
H. G. Wells, whom we had not seen for some seven years, turned up for lunch on his way to Churt to collogue with Lloyd George. 'He uses me as a super-press man,' he jovially remarked. H.G. has grown super-fat and wheezy, almost rivals Chesterton. This fatness accentuates the piglikeness of his features. (The pig face is uncommon in England – English are mostly dogs and birds – less often horses, cats and apes, but still fewer pigs.) . . . I was glad to see the genial old sinner . . . In his forthcoming novel he is said to have caricatured the lot of us. How he and Lloyd George will enjoy

themselves abusing the Labour government, inventing slogans for the next general election . . . They are two old buccaneers, out of joint with the world as it is, and impatient to see it altered to their likes, with themselves as the principal actors. But like ourselves and GBS they are voices from the past. Wherefrom will come the voices telling the future? . . .

M. K. Gandhi (1869–1948), the leader of the Indian nationalist movement, had just made his 'salt march' to the sea; he was among the 54,000 arrested for 'civil disobedience' offences.

*4 May.* [Passfield Corner]
Gandhi arrested; and now we shall see how deep-rooted is the following of the Indian saint, whether faith will move mountains of Indian disunity and inexperience and upset the British Raj! 'The only way of compelling the Englishman to get off the back of the Elephant is for the Elephant to make it damned unpleasant for him,' the nationalist Indian would answer. It is not prejudice in favour of autocratic British rule in the mind of the Labour Cabinet and the viceroy that blocks the way to granting immediate Dominion status, but sheer perplexity as to how on earth to do it without tumbling India into a state of civil war. We did it in Ireland by separating off the Ulster Protestants from the Free State Catholics and securing Ulster from any interference from the new Dominion. But how to keep the hostile races, communities and castes of India from trying to dominate one another seems to pass the wit of man! Whether it would be better for the people of India to be left to fight it out among themselves is another matter. But would the other white races and Japan leave India to fall into the state of China?

On 23 January 1930 Mosley, who had been asked to help J. H. Thomas combat unemployment, bypassed him and sent MacDonald a memorandum proposing reform. A Cabinet committee chaired by Snowden rejected these proposals. Before a third discussion on 19 May, Mosley told MacDonald he proposed to resign. After a powerful resignation speech in Parliament on 28 May he began to organize a breakaway party. Thomas was moved to the Dominion Office on 5 June, among other government changes.

*19 May.* [Passfield Corner]
Oswald and Cynthia Mosley here for the night, at a critical moment of his career. . . . Mosley says that the party is breaking up in the country,

that there will be a débâcle at the next election and that the party will be so disintegrated that it will not revive for a generation. It is fair to add that, except in the case of Thomas, Mosley does not abuse the leaders. About Thomas he is contemptuous . . . 'I've an 'ell of an 'ead,' Thomas was wailing at the last meeting, the quite obvious explanation being a night of boozing. . . . Mosley respects and likes Snowden but says that he has become conservative and anti-socialist without knowing it, largely owing to the 'classy' adventures into which Mrs Snowden has dragged him. She is reported to have said that she needs no friends because she is so intimate with the royal family. . . . About the participation of the Cabinet Ministers and their wives in Court and London Society functions, the Mosleys are far more acidly emphatic than I am . . .

*31 May.* [Guernsey?]
On the night of our departure for the Channel Isles Sidney reported an interview with MacDonald, who is struggling out of the depths of difficulties with the party. Sixty members had signed a demand for the dismissal of Thomas and the P.M. was considering how to find a way out for his old friend and colleague. Sidney played up and offered to clear out of either of one or of both his offices as Secretary of State for Dominions and Colonies. The P.M. expressed his appreciation, but two Secretaries of State would still be needed in the House of Lords. There was, however, the possibility of appointing a new Secretary for State for the Dominions leaving Sidney as Secretary of State for the Colonies, giving Thomas the Dominions . . . Sidney acquiesced . . . and came off for our fortnight's holiday in excellent spirits. . . .

*16 June.* [Passfield Corner]
A satisfactory holiday in the Channel Islands, wandering to and fro Guernsey, Sark and Jersey as 'Mr and Mrs Sidney Webb'. In both the hotels not recognized as 'personages' until the end of our stay – in each case there were guests who spotted us and at the end of each visit a letter or telegram giving Sidney's official name away, a blunder on the part of correspondents . . .

Before I left London I was 'vetted' by an accomplished woman doctor. Her report was that lungs, heart, kidneys, were all A.I. – and the arteries those of a young woman. But excessive whizzing in the ear and sleeplessness are chronic; she suggested specialists for each, including a psychologist for sleeplessness! Whether I shall take her advice I have not yet determined; each specialist will probably assure me that there is nothing the matter with me, except old age. 'Why do you want to work at your age?' the last medical man I saw asked me.

York House was the London residence of the Prince of Wales (1894–1972) who became Edward VIII for eleven months before he abdicated in December 1936.

*13 July.* [Artillery Mansions]
. . . an informal dinner at York House – my first introduction into the Court circle. The Prince, having devoted himself at dinner to the young Countess (Minto) and the middle-aged Duchess (Abercorn), settled down afterwards by the aged Baroness (Passfield) and opened out into an oddly intimate talk about his religious difficulties.

'What do you really believe, Mrs Webb?' he asked in an agitated tone. (I was there as Lady Passfield.) He is a neurotic and takes too much alcohol for health of body or mind. If I were his mother or grandmother I should be very nervous about his future. . . . the unhappiness of the Prince's expression, the uneasy restlessness of his manner, the odd combination of unbelief and hankering after sacerdotal religion, the reactionary prejudice about India and the morbid curiosity about Russia revealed in his talk interested me. The Anglican Church, whose services he said he 'had to attend', he clearly resented. He must be a problem to the conventional courtiers who surround him! Will he stay put in his present role of the most popular heir-apparent in British history? As I talked to him he seemed like a hero of one of Shaw's plays; he was certainly very unconventional in his conversation with a perfect stranger. . . .

But how I loathe London Society in all its aspects. . . . What I detest most of all are my own reactions to it – the stimulus it gives to latent personal vanity, contemptible in an old lady of seventy odd! . . . once Sidney is out of office I shall be quit of the whole business – in any case I intend to give up entertaining at Christmas and save the remainder of our official salary lest worse befall old England and our own little income. Again the desire to be 'thoroughly comfortable' in one's old age! Personal vanity curbed by greed! Alas! for human nature, I am of the old opinion still: I do not *like* human beings.

*2 August.* [Passfield Corner]
. . . Whether it is old age or the absence of personal ambition [Sidney] is ready to retire whenever J.R.M. no longer requires him, and certainly

will not join another Cabinet if by any chance Labour comes back to office after the next general election. Personally I think the Tories will romp back; the rot within the Labour Party is serious and there is panic among the well-to-do, not about the unemployed, but about the maintenance of the unemployed. At the back of the mind of the middle classes there is a settled conviction that if a man cannot be given work he ought not to be given food, at any rate not more than is necessary to prevent the scandal of deaths by starvation. The propertied classes are not yet prepared to accept the third alternative of maintenance under training or disciplined occupation. As this solution is also objected to by the uninstructed proletarian it is not likely to be adopted by either of the alternative Cabinets. Meagre unconditional outdoor relief is still the one and only device. Enlightened public opinion seems paralysed; both Front Benches refuse to think – they just drift between putting men on the dole or striking them off. The Labour government has put men on, the Conservative government will throw them off and try to solve unemployment by fiscal protection.

Grigory Sokolnikov (1888–1939), a Bolshevik since 1905, was Soviet Ambassador in London 1929–32. He was to die in prison, a victim of the 1937 Stalinist purge. Beatrice was much influenced by him and his wife.

*3 August.* [Passfield Corner]
The Soviet Ambassador and his wife here for a day and night, a singularly sympathetic man and woman. . . . They are refined and admirably mannered, quiet, dignified, straightforward and pleasant, not aggressive but very staunch in their upholding of Bolshevism in a hostile world. Of the two, she is the most outspoken. They had been in Glasgow and she observed the dull depressed attitude of the people in the streets. In Moscow everyone was excited and neurotic. England was healthier to live in but not so interesting. . . . Philip Snowden lunched here to meet them . . . He impressed Snowden favourably. Sitting after lunch in the loggia and discussing the Five Year Plan, Sokolnikov described the enthusiasm with which the Communist workers were accepting low wages and a relatively hard life in order to save money for capital improvements. 'That's sound,' said the British Chancellor of the Exchequer. 'I sometimes despair about the working class. . . .' 'Ah, Mr Snowden,' said I. 'You will never get the British workman to work harder on less wages when he sees the employing class enjoying leisure and large expenditure. It is the equality of income

that enables the Soviet government to ask and obtain increased energy and sacrifice from the manual working citizen. The workers know they are working not for other people's children but for their *own* children.'

*7 August.* [Passfield Corner]
Charlotte is presenting me with the complete edition of GBS's works and I am reading the volumes one by one ... GBS himself thinks that the elect of all times will read and reverence Bernard Shaw as they continue to do Plato, Dante, Shakespeare and Goethe. Not even his admirers take him at that valuation. But in sheer vitality of brain, other able persons – Sidney and I, for instance – are dwarfs beside him. ...

W. T. Cosgrave (1880–1965) was the moderate Premier of Ireland 1922–32.

*6 September.* [Passfield Corner?]
A week-end at the Viceregal Lodge [in Dublin] and three days with Lion Phillimore ... Should I or should I not curtsy? I compromised, curtsied on arrival and at the 'state' dinner party, but not otherwise. 'Their Excellencies' and the splendour of the Viceregal establishment (twenty-seven indoor servants, fifteen gardeners) seems an expensive anachronism for so small a community and will, I imagine, be dropped – the institution is clearly not popular with the citizens of Dublin. Republicans and Labourites refuse to recognize the Governor-General, and Belfast boycotts and is boycotted. ...

At the Viceregal Lodge we met the leading politicians, judges and foreign Ministers. At Lion's we saw the Cosgraves more intimately. The able group of young men now governing the Free State ... had much zeal and no 'side'. The quiet efficiency of their administrators made me ashamed of the long struggle for Home Rule, culminating in the disgraceful episode of the Black and Tans. The most notable impression left on my mind was the heavy hand of the Roman Catholic Church. In no other country have I become aware of the spiritual oppression of the common people by the fear of Hell. One almost began to feel this fear oneself. ...

There is much bitterness about the separation of Ulster. 'The Irish will never forgive, until that is put right,' one Cabinet Minister said to me. 'Sooner or later we shall fight for it,' he added. They feel that they have been 'done' by wily Englishmen ... Throughout our visit we were accompanied by an armed escort – an armed guard slept in the house with us when staying with Lion. Cosgrave's house was heavily guarded and everywhere he went he was attended by armed detectives.

*4 October.* [Passfield Corner]
A spate of high-class social functions this week . . . two lunches and an afternoon gathering in a little over twenty-four hours, and a Buckingham Palace state dinner on Friday. . . . The Buckingham Palace dinner centred round the delegates from the Dominions and their wives; it was part of the web of imperial destiny, and well wrought. The ceremony and its settings combined dull dignity with refined magnificence: there was almost a religious atmosphere as the 120 guests trooped up the stairs into the sumptuous range of reception rooms, each guest bending over the hands of the two Idols on the way to the inner temple of the banqueting hall – with the golden plate and crimson-clothed attendants. What spoilt the pageant was the dowdyism of the women guests, in marked contrast with the superb garments and jewels of the Queen and her aristocratic Court ladies. I, for instance, though I appeared as The Lady Passfield, wore a high-necked long-sleeved grey chiffon velvet which I have been wearing for six months at every dinner I have attended; Mrs Lunn, the Under-Secretary's wife, had donned a conventional black satin, obviously bought for the occasion from the local Co-op. Ethel Snowden, with a paste tiara and a cheap fashionable frock, was the intermediate link between we humble folk and the Court circle. . . .

After dinner the Queen [Mary] stood in one of the large reception rooms and we ladies grouped ourselves round the walls, a few being picked out and led up to the Queen by the Duchess of Devonshire for two or three minutes' perfunctory talk, I being one of them. The Queen is a fine figure of a woman: she holds herself well and is magnificently apparelled and bejewelled, the lines of her face extensively 'made up'; she is stiff in manner, curt in words and lifeless in expression, and really looks like an exquisitely executed automaton – a royal robot. I gather she is an honest and kindly soul, but curiously shy – she was painfully at a loss of what to say to me. . . . 'Where do you live?' was her only contribution. 'In a cottage near Liphook, Ma'am.' 'Liphook!' she said in a puzzled tone, and seeing another lady being prepared for an audience I back away. . . . About 10.30 o'clock the King and Queen and other royalties walked through the gallery and the King, who is far more homely and gracious than his royal mate, stopped in front of me and hoped 'that you are not too tired', to which

I mumbled some amiable reply. So ends my first and last appearance at the Court of St James's!

There was a rapid and fierce Zionist reaction to Sir John Hope Simpson's report on land settlement and the Passfield White Paper. 'It is really the work of the Office,' Sidney had written to Beatrice on 10 October when the draft was completed, but he had to take responsibility. In March 1931 MacDonald made some concessions to Zionist pressure.

*26 October.* [Passfield Corner]
Sidney, by the publication of the Hope Simpson paper, and the *Statement of Policy* accompanying it, has involved himself and the Labour government in a storm of anger from Jewry all over the world. . . . The *Statement of Policy*, by the way, is a badly drafted, tactless document – he ought to have done it himself. But so far as the Jews are concerned, that betterment of form would not have made it more acceptable. . . .

*30 October.* [Passfield Corner]
. . . For the next six weeks the P.M. and other Cabinet Ministers . . . will be absorbed in the Round Table conference to settle the fate of India, or rather of the British in India. Here in old England, dissolution is in the air in more sense than one.

Is it a further cause for pessimism, or a consolation tinged with malice, that other powerful races are rolling in tempestuous waters? The U.S.A., with its cancerous growth of crime and uncounted but destitute unemployed; Germany hanging over the precipice of a nationalist dictatorship; Italy boasting of its military preparedness; France, in dread of a new combination of Italy, Germany and Austria against her; Spain on the brink of revolution; the Balkan States snarling at each other; the Far East in a state of anarchic ferment; the African continent uncertain whether its 'paramount interest' and cultural power will be black or white; South American states forcibly replacing pseudo-democracies by military dictatorships; and, finally – acutely hostile to the rest of the world, engulfed in a fabulous effort, the success of which would shake capitalist civilization in its very foundation – Soviet Russia, struggling with fanatic fervour to bring about, for the first time in the history of the world, an equalitarian state, based on an uncompromising scientific materialism.

What a world has been opened up by the Great War!

*12 November.* [Passfield Corner]
We lunched on Thursday at the Soviet Embassy – a princely mansion in Kensington Palace Gardens with great reception rooms and large garden, its occupants looking, according to ordinary diplomatic standards of style and expression, strangely out of place. Indeed it was impossible to distinguish the Ambassador, his wife and staff from those serving them in what is here called a 'menial' capacity – ideas, manners and mutual relations being the same all through. This expression of the equalitarian state was unique and to me pleasing. . . .

The Sokolnikovs encouraged us to go to Russia, altogether denied that we should find it expensive if we arranged a trip through their Tourist Agency . . . We are the only 'Cabinet' members who have consorted with them. The Hendersons do not 'know them' socially, nor the P.M. . . .

~ 1931 ~

Stafford Cripps (1889–1952), the son of Alfred and Theresa Cripps, was an outstandingly successful barrister. In the 30s he was expelled from the Labour Party for persistently supporting left-wing causes. Malcolm Muggeridge (1903–1990), journalist and broadcaster, was married to Kitty, the daughter of Beatrice's sister Rosy.

*19 January.* [Passfield Corner]
A bevy of nephews and nieces during the Xmas holidays. . . . Malcolm Muggeridge, Kitty's husband, stayed two days. He is the most intellectually stimulating and pleasant-mannered of all my 'in-laws'; under thirty years of age, ex-teacher in India and Egypt, now writer on the *Manchester Guardian* and playwright. His first play, *The Three Flats*, is to be acted by the Stage Society in February. An ugly, but attractive and expressive face, a clever and sympathetic talker, ultra-modern in his views on sex, theoretically more than practically I think. A great admirer of D. H. Lawrence and his 'return to nature' . . . Yet I think Malcolm is a mystic and even a puritan in his awareness of loyalties and human relationships. . . .

And now Stafford Cripps enters the political arena as Solicitor-General and the winner, by a huge majority, of the Bristol seat. . . . He is the only one of the 155 nephews and nieces who might become a big figure in public life. . . .

*22 January.* [Passfield Corner]

My seventy-third birthday: a basket of flowers from the Soviet Ambassadress, a bunch of carnations and lilies from the Countess of Warwick, a few telegrams – one from Cynthia and Oswald Mosley. The trend of my reputation is clearly to the left and not to the right . . .

*2 February.* [Passfield Corner]

I started today on the first page of *Our Partnership*. I shall not take this venture so seriously as I did *My Apprenticeship*. That was a terrific labour, an agony of mind . . . Sometimes I cursed myself for becoming entangled in the self-conscious 'scribblings of a woman' (as Sidney once called the diary), and wondered how I could get out of printing it . . . The event proved, as it usually does, that neither inflated expectations nor neurotic forebodings are justified; the book had a *succès d'estime* but not a popular success, and my profit on the publication of these two years' effort, deducting the cost of the secretary, was a few hundred pounds – certainly not a livelihood for the author. . . .

*4 February.* [Passfield Corner]

. . . What I am beginning to doubt is the 'inevitability of gradualness' – or even the practicability of gradualness, in the transition from a capitalist to an equalitarian civilization. Anyway, no leader in our country has thought out *how to make the transition* without upsetting the apple cart. Sidney says 'it will make itself', without an acknowledged plan accepted by one party in the state and denounced by the other. We shall slip into the equalitarian state as we did into political democracy – by each party (whether nominally socialist or anti-socialist) taking steps in the direction of curtailing the tribute of rent and interest and increasing the amount and security of revenue of labour. But this cannot be done without transferring the *control* of the savings of the country, and I don't see how that is to be done gradually, or without a terrific struggle on clearly thought out lines. And no one is doing the thinking. . . .

*25 February.* [Passfield Corner]

An amazing act of arrogance, Oswald Mosley's melodramatic defection from the Labour Party, slamming the door with a bang to resound throughout the political world. . . . A foreign journalist at the Labour Party conference nicknamed him 'the English Hitler'. But the British electorate would not stand a Hitler. . . . I doubt whether he has the tenacity of a Hitler. He also lacks genuine fanaticism. Deep down in his heart he is a cynic. He will be beaten and retire. In the chaos of our political life today, there will be many meteors passing through the firmament. There is still Winston Churchill to be accounted for. Have there ever been so many political personages on the loose? Mosley's sensational exit will matter supremely to himself and his half-dozen followers but very little to the Labour Party . . .

Joseph Stalin (1879–1953) had just launched the first Five Year Plan. It was a major factor in winning support from socialists disillusioned by the failure of social democracy to cope with economic collapse. Beatrice had engaged Jean and Annie Smith in 1928. They remained at Passfield for the rest of her life.

*15 March.* [Hastings]
. . . If the Russian General Plan succeeds in proving to the world that production can be carried on successfully *without* the incentive of profit to the capitalist and the lash of starvation for the wage-earner, the lines will be drawn for either a great war against the dictatorship of the proletariat or the spread of Communist civilization by peaceful penetration throughout the political democracies of the world. That the barbaric Russia should lead the way to a new civilization is the most humiliating prospect for the cultured Frenchman, the scientific German and above all for 'God's Englishman'.

*19 March.* [Passfield Corner]
My week at Hastings, whither I had taken the older of my two servants to recover from an illness, was spoilt by a domestic brawl at Passfield between the Olivers and the younger sister, due to Mrs Oliver's overbearing temper and Jean's neurotic temperament . . .

I have had, in my long career as mistress – before marriage, of many servants, since my marriage, of two – only three absolutely trustworthy servants, Neale and Mrs Thompson in Father's household, and Emily Wordley in my own. All these have earned, by their trustworthiness, annuities, and they richly deserved them! Skill and industry one can buy, but perfect honesty and absence of all deception is priceless, and should be rewarded long after the service is at an end. It is interesting but depressing how quite intelligent and otherwise well-conducted servants will carry on an illicit and gainful business – take a commission from a tradesman or send parcels home, for instance. They seem actually to enjoy the risks of it: it is a form of gambling, and they have no notion of the eventual loss of confidence and gratitude on the part of the mistress, not to mention their own peace of mind! However, there is a far higher level of honesty today than there was fifty years ago when I started housekeeping, largely because servants and mistresses are on far more equal terms. There is more friendship between them, and no decent person cheats a friend. Small deceptions and peculations are, like personal cleanliness, largely a question of class or degree of education. Petty theft is like having nits in the hair and leaving them there. . . .

*27 March. Passfield Corner*
I shall be glad when Sidney retires, as the lonely life down here, with the alternative of days and nights in London (equally lonely during the day, and with the discomforts of the little flat and the noise and bustle of the streets), [is] beginning to prey on my nerves, and might end in a bad breakdown. I am beginning to feel the *helplessness* of old age, which with me is masked by will-power and physical activity. To other people I seem in full possession of my faculties, but in my own consciousness I am depressed and dazed; memory fails me and I worry about this thing and that. . . .

> Harold Nicolson (1886–1968) joined Mosley's New Party in March 1931 and became editor of the party's journal, *Action*. He was married to the poet and novelist Vita Sackville-West (1892–1962). John Reith, later Lord Reith, was the founding Director General of the B.B.C.

*1 April.* [Passfield Corner]
Leonard and Virginia Woolf here for the week-end. Leonard a distinguished Jew – a saint with very considerable intelligence; a man without vanity or guile, wholly public-spirited, lacking perhaps in humour or brilliancy but original in thought and always interesting. She stands at the head of literary women, fastidiously intellectual with great literary artistry, a consummate craftsman. (She is beautiful to look at.) Coldly analytical, we felt she was observing us with a certain hostility; she is also extremely sensitive – apt, I think, to take offence at unintentional rudeness. Among their intimate friends are the Harold Nicolsons, the ex-diplomat and present broadcaster, to whose persiflage we always listen on Friday evenings. He is a convert to Mosley and one of his prospective candidates. Reith of the B.B.C. is another disciple. Apparently Mosley is convinced that he will sweep the constituencies and become Prime Minister in the near future, and is already choosing his Cabinet! Which

argues megalomania. If he gets returned himself, he will be lucky. It is passing strange that so clever a man . . . should be so completely ignorant of British political democracy, of its loyalty and solid judgement, of its incurable dullness and slowness of apprehension of any new thought . . .

Virginia Woolf had met the Prime Minister at a small dinner of six persons, at which he seemed to be completely absorbed by Lady Londonderry. MacDonald's aloofness from his colleagues and open dislike and avoidance of all Labour M.P.s has become one of the standing jokes of British political life. . .

On 8 July 1930, Dora Russell gave birth to a daughter, Harriet. Although the father was a young American journalist, Griffin Barry, the child was registered in Bertrand Russell's name, a subject of long legal controversy. He succeeded to the earldom in 1931 on the death of his brother Frank. The Olivers had been dismissed and a new resident gardener named Miles installed in the bungalow with his wife and daughters. Sidney had written to MacDonald requesting permission to retire, certainly not later than October.

*21 April.* [Passfield Corner]
Bertrand Russell, now an Earl, lunched here on Sunday to talk over his new role as a Labour peer. I had not asked his wife. But in the course of conversation he remarked, 'My wife was so sorry she could not come, but she has the infant to attend to.' I accepted the apology and turned the conversation. Now it was the advent of the baby, advertised by her to her friends as another man's child and accepted by him as not his own, which had decided me to withdraw as Dora's acquaintance . . . What interested me was the change in Bertrand; he looked wretched. . . . Poor Bertie; he has made a miserable mess of his life and he knows it. He said drearily, when I asked him if he was going back to his old love – mathematical metaphysics – 'I am too old to write anything but potboilers'. . . .

*1 May.* [Passfield Corner]
Finished the first chapter of *Our Partnership* . . . Now that I have got over my domestic troubles and the beauty of the spring has arrived, with the birds singing from early morning to late in the evening, I am working better and enjoying life in my charming house. Also, I am looking forward to a happier autumn and winter, with Sidney by my side and a holiday abroad. . . . .

*1 July.* [Passfield Corner]
Five crowded days in London, including a day and night with Beveridge and Mrs Mair, her daughter and two young medical men, in Beveridge's bungalow in Wiltshire. Beveridge has in fact annexed the Mair family, minus the husband and father; what has happened to this unhappy man no one cares or knows. Clearly the arrangement is to everyone's advantage so long as you ignore Mair's right to his wife's devotion; but has he any rights? That question ought to have been settled long ago; it is that ambiguity that is unpleasant.

*13 July.* [Beachy Head Hotel]
*All Passion Spent,* by Vita Sackville-West; an exquisite description of old age in the setting of the British governing class, a perfect piece of crafts-manship, a real literary gem. . . .

> The Italian-born Humbert Wolfe (1886–1940), poet, translator and civil servant, was well known for his tart witticisms. Ellen Wilkinson's rela-tionship with the cartoonist and Labour M.P. J. F. Horrabin (1884–1962) ended with his marriage soon after this entry. She later had a complex attachment to Herbert Morrison. GBS spent a fortnight in Russia with Lord and Lady Astor. The visit provoked a sensation in the press.

*28 July.* [Passfield Corner]
Ellen Wilkinson and Charlotte Shaw down here for the week-end. Ellen has been tamed politically by being the loyal parliamentary private secretary of Susan [Lawrence], and is full of affection and admiration for her chief. Humbert Wolfe, the reactionary official of the Labour Department, better known as a poet, is insolent in his remarks about the subserviency of his chief (Margaret Bondfield) to his influence and direction. About Susan Lawrence, he observed that she was a 'virago intacta', which was as witty as it was true. Susan and Margaret, I sug-gested, are the last of their class of celibate women in public life . . .

On our long walk together Ellen asked me what I thought on these questions: was it reasonable to expect a woman in public life, who did not want to get married, to remain a celibate if she found a congenial friend who happened to have an uncongenial wife? I answered that I remained a puritan on such questions but that I was not dogmatically opposed to extra-matrimonial arrangements so long as they were not promiscuous, were founded on real companionship of heart and head, and also did not involve *cruelty* to others who had 'vested interests' of an emotional character. Ellen referred, I think, to her own relations with Horrabin. She is a strong, able and honest woman . . . and very self-sacrificing to her brothers and sister, who largely depend on her. I like her as a companion and respect her as a people's representative. But she has been hardened and a little coarsened by her life in Parliament . . . For good or for evil the political emancipation of women and their entry into public life has swept away the old requirement of chastity in the unmarried woman! The conventions (there is no code) are now the same for men and women.

Charlotte Shaw was in her usual beaming mood about the greatness of her great man; and brought batches of cuttings giving his paradoxical sayings and the universal homage of the Russian people. . . . Shaw's apparent wholesale approval of Russian Communism is a little discounted by his equally demonstrative admiration of Italian Fascism three years ago . . . However . . . I shall listen to GBS's testimony after his ten days' inspection of show institutions, surrounded with admiring crowds, with interest, and a bias towards taking his account at its face value – very different from my intense irritation when listening to his praise of Fascism!

In mid-May, the Kredit-anstalt bank in Vienna failed. In the ensuing rush for liquidity, British banks could not recover recent advances to Germany and were forced to meet their obligations in gold. A run on sterling began and substantial sums were lost, prompting a crisis of confidence in the government. In July, a committee set up by Snowden to propose economies produced a sensational report, advocating severe cuts in government expenditure. Many in the Labour movement objected; the crisis deepened through the summer. The proposed reduction in unemployment benefit was the sticking point. Unable to reach agreement, the Cabinet resigned, many believing MacDonald was resigning with them. MacDonald then formed an emergency National government which swept to power with 566 supporters in the autumn election. Labour saved only 52 seats. It took the Party years to recover.

*4 August.* [Passfield Corner]
. . . the Cabinet is really in a very tight place. The Report of the Economy Committee appointed by Snowden, made up of five clever hard-faced representatives of capitalism and two dull trade unionists, is a sensational demand for economy in public expenditure, not merely cutting down what they consider 'doles' but also health and education services. Luxury

hotels and luxury flats, Bond Street shopping, racing and high living in all its forms is to go unchecked; but the babies are not to have milk and the very poor are not to have homes. The private luxury of the rich is apparently not *wasteful expenditure*. A Cabinet committee has been appointed to consider it . . . But Snowden is responsible for appointing the committee. And he is really in agreement with the Report! . . .

*8 August.* [Passfield Corner]
GBS spent two nights here and gave his pleasant chatty address on Russia to the Fabian summer school. He was tired and excited by his visit to Russia; carried away by the newness and the violence of the changes wrought. Here is tragedy – comedy – melodrama, all magnificently staged on a huge scale. It *must* be right! The paradox of the speech: the Russian Revolution was pure Fabianism – Lenin and Stalin had recognized the 'inevitability of gradualness'! Also they had given up 'workers' control' for the Webbs' conception of the threefold state – citizens, consumers and produces' organization. What is not Webbism or Western is the welding together of all three by a *creed* oligarchy of two million faithful, dominating a population of 120 million indifferent, lukewarm or actively hostile. That is the crux of the controversy between those who approve and disapprove of Soviet Russia. . . .

*22 August. 4 a.m.* [Passfield Corner]
Sidney came back from the Cabinet meeting on August 20th – which had sat all day and was still sitting at seven o'clock when he left to catch his train – tired and depressed. He goes up this morning for another long day of critical meetings. The financial plight of Great Britain . . . is very serious . . . The only excuse for the Labour Cabinet is that no other group of men, whether politicians, businessmen or academic economists, whether Tory, Liberal or Labour, seem to understand the problem. No one knows either what the situation is or, assuming it is bad, the way out of it to sound finance. Even the fundamental facts of the situation are unknown. . . . Anyway, it is a sorry end to the second Labour Cabinet . . . they will leave the state of England worse than it was when they took office. . . .

*24 August. 6.30 p.m.* [Passfield Corner]
*The Fall of the Labour government 1929–31.* Just heard over the wireless what I wished to hear, that the Cabinet as a whole has resigned, J.R.M. accepting office as Prime Minister in order to form a National

Emergency government including Tories and Liberals; it being also stated that Snowden, Thomas and alas! Sankey will take office under him. I regret Sankey, but I am glad the other three will disappear from the Labour world; they were rotten stuff . . . A startling sensation it will be for those faithful followers throughout the country who were unaware of J.R.M.'s and Snowden's gradual conversion to the outlook of the City and London society. . . . So ends, ingloriously, the Labour Cabinet of 1929–31. . . .

*25 August.* [Passfield Corner]
Sidney came back early in the afternoon of our second Fabian Garden Party. He was exhausted, and rather upset by the queer end of the Labour Cabinet – but delighted to be out of it all. . . . One of the good results of the National government under Mac is that it unites, as no other event could, the whole of the labour movement under Henderson in determined opposition to the policy of making the working class pay for the mistakes of the financiers. . . .

*10 October.* Scarborough
Dull, drab, disillusioned but *not* disunited is the impression I got of the Labour Party conference of 1931. . . . What seems now to be the prevailing spirit . . . is a dour determination never again to undertake the government of the country as *the caretaker of the existing order of society* . . .

*28 October.* [Passfield Corner]
. . . Ponsonby and the Marleys and we two listened to the wireless from ten to two on Tuesday the 26th. Towards the end of the tale of Labour losses we became hilarious; the unfolding situation was so absurd! MacDonald, at once author, producer and chief actor of this amazing political drama, had shown consummate art. He had been aided and abetted with acid malignity by Philip Snowden . . . The Parliamentary Labour Party had not been defeated but annihilated, largely, we think, by the women's vote. . . . Whether new leaders will spring up with sufficient faith, will-power and knowledge to break through the tough and massive defence of British profit-making capitalism . . . I cannot foresee. . . . What undid the two Labour governments was not merely their lack of knowledge and the will to apply what knowledge they had, but also their acceptance, as individuals, of the way of life of men of property and men of rank. It is a hard saying and one that condemns ourselves as well as others of the Labour government. *You cannot*

*engineer an equalitarian state if you yourself are enjoying the pomp and cir-*
*cumstance of the city of the rich surrounded by the city of the poor.* . . .

*Christmas Day.* [Passfield Corner]
This day forty years ago I was at Box House . . . awaiting the death of the
dear one to tell my family that I was bound up in the vocation of continuous enquiry into social organization. A life, it proved to be, of
extraordinary happiness and some success. 'I knew my little Bee would
do well for herself,' I could hear dear Father saying, with his beaming
smile, if he came back to see. . . . Others of his daughters had greater
personal charm and good looks – 'but for sheer common sense give me
my little Bee,' he would have said. And I think he was right. 'Beatrice',
once said Leonard Courtney to Kate, 'has great general capacity. She is
not an intellectual. She merely applies this general capacity to certain
problems of the intellect.' And that is exactly what I want to do about
Russia. . . . For the next four months Sidney and I will be turning out a
textbook on Methods of Social Study – a good part of it written years
ago. But our main task will be preparing our mind for seeing as much of
Russia as we can afford strength and money to see. . . .

# The Promised Land

## January 1932–December 1937

*4 January.* [Passfield Corner]
Sidney and I have settled down to our old life of regular work . . . So far
as we ourselves are concerned it is a very happy, contented life. . . . Why
then does the world today seem such a gloomy place to live in? I think
it is because of the strange atmosphere of fear and hopelessness . . . Every
kind of social organization is on the defensive . . .

What, of course, is satisfactory to us, as socialists, is that those who
defend the present order of society, in the newspapers or over the wireless (the B.B.C. has been collared by the defenders of capitalist
enterprise), are at their wits' end as to how they can explain the present
world disaster – the worst collapse of profit-making enterprise the world
has ever seen. . . . Nor can the pundits of private enterprise tell us *what*
is the cause of this mad state of things. Some say it is the stupid use of
credit or currency; others, war debts and reparations; others, the denial
of free trade and free exchange between countries; others, too much
spending or speculation, whilst a few attribute it to rationalization and
too little spending. . . . Not one of these clever ones, not even Keynes,
dare say that the game is up for profit-making enterprise. Even the
Continental socialist parties hesitate to say it. Why? Because that way lies
Soviet Russia. . . . What attracts us in Soviet Russia, and it is useless to
deny that we are prejudiced in its favour, is that its constitution, on the
one hand, bears out our *Constitution for a Socialist Commonwealth* and,
on the other, supplies a soul to that conception of government which

our paper constitution lacked. We don't quite like that soul; but still it seems to do the job; it seems to provide the spiritual power. . . .

It is the invention of the religious order, as the determining factor in the life of a great nation, which is the magnet that attracts me to Russia. Practically, that religion is Comtism – the Religion of Humanity. Auguste Comte comes to his own. Whether he would recognize this strange resurrection of his idea I very much doubt. Of course the stop in my mind is . . . How can we combine religious zeal in action with freedom of thought? . . .

The *Listener* is a weekly journal published by the B.B.C.

*23 January. 3 a.m.* [Passfield Corner]
The three talks went off excellently – the last, on the capitalist system, its drawbacks and diseases, was the subject of much discussion at the B.B.C., and some perturbation. Committees sat on it: 'If it had not been Mrs Webb, it would have been censored,' I was told. Some objectionable passages were omitted from the *Listener*'s report; I had many letters from listeners. All the same, I doubt whether I shall be welcomed again – certainly not on Russia . . . And I also doubt whether I shall be able to stand the strain . . . after all, yesterday was my seventy-fourth birthday.

In the summer of 1930 Dora Russell engaged as a governess Marjorie 'Peter' Spence, an Oxford undergraduate whom Bertrand Russell married in 1936, after a complicated divorce.

*20 February.* [Passfield Corner]
Graham Wallas with us. It interests me that he and we are much nearer in opinion than we have been for many a long year. . . . And though he fears the suppression of free thought in politics under Communism, the Soviet system has his sympathy . . . Poor liberalism! Even aged Liberals are reconsidering their faith . . . Bertrand Russell, recently in the U.S.A. and here for lunch, agreed about Soviet Russia but maintained that in spite of all the corruption and violence of the U.S.A., its oppressions and cruelties, there was more hope there for the future . . . than in Great Britain. . . . Neither he nor we mentioned his wife, so apparently he accepts our refusal to associate with her.

(22 September. Alys tells me that they have separated as he has fallen desperately in love with a clever charming girl of twenty-five whom he insists must be recognized as his wife!) . . .

*28 April.* [Passfield Corner]
I attended the sectional meetings and dinner of the British Academy, of which I have been elected the first woman member. It is a funny little body of elderly and aged men, the aged predominating . . . The little crowd gave a lifeless and derelict impression – very Oxford-donnish and conventional in culture and tone. It is a mystery why anyone agrees to pay £10 entrance fee and £3 3s 0d a year. . . . Our availability is slightly increased by my auntship to Stafford Cripps, who is assumed to be the future leader of the Labour Party. It is certainly a strange family episode that there should have been two 'R.P.' sons-in-law in the two Labour Cabinets and that a grandson should be the heir apparent . . . Dear old Father would have chuckled over it in spite of his Toryism. Mother would have been more gratified by my fellowship of the British Academy and triple doctorate. Her daughter the perfected Blue Stocking! and her own lifelong absorption in book-learning amply justified – her ambition brought to fruition in one of the ten children whom she had, at the cost of her own career as an intellectual, brought into the world. Bless her.

> In a posthumous memoir (1984), Wells described how Moura Boudberg (d. 1975) came to London as his mistress, and his distress when he discovered her dubious relationship to the Soviet authorities.

*4 May.* [Passfield Corner]
A week-end at the Shaws. H. G. Wells with his son, Frank, and a friend, a Russian baroness, turned up to tea. The talk was fast and furious . . . H.G. denigrating Russian Communism . . . The Russian 'baroness' (the widow, we afterwards heard, of a Benckendorf killed in the war; she had escaped from Leningrad in 1923 by a faked marriage with a German, afterwards dissolved, and she is now acting as Gorki's secretary in Italy), a handsome, attractive aristocrat, took a lively part in defence of Soviet Russia. So did GBS and the Webbs. H.G. did not like being on the right of the Webbs . . .

*14 May. 4 a.m.* [Passfield Corner]
Our journey put off for one week owing to ice in Gulf of Finland, thus prolonging the worry of our elaborate preparations, alike in bodily comforts and the tutoring of our minds. . . . 'You must not become a monomaniac about Russia,' Sidney warned me. 'What does it matter what two "over-seventies" think, say or do, so long as they do not whine

about getting old and go merrily on, hand in hand, to the end of the road?', I answer back . . .

On 21 May, the Webbs set sail for Russia. The account of their two-month visit, which does not form part of Beatrice's personal diary, is summarized in the four-volume edition. All the evidence suggests that, though the Webbs were treated with great deference, theirs was very much a 'managed' tour. They returned to England in the last week of July.

*1 August.* [Passfield Corner]
Malcolm and Kitty Muggeridge here for a farewell visit before they settle down in Moscow. Kitty suddenly and unexpectedly turned up in Leningrad a few days before we sailed – she had come in the same boat as the Fabians – travelling 'hard' in a party of ninety, mostly workers of humble station. She was staying at the river-front hostel for sailors, sleeping ten in a room, and roughing it considerably in order, as she told us, to 'prospect' for work for herself and a resident's visa when she returned with Malcolm in September. Now she reports success. During her nine days in Moscow she devoted herself, apparently without any guide as she speaks a little Russian, to interviewing possible employers – and secured a provisional engagement on the *Moscow News* and a visa for continued residence. . . . 'I was hungry, hot and tired all the time but it was tremendously exciting to get out of a dead city like Manchester into a living – intensely living – world like Moscow,' she told us . . .

*9 August.* [Passfield Corner]
Graham Wallas dead; the first to go of ten persons, five men with their attendant wives all over seventy years of age, continually associated together in the last two decades of the nineteenth century in building up the Fabian Society, its doctrine and its propaganda. Edward Pease [(1857–1955)] in at its birth, January 1884, and for twenty-five years its general secretary . . . GBS 1884, Sidney Webb and Sydney Olivier 1885, and Graham Wallas 1886 . . . In one respect, it must be admitted, these five founders of the Fabian Society resembled each other; to a greater or lesser extent they all 'made good' according to Victorian tests of 'success'. They started poor men, without independent means or social status; they attained security and sufficiency of income in old age, from the £1,000 a year of Edward Pease's unexpected inheritance from an uncle, to the income of a millionaire earned by GBS. Four out of the five find

themselves in *Who's Who*, two became peers of the realm, whilst GBS rose to be the greatest international figure in literature. . . .

*20 August.* [Passfield Corner]
Meantime I am not getting on with my task of analysing all our material and getting the Russian documents translated. Partly because I have not yet recovered from the effects of the two months in Russia and there are many persons we have to see; but also because I ponder over our conclusions . . . And alas! I lack the self-discipline which I admire so much in the Communist teaching. . . . I am not satisfied with myself and wonder whether I am at the end of my tether, physically and mentally.

Beatrice gave a B.B.C. talk on her visit to Russia on 22 September.

*22 September. 9 p.m. Artillery Mansions*
I delivered my talk with verve, but I felt very unequal to the strain and came back with a racing heart . . . I spent two or three weeks preparing the talk and have been dizzy ever since, so much so that it required all my courage to come up and give it. . . .

*25 September.* [Passfield Corner]
*Too True to be Good*, which we saw on Friday night, is a farce spoilt by a sermon and a sermon spoilt by a farce, the farce being far better than the sermon. . . . The audience would also have been bored if they had not known that they were listening to GBS . . . Of course GBS, like all aged folk who are famous, lives in an atmosphere of affectionate tolerance from snobbish strangers which is disabling; it leads to a sort of mental flatulence in the victim. Even the old Webbs are slightly subject to it, but our output is tasteless fare, not to say indigestible, compared to GBS's sparkling and stimulating draughts. . . . He is far more fascinating as an old man than he ever was as a young one. He *was* impish; old age has made him statuesque.

Ivan Maisky (1884–1975) was Soviet Ambassador to London 1932–43. Sidney was writing a series of syndicated articles on the Soviet Union.

*24 November.* [Passfield Corner]
Maisky, the new Soviet Ambassador, and his wife, whom we invited to lunch to meet some Labour men at the London School of Economics on Thursday, telephoned that he would like to consult Sidney about the

negotiations for the new trade treaty, and motored down on Tuesday. He is a more accomplished diplomat and less ardent Communist than Sokolnikov – he was a Menshevik, a member of the Provisional government in 1917, but came over to the Bolsheviks after the October revolution . . . He takes a broad view of Soviet Communism as 'in the making' – the fanatical metaphysics and repression of today are temporary, brought about by past horrors and the low level of culture out of which the revolution started. . . .

*18 December.* [Passfield Corner]
As the year draws to a close, events at home and abroad get more and more gloomy. There is no sign, either in the U.S.A. or in Great Britain or on the Continent, of a definite revival of trade or of any diminution of unemployment . . . Nor is the news about the U.S.S.R. hopeful. Whilst Sidney has been writing optimistic accounts of its constitutions and activities, reports from friends as well as enemies reach us about the dearth of food and other consumable commodities; growing discontent among the peasants; fears about the next year's harvest owing to bad sowing; dissension, heresy hunts and purges within the Communist Party. . . . All of which makes thinking, reading, talking about the U.S.S.R., still more writing about it, horribly distracting. . . .

*28 December.* [Passfield Corner]
Sidney finished the tenth article yesterday, completing his planned output for the autumn months, yielding about £400, nearly all from the U.S.A. Considering his age, it has been a brilliant performance. He has been in excellent health, intensely interested in his subject, enjoying his talks with friends, his comfortable home and the company of his fast-ageing wife. For aged I have felt this autumn, always tired, teased with eczema, sleeplessness and noises in the ears and head. . . . 'Count your blessings,' is his refrain to my recurring self-pity! So ends 1932.

~ 1933 ~

*4 January.* [Passfield Corner]
We spent some time on New Year's Day, and after, in casting and recasting the plan of our book on Russia . . . whatever may be the fate of this adventure, it will give us a daily task . . . and, last but not least, it will

furnish matter for my early morning scribbling in this manuscript book, which I enjoy. It is my pet pastime, a gossip with an old friend and confidant, a sort of vent for my egotism. . . .

*22 January.* [Passfield Corner]
My seventy-fifth birthday. 'Mrs Webb retains to a remarkable degree her mental vigour and industry,' observed the *Evening Standard*! (Note, not her charm – 'able but not charming' – as John Morley said fifty years ago.) Telegrams and greetings, newspapers ringing me up for interviews, which I refuse. I don't feel mentally vigorous or industrious, but relatively to the senility usual at that great age, I suppose I am so. And Sidney certainly *is* so. . . .

> Beatrice had been treated with X-rays and doses of luminal for insomnia and skin irritation.

*14 February.* [Passfield Corner]
On the eve of a holiday trip to Portofino. The X-rays proved a false hope; the luminal gave me more sleep and reduced the eczema but I felt 'drugged' – also with Soviet books and papers and secretary surrounding me, I could not refrain from trying to get on with our task. . . . So, Sidney having finished his task of turning out articles and gathered in dollars, which more than paid for the Russian trip, we thought we deserved a real rest in sun and beauty, with no revolution to distract us and no thinking to weary our aged brains. Sidney suggested that he should begin the first chapter of the book, but I scowled at him and he desisted. . . .

*23 February. Portofino Villa*
So here we are, some thousand feet up, overlooking a long stretch of sea and mountain to the west and to the east a wonderful view; but alas! no sun, only mere feeble glimmers through snow-storms, with a biting north wind outside and no fires inside; the central heating fails to spread adequately, a condition made just bearable by an oil-stove in our bedroom. Otherwise the hotel is comfortable: no noise, good food and a pleasant little company of eight including ourselves. . . . Sidney and I walk along the mountain paths for an hour or two in the morning and lie on sofas reading in our rooms most of the afternoon . . . He sleeps a good deal and I try to sleep, but my bones ache and my head whizzes, so it is not exactly a successful venture . . .

*2 March.* [Portofino]

Into this octet of British tourists sprang, from out of a luxurious motor car, Lion Phillimore: an exuberant, generous and witty personality with her mop of black and grey hair, tall figure, handsome features but unhealthy skin, clad in furs by day and in velvet at night, fresh from the sophisticated society of the Rome of Mussolini and of the Vatican, full of admiration for the one and of denunciation of the other, wonderfully vital and dogmatic on all subjects and persons under the sun. We openly chaffed each other and amused all the other guests with our stroke and counter-stroke of intimate criticism. When she left five days after, 'bored stiff' by the grey cold sky and not over-comfortable room, there was a chorus of 'How you must miss her!' . . . . Lion pressed us to hasten to join her at Cannes, but we thought it better to stay in the high air and quiet of this place according to plan, spending only the arranged week at Cannes before we return home on the 13th. We solace our sunless solitude in the oil-stove-heated room with reading the novels in the hotel library, among them *A Modern Comedy* by Galsworthy, a remarkable description of England after the war. . . . The two books about Soviet Communism I brought with me I handed over to Lion, as I had not the slightest desire to read them.

Odette Keun (1888–1978), a writer and journalist born in Constantinople, had been living with H. G. Wells in his *mas*, Lou Pidou, outside Grasse, for some years, but their relationship was breaking up. Somerset Maugham (1874–1965), the novelist, lived at Cap Ferrat on the French Riviera.

*9 March. Cannes*

A suite of two bedrooms, bathrooms and a sunny sitting-room with a wide view of the sea and mountains, together with a motor car in constant attendance, awaited us here, with Lion as hostess, dispensing her kindness with generous gestures of concern for our comfort. . . . Lion and we two went to lunch with Odette at Grasse (H.G. was away), where we met Somerset Maugham. I expected a blatant personality in our hostess. Quite the contrary; a charmer appeared, an artiste skilfully turned out, just enough rouge, powder and pencilling to add an audacious chic without vulgarity to her expression; her garments were perfect in their harmony and fitness. The only blemish in our hostess was a too continuous rapid and inconsequent chatter, fatiguing to her guests; spells of silent and attentive listening would have been welcome to the Webbs! She and Somerset Maugham behaved with alarming unconventionality; they wrangled over some story about him she wanted to tell; he angrily forbade her; she ended the wrangle by lovingly embracing him! Whereupon Lion mischievously observed, 'Lord Passfield looks jealous.'

Somerset Maugham, whose novels we have always admired for their vivid imaginative artistry and unusual characters and backgrounds, seemed to me a coarse and unsavoury personality, exuding low motive and the suspicion of low motive in others. (We heard afterwards that he has a sinister reputation here as an addict in sodomy.) German Hitlerism, Soviet Communism and the decay of capitalist democracy and Christian morals, it is needless to say, were the subject-matter of our somewhat heated discussion, but S.M. contributed little but general cynicism. I fancy that he disliked us as much as we disliked him. 'Bought by the U.S.S.R. to propagate Communism,' was his surmise; indeed he went near to suggesting it, in an off-hand way. . . .

*29 March.* [Passfield Corner]
Malcolm's curiously hysterical denunciations of the U.S.S.R. and all its works in a letter to me have been followed up by three articles by him in the *Manchester Guardian*, drawing a vivid and arrogantly expressed picture of the starvation and oppression of the peasants of the North Caucasus and the Ukraine. . . . What Malcolm asserts, without apparently any evidence except hearsay for his assertion, is that the peasant population of the U.S.S.R. is today starving, and that this starvation will become catastrophic next year. What makes me uncomfortable is that we have no evidence to the contrary . . .

Adolf Hitler had become Chancellor of Germany on 30 January 1933.

*30 March.* [Passfield Corner]
Another account of famine in Russia in the *Manchester Guardian*, which certainly bears out Malcolm's reports. A melancholy atmosphere in which to write a book on Soviet Communism . . . Fortunately for the U.S.S.R. the attention of the capitalist countries is today concentrated on the Mad Dog of Europe – Hitler's Germany. Persecution of political democrats, combined with a ferocious persecution of the Jews – financiers and scientists, teachers and doctors, as well as money-lenders, multiple shop-keepers and Communists – offends the powerful capitalist democracies of the U.S.A., United Kingdom and France. . . .

*1 May. Ayot*

GBS and Charlotte in the best of health . . . He is writing a political play – at which we tremble. 'But what else can I do but write? It is my work and my play.' And so he writes on and on, just as we do in our duller way; aged folk become either scatter-brained or obsessed: he is the one, we are the other . . .

The tension between those who accept and those who denounce the U.S.S.R. increases day by day, and I am wondering whether Charlotte will not presently feel the cold draught. We should certainly feel it if ever we went out of the narrow circle of those who wish to see us, mostly friends of Russia. It is difficult to keep off the subject; it seems to poison the air of social intercourse. 'A country of wild beasts,' Beveridge muttered under his breath when we sat with him at lunch at the London School of Economics. Charlotte's solicitor 'foamed at the mouth' and hysterically refused to obey her instructions when she asked him to invest £1,000 in the Soviet 15 per cent loan. 'Your fellow citizens in prison!' he shouted at her. . . .

E. M. Forster was writing a biography of Goldsworthy Lowes Dickinson (1862–1932), humanist, historian and Hellenist, and Fellow of King's College, Cambridge.

*11 May.* [Passfield Corner]

. . . A glorious spring – the chorus of birds, the soft brilliance of leaf and bloom on earth, and the sun and cloud, sunset and sunrise. . . . altogether a good life and a pleasant one, in spite of being well on in the eighth decade and quite obviously on the downgrade in capacity. 'Speak for yourself,' I hear Sidney saying!

E. M. Forster came down to lunch and tea; a tall big-boned man with significant and attractive features and troubled expression, ultra-refined, exquisite hands (of which he is aware), interested in many things but uncertain as to ultimate values – aesthetic or social reformer, which is uppermost? Ostensibly he came to enquire about Lowes Dickinson's attachment to the London School of Economics . . . But we talked politics and economics – U.S.S.R., Germany, U.S.A., the state of mind of the young men at the university (he is a Fellow of King's Cambridge), a state of mind just at present which he admits is definitely revolutionary to the left or the right, Communist or Fascist. . . . We disputed the relative value of tenderness and loyalty in life; he valued tenderness. I retorted that without loyalty, tenderness might easily, as with D. H. Lawrence, be transformed into conscious cruelty, and that was almost worse than mere animalism . . . I would rather have a relationship of *polite consideration* between individuals, and nothing more, from start to finish, than a passionate friendship ending in hatred, malice and all uncharitableness. . . .

Lady Cynthia Mosley died of acute appendicitis on 16 May 1933.

*24 May.* [Passfield Corner]
. . . Bernard Shaw's personality is a work of art . . . But his thought is repetitive, and it seems to us today ugly and depressing . . . an unreasoning obedience to the superman's orders is the only way of salvation. But where is this superman? GBS answers – Mussolini or Mosley, though with the advent of Hitler he is a little shy about Mosley, so we avoided discussing that political showman . . . With the death of the charming Cynthia, he may seem less promising to GBS, as he certainly will to the rest of the political world. The British elector is too civilized to be taken in by Mosley, with his antics and his cocktails. . . .

*8 June.* [Passfield Corner]
. . . *The Passionate Pilgrim* by C. M. Williams is a telling biography . . . whatever may have been her sins and shortcomings, Annie Besant was the most wonderful woman of her century. Which brings me to a melancholy reflection. Looking back on half a century of contemporaries, *where oh! where are the distinguished women, relatively to men*, in art, literature, science, public affairs? I forgot. There is Amy Johnson; her record remains unbroken. But it is a record of muscle, nerve and sight . . . The few words she speaks or writes are records of the utterly commonplace. . . .

*1 August.* [Passfield Corner]
After reading through what he has written . . . Sidney is much encouraged about the value of the book. Also we are bucked up by reports of the bumper harvest in the U.S.S.R. . . . We are of course getting a good deal of help in our work which would not be open to other authors, either arranged and paid for by us from non-Bolshevik Russians resident in England or gratuitously from the U.S.S.R. authorities. What *we* contribute is our long experience in scheming the investigation and devising the scope and form of the product. . . .

Arthur Henderson was President of the Disarmament conference which opened in Geneva in February 1932. In September 1931 the Japanese had taken over Manchuria and in February 1933 began their long war against China proper. Germany had been arming secretly, even before Hitler came to power. In the summer of 1933 Hitler made a seemingly reasonable speech, and the British and French offered him the 'equality' he demanded by freezing and then cutting their own armed forces. But on 14 October Germany withdrew from the Disarmament conference and resigned from the League of Nations. The Socialist League was the successor to the I.L.P.

*5 August.* [Passfield Corner]
Dear Uncle Arthur here with his good little wife . . . he is still obsessed with the value of getting some concordat signed by the powers . . . To us it seems he absurdly overrates the binding value of *signed documents*, however vague the words are, whatever the character of the individuals who sign them . . . And when the individuals are obviously half-wits and scoundrels, like the Hitler group, can you expect other parties, who have been enemies, to take their signatures at face value? . . . Japan in the east and Hiterlism in the west have riddled, even ridiculed, Henderson's efforts for disarmament. . . .

I must add to this entry that Henderson is mildly concerned at the Communist obsession of the old Webbs, and he roared with laughter when I danced wildly to the strains of the 'Internationale' booming through the ether from Moscow's Red Square. 'When are you two going to tell us how to apply Communist theories to England?' 'We will leave that to the young folk,' I replied. . . .

*19 August.* [Passfield Corner]
Watching the milestones of declining strength. For the first two or three years of our life here – 1924–26 – the longest walk was eight miles or a little over; for the next five or six years, six to seven remained my limit. Yesterday I dared, for the first time for six months, the shorter Weavers Down round, which is five miles, and was over-tired in heart and muscle. So I doubt whether I shall do it again. Sidney could do more than I, but he claims that he is tired at five or six miles. But then he has the queer psychological habit of *sweating*, even in cold weather, so that he has to change underclothing, a habit to which I attribute his excellent health! With regard to brainwork, he goes steadily on writing and reading about the U.S.S.R. most of the working hours – he gains, relatively to past years, by having no other activity. He gives his whole mental energy to the work, which he has never been able to do before except in holiday times. . . .

*24 August.* [Passfield Corner]
Lunched with Lloyd George, this renewal of relations arising out of his hospitality to the Fabian summer school at Frensham Heights. As an 'over-seventy' he has not changed from his former self. He has still the same easy and oncoming way . . . But as of old he has no settled principles or values . . .

The Fabian school becomes every year more respectable and seedy, made up of ageing females or stray foreigners and a few younger folk who come for the bank holiday. Indeed, if it were not for Galton and the prospect of promised legacies, the jubilee year (1934) would seem an excellent date for winding up the society . . . So far as there is an activist group within the Labour Party it is the Socialist League, now presided over by Stafford Cripps, itself not a promising faction within the Labour Party, but at any rate a party of young people. . . .

The Labour journalist and M.P. Mary Agnes Hamilton (d. 1966) wrote the first biographical study of the Webbs.

*25 September.* [Passfield Corner]
Sidney and I have been mildly interested in Mary Agnes Hamilton's biography and the reviews of it we have chanced to see. Very kindly and flattering . . . The one criticism of us, made alike by the biographer and her reviewers – that the Webbs have 'limitations', even striking and challenging limitations – is obviously true. We are specialists, and in order to extract the utmost from our joint brains, we have cut ourselves off from many pleasant pursuits and pastimes which to us, intent on getting each job finished, would have been irritating and unrestful. Also we are, as I said in my diary when we were first engaged, 'second-rate minds'; neither of us is outstandingly gifted; it is the *combinat* that is remarkable. And this brings me to a criticism of the Webbs which seems to me simply funny. We are said to lack 'humanity', to be strangely inhuman. Why? Because we have continued to be devoted to each other and have worked together ceaselessly without friction! Why should an unblemished monogamy be considered 'inhuman'?

There is one charge against us, which opens up a big controversy as to the duty of man. It is complained that we have been indifferent, even callous, to issues such as the Boer War or war in general, that we have never shown moral indignation. Well, rightly or wrongly, we don't believe in moral indignation. . . . It may be your duty to intervene, either with words or deeds, to prevent wrong happening, but why be indignant? . . . it is doubtful whether the moral indignation of outsiders helps the cause of the oppressed. Thus we remained silent on the outbreak of the great war and, as Mary Agnes said, we seemed 'very little people'. But when you *are* of little consequence, why not hold your tongue?

The most notable over-estimation of the Webbs in the *Life* is that of our social position – a myth created by H. G. Wells in *The New Machiavelli*. Also, we have had a jolly good time of it and all the talk about 'disinterestedness' and self-sacrifice, etc. etc., is overdone. . . .

### 2 October. The Albany [Hastings]

Labour Party conference. I have been too unwell for the three nights we have been here to see much . . . But it is clear that the Labour Party is in a bad state in body and mind. . . . I doubt whether the old Webbs will be seen at another Labour Party conference. With our old friendship with Henderson and our friendly relations to our gifted nephew, we are in an awkward position; we cannot help, we may hinder. . . . British politics seem to me to have drifted into a morass of apathy and indecision. There is *no* group of men who are at once united and single-minded . . . Meanwhile . . . Whither the world? For upon that depends the fate of Great Britain. She is no longer mistress of her own destiny.

### 11 October. Hastings Hospital

The haemorrhage through the urine persisted and increased and my brain began to whiz. So I called in a medical woman, who diagnosed carbuncles at the opening of the bladder and advised me to go into hospital to be explored and operated on. . . . So here I am, recovering from five hours' unconsciousness and still suffering from frequency and the debris of extensive burning, the carbuncles being more extensive than expected, but my general health a good deal better than is usual at seventy-five . . . The long sleepless nights and hours of the day between Sidney's visits in my private room hang wearily on my consciousness. Also, the thought that I may not be able to regain sufficient strength to help with the book depresses me. I try to remind my resentful soul that Sidney and I have been singularly free from pain and disability during our forty odd years of work together . . .

### 24 November. [Passfield Corner]

I have spurts of capacity in the way of scheming the book . . . but I do little or nothing in its actual execution. Fortunately Sidney is thoroughly absorbed . . . This child is our last begotten, and we are as keen on it as we were forty years ago when we were explaining British trade unionism. . . . It is, in a sense, our last will and testament. But the sands – at any rate of my energy – are fast running out. I have a sense of working against time.

*16 December.* [Passfield Corner]
Haemorrhage returned, showing that the operation was not wholly successful – consequently I am beginning to regret my decision to have it at Hastings . . . a wasted thought, because the decision seemed the best at the time and may have been so . . . Today the haemorrhage is heavier than it was before the operation, which is disturbing to one's peace of mind . . . If only I can last out the writing of the book . . .

Man, it seems to me, has no case against death; if he has been thwarted in the past and is suffering pain in the present, death comes to him as a deliverer from all his woes. If he is among the fortunate ones as we have been, then he must accept the last phase, which need not be distressful if he wills to end it. . . .

*16 December.* [Passfield Corner]
Beveridge here for the night; back from the U.S.A. . . . He is in the depths of gloom, admits that the state of mind and state of things in the U.S.A. is far worse . . . than he had thought possible. And as he loathes Soviet Communism . . . he is depressed and hopeless. The callousness of public opinion about the Nazi persecution of the Jewish race, the unwillingness to save them from starvation, is also distressing him. The London School of Economics is, because of his skill and devotion, a brilliant success; he is in truth a second founder. . . .

~ 1934 ~

*3 January. Empire Nursing Home, Vincent Square*
. . . I am here, in this ultra-comfortable and rather costly home, for a thorough testing out of my trouble, with a view to cure, if that be possible to a worn-out body. Anyway, I am not yet senile – at least I don't think I am – and for that I ought to be grateful. And in some ways it is pleasanter to be treated as an invalid and give way to illness than to try to keep up the semblance of health and regular work when feeling rotten inside, as I have been doing the last year. So good luck to the old Webbs in 1934 and may I be alive to see it out!

*6 January.* [Empire Nursing Home]

. . . A growth in the right kidney is responsible for the bleeding – which, fortunately for the exploration, was copious, so that they could discern the source of it clearly. The only *cure* is the cutting out of the kidney – a serious matter for a woman of my age. And before doing that, the other kidney would have to be tested to see whether it will bear the burden. Death is so near at seventy-six that one wonders whether it is worth while risking immediate death in order to chance lengthening life a few months or years. I suppose I shall decide to have the preliminary test – an X-ray after injection, and then call in a second expert and abide by their joint advice. If only Sidney could be spared this time of anxiety. . . .

F. J. W. Barrington was a distinguished London urologist.

*7 January.* [Empire Nursing Home]

Decided to have the test today and abide by Barrington's advice . . . If one did not . . . and went on bleeding more and more, one would be in a constant state of anxiety and regret. Also, a lingering death would be worse for Sidney and for me; it would prolong the sorrow of the parting and make it more difficult for Sidney to work whole-heartedly at the book. If I recover from the operation I shall be fit to help him, at any rate to be a source of comfort and happiness. If I drop out he is still healthy enough to go on without me and make a new life for himself. Anyway, I have done the work I intended to do and lived the life I preferred. And the problem we have been seeking to solve for the last fifty years – poverty in the midst of plenty – is today being solved, and very much as we should have solved it . . . As I lie awake during the night listening to Big Ben's chimes and the hootings of the Thames steamers I recall, one by one, all our separate researches and the writing of those unreadable books, and meditate on our happiness and interest in the work. But if Soviet Communism had not arisen, all the work we had done would have seemed to have helped on the decay of capitalist civilization, without creating a new social order to take its place. Today we see the promised land, though not near at hand, so far as our own people are concerned. Still, there it is. . . .

*12 January. 2 a.m.* [Empire Nursing Home]

I spent two or three hours in the middle of last night drafting a scheme for the 'In Place of Profit' chapter, with which Sidney was delighted. It is easy to please him, poor dear, in his hour of anxiety. For me it whiled away the hours of awaiting the operation. I think I shall survive the ordeal. I have a wiry constitution, but if I don't I shall leave him with plenty of friends, a comfortable home, good health and a really exciting and creative task. We *have* been happy together and singularly at one in heart and intellect. . . .

*21 January. 3 a.m.* [Empire Nursing Home]
At last I do feel 'on the road to recovery', after twenty-four hours solid misery in being 'purged' more than was necessary. Sidney is down at Passfield for the week-end and I see him fast asleep in his little room . . . Dancing attendance on an invalid does not suit him, though he does it with devoted dutifulness. He feels awkward and lost at it. . . .

*25 January. 3 a.m.* [Empire Nursing Home]
Apparently most invalids hate being in nursing homes and complain about the management. This one seems exceptionally friendly and considerate. But still it is extraordinarily trying to the temper and nerves . . . As I sleep a bare three hours in the twenty-four I sometimes wonder whether it is worth while to go on with it. Courage old lady, courage; count your blessings! . . .

*29 January. 3 a.m.* [Empire Nursing Home]
A fortnight and two days since the operation; kidney working well, but still suffering from flatulence, occasional pain in the wound and sleeplessness . . .

'The function of the cheque is purely therapeutic,' Shaw wrote to Sidney on 30 January. 'Nobody can resist the bucking effect of a thousand pounds in a lump. . . . The minutest push towards recovery is so priceless that thousands are as twopence in comparison.' The United States had recently established diplomatic relations with the U.S.S.R.

*1 February.* [Empire Nursing Home]
I get up tomorrow for the first time and if all goes well leave here on Thursday with a nurse for the week-end to see me settled in at home. . . . Meanwhile our dear old friend GBS has eased the financial situation by a generous gift of £1,000. He and Charlotte came to see me separately; they are off for a three months' tour to New Zealand . . . their loyalty and generosity to the old Webbs is unassailable and continuous. . . .

*4 February.* [Empire Nursing Home]
Among other visitors Susan Lawrence came, full of her U.S. visit and in a great state of excitement over the 'boiling cauldron' she there witnessed, stirred this way and that by the Giant Roosevelt. . . . It is very much the same state of enthusiasm with which she lived in the first days of the General Strike of 1926. . . . Meanwhile the U.S.A. broadcasting authorities are arranging for reciprocal broadcasts with Moscow. 'Everyone is speaking pleasantly about the U.S.S.R.,' reports Susan, and 'It is Wall Street and the bankers who are the *bêtes noires* today.'

*7 February. 3 a.m.* [Empire Nursing Home]
. . . If I had to confess my sins, what sins should I confess . . . ? I smoke: it is an unhealthy and expensive habit. I am aware that I often take another cigarette when it actually hurts my tongue and throat, then throw it away, which is wasteful because I smoke an expensive German brand – 'nikotine unschadlich', 8s 6d a hundred. Otherwise I think my personal habits are hygienic. I have given up alcohol; in food I try to live according to plan, guided by experience and not according to appetite. Except for smoking I have a good conscience, or rather I accept my own limitations in intellect, character and manners, and don't feel called on to regret or alter them, especially at my time of life. . . .

*13 February.* [Passfield Corner]
With the departure of my nurse today, my illness comes officially to an end . . . The difficulty is to combine a go-easy attitude to work and exercise, as I am advised to do, while refraining from pernicious self-indulgence in cigarettes, an untimely cup of tea in the middle of the night or the use of narcotics. Meanwhile Sidney delights me with his placid satisfaction in writing the book, and his eagerness to 'listen in' to Moscow every night amuses me. . . .

> On 12 February civil war broke out in Austria when the Social Democrats were provoked into armed rebellion. After four days they were defeated, the party declared illegal and the Chancellor strengthened his authoritarian control.

*14 February.* [Passfield Corner]
How well I remember that eight days in Vienna in the spring of 1929, and our immense admiration for the little group of Viennese socialists who had made Vienna, with its admirable housing and other social

services, the mecca of evolutionary socialism. Here at last we witnessed the Will and the Way. . . . Today Austria seems ripe for absorption by the Third Reich, with the alternative of becoming a protectorate of Fascist Italy. All the tables are turned. As for liberalism – it has been smashed to smithereens and thrown on to the dust-heap in one country after another; even in Great Britain, the home of its first beginning, it is a despised and divided minority. . . .

*5 March.* [Passfield Corner]
If I cannot help I must not hinder. It is clear to me that Sidney ought to go to Moscow some time this year before we finish the book. . . . The most feasible plan is for Sidney to go . . . in September and to take Barbara [Drake] with him . . . I will stay quietly here . . .

Current political unrest was reflected by the behaviour of students at the L.S.E., where Communist literature circulated widely and appeals to revolt through resolutions in the Students' Union turned into an organized campaign of rebellion and vilification of the staff. Lionel Robbins (1898–1984) was professor of economics and a strong anti-socialist.

*12 March.* [Passfield Corner]
Beveridge turned up yesterday . . . full of the trouble about the misbehaviour of a knot of Marxists. . . . The trouble at the School is, I fear, destined to become worse during the next decade. Political and economic studies, carried on in London, one of the hubs of the political and financial world, by an assembly of some three thousand students of all races and professions . . . under the direction of a large and miscellaneous staff . . . is bound to develop heated antagonism of creed and class. Beveridge cites Laski, with his Labour Party journalism and his close association with political personages, as the centre of the mischief. Laski denounces Robbins and his group of fanatical individualists . . . And all this fanaticism will grow worse in the coming duplex struggle for power in country after country . . .

Herbert Morrison (1888–1965) had led the Labour Party to its first and long-lasting majority on the London County Council.

*14 March.* [Passfield Corner]
Labour wins London: Herbert Morrison is the organizer of victory, a long pull and a hard pull lasting twenty years, the final victory doing

endless credit to his doggedness, skill and masterfulness. He is a Fabian of Fabians, a direct disciple of the Sidney Webbs. . . .

*27 April.* [Passfield Corner]
. . . Sidney . . . says that for the first time he feels himself 'to be an old man'. . . . Meanwhile I drift through the days, enjoying the beauty of springtime sight and sound, doing very little creative work but glad to be alive. Every now and again I have a bright idea; sedulously I pick out, from my reading of the spate of books and U.S.S.R. periodicals, useful extracts for Sidney's use. . . . But except for the fact that my presence comforts and encourages him, I help little with the big task. The truth is that we are about ten years too old. . . .

John Cripps (b. 1912), the son of Stafford Cripps, was to accompany Sidney and Barbara Drake to Moscow. George Catlin (1896–1979) was professor of politics at Cornell University 1924–35. In 1925 he married Vera Brittain (1894–1970), the author of *Testament of Youth* (1933).

*3 May.* [Passfield Corner]
Dinner at the Drakes to introduce Barbara and John Cripps to the Maiskys . . . This jaunt to London, together with entertaining Catlin and his wife (Vera Brittain) the following day, left me a wreck so far as work is concerned . . . Catlin . . . is much improved: the former artificiality of manner and modish appearance diminished. But glibness and plausibility, shallowness of thought and feeling, remain. . . . Vera is a charmer, a competent writer and, it is said, a brilliant lecturer. F. W. Galton was swept away by her Fabian lecture. Her lips and nails delicate crimson, cheeks slightly and skilfully rouged; undoubtedly an attractive little body . . . She will succeed in life; her subjects – feminism and pacifism – are a trifle stale, but among women they still have a vogue. Her recent autobiography sold well. Next autumn she goes on a lecturing tour in the U.S.A., where she will carry all before her. . . .

*25 May.* [Passfield Corner]
. . . The Beveridge–Mair entanglement has become a hot-bed of intrigue and scandal at the School. The husband has considerately left England and settled in Australia; the children refuse to live at home; Beveridge has handed over his country cottage to Mrs Mair in order to regain his freedom during the recess, and rushes off to the Continent with his motor car. He recently moved out of his next-door Campden Hill house

to escape her attentions, but she followed him to a flat within sight of his new abode in the Temple, from which she spies on his movements. She also 'orders' Mrs Turin [Beveridge's secretary] to show her Beveridge's private correspondence and his bank book. . . . But apart from the miseries of Mrs Turin, the affair is a source of demoralization at the school, an ugly feature in a co-education institution . . . What interests me as a sociologist in this unsavoury episode, is the disintegrating effect of the combination of a legalized monogamy . . . with a practical condonation by public opinion of illicit relations . . . This contradiction makes possible emotional relationships between colleagues . . . If Beveridge and Mrs Mair were married they would not be Director and Assistant Director . . . The plight of our old and loyal friend worries me – I don't see a way out for him. The woman has become a Fury and is in control of his home and his work-place. For his own and the students' sake, Beveridge would do well to move off to other work. But no one is in a position to suggest it to him. . . .

*2 July.* [Passfield Corner]
GBS and Charlotte here for the week-end, as jolly as ever after their New Zealand tour. . . . I asked him why exactly he admired Mussolini, Hitler and Mosley; they had no philosophy, no notion of any kind of social reorganization, except their own undisputed leadership . . . what was the good of it all? He admitted that they had no economic principle – but they had *personality* and it was personality that was needed to save the world. . . . But Hitler's personality was a degraded one, I objected. He was returning to old primitive values – blood-lust, racial superstition, blind obedience. As for Mosley . . . he was dissolute and unprincipled . . . a charlatan.

'That was said of Mussolini and is said of Hitler; but they have secured the obedience and devotion of their people. Mosley is the only striking personality in British politics; all the others are nonentities,' he replied. . . .

He and Charlotte insisted on reading two chapters of the book . . . His main criticism was that we were *too* appreciative: 'If their methods are as effective as you suggest, why are not the results, measured in the standard of life of the mass of the people, better?' We agreed to tone down.

On 1 September Sidney sailed for a five-week visit to the U.S.S.R., where Soviet officials were to review and revise the draft chapters of *Soviet*

*Communism.* Barbara Drake later said that all through the tour, 'Sidney would whisper to me, with the relish of a scientist whose theoretical proposition has stood the test of practical experiment: "See, see, it works, it works."'

*27 August. 3 a.m.* [Passfield Corner]
As the time flies before the fateful September 1st I get into a . . . panic about Sidney's state of health – I think it must be a subconscious desire to stop his going which clothes itself in concrete fears . . . However, he stands firm and refuses to see a medical man. It will be a joyful day when I see him back in good spirits with new zest to finish the book . . .

*7 September.* [Passfield Corner]
I devour books about Germany: one wants to understand how it is that that gifted race has drifted into disaster . . . For after all, the Weimar Republican Germany was a full-blown political democracy (it had even proportional representation) supplemented by highly organized trade union and co-operative movements and a powerful socialist party. And yet the whole structure was swept away in a few days without the pretence of a struggle, without even a murmur of dissent – and replaced not by a shrewd personal dictator like Mussolini, working under an established constitution, but by a group of gangsters, led by a neurotic genius of an orator. This dictator has, in two short years, antagonized all the great international powers of the world: Jewry, the Roman Catholic Church, the working-class movements in all countries, and international finance, not to mention the four great powers – France, Great Britain, the U.S.A. and Italy. Incidentally, Hitler has raised the U.S.S.R. from being an outcast state into a leading guarantor of the peace of the world, courted by France, supported by Great Britain, accepted by the U.S.A. and finally offered a permanent seat on the Council of the League of Nations. And this is the regime which Hitler asserts will last a thousand years. . . .

*15 September.* [Passfield Corner]
'We are all in the best of health, the weather continues sunny in a cloudless sky,' writes Sidney, which comforts me. Today I start on my fortnight's holiday among nephews and nieces, ending with a stay with Molly Holt with her motor car at Bournemouth. It has been a melancholy time: clearing up the debris of our eighteen months' work on the book; looking at Sidney's chair in the study and wandering alone with

Sandy over the moors in the afternoon; anxious about his health. He also has felt the separation, in spite of the excitement of being again in Moscow. But one must not become 'maudlin' in old age. There remains the solid fact that all through our married life we have never before been separated for five weeks, and this separation is aggravated by the five-day post on both sides. However, there is the flashed message to and fro to fall back upon in case of disaster. Silence means continued safety. . . . But I doubt whether either of us would consent to be parted again. 'And then,' he writes, 'I shall be within a week of rejoining my Bee, not again to leave her until the end.'

*27 September. Royal Bath Hotel, Bournemouth*
I posted last night, to catch today's air mail, my last letter to Sidney, while he is staying in the new land of hope and glory! . . . Meanwhile I have been living a half-life without him, dragging my uneasy body and dulled brain through pleasant scenes and comfortable circumstances, but suffering acute emotional starvation . . .

*4 October.* [Bournemouth]
. . . Yesterday Betty Balfour came for lunch and the afternoon. . . . we embraced each other, and set out at once on a five hours' talk about old times at Whittingehame, the changing scene in British politics and finally about Soviet Communism, about which she is gently shocked but keenly interested. The background of her life – the Balfour clan – has lost its former ease and splendour and political importance. Arthur Balfour, when I first knew him, as Premier, was reputed to have £20,000 a year, with Whittingehame and Carlton House Terrace as his homes. Today Whittingehame is shut up, Carlton House Terrace with all its furniture sold, and what was left of his property was valued at £40,000. . . . Gerald and Betty keep a modest house at Fishers Hill, with aged Mrs Sidgwick as a helpless invalid and an old gentleman as a friendly lodger. Of the five daughters, only the eldest made a good marriage from the worldly point of view – and as Betty said, somewhat wistfully, 'Gerald (now over eighty) has to earn our living by attending board meetings two or three times a week'. . . . He thinks that the London School of Economics is a nest of revolutionaries. I tried to reassure her . . . I emerged out of this interview with a dear old friend somewhat exhausted but pleased with the reminder, if not the renewal, of an old tie of friendship. We are both of us too old and too occupied to see much of each other.

*5 October.* [Oxford]

I motored to Oxford and spent the night with another old friend – a very old and faithful one, Louise Creighton, now eighty-four. The visit saddened me. . . . Lousie is hopelessly crippled and creeps about the house. Her mind is clear, and old age and helplessness have softened her outlook on the world . . . But she is desperately lonely and bored with existence, hurt that the young people no longer care to come and see her. The plain truth is that the aged feel what their children and many of their friends are thinking about them, and sometimes even hinting at in conversation – 'If you are not enjoying life why don't you die and be done with it.' And the old person may feel that there is no answer, except that he does not want to die, or does not see any comfortable way of doing it. . . .

*10 October.* [Passfield Corner]

Barbara's voice from Hay's Wharf came through my bedroom phone, just as I had finished my coffee – 'Sidney is coming direct to the Carlton Hotel.' What a joyful moment, and then the meeting, Lion laughing at our glee. Once at Passfield that afternoon I collapsed in happy passivity – a whole day in bed. He is well and certain that the journey and separation was worth while, completely reassured as to the eventual success of the new social order. There is one dark spot – the lack of free expression among those intellectuals who are against the Communist creed . . . But this freedom for adverse propaganda can hardly be accorded, or rather would not be permitted by the government of any country so long as they do not feel secure against active revolt and deliberate sabotage . . .

*17 October.* [Passfield Corner]

Rosy Dobbs here for a week – strong in body and mind and happier than I have ever known her. . . . The secret of her happiness is her art, her freedom to go and do what she likes and make casual friends by the way, and, be it added, her control of the family purse. . . .

*25 October.* [Passfield Corner]

H.G. sent us his autobiography [*An Experiment in Autobiography*]. . . . it is fascinating reading, alike in its self-revelation and in its casual portraiture. The portrait of Arthur Balfour is perfect; the caricature of Haldane witty and apt. Towards the Fabian group he is friendly, if contemptuous; Graham Wallas was the one he liked best and learnt most from, perhaps because they shared common hatreds: the monarchy, the

Church and the manual workers' trade unions. H.G. was jealous of G.B.S.'s prestige and fame; he envied his attractive figure and personality; he was intuitively hostile to the Webbs' long-winded investigation of social institutions . . . H. G. Wells emerges from his autobiography a splendidly vital man: an explorer of man's mind, a critic, artist, derider and visionary all in one. In spite of deplorable literary manners and mean sexual morals, H.G. is to me a likeable and valuable man. He has been on the side of the angels . . .

The Shaws tell us that H.G. is today ill and worried; has parted with Odette, having endowed her with the Grasse villa and a small annuity. He has fallen to the charm of 'Moura', the aristocratic Russian widow of Nicolas Benckendorf, vividly described by the infatuated Bruce Lockhart in his *British Agent in Moscow*. 'She will stay with me, eat with me, sleep with me,' whined the lovesick H.G. to GBS, 'but she will not marry me.' H.G., aware of old age, wants to buy a 'sexual annuity' by marriage. 'Moura', looking back at his past adventures, refuses to give her independence and her title away. And no wonder!

## ～ 1935 ～

*1 January. 4 a.m.* [Passfield Corner]
I have had the forbidden cigarette to celebrate the New Year. Except for eczema and sleeplessness, I am much better than I expected to be this time last year. I can use my brain on the book and walk three or four miles. The first volume is in print; we are at work preparing the first three chapters of Volume II for the printer by the light of new material of Sidney's journey to the U.S.S.R. . . . .

*12 January.* [Passfield Corner]
We went to London to see the Shaws, both of whom have had alarming attacks – GBS, a collapse after producing one of his plays for the Vic before Christmas and Charlotte, a few days ago, blood-poisoning from a blow when packing up for their trip. They were glad to see us – Charlotte, who was still in bed, told Sidney that when GBS fainted in her arms she felt that if anything happened to Shaw she had only him to rely on. . . . we all dread the death of anyone of the quartet, and would feel responsible for the remaining partner. But they are both recovering and off they will go, in ten days' time, on their long ocean trip, in spite of our demurrer. . . .

*29 January. 2.30 a.m. Ventnor*

We came here for a long week-end. I was fed up with day after day on the book . . . I longed for the sea and a change of thought and feeling. Sidney was acquiescent . . . Cold blast of wind and snow for these last days throughout Great Britain, but here we have had sun and shelter from the north-easter: two mornings mild walking along the coast, two mornings motoring round the island and one evening at the cinema. It has been a refreshing change of scene, but alas, my worn-out body does not respond to unaccustomed circumstances, and the dizziness has come on again. My one abiding comfort is Sidney's wellness and happiness and self-confidence about finishing the book in good style. . . .

> The Webbs had planned to visit relatives to enable their maids to go on holiday.

*21 April. Easter Sunday.* [Passfield Corner]

A nervous breakdown has compelled – or shall I say enabled – me to cancel all the visits arranged for the four weeks out of our home . . . Sidney himself is considerably exhausted and looks a deal older; every day he slogs at the book all the long morning from 7.30 coffee to one o'clock lunch, and is reading and thinking about it the rest of the day. The task has been too big and too exciting for our strength – let us hope not for our reputation! . . .

*16 May.* [Hastings]

The X-ray examination which the clever young doctor insisted on my undergoing was cheerful news. There is no obstruction and no growth in the lower bowel; the trouble is weakness of the muscle of the colon and slight bulge out on the wrong side, which I suggested was due to the absence of the right kidney. The remaining kidney is O.K. . . . So that all that is needful for continued life for yet a while is strict diet and a quiet life, sufficient and not too much exercise. But my dependence on the right food etc. will make our vision of future journeys, to Scandinavia and the U.S.S.R., not to be fulfilled. It may well be that the attack means a lower level of energy, mental and physical.

> The Silver Jubilee of King George V's accession was celebrated on 6 May with street parties and pageantry.

*23 May. 12.15 a.m.* [Hastings]
... Though I enjoy looking at the sea by day and night from our pleasant rooms and fill up my time reading Tolstoy and Dostoyevsky and
listening to the wireless, I long to get back to Passfield, but have to wait
until the girls are back ... If only science would tell me what exactly I
ought to do! ... I tried two days' starvation and made the pain
worse. ...

While I have been suffering this setback, the National government has
been driving ahead, by the amazingly popular Jubilee celebrations, the self-
confident propaganda of 'returning prosperity' and the plans for aerial
rearmament, to meet the menace of Hitler's Germany. The international
situation gets steadily more hopelessly warlike – Italy v. Abyssinia, the
France–Soviet pact, the refusal of Hitler to have any dealings with the
U.S.S.R. and his menacing attitude towards Lithuania and Austria. There
is a certainty of immediate reconstruction of the National government,
with Baldwin as P.M. and an election within the next six months.
Labour seems to be losing heavily in the constituencies owing to its
ambiguous attitude about the monarchy, rearmament and revolutionary
socialism, and its poor and divided leadership. ... The only hopeful note
in the present position is the rising prestige of the U.S.S.R. ...

*30 May. 2.30 a.m. Passfield Corner*
Back again and feeling much better ... we are at work again ... If only I
could get four hours' solid sleep in the twenty-four, or make up my mind
to do without it. However, there is the chorus of birds to delight me ...

*Whit Monday, 10 June. 2.30 a.m.*
Yesterday Sidney made the first draft of the final paragraph of our book:
it will need redrafting, but it is 'The End'. A thrilling moment when he
read it to me! ...

*23 October.* [Passfield Corner]
... Arthur Henderson dead: Sidney's oldest and most continuous friendship and colleague in the labour movement of the last twenty years. He
was the exact opposite number to GBS. He had no intellectual distinction;
no subtlety, wit or personal charm. Nevertheless he was an outstanding
personality, because of his essential goodness ... He was immensely
respected by the party in the country, more so than any other leader. He
was disliked by the Court, the City, and London Society, which stands to
his credit. Non-smoker, teetotaller, chapel-goer, estimable husband, father

and friend, he was scrupulously honest, hard-working and incorruptible, and yet widely tolerant of other people's lapses and laxities. Henderson was a model puritan, dutiful without being censorious. . . .

Baldwin fought a quiet election, playing down the question of rearmament. Ramsay MacDonald was defeated in Seaham Harbour.

*15 November.* [Passfield Corner]
'I shall want plenty of whisky tonight,' observed Ponsonby as he joined us after dinner to listen to the election results. 'I am beginning to fear that we may get a majority.' We agreed. But as the meagre victories came through – not a hundred seats in all . . . they were a trifle depressing even to our cautious minds. . . . The Conservative Party has been left, with a 250 majority, securely in command of the British people for the next four years. Over the larger part of Great Britain there is not the remotest sign of any widespread discontent with the existing social order. . . . Meanwhile I am back at work on *Our Partnership*, an easy and comforting task . . .

*27 November.* [Passfield Corner]
The irreproachable and colourless Attlee elected chairman of the Parliamentary Labour Party and Leader of His Majesty's Opposition. . . . a somewhat diminutive and meaningless figure to represent the British labour movement in the House of Commons!

Clement Attlee (1883–1967) was also to be the victor in the 1945 Labour landslide. The Webbs always made their own printing and publishing arrangements, although trade editions were published through Longmans. Noting that cheap editions and early sales covered their costs, Beatrice remarked, 'All the same, we could not have done the job without an independent income (one up to the capitalist system!), to which must be added that no such glorification of "the other way" would have been permitted in the USSR.' The first edition of *Soviet Communism* had a question mark after the subtitle, *A New Civilization?* The second edition omitted it.

*15 December.* [Passfield Corner]
Our book has had a good Press. *The Times* gave it a column on the day of publication, flattering to the authors and hostile to the subject, and a sympathetic review in the *Literary Supplement*. Other papers followed suit . . . The most hostile review was that in the *Observer* . . . which

opened with: 'It is impossible to read this book with patience and com-
posure,' and went on to a two-column tirade against the U.S.S.R. as an
inhuman society of robots, whilst treating us with the respect due to the
misguided skill and industry of the aged Webbs. . . .

*20 December.* [Passfield Corner]
Two most agreeable gatherings – one at which we were hosts, the other,
the honoured guests – celebrated the publication of our book. Our
lunch at the London School of Economics . . . represented those who
had read and corrected the proofs. It was a lively affair but there were no
speeches. At the Soviet Embassy the Maiskys entertained at dinner some
forty admirers of the Webbs' work – half our own family and friends, the
others mostly Soviet officials, diplomatic and trade, with their wives. It
was equally informal and homely, with no ceremony or glamour – a sort
of family gathering of brainworking men and women inspired by a
common purpose. . . . Maisky, in proposing our health, and the wide cir-
culation of our book, described how as an undergraduate at St
Petersburg, he had bought the Webbs' *History of the English Working
Class* (Lenin's translation of the *History of Trade Unionism*) and forthwith
became a political revolutionary. . . . Who would have foreseen this
proletarian gathering – in sympathy, not in class – at the Russian
Embassy, with eminent Fabians as the central figures, in those pre-war
days when the Czarist diplomats were the wealthiest, the most sophisticated and the most accomplished aristocrats in London society. . . .

> The League of Nations had condemned Italy's invasion of Abyssinia and
> called for effective sanctions. The Labour Party supported this policy, but
> Baldwin's government was reluctant to risk a military confrontation in
> the Mediterranean. The British Foreign Secretary, Sir Samuel Hoare
> (1880–1959), concocted a peace plan with Pierre Laval (1883–1945), his
> French opposite number, which would have given Italy two-thirds of a
> country which had not yet been overrun. When these proposals were
> published, the outcry led to Hoare's resignation. This betrayal was gen-
> erally thought to have been the death-knell of the League. Anthony Eden
> (1897–1977) became Foreign Secretary.

*25 December.* [Passfield Corner]
The year ends with the Cabinet's mad muddle – the sudden and wholly
unexpected presentation to Italy, Abyssinia and the League of the disgraceful peace terms hastily devised by Laval and Hoare, dismembering

the victim of the war for the benefit of the violator of world peace . . . followed by the abject apology of Baldwin, the tearful resignation of Hoare and the triumphant emergence of the popular Anthony Eden as Foreign Secretary, pledged to carry out the sanctions even at the cost of war with the mad Mussolini. How and why all this happened no one knows and no one seems to care. . . .

## ∼ 1936 ∼

George V died on 20 January and was succeeded by his son Edward VIII.

*21 January.* [Passfield Corner]
About nine o'clock last night Sidney was rung up from Moscow and became entangled in a conversation with two Soviet officials who asked for a message from him glorifying Lenin on the twelfth anniversary of his death; the upshot, I gathered, was not satisfactory, as his many-syl-labled words were not understood at the other end, so he agreed to telegraph the message. At five o'clock this morning the girls were awak-ened by the continuous ringing of the front doorbell; the constable at Liphook brought a telephone call from London announcing the King's death and summoning Sidney to the Privy Council today to receive the new Sovereign. Old age and the absence of correct uniform is a sufficient excuse for staying at home.

Will Great Britain under the new King or the U.S.S.R. under the tes-tament of Lenin prevail during this century? . . .

*22 January. 4 a.m.* [Passfield Corner]
My seventy-eighth birthday – two years off eighty! I reflect. As a brain-worker I feel a wreck: I can read and I can walk two or three miles, but I can't think with sufficient clearness to write – if I try to do so I go still dizzier. *Our Partnership* must lie in its pamphlet box until we return from holiday in Majorca . . .

*17 March.* [Majorca]
Recovering tone and enjoying the complete change of scene . . . Our visit has been enlivened by Beveridge's companionship and made homely by the near neighbourhood of the Dobbses. The little group of British residents are wholly unconcerned with the life of the 'natives';

none of them can tell Sidney what is the constitution and working of the local government. . . . The main interest is gossip about the antecedents, quarrels, means or lack of means of the foreigners living here. The Dobbses, with their strangely scatterbrained life in their ramshackle but picturesque flat, are thoroughly at home here and they all three – father, mother and son – seem to enjoy the life, taking tea with the other foreign residents every day or entertaining them in their flat. Bridge and mountaineering are the relaxations, sharing each other's books and newspapers the cultural equipment. . . .

*2 April.* [Passfield Corner]
The three days' and two nights' journey from Palma through France completely exhausted me, and we shall certainly not go far abroad again. . . .

*10 April.* [Passfield Corner]
Foreign affairs, whether over the air or in the printed word, are like a bad dream: frustration of the peace-makers, success for the war-makers. Japan and Italy carry on their conquests by land, sea and air without hindrance. Germany breaks her bonds and rearms; all three aggressive powers openly glorify war as an instrument – as *the* instrument to settle the relation of one state to another. They even declare the conquest of other races . . . the most essential and holy of all human activities! The satiated and therefore pacific powers, hugging their possessions, go on arguing and protesting at Geneva and in their respective Foreign Offices, but nothing comes of it . . . Meanwhile the U.S.S.R. has notified Japan that if they invade Outer Mongolia it means war. The Bolshevik leaders at any rate mean business and know their own mind!

*22 April.* [Passfield Corner]
Nearly three weeks since we returned and I am still suffering from continual whizziness of ear and muzziness of brain, complicated during the first week by painful piles . . . So I am experimenting in a course of massage by an osteopath who calls himself a naturepathist . . .

Maisky's remarks were among the earliest hints that the Soviet Union might make its own settlement with Nazi Germany.

*11 May.* [Passfield Corner]
. . . The Maiskys came down Sunday morning . . . naturally Maisky was anxious to talk about the humiliating collapse of British–Franco policy

and the triumph of Mussolini over the League and collective security. He intimated that the Soviet government, though convinced that only by an enforced collective security against aggression could peace be secured, were beginning to doubt whether it was worth while binding themselves up with such half-hearted partners as the British government. It might be wise for them to withdraw and mind their own business. That would mean that Germany would absorb Austria and the German districts of Czecho-Slovakia.

*23 May.* [Passfield Corner]
. . . The annual visit of the Shaws. This winter's three months' cruising has left them the worse for it; like ourselves they are on the downward journey . . . He brought a new play – the very title of it, *Geneva*, made us apprehensive. We listened to it for well over an hour yesterday morning. It is another and worse example of the *Beggars' Opera* type . . . but alas! without the *Beggar's Opera* lightness and wit . . .

The one success of the visit was an expedition to Telegraph House, with its attractive vision of the elderly philosopher's charming young wife 'Peter Spence', who captured the hearts of GBS and Charlotte. Will this coupling of elderly genius (sixty-five) with youthful charm (twenty-five) endure to the end of the road? It is to be hoped that Bertie will die suddenly, while still a brilliant talker and a successful writer and lecturer, otherwise I should fear a solitary end for this ageing adventurer in matrimony. Amber Blanco White tells me that Peter worked her way up, from a poverty-stricken home and board-school education, through scholarships, to Oxford – where she met Bertie as lecturer. For four years she has been his companion and literary assistant; she suffers from the inferiority complex, alike in social origin and conventional ethics, but is wholly devoted to her great man. Amber has, I gather, helped her to get back her self-respect and self-confidence. Amber, a good wife and mother and clever thinker, lecturer and writer, with her own past experience, is the best of counsellors. . . .

*19 June.* [Passfield Corner]
Two nights and three mornings in London: lunch with Susan one day, with the Keyneses the next; the afternoons and evenings at Barbara's, Laski to dine, saw ten nephews and nieces, had a talk with the Maiskys in the morning at the Embassy . . .

But it was my lunch with the Keyneses that interested me most – for Keynes had, in his attractive way, boomed our book in his recent broadcast talk . . . He still refuses to regard the U.S.S.R. as anything more than an interesting experiment which has neither failed nor succeeded in providing a decent livelihood for its people. 'It is not more bread that people want, it is poetry, it is "mental equilibrium", it is "faith" . . .' I could get nothing more concrete than that; he even admitted that he himself had no faith and was still looking for one. . . .

*25 June.* [Passfield Corner]
A sad drive to the Haslemere dogs' home so that Sandy might be 'put to sleep', never to wake again. What with the coming of old age, aggravated by the hot weather, he had been unusually subject to gusts of passion; he had to be tied up whenever postmen or tradesmen came to the house; Annie dare no longer wash or even brush him; and on Saturday, when I touched his back inadvertently, he flew at me and mauled my leg badly. He has been a source of interest and companionship, especially when Sidney was away; he had a striking personality, extremely intelligent, but a rebel to all authority and with a violent temper alike with dogs and men. But for all that he was a lovable little brute . . . I doubt whether I shall get another dog. They add to the duties and risks of life, and neither the two old Webbs nor the two girls have any surplus energy to dispose of. And with dogs, if they live to become infirm, the parting from them is a real sorrow.

> Sir Josiah Stamp, later Lord Stamp (1880–1941), was an economist and businessman. Eileen Power (1889–1940) was professor of economic history at the L.S.E.

*12 July.* [Passfield Corner]
Josiah Stamp and his wife spent the week-end with us . . . The immediate reason for the meeting was the crisis at the London School of Economics. According to Stamp, who is chairman of the governors, there is a violent upheaval led by the representative committee of the professors on the Committee of governors against the Beveridge–Mair directorship or, as they style it, dictatorship. Mrs Mair will be sixty this year, the age of retirement, unless the governors extend it for four years or less. Beveridge insists that her term must be extended for the five years and threatens to resign if it is not. Robbins and his group – Laski and Eileen Power backed by their friends – in spite of their divergent views on politics and economics, unite to denounce such an extension, and threaten a scandal and wholesale resignation if Mrs Mair is retained. But this is not all. Outside authorities – the university inspectors (he showed

us a letter from Clapham) and the U.S.A. donors of funds – object to Mrs Mair. Sidney and I, in spite of our warm liking for Beveridge and desire not to break with him, agree that the crisis must be ended and *Mrs Mair must go.* . . .

*20 July.* [Passfield Corner]
Our old friends the Coles came for the night; middle-aged and thoroughly stabilized in all their relationships, endlessly productive of books, whether economic and historical treatises or detective stories, mutually devoted partners and admirable parents of their promising children, they lead their little troop of admiring disciples along the middle way of politics, rather to the right of the aged Webbs – a curious commentary on the would-be revolutionary Guild Socialist movements of the second decade of the twentieth century. . . .

The military revolt against the liberal government in Spain, led by General Francisco Franco (1892–1976), began on 19 July.

*24 July.* [Passfield Corner]
The forty-fourth anniversary of our marriage was spent at Parmoor . . . Meanwhile we listen with excited interest to the news about the Spanish revolution, broadcast from governmental and rebel stations. The civil war is developing into a definite class war; soldiers and sailors revolting against the rebel officers; the government arming the workers and peasants against the Fascist leaders and actively inciting the common soldier and sailor to depose their officers. Much depends in foreign affairs on what side wins in Spain . . .

Zinoviev had already been imprisoned for a year when Kamenev and thirteen other old Bolsheviks were tried and executed for conspiracy in the first of the show trials which accompanied the Stalinist purges.

*28 August.* [Passfield Corner]
For the defenders of Soviet Communism in foreign parts the sensational trial in Moscow, denounced by Trotsky as a monstrous lie, is a nasty shock. To re-open a criminal indictment concerning a particular episode when the principal individuals accused have already been tried, convicted and are in confinement, is repugnant to the British conception of jurisprudence. For the defendants to plead guilty, to refuse the aid of counsel, to vie with each other in abject confession of their crime and an

accusation of other persons – in the case of Zinoviev and Kamenev, a revolting exhibition of treachery to the government and to former comrades, of cringing cowardice and repetitive lying – lends a suspicion of torture behind the scenes, or of promises of pardon not fulfilled by the G.P.U., capped by the immediate execution of the whole sixteen of them after the verdict. Even if you desire to destroy your enemies, the violence of the prosecution, indictment and denunciation, and the savage demands for death sentences by workers all over the country, repeated night after night in Moscow broadcasts, is offensive to British calm and good manners. We blew our rebels from the cannon's mouth after the Indian Mutiny; we massacred crawling men, women and children at Amritsar not so long ago; we hung poor old Casement, shot the romantic Erskine Childers, slaughtered innocents by the Black and Tans in the Irish rebellion in the 20s, with an easy conscience; but we did not talk about it, or revel in reviling our victims.

Why the Stalin governing group decided on this melodramatic staging of their revenge . . . is impossible to understand and justify. My own explanation is that all the leading men in the U.S.S.R. have been brought up in the atmosphere of violent revolution, of underground conspiracies and ruthless killings, and they cannot get out of this pattern of behaviour. Those who have the power suspect all those who disagree . . . whilst some of those who dissent do actually revert to revolutionary practices – certainly Trotsky did, and the evidence is that Kamenev and Zinoviev were also conspiring against Stalin. But whether or not these dissenters were guilty of conspiracy to murder they were bound to be thought so, and treated according to the revolutionary principle of kill your enemies, otherwise you will not survive yourself. . . .

Kingsley Martin (1897–1969) became the editor of the *New Statesman* in 1930.

*14 September.* [Passfield Corner]
In old age it is one of the minor satisfactions of life to watch the success of your children, literal children or symbolic. The London School of Economics is undoubtedly our most famous one; but the *New Statesman* is also creditable – it is the most successful of the general weeklies, actually making a profit on its 25,000 readers, and it has absorbed two of its rivals, the *Nation* and the *Week-end Review*. Kingsley Martin, with his queer, shifting, alive intelligence, his careless hygiene, his miscellaneous ethical code (he is not a whisky addict which apparently the majority of

journalists are, especially the Americans; but he has got rid of his wife) and loose views about his neighbour's morals, has turned out a successful editor. . . . He has no philosophy of life; he flits from one viewpoint to another. He delights in gossip. That gives the *New Statesman* its variety of outlook – perhaps makes it popular in this dissolving world.

*20 October.* [Passfield Corner]
The reports of the Labour Party conference in the Press are hopelessly discouraging . . . The dark shade of the Spanish civil war, its hideous cruelties, the miserable failure of the non-intervention policy of Great Britain and France, the chance of this creed war spreading to France and leading to a world war, revealed the Labour Party without a decisive policy, not knowing, as in the case of Abyssinia last year, whether they were prepared to risk war in order to prevent gross injustice in the international sphere, and whether or not they would trust the National government with increased armaments. As it is the Fascist states are carrying all before them and look like continuing to do so . . . What seems inevitable is a world war.

*25 November.* [Passfield Corner]
The birthday of our biggest and most self-important child – *Soviet Communism* – certainly the best-seller of all our works. 20,000 in Great Britain, 5,000 in the first six months in the U.S.A.; penetrating into Japan, Australia, South Africa, New Zealand and India – so enthusiastic readers in those parts inform us . . .

Edward VIII's relationship with Mrs Ernest Simpson, a twice-married American, was reported in foreign newspapers and was generally known in London society. After Mrs Simpson's divorce on 27 October there was a long and discreet tussle between the King and Baldwin before the matter became public on 2 December. The King privately told Baldwin on 5 December that he proposed to abdicate, but there was much agitation before this was announced on 10 December. The King made a broadcast from Windsor Castle on the evening of 11 December, before leaving for France. His brother the Duke of York (1895–1952) became King George VI.

*5 December.* [Passfield Corner]
If the Queen Bee in a densely packed hive crawled out of her cell and wended her way towards the outer world, there could hardly be a bigger

buzzing in the company of bees than there has been among the humans of the British Empire about King Edward's proposal to marry Mrs Simpson. In Labour circles there are two strains of thought and feeling. The most spontaneous reaction is 'Why should not the King marry the woman he loves, even though she be a commoner, a foreigner and a divorcee?', reinforced by the openly expressed suspicion that the whole episode is a conspiracy against the King – the outcome of the reactionary government and the offended Church's hatred of a monarch who busies himself, not with Church and Court functions, but with the miseries of the common people and the way to end them at the cost of the rich. . .

What comes out of the whole business is that neither the Church nor the Court circle would have objected to a King's mistress – Edward VII had a succession of these, openly accepted by all concerned; what they do refuse to endure is a Queen who does not conform to Court usage, still more a King who dislikes conformity to Church rites and is on the side of the common people. If the King refuses to relinquish the proposed marriage, or to step down from the throne, the Cabinet will resign. The Opposition will refuse to take office, the scratch government he will get together (Winston Churchill, Lloyd George?) will have to dissolve, and the electorate will be divided according to distorted class bias. No one knows what will happen, except a vitiated and muddled public opinion expressed by a scratch majority. If he abdicates and York is proclaimed King, reaction will have won. If he withdraws the question of marriage and just 'carries on', he might win through. No Conservative government would risk a general election on the Cabinet's right *to compel a King to promise not to marry*, if he had the common people on his side. No one knows what are Edward VIII's opinions, except that he loathes the Anglican Church, associates with a bad-mannered lot, and cares for the comfort of the unemployed men. Whether he is atheist or tends to the Roman Catholic Church, Communist or Fascist is unknown. He may not know himself. Some say he is intimate with the German Embassy and is a reactionary: Rothermere and Mosley support him. He is neurotically excitable, obstinate, hates show and has a warm heart for the underdog; but he is not an intellectual. It is said that he is, in conversation and conduct, coarse and common. '*What do you really believe, Mrs Webb?*' in an earnest tone and with a nervous gesture, is the only sentence in his talk with me that I remember! What struck me as most certain is that he is an unhappy man who has not found as a royal personage a comfortable private life. Which is to his credit . . .

*12 December.* [Passfield Corner]
The events of the last week are the most superb manifestation of good manners on the part of the British governing class. To engineer the abdication of one King and the enthronement of another in six days, without a ripple of mutual abuse within the royal family or between it and the government, or between the government and the opposition, or between the governing classes and the workers, was a splendid achievement . . . An exquisite example of British calm, British solidarity, British kindliness and British common sense. What could be more convincing and disarming than Baldwin's homely and sympathetic account of his friendly remonstrances to the King about his disreputable appearance with his acknowledged mistress at home and abroad? A month later, the King asks, 'What about a morganatic marriage?' 'Impossible', answers Baldwin, after consulting the Cabinet. '*I intend to marry Mrs Simpson,*' answers Edward, 'and go', he adds. So he announces his abdication. The Cabinet begs him respectfully, even affectionately, to reconsider, etc., etc. He refuses. Hence the swift passage, in a single day, of the necessary Bill through both Houses of Parliament and, within a few hours, the proclamation of the new King and Queen; and then, that very evening, the touching farewell of Edward to his people over the air.

What behaviour could have been more suited to unite the House of Commons, to pacify the mob, to damp down, once for all, the upgrowth of a King's party? 'Manners maketh man,' is the old adage. 'Good manners hideth a multitude of sins,' is more to the point in British politics.

In April 1937 Beveridge accepted the headship of University College, Oxford. Mrs Mair accompanied him.

*31 December.* [Passfield Corner]
The last day of the year we had a painful visit from Beveridge. . . . He and Sidney had a long interview during which Sidney spoke of the 'impossible situation' at the School. Beveridge said he had never heard of the 'scandal'!!! But he looked tragic . . . We parted with affectionate words, but we are anxious about the effect of the visit on his and Mrs Mair's intentions. . . .

~ 1937 ~

*7 January.* [Passfield Corner]
Here we are, once again, at the opening of another year of the mad century.

So far as we are personally concerned, we are rather more comfortable than we were this time last year; for I am slightly more able-bodied and workable. But Europe and Asia are in the same cruel turmoil . . .

*Our Partnership* is growing steadily; four chapters are finished – so far as I can see at present, about half the first volume. But work on it is painfully tiring. But muddling through a couple of hours every morning, thinking about it and reading endless biographies and reminiscences the rest of the day, gives meaning to my life and interest to our talks together. . . .

*20 February.* [Passfield Corner]
Certainly the more one studies the verbatim report of the Moscow trials the greater is the puzzledom as to the psychology involved. Why did those intelligent and strong-willed men get involved in that crazy conspiracy at a fearful risk of death? . . . why, if it is a 'frame-up', the Soviet government should wish to publish to the world such a damaging libel on Soviet Communism and its strength, is utterly bewildering. *Unless the facts are true* the whole business is absolutely incomprehensible, whether on the part of the government or on the part of the accused but innocent victims. . . .

*15 March.* [Passfield Corner]
We motored over to Telegraph House . . . to the odd dwelling-place of two successive Earl Russells, distinguished for their gifts, heresies and unsuccessful matings and consequent poverty: both of whom have been our intimate friends. Poor Bertrand, today sixty-five, with a young wife and a coming child, with little or no income beyond what he earns, looked physically worn out and mentally worried. And well he may be. He would like a professorship, but he is past the age at which any British university could appoint him. His only hope is the U.S.A. But his particular subject, the philosophy of mathematics, is off the modern curriculum . . . Sidney and I have been revolving in our minds how we can help him. We owe him a debt of gratitude for his generosity in giving the London School of Economics five years' fellowship income in the early days of the School's career. . . . He ought to have a Civil List

pension, but what government would reward so distinguished a rebel against authority, human or divine?

*19 March.* [Passfield Corner]

What troubles me, in the task of building up successive chapters of *Our Partnership* . . . is twofold. How big is the work to be? . . . also many reflections about manners and morals, and more especially about religion, are not my present way of thinking: am I there and then to say so and give my present point of view? Finally there are the critical, sometimes the defamatory character of the notes about people, friends, acquaintances and enemies, observations which are often hasty and unwarranted, contradicted or modified by later impressions. Of course, I console myself with the thought that I can always leave out (or my literary executor can leave out) what is not desirable to print . . . But if that be so, why trouble to select? . . . This question I think suggests the answer . . . one could find a skilled editor to cut down the book to what was a desirable length and content according to the circumstances of the time. . . .

*18 April.* [Passfield Court]

. . . Our stay at Longfords . . . and the expedition to Standish, our old home, seemed like visiting a family graveyard . . . Longfords is today sold to be cut up into lots; the neighbouring woods and fields have been increasingly supplanted by little villas, each with its patch of garden and outbuildings. The enlarged mill has eaten up most of the beautiful garden and woods; what is left has fallen into disorderly decay. The whole neighbourhood has become urbanized: the nine-mile drive to Standish House is today through streets of little shops and rows of small houses, interspersed with new mills and little villas.

When we reached the old home, the house and its spacious gardens was the habitation, not of a family, but of 260 tuberculosis patients with a complete staff of medicals, nurses, mechanics and gardeners. When we introduced ourselves as the Webbs, 'a remnant of the Potter family', we were welcomed as honoured guests and allowed to wander about at our own sweet will – I, with queer memories associated with this room or that, this corner of the garden or that view of the valley of the Severn or the Standish woods. To outlive one's own generation, to realize that even the memory of these men and women has passed away – well, it all adds to the melancholy of old age, to which is added, in our case, the consciousness of decay in our own civilization, our own race, our own class, of the beloved and oneself! . . .

*14 May.* [Passfield Corner]

We listened in to the magnificent medieval pageant of the Coronation of George VI. How strangely Jewish, alike in the words (nearly all from the Old Testament), in the rites-of-human-sacrifice doctrine of the atonement, the priestly anointing, and above all in the dominating ideology of a divinely appointed King, of a chosen people, to rule by the sword, over the rest of mankind. So much for the Abbey service. The Alice in Wonderland of the procession, the gorgeousness of the scene, centred round two little robots in the glass coach, preceded and followed by the armed forces from all parts of the Empire – one long orgy of glorification of the imperial mission of Great Britain, manifested in five continents . . .

To me the revolting role in the massive spectacle served to the multitude is that of the Anglican bishops. Is it conceivable that these highly selected scholars and would-be philanthropists honestly believe in these rites and ceremonies, in this strange mixture of magic with the deification of force, pure and simple, as a way of organizing mankind for the glory of God? What about the pacifists, the secularists, the old evangelical Quaker element – why have they not protested? Why this ironic silence on the part of the intellectual élite, the total absence of moral indignation on the part of the followers of Jesus of Nazareth at this adoration of power and riches? . . .

*5 June.* [Passfield Corner]

Our dear old friends – GBS and Charlotte – spending a few days here, he visibly frail and in decline, distressed that he can no longer write his plays . . . He cannot visualize complicated social institutions and their reactions on individuals: his detail is all wrong and his philosophy not thought out. And he knows it! . . . They consulted Sidney about what to do with their respective fortunes; they want to endow (Charlotte brought a draft will endowment for the Irish Free State) 'culture' or, as GBS puts it, 'knowing *how to behave* in public administration, or in any other career' . . . What kind of testament he will sign, seal and deliver, heaven only knows. Sidney spent an hour or two drafting some description of what he thought GBS really wanted to do, in language which might be understood by an intelligent trustee, and another hour or so discussing with Charlotte her draft. In return GBS will go through the proof of the postscript to our chapters [for the revised edition of *Soviet Communism*]. So continues the old unbroken comradeship in work, started forty-five years ago, between GBS and the Webbs. . . .

Beatrice had arranged a reunion party for what she called 'the R.P. clan'.

*13 June. 4 a.m.* [Passfield Corner]
The family party . . . was a decided success. Over one hundred of the descendants of Richard and Lawrencina Potter assembled in our garden, with a few old friend outsiders . . . It pleased me to think how the seven sisters would have loved to be there and watch their descendants eagerly talking and laughing together. Dear old Father, how delighted he would have been at the thought of the successful careers of many of his descendants and their spouses. Three peers, four privy councillors, two Cabinet Ministers, two baronets and two Fellows of the Royal Society – a typical nineteenth- and twentieth-century upper-middle-class family, rising in the government of the country . . .

But it was an exhausting episode for the aged Webbs and their two girls, with the Mileses and my old servant Jessie and my secretary Gabrielle Irwin to help. I doubt whether this experiment of a large garden party will be repeated. The garden looked lovely, the three sitting-rooms were enlarged by a pavilion, the weather was perfect and there was a due consumption of tea and cakes and sherry and cigarettes. So all went well . . .

I wrote that the R.P.s had during the last fifty years risen in the world. But this is only true of half a dozen individuals . . . As a group, the R.P.s have become poorer. At the end of the nineteenth century the combined business and professional incomes of R. D. Holt, Daniel Meinertzhagen and the Crippses must have hovered somewhere near £100,000, whilst Henry Hobhouse, Arthur Playne and even Leonard Courtney (after he had been endowed by his wealthy brother-in-law Richard Oliver) reckoned their income in thousands, rising in the case of Henry Hobhouse and Arthur Playne to £5 or £6,000 a year. Only Rosy and I were at the £1,500 level and were considered by the other members of the clan to be 'poor', if we had children, which I had not. . . .

The Webbs spent a holiday at the Kurhaus at Beatenburg near Interlaken. After the death of Beatrice's sister Margaret, Henry Hobhouse had married his former secretary Anne Grant.

*12 July.* [Passfield Corner]
We enjoyed our first flight in the air to Basle and back again, an ideal way of travelling for an aged couple. Instead of the tiresome journey by rail and steamer . . . we motored to the Croydon aerodrome, where we

lunched, entered the plane at 1.45 and arrived at Basle 4.15, owing to a north-west wind which shortened the official time-table by one hour! The journey back was rather more exhausting . . .

The three weeks at Beatenburg at the Kurhaus was delightfully restful. George and Rosy Dobbs were with us for the first ten days and Rosy, as our guest, stayed on . . . Sidney and I wandered about in a honeymoon spirit . . . I returned home feeling much stronger . . .

While we were away, my aged brother-in-law Henry Hobhouse died. Throughout our lengthy relationship . . . he and we, though respecting each other, were not friends or associates. I think he disliked me: in the main because of my old intimacy with Margaret . . . But after her death and his remarriage he became very much attached to me – a sort of remorse, I think, for his detachment from his wife during the last days of painful illness. I grieve today that I did not go to see him last spring, when he begged me to come. . . .

*10 August.* [Passfield Corner]
When I read through the diaries, year after year, I wonder whether all our personal work (coupled with intrigue) to get this reform or that carried into law, to convert this group or that of men and women to our way of thinking, was worth while from the standpoint of the community? . . . judged by the state of Great Britain today . . . it looks as if we socialist reformers failed to stop the rot, as if our self-complacency was unwarranted. Sidney maintains his faith and contradicts my pessimism. . . .

Sir Alexander Carr-Saunders (1886–1966), a demographer, remained director of the L.S.E. until 1956.

*27 August.* [Passfield Corner]
Carr-Saunders, the new Director of the School of Economics, here with his wife alone. Sidney and he together the whole evening up till 12.30, Sidney telling him the story of the School and all its many difficulties with the four successive Directors, whilst I entertained the pleasant little lady for a suitable spell, both of us going early to bed. So far as we can see, Carr-Saunders is the right man for the job. . . . I doubt whether he is as able, either intellectually or administratively, as Beveridge; far less power of initiative and fulfilment, but he has more judgement and far better manners – 'the manners that maketh man'. To be the head of the London School of Economics with its 120 professors and lecturers and

its 3,000 students in these tumultuous times of mutually hostile political and economic creeds, held with religious fervour, is a difficult business. . . .

*7 September.* [Passfield Corner]
The world event which every day animates our evening listening to the news is the Sino–Japanese war. We have always been admirers of Japan, alike before and after our visit in 1911. But since the great war she has been an evil influence in the world, intensely imperialist, militarist, insincere in her religious faith, reactionary in her political and economic doctrine. Japan has, in fact, 'lost her head' and, I think, her soul. China, meanwhile, has been finding herself – a new self, patriotic and with an understanding of science and a growing appreciation of the new civilization of the U.S.S.R. Japan has, by her insolent aggression, thrown China into the arms of the Soviet government; the Chinese C.P. have enthusiastically joined Chiang Kai-shek in his defence of the homeland. . . .

MacDonald had resigned from the government at the end of May. On 5 November he set off for a holiday in South America, but died of heart failure during the journey. Lord Allen (1889–1939), a pacifist and Labour journalist, had been chairman of the I.L.P. 1922–26.

*11 November.* [Passfield Corner]
Sidney was rung up by various Press agencies and newspapers for appreciation of Ramsay MacDonald on his death at sea. Sidney 'begged to be excused'. Allen of Hurtwood gave a sanctimonious broadcast calling for honour and pity for the *lonely* soul of his past leader. J.R.M. *was* lonely, because he had no genuine feeling for causes or comrades. . . . From reports and the unkind snapshots appearing in the Press, MacDonald became in his last years a miserable man . . . His best friend must rejoice that he 'passed peacefully away'. History will not be kind to his memory. Arthur Henderson will stand out as the wisest and most disinterested of the labour leaders of 1906–36.

*29 November.* [Passfield Corner]
Sidney was slightly ailing. So I seized the opportunity to pick out a future medical attendant for the aged Webbs . . . I chose Ronald Gray, a youngish and reputed clever man, physician and surgeon. He overhauled both of us, reported us in first-rate condition considering our age: no blood pressure, good kidneys, healthy heart and lungs. . . .

*6 December.* [Passfield Corner]

Had to call in Gray again, as Sidney developed severe pain in the leg whenever he walked more than a few yards. Diagnosed an intermittent claudication – which means lack of elasticity in the artery, when subject to the increased call for blood produced by exercise: an infirmity characteristic of old age. However, Gray thinks it will yield to treatment, plus warmer weather. But for the time I have to take solitary walks – without even a dog to solace my loneliness. All the same, we two aged ones *are* fortunate. . . . The one drawback to happiness is the nightmare abroad and at home of war and the fear of war; the ghastly thought of what is happening in Spain and in the vast continent of China. There is also uneasiness as to the internal condition of the U.S.S.R., the continuance of conspiracy trials and executions, which we explain so plausibly to others but do not altogether accept as *inevitable* ourselves! There is always the lurking suspicion that Stalin and his clique *may* have lost their heads! . . .

In November, on a nominally unofficial visit, Lord Halifax (1881–1959), a leading exponent of appeasement, visited Hitler. The visit convinced Hitler that Britain would not check his territorial ambitions and persuaded Neville Chamberlain, who had replaced Baldwin as Prime Minister in 1937, that Hitler wanted a peaceful settlement in Europe. A few weeks later, dismayed at Chamberlain's conciliatory attitude, Anthony Eden resigned as Foreign Secretary.

*13 December.* [Passfield Corner]

The Maiskys here for a day and a night: he in good spirits, frank and talkative; she tired, and I think, depressed. Of course he is reserved about the arrests and rumours of arrests; justifies some, denies the fact of others . . .

Maisky talked mostly about foreign affairs: why could not the British government be sensible and come in wholeheartedly to a pact against the aggressors? . . . Many of the younger members of the government . . . want to do it. But the 'Cliveden coterie' . . . are die-hard pro-German . . . It was this set that sent Halifax to Germany; it was Eden who countered this movement by the visit of the French Minister to London. The P.M. holds the balance: he is a hard-headed businessman with no imagination; he is equally hostile to the U.S.S.R. and Germany. Above all, he wants to keep out of war. But unless some steps are taken by the British government to show a stern front against the aggressive nations, war there will be, and against the British Empire. . . .

*14 December.* [Passfield Corner]

I went up to London for Xmas shopping and lunched with Susan. Our old house reeked with escaping gas: gas cookers, gas fires, gas heaters, from the basement to the attic. Susan looked alarmingly changed: swollen figure and sallow face: Emily told me she had been seriously ill with swellings and sores, poor dear. . . .

To me, the old home with the roaring traffic, facing the Thames river with its barges and bridges, the old servant and the old friends and the old old gossip about the Labour world, was like ghost-land, the old Mrs Webb of eighty being the oldest ghost of the lot. I was glad to get back to our silent and comfortable cottage home with my old man. We too are ghosts of our former selves haunting this mad century with its tragic happenings; but we are happy ghosts, loving each other and always with a job in hand, like two aged craftsmen . . .

# Fallen on the Way

## January 1938–April 1943

*5 January.* [Passfield Corner]
Laski's hostile review of our second edition of *Soviet Communism* and its postscript in the *Political Quarterly* for January is only one more sign of the swing over from the Soviet Union on the part of the left intellectuals who claim to lead the rising generation. . . .

The old Webbs are distinctly out of favour with the intellectuals, whether right or left; but owing to their old age they are treated with kindly respect. We shall end as we began, in a small group of dissentients from the existing social order, the difference being that in the nineteenth century that order seemed stabilized, today it is in dissolution and everyone not only knows but proclaims it. . . .

*23 January.* [Passfield Corner]
Yesterday's eightieth birthday was entertained and distracted by the greetings of friends and relations. The *Spectator* had a two-column article by GBS, the *New Statesman* a short one from H. G. Wells and two long letters from Laski and Margaret Cole – all delightfully appreciative; even the *Evening Standard* and the *Observer* gave me a paragraph. There were three bouquets from the London School of Economics, from the students, teachers and staff, and an imposing one from the National Council of Labour; altogether a grand display from the left . . . We finished up the day by an afternoon concert at the Ponsonbys from the Booth quartet; and another bouquet and another testimony to the

Webbs. What amused me most was the singling out by H. G. Wells and some other friends of my capacity as a *manager*, or as H.G. called it, as a Great Lady – 'the greatest lady I have ever met', which seemed to me rather absurd, seeing my intensely bourgeois simplicity of life, and pre-occupation with what most people consider dreary drudgery of an ant-like type. . . .

*25 January.* [Passfield Corner]
The end of our partnership?

The inevitable has come, one of the partners has fallen on the way, the youngest and the strongest. He may lie there for a while, but we shall never march together again in work and recreation. I cannot march alone.

On Monday Ronald Gray saw and examined him: his leg was sufficiently cured to walk two miles and all seemed well, though I had been startled sometimes by his tired and woebegone look. Yesterday morning, when I knocked at his door at 6.30, his voice sounded queerly grim; when I returned from refilling my hot water bottle, he was standing by the bed seemingly puzzled how to get in – and then after he had gulped down his tea there was silence, with a twitching of the hand. He insisted on getting up for his breakfast downstairs, but when I joined him he was again silent and when he tried to answer me his answers were difficult to understand. But he seemed in no pain and did not complain. Ronald Gray gave the verdict: it was a stroke, a clot in the arteries on one side of the brain. It might pass away – but . . . So there he is lying in the bed of the south-west room with a day and night nurse in attendance. He will have care and love so long as I am strong enough to give it. Loneliness will not last long for the one that is left, and I would rather bear it than that he should. If only we could talk together. He tries over and over again and occasionally there will be a word, 'yes' or 'no', or some slight indication of a word, but then silence and a pained expression of frustration. But he smiles and nods his head when I kiss his hand and hold it in mine. Anyway I can spend hours petting him, telling him the news or talking about past times, or saying 'We have written the book,' which always makes him smile.

*3 February.* [Passfield Corner]
'I have been there before.' Over fifty years ago, one morning in the autumn of 1885, I began a life of waiting on a loved one: the routine of watching helplessness of body and mind, of dealing with affairs left unfinished by an active brain, of reorganizing the domestic doings to the

best advantage of a permanent invalid, without knowing what would happen in the future to him or to oneself. Today I am in the same plight. But this time the problems are easy ones: instead of large establishments in London and the country, countless business commitments of an international capitalist to settle up, eight sisters and their seven husbands all equally affected (one sister indeed living at home in a state of neurotic collapse), and my own career, intellectual and emotional, in the melting-pot, I live today in comfort in a small house with sufficient income for our needs and little financial responsibility, with no one to consider but the loved one . . .

*11 February.* [Passfield Corner]
It is clear that the only time I shall have for thought and its expression will be the early hours of the mornings; the remainder of my waking hours will be taken up with waiting on the beloved one, transacting business and dictating letters, intervals of outdoor exercise, and resting in the sitting-room over a book with, now and again, a bit of a cigarette. Aged and infirm, my thought is of doubtful value; I no longer have his mind to submit it to; and there will be the perpetual strain of watching helplessly his gallant struggle to make good. He is the best of the stricken, gentle and uncomplaining, with a pathetic resolute intention to get back his speech and handwriting in order to carry on. If only he could express himself fully: all he can do is to mutter words which are more often than not the wrong words, from which I try to gather his meaning. If I fail we sometimes laugh and kiss each other and I beg him 'wait till you are stronger'. Dr Gray assures me that unless he gets worse he will undoubtedly get better and might even return to normality, but on a low level of achievement. But for both of us it will be intellectually, though not emotionally, a lonely life. At present, I am isolated from friends and relations. The only person I have seen since he was struck down twenty days ago, outside my own servants, nurse and medical man, is Barbara Drake, who spent one night here and as always was affectionate, interesting and helpful. When Father collapsed at York House in November 1885 I had a period of utter loneliness, though with a far larger circle of relations and paid servants . . .

As a young woman of twenty-eight I heard around me a whispering, occasionally openly said: 'What a failure she has made of her life.' As an aged woman of eighty there is a tuneful chorus . . . singing of the successful achievement of the Webbs. When one is about to quit the stage of life, it is consoling to hear the applause of a great audience. Alas!

for human vanity in its most harmless form of delight in flattery. Is it wrong or is it right? . . .

*12 February.* [Passfield Corner]
Sidney is making a good recovery; his speech is coming back and he is practising his writing, but it will be a long time, if ever, before he can live a normal life without a constant attendant. And this necessity of adding another member to the household will be a source of worry to me. . . .

*22 February.* [Passfield Corner]
It is exactly a month this morning since Sidney showed signs of a stroke . . . He is undoubtedly better, but he is disabled and downcast – he broods over his condition, wondering whether he will recover. Would Dr Gray tell him, he asked me, what exactly he is suffering from? I told him that it was an affection of the arteries – I thought it better to be quietly frank – that it had affected his speech but that Gray thought he would get back ninety per cent of his strength, but would have to lead a quiet life . . . During the three or four hours we spend together we take little turns on the landing and the other bedrooms; I read to him or talk, or we listen to music over the wireless in his bedroom. We are very very happy together, those hours are my anchorage, my home – the rest of my life is lonely, especially the walks over commons or through woods where we have wandered together in the past fourteen years . . .

*23 February.* [Passfield Corner]
The general impression of the Eden–Chamberlain crisis is that the hard-grained commonplace narrow-minded capitalist Prime Minister is intent on keeping out of the war, preserving what he can of the British Empire and virtually joining, without saying so, the anti-Comintern pact so as to effectively isolate and discredit the U.S.S.R. and stop the spread of Communism in Europe and Asia. Franco is to win in Spain, and Japan in China, Italy in the more barren districts of Africa. Meanwhile the three Fascist powers will have exhausted themselves – bitten off more than they can chew – and Great Britain, with her piled-up armaments and submissive working class, will be impregnable. But don't talk about it – stick to the slogans: be strong, but keep out of war, extend your trade and isolate the U.S.S.R. I think Chamberlain will succeed in keeping public opinion on his side, in spite of the fact that all the talents and idealists are against him: Lloyd George, Churchill, Cecil; intellectuals like

Harold Nicolson, Boothby, as well as the Labour and Liberal parties . . .
When I saw Galton and GBS on a flying visit to London they were both
on the side of Chamberlain: GBS because of his admiration for
Mussolini and Galton because he wants to keep out of the war and
instinctively dislikes contact with the U.S.S.R. . . .

*9 March.* [Passfield Corner]
Every now and again I relapse into gloom: continued physical discomfort leading to a distaste for life. When I am with him, I am relatively
happy in giving care and love; it is when I wander alone in my morning
walk, or sit by the fire in the evening, listening to the news of war and
of fear of war, and latterly to the turbid revelations of the [latest]
Moscow trials, wondering what is the true meaning of all these horrors.
It is then that my poor old brain begins to whizz and ache and I feel
worn out, too old to live. Indeed one of the puzzles is: how far are my
aches and pains produced by thoughts, gloomy and disturbing? How far
are these unpleasant sensations the direct effect of my loneliness, fear of
losing my life companion and, last but not least, deep distrust of what is
happening in the U.S.S.R.? . . . The sickening vilification of all who
differ from the policy of the government clique, the perpetual fear of
innocent citizens of being wrongly accused and convicted, is a terrible
social disease . . . The poor Maiskys, what a life they must be leading!

Joachim von Ribbentrop (1893–1946), later Foreign Minister of Nazi
Germany, was executed as a war criminal: he was currently Ambassador
in London.

*12 March.* [Passfield Corner]
Sitting alone in an armchair by the fire, I listened last night to the French
news at eight o'clock, the English at nine o'clock and then turned to
Moscow. Tense and agitated was the French voice, tense but coldly composed was the English. Hitler had annexed Austria was the fact if not the
form of this amazing recorded happening. After that, the droned-out last
act of the Moscow trial was an insignificant item of scandalous news.
What did the so-called 'witch trials' of the far-off Eurasian continent
matter compared to the triumphant march of Hitler's Third Reich to a
German domination of central Europe – the very disaster that the great
war was waged to prevent! A comic anti-climax was the statement in the
'rest of the news' that von Ribbentrop had been received by the King and
lunched with Chamberlain that very morning . . .

*1 April.* [Passfield Corner]

Sidney is apparently happy and hopeful – he suffers no pain or discomfort, always excepting getting very tired towards the end of the day; he goes to bed directly after seven o'clock supper, wakes up in the night and reads for an hour or so and then sleeps again. When I come in at 6.30 a.m. he greets me with smiles and kisses and wants to have the last news or [hear] about any talk I have listened in to. The weather has been glorious and the chorus of birds in the morning consoling. The one tiny snag are the roaring army aeroplanes, many by day and some by night, reminding us of the coming war. . . .

*9 May. Eastbourne*

For the first three weeks of our stay I made no entry in the diary. The days pass here automatically without distinguishing one day from another. My dear man is enjoying the change of scene and diet; the drives every other morning in Lion Phillimore's car, the walks on the charming esplanade towards Beachy Head, which we know so well, the wireless, the browsing over the score or more books which we brought with us. He is, I think, a little stronger on his feet; but his powers of expression and speech are still too defective for him to enjoy the give and take of conversation with anyone but me and his nurse, who have learnt to understand him. Occasionally he wonders whether he will ever be back at his desk. His deep-down unselfishness and humility and kindly consideration of others are even more striking as an invalid than they were in active life. . . .

*19 May.* [Passfield Corner]

Our four weeks at Eastbourne was ended by Lola Holt motoring Sidney and nurse home whilst I travelled up to the lunch at the London School of Economics in honour of my eightieth birthday – an exciting and exhausting episode for the aged Beatrice Webb. Over eighty of the lecturers and one or two governors attended. . . . Eileen Power in a witty and charming speech and Carr-Saunders in a serious and kindly one, proposed my health and I responded, I was told 'brilliantly' (but how the aged are flattered!). . . . I described how the little Fabian group who started the School had benefited by the fact that the Fabians were not concerned with the great controversies which raged in the 90s and the first decade of the twentieth century: Irish Home Rule, Free Trade v. Protection, Imperialism v. Pro-Boer; Religious Education v. Secularism, Temperance v. Drink; and therefore were on friendly terms with the leaders of both parties. . . . Today the situation was completely changed. Intellectually we are all at each other's throats. But the School had fortunately maintained its reputation for being the middle way. . . .

*30 May.* [Passfield Corner]
Thirty-six hours away from Sidney, wandering in luxurious surroundings, chiefly seeing 'the Sacred Aged' (as the Chinese call all mortals who have survived the three score and ten). Actually I embraced three over eighty and one over ninety. (Actually embraced, and for the first time I kissed GBS!) First with Lola to Parmoor where, in the big house with its enormous rooms, lives the aged and somewhat senile brother-in-law . . . Then on to London, where I visited the aged Shaws in their luxurious flat and found GBS lying on the sofa with Charlotte bending over him with motherly affection, having persuaded him to be injected with insulin for the pernicious anaemia which had reduced him to a white-skinned shadow. He was full of wit and delighted to see his old friend. Then on to the L.C.C. palace on the river . . .

From the L.C.C. offices Barbara [Drake] motored me to the Macnaghtens, where I met and embraced warmly the ninety-year-old Mary Booth, my oldest living friend. We were genuinely glad to see each other once again . . .

Sidney met me at Haslemere. I told him that of all the aged mortals I had seen he was the least egotistical, and the best to live with for his attendant relative . . .

Jawaharlal Nehru (1889–1964), a leader of the Indian National Congress, became the first Prime Minister of India. His daughter Indira Gandhi (1917–1984) also became Prime Minister.

*3 July.* [Passfield Corner]
Nehru, the leader of the Indian Congress, and his lovely daughter spent some hours here on Saturday with Ponsonby to meet them. I had read and admired his autobiography and welcomed him warmly. He is the last word of aristocratic refinement and culture dedicated to the salvation of the underdog whether in race or class, but I doubt whether he has the hard stuff of a revolutionary leader. He is in theory a Communist; but doubts the possibility of the complicated Soviet organization among the mixed races of the Indian continent. 'Between two worlds, one dead and one powerless to be born' is a quotation which he recognized but did not agree with. He believes with fervour

that a united India can be born; is, in fact, being born, largely owing to the teaching of Gandhi, whose power as a saint and a missionary he realizes and admires, but whose economic proposals he dismisses as romantic remnants of the past. Nehru is convinced that the freedom of the individual, as manifested in the presence of opportunity to live the good life, cannot be secured without the organization of principal services and main industries deliberately for communal consumption and without the profit-making motive. Today the Indian people are too primitive for Soviet Communism. But they have been roused, not only by internal conditions of India but by the horrors of the invasion of China by Japan and their sympathy with other oppressed races. . . .

*10 August.* [Passfield Corner]
Beveridge here in high spirits, thoroughly enjoying his new life as Master of University College, Oxford: an easy job, within a cultured and well-mannered group; dignity and prestige without any particular responsibility or hard work . . . Also feels himself 'King of Unemployment Insurance' as chairman of the Unemployment Insurance Statutory Committee, telling Parliament what it ought to do about the insurance fund . . . What a change from the turbulent atmosphere and continuous work and friction of the London School of Economics. . . . Elspeth Mair is his housekeeper and Mrs Mair a constant visitor; she is also hostess of Avebury, his country home. So all is well with Beveridge.

*1 September.* [Passfield Corner]
Harold Laski here for five hours' talk before he goes for nine months' sojourn in the U.S.A. lecturing at universities, interviewing notables and ending with a visit to Roosevelt in Washington – so he says. His usual clever gossip and philosophic reflections. He is today completely convinced that the Soviet trials and executions were at once justified in fact and necessary to save the revolution from counter-revolutions . . . we found ourselves in complete agreement . . . all would be right when the new civilization was stabilized. . . .

After Austria was annexed, Hitler began to threaten Czechoslovakia. Believing that the Czechs must be sacrificed to preserve European peace, Chamberlain and the French Premier Daladier met Hitler and Mussolini in Munich on 30 September and agreed to dismember Czechoslovakia. Chamberlain returned to Britain claiming to have brought 'peace with honour . . . peace in our time', but relief soon gave way to the widespread conviction that before long war was inevitable, though the French had been demobilized, the Czech defences ruined, the Poles exposed to invasion and Russia left isolated.

*13 September. 4 a.m.* [Passfield Corner]
We listened last night to Hitler's passionate oration and the thunderous applause. His voice, its amazing volume and range of intonation, accounts for some of his potency in exciting mob devotion. So far as we could understand an unfamiliar language, he denounced western civilization: its capitalism, its political democracy, its religion and code of conduct, with almost equal passion as he did Bolshevism, with its 'Jewish commissars'. The fury and inconsequence of his words, without any definite commitment, left a strange impression of madness. Why should he denounce *capitalism*, which exists and is his ally in Germany, not to mention political democracy, which is certainly not Bolshevism? Why add to his enemies? Hitler and his followers have shown such a mania for persecution at home and aggression abroad that one wonders whether there is not an internal explosion coming and whether this craze for violence is not an attempt to divert the explosion away from revolution to patriotic aggression? It is inconceivable that the British government should not take up the challenge and defend the *status quo* in central Europe. . . .

*20 September.* [Passfield Corner]
For the last three days and nights, indeed ever since Hitler's excited oration, heightened by the sinister impression of Chamberlain's flight to sit at Hitler's feet, we have been living through a nightmare of foreign news. I try to take my own little mind off the horror and humiliation of the situation with the reflection, 'After all *we* are not responsible and never have been; why should we not continue to be mere lookers-on, just as one looks back on the horrors of history?' But . . . Czechoslovakia, the darling child, the creation of the British and French governments at Versailles in 1919, petted and praised for the last twenty years as the one sane political democracy in central Europe, neither pacifist nor Communist, and eminently well-behaved. And now handed over, in the course of three days, without any consultation with its government, by the British and French governments to Hitler with his pack of German Hun wolves. . . .

Well, well, need we think about it? And I try to get on with the book and Sidney, almost equally perturbed, turns to his old-fashioned novels.

But the nightmare persists, kept alive by the French and English broadcasts: 8.30 a.m., 12.45 a.m., 6 p.m., 7 p.m., 9.40 p.m. – all shamefaced, a queer tone in the announcer's voice – 'a horrid business, don't think *I* approve'; they all seem to mutter beneath the words they send over the air. . . .

*1 October. 3.30 a.m.* [Passfield Corner]
At 8.30 yesterday morning I heard over Paris radio that peace had been signed at Munich by Hitler, Mussolini, Chamberlain and Halifax. A sense of profound relief, or a consciousness of disgust for one's own out-look on life – which was the greatest? I think the sense of relief. Not in our time, O Lord! The wild enthusiasm of the reception of the two Prime Ministers in London and Paris proved that it was so with the man and the woman in the street. Chamberlain showed courage and will-power in taking the decisive step towards a Four Power pact with Hitler and Mussolini, excluding the U.S.S.R. in defiance of socialist political democracy and old-fashioned liberalism, with its pathetic faith in a League of Nations and collective security, not to mention the little group of British imperialists who see disaster in this one-sided alliance with the aggressive powers in search of new lands to conquer. Chamberlain deserves the gratitude of the Crown, the City and the Archbishops for his anti-Communism; he will get it from the bulk of the middle class of Great Britain because he has saved them from war . . . All the same, the victory of sheer force brutally expressed, and the abject repudiation by the French government of their oft-repeated guarantee of Czechoslovakia and their retreat from the Franco–Soviet pact, a terrible sign of weakness in the two European political democ-racies. It means the dominance of Germany in Europe through the threat of brute force. Taken with the acquiescence of the two great democratic powers, in Italy's conquest of Abyssinia and avowed help to Franco in Spain and Japan's barbaric invasion of China, it kills the League of Nations with its strivings for a reign of new international affairs.

*31 October.* [Passfield Corner]
The Maiskys here for five hours on Sunday afternoon and in good spir-its. He and I talked incessantly, Madame and Sidney intervening. . . . Maisky was convinced that Germany was immensely powerful in the air, 7,000 warplanes and another 3,000 in reserve with a capacity of manu-facturing 700(?) a month, England's being 100 a month. Her bluff could have been called by Great Britain, France and the U.S.S.R.: she could

not have fought a long war. But today she is far more powerful, and without the U.S.S.R. Great Britain and France could not protect themselves. He declared that Germany is going to demand back some if not all of her colonies within the next year and that Chamberlain and Halifax (and the Cabinet generally) intend to meet her wishes. Will the people of Great Britain stand it? . . . So long as Hitler has bloodless victories there will be no revolution in Germany. . . . He thought the British Empire doomed; and wonders when the British people would wake up and realize it. He had been amazed at the shortsightedness of Chamberlain, Halifax and Co. . . .

*1 November.* [Passfield Corner]
Annie exploded in a most unseemly way against Mrs Grant. As on other occasions she presented me with an ultimatum and lost her temper and her good sense. . . . Unless she mends her manners I am afraid she and Jean must go and I must get two Austrian or Czech servants. British women are no longer suited to domestic service in private houses, especially in the country . . . The plain truth is that the old standard upper- and middle-class home is no longer practicable. . . . Unfortunately at eighty years of age one cannot change one's social habits, and I have to see Sidney comfortably out of life and then disappear myself, leaving *Our Partnership* unfinished. Shall I succeed in doing so? If I drop out who will take care of my beloved? That is the question that worries me.

Walter Adams (1906–77) was secretary of the L.S.E. 1938–46 and its Director 1967–74.

*10 November.* [Passfield Corner]
A week of worry, enjoyment and work, with on the whole a comfortable conclusion. On 2 November, the day after the domestic upset, I was due in London to lunch with Carr-Saunders and his wife at the London School of Economics to fix up which room should be named after Sidney and Beatrice Webb, and to meet the new secretary, Adams, a remarkably able, pleasant and attractive young university man, exactly the sort for that key position. Then on to Barbara's for the family party on the next day: eighty R.P.'s turned up, all most kind to their aged aunt, and I talked incessantly that afternoon and also on the two evenings with one or other of them. . . .

*13 November.* [Passfield Corner]
The sinister madness of the Nazi persecution of the Jews, on a scale and with a publicity unprecedented in world history, has roused the U.S.A. from its isolation and also magnified the objection on the part of the British governing class to ceding colonies to Hitler's Germany. The Pope too is up in arms, some Nazi authorities declaring that when Judaism has been disposed of, the Roman Church will become the next victim of their insensate hate. There seems today something indecent in Chamberlain's friendliness to Hitler at Munich. And the P.M.'s refusal to tell the House of Commons whether or not he is prepared to discuss with Hitler the transference of mandated territories back to Germany is rousing Conservative M.P.s out of their complacency. . . .

*24 December.* [Passfield Corner]
A white but gloomy Christmas: the one bright spot in the world situation is the outspoken contempt of American statesmen and the American Press for Hitler's Germany and their helpfulness towards the Spanish Republican government on the one hand, the Chinese resistance to Japan on the other. Altogether Chamberlain's policy of 'appeasement' is proving a tragic absurdity – the aggressor states, far from being satisfied, are every day more outrageous in their demands, and war seems inevitable. It looks as if the governments of Germany, Italy and Japan *dare not stand still*: they must conquer or dissolve. Hitherto they have conquered, but at a terrible cost to their own people. . . .

*New Year's Eve.* [Passfield Corner]
. . . Looking back on 1938, in spite of Sidney's breakdown early in the year, my dominant feeling is one of gratitude that Our Partnership has survived, though on a lower level of activity. He is no longer an active partner, but he is still the beloved companion – in body and mind. He is happy and suffers no pain. He no longer reads anything but novels: he is interested in current works and reads reports and scholarly histories and biographies. Meanwhile I potter on with odd jobs. . . .

## ∼ 1939 ∼

*6 January.* [Passfield Corner]
We listened on Wednesday afternoon to that world performer President Roosevelt, addressing all the nations as to what is right and what is

wrong in public affairs at home and abroad. Religion, democracy, the acceptance of international law are the three fundamental principles of the good life. In voice and manner he is a great orator; he is self-convinced of the rightness of his cause and the essential superiority of the American civilization over all other civilizations. He has the added charm of belonging obviously to the aristocracy of that civilization. His foreign policy was accepted with enthusiastic applause by Congress at Washington – an applause which has no doubt been echoed by the millions of listeners in the British and French Empires, the U.S.S.R. and in little European democratic states.

*20 January.* [Passfield Corner]
A tiresome job for a tired brain! Elected President of the newly constituted Fabian Society merged with the New Fabian Research Bureau, under the direction of the Coles. I have to explain in an article in the February *Fabian News* the reasons for this amalgamation . . .

> On 10 March Chamberlain said that Europe 'was settling down to a period of tranquillity' and Samuel Hoare denounced 'jitterbugs' who were predicting war. On 15 March German troops occupied the rump of Czechoslovakia and declared it a protectorate. On 17 March Chamberlain began to turn foreign policy towards the resistance of Fascism. President Roosevelt announced a revision of the U.S. Neutrality Act to permit the sale of arms to countries resisting aggression.

*16 March.* [Passfield Corner]
The news last night of Hitler's crash into Czechoslovakia and the Halifax–Chamberlain shamefaced admission of it, in Lords and Commons, roused in me horror at the cruelty to Czechoslovakia, and a sort of grin – a contemptuous grin – at the imbecility a bare six months ago of the Munich episode. Also there was satisfaction that all notions of a Four Power pact with Germany and Italy were killed for good and all; that the U.S.S.R. has become our inevitable ally in its resistance to the aggressive states in the near future, and that the U.S.A. would be Hitler's Public Enemy No. 1, ready to help in supplying arms even if not ready to use them.

*18 March.* [Passfield Corner]
Chamberlain's unexpected oration over the air from the Birmingham Town Hall last night, with the thunderous applause of the ancestral

audience in the city of his birth and of the life of his great father, will certainly impress the world of listeners that, at long last, he and his government mean to resist Hitler's lawless use of force – at least against France and Great Britain. An honest man of limited intelligence and intense class consciousness, ugly in voice and manner, intent on pursuing peace for his own country at almost any cost except loss of territories by France and Great Britain. To preserve these Empires he would be ready to risk war. He looks across the Atlantic for the support of the great power in the West; he cannot bring himself even to glance at the other great power in the East.

In *The Holy Terror* Wells predicted the circumstances of Stalin's death fifteen years later. On 21 March the Germans made demands on Poland, including the recovery of the 'free city' of Danzig and part of the corridor dividing Germany from East Prussia. Poland appealed for help and on 31 March, with French support, Chamberlain gave Poland a military guarantee – an offer made without any attempt to involve the U.S.S.R., Poland's near (but disliked) neighbour.

*31 March.* [Passfield Corner]
. . . I lunched with H. G. Wells yesterday in his attractive and luxuriously fitted house in Hanover Terrace, Regent's Park. He has sent me his latest book, *The Holy Terror,* and begged me to come and see him – he wanted to know whether *we* had invented the term *industrial democracy* and what we meant by it. . . . He was obsessed with his own vague vision of a world order . . . But he utterly failed to make me understand what sort of social institution he had in mind. . . . Poor old Wells. I was sorry for him. I doubt whether we shall meet again – we are too old and tired. . . . GBS told me that 'Moura' has her own 'Russian house' but visits him daily. . . .

The following morning I called on the Maiskys: Madame Maisky was upset by the putting off, day after day, of the proposed interview of Maisky with Halifax about the threat to Poland. . . . Presently a message was brought in from Halifax asking Maisky to call at the Foreign Office at one o'clock: upon which I departed, after wishing them well. The Shaws, where I lunched, were in good spirits: GBS looking his best and obviously enjoying the success of *Pygmalion* on the films, and *Geneva* and *The Doctor's Dilemma* on the stage. There is a marked Shaw revival: his witty and unconventional cynicism, with its queer freedom from apparent bias for or against any of the current ideologies, is evidently refreshing to the public mind. . . .

On Good Friday (7 April) Mussolini attacked and annexed Albania, provoking the British and French governments to offer guarantees to Rumania and Greece. On 26 April the British government introduced military conscription for the first time in peace. Hitler, it was later revealed, had already decided to invade Poland; his Reichstag tirade of 28 April began the six-month build-up to war.

*8 April.* [Passfield Corner]
The Maiskys called here yesterday – they had driven out into the country to get some rest from the turmoil. Just before they left the Embassy the Ambassador had been called up by a friendly American journalist and informed of the Italian invasion of Albania (I had heard it over the wireless at 12.25). He shrugged his shoulders when I asked him what he thought of it, as if to say: 'What else can Chamberlain expect?' 'How do your people put up with him?' he asked me presently. He has proved to be disastrously wrong; why does the Conservative Party continue to trust him? He intimated that Moscow did *not* trust him and it was doubtful whether they would join a pact if he remained Premier. . . .

*8 April.* [Passfield Corner]
Meanwhile I have broken down in health. I can no longer walk because of sores on my shins, which compel me to keep my legs up. I can no longer sleep except by taking alonal, both of which treatments are laid down by Orr, our medical attendant. Also Sidney has been laid up, but is now getting back to normal. The book is laid on one side, and will not be resumed until we return, I hope rested, from our holiday in North Cornwall. Which is depressing. Have I not reached senile incapacity for further clear thought, I ask myself? Anyway, I am tired of living. I should welcome a painless death if I could take my beloved with me. He would think it hysterical, certainly unreasonable, to desire it, but I doubt whether he would resent it. He feels, as I do, that our living life is finished: we are merely waiting for the end.

*5 May. Polzeath, Cornwall*
A long and expensive journey here, with a night at Exeter . . . The one redeeming feature was Ella Pycroft's evening with us at Exeter. An aged and fragile but dear old lady, with her outstanding honesty, sympathetic intelligence and all-pervading kindliness still strong, in spite of loss of memory and tottering steps. She and I talked of old times, my work as rent-collector of East End dwellings, and her naive

response when I suggested that I might marry Sidney Webb: 'Oh! Beatrice, you couldn't.' . . .

*22 May.* [Cornwall]
Our stay here has been restful, the loneliness, the beauty – the strange beauty – of the Cornish coast has been a real relaxation for a troubled mind and tired and worn-out body. Whether I shall be able to continue my book I do not know. But what does it matter? . . .

*18 June.* [Passfield Corner]
Two nights at Barbara's, first to introduce the Carr-Saunders and Adamses to the Shaws at lunch, with a view of help from Charlotte for the new cultural library and lecturers to carry out GBS's variation of the principle 'manners maketh man'; secondly to attend a meeting of the newly constituted Fabian Society and, incidentally, to lunch with the Maiskys to meet Harold Nicolson, with family gatherings thrown in. . . . Meanwhile the news from the Far East looks like Japan joining the Axis in war with Great Britain – for which we are all preparing.

> Charlotte endowed the Shaw Library at the L.S.E. King George VI and Queen Elizabeth had just made the first visit by reigning British monarchs to the United States.

*24 June.* [Passfield Corner]
How amazingly personal the world has become: the mob idolizing particular individuals instead of claiming, as they did in the nineteenth century, the right of groups to govern themselves . . . And this idolization of persons on account of their assumed and exceptional goodness and infallible wisdom is not confined to the so-called totalitarian states. The British people, with their genius for compromise, have lit on the device for a robot King and his wife – who have no power but are treated with extreme deference and arouse in the mob worshipful emotion. The efficiency of the device has been shown by the enormous success of the British King and Queen not only in Great Britain but in Canada and the U.S.A. They are ideal robots: the King kindly, sensible, without pretension and with considerable open-mindedness, and the Queen good-looking and gracious and beautifully attired, who blows kisses to admiring Yankees in New York but looks the perfect dignified aristocrat in London. Is this turn towards idolizing particular human beings characteristic of the last two decades, the reaction from a loss of

faith in a supernatural god or gods? This mania for a *leader* seems a similar instinct to that shown by wolves – and even by dogs, when the dogs have lost contact with the idolized man. It is clearly a dangerous human instinct when manifested towards men who exercise personal power over multitudes of their fellow men, as do Hitler and Mussolini. . . .

*28 June.* [Passfield Corner]
Alike in France and Great Britain, the governments and the inner circle, war is expected to break out in July, August or September . . . The only excuse for Munich put forward by those in authority is that Great Britain and France had shamefully neglected to arm themselves for the inevitable struggle with the Fascist states. That, obviously, was the fault of the Conservative governments who have ruled Great Britain for the last twenty years, except for the short interlude of the two minority Labour governments . . . neither the one nor the other controlling Parliament. The root of this disaster lies in the hatred and fear of Soviet Communism on the part of the all-powerful capitalist and landlord class, reinforced by the dislike of public expenditure. And dearly will they pay for it!

*13 July.* [Passfield Corner]
Sidney's eightieth birthday. . . . Testimonies of affection and respect drifted in during the day. Sidney happy and peaceful, pleased with his past life of successful adventure in public administration and the writing of books, content with the comfort and friendly consideration which envelops his old age, above all the continuous comradeship with his aged but loving wife. So all is well with the Webbs. If only I could get on with the book! . . .

*23 July.* [Passfield Corner]
Forty-seven years today we were married in the shabby little office of the Registrar of St Pancras Workhouse – a fitting spot for the opening of our recognized partnership, dedicated to the abolition of poverty in the midst of riches. Since that date we have been one and indivisible, in work and rest, at home and abroad, in our private life and our public career. Looking back on those forty-seven years of companionship in thought and action, I remember no single note of discord. In stating our conclusions we have sometimes disagreed, but it has ended either in a compromise or in the dismissal of the problem from our thoughts . . .

Today Sidney and I have ceased to work together. But we love each other more and more, and when one dies, I think, the other will die too. . . .

British and French negotiations with the U.S.S.R. had continued all summer, with distrust on both sides making them both dilatory and inconclusive. Suspecting that the Western Powers might be seeking to embroil him in war if Hitler attacked Poland, Stalin turned the tables and, on 23 August, signed a non-aggression pact with Germany. S. P. Turin (1882–1953), a lecturer in Russian economics at the L.S.E., had translated Soviet documents for the Webbs. He and his wife Lucia were Soviet émigrés.

*25 August. 4 a.m.* [Passfield Corner]
The German–Soviet pact seems a great disaster to all that the Webbs have stood for. Even Sidney is dazed and I am, for a time at least, knocked almost senseless! The manner of its making is even worse than its meaning. If the Soviet statesmen had, after the breakdown of collective security (professed to be the policy of Great Britain and France), retired from European politics, and then entered into non-aggression pacts with other countries, even with Germany, or insisted that they would remain neutral (like the Scandinavian government), they would have retained the respect of the world. But to become fervent supporters of collective security, to be missionaries of resistance against aggression and all attempts to extend territories by force, to be leaders all over the world of anti-Fascist and anti-Nazi movements, and then to conclude suddenly and secretly an alliance with Hitler's Germany, is a terrible collapse of good faith and integrity. Further, if Stalin and his colleagues were, during the last four months, turning towards Hitler and actually secretly discussing this alliance, they ought not to have been discussing with British and French diplomats, openly and apparently sincerely, an alliance against Germany in her march towards European domination. The military discussion, involving intimate exchange of military information, was especially dishonourable. To continue these discussions to the very night of the signature of the Soviet–German Pact was a disgraceful proceeding. . . . I console myself with the thought of how rapidly currents of thought and feeling throughout the world change their course. . . .

*27 August. 3 a.m.* [Passfield Corner]
The Turins here for a night. She is hard at work as Carr-Saunders' secretary, packing up at Houghton Street so as to move to Peterhouse

College, Cambridge, if war breaks out: the Foreign Office taking over the London School of Economics' building. . . . We and they listened over the wireless to the final stages of the fateful decision of the British Cabinet on Sunday and today. Shall it be peace or war?

I am in a state of utter exhaustion . . . haunted by the agony of the world we live in, this terrifying vision of herds of human beings being prepared for mutual slaughter in their millions. . . .

*1 September.* [Passfield Corner]
Owing to Annie's skill and industry, with Jean's help, we have solved the blacking-out of our little abode successfully. . . . I try to get on with the book. So I must limit my entries in the diary to other people's thoughts, and not waste my minute energy in expressing my views. . . .

> Despite last-minute attempts to avert war, Germany invaded Poland early in the morning of 1 September. After Parliament and the House of Commons met on the evening of Saturday 2 September, Chamberlain said that everything he had hoped and wished for in his public life had 'crashed in ruins'.

*3 September.* [Passfield Corner]
Listened at eleven this morning to Chamberlain's admirably expressed declaration to the House of Commons of war with Germany. His voice, amplified by the wireless, was strikingly like his father's. In his sorrowful admission of the failure of his policy of appeasement and sombre but self-controlled denunciation of Hitler and his monstrous ways, he was at once appealing and impressive. Now that we are at war – a war during which we personally can take no part – I feel detached and calm; the strain has ceased . . .

*7 September.* [Passfield Corner]
Our first air raid, which turned out to be a false alarm; the enemy aeroplanes never got beyond the east coast. A banging at the front door and a grim voice calling 'Air raid'. I had just come from my bath and looked out of my window. There stood a man with a bicycle, his gas mask slung over his shoulder, who explained that a warning had been given from Portsmouth that German aeroplanes were in the neighbourhood. A few minutes later, I went into Sidney's room and saw him sitting up with his gas mask on! I suggested that he should take if off, which he promptly did. Mrs Grant had been in and was angry. '*You have no right*

to tell Mr Webb to take his off,' she said in a menacing voice. 'Pardon me,' I laughed. 'I am his wife and the mistress of this house. Keep yours on if you like. It is damned nonsense putting on gas masks out in the countryside. The Germans won't waste their gas on us. Our only danger – if there is one – is an explosive bomb. Even a quarter of a mile off I am told it might bring our house down!' Annie and Jean were slightly excited and interested, but went on with their work. In two hours' time the all-clear was sounded. We who live round about the camps – there is a firing-range for tanks a quarter of a mile away – are fortunate in being in a *neutral* area – neither so dangerous for our own children to be evacuated nor sufficiently safe for strange children to come. We are free from lodgers and yet, for sensible folk, not subject to panic. So all is well. . . .

*18 September.* [Passfield Corner]
Satan has won hands down: Stalin and Molotov have become the villains of the piece. Molotov's broadcast to the peoples of the U.S.S.R. justifying the march of the Red Army into Poland is a monument of international immorality, cloaked in cynical sophistry. At twelve o'clock we listened in to the news over the wireless: at three o'clock a telephone message from the Soviet Embassy that the Ambassador was detained in London – Madame Maisky hoped they might be able to come later on. Poor Maiskys, we shall never see them again: if we did we should not know what to say to them, nor they to us. With their friend Litvinov they will disappear, let us hope safely, somewhere in the background of that enormous and enigmatic territory. The aged Webbs will fade out presently: but the horror of a raging war, which can neither be lost nor won, will destroy the old without bringing the new civilization within sight of this generation. Owing to the lust for the old territories of Czarist Russia to be won by force, the statesmen of the U.S.S.R. have lost not merely moral prestige, but also the freedom to develop the new civilization, whilst the old western civilization was being weakened and perhaps destroyed by war. To me it seems the blackest tragedy in human history. Sidney observes that, within a century, it may be 'a forgotten episode'. He refuses to be downcast.

*2 October. 4 a.m.* [Passfield Corner]
Winston Churchill (as First Lord of the Admiralty)'s broadcast on 'The First Month of the War' is a notable event. His reference to the U.S.S.R. ought to revive the spirit of downcast friends of the Soviet

Union. If only our old acquaintance were the Prime Minister in the place of the reactionary and mechanical-minded Chamberlain, the prospect of a right and rapid ending of this murder and waste of the war would be more hopeful. Anyway, he becomes the leader of the progressive forces in Great Britain, and the leaders of the Labour Party will have to follow suit or lose their influence on public opinion, owing to their attitude to the Soviet Union . . .

*5 October.* [Passfield Corner]
. . . Everyone I speak to seems utterly bewildered and downcast – far more so than in the early days of the great war. There is no war enthusiasm – at best, a dull acquiescence. The imminence of air raids, the black-out at nights, the evacuees and their parents, the heavy taxation and drastic rationing of light, heat and food already enforced, and a hundred other grievances, irritate and depress the spirit of the nation.

*8 October.* [Passfield Corner]
An hour with the Booths at Funtingdon Lodge. George and Margy looked tired and strained. The old nurse who lived with them had died a few weeks ago; and now my old friend Mary Booth, and much-loved mother of a devoted family, has passed away in her ninety-second year. . . .

*27 October.* [Passfield Corner]
I journeyed up to London in a train crowded with officers in uniform and youths looking sad and distraught, saying farewell to mothers and sweethearts, and a few older men to wives and children at the stations – to lunch with Barbara and meet the Leonard Woolfs. They had expressed a desire to meet me again. Leonard was looking terribly ill with his trembling hands, but was as gently wise as ever. . . . Virginia seemed troubled by an absence of any creed as to what was right and what was wrong. I asked her whether she was going to write a second volume of [*The*] *Years.* I longed to hear how the family she described so vividly would respond to this new war. Would they be as unconcerned as they were during the great war of 1914–18? She gave me no answer except that she did not know her own mind about what was happening – so how could she describe the mind of others! . . . This gifted and charming lady, with her classic features, subtle observation and symphonic style, badly needs a living philosophy. Brought up in the innermost circle of the late Victorian intellectuals, in revolt against the Christian religion with its superstitions

and its hypocritical conventions, they were between *laissez-faire* and *laissez-aller* in all the circumstances of life. *Absence of restraint* was to them the one and only meaning of liberty, for they personally enjoyed the presence of opportunity to lead the life they liked, or thought they liked. Virginia Woolf realizes that this creed has broken down; but she sees no way out . . . We all aim at maximizing human happiness, health, loving kindness, scientific certainty and the spirit of adventure together with the appreciation of beauty in sight and sound, in word and thought. Where we differ is how to bring about this ideal here and now. . . .

Finland resisted the Soviet attack until March 1940.

*1 December.* [Passfield Corner]
Another shock for the friends of the Soviet Union! the march of the Red Army into Finland and the bombing of the towns by a Red Air fleet. As before it is the *manner of doing it* – the working-up of hard hatred and parrot-like repetition of false – glaringly false – accusations against poor little Finland, which is so depressing. . . .

*Christmas Day.* [Passfield Corner]
On Friday the Maiskys telephoned that they would like to come down to tea and supper on Sunday. As we had heard . . . that the Allies were going to break off diplomatic relations with the U.S.S.R. we assumed that it was a farewell visit. . . .

What Maisky did not realize, or at any rate would not admit, is that the war in Finland is the main issue; the Finnish people and their constitution are idealized by British liberal and conservative intellectuals . . . We parted with the Maiskys affectionately. . . . They both declared that the happiest times of their presence in Great Britain have been their visits at the home of Sidney and Beatrice Webb. . . .

### ∾ 1940 ∾

*8 January.* [Passfield Corner]
H. G. Wells has sent me his latest work – *The New Moral World*, a continuation and repetition of *The Fate of Homo Sapiens*, published a year ago. He has become a revivalist preacher, warning men that they are rushing headlong to extermination and showing them the narrow way of salvation. His God is Science, served by countless public-spirited

scientists; his Devil is Religion, or more precisely the Roman Catholic Church with its infallible Pope (Protestantism he dismisses as the halfway house to Secularism) . . .

> Beatrice had put *Our Partnership* aside to attempt a short, popular book, *Our Pilgrimage* in three parts: Fabian socialism, the decay of capitalism, and the new civilization. The book was never completed.

*22 January.* [Passfield Corner]
My eighty-second birthday: two years since Sidney was on the eve of the stroke which withdrew him from a working life. Two years more and we shall be in our Jubilee year, when I want to publish my last literary work, *The Three Stages of Our Pilgrimage.* In the last year I have only accomplished three chapters out of five of *First Stage: Fabian Socialism.* If I could finish the other three this coming year I could do it: assuming that I cut down the last stage to one chapter on Soviet Communism. Of course there is a possibility that the U.S.S.R. may collapse and the *New Civilization* appear as a dream dreamt by the aged Webbs. . . .

*29 February.* [London]
. . . Barbara and I went to hear Attlee lecture on War Aims at Canterbury Hall, Cartwright Gardens – the London centre of the London School of Economics. He was rather unfriendly to me at the reception before the lecture. His hour's lecture was pitiable: he looked and spoke like an insignificant elderly clerk, without distinction in the voice, manner or substance of his discourse. His address was in fact *meaningless*; there were neither statements or arguments that you could take hold of, whether to accept or to deny . . . Altogether a hopeless failure. I doubt whether anyone in the audience – they were mostly middle-aged men – had any notion of what he actually advocated, either about the desirable peace or about the internal social organization after the war. To realize that this little nonentity is the Parliamentary Leader of the Labour Party, the representative of His Majesty's Opposition at £2,000 a year, and presumably the future P.M., is humiliating. . . .

*14 March.* [Passfield Corner]
It is with relief I listened to the doleful admission by the British and French wireless that Moscow had made a triumphant peace with Finland. Sidney admitted that he also welcomed the news. . . . The neutral world, however prejudiced against Soviet Communism, observes

that the Red Army has done its job, whilst the French and British armies are still peacefully contemplating the Siegfried Line. . . .

*20 March.* [Passfield Corner]
Now that the U.S.S.R. with its 'new civilization' is out of the war, I can turn to and concentrate on *Our Pilgrimage*. . . .

*3 April.* [Passfield Corner]
. . . I creep along with my work, tired by day and sleepless by night, looking after my dear one except when I go with Peter [her new dog] for a walk of two or three miles (I exhausted myself yesterday with a four-mile walk) whilst Sidney goes with Mrs Grant for one or two miles, sitting down on the camp-stool which she carries. One day passes into another night rapidly; the week seems ended unexpectedly; the only time that drags are the hours in the night – that is why I scribble in this diary with which I deaden my dislike of living . . . If I succeed in writing a thousand well-chosen words to add to my Chapter I am satisfied – even if I have to re-write it the next day! And so I creep on until Saturday when Miss Burr comes and I dictate the net result and deal with the week's correspondence. . . .

On 9 April Germany occupied Denmark and, despite British intervention, began an invasion of Norway. In a parliamentary debate about Norway on 7–8 May, Chamberlain was seen to have lost the confidence of his party. On 10 May Hitler invaded Holland and Belgium. That evening, Churchill agreed to form a coalition government. Chamberlain remained in the Cabinet until 30 September, when he resigned due to ill health. He died on 9 November.

*10 April.* [Passfield Corner]
Denmark conquered; then parts of Norway seized, Sweden threatened unless she accepts the protection of Germany. Such are the activities, within a few hours, of Nazi Germany – nominally in answer to our laying of mines in Norwegian territorial waters, but actually prepared and even begun before that event. The lightning speed of German aggression and its ruthless efficiency is amazing. . . . It took the Red Army six months and hundreds of thousands dead and wounded to grab a small part of Finland. *In six hours, with no loss of life*, Germany has annexed the whole of Denmark and is in control of the capital and southern ports of Norway. A sinister warning for Moscow, and a

dramatic challenge to the Allies' blockade and their confidence in ultimate victory.

*11 May.* [Passfield Corner]
At long last we are actively at war. There will be no more French communiqués – All quiet on the Western front. We have the invaded Holland and Belgium on our side, not yet defeated, fully prepared to resist, with the defeated Czechs, Poles, Norwegians and I assume Danes as our allies; which means the navies and shipping of six European naval powers under our command. There are signs that the U.S.S.R. will not be against us – the Kremlin offered a mutual defensive pact (against German aggression) to Sweden and Finland! His Holiness the Pope has denounced this new wickedness on the part of pagan Germany; the American President will doubtless do likewise. . . . Chamberlain is no longer Premier; Churchill is our Champion, and the Labour Party have accepted office. All of which we heard over the wireless yesterday . . . I felt converted to fighting Hitler to the bitter end. His mad aggression has become irredeemable: '*Il faut en finir*' the French are reported to be saying. And the Soviet Union is left standing more or less on one side. . . .

The French government led by Paul Reynaud (1878–1966) refused Churchill's dramatic offer of an Anglo-French union, and then capitulated. General Weygand (1867–1965) became the French commander-in-chief. Marshal Pétain (1856–1951) became the head of the collaborationist Vichy regime, which sued for peace on 17 June and ceased fighting on 25 June.

*22 May. 2 a.m.* [Passfield Corner]
The literally and unmistakably *awful* news last night, which we listened to over the French wireless at 7.30, may mean disaster to France and perhaps to Great Britain. Reynaud's speech to the French Senate came over the air in a tragically excited voice. The French army had failed to destroy the bridges over the Meuse . . . Gamelin, the French generalissimo, was not mentioned; but he was suddenly superseded by General Weygand and eighty-year-old Marshal Pétain, the hero of Verdun, was to be deputy premier to Reynaud! . . . But will there be time to save France with Italy coming in in the Mediterranean tomorrow! And if France is overrun, what will happen to Great Britain: will the British Expeditionary Force get back across the Channel before they are mopped up by the victorious Germans? . . .

This is the last meeting with the Shaws that Beatrice records in the diary. Charlotte became increasingly immobilized with lumbago; she died on 12 September 1943, aged eighty-six. Shaw lived on until 1950.

*24 May.* [Passfield Corner]
Yesterday we drove up to lunch with the Shaws at Whitehall Court. Sidney insisted on doing so: he had not seen them for two and a half years and wanted badly to see them 'once again' and to speak to Charlotte about endowing the London School of Economics, which he did and was comforted to hear that she had sent £1,000 to Carr-Saunders for the teaching of 'good manners and general culture' to the students. They were delightfully affectionate. . . .

Stafford Cripps was dispatched to Russia to negotiate a trade treaty. He remained there as Ambassador until the German invasion in 1941 led to a formal alliance.

*28 May.* [Passfield Corner]
. . . Yesterday's news. Stafford departed by air for Moscow; leading article in *The Times* approving of his visit. 'Increasing gravity of the situation' reported with the usual spate of stories of the marvellous heroism and skill of our air crews. Concentration on home defence and evacuation of eastern ports. *The invasion of Great Britain* threatened from France, Belgium and the Dutch ports. And our intellectuals have been spending their time in discussing what exactly should be the terms of a *dictated* peace imposed on Germany! While the French and British armies sat confidently behind the Maginot line, leaving the neutral frontiers wholly undefended; and yet threatening to send an expeditionary force to beat back the Red Army in far-off Finland and add the U.S.S.R. to our enemies. There is a sinister comedy in the doings of the Chamberlain Cabinet during the last five years. For comfort we fall back on historical precedent. Great Britain has always begun her great wars with defeat and ended in victory.

*29 May.* [Passfield Corner]
Reynaud's dramatic broadcast following the 8 a.m. British news, reporting capitulation of the Belgian army, was a dead stop to the morning's mite of work. It means, I assume, the evacuation of the B.E.F., under German fire, either back to an English port or to a French port in Western France?

On 20 May German units reached the Channel coast, cutting off all the British army and part of the French. On 29 May an improvised ferry service from the Dunkirk beaches began to rescue the remains of the B.E.F. and the French troops. By 1 June four-fifths of the British army had been saved. Churchill's speech in the House of Commons on 4 June ended with the words: 'We shall fight on the beaches, we shall fight on the landing grounds, we shall fight in the fields and in the streets, we shall fight in the hills; we shall never surrender. . . .'

*5 June. 1 a.m.* [Passfield Corner]
Churchill's remarkably frank and rhetorically eloquent speech summing up the events of the last five days will echo round the world. Over three hundred thousand Allied troops have been brought over the Channel from Dunkirk to English ports under perpetual German bombing and gun-fire, by some thousand ships and boats of all sorts and kinds escorted by the navy and air force. The B.E.F. leaves behind them thirty thousand dead, wounded and missing. We have lost the whole of our armaments – guns, transport, tanks. Our small air force has proved itself, man for man, machine for machine, far superior to the Germans, who have lost four to one in the battle in the air. In a sense it is a glorious adventure; but from a realistic standpoint, Winston admits it, it is the greatest military disaster which has ever overtaken the British army. Today we have to defend our own island from invasion; he thinks that in this homely task we are invincible. But the French army – can it stand up against the German hordes, possibly reinforced by the Italians? That is left in doubt. . . .

Roosevelt's promise to make the United States 'the arsenal of democracy' was followed up by the immediate transfer of much-needed destroyers, by accelerated shipments of arms and, in 1941, the helpful financial provision of the Lend-Lease agreement.

*11 June. 4 a.m.* [Passfield Corner]
Six o'clock news: Mussolini declares war on France and Great Britain . . . Awake and restless I slipped down at twelve o'clock to hear Roosevelt's promised oration at 12.15 a.m. . . . The subject was the future of America and the outlook for her youthful citizens. This war was a crisis – perhaps the greatest in history of a freedom-loving democratic self-governing country confronted with a mortal enemy, i.e. dictators aiming at world dominion through brutal force. . . . Applause of a wild character echoed

across the aerial waves of the Atlantic. Short of declaring war on Germany and Italy the oration could not have been more helpful to the Allies.

Paris had been occupied on 14 June. The undefeated but outflanked French armies on the Maginot line surrendered on 17 June.

*18 June. 15 Sheffield Terrace*
I travelled up to London to attend the annual meeting of the Fabian Society. Over the wireless had come the news that the French government had asked for an armistice. The train was crowded with soldiers and officers and civilians on government business: all were silent as if they were going to a funeral. Opposite me the handsome young private, travelling first class, looked tragically wretched; two ugly businessmen were talking about some war business in a morose murmur. Bardie [Barbara Drake] received me with her usual affectionate greetings and abuse of our ruling class. There were about fifty persons present at the little reception at the Fabian office, among them the ever-present Coles, Ellen Wilkinson, Susan Lawrence, Leonard Woolf and some younger men who seemed pleased to be introduced to me. I made my little speech as President in a nearby hall, extolling the Society and its combination of intellectual tolerance and research, and pointing out the problem to be solved if we survived as an independent country. No one I spoke to saw hope; the general feeling was anger at the government, humiliation and fear – sometimes one, sometimes another uppermost. Bernard [Drake] looked desperately unhappy, but he still asserts we shall hold out, even if the French army and fleet surrendered. . . .

In a broadcast on 18 June Churchill warned that a German attack was imminent. 'Let us therefore brace ourselves to our duties, and so bear ourselves that, if the British Empire and its Commonwealth last for a thousand years, men will still say: "This was their finest hour."'

*25 June.* [Passfield Corner]
. . . Winston's message to the peoples of Great Britain and France yesterday was admirably conceived and perfectly expressed: he is wise and eloquent, a great wielder of words. The behaviour of the Bordeaux government proves the internal rottenness of France; and the panic fear of the inner set of financiers and landed proprietors of ruin and

revolution – the preference for the Nazi domination to the loss and suffering of defeat without surrender accepted by the Dutch and Norwegians. . . .

*27 June.* [Passfield Corner]
The first night of what will be continuous air raids over this neighbourhood of camps, aerodromes and searchlights: they began about 11 p.m. and stopped about 4 a.m. Sombre humming of the planes overhead . . . an occasional booming of guns. I looked out at the sky, and watched the searchlights playing up and down the clouds – sometimes to the west, sometimes the east – or north – and felt comforted that they were not shining overhead. I suppose as the weeks go on we shall cease to be interested, unless the noise becomes thunderous and we take refuge at the back of the dining-room. Mrs Grant wanted Sidney to go downstairs the first night, but he refused. The danger of another stroke through over-excitement and fatigue is far greater than the house being bombed or even the windows shattered. 'If *you* like to sit downstairs, by all means do.' And that settled it.

*2 July.* [Passfield Corner]
The amazing beauty of this spring and summer, the sheer delight of the morning walks in the woods and on the moorland, is a strange background to the ever-present prospect of invasion from the air and the probable entry of armed men on the roads. We have dug-outs and trenches at our gates and have bombs dropping and guns booming almost every night; we are warned over the wireless that these isolated flights are merely the forerunners of more formations of enemy bombers later on; as Hitler must win now or never. . . .

A series of defiant broadcasts by Churchill did much to rally opinion during the Battle of Britain, which began on 10 July. He made a world broadcast on 14 July. The novelist J. B. Priestley (1894–1984) began a series of talks after the nine o'clock radio news on Sundays which combined patriotic nostalgia and aspiration for social change. The talks were curtailed after Tory critics – including, it was said, Churchill himself – complained.

*15 July.* [Passfield Corner]
Assuredly personality has an enormous opportunity owing to wireless: Churchill's broadcast on Sunday night was a model of wisdom, courage

and decisive leadership, a perfect manner and impressive voice. J. B. Priestley's postscript, describing Margate in brilliant sunshine – intact but deserted, noiseless and empty, a mysterious and beautiful vision, with a background of memories of the crowded beaches, hotels and cinemas, shops and stalls, of laughter and shouting, swimming and scrambling in the sea and on the sand, of men, women and children in the mass – was a fitting contrast and emotional relief from Churchill's sincere appeal to statesmen, thinkers and citizens of all countries, to have a faith in the British will and capacity to beat the evil power of Hitler's barbarous Germany. The one drawback to the B.B.C.'s daily emissions is its romantic optimism about British exploits on the sea and in the air, an optimism which has hitherto been contradicted by the event. . . .

*20 July.* [Passfield Corner]
Roosevelt accepts nomination for a third term; and asserts the American detestation of the brutal aggression of godless Germany against the independence of Christian democracies. Hitler's address to the Reichstag gives the oft-told story of the humiliation of the German people by the Versailles treaty and their emancipation by his leadership, and ends by offering the immediate negotiation of peace with Great Britain. Meanwhile, as a minor incident, Stafford has a friendly talk with Stalin which *The Times* reports with approval. Hitler's peace overture is indignantly refused in the Press of Great Britain and contemptuously rejected in the U.S.A. So we may expect a 'blitzkreig' within a few days or weeks. To keep up his almost super-human reputation with his own countrymen and his allies he has to smash Great Britain's resistance. . . . I am so unutterably tired of living that I am free of all fear of being destroyed. . . .

Ernest Bevin (1881–1951), former secretary of the Transport Workers' Union, was Minister of Labour. On 13 August the Germans began a full-scale attack on the airfields and radar stations in south-east England.

*11 August.* [Passfield Corner]
. . . Poor Beveridge was in a state of collapse. I have never seen him so despondent about public affairs, so depressed about his own part in bettering them. . . . his services as an administrator have not been requisitioned – all that has happened is that Bevin (I think at Cole's suggestion) has appointed him as *adviser* (not as administrator) in respect of the organization of manpower for the supply of munitions and carrying on the war. . . . He agrees that there must be a revolution in the

economic structure of society; but it must be guided by persons with training and knowledge – i.e. by himself and those he chooses as his colleagues. . . .

*14 August.* [Passfield Corner]
Yesterday morning, as I was enjoying my hot bath, there opened a roar of aeroplanes overhead, then machine guns and rapid explosions, shaking the walls and the roof. 'I must not be found naked,' I thought, and hurriedly put on my underclothing. Mrs Grant, white and trembling, was downstairs and stationed herself in the back kitchen with white face and her hands folded: whilst Annie went about her business preparing our breakfast. Apparently there was a battle in the air between seventy German aeroplanes and the Longmoor and Bordon air defences. The roar overhead raged for half an hour and then slowly died away. At one o'clock the B.B.C. mentioned the Hampshire camps as one of the targets for the four hundred German invading aeroplanes. The usual disproportionate German losses were announced during the day. . . . The best we can hope for is that *we* shall not be conquered, that Germany will become more hopelessly paralysed by the battles in the air than we shall be. . . . Anyway there is a growing anger against Germany – not only within the armed forces but among ordinary men and women carrying on the civil life of the nation. Disillusioned but determined to best the invader sums up my impression of the national consciousness. Those who desire to make peace with Hitler before we have beaten his dream of conquest decisively are a tiny minority of the governing class and they judge it better to be silent. . . .

*20 August.* [Passfield Corner]
Another night of bomb explosions, but not the furious roar of German planes and attacking British planes overhead we experienced on Friday. But sleep is impossible and poor Mrs Grant is crouching in the back of the kitchen, comforted by Annie, whilst Sidney and I keep to our beds; and I try to get on with my chapter, without having the strength to do so. . . . Sidney remains philosophical in mind and physically comfortable, reading incessantly newspapers, official documents, propagandist literature, and his bevy of books from the London Library and *The Times* Book Club. . . .

Leon Trotsky was assassinated by a Spaniard, Roman Mercader – an agent of Stalin – in Mexico, where he had been living in exile since 1936.

*25 August.* [Passfield Corner]

Trotsky murdered. . . . That tiny event compared with the war raging over Europe and Asia ends the most disastrous episode in the history of the counter-revolutionary upheavals in the U.S.S.R. of the 20s and 30s – so damaging to the reputation of the 'New Civilization' within the labour and socialist movements of the western democracies. How will the Soviet Press report it? If they are wise they will report it accurately, without abuse of Trotsky, as an event of no importance to the present government of the country. Our Press, including the *New Statesman,* suggests that in spite of the evidence to the contrary, the murderer was an agent of Stalin! How the educated public opinion in Great Britain hates the increasing prestige of the Soviet Union. . . .

*9 September. 4 a.m.* [Passfield Corner]

Every night the battle over the air begins about nine o'clock and ends in the early morning. I thought I heard the 'all clear' half an hour ago; but now the war has started again, judged by the roar of the aeroplanes overhead and the searchlights playing about the sky when I put the light off and look out of the window. Sidney and I are little disturbed by it; but Mrs Grant and the girls are up most of the night, which means fatigue and irritated tempers throughout the day, and I have to live in a state of uncertainty as to whether my little group will hold together . . . Certainly other citizens are suffering far more than the few inhabitants of Passfield Corner!

On 7 September the Germans turned their attack on to London and away from the fighter bases in Kent – a disastrous tactical error. London was bombed every night from 7 September to 2 November. The City of London and the East End were devastated.

*15 September. 3 a.m.* [Passfield Corner]

Since the sustained attack in London opened, we here have had a relatively quiet time – air warnings and all-clear notices happening during day and night, but few and distant bombs or gunfire. Letters from Barbara and Alys Russell and B.B.C. and newspaper reports describing the noise and danger, destruction of homes, hospitals and churches, of deaths and woundings of men, women and children, illustrated by pictures, lend a background of continuous tragedy, which even the good-tempered heroism of the cockney and his perpetual sense of humour does not cancel out. J. B. Priestley's broadcasts on Sunday evenings stand out as superlative expressions of all that is good and helpful. Meanwhile the crisis in my household has petered out; and our triplet staff is at peace. Mrs Grant has got over her panic, and realizes how fortunate she is to evade ill-paid service in a hospital and enjoy well-paid service and an easy life in a comfortable home. Annie and Jean are reconciled and behave to me with due kindness and respect . . . I crawl on with my chapter. . . .

*9 October.* [Passfield Corner]
Churchill's eloquent but sombre speech to the House of Commons yesterday dismisses pessimistic defeatism and foolish optimism with equal force. . . . All that is clear is that we are in for a long war; and that while we have resisted successfully German invasion there is as yet no decisive turn of the tide in Europe, Africa or Asia. . . .

On 21 October Churchill broadcast in French as well as in English to rally the French nation. The Italians had now attacked Greece from their base in Albania. In mid-November Beatrice was asked to write an article for a Communist publication to refute allegations that the U.S.S.R. was a dictatorship.

*22 October.* [Passfield Corner]
Churchill's address to the French people was admirable in its attitude towards the French people themselves, but brutally abusive of Hitler and contemptuous of Mussolini. But what is the meaning of the last words: 'Long live the forward march of the common people in all lands towards their just and true inheritance'? Is it mere rhetoric on the part of the recently elected chief of the Conservative Party? Or is it a realization, deliberately expressed, that the old order is doomed and a new social order must be created? . . .

*9 November. 4 a.m.* [Passfield Corner]
The victory of Roosevelt and the gallant resistance of Greece are two signs of the turning of the tide; also the failure of the Italian air force, army and navy to fight effectively – if the reports are true – is the third necessary condition of victory. Meanwhile my decrepitude increases: sleeplessness, whizzing of the brain and the worsening of the frequency due to chronic cystitis, above all the incapacity even to crawl on with the book, makes me long for release from life, especially during the night. . . .

*9 December.* [Passfield Corner]
I am hard at work, with my decrepit intellect, writing that d——d article for the *Anglo-Soviet Journal* to be published in its January number. I
have finished the first part – Is Stalin a legalized dictator as Hitler and
Mussolini are? – and I am now wrestling with the second question. Is the
Soviet Union a political democracy? . . . How can I combine an admiration for the constitution and activities of Soviet Communism with a
frank admission of its defects . . . What is happening, for instance, in the
Soviet part of former Poland? According to a pamphlet issued by *Free
Europe,* the occupation of the Red Army and the establishment of the
Soviet regime has not only been brutal to the old governing class, but
wholly unsuccessful in giving the means of subsistence to the people,
leave alone culture and the consciousness of self-government. According
to the *Moscow Weekly News,* the people of the new provinces are revelling
in the better conditions of life and the sense of emancipation. Where lies
the truth? . . .

~ 1941 ~

The Webbs were in fact able to issue a wartime edition of *Soviet
Communism,* using Beatrice's article for the *Soviet Journal* as the basis of
a new introduction.

*15 January.* [Passfield Corner]
We have had a shock. In the devastating German raid on London on
29 December all our books, bound and unbound – seven thousand
volumes – were destroyed. At first I was downcast, but Sidney was
more philosophical: he reckoned that our present income from books
was only £200 to £300 a year and would dwindle year by year, and that
had to be cut by 9*s* in the pound taxation – also it might lead to the
surtax on surplus income. When in the six o'clock B.B.C. news we are
told that five million books had been swept away, I was consoled by
the feeling that 'we are all in it', and had no reason to feel specially
injured. . . .

*21 January.* [Passfield Corner]
I often wonder whether I shall survive this year? Tomorrow I shall be in
the eighty-fourth year of my too long life. . . . What is clear is that *if* I
drop out of the scene, Barbara will have to arrange for Sidney to go, with

his maid-valet, to a residential hotel; and either shut this house up or let it to someone connected with the L.S.E. Indeed I may have to do that myself – whether to save expense, or, more likely, to save my own peace of mind and therefore prevent a breakdown. However, sufficient for the day is the evil thereof – we may be bombed out, or we may lose the war, or all be ruined in winning it. . . .

*19 March. 4 a.m.* [Passfield Corner]
A terrific battle is going on to the south; the roar of the aeroplanes, widespread gun-fire, searchlights and bursting shells in the moon and starlit sky – perfect weather for the invasion about which Herbert Morrison warned us over the wireless last night, as if it were imminent. Our bored troops would welcome it; also it would prove that Hitler was desperately intent, at the risk of the destruction of his army, to strike before the advent of America's overwhelming strength. But we shall have a nasty but exciting time – to relieve the boredom of the whizzing head. . . .

Leslie Stephen (1832–1904), man of letters, was the founder and editor of the *Dictionary of National Biography*.

*7 April.* [Passfield Corner]
In the morning news: 'Mrs Virginia Woolf, missing from her home since Friday 28th . . . assumed drowned in the river Ouse.' During the day and for some days afterwards, ghosts from the past haunted me – that tall, talented woman with her classic features, her father Leslie Stephen, also tall, good-looking, highly cultured, with whom in the 80s I used to discuss English history in the house of Alice Green in Kensington Square. An old man, seemingly kind and courteous to a young writer but pictured as a supreme egotist towards his family by his daughter with a bitter pen in *To the Lighthouse*, perhaps her most successful novel.

Virginia was a beautiful woman and a writer of great charm and finesse – in her *uniqueness* the most outstanding of our women novelists. The Woolfs stayed with the Webbs, and the Webbs with the Woolfs, and Leonard was one of Sidney's most intimate colleagues in international propaganda during the great war; but we never became sympathetic friends. I think we liked them better than they liked us. In a way which I never understood, I offended Virginia. I had none of her sensitiveness, her understanding of the inner life of the subjective man, expressed in the birth, life and death of social institutions. Also we clashed with

Leonard Woolf in our conception of what constitutes human freedom: the absence of restraint for the intellectual or the presence of opportunity for the ordinary man – which element was to be the foremost object of the social reformer? In particular, he abhorred Soviet Communism. But in spite of this mental aloofness from the Woolfs I am pained by the thought of that beautiful and brilliant Virginia yielding to the passion for death rather than endure the misery of continued life. Twenty years ago her devoted husband had nursed her through a period of mental derangement and suicidal mania. In middle age she became a vigorous and seemingly self-assured woman, an eminently successful author and a devoted companion to her distinguished husband. What led to the tragedy? And what is happening to the ultra-refined, public-spirited and gifted Leonard Woolf? The last time I saw them both was at a luncheon at Barbara's about eighteen months ago. Her last words to me, as she and Leonard met, were 'I have no living philosophy' – which may probably account for her voluntary withdrawal from life. Can man continue happy without some assured faith as to what should be the right relation of man to man, also of man's relation to the universe? On the first I have a clearly defined conclusion; on the other I am a religious agnostic. I do not know, I only have an emotional feeling that there *is* a spirit of love at work in the universe, and I pray from time to time that it may help me to act rightly to my fellow men. But if I were not supremely fortunate in my circumstances, would that vague and intermittent faith save me from despair during these days of death and destruction, by day and by night? . . .

*20 April. 3 a.m.* [Passfield Corner]
These two last nights have been the most fearful of the war. The Battle of Britain is raging round us. Tonight continuous bombing and gunfire has shaken the house. A huge fire has lit up Aldershot and Farnham to the east; whilst gunfire and flares light up Bordon and the south coast. Mrs Grant is cowering downstairs in the kitchen; I find Sidney reading, but glad to have a cup of tea. Neither he nor I are perturbed; Annie wanders up and downstairs, looking out for fire bombs. I tell her that the Germans won't waste any on us in a non-built-up area; and anyway if a fire bomb falls on the house and gets through the roof, we should hear it. Meanwhile, last night, London has had a terrific attack. . . . Can we and the Americans keep the Allied shipping safe across the Atlantic? That is the question. If we repel invasion and safeguard our supplies across the Atlantic, Great Britain will survive, but we shall owe our survival not to our own strength but to help from the U.S.A. We may

save Egypt and retain control of the Suez Canal and Gibraltar. But we are a long way off recovering the freedom of Europe from the rule of Hitler's Germany. What blind fools our governing class of aristocratic and wealthy men have been in their foreign policy since 1931. First appeasing Japan, Italy and Germany by refusing to condemn their military aggression in Manchuria, Spain, Abyssinia and Central Europe; then declaring war on account of the invasion of Poland with its two million German inhabitants and guaranteeing other small states we could not reach, like Norway, with our armed forces. Lastly increasing the hostility of the U.S.S.R. by threatening to send an army to Finland – all through fear of the spread of Soviet Communism. . . .

So I return to my task of finishing the Introduction before Sidney and I drop out of existence. The nights of battle and days of peace are the strangest sort of life the British people have ever experienced. Just as I feel that we and our generation are, through old age, on the verge of non-existence, so do I envisage that the present-day Great Britain and her ruling class are doomed to disappear within the next few years. Our little island will become subordinate – either to the U.S.A. and the Dominions or to Germany, or to the U.S.S.R. and its new civilization, creeping over the world. As we happen to believe in the *rightness* and eventual success of Soviet Communism, we are not despondent about the future of mankind. . . .

After a series of visits and letters, the officials of the Society for Cultural Relations with the U.S.S.R. tried to persuade Beatrice to remove critical statements from her article. She refused, and withdrew it. C.E.M. Joad (1891–1953), who taught philosophy at Birkbeck College, London, made a wartime reputation as part of the radio 'Brains Trust'.

*18 May.* [Passfield Corner]
A correct little note from Beatrice King closes the episode of writing an article for the *Anglo-Soviet Journal*: the Russian representative of *Voks* could not tolerate the suggestion that Soviet Communism had *any* 'infantile diseases', refused to admit that Lenin and Stalin had been 'idolized' or that there was any restriction on free criticism of Stalin's policy by word or by script. So the printers first sent off the proofs with my signature *without* the final paragraph of criticism, and when I telegraphed that I must have that part printed before passing it for publication, the editorial committee sent the editors down here to persuade me to omit it. . . .

*31 May.* [Passfield Corner]
Kingsley Martin, with his life companion Dorothy Woodman, a well-known left-wing and former Quaker journalist and organizer, here for a couple of hours. Our old friend was exactly the same genial, intellectual scatter-brained clever editor of the *New Statesman* whom we knew so well in the 20s, but whom we had not seen for five or six years. He told us about the new intellectuals – the extraordinary vogue, through their success as broadcasters, of Priestley and Joad, who find themselves leaders of the young generation, bombarded with letters and able to attract large audiences wherever they go, but both alike with no clear vision of what they want to happen in Great Britain or in the world after the war. . . . He is pessimistic over Great Britain after the war, and agrees that even if we win the war (he thinks official public opinion is unduly optimistic, or at any rate pretends to be so), Great Britain will become a fortified outpost of the American Confederation of English-speaking Republics. He is not hostile to the U.S.S.R. and is friendly with the Maiskys, but is not an admirer of its present internal organization. Stalin is a dictator. . . . The U.S.S.R. is no longer honestly Communist in the distribution of the wealth of the nation. There are all sorts of evils – poverty, scarcity, corruption, intolerance are rife here, there, and everywhere. . . .

Kingsley Martin agreed that there was no unity within the ranks of those who wanted, or said they wanted, a 'New Social Order'. He felt that he himself changed his opinion from day to day as to which policy was 'the lesser or the greater evil' and was at a 'loose end' as to what constituted the good, the beautiful and the true in social organization. . . .

Stafford and Isobel Cripps had returned to London. He had already warned Russia that Hitler was about to attack. The Germans invaded Russia on 22 June. Despite repeated warnings from the British government and Soviet intelligence agents, Stalin suspected a trap and failed to deploy his forces properly; they were surprised and heavily defeated in the early battles.

*14 June. 2 a.m.* [Passfield Corner]
A year ago, I journeyed up to London on the day of the collapse of France, 14 June 1940, to stay with Barbara . . . I witnessed the horrified silence of my fellow travellers as to what was the meaning of the terrific fact of a beaten France. Yesterday, 13 June 1941, I was again at Barbara's a little after noon. She greeted me with, 'Stafford thinks the crisis will

come this Sunday; we shall know whether it is war between Germany and Russia or peaceful surrender of Stalin to Hitler.' . . . Stafford had had long and confidential talks with Churchill, who was in first-rate form; a splendid leader for the purpose. The sensational and much advertised meeting of the day before, of 'the Allies' – Great Britain and the representatives of the conquered countries – when Churchill made his oration damning 'that bad man Hitler with his ragged lackey, Mussolini' and vowed war 'to destroy Hitlerism', was staged in order to encourage Stalin to resist, to satisfy him that the U.S.S.R. would not be betrayed by the Allies, through a negotiated peace with Hitler. . . .

*23 June.* [Passfield Corner]
Yesterday, Sunday morning, over the nine o'clock news, came the momentous – or shall I write *monstrous* – proclamation by Hitler of a state of war with the U.S.S.R. – as usual with a vilification of his victim, not only for acts hostile to Germany, but guilty of the sin of Communism, the devil at work in the world today. This ultimatum had been handed to the Soviet Ambassador in Berlin at 5 a.m. after the German air force had bombed Kiev and other Russian cities. Finland and Rumania were announced as Hitler's allies and were also on the march into the Soviet Union. Molotov's matter-of-fact broadcast to the Russian people at twelve o'clock added little to the scene. Then at nine o'clock that evening, we had Churchill's sensational oration to the world, especially designed for the U.S.A. with its anti-Communist prejudice. . . . It is the full co-operation of the U.S.A. which is the crucial event of today and tomorrow if we are to beat Hitler and the German people to their knees, as Churchill says we must. On balance, in spite of the danger of a routed Russian army, Sidney and I welcome this declaration of war on the U.S.S.R.: it saves Great Britain from defeat or a stalemate peace. . . .

*25 June. 2 a.m.* [Passfield Corner]
The House of Commons debate with Foreign Secretary Eden announcing, in the most friendly words, a whole-hearted alliance with the Soviet government, as one more victim of Hitler's barbarous aggression, was yet another avowal of the staggering world event – this time wholly in the right tone from the standpoint of the Webbs. He explains in the most courteous phrases that the British people had a different creed from that current in the U.S.S.R.; but that was equally true of several of their old allies, and need not interfere with a loyal co-operation in foreign affairs. . . .

*3 July.* [Passfield Corner]
Over midday wireless we heard of Alfred's death [Lord Parmoor] . . .
Among my brothers-in-law when I was a young woman, he was the one
I liked best, and he was undoubtedly Father's favourite son-in-law . . .
His death is another 'passing over' of the world I have lived in, and adds
to my ghost-like consciousness during these terrible days of world
war. . . .

> The B.B.C., which played all the anthems of the Allies on Sunday
> evenings, had so far failed to include the 'Internationale' – it was
> rumoured that the Foreign Office had objected until all the formalities of
> alliance were complete.

*14 July.* [Passfield Corner]
Yesterday on the one o'clock news, the announcer stated solemnly that
at two o'clock an important statement on foreign affairs would be made.
'That will be an whole-hearted alliance with the U.S.S.R.,' said I to
Sidney. 'I don't think so, it will be about America,' he answered. At two
o'clock came the terms signed by Molotov and Stafford. 'That means
that we shall have the Internationale tonight.' 'Wait and see,' he
observed, and he was right.

*30 July.* [Passfield Corner]
Isobel sent me a batch of letters from Stafford, a day-to-day account of
his doings, intensely interesting, culminating in the big achievement of
the Anglo–Soviet pact, which he and Stalin negotiated and he and
Molotov signed. He likes Stalin, with whom he is now on intimate and
confidential terms. From his picture, he seems a singularly direct and
honest-minded man, with no pretentiousness, no sign of wishing to be
a personage; not too optimistic – in short, a *business man*, completely
absorbed in carrying out scientific humanism . . .

*8 August.* [Passfield Corner]
In the last ten days I have had a nightmare of a life of physical and
mental exhaustion. . . . What is significant is the suddenness and magnitude of the change in public opinion; from refusal, even on the part of
the left wing, to see anything that is good in Soviet Communism, to the
equally sudden waking up of the ordinary conservative-minded man to
a lively interest in the surprising courage, initiative and magnificent
equipment of the Red armed forces – the one and only sovereign state

that has been able to stand up to the almost mythical might of Hitler's Germany. . . .

The new edition of *Soviet Communism* brought a lot of publicity for the Webbs.

*11 September.* [Passfield Corner]
I am being drugged by Orr, to secure rest for my exhausted brain, whilst the Press and periodicals are advertising the Introduction. *Picture Post,* the *Tablet, Reynolds News* and the *New Chronicle* and the *Journal of the National Association of Local Government Officers* are publishing pictures and accounts of the aged Webbs – *Picture Post* with letterpress by GBS. I was somewhat shocked but also amused by the caricature in a close-up photograph of the aged woman in *Picture Post,* for it represented my present plight of utter exhaustion. How far will this pre-publication and gratuitous advertisement of the book help its immediate sale? is the question we ask each other. And when shall I be fit and free to get back to the book? I am at the end of my wits, except for writing in my diary – an old habit which I can't cure, any more than Rosy can her passion for sketching. . . .

Stephen Potter (1900–1969) later became known for his book *Lifemanship.* Madame Chiang Kai-shek (b. 1898), married to the Chinese leader, herself played an active part in public life. Marie Curie (1867–1934) was, with her husband, one of the discoverers of radium. She won two Nobel prizes and was professor of physics at the Sorbonne. Alexandra Kollontay (1872–1952) was an old Bolshevik and campaigner for women's rights.

*27 September.* [Passfield Corner]
Stephen Potter, a friend of Barbara's, tall, good-looking and a clever talker, a B.B.C. official of three years' standing, came down to interview me. He is proposing a series of biographic broadcasts on eminent men of today who represent the happenings in Great Britain of the last fifty years – artists, scientists and literary men. Not statesmen, I gather. The B.B.C. wanted a woman so they picked me out as old, distinguished and writing – also to our being the leading exponents of Soviet communism 'in the news'.

It is odd how few distinguished women there are today in Great Britain and elsewhere. I suggested to my interviewer that Madame Kai-shek was the only outstanding woman: why not get the Chinese Ambassador to get a record from her flown from Chungking? Madame Curie is dead, Virginia Woolf – who was, at any rate, *unique* in literary gift, though her particular type was not impressive – is also dead. How few women have been or are distinguished except in their personal relation to men – how few have influenced public opinion and public activities, independently to their sexual relationship to men? There have been and are today distinguished actresses and dancers, singers and other types of musicians, but no musical composers, painters or architects. In the art of writing there have been two great novelists, George Eliot and George Sand – today there is no woman who is the equal of H. G. Wells as a novelist, or GBS as a playwright. No scientist or philosopher; there has never been a great poet, except in mythical Greece, or dramatist. What about the two great women who have been the acknowledged heads of Sovereign States – Elizabeth of Great Britain, Catherine the Great of Russia? No one would suggest that Queen Victoria was a distinguished personality – she was utterly commonplace in intellect and conventional in conduct.

And so the B.B.C. has to fall back on the aged Beatrice Webb for a contemporary notable woman, just as the British Academy had to a few years ago. But even here it was a personal element that gained me the prestige – it was *My Apprenticeship* that has singled me out today just as it was *The Diary of a Working Girl* in the first years of authorship. The most striking case of the absence of distinguished women has been in politics and administration. There is no outstanding woman M.P. either in Great Britain or elsewhere. In the U.S.S.R., where women are admitted to all vocations, even to command in the army, navy and air force, no woman stands out as influential except perhaps Kollantay, the Soviet Ambassadress in Sweden. But she owes this celebrity largely to having been an intimate friend of Lenin, and through this friendship becoming the first woman to be an Ambassadress to a foreign power. . . .

*6 October. 2 a.m.* [Passfield Corner]
. . . Yesterday afternoon, when he and I were sitting in the garden, I asked Sidney: 'Do you wish to go on living?' He sat silent, surprised at the question, then slowly said '*No*'. He is physically comfortable, he is always reading and not actually bored; he loves and is loved, he is mildly interested in other people and keen to hear the news. But he resents not being able to think and express his thoughts, and thus help the world he lives in. . . .

The German armies had now surrounded Leningrad and were driving on towards Moscow. Russian losses of men and material had been immense.

*26 October.* [Passfield Corner]
The Maiskys came to tea and talk yesterday afternoon. Outwardly they were exactly the same cheerful friendly couple . . . But from the tenor of his talk . . . I gathered they were pessimistic about the successful resistance of the allied forces if the Germans penetrate into the U.S.S.R. They were disappointed by the inadequacy and delay in military help from Great Britain and the U.S.A. Though they (especially Madame Maisky) were certain that Stalin and the Soviet Union would fight on, and, come what may, that the German hordes would be beaten back, it would be after an amount of destruction of the lives and property of the Soviet people unparalleled in the history of the human race. . . .

*20 November.* [Passfield Corner]
Longman writes that they have already disposed of seven hundred copies of the book, which is heartening to my satisfaction and will enable us to live within our income in the coming years. . . .

*24 November.* [Passfield Corner]
Another distracting row in my little household with the Smiths and Mrs Grant on food for Peter, about whose treatment I found Mrs Grant weeping, and Annie in a state of angry denunciation of Mrs Grant's unjustified activities and demands. I am suffering badly from cystitis and long to disappear from the scene, if I could only take the beloved one with me. . . .

Early on the morning of 7 December Japanese aircraft launched a surprise attack on the U.S. base at Pearl Harbor in Hawaii. The United States now declared war on Japan, Germany and Italy. Churchill went to Washington to co-ordinate plans with Roosevelt and addressed Congress on 26 December.

*9 December. 3 a.m.* [Passfield Corner]
Roosevelt's authoritative and admirably delivered address to Congress – broadcast at 6.30 p.m. – and the long continued and deafening applause by the Congress announcing the treacherous and pre-arranged attack on American islands in the Pacific, involving

serious military and naval losses, is a landmark in world history. . . . All
the Great Powers will be at war . . . What a world war! Does it mean
the temporary debasement of the human race, or its rise with the next
generation into a New Civilization, intent on realizing the good, the
beautiful and the true – human ethics, art and science? That is the
issue to be decided in 1942–43. Meanwhile we are all in for a hard time
of it. . . .

*26 December.* [Passfield Corner]
Sidney, Barbara and I listened yesterday at 6.30 p.m. with an all-out
admiration to Churchill's oration to the Congress of the United States at
Washington. The applause before and after the speech was deafening. His
opening allusion to his American mother was perfect in its tact; the summary of past events, of present difficulties, of future prospects, of the
supreme dominion, in deciding the fate of the world, of the U.S.A. and
the British Empire, was all exactly suited to the occasion. . . . The speech
was, in fact, wise, eloquent, perfectly phrased and admirably delivered in
its tone and timing of one sentence after another. . . . Its one weak
point . . . was the tacit refusal to recognize the Soviet Union as the equal
to the U.K. and the U.S.A. in determining the terms of the eventual
peace . . .

## ～ 1942 ～

*7 January.* [Passfield Corner]
During the next weeks I have to decide whether to reprint the
Introduction, GBS's Preface and the Constitution of 1936 as a booklet
on what paper is available. . . . But with a whizzing brain, a failing
memory and above all painful intestines and sleeplessness, it is unlikely
that I shall be fit to do it. This year will decide whether the aged Beatrice
Webb is worn out as an author. . . .

*22 January. 3 a.m.* [Passfield Corner]
My eighty-fourth birthday. . . . The weather is depressing, bitterly cold,
snow piled up on the lawns and roads which makes walking difficult.
The news from the Far East front is alarming and public opinion is
indignant at the lack of preparedness and the foolish underrating of
Japan's strength, which has meant humiliating defeat for the U.K. and
the U.S.A. in the first stages of the war. . . .

*22 February.* [Passfield Corner]
Yesterday I journeyed up to London, in bitter cold weather, to meet the Cripps' at a Lunch at St Ermin's Hotel given us by Barbara.

On Thursday evening we had heard over the wireless that Stafford had had an audience with the King and had stayed to lunch; on Friday the papers announced that Churchill had reorganized his War Cabinet and appointed Stafford as 'Leader of the House of Commons' – virtually second in command. . . . Time will show whether he will succeed or fail in becoming the leader of the British people . . . We have never been intimate with Stafford as we were with Haldane and Balfour or Arthur Henderson and many other politicians and civil servants. He has been affectionate and respectful to his aged uncle and aunt: that is all. . . . The most significant and unusual fact about him is that he belongs to *no political party* and shows no sign of joining one that already exists or of creating a new one. . . .

*24 February.* [Passfield Corner]
Confronted with a domestic dilemma. The heroic Annie is suffering from influenza and her gall-bladder is affected – Jean in bed with a similar attack. Mrs Grant maintains her egotistic aloofness and I am at once ignorant of all domestic service and somewhat unsafe in the use of my hands and feet through old age. If only I had been brought up to know how to cook and clean. Rosy can do it, but I can't and I am too feeble to learn; nor could any of my older sisters. Music and painting, languages and literature, the four rules of arithmetic and a smattering of mathematics and philosophy were imparted to us by resident governesses, and visiting minor Canons of the nearby Cathedral town. But we were not even taught to mend our clothes, leave alone to make them. Today, even the daughters of noblemen and wealthy businessmen are taught and practise the domestic arts – cooking, cleaning, the use of electric, gas and Aga stoves, washing and mending the clothes – because of the difficulty of getting servants or because they no longer can afford them.

Lady Whitley was the wife of Edward Whitley (d. 1945), a prosperous research chemist and supporter of the Poor Law Campaign.

*28 February.* [Passfield Corner]
Took Sidney and Lady Whitley and Mrs Grant to see a film of Bernard Shaw's *Major Barbara*. When the play was first performed early in the

1900s the character of Undershaft, the glorification of the Maker of Munitions, the triumph of his philosophy of life, the dismissing of the Christian faith, the ultra-cynicism, sounded out of keeping with the progressive thought of the time . . . Today it is dramatically - topical. . . .

*30 March.* [Passfield Corner]
*The Times* yesterday announced the death of the Countess of Balfour after a short illness. She was the only woman, outside the family group, I loved and cared to see and write to. . . . To me a light has gone out of the world I live in. Poor old Gerald! an ailing decrepit man. I always liked and respected him. . . .

*17 April. 2.30–3.30 a.m.* [Passfield Corner]
The raids begun again: the wailing of the siren, the bombs dropping nearby, which gives me an extra excuse for this cup of tea and writing in the diary. Rosy here for a week's holiday from nursing George, cooking and cleaning, looking after grandchildren. . . . A wonderfully active old lady, but a rather troublesome guest to the household she visits, scattering papers and prints, clothes and books, ideas and requests, and using other people's belongings wherever she stays or goes. But as the two last of the Potter sisters we have a certain permanent relationship in affections and remembrances which I respect, and my household accepts if it is limited to a week's visit here twice a year. . . .

*13 June.* [Passfield Corner]
Lloyd George . . . paid us a surprise visit yesterday afternoon. We had not seen him since we lunched with him eleven years ago on the eve of the election of 1931. . . .
  Today the great statesman of 1914–22 is a picturesque aged elder with flowing white hair, excited gestures and vehement opinions, hating Churchill's government. . . . gloomy about the future of the British Empire. . . . We parted the best of friends. Poor old man. The Wizard of Wales, who ruled the Great Britain that won the war of 1914–18 and lost the peace in 1918–21 seemed to me to be, like the aged Webbs, a ghost from the past wandering about the ruins of his old home – the British Empire of the nineteenth century. . . .

Tobruk had fallen to Rommel's forces on 20 June, provoking a vote of no confidence in the government.

*2 July.* [Passfield Corner]

Listened yesterday evening to an almost verbatim account of Churchill's frank and eloquent speech in his own defence as to supreme authority in the waging of the war – on the motion of no confidence, owing to the fall of Tobruk. He did not attempt to deny the extent of the disaster, or the fact that it was the result of military incapacity . . . What he did prove was that any disunity on the part of the British people – any change of government, or even any lessening of the prestige of the Prime Minister – would be an even greater disaster. So he got a vote of 476 to 25, with some 50 abstentions, which was sufficient for achieving his purpose . . . The opposition to Churchill's leadership is made up of hard-grained Tories . . . clever but inexperienced left-wing Labour men . . . one or two Liberals and newly elected 'independents' of no importance. There is no one in the official Conservative or Labour parties who has the qualifications for supreme leadership as Lloyd George had in the great war of 1914–18. . . .

*14 July.* [Passfield Corner]

Again I am feeling desperately ill, troubled with my intestines, which keeps me awake at night and in discomfort all day – doubtful whether I ought to eat or not and what I ought to eat – made more difficult by rationing. Also trouble in my little staff: Annie and Jean continually quarrelling with Mrs Grant and vice versa. Friends and relations turning up to tea which compels me to walk and talk more than I am equal to. As everyone seems to be suffering a similar if not worse strain than I am, with mass murder going on over the whole world, I try to compel myself to be indifferent to my own troubles. . . .

*25 July.* [Passfield Corner]

Yesterday our golden wedding. I had not notified it to my relatives and friends. But the Press discovered it. The *Daily Herald* and *News Chronicle* phoned the day before to ask whether the editor or his representative could come down to interview us, a proposal which I politely refused. The *Daily Telegraph* rang me up on the day: they wanted me to answer the question, 'How does the state of the world war today differ from that of the day of your silver wedding twenty-five years ago (1917)?', a question to which I tried to give an impromptu answer. A few telegrams and letters trickled through . . . But my own family were not aware of it, and as they do not read the *Daily Herald,* the one paper to publish it, they did not trouble me with telegrams or letters to answer. . . .

. . . Our booklet is selling out rapidly . . . The British Embassy at Kuibishev has applied . . . for an article by the veteran Webbs for their new weekly *Our British Ally* . . . which will keep me busy for the next few mornings. So it looks as if I am still useful. . . .

> Churchill had sent Cripps to India on 22 March to try to win over Indian opinion in view of the increasing threat from Japan, but by 10 April the talks had broken down and Nehru joined Gandhi in passive disobedience. Early in August Churchill flew to Cairo, a visit which resulted in the appointment of General Alexander (1891–1969) and General Montgomery (1887–1976) in North Africa. He went on to Moscow to tell Stalin of the proposed landing in French North Africa. After widespread demonstrations, Nehru was detained in October until Japan was defeated. He was not a Communist, though sympathetic to the Soviet Union.

*11 August.* [Passfield Corner]
India has become the black spot in the news about Great Britain. There is a rumour that Churchill is in Moscow to discuss with Stalin about the Second Front and also about India. . . . Gandhi stands out as one of the great personalities in world affairs. . . . To me his saintly egotism and clever contortionist policy, his absurd economic dreams of a return to hand-work in the work-shop and the field, makes him a repulsive figure. But he has built up a revolutionary movement in India, which means, sooner or later, the withdrawal of the British supremacy, over the portions of India which are governed by the British . . .

The India conquered by Great Britain is an impossible unit for a sovereign state, with its powerful eighty million Mohammedan population, its princely provinces, its discordant religious sects and castes. Even within the Congress itself there is no common living philosophy – Nehru is a Communist, Gandhi is a visionary of a fantastic type, the majority being just ordinary profit-making businessmen, or rent-receiving landlords, with a medley of inexperienced reformers of the democratic brand, and a smattering of orthodox and pious Hindus belonging to different sects who would be dead against democratic government, political and industrial, liberal or socialist.

*26 August.* [Passfield Corner]
. . . I am using up my dwindling faculties in sorting out our correspondence . . . [it] is distinctly valuable for future histories of the last fifty years . . . At times I think that I am no longer fit for continued

authorship for publication and that it would be wiser to give it up and merely go on reporting events in the diary. . . . Authorship seems to be a profession from which you cannot retire – you long to carry on, however unfit you may be to do so. GBS and H. G. Wells cannot stop writing; they will die with an unfinished book on their desk. And I shall die with my diary, pen and ink in a drawer by the side of my bed.

Dr Hodgkinson now replaced Dr Orr as the Webbs' doctor.

*13 September. 2 a.m.* [Passfield Corner]
I have been feeling desperately ill for the last week or so, longing for an escape from life and yet fearing its effect on Sidney. I have just discovered blood in my urine – which is, I think, the sign of my remaining kidney going rotten, with death round the corner. So I shall call up Hodgkinson and ask him to come and tell me what lies before me . . . What haunted me during the night was not the prospect of death but the presence of pain.

*13 September. 11 a.m.*
Hodgkinson gives me hope that it is only an inflamed bladder that is troubling me and that if I drink liquid – whether china tea or citrine-tempered water – and stay in bed and keep warm, the chances are that I shall recover . . .

*17 September.* [Passfield Corner]
Hodgkinson came to see me yesterday. He had consulted Orr, our late medical man, who has been called up for service in India. They advised me to spend a night in the Haslemere Nursing Home in order that they may examine my bladder, to find whether or not it is the source of the bleeding. If there be a growth there it can be removed, and Orr is an accomplished surgeon. The operation will not be dangerous and will need only a slight anaesthetic and I can return here in the afternoon. If the bladder is clear there is nothing that can be done. . . .

*22 September.* [Passfield Corner]
Hodgkinson reported today that Orr was leaving for service abroad on Friday and would not be able to carry out the operation on Thursday morning. Hence it would involve my getting up to London. Also the operation would have to be more extended and injurious to my strength than a mere examination of the bladder; it would involve

investigating the condition of the kidney before it could be settled whether or not I was likely to live or die in the near future. So we decided against it on the ground that you cannot cure old age, and a lengthy period of increased disability would be worse than a peaceful death.

John Parker (b. 1906), a Labour M.P. since 1935, was the longest surviving member of the House of Commons when he retired in 1983.

*25 September.* [Passfield Corner]
On hearing that I am seriously ill Barbara Drake came down for the night, and I and she discussed the disposal of the Webb property, as Sidney and I were adding a codicil to our will, appointing two trustees in place of two who were no longer desirable. The trustees under the present will are Barbara Drake, Carr-Saunders, Laski, C. M. Lloyd and Herbert Morrison. Lloyd is dying of cancer; and Herbert Morrison has become reactionary and anti-Soviet. So we are appointing, at her suggestion, John Parker, M.P. (general secretary of the Fabian Society) and Margaret Cole, who will represent G. D. H. Cole and herself, who practically share our views as to the future organization of society, national and international . . . The only question we did not discuss was what should be done about our own books and the various pamphlets we have written; and how my diaries and my unfinished *Our Partnership* and *The Three Stages of Our Pilgrimage* are to be dealt with. It is clear that I shall not be able to finish either the one or the other for publication before or after my disappearance from the scene. . . .

*30 September.* [Passfield Corner]
Hodgkinson and I had a final talk about my state of health and he will not come again unless I send for him. He tells me to eat more, lead as normal a life as I have strength to carry out. . . .

On 4 November the British 8th Army won the decisive battle of El Alamein and began to drive west towards the Anglo-American force which had landed in Morocco. The Soviet Union was about to launch the massive offensive which led to a German disaster at Stalingrad. The tide of war was beginning to turn.

*9 November.* [Passfield Corner]
The amazing victory of the British armed forces in Egypt and the successful invasion of North Africa by the American army, reinforced by

British air and naval units, have been the outstanding news of the last
few days. . . .

*11 November.* [Passfield Corner]
Carr-Saunders spent three hours here on Friday afternoon to be
informed about our will as one of the five trustees, and to look over our
house and grounds and furniture and books, all of which are to go to the
L.S.E. when we are dead. . . . He is a conscientious and kindly man,
quite oddly *neutral* towards other people's opinions . . . So far as I can
judge he is mildly conservative in politics and agnostic in religion . . .

> Appointed chairman of the Inter-Departmental Committee of Social
> Insurance and Allied Services, Beveridge had drafted a comprehensive set
> of social security measures from the cradle to the grave. Conservative
> opposition to the Beveridge Report merely enhanced its popularity as the
> first earnest of postwar reconstruction. Sir William Jowitt (1885–1957), a
> prominent lawyer, became Lord Chancellor in 1945. The four freedoms –
> of speech and worship, from want and fear – were incorporated in the
> Atlantic Charter Roosevelt and Churchill signed at sea in August 1941.
> Mrs Mair's husband having died on 21 July, she was at last free to marry
> Beveridge. He had been knighted and became a peer in 1946.

*6 December.* [Passfield Corner]
The publication of the Beveridge Report, the endorsement of it by Sir
William Jowitt and the House of Commons, the extraordinarily
favourable reception of it by public opinion, by *The Times* and other
papers, and by the B.B.C. in its news bulletins, is a striking testimony to
Beveridge's outstanding capacity for invention and argument. . . .
Beveridge himself calls it a revolution, though a peaceful one. But it is
based on what seems to me a radically false hypothesis: that it is consistent with the continued existence of the capitalist and landlord as the
ruling class . . . if Beveridge's scheme is adopted as the law of the land, we
shall have a catastrophic increase in the number of unemployed persons
together with a collapse of the means of maintaining them. The more
carefully the scheme is examined, the more it will be condemned both by
the capitalists, who will be keeping low profits, and by whole-hearted
believers in the four freedoms of the Atlantic Charter. Hence it is destined
to fail. It will either be rejected, which I think is the most probable result,
or if accepted and applied will be catastrophic in its results – and in
both cases it will divide the country into two political parties, those who

insist on maintaining our present capitalist civilization and those who would substitute the new civilization of Soviet Communism.

*9 December.* [Passfield Corner]
Beveridge's crowded meeting at Oxford yesterday, with the extraordinary applause of the audience of some two thousand and of crowds outside, has added to his reputation as an agitator for his scheme . . . The increasing prestige of Beveridge's Report . . . resulted in a request to me from the *Cooperative News* to review it, which I shall try to do, in spite of being incapacitated by an attack of intestinal trouble, swollen feet and tingling legs, which has kept me in bed for ten days under the orders of my kind and clever medical adviser, Dr Hodgkinson. I am still in a state of mental depression, a feeling that I am too ill to live, let alone to give interviews and write articles for the Press. However, we live in the most comfortable home, and owing to Annie's kindness and care, I can just carry on! . . .

*15 December.* [Passfield Corner]
Today Beveridge married Mrs Mair. He wrote some time ago to tell me of the coming event and I sent him our warm greetings . . . It is to be hoped that the past will be forgotten and that Lady Beveridge will be accepted by the world they live in in London and Oxford.

*19 December.* [Passfield Corner]
*The Times* gave a list of peers and peeresses, Ambassadors and their wives and eminent politicians who attended the Beveridge–Mair marriage luncheon . . . It is rumoured that Churchill favours the Report; the Liberal Party has endorsed it enthusiastically, and the Labour Party has accepted it with qualifications, and demanded that it should be passed into law at once . . .

*Xmas Day.* [Passfield Corner]
Over the wireless comes, day after day, the cheering news of continuous victories on the Soviet front of a thousand miles; the collapse of the German armies, the taking of huge quantities of munitions, and above all the surrender of thousands of German soldiers to the Red Army. As this coincides with the retreat of the Germans in North Africa and the air supremacy of the Americans and British in the Mediterranean, it looks as if victory were bound to come. Meanwhile the Japanese are on the defensive . . .

~ 1943 ~

*14 January. 4 a.m.* [Passfield Corner]
The worst night of unremitting abdominal pain compelled me to call up
Annie to help me to bear it. I had some soup for supper, made of vegetable
boiled with a mutton-bone, in which I had soaked a piece of toasted
bread. When she was with me I belched up wind and was sick – the soup
had evidently not agreed with me. She stayed with me, sleeping on the sofa
until near five o'clock. I had done a morning's work, answering letters and
keeping others to dictate to Miss Burr on Thursday. . . .

*4 January. 12 p.m.*
Hodgkinson came and told me that gastric dysentery was everywhere,
and all his own household had been suffering from attacks of sickness –
which comforted me. . . .

*22 January. 5.30 a.m.* [Passfield Corner]
My eighty-fifth birthday! I have a swollen foot, painful intestines, but an
active brain. The two aged Webbs are still in request – we have a stream
of visitors and I have a big correspondence with people who want to
know about Russia or our opinion of the Beveridge Report, which interests numberless people here and in the U.S.A. . . . Sidney is well and
happy, and I am, in spite of my rather painful existence, interested in the
world we live in . . .
    The amazing success of the Soviet people in beating back Hitler's pow-
erful army is delightful news over the radio and in the newspapers, and
makes life worth living to those who believe in the living philosophy of scientific humanism . . . I sometimes wonder whether I shall be alive this day
twelve months hence. I should be glad to be spared the pain of living, but
so long as my dear one lives on, I wish to be here to look after him.

    The critic Raymond Mortimer (1895–1980) was for some years the liter-
    ary editor of the *New Statesman*.

*12 February.* [Passfield Corner]
Kingsley Martin and Raymond Mortimer here for tea and talk. K.M.
was most affectionate to the aged Webbs . . . Raymond Mortimer is an
attractive and successful literary journalist . . . He has come down with
K.M. because he was a great admirer of *My Apprenticeship* – he and
Kingsley Martin wanted me to contribute extracts from my diary about

Bernard Shaw. I told them that would be undesirable. Our relations with GBS had been those of warm friendship and courteous co-operation, but nearly all the entries in the diaries were about our brilliant friend's troublesome antics . . . I preferred to abstain from any quotation from the diaries until both the Shaws and the Webbs were no longer living personalities . . .

*20 February.* [Passfield Corner]
Over the wireless came the news of Sidney Olivier's death at Bognor Regis, not far from here. He was Sidney's oldest intimate friend and colleague of more than fifty years' standing. . . . A year older than Sidney and a few months younger than I am, he had become an aged but rather worn-out figure, still intent on furthering the cause of racial equality within the British Empire, but not a very comfortable companion for his wife.

*24 February.* [Passfield Corner]
Hodgkinson turned up on Monday morning to see how I was after being dosed with the liquid narcotic. I complained that though I slept a little longer in the night, I was comatose all the day and too tired to go for my usual walk. So he ordered me to return to the taking of two alonal and two veganin at ten o'clock at night. After three days I am much better. So I get four or five hours' sleep at nights and can work and walk better during the day. Which is hopeful. . . .

*9 March. 6 a.m.* [Passfield Corner]
I was awake when at 2 a.m. there sounded the loudest alarm we have had – from Bramshott I think – followed by gun-fire, which shook the door. I looked behind the curtain, there were searchlights and the shining of flickering lights in the skies over to the South-East. Presently there appeared eight brilliant stars from which dropped endless streams of incendiary bombs over one particular spot which remained stationary . . . The raid lasted for two hours, concentrated on the camps and munition works on the way from the south coast to Woking and London. That made me feel slightly ashamed of myself. It had interested me, and in that spirit of exhilaration I forgot that it might mean hundreds of dead and wounded, while we, being a mile or two off the target, might be exempt from the danger of being involved. With my continuous discomfort – or even pain – it is a queer distraction from physical pain and mental depression!

*10 March. 10 p.m.* [Passfield Corner]
This morning's papers report that . . . three enemy bombers were
brought down and the crew of two killed, with one wounded pilot who
became a prisoner of war. What *did* happen, bringing an interesting
souvenir to the Webb household, was the fall of a German balloon [a
parachute] and the acquisition of enough white silk to furnish all the
household with silk night-gowns. The balloon – with its yards of silk
and its long cords of white rope, at the end of which were the empty
containers of the flares – I had noticed in the sky. . . . Unless the government claims them we shall keep them as a record of the second great
war . . .

*11 March.* [Passfield Corner]
The return to a bleeding bladder – the pain by day and night bringing
a depressing mental state . . .

*25 March.* [Passfield Corner]
Dead tired with dictating some dozen letters and settling with
Longmans about the telegrams I have had to answer from rival New
York publishers for permission to publish *The Truth About Russia*, one
offering us a 2,000 dollar advanced royalty, another wanting to publish
it for the South American states. . . . It is satisfactory to our pride, but
with other demands on my exhausted brain and a painful intestine, it
has made my desire to leave life still more dominant. We have lived the
life we liked and done the work we intended to do . . .

*2 April.* [Passfield Corner]
Another trouble in my household. The devoted Annie exploded with
Jean yesterday afternoon and shouted abuse at me! All because I asked
them for some information for Miss Burr, but really because they dislike
Mrs Grant and think she has too easy a time of it! I begged them not to
go on shouting abuse, but in spite of my dizzy head and the smarting
state of my feet and hands they shouted while I was making tea for
Sidney and myself. It is partly due to the strain of being at war – a war
which the news over the B.B.C. and in the papers tell us will be long,
and perhaps last until 1944–45 . . . I suggested that if they went, Sidney
and I, with Mrs Grant and Peter, would go to a hotel – which neither
Sidney nor I would like but which would exactly suit Mrs Grant. I
think that impressed them and they became good and devoted servants
again!

*9 April. 1 a.m.* [Passfield Corner]

Last night I was desperately tired – I wondered whether my brain was going and I was likely to become insane tonight. So I went to bed at 8.30 and took one alonal. What tired my bewildered brain was going up and downstairs for the nine o'clock news, which is generally a repetition of the six o'clock. So I think I shall go to bed earlier. What suits me is to spend more time in bed in my room, and less downstairs. If I leave Sidney down in the library alone, of course it gives Annie and Jean more to do and Mrs Grant more to do as they have to see to his comforts. But Annie and Jean want me to do it and it is Mrs Grant's job to look after Sidney, which she does not object to doing except on Thursdays. But I feel very tired.

*19 April. 7 a.m.* [Passfield Corner]

My present state of body and mind is a combination of physical discomfort and mental satisfaction. I find living a painful experience. Severe cystitis and a paralysed colon means physical pain by day and by night. But it is clear that so long as Sidney is alive I could not leave him. When he is dead I shall at once disappear gladly and by my own act. It will suit the public interest; as it would be easier for our trustees . . . to wind up our affairs. This house, with its comfort inside and beauty and usefulness in its twenty-one acres, will be able to be returned to the public advantage.

This is Beatrice's last entry in her diary.

*19 April. 7 p.m.* [Passfield Corner]

The most amazing fact is that the history of mankind is happening as I write these words. Tonight when we were listening to wireless the B.B.C. broadcast and the electric fire suddenly ceased. Sidney and Mrs Grant and Annie all asserted that it was accidental. But presently (as I write these words) the B.B.C. ceased its activity and my cup of tea went cold – so did Sidney's glass of sherry. Annie came to tell me that two British air-machines had passed low over our house and they had suddenly disappeared. At the same time I felt that I must go to the water closet and I had an action which seemed to clear away all unnecessary excreta, and I couldn't for the next few hours get my feet warm and comfortable. But suddenly I ceased to exist. So did Annie and Jean and Mrs Grant and Sidney. So we are having a painless death as I had longed for. For if my reasoning is right we shall all disappear, including the *Germans themselves from the territory which they have conquered.* There will be no Jews, no conquered peoples, no refugees. The garden will disappear and all our furniture, the earth and the sun and the moon. God wills the destruction of all living things, man, woman and child. We shall not be frozen or hurt. We should merely – not exist (never even have existed). It all seems incredible and therefore is worth noting. Even Churchill and Roosevelt, states and kingdoms, would disappear! No one would fear, it will be sudden and complete, so no one need worry, and we can go on as long as we are conscious that we do exist. It is as ridiculous as it is terrifying. Annie as she left me said she would bring me my breakfast, and even offered to stay with me during the night so that I should not be lonely. So I kissed her and said good-night. I thought it kinder not to tell Sidney and Mrs Grant. We shall none of us suffer pain and discomfort; it will be sudden, complete, as the wireless set was in its broadcast, and the fire and the electric light, the chairs and the cushions, and the kitchen, the dining-room, the study and the sitting-room. What an amazing happening, well worth recording in my diary, but that also will suddenly disappear even if I went on with this endless writing. As I turn out the light and heat up my tea kettle and hot water bottle, so my stomach may no longer pain me, I feel that this is *inconceivable – and therefore that it will not happen.*

Beatrice Webb died of renal failure eleven days later, on 30 April 1943. She was cremated. On 13 October 1947, Sidney died. On his death Shaw wrote to *The Times* suggesting that 'to commemorate an unparalleled partnership' the remains of the Webbs should not lie in the garden at Passfield (as they had directed), but in Westminster Abbey. On 12 December 1947, in the presence of a Labour Cabinet which contained a majority of Fabians, they were interred together in the Abbey, the first wife and husband to be so honoured. A memorial stone with the name 'Beatrice' stands in the wood at Passfield Corner.

# Chronology

**1873** Visit to America. Marriage of Georgina to Daniel Meinertzhagen
**1874** Introduced to London society
**1875** At school in Bournemouth
**1876** 'Comes out' in London Season
**1877** Interest in religion, concern about her own future
**1878** Extended trip through Europe with the Playnes
**1879** At Rusland
**1880** Marriage of Maggie to Henry Hobhouse. Autumn trip to Italy
**1881** Return from Europe in the spring. Marriage of Theresa to Alfred Cripps
**1882** *April* Death of Lawrencina Potter *June* Beatrice makes her will. Visits to Germany and Switzerland with Richard and Rosy Potter and Herbert Spencer during the summer
**1883** *February* Richard Potter rents 47 Prince's Gate *March* Marriage of Kate to Leonard Courtney *April* Beatrice joins Charity Organization Society *June* Meets Joseph Chamberlain *Autumn* Visit to The Argoed *November* First visit to Bacup
**1884** *January* Chamberlain visits The Argoed. Beatrice returns visit to Highbury *April* Richard Potter takes York House as London residence *September* Beatrice writes a second testimentary note. Holidays in Bavaria with Margaret Harkness *December* Starts work in Katherine Buildings
**1885** Works at Katherine Buildings *November* Richard Potter has a stroke
**1886** *January* Beatrice makes another will. Living in Bournemouth lodgings with her convalescent father *February* Unemployed riot in Trafalgar Square. Article on unemployed in *Pall Mall Gazette*. Letter to

Chamberlain about unemployed   *March* Joins Charles Booth's survey of London. Chamberlain's defection from Liberals   *October* Beatrice visits Highbury. Visits Bacup

**1887** *March* Visits Liskeard. Study of dock labour   *August* Final break with Chamberlain after his visit to The Argoed   *September* Gives up York House   *October* Publishes dock labour article in *Nineteenth Century*. Decision to study sweating

**1888** *April* Works in East End as trouser-hand   *May* Gives evidence to House of Lords on sweating   *August* Marriage of Rosy to Dyson Williams *September* 'The Pages of a Workgirl's Diary' published in *Nineteenth Century*   *November* Chamberlain's marriage

**1889** Works on history of Co-operation   *June* Visits Co-operative Congress in Ipswich   *August* London dock strike   *September* Attends Trade Union Congress in Dundee   *October* Moves to Box House

**1890** *February* Meets Sidney Webb   *May* Attends Co-operative Congress in Glasgow   *June* Holidays in Bavaria and Italy with Alice Green   *December* Breaks with Sidney Webb

**1891** *April* Lectures on Co-operation at University Hall   *May* Reconciliation with Sidney Webb. Engagement. Attends Co-operative Congress in Lincoln   *June* Holidays in Norway with Sidney Webb and Graham Wallas. Sidney Webb resigns from Colonial Office

**1892** *July* General election results in Liberal majority. The Webbs marry and honeymoon in Ireland and Scotland   *October* The Webbs settle in Netherhall Gardens, Hampstead. Sidney chairman of Technical Education Committee, L.C.C.

**1893** *January* Independent Labour Party founded   *February* Gladstone introduces second Home Rule Bill   *May* Beatrice's sister Theresa dies. The Webbs spend summer at The Argoed; Shaw and Graham Wallas visit *October* The Webbs move to 41 Grosvenor Road   *November* 'To Your Tents, O Israel' appears in the *Fortnightly Review*

**1894** *March* Gladstone resigns as Prime Minister and leader of Liberal Party. Rosebery replaces him. Sidney drafts Minority Report of the Royal Commission on Labour Disputes   *May* *The History of Trade Unionism* published. The Webbs holiday in Italy   *July* The Webbs rent Borough Farm, Surrey. They hear of the Hutchinson legacy and conceive of the L.S.E.   *December* Progressives defeated at Westminster Vestry elections

**1895** *March* Sidney re-elected for Deptford in L.C.C. elections   *April* Hewins chosen as director of L.S.E.; Sidney writes Minority Report of the Royal Commission on the Aged Poor. The Webbs spend Easter at the Beachy Head Hotel with Shaw and Wallas   *July* Tories returned in general election; Lord Salisbury Prime Minister

**1896** *February* Offenders in Jameson Raid charged at Bow Street   *April* The Webbs holiday in the Lake District   *May* Select Committee enquires into

Jameson Raid. The Webbs at The Argoed *June* The Webbs visit the
Russells *August* The Webbs rent Suffolk rectory; Shaw and Charlotte
Payne-Townshend visit *October* L.S.E. opens at Adelphi Terrace

**1897** *February* Beatrice addresses women students at Girton and Newnham,
Cambridge *May* Shaw elected to St Pancras Vestry. The Webbs take
house for three months with Charlotte Payne-Townshend; Shaw visits.
Long Strike of engineering workers begins in support of eight-hour day
*June* Queen Victoria's Diamond Jubilee *July* House of Commons debate
following report on Jameson Raid

**1898** *January* Wallas marries Ada Radford *March* Progressive victory at
L.C.C. elections. The Webbs leave on 'sabbatical' journey, returning in
December

**1899** *February* The Webbs start work on series of volumes on English local
government *April* Beatrice visits Bradford and Leeds on investigative tour
*September* The Webbs visit Manchester, Liverpool and Lake District
*October* The Boer War begins

**1900** The Webbs in Devon for research *February* Boer victories followed by
the relief of Ladysmith. Labour Representative Committee formed to
establish a Labour Party in Parliament *May* The relief of Mafeking *July*
Beatrice meets Chamberlain in House of Commons *August* The Webbs
in Tyneside for research and holiday at Bamburgh *October* Tories retain
parliamentary majority in 'khaki' election

**1901** *January* Queen Victoria dies. Publication of Fabian tract 'The
Education Muddle' *March* Progressives win L.C.C. election *April* The
Webbs holiday at Lulworth, Dorset *July* The Webbs visit the Russells near
Oxford *September* Sidney's article 'Lord Rosebery's Escape from
Houndsditch' published in the *Nineteenth Century.* The Webbs holiday in
the Yorkshire Dales. Beatrice becomes interested in food reform
*December* Lord Rosebery makes important speech in Chesterfield

**1902** *February* The Webbs meet H. G. Wells. The Liberal League is formed
*March* The Education Bill introduced in Parliament *April* The Webbs at
Crowborough, Sussex *May* Boer War ends. The Webbs stay with the
Russells at Friday's Hill. Permanent building for the L.S.E. opens *July*
Beatrice takes Alys Russell to Switzerland. Lord Salisbury resigns; A. J.
Balfour becomes Prime Minister *August* Edward VII crowned *September*
The Webbs at Chipping Campden *December* The Education Act is
passed

**1903** *January* The Webbs in Norfolk with the Shaws and Wallases *February*
Beatrice visits Herbert Spencer in Brighton *May* Chamberlain advocates
imperial preference and tariff reform *June* The Webbs in the Cotswolds.
Sidney appointed to Royal Commission on Trade Union Law *September*
The Webbs cycle in Normandy and visit the Russells *October* Sidney
writes 'London Education' for the *Nineteenth Century.* The London

Education Act passed  *November* Hewins resigns; Mackinder replaces him as director of L.S.E.  *December* Herbert Spencer dies

**1904** *March* Shaw beaten at St Pancras in L.C.C. elections  *April* The Webbs visit Wells at Sandgate  *May* The Webbs in Hampshire near the Meinertzhagens  *August* War breaks out between Japan and Russia

**1905** *May* The Webbs spend three weeks at Longfords and visit Wells  *June* Blanche Cripps commits suicide. The Webbs at Aston Magna and Beachy Head  *August* The Webbs spend two months in Scotland and visit Willie Cripps  *November* Beatrice appointed to Royal Commission on the Poor Law  *December* Arthur Balfour resigns. Campbell-Bannerman becomes Prime Minister. Russo-Japanese war ends with revolutionary outbreaks in Russia

**1906** *January* Great Liberal victory in general election  *February* H.G. Wells makes a bid to take over the Fabian Society  *May* Death of Lawrencina Holt  *November* Beatrice withdraws her opposition to women's suffrage  *December* Defeat of Wells over Fabian reform

**1907** *March* Sidney Webb again returned for Deptford in L.C.C. election  *June* The Webbs in Scotland  *July* The Webbs staying at Ayot St Lawrence  *September* Mary Playne has operation for cancer

**1908** *January* Charles Booth resigns from Poor Law Commission  *April* Death of Campbell-Bannerman. Asquith becomes Prime Minister. Beatrice in Ireland  *May* W. Pember Reeves appointed director of L.S.E.  *August* The Webbs at Fabian summer school near Harlech

**1909** *January* End of Royal Commission  *February* Publication of Majority and Minority Reports  *March* The Webbs on holiday in Italy  *April* Introduction of the 'People's Budget' by Lloyd George  *May* The Webbs start campaign for the break-up of the Poor Law  *June* The suffragettes step up militancy with hunger strikes and violent reactions to forced feeding  *July* Beatrice receives honorary degree from Manchester University  *August* Affair of Wells and Amber Reeves becomes public  *December* Publication of *Ann Veronica*

**1910** *January* Liberal victory in general election  *March* Sidney Webb resigns from the L.C.C.  *April* Budget passed in House of Lords  *May* Death of Edward VII  *June* The Webbs in Switzerland  *July* Railway strike  *September* Strike in Lancashire cotton industry  *November* Publication of *The New Machiavelli*. Strike and riots in South Wales coalfields at Tonypandy. Parliament dissolved  *December* General election gives renewed mandate to Liberals

**1911** *February* Parliament Bill introduced  *June* The Webbs leave for tour of Japan, China and India. Coronation of George V. Seamen's strike  *August* Parliament Act passed. Dock and railway strikes. Rioting in Liverpool. Troops called out  *October* Rebellion in China and republic proclaimed  *November* Balfour resigns. Bonar Law replaces him as leader of the Tories.

National Insurance Bill passed. Renewed suffragette protests. King and Queen visit India

**1912** *February* Coalminers strike for a national minimum wage. Defeat of Suffrage Bill  *April* Introduction of third Home Rule Bill.  *May* The Webbs return from Asian tour. Strike of dockers and transport workers  *June* R. B. Haldane becomes Lord Chancellor  *July* Insurance Act comes into force. Intensification of suffragette militancy led by Christabel Pankhurst  *September* Threats of rebellion from Ulster Irish against Home Rule Bill  *October* Beatrice founds Fabian Research Department

**1913** *April* First issue of the *New Statesman*. Introduction of the 'cat and mouse' Act to deal with suffragettes on hunger strike  *September* The Webbs at Fabian summer school in Lake District

**1914** *January* The Triple Alliance formed between miners, railway and transport workers for co-ordinating disputes  *March* Curragh mutiny in protest against government policy in Ulster  *July* Death of Joseph Chamberlain  *August* Outbreak of war. MacDonald resigns as leader of the Parliamentary Labour Party  *September* Formation of Union of Democratic Control  *October* First Battle of Ypres. Turkey enters war against the allies  *November* Georgina Meinertzhagen dies  *December* First Zeppelin raids over Britain

**1915** *April* British troops attack Gallipoli. Air bombardment of London. Second Battle of Ypres. First use of poison gas by the Germans  *May* Asquith forms a coalition government. Arthur Henderson represents Labour. Sinking of the *Lusitania*  *November* Haig replaces French as commander-in-chief  *December* Gallipoli evacuated

**1916** *January* Military Services Act imposes compulsory recruitment for unmarried men aged eighteen to forty-one with allowance for conscientious objectors  *February* Battle of Verdun begins  *April* Surrender of British at Kut. Rebellion in Dublin  *May* Battle of Jutland. Military Service Act for married and unmarried men up to forty-one  *June* Kitchener drowned. Lloyd George becomes Secretary for War. The Webbs at Wyndham Croft, Sussex  *July* Battle of the Somme  *October* Shaw resigns from *New Statesman*  *December* Lloyd George replaces Asquith as Prime Minister and reorganizes the coalition

**1917** *February* Beatrice joins Reconstruction Committee  *March* Revolution in Russia  *April* America declares war. Battle of Arras  *May* Henderson visits Russia as representative of War Cabinet  *July* Third Battle of Ypres  *August* Henderson resigns from government  *November* Bolsheviks seize power and make armistice with Germany. First tank battle on Western Front

**1918** *February* Introduction of food rationing  *March* Germany makes a new offensive on the Somme  *May* Death of Leonard Courtney  *June* Representation of the People Act (women's vote) becomes law  *October*

Germany appeals to President Wilson for an armistice  *November* End of war with Germany  *December* Victory for Lloyd George in 'coupon' election

**1919** *February* Triple Alliance resumed  *March* Miners' strike. Sidney Webb appointed to Sankey Coal Commission  *June* Treaty of Versailles signed. Sankey Commission reports. William Beveridge chosen as director of L.S.E.  *September* Railway strike  *October* Woodrow Wilson has a stroke

**1920** *February* George Lansbury goes to Russia  *July* Sidney Webb nominated as Labour candidate for Seaham. Formation of Communist Party  *August* Second International meets at Geneva  *October* Miners' strike

**1921** *March* Death of Margaret Hobhouse  *April* Miners' strike and 'Black Friday'. Massacre at Amritsar in India. Beatrice starts the Half-Circle Club. Unemployment passes two million  *June* Truce in Ireland  *October* Conference on Ireland  *November* Washington Conference on naval affairs and Far East  *December* Treaty with Ireland marks the end of Irish unity

**1922** *August* The Webbs spend summer at Presteigne  *October* Tories meet at Carlton Club and bring the coalition government to an end  *November* Tory victory in general election. Sidney Webb returned as Labour M.P.

**1923** *March* Death of Arthur Playne  *April* Lady Warwick offers Easton Lodge to the Labour Party  *May* Bonar Law resigns and is replaced by Stanley Baldwin  *August* The Webbs buy cottage at Liphook, Hampshire  *October* Deaths of Bonar Law and Mary Playne  *November* The Webbs move into Passfield Corner  *December* General election results in first Labour government

**1924** *January* First Labour government appointed after a general election in December 1923. Sidney Webb appointed President of the Board of Trade  *April* British Empire exhibition at Wembley. Publication of the Dawes plan  *July* Inter-allied conference in London. Beatrice receives honorary degree at Edinburgh  *August* Breakdown of Russian trade negotiations. Editor of *Worker's Weekly*, J. R. Campbell, arrested on charge of incitement to riot  *September* MacDonald scandal over McVitie & Price shares. Tory motion of censure on Campbell case and vote of no confidence in government  *October* General election. Zinoviev letter  *November* Tory government with Stanley Baldwin as Prime Minister

**1925** *February* The Webbs make arrangements to share 41 Grosvenor Road with Susan Lawrence  *April* Britain returns to the gold standard. Beatrice at Freshwater with Kate  *June* Coal-owners cancel existing wage agreements  *September* Royal Commission on mining industry appointed  *October* Locarno Pact

**1926** *January* The Webbs holiday in Sicily  *February* Publication of *My Apprenticeship*  *March* Publication of Royal Commission report on mining industry  *April* Deadlock over negotiations between miners and mine-

owners  *May* General Strike  *August* Labour Party garden party at Passfield
*September* The Webbs at T.U.C. Bournemouth  *December* B.B.C. charter
as public corporation

**1927** *May* Trades Disputes Act. End of trade agreement with Russia  *October*
Death of Jane Wells

**1928** *January* Beatrice's seventieth birthday. Floods at Grosvenor Road
*February* Death of Asquith  *July* The Webbs on holiday at Val d'Isère
*August* Death of R. B. Haldane. Kellogg–Briand pact. Beatrice tours
mining districts of South Wales  *December* The Webbs' Poor Law history
concluded. Vote given to all women over twenty-one

**1929** *January* Webb portrait presented to the L.S.E.  *March* Death of Kate
Courtney. Beatrice makes her first broadcast  *April* The Webbs on holiday
in Greece and Turkey  *May* The Webbs receive honorary degree in
Munich. General election  *June* Second Labour government. Sidney
becomes Secretary of State for the Dominions and Colonies and goes to
the House of Lords  *August* The Webbs take first flight  *September* The
Webbs give up Grosvenor Road and move to Whitehall Court.
MacDonald in America to discuss naval disarmament  *October* Wall Street
crash

**1930** *January* Mosley's economic proposals rejected by the government  *April*
Gandhi arrested for civil disobedience. The Webbs move to Artillery
Mansions  *May* Mosley resigns from the government  *June* Thomas takes
over the Dominions. The Webbs holiday in the Channel Isles  *July* The
Webbs dine with Prince of Wales  *October* Imperial conference. Crash of
R101

**1931** *February* Beatrice starts *Our Partnership*. Mosley resigns from the
Labour Party  *April* May Committee set up  *May* Failure of the Kredit-
anstalt bank  *July* May Committee reports. GBS visits Russia  *August*
Crisis in Labour Cabinet and fall of Labour government  *September* Japan
invades Manchuria – the first violation of peace since the war  *October*
General election and formation of the National government

**1932** *February* Disarmament conference opens at Geneva  *April* Beatrice
elected to the British Academy  *May* The Webbs visit Russia  *July* Webbs
return from Russia. I.L.P. disaffiliates from Labour Party  *August* Death of
Graham Wallas

**1933** *January* Hitler becomes Chancellor in Germany  *February* The Webbs
on holiday in Italy. Japan invades China. Oxford Union motion on
whether to fight for 'King and Country'  *October* Germany resigns from
the League of Nations and withdraws from disarmament conference. The
Webbs attend Labour Party conference in Hastings. Beatrice undergoes
operation on her bladder at Hastings

**1934** *January* Beatrice undergoes second operation for removal of kidney
*February* Civil war in Austria  *June* Baldwin takes over from MacDonald.

The 'night of the long knives' in Germany *September* U.S.S.R. joins the
League of Nations. Sidney Webb visits Russia *October* Sidney returns
from Russia. Death of Ada Wallas

**1935** *January* The Webbs in Isle of Wight *April* The Webbs in Hastings
*May* George V's silver jubilee *June* The Peace Ballot *October* Italy invades
Abyssinia *November* General election resulting in Conservative
government under Baldwin. Attlee elected leader of the Labour Party
*December* The Hoare–Laval Pact

**1936** *January* Death of George V *March* Hitler invades Rhineland. The
Webbs on holiday in Majorca *July* Spanish civil war begins. Purge trials in
Russia *December* Abdication of Edward VIII

**1937** *January* Labour Party expels Socialist League *April* Beveridge appointed
head of University College, Oxford *May* Neville Chamberlain becomes
Prime Minister *July* The Webbs in Switzerland. Death of Henry
Hobhouse *October* Carr-Saunders becomes the new director of the L.S.E.
*November* Death of Ramsay MacDonald

**1938** *January* Beatrice's eightieth birthday. Sidney has a stroke *February* Eden
resigns as Foreign Secretary. Ribbentrop becomes Foreign Minister in
Germany *September* Hitler's speech at Nuremberg. Chamberlain makes
peace agreement with Hitler at Munich *October* Hitler takes over
Sudetenland

**1939** *March* Hitler occupies Czechoslovakia. British give guarantee to Poland
*April* Mussolini attacks Albania. Conscription introduced *August*
Soviet–German pact *September* Germany invades Poland. Britain declares
war *December* Russia invades Finland

**1940** *April* Germany occupies Denmark and Norway *May* Germany invades
Holland and Belgium. Churchill replaces Chamberlain as Prime Minister
and forms a coalition government *June* Paris occupied. French army
surrender. Vichy government sues for peace. British Expeditionary Force
evacuates at Dunkirk *August* Trotsky assassinated *September* Climax of
the Battle of Britain *November* Death of Neville Chamberlain

**1941** *April* Death of Virginia Woolf *June* Hitler invades Russia *July* Death of
Lord Parmoor *December* Japanese attack Pearl Harbor. America declares
war

**1942** *March* Death of Betty Balfour *June* Fall of Tobruk *July* The Webbs'
golden wedding *November* Victory at El Alamein *December* Publication
of Beveridge Report

**1943** *April* Death of Beatrice Webb

# List of Illustrations

*Acknowledgements and thanks are due to the individuals and institutions listed in brackets below.*

1. Beatrice with her parents (Lord Parmoor)
2. Herbert Spencer, *c.* 1875 (Passfield Papers)
3. Portrait of Sir Charles Booth by William Rothenstein, 1908 (The University of Liverpool)
4. Family Group, 1865 (Passfield Papers)
5. Standish House, Vale of Severn (Passfield Papers)
6. The Argoed, 1982
7. Joseph Chamberlain
8. Beatrice Webb, aged about 27
9. Sidney Webb, 1885 (Passfield Papers)
10. 44 Cranbourne Street, WC2 (Archives, Westminster City Library)
11. Bernard Shaw, *c.* 1901 (Hulton Getty)
12. Charlotte Payne Townshend on bicycle, *c.* 1896 (Passfield Papers)
13. Beatrice and Sidney Webb, photographed by Shaw (London School of Economics)
14. The Potter sisters at Standish (Kitty Muggeridge)
15. 41 Grosvenor Road (Passfield Papers)
16. Adelphi Terrace (LSE Archive)
17. A.J. Balfour, 1898 (Hulton Getty)
18. 'The Wire Puller' (*Manchester Evening News*) (Passfield Papers)
19. Fabian Summer School (Passfield Papers)
20. Winston Churchill (Mansell Collection)

# Index

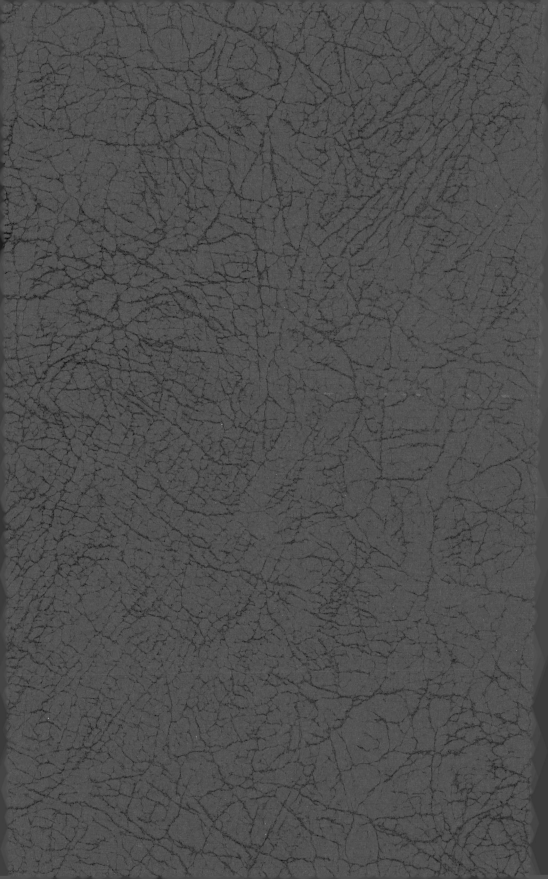